THE OXFORD HANDBOOK OF

AMERICAN ISLAM

THE OXFORD HANDBOOK OF

AMERICAN ISLAM

Edited by

YVONNE Y. HADDAD

and

JANE I. SMITH

OXFORD
UNIVERSITY PRESS

OXFORD
UNIVERSITY PRESS

Oxford University Press is a department of the University of Oxford.
It furthers the University's objective of excellence in research, scholarship,
and education by publishing worldwide.

Oxford   New York
Auckland   Cape Town   Dar es Salaam   Hong Kong   Karachi
Kuala Lumpur   Madrid   Melbourne   Mexico City   Nairobi
New Delhi   Shanghai   Taipei   Toronto

With offices in
Argentina   Austria   Brazil   Chile   Czech Republic   France   Greece
Guatemala   Hungary   Italy   Japan   Poland   Portugal   Singapore
South Korea   Switzerland   Thailand   Turkey   Ukraine   Vietnam

Oxford is a registered trademark of Oxford University Press
in the UK and certain other countries.

Published in the United States of America by
Oxford University Press
198 Madison Avenue, New York, NY 10016

Library of Congress Cataloging-in-Publication Data
The Oxford handbook of American Islam / edited by Yvonne Y. Haddad and Jane I. Smith.
pages cm
Includes index.
ISBN 978-0-19-986263-4 (cloth : alk. paper)   1. Islam—United States.   2.   Muslims—United
States I.   Haddad, Yvonne Y.   II.   Smith, Jane I. 1935–
BP67.U6O94 2015
297.0973—dc23
2014007963

1 3 5 7 9 8 6 4 2
Printed in the United States of America
on acid-free paper

Contents

PART II. INSTITUTIONALIZATION OF ISLAM IN NORTH AMERICA

PART III. INTEGRATION AND ASSIMILATION OF MUSLIMS

Contributors

Asma Afsaruddin is professor of Islamic studies and chairperson of the Department of Near Eastern Languages and Cultures at Indiana University, Bloomington. She is the author of the recently published *Striving in the Path of God: Jihad and Martyrdom in Islamic Thought* (2013).

Ihsan Bagby is associate professor of Islamic studies at the University of Kentucky and most recently authored a series of three monographs on American mosques: *The American Mosque 2011: Basic Characteristics; The American Mosque 2011: Activities, Administration and Vitality;* and *The American Mosque 2011: Women and the American Mosque.*

Jocelyne Cesari is senior research fellow at the Berkley Center for Peace, Religions and World Affairs at Georgetown University and director of the Harvard-based Islam in the West Program. Her most recent book is *Why the West Fears Islam: Exploration of Muslims in Liberal Western Democracies* (2013).

Sara J. Chehab is assistant professor of international relations at Zayed University in Dubai (UAE). Her research focuses on the political economy and society of the United Arab Emirates and US foreign policy in the Middle East. She holds a PhD in political science and international relations from the University of Delaware, which she obtained in May 2011.

Sylviane A. Diouf, an award-winning historian, is the author, notably, of *Servants of Allah: African Muslims Enslaved in the Americas* (1998 and 2013) and has contributed several book chapters on African Muslims. She is a curator at the Schomburg Center for Research in Black Culture, The New York Public Library.

Susan L. Douglass is education outreach consultant for the Alwaleed bin Talal Center for Muslim–Christian Understanding and has managed several grant projects for the Ali Vural Ak Center for Global Islamic Studies as a doctoral candidate at George Mason University. She is the editor and chapter author of the volume *Rise and Spread of Islam: 622–1500 CE* (2002) and several online and print teaching resources for world history and Islamic education.

Peter Gottschalk is professor of religion at Wesleyan University. His research explores both Hindu–Muslim relations in India and Islamophobia in the United States, and his most recent book is *American Heretics: Catholics, Jews, Muslims and the History of Religious Intolerance.*

Yvonne Y. Haddad is professor of history of Islam and Christian–Muslim relations at the School of Foreign Service, Georgetown University. She is a past president of the Middle East Studies Association. Her publications have focused on Muslims in the United States, Islamic revolutionary thought, women in Islam, Christian–Muslim relations, and Arab intellectuals.

Juliane Hammer is an associate professor of religious studies and the Kenan Rifai Scholar of Islamic Studies at the University of North Carolina at Chapel Hill. She is the author of *American Muslim Women, Religious Authority, and Activism: More than a Prayer* (2012) and co-editor of the *Cambridge Companion to American Islam* (with Omid Safi; 2013).

Marcia Hermansen is director of the Islamic World Studies Program at Loyola University, Chicago, where she is a professor of Islamic and religious studies in the Theology Department. She recently co-edited *Muslima Theology: The Voices of Muslim Women Theologians*, with Peter Lang, 2013.

Altaf Husain is an assistant professor in the School of Social Work at Howard University. He recently authored a chapter on "Muslim Leadership in the U.S. context" which appeared in *Religious Leadership: A Reference Handbook*.

Munir Jiwa is founding director and associate professor at the Center for Islamic Studies at the Graduate Theological Union in Berkeley. His work focuses on Islam and Muslims in the West, media, aesthetics, secularism, and religious formation. He is the recipient of grants from Ford, Mellon, Carnegie, and Luce foundations.

Akel Ismail Kahera currently serves as professor of architecture and associate dean of the College of Architecture, Art and Humanities at Clemson University. He is the author of *Deconstructing the American Mosque* (2002) and *Reading the Islamic City* (2011).

Rabia Kamal is an adjunct professor at the University of San Francisco. Her areas of expertise include cultural and visual anthropology, American Islam, cultural and racial politics in the US and the use of social media and new technologies for identity formation and political engagement. She is the author of "Pakistani America: History, People, and Culture," which appeared in the *Encyclopedia of Asian American Folklore and Folklife*.

Nadia Khan is a doctoral student in Islamic Studies at the University of Chicago's Divinity School.

Charles Kimball is presidential professor and director of the Religious Studies Program at the University of Oklahoma, Norman. He is author of five books, including *When Religion Becomes Evil: Five Warning Signs* (2002, 2008) and *When Religion Becomes Lethal: The Explosive Mix of Politics and Religion in Judaism, Christianity, and Islam* (2011).

Lance D. Laird is assistant director of the Master of Science Program in Medical Anthropology and Cross-Cultural Practice at Boston University School of Medicine. He is the author of numerous articles on American Muslims' health, medicines, and interactions with health-care institutions, in journals ranging from *The Muslim World* to *Archives of Disease in Childhood*.

Peter Makari has served Global Ministries of the United Church of Christ and Christian Church (Disciples of Christ) as executive for the Middle East and Europe for the Common Global Ministries Board since July 2000. He is the author of *Conflict and Cooperation: Christian-Muslim Relations in Contemporary Egypt* (2007).

Peter Mandaville is professor of government and politics and director of the Ali Vural Ak Center for Global Islamic Studies at George Mason University. He is the author of *Transnational Muslim Politics: Reimagining the Umma and Islam and Politics*.

Kathleen M. Moore is professor and chair of religious studies at University of California Santa Barbara. She is author of *The Unfamiliar Abode: Islamic Law in the United States and Britain* (2010), co-author of *Muslim Women in the United States: The Challenge of Islamic Identity Today* (2011), and collaborator on various projects about shari'a and gender in the United States and western Europe.

Hussein Rashid is an independent scholar, most regularly affiliated with Hofstra University. He has published several academic articles on American Muslims and popular culture, in addition to writing about religion in many mainstream media outlets.

Carolyn Moxley Rouse is professor of anthropology at Princeton University. She is the author of *Engaged Surrender: African American Women and Islam*.

Randa B. Serhan is a assistant professor of sociology and director of Arab World Studies at the American University in Washington, D.C. She co-edited *American Democracy and the Pursuit of Equality*.

Muzammil H. Siddiqi is adjunct professor of Islamic studies at Chapman University and chairman of the Fiqh Council of North America. He is also religious director of the Islamic Society of Orange County, Garden Grove, California.

Abdulkader H. Sinno is associate professor of political science and Middle Eastern studies at Indiana University, Bloomington. He is the author of books and articles on Muslim minority political representation in Western liberal democracies, public sentiment toward Muslim immigration, the Arab Spring, conflict processes, and Islamist parties' participation in elections.

Jane I. Smith retired in 2012 as associate dean for academic affairs and senior lecturer in Islamic studies at Harvard Divinity School. She is the author of a number of books on such topics as Islam in America, Christian–Muslim dialogue, women in Islam, American Muslims and education, and minority Muslim communities in America.

Harvey Stark is a visiting assistant professor at Wabash college and is completing his PhD dissertation at Princeton University on the Muslim American chaplaincy. He is author of "Religious Citizens After September 11th: The Impact of Politics on the Jurisprudence Concerning Muslim American Military Service."

Liyakat Takim is the Sharjah chair in global Islam at McMaster University in Hamilton, Canada. He is author of numerous scholarly works, including *Shi'ism in America* (2009) and *The Heirs of the Prophet: Charisma and Religious Authority in Shi'ite Islam* (2006).

Susan Van Baalen recently retired from the Federal Bureau of Prisons, where she was responsible for the development and implementation of policies and procedures to accommodate the religious beliefs and practices of more than 200,000 inmates in 110 institutions. She produced a sixty-session video series, *Islam's Place and Practice of Worship in the Correctional Environment*. In 2013, she contributed a chapter on Religious Programming in Peter M. Carlson, ed., *Prison and Jail Administration: Practice and Theory*.

Marvin R. Whitaker, Jr., is a PhD candidate at the University of Delaware in the Department of Political Science and International Relations. His most recent co-authored work (with M.A. Muqtedar Khan) is *Islamic Reformers in North America*, in *Religious Leadership: A Handbook*, Volume 2 (2013).

Timur R. Yuskaev is assistant professor of contemporary Islam, co-editor of *The Muslim World* journal, and co-director of the Islamic chaplaincy program at Hartford Seminary. His forthcoming book, *Speaking Qur'an: The Emergence of an American Sacred Text*, examines contemporary American Muslim interpretations of the Qur'an.

THE OXFORD HANDBOOK OF

AMERICAN
ISLAM

INTRODUCTION

COULD a Muslim become president of the United States? Thomas Jefferson thought so, though few other American leaders have even contemplated such an occurrence. President Barack Hussein Obama struggled mightily during his 2008 election campaign to assure the voting public that, despite his Arab-sounding name, he was not a Muslim, although his father was. A few asked whether it would have mattered if he were a Muslim, but for most people the answer was clear: Yes, it would have mattered a lot.

Not many Muslims in today's United States aspire to such a high office, but Muslims are increasingly recognizing that election to public office is an important step in the ongoing story of the indigenization of Islam. The same is true for their emergence as leaders in education, science and technology, arts and music, and virtually all other fields of American endeavor. The image of American Islam is constantly in flux as new people join the community, new information becomes available, and Muslim leaders help develop new interpretations of the faith and new ways in which Islam can be practiced in a pluralistic society.

Implicit in the question of whether a Muslim can be president is another question that has always existed under the surface and has come to the forefront since the events of 9/11: "Are Muslims *real* Americans?" To this have been added other concerns, such as whether Muslims might constitute a fifth column, or whether they seek the destruction of America by insisting on implementing *shari'a*. Similar questions have arisen whenever Americans have felt threatened by ethnic or minority groups that challenge the white Protestant establishment. Jewish and Catholic immigration to the United States sparked similar concerns. It is the unique American "melting pot" that has indigenized these religious communities. That six of the jurists on the Supreme Court today are Catholic and three are Jewish is a testament to American pluralism.

The kinds of concerns that some Americans have raised about Muslims have been particularly evident during those times in which the United States has been involved in overseas military engagement. The atrocities of 9/11 have posed a particular challenge as Muslims have had to "prove" their right to be citizens at the same time that they maintain a religious identity that has become inextricably intertwined with terrorism in the perspective of many Americans. The essays in this volume illustrate the many ways in which American Muslims today are rising to that challenge.

PART I: FORMATION OF THE MUSLIM COMMUNITY IN NORTH AMERICA

The first Muslims to cross over to the American shores did so unwillingly. They were primarily West African Muslims brought as slaves to support the American cotton industry. Sylvianne Diouf describes ways in which they maintained their faith and shows how their legacy still can be discerned in various ways. One of those ways is American music, as they have been pioneers in doo-wop, jazz, hip-hop, and rap. Both Diouf and Carolyn Moxley Rouse trace the development of these first Africans in America, from the rise of Black nationalist movements, which grew in response to dehumanizing slavery, to the expansion of the powerful Nation of Islam, and concluding with contemporary manifestations of African American Islam. Rouse emphasizes that the adoption of Islam by African Americans is a clear response to white supremacy and that their struggles for equal citizenship in America reflect many of the same issues of belonging that immigrant Muslims have had to deal with throughout their history in the United States.

Middle Eastern Christians and Muslims first came to the United States in the latter part of the nineteenth century, at a time when only white or African American males were allowed citizenship. They were primarily labor migrants, single men not intending to stay longer than it took to earn enough money to return home and start businesses. Those who did decide to stay faced the reality of noncitizenship, which they had to endure until 1924, when they were deemed by the U.S. Courts to be white and thus eligible to become "real" Americans. It was not until 1965, with the change in immigration legislation, that significant numbers of Muslims began to arrive from various parts of the world. Randa Serhan looks at the overall question of Muslim immigrant presence in America within the framework of immigration literature, including issues of gender and sexuality.

After 1965, there was a new influx of Muslim immigrants, mostly from the Middle East and South Asia. Initially, they were mostly students looking for advanced education in such fields as science, engineering, and medicine. They came from newly independent nation states and brought with them vivid memories of Western imperialism in which bureaucrats, missionaries, teachers, and others were seen as having attempted to inculcate in them Western secular values to replace their own Islamic beliefs. Many of them tried to develop a distinctive Islamic community in America, one with its own religious, cultural, and social values implanted onto the American landscape. Tension existed between those who believed that their primary commitment was to be Muslim in America with a separate identity and an allegiance to a transnational community and those who wanted to be seen as Muslim Americans, full partners in American society. Increasingly, the second option appears to be prevailing. More recently, as we shall see, new options for American Islamic identity are being developed.

While the majority of Muslim immigrants have been Sunni, reflecting the dominance of that branch in the world, significant numbers of Shi'ites and other groups have sought refuge on American shores since the early part of the twentieth century. Liyakat Takim describes how Twelver Shi'ism has developed in the American context, detailing its structures, rituals, and the overall formation of the community out of disparate ethnic groups. The challenge for Twelver Shi'ites, he argues, is to reconstitute themselves less as ethnically determined groups and more as Islamic institutions in the American context. Currently, the second largest Shi'ite group in the United States is the Nizari Isma'ilis, described by Yvonne Haddad and Jane Smith along with the Ahmadiyya, the Druze, and the Qur'anists, three other sectarian groups with historically strong international ties now struggling to define themselves with an American religious identity.

An important strand of international Islam that cuts across sectarian ethnic identities is Sufism, the more pietistic and spiritual branch of the faith, which has been present in the United States for well over a century. In the middle part of the 1900s, Sufi groups became part of the "cult culture" that welcomed various religious practices to America. In recent decades, American Sufis have looked for leadership specifically to the long-established Sufi orders in the Middle East, the Indian Subcontinent, and Africa. Marcia Hermansen describes contemporary manifestations of American Sufism, including organizations, the influences of Sufis on contemporary American Muslims, and the global rise of Islamic authenticity.

PART II: INSTITUTIONALIZATION OF ISLAM IN NORTH AMERICA

Muslim leaders, often working on a volunteer basis, have tried to create a place for Islam in the American mainstream. Beginning with the influx of students in the 1960s, efforts were made to establish organizations that incorporated Islamic identity in a Judeo-Christian environment. The Muslim Student Association (MSA) was started in 1963. Disenchanted with the secularism and socialism preached in the Muslim world, as well as with Islamic modernism popular in the Middle East, students tried to develop a culture with a clear Islamic identity. From the MSA grew what is now the largest American Muslim organization, the Islamic Society of North America (ISNA), which has established institutions similar to those of other American religions. Jocelyne Cesari describes these organizational beginnings, going on to talk about the dramatic way that 9/11 has brought about a change in emphasis from ethnic and cultural diversity to recognition of the political consequences of the rise of Islamophobia. Meanwhile, other Islamic youth movements in the United States have continued to grow and proliferate, as described by Rabia Kamal, and like other American Muslim institutions they have been transformed in clearly identifiable ways as a result of 9/11. Altaf Hussein enhances this picture by showing how Muslims, especially youth and often through organizations like MSA, have volunteered to address complex social issues in the United States and abroad.

With greater numbers of immigrants arriving in America from literally all over the world in the last several decades, and with African American Muslims increasingly visible as full participants in the pursuit of the Islamic faith, new definitions of what constitutes the American *Ummah* (community) have been constantly in the making. The American Muslim community has become the most heterogeneous in the world, raising questions of leadership, governance, law and interpretation, practice, education, changing roles for women, and more. Still, Americans born into Muslim families since 1965 are citizens by right of birth and have not, like their immigrant parents or grandparents, been raised in the context of a foreign Muslim culture. They are truly bicultural, growing up American but with awareness of their family's home culture, learning early how to negotiate the marked boundaries that this double identity represents. African American Muslims, meanwhile, have for the most part left nationalist-oriented and isolating communities such as the Nation of Islam. They are facing their own sets of identities as Blacks, Americans, and Muslims and are not free of the fear of being associated with the actions of militants overseas.

Despite the various ethnic, national, racial, linguistic, and other differences among Muslims, they share a common faith and prescribed practices that, despite some variations, are somewhat uniform. Muzammil Siddiqi lays out the common elements of Islamic faith and practice, suggesting some ways in which minor adaptations have been made to accommodate contemporary American culture. The primary way in which Islam has been expressed collectively in America is through its mosques, argues Ihsan Bagby, symbolizing Muslims' commitment to affirm their place as a worshipping community. The construction of purpose-built mosques, to serve alongside buildings converted for worship use, has contributed to a change in the landscape of America. But who is to serve as the leadership of mosques and Muslim communities? Muslims face a major challenge because there is technically no clergy in Islam. Until recently, American Muslims have had to rely either on untrained Imams or on trained leadership from foreign cultures. Currently, the community is experiencing a gradual transition to the appropriate education and training of Americans to perform these roles. The steps involved in this transition are spelled out by Timur Yuskaev and Harvey Stark in their treatment of Imams and chaplains as American religious professionals. The authors emphasize that it is important to understand the difference between these two kinds of religious leaders, although they may receive similar education in subjects such as law, ethics, and cultural practices. Creating professional standards is essential to meeting the different needs of the Muslim community, with particular attention to its younger American generation.

The diverse nature of Islam in the United States with its many national, ethnic, and cultural constituents, has raised questions for first-, second-, and third-generation American Muslims about whether traditional schools of law should still be considered authoritative or whether and how *shari'a* and *fiqh* have efficacy at all in this technically secular nation. Asma Afsaruddin highlights internal debates, discussions with international jurists, and the development of American organizations to initiate innovative legal reasoning based on the Qur'an and classic legal formulations.

Key to the development of an American Islam distinct from, yet strongly connected to, all the culturally defined Islams that go into its making is the importance of new roles and opportunities for women. Writing on American Muslim women, Kathleen Moore discusses movements such as progressive reformism, which argues that Islamic practice should be reformulated based on reengagement with the primary sources of Islam and that it is necessary for both women and men to be able to read and interpret the Qur'an and Islamic texts. Along with this, Moore says, comes the importance of rethinking Islamic rituals, claiming religious and communal authority, and challenging the ways in which Muslim women have been represented in the media and in other public venues in the United States.

Related to the topic of changing roles for American Muslim women is Juliane Hammer's treatment of discourse and practice with regard to marriage and family life. Hammer looks at Muslims as a minority within the American context but also connected to transnational Muslim communities with their own traditional marriage and family customs. Such customs, she argues, must be seen as part of the religious discourses and practices in relation both to changing Muslim attitudes about gender roles and to their importance to the public perception of Islam in the United States.

One of the most important issues facing Muslim families today is education, both secular and religious. The transmission of knowledge about Islam, and learning in general, is of crucial importance to Muslims, argues Susan Douglass. She discusses a variety of forms of education in the American Muslim community, including home-schooling, organized education, instruction in mosques and Islamic centers, the founding of special Islamic schools, writing and publishing, and new forms of media, focusing primarily on the current status of education related to Islam and Muslims in North America in the twenty-first century.

Education about Islam has also been a primary focus in the long-standing Muslim effort to bring new members into the Islamic community as well as to call back those who may have strayed from "the straight path." *Da'wa*, or "call," as Kathleen Moore explains, refers not only to restricted missionary work and efforts to convert non-Muslims but also to reinforcing greater piety on the part of Muslims themselves. Moore traces the importance of *da'wa* activity in the United States from the influence of Muslim scholar/teacher Isma 'il al-Faruqi to the most recent interpretations on social media and via the Internet. Education and *da'wa* are both important elements in the efforts of Muslims to reach out to those who are incarcerated in American prisons. Susan Van Baalen traces the history of prison Islam in the United States and the growing number of Muslims who are part of that system. She looks at program accommodations to protect prisoners' religious rights, as well as interactions between sectarian and religious groups in the prison system, and what that means for conversion to Islam and public perceptions of Muslim inmates.

Lance Laird describes the development of medicine in America as practiced by and reflected on by Muslim physicians, clinicians, and practitioners. A substantial number of Muslim immigrants have been medical professionals who eschew medications that contain alcohol or lard byproducts. Laird shows how scripture, tradition, legal practice, ritual, traditional herbal and physical remedies, biomedical science, and technology combine to provide a range of alternative medical systems for Muslims. He demonstrates how Muslims can be given appropriate care by non-Muslim health professionals, how Muslim physicians can improve their professional medical practices, and how public health—both Muslim and non-Muslim—can be promoted in the United States.

Part III: Integration and Assimilation of Muslims

In one way or another, most, if not all, of the essays in this volume deal with the reality of 9/11 and the impact of the events of that day on the Muslim community in America. The terrorist attacks changed life in some basic ways for Americans, with the most severe consequences for Muslims. The attacks of 9/11 served to awaken Americans' long-standing reservations and even fear of Muslims and of the violence long associated with Islam in the West.

As a consequence, the "American-ness" that Muslims gradually established over the course of the twentieth century came to be challenged as Islam was increasingly viewed as a threat to America and its security. Many of the rights granted by the U.S. Constitution were suspended through such decisions as the passing of the USA PATRIOT Act and the intensification of monitoring Islamic mosques, institutions, and web sites. Even internment camps to hold Muslim citizens seen to be enemy combatants were contemplated. Several voices raised the question of whether Muslims should be granted citizenship.

President Bush and others in the American government quickly called for and attempted to institute policies that promote the emergence of a "moderate" Islam, antithetical to the violence perpetrated by the terrorists on 9/11. Many within the Muslim community itself came to recognize that even repeatedly denouncing the perpetrators of 9/11 was not sufficient; it was clearly necessary for Muslims to embody a new kind of identity and consciousness. In this process many felt that they needed to alter some of the identity that they had fostered during the last decades of the twentieth century in favor of creating a moderate Islam that appropriated American values, standards, and norms. The primary identity to be promoted was American, with Muslims and the government working toward the same goal of transforming Muslims living in the United States into Muslim Americans.

Several articles in this volume deal specifically with American fear of Islam and the "war on terror" that was unleashed after 9/11, and most interpreters understand these realities to underscore the development of virtually all aspects of Islam in the United States today. Charles Kimball looks specifically at the war on terror and how it has affected American Muslims, in both negative and positive ways. Government surveillance programs aimed at Muslims, along with growing fear of Islam and Muslims, have resulted in the creation of Islamic organizations to monitor and give information about hate speech and hate crimes against Muslims. Positively, Muslims have undertaken many new forms of educational initiatives, including interfaith activity, to provide accurate information about Islam. In the same vein, Peter Gottschalk looks at Islamophobia and anti-Muslim sentiment, considering the long history of antipathies between Islam and Christianity. He argues that while the term "Islamophobia" may have been recently coined, the sentiments are long-standing and simply have been exacerbated by current social, economic, political, and military encounters.

For the majority of Muslims born in the United States, fear and demonization of Islam by other Americans did not lead them to conceal their faith. Rather, it led to efforts to affirm Islam as a religion of peace and to help educate non-Muslims (as well as other Muslims) about the true nature of Islam as both democratic and pluralistic. Among the various activities undertaken by American Muslims since 9/11 is increased participation in political life at the local and even national levels. Muslims have voted more regularly, organized registration drives, and served as and supported Muslim candidates for public office and have expressed their eagerness to be part of the political system so as to be heard from and taken seriously. Abdulkader Sinno gives us an inside look at the politics of Muslims in America, considering ways in which Muslims choose their level of activity in the political arena, their voting practices, success in running for office, and how politics can serve to foster and support particular Muslim causes.

As part of the effort to showcase an Islam that fits well into the American pluralistic paradigm Muslims have expended great effort to show that Islam itself is pluralistic and open to other religions. Muslims have willingly participated not only in talking about Islam in as many public venues as possible but also in taking part in numerous local and even nationally based interfaith dialogue sessions. Sometimes these are broadly interfaith, sometimes "Abrahamic" conversations involving Muslims, Christians, and Jews, and sometimes they are focused specifically on Christians and Muslims who struggle to understand not only each other but also their long history of difficult relations. Peter Makari lays out the context for these kinds of engagements, focusing on what he sees as constructive efforts and initiatives that may bode well for improved understanding and effective community-building. Makari also explores the intersection of the U.S. domestic context with the global context of Christian-Muslim relations and their mutual impact.

As change takes place in the community, it is possible to envision a three-pronged process to the efforts of Muslims to understand Islam and to make it understood. One is their effort to present an America-friendly version of a tradition in which East and West have often been pitted against each other. A second is the serious effort, especially but not only on the part of young Muslims, to rethink their faith for themselves in the light of their citizenship in the United States. A third involves the intellectual effort to retrieve the artifacts of their faith, so to speak, in the study of Qur'an, tradition, and other Islamic texts and to test them against the realities of their contemporary life. Sara Chehab and Marvin Whitacre examine a few of the intellectual contributions of American Muslim scholars. The authors highlight five representatives of such scholarship, showing how they have struggled to shed light on issues such as individual interpretation, law, gender equality, human rights, democracy and reform, and interfaith dialogue. This scholarship, they argue, is of great help to today's American Muslims as they attempt to see the possibilities for a true reformation of Islam in the Western context.

While the predominant interpretation of Islam before 9/11 sought to ground the American experience in terms of the cultures from which immigrants came, traditional Islam was, in a very real sense, simply transplanted into American soil. Efforts after 9/11 to affirm the kind of moderate Islam that America was demanding relied primarily on a continuation of that transplantation and grounding. A new phase appears to be in the process of overtaking American Muslims, especially characterized by the activities of the young. Rather than keeping Islam in the background and foregrounding their citizenship as "real" Americans, today's young Muslims are taking charge of their own identities in the effort to create a distinct American Muslim culture. This change involves ingenuity in a great range of fields, including art and architecture, music, films, novels, and new forms of media. The effort often involves the appropriation of existing American cultural practices and making them Islamic. The Muslim young people of today are trying to validate their experience as truly American, reclaiming the right to practice their faith as they understand it.

In the process, young Muslims have been at the forefront of Internet innovation in America. Nadia Khan writes about the age of new media and how it has been used by American Muslim activists to change the discourse about Islam. The Internet is now used by American Muslim religious leaders and institutions as well as by individuals seeking to learn and talk about the religion. A multitude of websites give Muslims access to everything from instruction on how to home-school children to purchasing Islamically inspired clothing. Khan emphasizes the way in which the Internet connects Americans with Muslims around the world, and serves as a critical tool in the efforts of Muslims to emphasize their identity as law-abiding American citizens.

Nowhere are the interests of young Americans in creating a truly Islamic American culture more evident than in various manifestations of the arts, including music, film, novel and poetry writing, architecture, and even Islamic dress. Muslims appropriate existing American practices and make them Islamic by style and interpretation. Muslim youth want to reclaim their right to individuality and identity as guaranteed by the American Constitution. Muslim authors increasingly write for a general American audience and not simply for other Muslims. Biographies and memoirs, poetry, novels, and plays attempt to counter, with the voice of reason, the negative portrayals of Islam that have come from American commentators particularly since 9/11.

Munir Jiwa reflects on his own ethnographic fieldwork among urban Muslims, considering artistic practices and identity in various contexts and looking at the distinctions between religious and secular Muslim art. He describes the work of a series of American Muslim artists, providing insight into the processes of art making and creative expression so as to help the reader appreciate the diversity of commitment and artistic practice, both aesthetic and theological. Taking the discussion of Muslim art in the United States into the realm of architecture, Akel Kahera examines the taxonomy of images that define the American mosque. He considers the problems attendant on various kinds of ideologies of style, providing case studies of four prominent mosques in the United States to illustrate how these styles are represented.

In some cases young Muslims have attempted to engage American society by writing and directing film as a form of Islamic media. Through it they can articulate new ideas and interpretations of what it means to live as Muslim in America. Hussein Rashid considers the history of the American film industry and the ways in which it has portrayed Muslims. He then examines some of the means by which Muslims are using film to define who they are, concluding that film can be used as an important medium in establishing Muslims in the American national narrative. Film allows for an examination of what it means to belong in America and how Muslims can be integrated into the American story.

One of the ways in which Muslims have been most visible on the American scene is through the range of styles of clothing that they adopt, especially women. Regardless of whether they are influenced by clothing style and legislation in cultures elsewhere, American Muslim women in general, and African American women in particular, have clearly been at the forefront of defining what they consider to be both attractive and appropriate in terms of dress. They have developed very creative ways to dress within their understanding of the boundaries of Islamic modesty, creating new styles such as a combination of American jeans with Islamic headdress or flowing top. Rabia Kamal ties the growing interest in Islamic dress and fashion to various diasporic trends, Muslim women's exposure in the media, and changes in global politics and economy. She considers the many factors that have helped American Muslim women (and men) determine what is appropriate to wear and chronicles the development of a growing Islamic fashion industry.

The story of Islam in America, then, is one of recurrent attempts on the part of Muslims to find their place as legitimate members of the extremely diverse American public. As Muslims wonder whether they will be able to uphold whatever elements of the faith they choose to, if any, they face the reality that the *shari'a* is increasingly demonized by much of conservative American society, with some states explicitly banning it. Such activity is as an expression of the wide-ranging Islamophobia that does not appear to be disappearing. Muslims today are trying to make sure that American society is open to Muslim participation and incorporation *as Muslims*, and not simply as citizens who happen to be Muslims.

One of the questions often raised by Americans, particularly as events around the world continue to underscore the fact that certain elements of global Islam appear to promote violence, is the relationship between American Muslims and global Islam. Essays throughout the volume make reference to this connection in a variety of ways. In the final essay, Peter Mandaville helps readers better understand the interplay between Muslims living in the United States and the Islamic world at large. He argues that the very diversity of the Islam practiced and advocated in most of the cultures of the world makes it very difficult to even talk about what is meant by "global Islam." Nonetheless it is true that many American Muslims today are either aware of, or have some engagement with, Muslim groups and organizations outside the United States. As this volume has suggested, nearly every major global community or movement that has originated in the Muslim-majority world finds representation in America. Increasingly, what Mandaville calls "interlinked discursive spaces" such as the Internet, social media, and satellite television allow for Muslims of a range of ethno-national backgrounds and theological orientations to come together to debate the meaning of Islam and the future of their faith in the American context.

This handbook is being published at a unique time in American history. The United States is still recovering from the shock of 9/11, when 3,000 Americans died because of an attack by Muslim extremists, in the meantime trying to extricate itself from two wars on two Muslim nations: Iraq and Afghanistan. These are troubling times for those who share the faith of the perpetrators of the attack. American Muslims remember the treatment of the Germans during World War I, the Japanese during World War II, and those suspected of being Communists during the Cold War, and they fear for their own future. The American government is attempting to strike a balance between security. on the one hand. and, on the other, America's commitment to freedom of religion and the promise made to citizens of all faiths that they will be able to thrive under the Constitution that is the very foundation of America.

The handbook illustrates how much the Muslim community has been able to achieve in the United States. It also reveals its growing pains, the shock to its very foundations caused by the events of 9/11 and the efforts of young American-born Muslims to maintain their commitment to the American values of freedom of religion and speech as well as to social justice and service to the larger community. The Muslims of America are very much in flux as they adjust to the reality of Islamophobia at the same time that they try out new ways in which to understand and express themselves. Immigrant and African American Muslims have struggled with their sense of belonging in America very differently, but today are beginning to come together more often as they affirm their religious identity in a secular culture. Despite their struggles Muslims continue to believe in the American commitment to justice, and hope for a future in which they will be fully accepted and incorporated into the social fabric of the country of which they are a growing body of citizens.

PART I

FORMATION OF THE MUSLIM COMMUNITY IN NORTH AMERICA

CHAPTER 1

....

THE FIRST
STIRRINGS OF
ISLAM IN AMERICA

....

SYLVIANE A. DIOUF

Islam and Muslims have had a continuous presence in the United States from the time of the first thirteen colonies until the present. There is probably no one period in the country's history when Muslims have not been part of its fabric. But the manifestations and interpretations of the religion have been quite diverse, as have the various stories of its followers.

The first Muslims came—under force—to the United States from West Africa, and for more than 200 years left numerous traces of their sojourn here. Their presence is attested by their own writings, their portraits, Arabic vocabulary in the Gullah language of the Sea Islands, slaveholders' books, various correspondence, memoirs, newspapers advertisments for runaways, and abolitionist literature. Their absence from the American historical narrative, of course, would have been perplexing, since the areas from which they came were the first to be Islamized and also the first to be victimized by the transatlantic slave trade. Africans south of the Sahara had been familiar with Sunni Islam since the eighth century through their contacts with Berbers and Arabs from the north, with whom they traded gold, salt, horses, and captives. But Islam really started to take hold after around 1010, when two rulers—Wardjabi, who transformed the kingdom of Tekrur in northern Senegal into an Islamic state, and Jaa Kosoy of Gao, Mali—were converted to the faith.[1] Within a few decades Islam, which was spread by indigenous traders, clerics, and rulers, had become the religion of a sizable minority from Senegal to Lake Chad, and it reached northern Nigeria in the fourteenth century.

The Portuguese, the first Europeans to sail down the West African coast in 1444, discovered that Islam was already firmly rooted in Senegal and Gambia. A century later Ahmed Baba (1556–1627), a well-known scholar and jurist from Timbuktu, ruled that people from Bornu and Kano (Nigeria) and Songhay and Mali should not be enslaved because they were Muslims. "As for the Djilfos [Wolof from Senegal] they are Muslims according to what we have learnt," he wrote, "this has been proved; there are among them *tolba* and *fuqaha* and people who know the Qur'an by heart."[2] In 1606, a hundred years after the start of the slave trade to the West, Jesuit Father Barreira could only note with frustration that the Fulani, the Wolof, the Mandinka, and others followed "the sect of Mahomet."[3]

MUSLIMS IN THE TRANSATLANTIC SLAVE TRADE

Islamic law did not allow the enslavement of Muslims for crimes and misdemeanors, contrary to what occurred in other societies. This particularity eliminated from the international slave trade Muslim debtors, offenders, and criminals. As a result, those deported to the New World were generally prisoners of war. These wars were sometimes religious in nature, as was the case with a number of jihads that changed the sociopolitical-religious landscape of Senegambia, Guinea, and Nigeria in the eighteenth and early nineteenth centuries by establishing Muslim theocracies. Others were political and/or economic wars, dynastic conflicts, and wars and raids whose objectives were to round up captives for the slave trade across the Sahara and the Atlantic Ocean.

Other Muslims were victims of kidnappings. They were abducted by bandits, soldiers, and sometimes people looking for someone to sell or exchange for the freedom of their loved ones held in the slave pens on the coast. Muslims were particularly vulnerable because of their occupations as long-distance traders, pilgrims, itinerant teachers and religious leaders, or students and teachers en route to reputed centers of Islamic higher learning or to coastal towns to buy supplies for their schools. In 1731 Ayuba Suleyman Diallo (known in the West as Job ben Solomon) from Senegal was kidnapped and sold at a British post by the Gambia River, where he had gone to buy paper and sell slaves. He landed in Annapolis, Maryland.[4] Salih Bilali from Mali was about fourteen years of age when he was seized, and he remained enslaved for fifty-nine years in Georgia. Lamine Kebe of Futa Jallon in Guinea was abducted while on a trip to buy paper for his students. He spent the next thirty years in the American South.[5] As was true in West Africa (and subsequently among Africans in the New World), many Muslims were Sufis and followed the *Qadiriyya tariqa*, which inspired jihad throughout the region from Senegal to Nigeria.

The latest scholarship on the origins of the Africans deported to the Americas puts the total number at 12.5 millions of whom 10.7 million survived the Middle

Passage.[6] Half came from West Central Africa (Angola and Congo), where Islam was unknown. About 400,000 Africans (4 percent of the total) entered the British mainland. Among them were an estimated 92,280 (or 23.8 percent), both men and women, from West Central Africa. People from Senegambia, the most heavily Muslim area of West Africa, were almost as numerous, 91,600, or 23.6 percent, although of course not all Senegambians were Muslims. Besides them, Muslims from Guinea, Sierra Leone, Northern Côte d'Ivoire, and Ghana as well as Nigeria were also present in North America. Thus based on the high representation of Senegambians and additional numbers from other regions, it appears that the percentage of Muslims was higher in North America than anywhere else in the Western Hemisphere, although their total numbers were greater in Brazil.

Maintaining Islam in America

To arrive, enslaved, in a foreign land as a Muslim is one thing, but to maintain one's faith in the face of daunting obstacles is quite another. However, studies have shown that Islam continued to be practiced on farms and plantations. Its manifestations were varied. The first visible indicator of the Africans' continued identity as Muslims was their appearance. Some were able to circumvent the degrading and uniform slave dress code by adding accessories indicative of their religion. On the Sea Islands, some women wore white veils, as their descendants and others attested in the 1930s.[7] Bilali Mohamed—a Fulani from Timbo in Guinea's Futa Jallon region—the patriarch of Sapelo Island, wore a fez, and other men wore white turbans. Omar ibn Said was photographed with a skullcap and was also known to wear a white turban. Yarrow Mamout, enslaved in Maryland, was painted by Charles Peale in 1819 very much covered and wearing a bonnet typical of African Muslims. Mamout, who had freed himself, not only retained his name but used to pray in public and sing praises to God in the street.[8] When Diallo's portrait was painted in London in 1733, he was immortalized in a white turban and a white *boubou* (robe). Although he wore European clothes at that time, he had insisted on being painted in that manner and had to describe these Islamic garments to the artist.[9]

While they had no say about their diet, it has been recorded that some Muslims refused to eat pork, as was the case with Diallo. Nero, in South Carolina, had earned the right to get beef instead of pork.[10] In contrast, a Muslim from Mali enslaved in Mississippi lamented the fact that he had to eat the forbidden meat but stressed he never drank alcohol.[11] When the runaway Diallo was interrogated after his capture, he refused the wine offered to him. Ibrahima abd al Rahman did not drink alcohol either, and Yarrow Mamout used to say, "it is not good to eat Hog—& drink whiskey is very bad."[12] To retain a particular dress and continue to adhere to a specific diet may appear trivial, but those were difficult traditions to maintain precisely because they were visible and were the domains of the slaveholders, who distributed clothes and rations.

Praying was an easier endeavor, as one could do it in secret or in the intimacy of a home. Yet Yarrow Mamout, for example, was known to pray in the street. The Muslims prayed and had what was required to do so properly, as was evident in the case of Bilali Mohamed and his family. One of his descendants mentioned that he and his wife as well as a man named Israel had little mats to pray on.[13] Besides the rug, an indispensable item of the Islamic prayer is the *tasbih*. Resembling a rosary, it is made of round beads and has an elongated bead in lieu of a cross. Katie Brown, interviewed by the Works Progress Administration in the 1930s, remembered that Bilali Mohamed, her great-grandfather, had one: "Duh beads is on a long string. Bilali he pull bead an he say, 'Belambi, Hakabara, Mahamadu.'" Shadrach Hall mentioned that his grandmother Hester, a daughter of Bilali, as well as other Muslims would "sho pray on duh bead. Dey weah duh string uh beads on duh wais. Sometime duh string on duh neck."[14]

Muslim men and women further succeeded in respecting one of the most con-straining Qur'anic commandments: the fast, or *sawm*. The Fourth Pillar of Islam is meant to remind the believer of the hard lot of the poor and of the compassion of God, who gives people their sustenance. It is also intended to enhance self-discipline. The Muslim fast lasts twenty-nine or thirty days, during which one may not eat or drink between sunup and sundown. Enslaved people were, as a rule, underfed and overworked. These extremely brutal conditions notwithstanding, some Muslims fasted. Salih Bilali of Saint Simons Island was one of them. According to planter James Hamilton Couper, he was "a strict Mahometan; [he] abstains from spirituous liquors, and keeps the various fasts, particularly that of the Rhamadan."[15] Bilali Mohamed and his large family also fasted, and Ayuba Suleyman Diallo's "religious abstinence" was noted by Thomas Bluett, his biographer. Omar ibn Said was described as a "staunch Mohammedan, and the first year at least kept the fast of Rhamadan with all great strictness."[16]

While paying a tax (*zakah*) is the Third Pillar of Islam, freewill offerings are not mandatory but are strongly recommended. One particular tradition, widespread in the Sea Islands, reveals that Muslim women remained faithful to their religion's admonitions and one of its African gendered expressions. They made rice cakes and gave them to the children on important occasions.[17] The word associated with them was *saraka*, and the children grew up thinking that saraka was the "African" name of rice cakes. The same rice cakes are the charity traditionally offered by West African women on Fridays. It is a *sadaqa* (the Arabic has been transformed into saraka, *sarakh*, and *saraa* in West Africa), a freewill offering consisting of anything that the believer wishes to offer. It is recommended that the gift be accompanied by a sup-plication to God; therefore in West Africa—and on the Sea Islands—as women hand out the cakes, they say it is a sadaqa. Despite the harsh conditions slavery imposed on them, Muslim women continued the Islamic tradition of sadaqa, which was true to the authentic spirit of freewill offering, since it is stated that the best sadaqa is the one given by a person who owns little. A Gullah song carried the memory of the saraka into the twentieth century:

> Rice cake, rice cake
> Sweet me so
> Rice cake sweet me to my heart.[18]

It is, fittingly, a children's song, since they were the beneficiaries of the Muslim women's charity.

LITERACY

The Muslims shared a characteristic that distinguished them from most of their enslaved companions and from a good percentage of white people as well: literacy. Those who had started their Qur'anic education at age seven and had been deported in their mid-twenties could have been through several years of schooling. Among them were Qur'anic teachers like Lamine Kebe, Omar ibn Said, and Ayuba Suleyman Diallo.

Diallo owed his freedom to his literacy. Several months after he arrived in Maryland, he wrote a letter in Arabic to his father asking him to arrange for his release. He gave it to a slave dealer with instructions to forward it to the slave captain who had brought him over. It ended up in London with James Oglethorpe, the deputy governor of the Royal African Company, who had it translated and set out to help free the young father of four. In June 1732, after nineteen months of servitude, Diallo left Maryland. Once in London, he wrote three copies of the Qur'an by rote before sailing back to Senegal.[19]

Ibrahima abd al Rahman, a son of the ruler of the theocracy of Futa Jallon in Guinea and a prisoner of war enslaved in Mississippi, wrote a letter in Arabic that was sent to the sultan of Morocco, who subsequently inquired about the fate of his coreligionist. A US senator, a consul, Secretary of State Henry Clay, and President John Quincy Adams were all involved in his release following this fateful letter.

As a number of their enslaved coreligionists did in the rest of the Western Hemisphere, some men in the United States wrote manuscripts in Arabic. Bilali Mohamed produced a thirteen-page document in Arabic and gave the skin-covered manuscript to author Francis Robert Goulding. The text was an excerpt from a tenth-century *Risala* (message), written by the Tunisian Abu Zayd al Qairawani, which was part of the curriculum of higher studies in West Africa. Bilali's manuscript includes the title page, passages of the introduction, and excerpts of chapters dealing with ablutions and the call to prayer.[20]

Omar ibn Said produced several manuscripts, but his main work was his 1831 autobiography, in which he subtly denounced his continued enslavement. The first sentences come from *surat al-Mulk*: "Blessed be He whose hand is the *mulk* and who has power over all things. He created death and life that He might put you to the proof and find out which of you had the best work: He is the most Mighty, the Forgiving One" (67: 1–2). As a translation by Ala Alryyes has shown, "The noun al-mulk comes from the tripartite Arabic root *malaka*, meaning both 'to own' and 'to have dominion.' The title of the *surah* is, therefore, the perfect allusion to slavery."[21] with a passage describing hell for those who were warned but did not believe (67: 7–10). Omar depicted himself as the man who brought the message of Islam, for which he suffered a great deal, and his unbelieving owners as those who would in turn suffer judgment.

RELATIONS WITH NON-MUSLIMS

As they tried to maintain a religious and cultural continuity, Muslims interacted with non-Muslims. Information about the relationship between them shows what has sometimes been labeled as a divide between the two groups. But the description of an annual celebration that took place in the Sea Islands during slavery evidences not so much a divide as mutual respect among the participants regarding their different religious ways within a common endeavor, which was meant to reinforce the cohesion of the community.[22] The festivity marked harvest time and its function was to "thank for the crops." Formerly enslaved men and women mentioned to the Works Progress Administration that the festivity included prayers and dance and lasted all night. Although everyone agreed on this framework, some variations can be detected in the recollections of the respondents.

Rachel Anderson, whose great-grandmother was a Muslim, remembered that people did the "shout"—a counterclockwise religious "dance"—all night, and at sunrise they prayed and bowed low to the sun. Another descendant of Muslims, Rosa Grant, said that they shouted all night and at sunup sang and prayed. Harvest time for the Muslims appears to have meant chanting all night, a widespread Sufi tradition, ending with a prayer at sunrise, as is customary. People who were not associated with Islam gave a different version of the feast. Nero Jones of Sapelo Island remembered that they prayed and sang all night, and when the sun rose, they got out and danced. Hettie Campbell and Henry Williams of Saint Mary's both said that the people shouted and sang all night and started to dance when the sun rose. Catherine Wing stated that they went to church with their first crop, prayed, and danced.[23]

The three versions of the same event attest that even though the community as a whole commemorated harvest time, each group did so in its own way. The Christians went to church, the followers of traditional African religions celebrated with prayers and dances at daybreak, and the Muslims chanted and prayed to the east at sunrise. Despite differences in the celebrations, all shouted, a rite that may have been created by the Muslims and borrowed by the others. It has been suggested that the southern "shout" was a re-creation of the *sha'wt*, the counterclockwise circumambulation of the Kaaba during the *hajj* or pilgrimage to Mecca, the Fifth Pillar of Islam.[24]

THE LAST AFRICAN MUSLIMS

The last formerly enslaved African Muslims died out in the 1880s–1890s, but the illegal slave trade—beginning after January 1, 1808—secretly introduced thousands of West Central Africans as well as men and women from West Africa. The *Clotilda*, the last documented slave ship, landed in July 1860 in Alabama. At least one Muslim, Zuma (from *al-Jumaa*, or "Friday" in Arabic), a Nupe from northern Benin, was on board. She died between the late 1910s and 1922. Thus there were African Muslims in the country at least until the end of the nineteenth century and probably a handful afterwards. Yet there is no indication that their children, let alone their grandchildren, followed their religion. Notwithstanding their forefathers' and foremothers' visible display of religiosity, the Muslims' descendants interviewed in the 1930s in the Sea Islands did not seem to know anything about Islam, although they recalled their relatives and others having books (Qur'ans), prayer mats, prayer beads, turbans, and veils. They mentioned that their grandparents prayed at sunrise and sunset, but some linked their prayers to a worship of the sun and the moon.[25]

Even in Brazil, where Muslim communities were large and well organized, the transmission of Islam to a country-born generation did not succeed. One obstacle was the low number of Muslim women. Men often had non-Muslim spouses and—owing to the reality of slavery, which separated families through sales and also because couples often resided on different farms and plantations—had much less impact on their children than their mothers did. After emancipation, churches launched successful campaigns to convert people who up to then had had little Christian instruction. In this context, to be a Muslim was to singularize oneself and also to be linked with what people saw as a "primitive" African religion.

THE MUSLIMS' LEGACY

Despite having virtually disappeared as a religion, Islam was a central part of the West Africans' legacy. But it is in music that the Islamic influence on American culture has been the strongest. The music of the African Muslims is noticeably different from the musical styles carried over by the people of West Central Africa and the non-Muslim areas of West Africa, who favor rapid polyrhythmic drumming, call and response, group singing, and short melodic lines. In contrast, the typical song of Islamic West Africa is a solo that blues expert Alan Lomax has called a "high lonesome complaint."[26] It derives from the recitation of the Qur'an and the call to prayer, with vibrato, pauses, elongation of the notes, humming, and melisma (singing a syllable over several notes). In North America, that musical style, by chance, was able to survive better than the music of the more numerous non-Muslims. The reason can be found in the 1739 revolt led by people from the kingdom of Kongo at Stono, in South Carolina. The insurrectionists marched with drums beating to rally and galvanize their troops. Thereafter, drumming was forbidden by law in the South, which was never the case in French and Spanish colonies or in the British Caribbean. Thus, in America, contrary to what happened in the rest of the Western Hemisphere, Muslims who had not relied primarily on drumming and collective singing and dancing but had played a variety of string instruments and sung solo were able to maintain and continue developing their musical traditions openly, while West Central Africans could not. The latter "covered" their drumming by marking rhythms on their bodies by slapping their arms, thighs, and legs.

One style that evolved on the plantations and can be traced to West African traditions is the field holler, always sung solo. It progressively replaced the work song and became a constituent of the blues. Frederick Law Olmsted, traveling through South Carolina in 1853, heard a man raise a "long, loud, musical shout, rising and falling and breaking into falsetto, his voice ringing through the woods in the clear, frosty night air, like a bugle call."[27] What Olmsted described matches almost exactly the *adhan*, the Muslim call to prayer. When the adhan sung by a West African muezzin is juxtaposed with the "Levee Camp Holler" recorded by Alan Lomax in a Mississippi penitentiary in the 1930s, the similarities are particularly striking.[28] But this song is not the only one to evoke the adhan. Other hollers and early blues have the same ornamented and elongated notes, wavy intonations, pauses, and melisma. Horace Sprott, a singer born in 1890 in Alabama, used those techniques and explained that this was the way in which the elders—former slaves—sang. Musicologists have also noted that blues guitarists and banjo players use their instruments in the same manner as West African Muslim musicians do the *kora* (a sort of harp) and the many types of lutes derived from North African instruments.

With time, Africans from non-Muslim areas and people born in the United States became familiar with and used the styles brought by the Muslims, adding their own marks. Still, as musicologist and blues expert Gerhard Kubik emphasizes, "most of the blues tradition in the rural areas of Mississippi has prevailed as a recognizable extension in the New World of a west central Sudanic style cluster."[29]

ISLAM IN THE EARLY TWENTIETH CENTURY

As the last West African Muslims brought by the transatlantic slave trade died out, new movements that presented themselves as Islamic appeared in northern cities during the Great Migration (1916–1930.) The first African American to launch an indigenous Islamic movement was Timothy Drew, born in 1886 in North Carolina. Taking the name Noble Drew Ali, he started the Canaanite Temple in Newark, New Jersey, in 1913, before founding the Moorish Holy Temple of Science in Chicago in 1925. It became the Moorish Science Temple of America (MSTA) three years later. His followers were mostly recent southern immigrants to Philadelphia, Pittsburgh, Detroit, and Chicago. Ali, who called himself a prophet, produced a sixty-page "Holy Koran" in 1927, which mixed some notions of Islam, Christianity, and freemasonry. It proclaimed that African Americans belonged to the Asiatic race and were part of the Moorish nation, whose original religion was Islam. Ali denounced the terminology "Negro," calling blacks "so-called Negroes." His teachings essentially formed the basis of a black nationalist movement of the oppressed that exalted black pride by actually negating blackness in favor of an Asiatic/Moorish identity. In lieu of what they considered slave names, his disciples adopted surnames such as Bey and El. Besides providing new identities to its followers as heirs to a glorious past and a nonblack "race," the MSTA promoted entrepreneurship as a way toward social and financial independence. Ali died in 1929, in unclear circumstances, as his movement was rife with internal strife, which had led to the killing of his business manager.

Another incarnation of Islam among African Americans was the Ahmadiyya Movement in Islam, founded in India (now Pakistan) by Mirza Ghulam Ahmad in 1889. Ahmad presented himself as a renewer of Islam, the Messiah and Mahdi all in one, which put his movement in opposition to most Muslims, who consider Muhammad the last prophet. The Ahmadiyya sent missionaries to the United States in 1920. Under the leadership of Mufti Muhammad Sadiq, it established its headquarters in Chicago and founded the first Islamic journal in the country, *The Moslem Sunrise*. Although the movement was multiracial, given the climate of racism that Sadiq encountered and his disappointment with the negative reception he had received from the white population, the Ahmadiyya's strongest proselytizing efforts were directed toward African Americans in Detroit and Chicago. They were largely represented among the 1,025 converts registered between 1921 and 1925, at a time when the MSTA was very active in the community and also, a few years later, the Nation of Islam.[30]

The Ahmadiyya made converts in what was the largest black secular organization in the country, Marcus Garvey's Universal Negro Improvement Association. Both movements offered an internationalist outlook, pan-Africanist for the latter and anticolonialist and nonwhite for both. Although deemed quasi heretical by some in the Muslim world, the Ahmadiyya introduced a more mainstream Islam to African Americans by providing Qur'ans and other Islamic literature in English. But starting in the 1950s, it lost ground in the black community. According to Aminah McCloud, African Americans came to resent their lack of upward mobility and the little consideration given to their particular history and culture. This realization led to disaffection to the benefit of homegrown Islamic movements that addressed the believers' concerns about racism, discrimination, and identity.[31] For Richard Brent Turner, the split came about because some African Americans did not want to study the religion seriously or were disenchanted with the Ahmadiyya's multiracial agenda, while some turned to Sunni Islam in an effort "to Arabize their identities to escape the stigma of their blackness. Others went to the Nation of Islam because they were attracted to its nationalist agenda."[32]

Notwithstanding its decline, the Ahmadiyya had a significant influence on the early African American Islamic landscape as well as on the founder of the Nation of Islam, known variously as Farad Mohammed, F. Mohammed Ali, Wallace D. Fard, Wally Farad, and W. D. Fard. His origin has remained a mystery. He claimed to have come from Saudi Arabia, but some of his followers believed he was a Syrian, a Palestinian, an Iranian, a Jamaican, or a Turk. The FBI suspected that he had arrived from New Zealand in 1913. Wallace Dodd Ford, as his real name is believed to have been, first settled in Portland, Oregon. After serving three years in San Quentin Prison for drug dealing, he first made his appearance in the black community of Detroit in 1930 as a silk peddler. In this city of strong immigration from Mississippi, Alabama, and Tennessee, he became known as Wallace D. Fard and founded the "Lost-Found Nation of Islam in the Wilderness of North America." Fard produced manuals to explain his religious teachings, *The Secret Ritual of the Nation of Islam* and *Teaching for the Lost-Found Nation of Islam in a Mathematical Way*. Following several arrests, he moved to Chicago in 1933, was briefly jailed there, and returned to Detroit, from whence he disappeared in 1934. Rumors circulated as to his whereabouts, some believing that he had been killed by the police or by his second in command, Elijah Muhammad. The Nation of Islam's official version was that he had gone back to Mecca.

Fard's teachings were in some points similar to Noble Drew Ali's. He too rejected the label "Negro," affirming that African Americans were Asiatics and that their true religion, before they arrived in America, was Islam. He asserted that whites were fundamentally evil, whereas Asiatics were good. Such views bolstered self-confidence and self-esteem among those converts who, hoping for the Promised Land, had left the Jim Crow South of rigid segregation and racial violence and found themselves discriminated against and looked down upon in the North as well. Fard's preaching of racial separation from whites gave his followers a sense of free will in defining the social landscape rather than being subjugated by it. *They* made the decision to keep themselves apart.

After Fard's disappearance, Elijah Muhammad became the leader of the NOI. A southern migrant, he was born Elijah Poole in 1897 in Sandersville, Georgia, the son of William Poole, a Baptist preacher. Poole, Clara Evans, his wife, and their children migrated to Detroit in 1923. He worked at a number of jobs until the Great Depression of 1929 when, like millions of others, he became unemployed. Poole met Fard in 1931, converted, and was soon his trusted second.

THE NATION OF ISLAM UNDER
ELIJAH MUHAMMAD

Under Elijah Muhammad's leadership, the NOI encouraged self-reliance and self-sufficiency, encouraging its followers to open stores, restaurants, and other small businesses. It advocated pride, self-assurance, economic empowerment through entrepreneurship, and the creation of a separate state for black people, in the United States or elsewhere. As the people of the MTSA did, its followers shed what they referred to as their slave names; adopting X as their surnames. However, the religious teachings in which the NOI couched its philosophy were in contradiction with the faith it claimed. Among other heresies, The Honorable Elijah Muhammad, as he was called, asserted that Fard was God and he was his prophet. He also created a foundational myth alien to Islam. It alleged that earth was originally peopled by blacks who lived in Mecca and ruled the world until Yakub, a black scientist under God's authority, transformed a few selected blacks through the process of "grafting" into the white man. The process took 600 years and culminated 6,000 years ago with the appearance of blue-eyed whites who came to dominate the world and enslave blacks. This kind of racialization of the religion was foreign to the basic precepts of Islam.

Over the years the NOI gained a significant following, opened up dozens of temples or mosques; it also started schools in forty-seven cities. The movement was highly visible in the prison system. It consolidated its business enterprises; ran a farm; acquired land in Alabama, Georgia, and Michigan; and had interest in a bank. It had become a fixture of the black social scene and was a strong influence on black popular culture.

The movement was deeply rooted in the particular history of African Americans and revolved entirely around its leader's teachings. As Edward Curtis IV has summed up, "by offering his own interpretations of Islam, [Muhammad] effectively ended any possible debate and asserted his own prophetic authority. He embraced a particularistic form of Islam that he could control."[33] That leadership, these specific interpretations, and the NOI's noninvolvement in politics were contested in the 1960s, particularly by Malcolm X (Malcolm Little), who converted while in prison in 1952. Malcolm X had become a minister of Temple 7 in New York in 1954 and had worked tirelessly to expand the NOI's reach. Suspended from the organization in December 1963, he eventually founded the Muslim Mosque, Inc., changed his name to El-Hajj Malik El-Shabazz after his pilgrimage to Mecca in 1964, and founded the secular Organization of Afro-American Unity to rally non-Muslim African Americans around his program. The NOI, as well as the FBI, were alleged to be involved in his assassination on February 21, 1965. Despite these suspicions and his avowed moral turpitude, Elijah Muhammad remained in control of the NOI until his death on February 25, 1975.

The Early African American Islamic Experience

Scholars have called the MSTA and NOI proto-Islamic movements, but evidently, since these movements did not precede Islam, it is more correct to refer to them as proto-American Islamic movements, not only for the sake of historical accuracy but also because they were, more than Islamic, American. In their quest to inscribe African Americans' history into the history of Islam, leaders dispensed to their follow-ers a number of historical and religious myths and some outright fallacies. Contrary to their key assertion, Islam was evidently not the Africans' original faith. Such a belief presumed that they did not have any religion before the seventh century. Ironically, that very claim was one of the bases upon which the Catholic Church had justified the slave trade. Furthermore and paradoxically, none of these movements mentioned the presence in the United States of the deported West African Muslims who had intro-duced and practiced Islam in the New World for centuries. The only historical link that could thus be made between Muslim African Americans in the twentieth century and Africans as Muslims in the centuries before was ignored by both the MSTA and NOI. From a religious point of view, their extreme claims about their leaders and their prophets were fundamentally opposed to the most basic Islamic creed. They were, by definition, blasphemous, committing what in Islam is an unforgivable sin.

But these movements were nonetheless successful insofar as they responded to the needs of African Americans in the present as well as their aspirations for the future. They connected them to a real but also an imagined past and offered them an identity not merely attached to slavery and discrimination but to a glorious history preceding slavery. According to Sherman Jackson, who notes that problems compa-rable to these movements' "omissions and outright blasphemies" were also present in the early history of the Muslim world, by being rooted in the history and religion of the black community, "Their ignorance and excesses notwithstanding, through their marriage of 'Islam' with Black religion, men like Noble Drew Ali and the Honorable Elijah Muhammad succeeded in appropriating Islam for Blackamericans and in so doing created a psychological space through which millions of Blackamericans would subsequently enter the religion."[34]

What the MSTA and NOI succeeded in doing was to cobble together out of vari-ous secular and religious strands new African American religious movements that had little to do with orthodox Islam but, like it, could be used as conduits to mental emancipation, self-determination, and social justice.

Notes

1. Nehemia Levtzion, "Islam in the Bilad al-sudan to 1800," in *The History of Islam in Africa*, ed. Nehemia Levtzion and Randall L. Pouwels (Athens: Ohio University Press, 2000), 63–85.

2. René Luc Moreau, *Africains musulmans* (Paris: Présence Africaine, 1982), 127–129.

3. Nize Isabel de Moraes, *A la découverte de la Petite Côte au XVIIe siècle* (Dakar: Université Cheikh Anta Diop, 1995), vol. 1, 111–119.

4. Thomas Bluett, *Some Memoirs of the Life of Job, the Son of Solomon, the High Priest of Boonda in Africa* (London: Richard Ford, 1736).

5. Theodore Dwight, "Condition and Character of Negroes in Africa," in *The People of Africa: A Series of Papers on Their Character, Condition, and Future Prospects*, ed. Henry Schieffelin (New York: A.D.F. Randolph, 1871), 52–53.

6. *The Trans-Atlantic Slave Trade Database*. Available at: www.slavevoyages.org (accessed 4/20/2013)

7. Works Progress Administration. *Drums and Shadows: Survival Studies among the Georgia Coastal Negroes* (Athens: University of Georgia Press, 1986), 162.

8. Charles Wilson Peale's *Diary* in Allan D. Austin, *African Muslims in Antebellum America: A Sourcebook* (New York: Garland, 1984), 69–70.

9. Bluett, *Some Memoirs of the Life of Job*, 50.

10. Terry Alford, *Prince Among Slaves* (New York: Harcourt Brace Jovanovich, 1977), 59.

11. Edward Teas, "A Trading Trip to Natchez and New Orleans in 1822: Diary of Thomas Teas," *Journal of Southern History* 7 (August 1941): 388.

12. Austin, *African Muslims*, 69–70.

13. Works Progress Administration, *Drums and Shadows*, 38.

14. Ibid.

15. *William Brown Hodgson, Notes on Northern Africa, the Sahara and the Soudan* (New York: Wiley & Putnam, 1844), 69.

16. William Plumer, "Meroh, a Native African," *New York Observer*, January 8, 1863, 1.

17. Sylviane A. Diouf, *Servants of Allah: African Muslims Enslaved in the Americas* (New York: New York University Press, 2013), 92–94.

18. Mason Crum, *Gullah: Negro Life in the Carolina Sea Islands* (1940; reprint, New York: Negro Universities Press, 1968), 265.

19. Bluett, *Some Memoirs of the Life of Job*, 48.

20. Joseph Greenberg, The Decipherment of the 'Ben-Ali Diary': A Preliminary Statement." *Journal of Negro History* 25, 3 (July 1940): 372–375.

21. Ala Alryyes, ed., *A Muslim American Slave: The Life of Omar ibn Said* (Madison: University of Wisconsin Press, 2011), 18.

22. Diouf, *Servants of Allah*, 269–270.

23. Works Progress Administration, *Drums and Shadows*, 141, 165, 174, 187.

24. Lydia Parrish, *Slave Songs of the Georgia Sea Islands* (1942; reprint, Athens: University of Georgia Press, 1992), 54; Lorenzo Dow Turner, *Africanisms in the Gullah Dialect* (1949; reprint, New York: Arno Press/*New York Times*, 1969), 202; Sylviane A. Diouf, *Servants of Allah: African Muslims Enslaved in the Americas* (New York: New York University Press, 1998; 2nd ed., 2013), 96–97.

25. Works Progress Administration, Drums and Shadows, 76,106,141,156,166,179

26. Alan Lomax, *The Land Where the Blues Began* (New York: Bantam/Doubleday, 1993), 233.

27. Frederick Law Olmsted, *The Cotton Kingdom*, vol. 1 (New York: Mason Brothers, 1861), 214.

28. Diouf, *Servants of Allah*, 275.

29. Gerhard Kubik, *Africa and the Blues* (Jackson: University Press of Mississippi, 1999), 203.

30. Richard Brent Turner, *Islam in the African-American Experience* (Bloomington: Indiana University Press, 1997), 124.

31. Aminah B. McCloud, *African American Islam* (New York: Routledge, 1995), 21.

32. Turner, *Islam*, 140.
33. Edward Curtis IV, *Islam in Black America: Identity, Liberation, and Difference in African-American Islamic Thought* (Albany: State University of New York Press, 2002), 84.
34. Sherman Jackson, *Islam and the Blackamerican: Looking toward the Third Resurrection* (New York: Oxford University Press, 2005), 47.

References

Alford, Terry, *Prince Among Slaves*, 2nd ed. (New York: Harcourt Brace Jovanovich, 1977 New York: Oxford University Press, 2007).

Alryyes, Ala, *A Muslim American Slave: The Life of Omar Ibn Said* (Madison: The University of Wisconsin Press, 2011).

Austin, Allan D., *African Muslims in Antebellum America: Transatlantic Stories and Spiritual Struggles* (New York: Routledge, 1997).

——. *African Muslims in Antebellum America: A Sourcebook* (New York: Garland, 1984).

Clegg, Andrew C., *An Original Man: The Life and Times of Elijah Muhammad* (New York: St. Martin's Press, 1997).

Curtis, Edward IV, *Islam in Black America: Identity, Liberation, and Difference in African-American Islamic Thought* (Albany: State University of New York Press, 2002).

Dannin, Robert, *Black Pilgrimage to Islam*, 2nd ed. (New York: Oxford University Press, 2002).

Diouf, Sylviane A., *Servants of Allah: African Muslims Enslaved in the Americas* 2nd ed. (New York: New York University Press, 2013).

Jackson, Sherman, *Islam and the Blackamerican: Looking toward the Third Resurrection* (New York: Oxford University Press, 2005).

McCloud, Aminah B., *African American Islam* (New York: Routledge, 1995).

Turner, Richard Brent, *Islam in the African-American Experience* (Bloomington: Indiana University Press, 1997).

....

CHAPTER 2

MUSLIM IMMIGRATION TO AMERICA

....

RANDA B. SERHAN

THE notion of Muslims in America as a distinguishable or coherent group is a by-product of the September 11, 2001, terrorist attacks. It is a recent historical phenomenon that has been an imposition upon disparate segments of the native and immigrant population. This raises several key questions: Who are American Muslims? How many Muslims live in America? And how does one define a Muslim?

The answers given to each of these questions determine which population or group is being focused on. In other words, it is extremely difficult to speak about Muslims in America without giving one group or one era precedence over another. Therefore much of the scholarship since 2001 has been preoccupied with the racialization of Muslims or assessment of any potential terrorist threat Muslims may pose (Cainkar 2008, Elver 2012, Kohut and Lugo 2011, Naber 2008). These two topics are interrelated, since racialization, through processes of surveillance and suspicion of a particular group, is often an outcome of terror assessment.

Notwithstanding these critical questions, the present chapter takes a different look at the Muslim presence in America—namely, within the framework of incorporation common in the immigration literature. This approach allows for both casting a wider net historically and more contextualization of the role of religion in America.

Prior to delineating the parameters of immigrant incorporation and the role of religious institutions in that process, it is essential to answer the demographic queries posed earlier: Who are the American Muslims? How many are there? And how is a Muslim defined?

The census has not collected data on religious affiliation since 1936,[1] which means that any figures on the number of Muslims in America are necessarily estimates. The current estimates are between 2 and 7 million based on sources ranging from Muslim to nonpartisan and conservative nongovernmental organizations. At the lower end of the scale are figures by the Pew Forum on Religious and Public Life, a nonpartisan polling research center, which sets the number of Muslims in 2010 at 2.6 million, or 0.8 percent of the US population. At the higher end are figures produced by those with more vested interests, namely some Muslim associations and conservative groups (CAIR, 2012; Elver 2012; Johnson 2011). All of these estimates are based on surveys and polling conducted by these various organizations.

The largest three racial/ethnic groups represented among Muslims in America are South Asians, Arabs, and African Americans. At times African Americans are omitted from works on post-9/11 backlash since the targeted groups have comprised anyone who looks "Middle Eastern" (Bakalian and Bozorgmehr 2009, Gotanda 2011, Jamal 2008, Volpp 2002). Prior to 9/11, works on Muslims often conspicuously left out the Moorish Science Temple and the Nation of Islam as being too unorthodox and unrecognized by the wider Muslim community as coreligionists. Finally, a closely related issue is the question of who gets counted; this is a tricky issue for religion because it is a very personal matter. Are people counted by membership, attendance at mosques, by birth, or by place of origin? Interestingly enough, in the case of Muslims in America, it is often deduced by place of origin even when these places may have sent more non-Muslim than Muslim immigrants to the United States (a case in point is the Levant at the turn of the twentieth century).[2] In one account, India is included in this estimate despite the fact that it is not a majority Muslim country and that most of the immigrants at the turn of the century were Sikhs with a few Muslims peppered in (Bakalian and Bozorgmher 2009, Ghanea Bassiri 2010). Numbers conflict greatly, and the further back one goes the more speculative the figures are. Self-identification is lost, for most people considered to be Muslim because of the absence of such a question on the census.

Undoubtedly this is a deeply politicized matter; otherwise there would be little interest in gathering data on the number, location, age, income, belief, and membership of Muslims. It is perhaps safe to say that the general perception was that minority religions, and Islam in particular, did not have the ability to affect the American landscape until 2001, as illustrated by the establishment of the Pew Forum on Religion and Public Life and the extension of the Hartford Institute for Religion Research to include Islam in that same year. In fact, most immigrants continue to be Christian or to convert to Christianity soon after their arrival. For the purposes of this chapter, the category of "Muslim" is used loosely, but with the qualification that self-identification is central. This necessitates the inclusion of the Moorish Science Temple and, more significantly, the Nation of Islam as the earliest organized Muslim groups. By using a more loosely defined category, this chapter intends to compare modes of incorporation at different historical moments. There were six migration flows of Muslims to the United States, both involuntary and voluntary. The estimate for each flow is presented in the Table 2.1 (keeping in mind that records were even more scarce and sporadic during earlier eras than in recent decades).

Table 2.1 Muslim Migration Flows to America

Muslim Migration to America

Period	Estimate	Place of Origin	Sources
Involuntary			
Pre-Columbus/ Columbus	Few dozens on merchant ships	North Africa	Biographies and diaries[a]
Antebellum	Few thousand to tens of thousands on slave ships	West and North Africa	Research on slavery routes, newspaper accounts, diaries[a]
Voluntary			
1870–1914	4,300, mainly men Few thousand, mainly men	Levant (Greater Syria—Lebanon, Syria, Palestine) India, Albania, Ottoman Turks, Eastern Europe	Ethnicity and census data based on place of birth (Majority said to have returned after fall of Ottoman Empire; Indians returned—independence)[b]
1936–1939	250 to ~2,000/year; families	Mandate Palestine	Immigration records[c]
1947–1949	Unknown, women and children	Palestine, Israel, Jordan	Immigration records[d]
World War II–1965	Nonimmigrants, student visas	Diversity of nations, growing number of Iranian Muslims	Immigration records[e]
1965–present	2 to 7 Million	77 national and ethnic groups, numerous denominations	Estimate—place of origin, private organization, national surveys and polling[f]
Converts and those reclaiming Islam (internal shifts)			
Interwar period	Few to tens of thousands African American	Moorish Science Temple, Nation of Islam, Sunnis	Estimates based on membership in temples[g]
WWII–present	Few thousand annually	Women (white) converting after marriage, African American converts	Surveys on religious associations and mosques[h]

[a.] Gomez, M., "Muslims in Early America," *The Journal of Southern History* 60, 4 (1994), 671–710.

[b.] Haddad, Y., *Becoming American?* (Waco, TX: Baylor University Press, 2011); GhaneaBassiri, K., *A History of Islam in America* (New York: Cambridge University Press, 2010).

[c.] Naff, A., *Becoming American.* (Urbana: Southern Illinois University Press, 1985).

[d.] Al-Tahir, A., "The Arab Community in the Chicago Area," unpublished dissertation (Chicago: University of Chicago, 1952); Cainkar, L., *"Palestinian Women in the United States,"* unpublished dissertation (Evanston, IL: Northwestern University, 1988).

[e.] Ghayur, A., "Muslims in the United States: Settlers and Visitors," *Annals of the American Academy of Political Science* 454(1981): 150–163; Haddad, Y., "A Century of Islam in America," *HambardIslamicusXXI*, 4 (1997).

[f.] Johnson, T., "Muslims in the United States," *Council on Foreign Relations* 2011. (online); Moore, K., "Muslims in the United States: Pluralism under Exceptional Circumstances," *Annals of the American Academy of Political and Social Science*, 612 (2007): 116–132; Mohamed, Besheer, "Demographic and Economic Profile of Muslim Americans" (Washington, DC: Pew Research Center, 2012); FBI, "The Nation of Islam: Antiwhite, All-Negro Cult in United States" (Washington, DC: Central Research Section, United States Department of Justice, 2012). Available at http://vault.fbi.gov/Nation%20of%20Islam/Nation%20of%20Islam%20Part%201%20of%203/view

[g.] GhaneaBassiri, K., 2010; Gardell, M., "The Sun of Islam with Rise in the West," in *Muslim Communities in North America*, edited by Y. Haddad, and J. Smith (Albany: State University of New York Press, 1994).

[h.] Bagby, I., "The American Mosque 2011," *Hartford Institute for Religion Research* (2012); Ghayur, A. 1981.

The immigration literature maintains some of the essential arguments about the significance of religion and religious institutions but posits them outside of the primary modes of incorporation (Min 1992, Portes and Rumbaut 2006). The agreed upon social functions of religion are to provide a sense of community, give status, and offer social services (in the American model) (Connor 2011, Min 1992). As important as these functions are, we are told, "religion does not determine by itself any of these contextual elements" (Portes and Rumbaut, 2006, 304). The contextual elements are the three modes of incorporation: *governmental reception, public reaction toward newcomers, and the preexisting community*. As a migration and ethnicity sociologist, I am inclined to focus on the three modes of incorporation and think of religion or, in this case Islam, as a factor to be considered within this framework rather than as an independent variable. This is not to suggest that a particular migration group or flow may not be identified first by its religion, since obviously this has been occurring since the 9/11 backlash. Rather, it is to point out that religiosity (manifest) could be a reaction to discrimination, and its place in immigrants' life cannot be determined a priori.

HISTORICAL OVERVIEW OF MUSLIM MIGRATION TO THE UNITED STATES

Table 2.1 demonstrates two primary precepts: that Muslim migration to the United States has a very long history and that quantifying these disparate populations has been less systematic than speculative.[3] The earliest migrants were brought to the Americas under coercion from North and West Africa on slave ships. It was several decades before voluntary immigrants began to trickle into America from parts of the Ottoman Empire, Eastern Europe, and India. However, among this migration flow the majority were Christian from the Syrian provinces of the Ottoman Empire; much smaller numbers arrived from Albania, Anatolia, Poland, and India (Ghanea Bassiri 2010). After national origin quotas were established in 1924, only a trickle of migrants came from non-European regions. Several hundred Palestinians arrived annually during the Peasant Revolt between 1936 and 1939 (Naff 1985). Thus until World War II, there were few newcomers, and those who were already in the United States began to institutionalize their associations. Also during this period, African American nationalists began to call for the reclaiming of African heritage and culture, including Islam.

At the end of World War II, another migration flow of Palestinians arrived on Americans shores (in small numbers) as a result of the creation of the State of Israel (Al-Tahir 1952). It was only after the 1965 removal of national origin quotas that steadily growing flows of immigrants from predominantly Muslim countries were making the United States their destination and new home. As can be seen in the table, the numbers went from a few hundred thousand in the 1960s to an estimated 2 to 7 million in 2011.

What has this meant for these recent immigrants? How can we assess their level of incorporation and their place in the American polity? For this we must turn to the immigration literature to understand the modes of incorporation for earlier ethnic immigrants. Although religion is not considered one of the major modes of incorporation, it has been treated as a lynchpin for assimilation by some scholar or at the very least a facilitator to incorporation.[4] The theories on the role of religion in American life are discussed in the next section.

It is beyond the scope of this chapter to thoroughly examine each migration flow along the three structural modes of incorporation and how religion served to facilitate or inhibit the acculturation or assimilation of Muslims. Nonetheless a preliminary assessment is attempted in order to provide a broad understanding of the historical place of those individuals whom we are now identifying as Muslim.

ANTEBELLUM AMERICA

As mentioned previously, very little is known about the precise number of Muslims among the involuntary migrants who came during slavery. The very circumstance that brought the 400,000 to 523,000 Africans to America alludes to their reception and the public reaction to them (Ghanea Bassiri, 2010). Since they were the first Africans to be shipped to America, the third mode of incorporation is moot. It has been abundantly documented that slaves were denied their humanity and stripped of their culture, heritage, and religion (Ghayur 1981, Gomez 1994). Whatever religion the different groups practiced at the time was dismissed summarily. Their histories were obliterated to the point where scholars have had to trace the slave ship trade routes to try to situate their regions of origin, tribal affiliations, and religion. One widely cited scholar, Michael Gomez, studied both the spread of Islam in Africa from the fifteenth through nineteenth centuries and the source regions of those captured and brought to the Americas (1994). According to his estimates, there were six primary regions in West and North Africa from which most of the original African Americans came, and 50 percent of these areas had Muslims as minority populations. Gomez concluded that thousands or tens of thousand of Muslims were on those ships (1994). This point becomes significant subsequently as African Americans try to reconstruct their histories.

1870–1914 MIGRATION FLOW

Voluntary migration from provinces of the Ottoman Empire, India, and eastern Europe began in the late nineteenth century. They were initially received as "Turks," then as "Asians," and eventually, for those from the Levant (Syria, Lebanon, and Palestine), as "whites or Caucasians" (Bakalian and Bozorgmehr 2009, Hooglund 1987, Naber 2000, Naff 1985, Samhan 1999, Younis and Kayal 1995). As for Turks and Indians, they were both labeled Asians, and Eastern Europeans were included in the categories of European and white. The inclusion under "white" was not immediate and involved numerous legal battles (Elver 2012, Gualtieri 2001). The arguments used by lawyers on behalf of the "Syrians" invoked Christianity as one of the main reasons for naturalization (Gualtieri 2001). Reportedly Christianity was not taken into consideration, whereas arguments for proximity and interaction with Europeans were. However, it has also been noted that in at least one case, when the person was Arab but of darker skin, his status as Caucasian was questioned and his application rejected. The Immigration and Naturalization Service (INS) overturned this decision the following year, and 1920 has been marked as the year when Arabs were recognized as white and could secure their naturalization (Gualtieri 2001).

There is insufficient evidence to draw strong conclusions from the citizenship cases. However, a closer look at the religious composition of the immigrants and their claim to religion may suggest that being majority Christian (Catholic and Greek Orthodox) may have facilitated their incorporation into American society (Aruri 1969, Kayal and Kayal 1975, Naber 2000). Christians from the Levant initially frequented Catholic churches until they had the means to establish Melkite, Maronite, and Eastern Orthodox churches (Hagopian 1969, Hitti 1924). Also, Christians came as families hearing tales about the new world from missionaries who had gone to Jerusalem, Damascus, and Mount Lebanon (Khalaf 1987, Orfalea 1988). Their Muslim counterparts had arrived as young men. Either they had no intention of settling down or, if they did, they tended to marry Christian American women (Gualtieri 2001, Haddad 2011). They had no religious demands and showed no outward signs of piety. At the eve of World War I, most of these immigrants were concerned with independence movements and politics in their homelands. Arab, Albanian, Turkish, and Indian nationalism trumped religious affiliations (Bakalian and Bozorgmehr 2009, Mazrui 1996). In fact, when a Muslim missionary arrived in the United States in 1921, he wrote an open letter expressing his dismay that the Muslims there were only Muslim in name and none were practicing (Ghanea Bassiri 2010). Records suggest that the first "signs" of Muslim institutions came about when groups bought plots of land to bury family members who had passed away (Ghanea Bassiri, 2010). It is not clear if this was for religious observance or if they were rejected from other cemeteries. In any case, at least with this migration flow, their religiosity did not appear to increase with time, and being Muslim was not a primary facilitator/inhibitor of their incorporation.

INTERWAR PERIOD: NEW IMMIGRANTS AND CONVERTS

Immigration from non-European countries came to a near halt with the 1924 national quotas. Yet it was during this period that Islam came on to the scene and gained visibility in the United States. Internally, a native population with a long history in America began to mobilize to reclaim the denied history mentioned in the first wave, namely that of slaves. Marcus Garvey was credited for starting the Black Nationalist movement in the United States (Blake 1969). While he was not preaching or claiming Islam, two individuals influenced by his teaching, Noble Drew Ali and Fard Muhammad, started the Moorish Science Temple around 1913 and the Nation of Islam in 1930, respectively (Berg 2005, Beynon 1938, Gardell 1994, Haddad 1986, 1994, Tinaz 1996). Both Noble Drew Ali and Fard Muhammad preached to their followers that African Americans were robbed of their history and needed to reclaim their African languages, culture, and natural religion—Islam (Berg 2005). Humanity began with the black race, and Fard Muhammad saw the white race as evil.

According to Noble Drew Ali, Moors could not be slaves legally. Part of the problem of African Americans, he said, is that they have forgotten their roots in the Moorish (Moroccan) Empire (Beynon 1938). Fard Muhammad, on the other hand, asserted that he was born in Mecca and a descendant of Prophet Muhammad's clan. Returning to the original religion of Islam would free all African Americans because in Islam people of all races are equal and all humans are slaves only to God and not to other human beings (Beynon 1938, Gardell 1994). Both preachers believed that Christianity was for the white race and Islam for blacks. Beyond these links to Islam, the two movements were largely interpretations of Ali and Muhammad, who assumed prophet status and made religious practice secondary to the movement (Berg 2005). They both believed in separation. The Nation of Islam taught that Muslims could not serve in the armed forces and could not pledge allegiance to a flag that had oppressed African Americans for so long (FBI 1960, Gardell 1994). Noble Drew Ali died in 1929 and Fard Muhammad disappeared in 1934 (FBI 1960). The Nation of Islam grew rapidly, with an estimated 8,000 followers before Fard Muhammad's disappearance (Beynon 1938). Elijah Muhammad, in the meantime, had become Fard's main student and took over as prophet and leader of the Nation of Islam from the 1934 onward (Gardell 1994).

Although Noble Drew Ali and Fard Muhammad saw themselves as prophets of Islam, they were clearly an outgrowth of the Black Nationalist movement (Gardell 1994, Marable 1998). They built temples and advocated for economic independence, established schools, and, in the case of the Nation of Islam, formed a brigade to monitor and protect the nation (FBI 1960, Gardell 1994, Tinaz 1996). This attracted the attention of authorities and the media, which often described them as a "voodoo cult," "Muslim Cult of Islam," "savages," and "primitives" (Beynon 1938, FBI 1960, Tinaz 1996). They were placed under FBI surveillance (it is unclear when this ended). Leaders and members of the movement were often arrested and spent time in prison for sedition and refusing to enlist for service (Mazrui 1996, Tinaz 1996). Nearly all Nation leaders disappeared under uncertain circumstances. Overall, the first institutionalization of Islam in the United States came out of a resistance movement and was defined in racial terms by its adherents. In the next period, the Nation of Islam grew in notoriety and expanded its reach.

WORLD WAR II TO 1965

A new wave of Palestinians arrived in the aftermath of the creation of the State of Israel in 1948 (Al-Tahir 1952, Seiklay 1999). They were listed as Palestinian on immigration records until 1952 (Cainkar 1988). The reception was not warm, but this had more to do with American support for the creation of the State of Israel and less with whether the Palestinians arriving were Muslim or Christian (Haddad 2011, Marvasti and McKinney 2004). These newcomers benefited from the fact that previous coethnics had already won the right to citizenship.

Institutionalization of Islam continued, but in an assimilationist form, when an honored veteran of Lebanese origin requested that President Eisenhower allow Muslim soldiers to be identified as such on their dog tags, like other religions. During World War II, these soldiers' dog tags had been left blank (Haddad 2011). This same veteran formed the Federation of Islam in America in 1953 (Ghanea Bassiri, 2010). A decade later, international students from the United States and Canada met at the University of Illinois—Urbana-Champaign to form the Muslim Students' Association (Ghayur 1981). These two organizations represented the two main Muslim organizations in the United States prior to the 1965 change in immigration laws. In fact, most Muslim organizations did not appear until the 1990s (Bakalian and Bozorgmehr 2009).

The government and popular opinion were more concerned with the Nation of Islam. Malcolm X had been recruited to the Nation while he was serving a prison term in the late in 1940s. He became the Nation of Islam's best-known speaker, at times commanding more attention than Elijah Muhammed (Blake 1969, Tinaz 1996). The 1950s and 1960s saw growth in the organizational sophistication of the Nation of Islam, which caused alarm, and reportedly led the FBI to turn from surveillance to infiltration and internal agitation to get the group to split (Gardell 1994). Interestingly, in earlier FBI reports, the five pillars of Islam were defined and the Nation of Islam was considered to be an aberration. Later reports drop the "cult" label and the distinction and refer to the Nation of Islam and its members as Muslim (FBI 1960).

Elijah Muhammad led the Nation of Islam until his death in 1975, maintaining his interpretation of Islam. Although Sunni and Shi'a Muslims in the United States never accepted his interpretation, Muhammad was invited to Egypt, Libya, and Saudi Arabia (Ghayur 1981, Tinaz 1996). Malcolm X was sent on one of these trips to represent the Nation of Islam. In Saudi Arabia, Malcolm X performed Hajj (pilgrimage) and returned with a change of heart about the role of Islam in race relations. He preached that under Islam all races could work together to find justice, demonstrating his move closer to Sunni and "orthodox" Islam and away from the version propagated by the Nation of Islam (Berg 2005, Gardell 1994). Malcolm X was dismissed from the Nation of Islam and soon after assassinated. Claims about who was responsible vary greatly from members of the Nation of Islam to FBI operatives, but that is beyond the scope of this chapter. In any case, his version of Islam and preaching were unwelcome. What is of significance to this chapter is that the Nation of Islam was already suspect in the United States and, during its period of expansion, began establishing ties with leaders in the Arab world.

Warith Deen Muhammad, Elijah's son, took control of the Nation of Islam in 1975, upon his father's death. He preached a more moderate interpretation that was not antagonistic to the government and social polity, marking a shift to Sunni Islam (Berg 2005, Haddad 1986). Defections began and eventually Louis Farrakhan seized power over the Nation of Islam and restored Elijah Muhammad's original teachings of separatism. Farrakhan remains the leader of the Nation of Islam and a controversial, if not disliked, figure in American politics. He was also purported to have received large sums of money from Libya's Muammar Qaddafi, estimated at anywhere between several hundred thousands to a billion dollars (Berg 2005, Gardell 1994, Mazrui 1996). The connection of the African American movement and Islam to the Arab world and a wider Islam was established in the 1960s to 1970s in the government's perspective. Warith Deen Muhammad (d. 2008) formed the American Muslim Mission, which, after having undergone a variety of name changes, is now known as American Society of Muslims (Berg 2005, Haddad 1986, Tinaz 1996).

1965 TO THE PRESENT

The period since 1965 has brought the population that is most commonly identified as *the* Muslim Americans into political realms, policy, media, popular imagination, and social science research (largely in response to the aforementioned fields). The removal of national origin quotas and replacement with merit-based (and family reunification) immigration under the 1965 Immigration Act opened the doors to many previously inadmissible populations. Equally significant were the changes, in the previous year, that came with the Civil Rights Law, which gave minorities and ethnic groups increased rights and opened the way for identity politics (Alba and Nee 1997, 2003, Brubaker 2001, Glazer 2004, Steinberg 2001). Together these changes established an atmosphere of pluralism and tolerance that was enjoyed by many newcomers.

Arabs were the major exception to this generally amiable governmental reception and public reaction. The Israeli occupation of the West Bank and Gaza in 1967 obscured the benefits of the recent changes in US policy. In 1967, according to the Gallup Poll, 56 percent of Americans were sympathetic to Israel, 4 percent to Arabs, 25 percent to neither, and 15 percent had no opinion (de Boer 1983). Public opinion on the Arab-Israeli conflict was consistently in favor of Israel between 1967 and 1982 (de Boer 1983, Suleiman 1994, 1999, Trice 1978). The hostility toward Arabs and categorical siding with Israel set Arab immigrants and Arab Americans apart from the rest of the population (Abraham 1994, de Boer 1983, Shaheen 1984, Suleiman 1994, Stockton

1994, Trice 1978). Arabs were targeted as Arab, even if at times "Arab" was conflated with "Muslim." Arab Americans, not surprisingly, mobilized as Arabs first.

ARAB IMMIGRANT TRAJECTORY

Arabs arriving after 1965 came with well-defined national identities to a setting that also had well-delineated views of them based on international political developments. The new immigrants did not have the clout or legal facilities to defend themselves. However, Arab Americans who were already in the second and third generations were galvanized to fend off the negative imagery. One of the first responses came from several notable Arab American scholars and professionals who formed the Association of Arab American University Graduates (AAUG) in 1967 (Abraham 1994, Haddad 2011, Shain 1996). The AAUG was "dedicated to fostering better understanding between the Arab and American peoples, and promoting informed discussion of critical issues concerning the Arab world in the United States" (excerpted from the front cover of AAUG publications). Other organizations were established in later years around Arab issues and identity: the National Association of Arab Americans (1972), the Arab-American Anti-Discrimination Committee (ADC, 1980), and the Arab American Institute (AAI, 1985). Some observers noted that the Palestinian issue awakened a pan-Arab identity in the United States (Christison 1989, Suleiman 1999). Conversely, critics accused Palestinians of hijacking the Arab American identity (Shain 1996). The ADC and AAI continue to represent Arab Americans and are run mainly by the earlier generations of Arab American immigrants. The newer migration flows are just beginning to reach second and third generations.

There were too many events and moments when the government actively targeted Arabs and Arab Americans and the media demonized Arabs to discuss in detail. However, the most salient episodes include the 1973 surveillance and deportation of politically active Palestinians (Akram and Johnson 2004, Hagopian 1976); Arabs placed under surveillance after the Israeli invasion of Lebanon in 1982 (Abraham 1994); the 1986 arrest of the "LA-8" (seven Palestinians and a Kenyan) for distributing materials in support of the Popular Front for the Liberation of Palestine; and surveillance and investigation of Arabs during the first Gulf War (1990–1991) and after the first bombing of the World Trade Center by Osama bin Laden (1993). Arabs were even placed under surveillance after Timothy McVeigh's terrorist attack on a federal building in Oklahoma (1995) (Abraham 1994, Akram and Johnson 2004, Elver 2012, 2004, Naber 2000, Shain 1996). In response to McVeigh's attack, the Clinton administration passed the 1996 Antiterrorism and Effective Death Penalty Act, targeting foreigners and noncitizens (Elver 2012, Gotanda 2011, Moore 2007). Aside from politically active Arab Americans, it has been contended that Arab Americans were virtually invisible and left to their own devices in the 1970s and 1980s (Naber 2008).

Over the years, Arab immigrants came from countries beyond the traditional sending nations in the Levant (Syria, Palestine, Lebanon). Palestinians and Lebanese have among the highest rates of immigration to the United States but have increasingly shared this position with Egyptians and Iraqis (Bakalian and Bozorgmehr 2009). The Arab American identity has been shifting in the past several decades away from the pan-Arabic and toward fragmentation, as newcomers displayed divergent political concerns and often more religious identifications.

SOUTH ASIAN IMMIGRANT TRAJECTORY

South Asian Muslim immigrants present a dilemma for scholars, especially in their first decades of migration. The difficulty lies in their initial small numbers and their categorization as Asian American. South Asians from predominantly Muslim countries, namely Bangladesh and Pakistan, trickled into the United States in the mid-1960s through 1970s. There are no figures for Bangladeshis until 1975–1979, when reportedly 2,921 immigrants made their way to the United States (INS figures quoted in Bakalian and Bozorgmehr 2009). In that same period (1965–1974), there were 13,932 Pakistani immigrants. Both groups grew dramatically in the 1990s and the early 2000s, whereby in 2004 there were 109,990 Bangladeshis and 273,143 Pakistanis (Bakalian and Bozorgmehr 2009). These figures surpassed those of Iraqi and Egyptian immigrants respectively.[5]

Phenotypically and legally, South Asians are racially separate from Arabs. However, these distinctions did not affect their incorporation process in the initial period. In fact, they were more likely to be included under the "model minority" label, along with Indians and other South Asians (racially and because of their high human capital) (Ghayur 1981, Gotanda 2011). If Arab Americans were considered invisible despite the negative stereotyping, then South Asian Muslims were nonexistent in comparison. This "visible invisibility" privileged South Asian Muslims in the 1970s and 1980s, when they were able to focus on their economic upwardly mobility (Moore 2007). Paradoxically, since *Muslim* was conflated with *Arab* in the media, South Asian Muslims were afforded the space to identify as Muslim first and in turn to establish Muslim associations and centers in greater numbers (Warren 2000).

South Asian Muslims established their own mosques and associations to serve their own population, just as Arab Muslim, Turkish Muslim, and Iranian Muslim mosques had done. There were very few national Muslim associations, but where they developed South Asian Muslims became active members. The most visible organizations now are the Islamic Society of North America (1982), the Muslim Public Affairs Council (1986), the American Muslim Alliance (1989), the American Muslim Council (1990), and the Council on American Islamic Relations (1994) (Ghanea Bassiri 2010, Haddad 2011).

For the greater part of their tenure in the United States, South Asian Muslims seem to have commanded little negative attention as Muslims. Yet since 9/11, they have increasingly been placed under scrutiny and their activities and their place in US society has assumed more centrality in discussions of Arabs and Muslims.

According to Pew and Gallup data for 1910, the largest Muslim national group is Pakistani at 9 percent of all Muslim Americans. Collectively, Arab Muslims make the largest regional group at 23 percent of all Muslim Americans (Kohut and Lugo 2011, Younis 2009). All in all, since 1965, Muslims have represented seventy-seven ethnicities; they are racially mixed and are comparable to other Americans in terms of education and economic standing. African American Muslims are often left outside analyses of Muslim Americans, although they are included in the general statistics. African Americans constitute one third of all Muslims in the United States. When African Americans are excluded, Muslim Americans fare better than average on income and education compared with the rest of Americans (Mohamed 2012).

Islam and Incorporation into American Life

It becomes readily apparent that Islam and Muslims do not have a singular trajectory of incorporation into US society. In fact, it is not clear that Islam had much to do with immigrant incorporation until 9/11. Nonetheless, if one only looks at the post-9/11 period, it is easy to miss some of the historical precursors and nuances that make Islam stand out so drastically from other religions in recent decades. Stephen Warner suggests that religion should be studied as an independent variable to incorporation (2007). Some scholars have tried to make those links, for instance, Sarah Gualtieri proposed that Arab Muslims in the first voluntary wave were given a more difficult time than Arab Christians because of their religion (2001). There were too few cases and limited evidence to suggest it was anything but a matter of race and skin color. Other scholars have also tried to draw links between the first involuntary Muslim migrants brought on slave ships and Muslims immigrants post-1965 (Elver 2012, Gotanda 2011). While these studies provide intriguing propositions, the historical context for each group of Muslims was drastically different. Enslaved African Muslims were stripped of every aspect of their humanity, and it is not clear that there was any recognition or interest in their religious beliefs. Second, Arabs were treated as Asians and Turks before they were accepted as white, and this had very little to do with religion. As such, religion cannot act as an independent factor to explain the complex histories of waves of immigrants and native-born Americans.

Among the key threads deduced from the earlier flows of Muslims is the fact that participating in religious community or establishing a "congregation," both for immigrants and internal migrants, does not necessarily make groups more American or assist in their incorporation (Hirschman 2004, Warner 2007). Charles Hirschman's theory on "congregationalism" is one of the most cited works on immigrants and religion, and thus it is worth pausing to assess how it applies to Muslims. One of the main conclusions of congregationalism is that institutionalization of religion to replicate the Protestant church model is a sign of Americanization of all religions. African Americans were citizens fighting for their rights after emancipation when Noble Drew Ali and Fard Muhammad founded their religious groups to reclaim Islam as an African religion. The Moorish Science Temple and the Nation of Islam were the first instances of institutionalization of Islam in the United States. Their relationship with the FBI was contentious from the very beginning and remains tenuous. The preaching mattered more than the structural organization of the religion and its temples.

Between 1965 and 1990, it seems that congregationalism worked for South Asian and some Middle Eastern Muslims. Islamic centers and mosques were established as nonprofit organizations subject to US rules and regulations about voluntary membership, including a board and a lay leadership, and less formal attributes like becoming multifunctional, raising funds, and holding activities on Sundays (Haddad 2011, Warner 2000). However, it was some of these very same attributes that came under scrutiny in the 1990s and have done more so since 2001. Muslim mosques and foundations were investigated concerning their fundraising under the pretense that they might be funding terrorism abroad (Akram and Johnson 2004). The community center functions of mosques also became suspect, seen as potential spaces of recruitment of terrorists (Cainkar 2008). Thus religion and its practice are not reliable enough to measure the level of incorporation.

This is not to dismiss the significance of religion, especially when Islam has been associated with terror, violence, and treated as suspect in the popular imagination since 2001. Rather, it is to situate it in its rightful place as a facilitator or inhibitor to incorporation (Portes and Rumbaut 2006). As stated earlier, the three modes of incorporation according to immigration sociologists Alejandro Portes and Ruben Rumbaut are governmental reception, public reaction toward newcomers, and the preexisting community (2006). The three modes of incorporation are able to more thoroughly explain Muslim incorporation in the United States with one qualification: the group does not have to be "newcomers." In fact, it seems with Arab and Muslim Americans that after they were already acculturated they were pushed out and asked to return with a new Muslim identity to prove its allegiance to the United States. In each migration flow, the government's reception or reaction to ethnic groups, in this case Muslims, had an immense effect on public responses to the "newcomers." At times, public reaction has been exaggerated beyond the government's reaction, as has been the case since 2001. The government has continuously tried to placate the public, but opinion polls remain stacked against Arab and Muslim Americans (AAI, 2010). Nonetheless, it is important to remember that public opinion does not arise in a vacuum.

Finally, the third mode of incorporation seems particularly pertinent in the story of Muslim Americans. For African Americans, the history of their arrival on slave ships mattered. For Arab Americans, religion did not play a major role. Instead, when more Arab Muslims began to arrive to the United States, the older secular and Christian Arab Americans helped integrate them into a pan-Arab identity and organizations. In the case of South Asian Muslims, they did not have a preexisting community. Interestingly, this allowed them the freedom to identify as Muslims while still being seen as members of the new immigrants with high human capital—that is, the model minority.

What does this mean for current and future Muslim Americans? In the simplest terms, it means that incorporation is neither linear nor ever complete. If the first two modes of incorporation are compromised or become negative for any reason, then the group has to prove its belonging. On a more positive note, there are sufficiently large numbers of preexisting Muslim communities from all ethnicities who are organizing and mobilizing to secure their place in US social polity. The most recent migration flow of Muslims is quick to naturalize, comes with high human capital, and has income levels that are above the national average. All these attributes are assets that will keep Muslims from being racialized to the extent that activist scholars argue and will help to incorporate newcomers despite the added governmental and public scrutiny.

NOTES

1. Data were collected on religion in 1957 in the Current Population Survey, where it was established that 95 percent of Americans were Christian. The categories were Protestant, Catholic, Jewish, and other religion or nondeclared. There was no mention of Muslims. In the 1936 census, American Mohammedan Society and the American Moslem Brotherhood were mentioned as small sects or cults that were unorganized and too small to be counted (Mueller and Lane 1972, Murphy 1939).
2. The Arab American Institute and Arab American Anti-Discrimination Committee continue to publish estimates where the majority of Arab Americans are Christian.
3. The Pew Forum on Religion and Public Life claims to have conducted the first national survey of Muslim Americans in 2007, where it estimated that there were 2.35 million Muslims in the United States at the time of the survey.
4. Religion and select migration scholars contend that it is an underestimated and undertheorized. For examples see Warner, S., "Religion and new (post-1965) Immigrants: Some Principles Drawn from Field Research," *American Studies*, 41, 2/3 (2000): 267–286; Hagan, J., and Ebaugh, H.R., "Calling Upon the Sacred: Migrants' Use of Religion in the Migration Process," *IMR* 37, 4(2003): 1145–1162; and Connor, P. "Religion as a Resource: Religion and Immigrant Economic Incorporation," *Social Science Research* 40 (2011): 1350–1361.
5. Iraqis totaled 104, 796 and Egyptians totaled 137, 352. Pakistanis saw the greatest population growth only exceeded by Iranians at 362, 577 (predominantly Muslim) (Bakalian and Bozorgmehr, Y. Haddad, and J. Smith 2009). Afghanis began arriving in the 1980s, but their numbers had not exceeded 52,000 by 2004.

REFERENCES

Abraham, Nabeel, "Anti-Arab Racism and Violence in the United States", in *The Development of the Arab-American Identity*, edited by Ernest McCarus (Ann Arbor, MI: Michigan University Press, 1994): 155–214.

Akram, Susan M., and Kevin R. Johnson, "Race and Civil Rights Pre-September 11: The Targeting of Arabs and Muslims", in *Civil Rights in Peril: The Targeting off Arabs and Muslims*, edited by Elaine Hagopian (Ann Arbor, MI: Pluto Press, 2004): 9–25.

Al-Tahir, Abdul Jallil, "The Arab Community in the Chicago Area: A Comparative Study of the Christian-Syrians and the Muslim Palestinians", Ph.D. dissertation (Chicago: University of Chicago, 1952).

Alba, Richard, and Victor Nee, "Rethinking Assimilation Theory for a New Era of Immigration", *International Migration Review* 341 (1997): 826–874.

Aruri, Naseer, "The Arab-American Community in Springfield, Massachusetts", in *The Arab-Americans: Studies in Assimilation*, edited by Elaine Hagaopian and Ann Hagopian (Wilmette, IL: The Medina University Press, 1969): 50–66.

Bagby, Ihsan, "The American Mosque 2011: Report Number 2", *Hartford Institute for Religion Research*, May 2012. Available at http://www.hartfordinstitute.org/The-American-Mosque-Report-2.pdf (Accessed February 25, 2013.)

Bakalian, Anny, and Mehdi Bozorgmehr, *Backlash 9/11: Middle Eastern and Muslim Americans Respond* (Berkeley: University of California Press, 2009).

Berg, Herbert, "Mythmaking in the African American Muslim Context: The Moorish Science Temple, the Nation of Islam, and the American Society of Muslims", *Journal of the American Academy of Religion* 73, 3 (2005): 685–703. Available athttp://religion.ua.edu/pdf/bergjaar.pdf(Accessed March 1 2013.)

Beynon, Erdmann D., "The Voodoo Cult Among Negro Migrants in Detroit", *American Journal of Sociology* 43, 6(1938): 894–907.

Blake, J. Herman, "Black Nationalism", *The Annals of the American Academy of Political and Social Science* 382 (1969): 15–25.

Brubaker, Rogers, "The Return of Assimilation? Changing Perspectives on Immigration in France, Germany, and the United States", *Ethnic and Racial Studies* 24, no. 4 (2001): 531–548.

CAIR (Council on American-Islamic Relations), "About Islam and American Muslims", 2012. Available at http://sun.cair.com/AboutIslam/IslamBasics.aspx (Accessed January 22, 2013.)

Cainkar, Louis, "Palestinian Women in the United States: Coping with Tradition, Change, and Alienation", Ph.D. dissertation (Evanston, IL: Northwestern University, 1988).

——, "Thinking Outside the Box", in *Race and Arab Americans Before and After 9/11: From Invisible Citizens to Visible Subjects*, edited by Amaney Jamal and Nadine Naber (Syracuse, NY: Syracuse University Press, 2008): 46–80.

Connor, Phillip, "Religion as Resource: Religion and Immigrant Economic Incorporation", *Social Science Research* 40, 5 (2011): 1350–1361.

De Boer, Connie, "The Polls: Attitudes Toward the Arab-Israeli Conflict", *The Public Opinion Quarterly* 47(1983): 121–131.

Elver, Hilal, "Racializing Islam Before and After 9/11: From Melting Pot to Islamophobia", *Transnational & Contemporary Problems* 21, 119 (2012): 119–174.

FBI, Central Research Section, "*The Nation of Islam:* Antiwhite, All-Negro Cult in United States" (October 1960).

Gardell, Mattias, "The Sun of Islam Will Rise in the West: Minister Farrakhan and the Nation of Islam in the Latter Days", in *Muslim Communities in North America*, edited by Yvonne Haddad and Jane Smith (Albany, NY: State University of New York Press, 1994): 15–49.

Ghanea Bassiri, Kambiz, *A History of Islam in America*. (Cambridge, UK: Cambridge University Press, 2010).

Ghayur, M. Arif, "Muslims in the United States: Settlers and Visitors", *Annals of the American Academy of Political and Social Science* 454 (March 1981): 150–163.

Glazer, Nathan, "Assimilation Today: Is One Identity Enough?" in *Reinventing the Melting Pot: The New Immigrants and What It Means to Be American*, edited by Tamar Jacoby (New York: Basic Books, 2004): 61–74.

Gomez, Michael A., "Muslims in Early America", *The Journal of Southern History* 60, 4 (1994): 671–710.

Gotanda, Neil, "The Racialization of Islam in American Law", *The Annals of the American Academy of Political and Social Science* 637, 1 (2011): 184–195.

Gualtieri, Sarah, "Becoming 'White': Race, Religion and the Foundations of Syrian/Lebanese Ethnicity in the United States", *Journal of American Ethic History* 20, 4, (2001): 29–58.

Haddad, Yvonne, "A Century of Islam in America", *The Muslim World Today* 4 Washington, DC: The Middle East Institute, 1986.

——, *Becoming American?: The Forging of Arab and Muslim Identity in Pluralist America* (Waco, TX: Baylor University Press, 2011). Available at http://www.baylorpress.com/Book/291/Becoming_American_.html

Hagan, Jacqueline, and Helen Ebaugh, "Calling Upon the Sacred: Migrants' Use of Religion in the Migration Process", *International Migration Review* 37, 4 (2003): 1145–1162.

Hagopian, Elaine, "The Institutional Development of the Arab-American Community of Boston", in *The Arab-Americans: Studies in Assimilation*, edited by Elaine Hagopian and Ann Paden (Wilmette, IL: Medina University Press, 1969): 50–66.

——, "Minority Rights in a Nation-State: The Nixon Administration's Campaign Against Arab Americans." *Journal of Palestine Studies* 5, 1/2 (1976): 97–114.

Hirschman, Charles, "The Role of Religion in the Origins and Adaptation of Immigrant Groups in the United States." *International Migration Review* 38, 3 (2004): 1206–1233.

Hitti, Philip, *The Syrians in America* (New York: George H. Doran, 1924).

Hooglund, Eric, *Crossing the Waters: Arabic-speaking Immigrants in the United States before 1940* (Washington, DC: Smithsonian Institution Press, 1987).

Jamal, Amaney, "Civil Liberties and the Otherization of Arab and Muslim Americans", in *Race and Arab Americans Before and After 9/11: From Invisible Citizens to Visible Subjects*, edited by Amaney Jamal and Nadine Naber (Syracuse, NY: Syracuse University Press, 2008).

Johnson, Toni, "Muslims in the United States". *Council on Foreign Relations* 2011. Available at http://www.cfr.org/united-states/muslims-united-states/p25927

Kayal, Philip, and Joseph Kayal, *The Syrian-Lebanese in America: A Study in Religion and Assimilation* (New York: Twayne Publishers, 1975).

Khalaf, Samir, "The Background and Causes of Lebanese/Syrian Immigration to the United States before World War I", in *Crossing the Waters: Arabic-Speaking Immigrants in the United States before 1940*, edited by Eric Hooglund (Washington, DC: Smithsonian Institution Press, 1987).

Kohut, Andrew, and Luis Lugo, "Muslim Americans: No Signs of Growth in Alienation or Support for Extremism", *Pew Research Center*, August 2011. Available at http://www.people-press.org/files/legacy-pdf/Muslim%20American%20Report%2010-02-12%20fix.pdf (Accessed January 22, 2013.)

Marable, Manning, *Black Leadership* (New York: Columbia University Press, 1998).

Marvasti, Amir, and Karyn McKinney, *Middle Eastern Lives in America (Perspectives on a Multiracial America)* (Lanham: Rowman & Littlefield, 2004).

Mazrui, Ali A., "Between the Crescent and Star-Spangled Banner: American Muslims and US Foreign Policy", *International Affairs* 72, 3 (1996): 493–506.

Min, Pyong G., "The Structure and Social Functions of Korean Immigrant Churches in the United States", *International Migration Review* 26, 4 (1992): 1370–1394.

Mohamed, Besheer, "Demographic and Economic Profile of Muslim Americans" (Washington, DC: Pew Research Center, 2012). Available at http://www.aicongress.org/wp-content/uploads/2012/04/FMP-Pew-Demographics-AIC.pdf (Accessed: January 22, 2013.)

Moore, Kathleen M., "Muslims in the United States: Pluralism under Exceptional Circumstances", *Annals of the American Academy of Political and Social Science* 612 (2007): 116–132.

Naff, Alixa, *Becoming American: The Early Arab Immigrant Experience.* (Urbana, IL: Southern Illinois University Press, 1985).

Naber, Nadine, "Ambiguous Insiders: An Investigation of Arab American Invisibility", *Ethic and Racial Studies* 23, 1 (2000): 37–61.

——, "Introduction: Arab Americans and U.S. Racial Formations", in *Race and Arab Americans Before and After 9/11: From Invisible Citizens to Visible Subjects*, edited by Amaney Jamal and Nadine Naber (Syracuse, NY: Syracuse University Press, 2008).

Orfalea, Gregory, *Before the Flames: A Quest for the History of Arab Americans* (Austin, TX: University of Texas Press, 1988).

Portes, Alejandro, and Ruben Rumbaut, *Immigrant American: A Portrait* (Berkeley: University of California Press, 2006).

Samhan, Helen, "Not Quite White: Race Classification and the Arab-American Experience", in *Arabs in America: Building a New Future*, edited by Michael Suleiman (Philadelphia: Temple University Press. 1999).

Shaheen, Jack, *The TV Arab* (Bowling Green, OH: Bowling Green State University Popular Press, 1984).

Shain, Yossi, "Arab-Americans at a Crossroads", *Journal of Palestine Studies* 23 (1996): 46–59.

Steinberg, Stephen, *The Ethnic Myth: Race, Ethnicity, and Class in America* (Boston: Beacon Press, 2001).

Stockton, Ronald, "Ethnic Archetypes and the Arab Image", in *The Development of the Arab-American Identity*, edited by Ernest McCarus (Ann Arbor, MI: Michigan University Press, 1994): 119–153.

Suleiman, Michael, "Arab Americans in the Political Process", in *The Development of the Arab-American Identity*, edited by Ernest McCarus (Ann Arbor, MI: Michigan University Press, 1994): 37–60.

Tinaz, Nuri, "The Nation of Islam: Historical Evolution and Transformation of the Movement", *Journal of Muslim Minority Affairs* 16, 2 (1996): 193–209.

Trice, Robert H., "Foreign Policy Interest Groups, Mass Public Opinion and the Arab-Israeli Dispute", *The Western Political Quarterly* 31, 2 (1978): 238–252.

Volpp, Leti, "The Citizen and the Terrorist", *UCLA Law Review* 49 (2002): 1575–1600.

Warner, Stephen, "Religion and New (post-1965) Immigrants: Some Principles Drawn from Field Research", *American Studies* 41, 2/3 (2000): 267–286.

——, "The Role of Religion in the Process of Segmented Assimilation", *The Annals of the American Academy of Political and Social Science* 612 (2007): 100–115.

Younis, Adele, and Philip Kayal, *The Coming of the Arabic-Speaking People to the United States* (Staten Island, NY: Center for Migration Studies, 1995).

CHAPTER 3

IMAMS AND CHAPLAINS AS AMERICAN RELIGIOUS PROFESSIONALS

TIMUR R. YUSKAEV AND

HARVEY STARK

IN the summer of 2010, Bilal Ansari, an experienced prison chaplain and an imam from a long lineage of African American Muslim and Christian religious leaders, was asked to serve as a chaplain in a federal correctional facility for women. At the time of this request, two other Muslims were acting as volunteer part-time chaplains in this prison, but they were female and could not, in their and the predominant Muslim view, lead the Friday congregational prayer for the prison's seventy Muslim inmates. Ansari was asked to serve specifically as the imam for the women's Friday prayer.

This request was a result of an ongoing legal challenge faced by the prison officials. Twelve years before Ansari arrived there, a Muslim inmate filed a petition with a US district court to compel the administration of the facility to accommodate her religious practice. She won the case and the administration met two out of her three demands: she was no longer subjected to cross-gendered pat searches and could be photographed with her head scarf on. Her third request was to accommodate what she believed was her constitutional right and religious obligation—to attend the weekly Friday congregational prayer (*jumuʻa*). Time and again the facility's two full-time chaplains, who happened to be Christian, reached out to male Muslim leaders, imams, to solicit their services. Time and again these imams turned down the request. Their answer was grounded in a widespread understanding of the Islamic law (*shari'a*): they informed the prison administration that their services were not really needed from the point of view of Islamic law because Muslim females are not required to attend a *jumu'a* and, in addition, female-only gatherings do not meet the legal requirements for congregational prayer; a proper *jumu'a*, they said, has to include a certain number of male worshippers.

The female inmate at the center of the case and many other Muslim women in the facility did not accept this opinion. To them, the inability to have access to a *jumu'a* violated their US constitutional rights as well as their sense of Islamic justice. The petitioner persisted in filing complaints while the prison officials grew increasingly frustrated and saw her as a difficult inmate with unwarranted passive-aggressive behavior. After September 11, 2001, she was perceived as a Muslim radical, which led to extended confinement in segregated housing units and frequent strip searches. By 2010, the situation grew increasingly tense. A law firm stepped in to mediate the conflict and reached out to Imam Ansari.

This request confronted Ansari with a profound dilemma: Would he follow or go against a long-standing and commonly asserted Islamic legal practice? The problem was that, by accepting it, he would violate his sense of Islamic ethics. However, by following these ethical principles, he would, in the eyes of many of his peers, violate Islamic law (*shari'a*). As Ansari expressed it, "the question for me was—would I continue the dominant view of the Muslim community or would I 'innovate' under a new view." Needless to say he accepted the contract.

Ansari's decision centered on issues of professionalism, gender equity, and law and ethics (both religious and secular). Key to all these questions was the fact that Ansari took seriously the context of his work. After all, he was called to serve a particular community of women incarcerated within the American prison system. As often happens, it was the institution and constituency that framed the type of religious leadership and spiritual guidance needed. Setting, then, was a determining factor.[1]

AMERICAN MUSLIM RELIGIOUS LEADERSHIP: NEW PROFESSIONS

The poignancy and immediacy of Ansari's dilemma highlights many issues central to the ongoing development of Muslim religious professionals in America. It reflects a moment of change, negotiation, and decision making that is characteristic of Muslim life in American contexts. In addition, Ansari's institutionally recognized role as both a chaplain and an imam points to the professionalization of two new vocations in the history of religion in the United States.

This chapter examines the trends and challenges that have come to define American Muslim religious leadership as represented by Bilal Ansari and his male and female colleagues over the past forty years. Through specific examples, it highlights the roles imams and chaplains have played within the communities and institutions they serve. The goal is to present a picture of a historically new and evolving understanding of imams and chaplains as religious professionals. Although there is a direct, fluid, and organic connection between the titles of imam and chaplain, the importance of differentiating one profession from the other, in terms of the contexts in which they work and the responsibilities they carry out, cannot be overstated. With that in mind, this chapter proceeds with separate introductions to each vocation and culminates with an analytical reflection on the broader significance of the issues of context, professionalization, and gender.

For both imams and chaplains, the process of professionalization has been a slow and steady shift from part-time, volunteer, and ad hoc leaders to full-time paid professionals, recognized as such by the institutions they work in, the communities they serve, and society at large. The shift to full-time paid professionals has paralleled a similar shift in the demographics of the American Muslim community. The period between 1965, with the signing into law of the Hart-Celler Immigration Act, and the mid 1970s, with the ascension to leadership of Imam W. D. Mohammed, saw the beginnings of tremendous population growth among immigrant and American-born Muslims. With this growth in population came increased Muslim participation in American secular and religious life, a dramatic increase in the number of Muslim congregations, and the institutionalization of Muslim religious professionals. Taking this historical backdrop as a foundation, this analysis considers the four decades between the mid-1970s and mid-2010s as a formative phase in the development of American Muslim religious leadership, a phase that helps to explain the current state of that leadership and leads to a better understanding of narratives that parallel Ansari's story.

More than just religious functionaries, chaplains and imams are a central part of the leadership of the Muslim American community. This leadership is primarily shared among five main overlapping types: local administrative mosque leaders, leaders of national and regional organizations, public intellectuals, imams, and chaplains. From among these types, chaplains and imams constitute a Muslim parallel to other members of the American clergy, understood here as a category that encompasses religious professionals from a variety of American faith groups who are employed to carry out liturgical, educational, and counseling functions within religious and nonreligious institutions. In the American context, imams typically work within the congregational setting of mosques. Chaplains, on the other hand, serve Muslim and non-Muslim constituencies outside of the congregational setting, in most cases in non-Muslim institutions such as the military, the prison system, hospitals, universities, and colleges.

While the term *clergy* is considered here as a useful American shorthand for Muslim religious professionals, it does not fully encompass the diversity inherent in Islamic religious leadership. The importance of acknowledging the limitations of the term *clergy* is to recognize that the Islamic model of religious leadership does not fit neatly into the American perception of that leadership. For example, despite the fact that in American parlance the term *imam* is seen as the corollary of an American priest, pastor, or rabbi, this vision is a construct specific to an American setting. So while the term *imam* can refer to the official or unofficial "head" of a mosque, there are scholars and preachers outside of this context serving as imams whose leadership and authority rest primarily with the recognition of a given community or communities.[2]

Communal perception as to what qualifies a person as an effective leader in a specific context is a crucial aspect of this recognition. For example, in the case of Imam Bilal Ansari, his authority and ability to serve were governed by several overlapping communities and/or parameters, including the community of incarcerated women, the officials representing the prison, the Muslim religious authorities consulted regarding Islamic practice, and American constitutional law. Ultimately what was needed was a religious officiant with the ability to lead these women in a Friday congregational prayer. That meant a person who was qualified to do so in terms of his religious knowledge, but it also meant that this person had to be male because, in terms of scholarly consensus, a Friday congregational prayer would not be valid were it not led by a male imam. At the same time, this person had to be sensitive to the particular institutional circumstances and had to have the knowledge of an experienced prison chaplain. Ansari met all of these qualifications and in turn was empowered to negotiate between a long-held Muslim legal view that a Friday congregational prayer had to include male worshippers and the sense of justice held by group of women incarcerated in a US prison. In this case, Ansari established a Friday prayer exclusively for these women. The context prompted his experimentation, and the authority to proceed in this manner rested with his multiple roles as a scholar, imam, and professional chaplain.

So what was the trajectory of professionalization for American imams and chaplains that led to and defined Ansari's leadership? In the case of Muslim chaplains, it is somewhat easy to trace. As the name suggests, Muslim chaplains are part of an originally American Christian profession whose parameters were established by US clergy in the military, prisons, and other institutions. As chaplains from a minority religious group, Muslim chaplains follow the lead of Catholics and Jews, who were officially recognized as military chaplains in the 1840s and 1860s respectively. Along with other religious minority groups—such as Hindus, Buddhists, and Wiccans—Muslim chaplains have become part of the American institutional landscape over the past forty years.

The first officially recognized and publicly identifiable Muslim chaplain in the United States, Imam Warith Deen Umar, began his service in 1975 in the New York State Department of Corrections. Since then, the US military, hospitals, colleges, and universities have all hired Muslim chaplains. In 1993 Abdul-Rashid Muhammad was commissioned as the first Muslim chaplain in the US Armed Forces. In addition, the first decade of the twenty-first century witnessed a spectacular growth specifically in the fields of hospital and university chaplaincy. This growth was precipitated by the hiring of the first Muslim college chaplain, Imam Salahuddin Muhammad, at Bard College in 1995. Thereafter, in 1999, the hiring of Imam Yahya Hendi by Georgetown University marked the creation of the first full-time Muslim university chaplaincy position. Since September 11, 2001, at least thirty other colleges and universities have hired Muslim chaplains, most of them on a part-time basis but a significant number—approximately a dozen—full time.

On the other hand, to understand the historical trajectory of the professionalization of imams, one has to take into consideration the development of the American mosque. The *American Mosque 2011* study found that the visibility of the mosque on the American religious landscape was a relatively recent phenomenon, and so were the roles and responsibilities that came to define the profession of an American imam. As Ihsan Bagby, the report's author, points out: "The American mosque is a remarkably young institution: over three-fourths (76%) of all existing mosques were established since 1980."[3] Among the 2,106 mosques counted in 2011, close to half were established after the year 2000.[4] In addition to the relatively recent history of the American mosque, this research highlights the ongoing process of institutionalizing imams as mosque "leaders." Suggestive of this fluidity of leadership was the fact that in 2011 a full 49 percent of all mosque imams were volunteers.[5] In other words, they were not yet professionals in the sense of being compensated for their services. That being said, the fact that close to half of American mosques had hired part- or full-time imams speaks to the developing recognition of their professional status.

What does this mean in the American context and how does it compare with the situation for chaplains? To put it in other terms, where would a Muslim religious professional like Ansari find employment and what are the expectations of his potential employers? To answer these questions and to illustrate the specific roles and responsibilities performed by imams and chaplains, we turn to two employment announcements, one for a mosque imam and the other for a prison chaplain.

AMERICAN IMAMS

In the May/June 2010 edition of *Islamic Horizons Magazine*—a publication of North America's largest Muslim organization, the Islamic Society of North America (ISNA)—the Islamic Center of New England posted an advertisement "for a qualified and dynamic Imam."

The first among the required qualifications noted by the potential employer was the ability to perform liturgical functions, such as leading the Friday congregational and other prayers as well as recitation of the Qur'an. The advertisement also stressed that the qualified person should have an "excellent" knowledge of the Islamic sciences, including Qur'an, Hadith, and Fiqh, with a degree from "a *recognized* Islamic institution." In addition, other required and desired qualifications included "the ability to interact with the youth, English fluency, knowledge of Arabic, the ability to participate at inter-faith forums, some experience in pre-marital and marital counseling, experience in conflict resolution, and the ability to lead marriage ceremonies and funerals."[6]

In many respects, this advertisement typifies the evolving expectations of a mosque imam's responsibilities. Its stress on the imam's ability to perform liturgical duties speaks to his primary function in any mosque. "Knowledge of Islamic sciences" points to the desire of the institution to employ a person who is a member of a community of Muslim scholars, or 'ulama, and is trained in interpretation of the texts that constitute the crux of the discursive tradition of Islam. In this respect, the advertisement reflects—through the mosque board—the congregation's perceived need to carry on this tradition of Muslim scholarship in the United States. At the same time, there is a telling ambiguity in the announcement's use of the phrase "*recognized* Islamic institution." What a recognized Islamic institution is and who recognizes it as such is left open to interpretation.

This ambiguity points to several closely connected phenomena related to the state of Islamic education in the United States. First, it acknowledges the fact that there are institutions of Islamic learning, such as al-Azhar in Egypt or the network of seminaries in Qum, Iran, which have widely accepted legitimacy among Sunni and Shi`i Muslims. Second, it points to an understanding and even acceptance of the fact that despite the legitimacy of these historic centers of learning, professionalization in the United States requires the formal establishment of educational criteria. Finally, it speaks to a hesitancy regarding the rigidity of accreditation; the requisite knowledge to be an imam or chaplain is relatively fluid and in the United States has thus far not been confined to a specific curriculum or institution.

This, in turn, reflects the simultaneous desire to establish formal Muslim run seminaries in the United States with the existence of more informal modes of learning that have a long tradition in Islam. For example, the *All Dulles Area Muslim Society* (ADAMS Center) in Northern Virginia offers classes for aspiring imams and *khatibs* (preachers). This is replicated in many other large and sometimes small mosques in the United States. In addition, there are several educational institutions in the United States that are not accredited as formal theological schools carrying out rigorous training for male and female `ulama. Some of their students are hired as imams in the United States and abroad. One such place is Darul-Uloom Al-Madania in Buffalo, New York, which has its roots in the South Asian Sunni model of theological education. There have been attempts to establish Shi`ite seminaries in the United States as well, exemplified by the Islamic Institute of New York in Queens. In the 1990s the International Institute of Islamic Thought established the Graduate School of Islamic and Social Sciences to train imams and chaplains. Perhaps the best known such institution is Zaytuna College established in 2008, which gained prominence in the United States and abroad because of its online presence. Until its recent transformation into an Islamic Liberal Arts college, Zaytuna attempted to serve as a Muslim seminary. Finally, in 2010, the Muslim Endorsement Council of Connecticut was established and, in turn, created the Islamic Seminary Foundation, whose goal it is to establish a Muslim seminary in America that trains imams and chaplains.

The impetus to establish a Muslim seminary in the United States recognizes the fact that while there are established institutions like Al-Azhar, there is still a need to centralize, formalize, and facilitate the education and training of American imams locally. It is understood that to fully serve the Muslim community in the United States and appreciate the context of life in America, Muslim religious leaders must be at least in part locally educated. As Ingrid Mattson, former President of ISNA and founder of Hartford Seminary's Islamic Chaplaincy program, has noted, "[because] there is no ordination in Islam and no universally recognized body that legitimizes scholars, scholarly authority is always relational."[7]

It is this relational aspect that highlights the locally specific needs of a congregation. In the advertisement mentioned above, this comes across in the emphasis on the prospective imam's fluency in English and ability to work with "the youth." This shows a desire to respond to the changing cultural dynamics of the congregation, where a growing number of its members have either been born or raised in the United States. The additional requirements of participation in multifaith activities, ability to counsel families, and experience in conflict resolution further highlights the desire to employ a religious leader who can comfortably fit into the role of an American clergyperson. Finally, there is a clear focus here on hiring an individual with the skills to reach out to both the connected and disaffected parts of the Muslim community, specifically through the ability to "interact with the youth and provide for their spiritual growth."

These are qualities and expectations that a new cadre of Muslim religious leaders, such as Bilal Ansari, are trying to fulfill. Suhaib Webb is the imam of the Islamic Society of Boston Cultural Center, a center not wholly unlike the Islamic Center of New England. He is a leader who meets these expectations in ways similar to Ansari. A white convert to Islam, Webb was born in Oklahoma, studied education at the University of Central Oklahoma, and completed the Islamic studies curriculum at al-Azhar. He is known as a dynamic preacher. His admirers particularly appreciate his uncanny ability to fuse Islamic and American cultural idioms, exemplified by the writings and speeches posted on his website, SuhaibWebb.com, which also goes by the title "Your Virtual Mosque." His congregation values him as uniquely qualified to address the needs of their diverse and increasingly American-born and English-speaking community. As Nancy Khalil, a board member of the mosque said in an interview with the *Boston Globe*, "There's a huge dearth of qualified imams in this country.... We wanted somebody who could relate to a diverse congregation."[8] Although a 2000 mosque study showed that the number of mosques where one ethnic group dominates is as high as 64 percent, Khalil's quote obviously places emphasis on the growing diversity of the Muslim population in her community.[9]

The advertisement examined here describes an imam with such a multitude of skills that he could only be a generalist. However, within the job posting, some of the specific fields of expertise that the imam is expected to fill require specialization. Increasingly, one of the skills expected of imams, as with other religious leaders in the United States, is the ability to counsel members of the community, be it tending to the needs of the youth or to those of married couples. This expectation is not unique to large and diverse congregations, such as Imam Webb's or the Islamic Center of New England. A parallel example was documented in a *New York Times* profile of Shaykh Reda Shata, a Brooklyn-based Egyptian imam, who served an Arabic-speaking community in the early 2000s. Counseling took on a lion's share of his day-to-day activities.[10] Studies of American mosques corroborate such examples. Bagby, for example, notes that counseling, and "especially marital counseling, is a regular duty (burden, many imams would say) of mosque leaders—over three-fourths of mosques do some form of counseling."[11] Other research found that some three quarters of imams express the need for training in social work and counseling and lament that they have "little formal training" in such fields."[12] As a result, specialists among American Muslim religious professionals have emerged. Paramount among them are Muslim chaplains.

Muslim Chaplains

In July 2012, the California Department of Corrections and Rehabilitation (CDCR) posted the following advertisement for the position of a Muslim prison chaplain:

> Minimum Qualifications: Currently in good standing with the American Muslim Community, verified and approved by the local resident Imam where the applicant attends as a member. All candidates must attach to their application a letter of certification of good standing issued by the local resident Imam. Education: Completion of at least two years of Islamic Religious studies, including Islamic History, the Holy Quaran, Principles of Faith and Articles of Faith in any masjid or college. Experience: Completion of the equivalent of one year of full-time supervised clinical or field training in the community. Such training to include Islamic religious counseling and guidance, religious education, and the care and welfare of the family as it relates to religious education. Completion of no less than two years experience as an Imam or Instructress in the Islamic religion in a public or private institution or masjid.[13]

In many respects, this description of a prison chaplain parallels that of an imam in a Muslim congregation. The one significant difference is that this position is open to both men and women, "an Imam or Instructress"; as a consequence there is no mention of the ability to perform liturgical services (although knowledge and facilitation of such services is usually implied). While the advertisement does not specifically outline the day-to-day activities of a chaplain, its primary focus is on two areas of responsibility: education and counseling. Here the overlap between imams and chaplains is unmistakable. Like an imam, the chaplain sought by the CDCR was expected to have a level of religious education qualifying him or her to teach and, perhaps, provide interpretation of Muslim texts and practices. In other words, this professional had to have a command of Islamic scholarship that, in the eyes of the prison constituency, placed him or her within the community of American ʿulama. In addition, as with the imam job description, the CDRC advertisement stresses that the candidates should have counseling experience. However, here the professional qualifications as a counselor are more specific, including the "completion of full-time supervised clinical or field training in the community" with a specific ability in "Islamic religious counseling."

The overall ambiguity and flexibility of this job description highlights the fact that, at the time of this posting, in this and other settings, professional standards for the Muslim chaplaincy were still in development. In addition, the advertisement speaks to the relatively high demand for prison chaplains in state and federal prison systems— owing to the large number of Muslim inmates or those who convert to Islam during their incarceration—alongside the relative lack of qualified candidates. Because of this demand, the CDCR appears to remain flexible and casts a wide net that is likely to attract a significant number of applicants. This elasticity is evident in the confluence of the terms *masjid* (mosque) and *college* and the apparent absence of any mention of an accredited training program where a candidate is expected to complete his or her studies. As was the case with the imam posting, here again there is hesitancy regarding educational formalization paired with a desire for a clearer delineation of responsibilities and training.

For example, the "completion of one year of full-time supervised clinical... training" signals that the agency prefers a candidate who has gone through a course of clinical pastoral education (CPE) as is typically carried out by centers accredited through the Association of Clinical Pastoral Education. This requirement is standard for members of the clergy from faith groups with a much longer history of participation in the institution of chaplaincy. The fact that Muslim chaplains are either required or strongly encouraged to complete similarly accredited training is a sign of the evolving professionalization of Islamic chaplaincy. In other settings, such as the Federal Bureau of Prisons, the New York State Department of Corrections, and the US military, this requirement was obligatory at least a decade before the CDCR's posting.

Because CPE is typically carried out in hospital settings, its completion is also required of full-time Muslim hospital chaplains. In fact, the hospital setting is instructive in considering the trend toward the professionalization of Muslim chaplains.

As of 2013, the number of full-time Muslim hospital chaplains was limited—about twenty individuals across the United States. To fill the need for religious services and counseling, hospitals relied mostly on volunteers from surrounding communities, typically local imams. Nonetheless, the number of professional hospital chaplains did grow from 2000 to 2013. A pioneering effort in this respect was the establishment in 2011 of Muslim Spiritual Care Services (www.muslimhealth.org), a network of professional and volunteer Muslim chaplains, which promotes the need for professional training in Islamic chaplaincy.

National, regional, and local professional organizations, such as the Association of Muslim Chaplains (www.associationofmuslimchaplains.com), are essential to the professionalization of Muslim chaplains. Tellingly, the majority of the founding members of this and other Muslim chaplain organizations were graduates or students of Hartford Seminary's Islamic chaplaincy program, founded in 1999. As this was the first Muslim chaplaincy program accredited by the agencies that recognize similar training for other American clergy, such as the Association of Theological Schools, the Hartford Seminary program has helped establish an educational rubric for the training and professionalization of Muslim chaplains.

As of 2013, the program offered by the Hartford Seminary was the only one officially recognized by the US military and the Federal Bureau of Prisons as qualified to train Muslim chaplains. Its curriculum consists of seventy-two credit hours of theological education as well as one unit of CPE and practical field education. It is therefore equivalent to the master of divinity degree granted by Christian and Jewish theological schools. In the first decade of the Hartford Seminary's existence, the program graduated twenty-one individuals, among whom thirteen were employed as chaplains and three worked in positions that could be characterized as community chaplaincy. This field of chaplaincy was developed initially by the program's first graduate, Nurah W. Amat'ullah (Rosalie P. Jeter), the founding director of Muslim Women's Institute for Research and Development, a community service organization in the Bronx, New York. Following Hartford Seminary's model, several other institutions began training Muslim chaplains in the United States and Canada. Notable among them are Bayan Claremont, a graduate program at Claremont Lincoln University, in Claremont, California, and the Muslim Chaplaincy Program at the Ecumenical Theological Seminary in Detroit, Michigan.

At the time of the CDCR's posting, programs like those at Hartford Seminary and Claremont Lincoln University were still relatively new. The CDCR's language was clearly written to allow for applications from individuals who did not have formal and accredited training. In place of a specific requirement for seminary or otherwise accredited training, the advertisement includes strict guidelines that the candidate be in "good standing with the American Muslim Community, verified and approved by the local resident Imam," and that he or she provide "a letter of certification of good standing issued by the local resident Imam." One would be hard pressed to find a similar stipulation for a Catholic or Jewish chaplain. Several factors may have contributed to this requirement. In the absence of seminary training, the certification by a local imam and recognition from the local Muslim community is one way for CDCR to make sure that the candidate meets the minimum criteria and standards set by other faith groups. In addition, the candidate's connection to a local community may help in his or her work with incarcerated individuals seeking a community of support after their release from prison.

Aside from these two considerations, another pressing concern specific to the work of Muslim chaplains has arisen as a result of the events of September 11, 2001. In the decade following the 9/11 attacks, prison authorities in the United States were deeply focused on the possible radicalization of Muslim inmates, as evident in the classification of the female inmate at the heart of Ansari's story. As a result, there has been an undercurrent of suspicion, with chaplains seen as potential conduits for this radicalization. A particularly indicative example of this phenomenon was the firing of Warith Deen Umar in 2003 after he made controversial remarks regarding the 9/11 attacks. Accusations of radicalization extended to endorsing agencies as well. For instance, prior to the signing of the Patriot Act in October 2001, ISNA was the primary endorser for Muslim chaplains in the Federal Bureau of Prisons (FBOP). However, under the Patriot Act, ISNA was named as an unindicted coconspirator to terrorism, and subsequently the FBOP stopped accepting endorsements from it.

Another case that attracted media attention was that of Captain James Yee, who served as an army chaplain at Guantanamo and in September 2003 was accused of conspiring with the facility's detainees. The charges were eventually dropped, but the concern about Muslim chaplains as potential agents of radicalization remained. By seeking to ensure that the candidate they hired was "of good standing with the American Muslim community," the CDRC was attempting to mainstream its applicants, seeing this as a counterbalance to radical fringe or freelance clerics. Other agencies, such as the New York Department of Corrections, did this by solidifying their requirements for accredited training.

The CDRC posting was obviously specific to a particular environment and emphasized certain qualifications over others. In other settings a chaplain's role may be broader but more clearly defined. For example, at the same time as the CDCR made its announcement, Trinity College and Wesleyan University, both in Connecticut, advertised a full-time Muslim university chaplaincy position to be shared between the two institutions. This advertisement was more detailed, primarily because the position had been in existence for several years, occupied by both Marwa Aly and Sohaib Sultan, the second of whom later became Princeton University's Muslim chaplain. The responsibilities for the Trinity-Wesleyan position paralleled those of other university chaplains. A chaplain would, for example, cooperate with "other campus ministers and chaplains" in developing interfaith programs and providing counseling and pastoral care to students. Although the priority was the support of the universities' Muslim constituencies, the chaplain was also expected to counsel "all members of the campus communities, and [serve] among chaplains and campus ministers of all faiths who share in providing spiritual formation and religious instruction for students." Service to all constituents within an institution, regardless of faith, is expected of Muslim chaplains across institutions. At the same time, as much as the Trinity-Wesleyan posting attempted to be specific, it still left room for flexibility. Although the posting stated a preference for a "post-baccalaureate training in pastoral care, arts of ministry and multi-faith relations," it left the issue of accreditation open, signaling both the novelty of the Muslim chaplaincy and the desire to define professional standards as the field developed.

GENDER, CONTEXT, PROFESSIONALIZATION

The previous section briefly mentions the CDCR's stated openness to hiring either male or female candidates. This is indicative of the general trend toward inclusion of women in the institution of Islamic chaplaincy in the United States. There are, of course, parallel examples of Muslim women scholars and leaders in settings outside of the United States. In most such settings, however, women function within gender-segregated institutional environments: as teachers in all-female seminaries in Iran, as prayer leaders and teachers in female mosques in China, and as murshidas, or spiritual guides, to women in Morocco. In the United States there are certainly cases where the gender of a chaplain corresponds to the population being served. For example, Sana Yusra Shabazz, one of the first female Muslim chaplains, served as a prison chaplain at Beacon Hill Correctional Facility for Women in New York State. However, in other institutional contexts, female chaplains work with both male and female populations. This is particularly widespread in universities and hospitals. In university contexts, as of 2013, about one third of all chaplains were female, most of them in coeducational institutions.

The development of Islamic chaplaincy as a new model of religious leadership that is open to women and men is representative not only of a trend among Muslim chaplains but also of the overall trend toward greater participation of women in Muslim institutions, be it mosques, community associations, or nonprofit organizations. As such, it follows certain trends toward the greater inclusion of women in the affairs of American religious organizations across a variety of faiths. As with other communities, such inclusion can entail practical day-to-day negotiations between perceptions of what is traditional or orthodox and what is necessary for the well-being of a local community. One such example is the growth in women's participation in immigrant Buddhist organizations, typically as volunteers.[14] Similarly, for American Muslim women, the path to greater participation and religious authority has often been through volunteerism. Chaplaincy can then act as the next step for women activists. This is most evident in the emergence of community chaplaincy, pioneered by Nurah W. Amat'ullah, who in 1997 established her Bronx-based organization focusing on emergency hunger relief, health education, and the transitional needs of new immigrants. After graduating from Hartford Seminary with a graduate certificate in Islamic chaplaincy, she incorporated her expertise in pastoral care into her work with Muslims, Christians, and constituents from other faith groups.

The path toward the recognition of Muslim women as chaplains and religious leaders has not been easy. The challenge comes from all sides: the non-Muslim institutions that hire Muslim chaplains as well as the chaplains' Muslim constituents. As of 2010, some 80 percent of all professional Muslim chaplains in the United States were male.[15] In the US military, there were eleven Muslim chaplains, none of whom were women. In 2005, Major Shareda Hosein, an officer in the US Army and a graduate of Hartford Seminary's Islamic Chaplaincy Program, attempted to become the first female Muslim military chaplain. Despite endorsement from the American Muslim Veteran's Affair Council, the army refused her application. At the heart of this refusal was the army's insistence that they needed a chaplain who could provide all religious services, including formal prayer leadership for male and female Muslim personnel. In other words, as in the case of Bilal Ansari, the institution demanded the services of a male imam who was also a chaplain. Hosein's argument, which she articulated in the ensuing litigation, was that chaplains do not need to be imams. She argued that their role is to facilitate religious services, not necessarily lead them; she also pointed out that prior to this the army had already recognized her as a lay religious leader. In that capacity she reported to the base chaplain and brought in a local imam to lead prayers and give Friday sermons. Whenever needed, she also wrote sermons that were delivered by male khatibs during Friday congregational prayers.[16]

Hosein's case highlights the significance of institutional culture and even bias, which determines the prerequisites for religious leadership within a given institution and creates a gray area for Muslim chaplains. For example, similar standards are present in the army's position with regard to the Catholic military chaplaincy. Catholic chaplains are exclusively male because of the stipulation that they be ordained priests able to provide a full range of Catholic liturgical services. In addition, what Hosein and Ansari's cases make clear is that although there is a stated professional distinction between chaplains and imams, male chaplains and imams often move freely between the two roles. Ultimately, for chaplains like Hosein and Ansari as with other Muslim American religious leaders, each setting provides its own specific challenges.

In defining and delineating the Muslim chaplaincy, institution is not the only challenge that Muslim chaplains face. Because Islamic chaplaincy is a new profession, the first hurdle that many encounter is with the title *chaplain* itself. As is clear from the following anecdote, related by Mary Lahaj, a hospital chaplain in the Boston area, the challenge is particularly acute for women chaplains:

Presenting myself to Muslim patients as "the chaplain," with no predecessor, role model, or handbook of instructions, gave rise to some embarrassing moments for

me. For example, there is no word in Arabic for chaplain. I remember being introduced to a Kuwaiti patient by an Arabic interpreter as "the imam." The look of disbe-
lief on the patient's face was ludicrous. After that, I decided to introduce myself as "a
Muslim sister on the staff." Then I would just go into action, ensuring that the patient's
religious (and comfort) needs were met.[17]

The Arabic interpreter who introduced Lahaj could not find an Arabic equivalent
for the word *chaplain* and so instead turned to a particularly ubiquitous leadership
model, the imam. The difficulty was that an imam is always—or almost always—male.
Therefore, as Lahaj explained, she had to keep in mind that she "needed to describe
[the chaplain's] and the imam's role as two distinct jobs." It is significant that Lahaj's
argument about the role of a chaplain mirrors Hosein's. For both Hosein and Lahaj,
the position of the Muslim chaplain was as counselor and religious professional, one
who could listen to constituents' concerns, provide spiritual care, and, when needed,
refer them to the appropriate service providers.

Hosein's definition of chaplains, as facilitating but not necessarily leading religious
services, highlights their role as professionals who establish a place for religiously
observant Muslims in secular institutions. Islamic chaplaincy is thus a conduit for
the transformation of America's key institutions, such as the military and universities. While the numbers of Muslim chaplains is relatively limited, their influence
on the reshaping of institutionalized models of religious accommodation and pluralism is significant. At the same time, Lahaj's emphasis on the distinction between
chaplains and imams reflects the way in which chaplains are reshaping Muslim and
non-Muslim perceptions of the function and gender of Muslim religious leaders. For
the constituents of female Muslim chaplains, the class of American 'ulama undeni-
ably and obviously includes women.

Consider the example of Marwa Aly, the former chaplain at Trinity and Wesleyan.
As a chaplain, she was the most visible representative of the Muslim community on
campus. A skillful public speaker, she spoke regularly at various events for Muslims
and the broader campus community. However, when it came to the *jumu'a*, she
facilitated the weekly prayer by arranging for a male to serve as the imam for the
occasion. Unlike the cases of the CDRC advertisement, in which a chaplain needed
to be approved by a local imam, or Hosein who facilitated prayer by inviting a local
imam to lead it, the imams at the Trinity-Wesleyan prayers were students taught by
Aly herself.

Referring back to Bilal Ansari, this example also highlights the type of negotiation
and experimentation that is happening through the Islamic chaplaincy. In Aly's case,
her actions resulted in the expansion of a form of leadership and authority being
carved out by Muslim women. It is important to stress the organic, subtle, and everyday nature of this process. Muslim chaplains should not be seen as rebelling against
Islamic practice. The very nature of their work—which is centered on the needs of
their constituents, the primacy of pastoral care, and the preservation and restoration

of harmony within their communities—goes against any type of radical nonconsensual change. For chaplains to meet the challenge of their calling, they have to connect with their Muslim constituents and represent Muslims in broader settings. It is the contextually specific needs of their constituents and the institutions in which they work that create possibilities for change. As Aly explained to one of the authors, "My whole purpose is to empower the students on campus. Upon graduation they'll have the skills to give a *khutba* [sermon]." "But," she added, "hopefully, they'll remember that the one who taught them was a woman."

Within the Muslim chaplaincy, contestations with regard to gender play an important role in the development of new and contextually driven delineations of what it means to be a Muslim religious professional. "Chaplains are not imams and imams are not chaplains," is an often heard refrain of American Muslim leaders. This intended delineation is complex and fluid, yet it has not only helped to shape the understanding of what a Muslim chaplain is but also facilitated a reshaping of the role of an imam as American religious professional.

As the professions of imam and chaplain become institutionalized within Muslim communities and non-Muslim organizations, specific sensibilities arise regarding what the class of American Muslim religious professionals should look like. For non-Muslim institutions they become a part of the larger category of American clergy. For American Muslims, both professions become key models for the development of the American 'ulama. In both cases, whether speaking about the American 'ulama or the American Muslim clergy, communities and institutions will ultimately have to negotiate the roles of imam and chaplain with respect to institutional context, professionalization, and gender.

NOTES

1. For a detailed analysis of Ansari's engagement with Muslim legal discourses that relate to this issue, see his master's thesis: Bilal Ansari, "The Foundations of Pastoral Care in Islam: Reviving the Pastoral Voice in Islamic Prison Chaplaincy" (Hartford, CT: Hartford Seminary, 2011). As of July 2013, Ansari was serving as the Muslim chaplain at Williams College.
2. Patrick Gaffney, *The Prophet's Pulpit: Islamic Preaching in Contemporary Egypt* (Berkeley: University of California Press, 1994), 31.
3. Ihsan Bagby, *The American Mosque 2011: Basic Characteristics of the American Mosque Attitudes of Mosque Leaders*, Report Number 1 from the US Mosque Study, by (Washington, DC: Council on American Islamic Relations, 2011), 4. Available at: http://faithcommunitiestoday.org/sites/faithcommunitiestoday.org/files/The%20American%20Mosque%202011%20web.pdf(Accessed July 25, 2013.)
4. Ibid.
5. Ihsan Bagby, *The American Mosque 2011: Activities, Administration and Vitality of the American Mosque*, Report Number 2 from the US Mosque Study (Washington, DC: Islamic Society of North America, 2012), 12.

6. *Islamic Horizons,* May/June 2010, 45.
7. Ingrid Mattson, "Can a Woman be an Imam? Debating Form and Function in Muslim Women's Leadership," Available at: http://thepurestfaith.files.wordpress.com/2012/03/muslim-womens-leadership-dr-mattson.pdf (Accessed October 28, 2013.)
8. Omar Sacirbey, "With a New Imam, a New Outlook," Boston Globe, December 3, 2011. Available at: http://www.suhaibwebb.com/miscellaneous/announcements/boston-globe-with-a-new-imam-a-new-outlook/ (Accessed July 26, 2013.)
9. Ihsan Bagby, Paul M. Perl, and Bryan T. Froehle, *The Mosque in American a National Portrait* (Washington, DC: Council on American Islamic Relations, 2001), 19.
10. Andrea Elliot, "An Imam in America: A Calling Beyond Brooklyn (a Three Part Series)," *New York Times*, March 5, 6, 7, 2006.
11. Ihsan Baghby, "The Mosque and the American Public Square," in *Muslims' Place in the American Public Square: Hopes Fears and Aspirations*, eds. Zahid H. Bukhari, Sulayman S. Nyang, Mumtaz Ahmad, and John L. Esposito (Walnut Creek, CA: Altamira Press, 2004), 331.
12. Osman M. Ali, Glen Milstein, and Peter M. Marzok, "The Imam's Role in Meeting the Counseling Needs of Muslim Communities in the United States," *Psychiatric Services Online* 56, no. 2 (February 2005), 203. Available at: http://ps.psychiatryonline.org/data/Journals/PSS/3635/202.pdf (Accessed July 26, 2013.)
13. For the posting see: http://jobs.spb.ca.gov/wvpos/more_info.cfm?recno=494066 (Last accessed on July 7, 2013.)
14. See Wendy Cage, "Gendered Religious Organizations: The Case of Theravada Buddhism in America," *Gender and Society* 18, 6 (2004): 777–793.
15. Betsy (Mumina) A. Kowalski, "A New Profession: Muslim Chaplains in American Public Life," master's thesis (Hartford, CT: Hartford Seminary, 2011).
16. "A Soldier of Faith," *Washington Post*, January 20, 2008. Available at: http://www.washingtonpost.com/wp-dyn/content/article/2008/01/16/AR2008011603131.html (Accessed July 24, 2013.)
17. Mary Lahaj, "Making It Up as I Go Along," *Reflective Practice: Formation and Supervision in Ministry*, vol. 29 (2009): 148–153. Available at: http://journals.sfu.ca/rpfs/index.php/rpfs/issue/view/47 (Accessed July 24, 2013.)

Bibliography

Ahmed, Sameera, and Mona M. Amer. *Counseling Muslims: Handbook of Mental Health Issues and Interventions* (New York: Brunner-Routledge, 2011).
Antoun, Richard T. *Muslim Preacher in the Modern World: A Jordanian Case Study in Comparative Perspective* (Princeton, NJ: Princeton University Press, 1989).
Beasley, Vanessa B., *Who Belongs in America? Presidents, Rhetoric, and Immigration.* Presidential Rhetoric Series. (College Station: Texas A&M University Press, 2006).
General Office of the Inspector, "*A Review of the Federal Bureau of Prisons Selection of Muslim Religious Providers*" (Washington, DC: US Department of Justice, April 2004).
Haddad, Yvonne Yazbeck, Jane I. Smith, and Kathleen M. Moore, *Muslim Women in America: The Challenge of Islamic Identity Today* (New York: Oxford University Press, 2006).

Hammer, Juliane, *American Muslim Women, Religious Authority, and Activism: More Than a Prayer*. Louann Atkins Temple Women & Culture Series (Austin: University of Texas Press, 2012).

Karim, Jamillah, *American Muslim Women: Negotiating Race, Class, and Gender within the Umma* (New York: New York University Press, 2009).

Khoja-Moolji, Shenila S., "An Emerging Model of Muslim Leadership: Chaplaincy on University Campuses." Ed. The Pluralism Project (Cambridge, MA: Harvard University Press, April 2001).

Morgan, John H., *Muslim Clergy in America: Ministry as Profession in the Islamic Community*. Expanded 2nd ed. Lima, OH: Wyndham Hall Press, 2010.

Slomovitz, Albert Isaac, *The Fighting Rabbis: Jewish Military Chaplains and American History* (New York: New York University Press, 1999).

SpearIt. "Facts and Fictions About Islam in Prison: Assessing Prisoner Radicalization in Post-9/11 America" (Washington, DC: Institute for Social Policy and Understanding, January 2013).

Sullivan, Winnifred Fallers, *Prison Religion: Faith-Based Reform and the Constitution* (Princeton, NJ: Princeton University Press, 2009).

Yee, James, and Aimee Molloy, *For God and Country: Faith and Patriotism under Fire* (New York: Public Affairs, 2005).

Zaman, Muhammad Qasim, *The Ulama in Contemporary Islam: Custodians of Change*. Princeton Studies in Muslim Politics (Princeton, NJ: Princeton University Press, 2002).

CHAPTER 4

ISLAMIC ORGANIZATIONS IN THE UNITED STATES

JOCELYNE CESARI

INTRODUCTION

For Muslims in the United States, unlike their counterparts in Europe, there is a "before 9/11" and an "after 9/11." Before 9/11, although Islam was already perceived as an international political threat, it rarely came under attack or scrutiny as a danger for American civil liberties or political values. There were, of course, controversies over the wearing of headscarves, particularly in the business world. But the United States' strong judicial tradition of defending religious freedom worked in favor of Muslims, without turning each legal case into a nationwide debate.

Such invisibility has disappeared since 9/11. An entire religion is subjected not only to widespread public suspicion but also to government surveillance of its activities and associations. The actions carried out in the name of the War on Terror include police searches of organizations' offices and arrests of people accused of belonging to militant Islamic organizations, and these actions have been denounced by Muslim leaders and others as just so many attacks on civil liberties. With the election of President Obama in 2008, the situation has been further exacerbated. Since then, anti-Islamic activist groups have initiated campaigns against the building of mosques, backed anti-Sharia bills, and supported other acts of hostility against the visibility of Islam in public spaces. This public scrutiny of Islam brings together for the first time the American and European experiences.

This before and after 9/11 situation has influenced the development and strategy of Islamic organizations. Before 9/11, ethnic and cultural features were as powerful as Islam in the mobilization of Muslims through associations or organizations. In other words, Pakistani American, Arab American, and African American organizations were as important as Islamic ones. Even the places of worship were strongly influenced or dominated by one ethnic or cultural group (Cesari, 2004). After 9/11, the Islamic factor disconnected from its multiple cultural backgrounds has been increasingly more influential in the public perception of Muslims and in the way that Muslims present themselves in social and political interactions on the American public scene. It has not, however, completely erased the racial and social divides between African American and immigrant Muslims.

ISLAMIC ORGANIZATIONS VERSUS CIVIC ORGANIZATIONS

The emergence of a Muslim minority within American society is fairly new. One reason for this delayed mobilization is that, despite the considerable number of African American converts to Islam, African Americans are more commonly defined by their skin color or ethnicity rather than by their religious practice and beliefs. This perception is partially explained by the fact that the Nation of Islam, as well as other, more short-lived organizations such as the Islamic Party, have always advocated for segregation and rejection of American core political values. The founder of the Nation of Islam, Elijah Mohammed (1897–1975), was imprisoned during World War II for having exhorted the black population not to vote or serve in the military. The acceptance of an African American role in mainstream politics is a relatively recent phenomenon. Among those black leaders who have been influential in American civil society was Warith Deen Mohammad (1933–2008), the head of the Muslim American Society.[1] One of the largest Muslim organizations in the United States, did not survive the resignation and then the death of its leader. The second reason for the relatively recent emergence of the American Muslim minority is that Arabs or other Muslims who immigrated to America from the 1920s through the 1950s were for the most part progressively assimilated into American culture.

It was only after 1967 that Islam became a central element of collective identity in the United States. For immigrants who entered the country after 1965, Islam was the primary means of cultural and political identification—in contrast to their predecessors, who had built their identity more on the basis of Arab nationalism. Thus, Arab activists, formerly concerned with issues related to the Middle East, and to Palestine in particular, have begun instead to form Islamic associations. The Federation of Islamic Associations (FIA), founded in 1953, played a pioneering role in this area but never quite succeeded in overcoming the tensions between first- and second-generation immigrants.

Since then, Muslims have taken one of two paths to inclusion in American civil society: Islamic associations and civic activism.

Religious Organizations

The late 1970s and the 1980s witnessed the construction of an active movement for the cause of Islam in the West and an increase in American Muslims' concern with domestic issues and involvement in American society. Settling in America required undertaking a conscious effort to create the psychological space and institutional infrastructure for a permanent Muslim presence.

The Islamic Society of North America (ISNA) was created in 1982 as a result of the diversification and specialization within the Muslim Student Association (MSA).[2] It was established to address the changing needs of the MSA constituency, which at the time was largely made up of immigrant students residing temporarily in the United States. As these members graduated from colleges and universities across the country, started families, joined the workforce, and otherwise begin to make permanent their stay in America, their needs outgrew the resources and purpose of the MSA. It was this need for institutions that could serve expanding religious, social, civic, and professional interests that led MSA leadership to create ISNA. Now an umbrella organization, ISNA has come to supersede its parent entity in both size and activity. It is a coalition of different types of local organizations, including Islamic centers and professional associations (such as lawyers' or physicians' groups).

According to the organization's mission statement, "ISNA is an association of Muslim organizations and individuals that provides a common platform for presenting Islam, supporting Muslim communities, developing educational, social and outreach programs and fostering good relations with other religious communities, and civic and service organizations" (ISNA, 2012).

Organizationally, ISNA consists of the Majlis al-Shura (policy-making board), the Executive Council, and the General Secretariat, which handles administrative and financial affairs. ISNA divides its continental US and Canadian constituency into five zones, each with a representative who sits on the executive board. Affiliated groups function with their own boards and committees. The Majlis al-Shura and the Executive Council are composed of both elected and appointed members, whereas the General Secretariat consists of full-time paid employees. Members and staff in these institutions come from a diverse background, which includes but is not restricted to immigrants of Arab, European, African, and Asian origin; second-generation children of immigrants born in the United States; and indigenous white, black, and Latino Americans who were either born of Muslim parentage in the United States or have adopted the Islamic faith as an individual choice.

Ilyas Ba-Yunus was the first president of ISNA (1983–1985), during whose term ISNA acquired and expanded on many of the predecessor organization's programs and resources. Ingrid Mattson became the first woman to occupy an Executive Council position when she was elected Vice President. Mattson again made history in 2006 when she was elected as president of ISNA, the first female and indigenous Muslim convert to hold this position atop one of America's largest and most influential Muslim organizations.

ISNA represents a traditionally based orientation of Islam. Its membership and leadership come from a range of schools of thought and sects within Islam, although the majority are Sunni. ISNA is advised in matters of Islamic jurisprudence by the independent Fiqh Council of North America (FCNA). FCNA is a body of sixteen scholars from difference religious persuasion within Islam who study religious questions as they arise and issue *fatwas* (rulings). FCNA does not subscribe to any one of the five major schools (four Sunni and one Shi'a) of law exclusively but seeks to address novel conditions that emerge as a result of a unique North American–Islamic convergence in light of historically accepted and honored legal methodology.

Today, some 300 Islamic centers and professional organizations are affiliated with ISNA. Founding constituents of ISNA include the Association of Muslim Social Scientists (AMSS), the Islamic Medical Association of North America (IMANA), the Association of Muslim Scientists and Engineers (AMSE), the Muslim Students Association of the US and Canada (MSA), and the North American Islamic Trust (NAIT), which was established to hold titles of mosques, community centers, and schools required by the growing number and religious devotion of Muslim families. In addition, the Council of Islamic Schools in North America (CISNA), the Muslim Youth of North America (MYNA), and the Islamic Media Foundation (IMF) are also represented on ISNA's Majlis al-Shura. In 1973, NAIT founded the American Trust Publications (ATP) to publish Islamic educational material that was also relevant to the unique American context. Since its founding, ATP has published more than 260 titles that include both Islamic literature developed in America and classic religious texts. ISNA publishes a bimonthly magazine, *Islamic Horizons*, with a circulation of 60,000.

A few of the many services ISNA provides are the Speaker's Bureau, matrimonial services, *shahadah* and Islamic marriage certificates, ISNA Zakat fund, Islamic *da'wah* literature, inheritance distribution counseling, and the Islamic Book Service. ISNA's annual convention, the largest annual Muslim event in America, attracts an average of more than 30,000 attendees. Similarly, AMSE, AMSS, and IMANA hold conventions each year. ISNA also regularly hosts specialized conferences including but not limited to "Islam in America," "Islamic Education Forum," "Community Development Conference," "Islamic Perspectives on Counseling," "Islam in American Prisons," "Muslim Refugees in America," and "Seminars on Conflict Resolution and Domestic Violence," which bring together Muslim and non-Muslim academicians and experts to address and collaborate on related concerns emerging within

American Muslim communities. The North American Islamic Trust was established in 1973 by the MSA as a not-for-profit Saudi-backed endowment that seeks to serve Muslims within the United States. It supports services and has close relationships with ISNA, MSA and their affiliates, and other Islamic institutions within the United States. As an Islamic endowment, the organization is interested in funding real estate associated with mosques, Islamic schools, and Muslim community projects, as well as developing financial products (such as mutual funds) that are compatible with Islamic and American law.[3]

The organization has been recognized by the American government as a means to connect with and develop a relationship with its Muslim constituency. In 2005, Undersecretary of State for Public Diplomacy Karen Hughes addressed the community at ISNA's annual convention. The Deputy Secretary of Defense, Gordon R. England, also spoke to the meeting participants on September 1, 2006.

ISNA was one of the first among major Muslim American and Canadian organizations to issue statements of condemnation hours after the terrorist attacks of 9/11. The organization reaffirmed its claim continually in subsequent years and was a signatory of the Fiqh Council of North America's *fatwa* reiterating the illegality of terrorism issued in 2005. It has recently established the ISNA Office of Interfaith and Community Alliances (IOICA) in Washington, DC, in an effort to build avenues for dialogue and inter-religious harmony. The president of ISNA at the time of this writing, Imam Mohamed Magid has been particularly involved in the denunciation of radicalism. He has actively cooperated with the FBI and law enforcement officers (ISNA, 2012) to report any suspicious activity or person in the proximity of mosques or Islamic organizations.

The issue of women's involvement in Muslim public space has also been a point of concern for ISNA. The reality of female exclusion and severe segregation in, for example, mosque prayer space and governing bodies have led to an outcry against a patriarchal domination in Muslim communities and institutions. An initiative undertaken by the ISNA Leadership Development Center seeks to combat this trend and endorses new guidelines for women-friendly mosques. In June 2005, it published and widely distributed "Women Friendly Mosques and Community Centers: Working Together to Reclaim Our Heritage" jointly with the Islamic Social Services Associations (ISSA) and Women in Islam (WII). The report makes an argument for visible and equal female participation and engagement within the public realm based on Quran and *sunnah*, which ISNA hopes to promulgate among its constituency (Haddad, 1993, pp. 16–18; Smith, 1999, pp. 170–1).

The ICNA is the other major Muslim umbrella organization in the United States. It was inspired by the Islamic party Jamaat-Pakistani Islamiyya.[4] Prior to its official formation as ICNA in 1971, it was inaugurated in September 1968 with the Urdu name of *Halqa Islami Shamali Amrika*, which translates in English as the Islamic Circle of North America. The organization is an example of Muslim social and cultural integration in the West and illustrates the adaptation of the Pakistani Jamaat-I Islami methodology to the American context with its focus on the development of civic activities rather than the claim for an Islamic state (Leonard, 2003b).

ICNA is headquartered in Jamaica, New York, with regional offices in Detroit, Michigan, and Oakville, Ontario. It is a nonpolitical social organization dedicated to religious education, social services, youth development, and the overall strengthening of Muslim identity among American Muslims. The organization's self-proclaimed goal is "to seek the pleasure of Allah (God) through the struggle of *Iqamat-ud-Deen* (establishment of the Islamic system of life) as spelled out in the Qur'an and the Sunnah of Prophet Muhammad." ICNA copied from the methodology of Jamaat-I Islami—to facilitate the establishment of an Islamic society by way of education, welfare work, social reform, and due engagement with political processes.

Organizationally, ICNA is led by an *ameer* (president), secretary general, vice president, executive council, eight zonal representatives, and a consultative body called the *Majlis Ash-shura*. It has three divisions: the ICNA Sisters Wing, Young Muslims, and Young Muslims Sisters. All divisions work semi-independently but also have representatives on ICNA central Shura Council, which oversees the organization as a whole. ICNA is primarily concerned with *dawah* (proselytizing) and *tarbiyyah* (religious learning), interested principally with character-building of individual Muslims and facilitating easy access to information on Islam for a non-Muslim community. It is heavily involved in interfaith work. ICNA's multitiered structure is founded on the local level with its "neighbor-nets," which hold monthly meetings and study circles. Neighbor-nets are conglomerated in city/town chapters, then state, and finally regional bodies. On an individual level, members are required to dedicate 2 hours weekly to a social or civic service. For this reason, ICNA members have become well known for their community volunteer work within both Muslim and non-Muslim communities.

Sociologically, founders and current members are largely immigrants of South Asian background, a majority of them being Indian and Pakistani immigrants or recent descendents. However, membership is open to any Muslim woman or man agreeing to the organizations goals and initiatives. ICNA is most active in the Northeastern region of the United States, but its members are spread throughout the United States and Canada. Currently, there are an estimated 100 regular monthly study groups, and approximately 10,000 participants attend its annual convention. ICNA also claims more than a dozen affiliated mosque communities.

Due to its links with Jamaat Islamiyaa, accusations have been levied against ICNA as a US-based front for more radical actions. These accusations have been repeatedly denied by the organization, and inquiry into the organization has successfully removed the group from suspicion and formal charges against it by government agencies have been dropped, as the latest release from terrorism financing scrutiny reaffirms. In December 2003, the US Senate Finance Committee sent a letter to the Internal Revenue Service requesting financial histories and details on 25 organizations, including ICNA. Nearly 2 years later, in November 2005 after a stalled and

informal investigation, the organization was cleared of all suspicion of financing terrorist groups and activities. The Committee acknowledged that nothing indicated
such misgivings were appropriate or that further investigation was warranted.

Furthermore, given the fact that Muslims are a minority in the United States,
ICNA activism diverges dramatically from the political goals of the Jamaat-I Islami
in Pakistan. An active political force in Pakistan, the Jamaat has been a dynamic
actor in government, running in elections, occupying cabinet posts, and influencing
the formulation of state policy. ICNA does not maintain aspirations of establishing
Islamic governance in the United States; rather it tries to reinforce religious practices
and identity among American Muslims.

Subsequently, founding members of ICNA set out to establish local study groups
and focus on community development. As a result, ICNA programs include the
establishment of Islamic information hotlines, wide-scale production and distribution of religious literature, establishment of soup kitchens, and outreach to prisons,
campuses, media via direct contact, mailings, electronic mailings, and web-based
information sites and publication. It also established one of the first shelters for
Muslim women in the United States. Educational programs focus on weekly community study circles and periodic religious conferences and retreats. ICNA's participation in the American political sphere is minimal, and individual members are left
to speak for and by their own accord. While ICNA takes no direct or formal political
stands, as it cannot given its 501(c)3 IRS-approved tax-exempt status, it does encourage the political awareness, education, and participation of its membership.

Over the past few years, ICNA has begun to play a more vocal role in political and
intellectual discussions emerging in and around the Muslim American community.
Among the most noteworthy are full political participation, advocacy of civil liberties,
and unequivocal condemnation of violence and terrorism. Their 2003 annual convention was themed "Muslims: Citizens of the West: Rights, Duties and Prospects"
and included sessions on history and process of the American political system and
media relations and was addressed by then presidential candidate General Wesley
Clark. ICNA has also become more conscious of civil liberties and responsibilities. At
the hands of its head civil rights advocate, Adem Carroll, ICNA has collaborated with
the Council on American-Islamic Relations to sponsor informational seminar and
provide legal counsel in major cities such as New York, Philadelphia, and Houston. In
July 2005, ICNA was among 144 other Muslim American organizations and religious
leaders to cosign the *fatwa* (formal legal opinion) issued by the Fiqh Council of North
America condemning terrorism.

ICNA is part of the Islamic Shura Council of North America (ISCNA) (1993), a
conglomerate of four of the largest and most representative Muslim organizations in
the United States: ICNA, ISNA, American Muslim Association formerly under the
leadership of Imam Warith Deen Mohammed, and the community under the leadership of Imam Jamil Al-Amin. ISCNA is most noteworthy on two counts: its col-
laborative efforts between the major indigenous and immigrant Muslim American

organizations and its part in facilitating the joint observance of Ramadan and the two Islamic holidays among the majority of US Muslims. The dates for these holidays are determined by the sighting of the new moon. and methodological differences have led to the observance of these holidays on different days within the same or nearby regions. ICNA is also a member organization of the American Muslim Taskforce for Disaster Relief (AMTFDR), which was originally formed in response to Hurricane Katrina (Southeast USA, 2005). AMFTDR was made permanent with its efforts to also provide coordinated and efficient relief to South Asia following the 7.6 magnitude earthquake of October 2005 whose epicenter was in the Pakistan-administered disputed region of Kashmir. Through it, ICNA collaborates with ISNA, Council on American-Islamic Relations (CAIR), Islamic Relief Worldwide, American Muslim Society, Muslim Public Affairs Council, and North American Islamic Trust, among others. ICNA joined other major Muslim American organizations in their condemnations of the terrorist attacks of 9/11 (United States) and July 8, 2005 (United Kingdom).

ICNA is a very active interfaith participant. ICNA Relief is a member of the New York Disaster Interfaith Service (NYDIS) and the National Voluntary Organizations Active in Disaster (NVOAD). Mohammad T. Rahman of ICNA Relief serves as a vice president on the 2006 board of directors for NYDIS among other officers, staff, and members of Christian, Jewish, Sikh, and Buddhist faiths. The American Red Cross and the Salvation Army are also members of NVOAD. ICNA has campaigned for and spoken out on a number of shared concerns among America's faith based communities through its interfaith partnerships. It is a signatory of the Catholic Relief Services' (CRS) Interfaith Statement in Support of Comprehensive Immigration Reform (October 2005). The CRS operates on five continents and in 99 countries. Other signatories include the Anti-Defamation League and the Institute on Religion and Public Policy. With the Committee on Ecumenical and Interreligious Affairs, ICNA has participated in the Mid-Atlantic Catholic-Muslim Regional Dialogue for the past six years. As a result, a joint statement on the state of marriage and family life in America is published in 2006, intended to assist both religious and lay workers in maintaining strong faith-based relationships for those under their care. ICNA's regional chapters are also active in interfaith work on the local level. In July 2004, the Houston community established the Apache Indian Bus Fund to assist the Jumano Apache Indian Tribe purchase school resources and supplies.

The *Message International Magazine* is published by ICNA monthly. The content covers issues pertaining to the Muslim world such as relationships between the West and Muslim countries. Increasingly, it covers emerging concerns of the North American community including intergender relations and dating for Muslim youth, banking with respect to Islamic principles, and moon-sighting techniques for such religious enormities as the dating of Ramadan. The magazine is published separately in the United States and Canada with a combined circulation of 25,000 copies.

ICNA has been active in the area of literature and audiovisual production. The ICNA Book Service was established with the purpose of providing high-quality

Islamic literature to Muslims living in North America. ICNA's Sound Vision department offers an estimated 1500 items, including audiotapes, videotapes, and computer programs that are purchased by consumers across the United States, Canada, and England. ICNA provides a variety of literature in numerous forms, including written, audiovisual, and multimedia. Topics range from fiction written for American-born Muslim adolescents, art and architecture, family and marriage, to hadith and Qur'an sciences (sayings and actions of Muhammad) collections, Qur'anic commentary, and history. Sound Vision has also been at the forefront of creating a new genre of English-language mainstream music for Muslim youth such as rap artists of African, South Asian, and Arab decent who perform lyrics written about religious practice in the United States. It has garnered much popularity because of its work with Dawud Wharnsby Ali. Ali was one of the first serious singers-songwriters to develop the genre of English-language *nasheeds* (Islamic spiritual songs).

Among its more specific religious and cultural activities is the growingly popular "Great Muslim Adventure Day" held at Six Flags Great Adventure in New Jersey and first organized in 2000. For this annual event ICNA with a number of co-sponsors rents the park and with the intention of accommodating the Muslim family. This includes the performances of Islamic music groups, *halal* food (prepared according to religious law) at food stalls, public declaration of the *adhan* (call to prayer) for four of the five daily prayers, and speeches by popular Islamic scholars such as Zaid Shakir.

ICNA Relief is a division of ICNA with the objective of providing humanitarian aid to Muslims abroad as well as establishing services in poor neighborhoods in cities across North America. From it has emerged family counseling centers, women's shelters, soup kitchens, and blood drives, which were increased in the aftermath of the terrorist attacks of 9/11.

Neither ISNA nor ICNA is representative, however, of all the currents of American Islam. Despite the ecumenical claims of its successive presidents, ISNA has never been able to reunite the American Muslim community. In past years, it has come under criticism for insufficient inclusion, appreciation, and participation of African American Muslims. While ISNA's membership includes a wide range of immigrant and indigenous, first- and succeeding-generation American Muslims, and multiethnic populations, African Americans have not always felt fully understood or accepted by ISNA's general body and sometimes held that the content of ISNA's conventions, publications, and initiatives do not address the unique experiences of the black community. As such, it is still largely perceived as an immigrant organization. However, as more African American scholars and professionals assume leadership positions in the organization (Majlis As-Shura), and younger-generation Muslims born and raised in the United States become members, the incongruence is decreasing.

ISNA has also been criticized for leaning too much to the right in terms of Islamic interpretation. The majority of books and tapes sold at the ISNA's Annual Convention are indeed strongly biased toward the Salafi movement and leave little space for more liberal or progressive options. This criticism is also a reflection of the absence of representation within ISNA of minority movements, such as Shi'ite or Sufi Islam, and sectarian groups such as Ahmadiyya. In other words, ISNA until now reflects the image of the Muslim immigrant elite: conservative, Sunni, and responsive to the messages of Saudi/Wahhabi Islam or of the Muslim Brotherhood.

Muslim Lobby Groups

Since the 1980s, there has been a growing number of Islamic organizations active in US political life. Liberty of conscience and freedom of expression being the cornerstones of American civil society, Muslims express themselves with a freedom unknown to European Muslims, and, *a fortiori*, to those living in the Muslim world.

As a consequence, a considerable number of organizations, journals, and institutes have been created in the past 15 years to counteract the prevailing demonization of Islam in American public sphere. The efforts of the Council on American-Islamic Relations (CAIR) have been particularly representative, in this respect, of the emerging Muslim voice. The Council was created in 1994 in order to document instances of bias against Muslims and Islam and to confront anti-Muslim prejudice. According to its mission statement, CAIR aims to encourage dialogue and enhance the understanding of Islam in a way that protects civil liberties and empowers Muslim Americans. CAIR also seeks to empower the American Muslim community by educating it about legal rights and responsibilities and insisting that Islamic identity and full participation as American citizens can legitimately be synthesized.

Their lobbying efforts have consisted of using existing public laws to defend the rights of Islam, including the right to practice Islam in the name of religious freedom.[5] CAIR has brought numerous lawsuits before the courts in defense of Muslims— against the government, businesses, and the media—on First Amendment grounds, as well as those of the Civil Rights Act of 1964 and Equal Opportunity laws. The organization has won countless victories in high-profile lawsuits against corporations such as Nike and Budweiser that were convicted of having used Islamic images to attack the beliefs of Muslims or of treating Muslim employees in a discriminatory fashion. After 9/11 the group's primary focus has been the struggle against anti-Muslim discrimination in the name of the "War on Terror."

CAIR is the largest Islamic civil rights and advocacy organization in America and has thirty-two regional chapters throughout the United States and Canada. The relationship between CAIR's national and regional offices is flexible and indefinite, with the national office maintaining minimal control over daily operations. All chapters maintain separate executive boards, staffs, and web pages. Financially and legally, chapters are independent entities. The CAIR national office currently has departments focused on civil rights, media, government affairs, research and mediation, and legislative counsel.

As a civil rights defense organization, CAIR has played a central role in identifying and responding to cases of religious discrimination, defamation, and hate crimes perpetrated against Muslims. Their Civil Rights Department focuses on education and defense of the constitutional liberties of American Muslims. CAIR's Government Relations Department monitors legislation and government policies and seeks to present Muslim responses to developments of concern as well as to advise legislators and executives on issues of sensitivity regarding the Muslim community. CAIR's Communications Department monitors media portrayal of Islam and Muslims on the local, national, and international levels.

Among CAIR's most notable achievements are the 1996 Simon and Schuster publishing company's recall of a world religion textbook in which the Prophet Muhammad was inaccurately and offensively represented and the 1998/99 redesigning of a Nike shoe on which the Arabic word for "God" was positioned on the heel. CAIR has also played an active role supporting religious accommodation in the workplace. In May 2001, under pressure by CAIR, United Airlines reformed its dress code allowing for the donning of "a company sanctioned hijab, turban, or yarmulke as part of [their] uniform."

CAIR is an active community participant. It regularly works with a variety of Muslim, civic, political, human rights, and civil liberties organizations with whom it shares interests and concerns. In 1996, CAIR joined with other advocacy groups in a grassroots campaign to get out the American Muslim vote. As part of this effort they began to survey their constituencies about their political views. For the 2000 presidential elections, a CAIR poll reported a preference for Bush, with 33 percent of the Muslim interviewees backing him against 28 percent in favor of Gore (Rose, 2001). These numbers shifted drastically in the 2004 election, where a CAIR poll found that 93 percent of interviewed American Muslims voted for John Kerry (Poole and Ali, 2005).Since then, Muslims have been voting consistently for Democratic party candidates. For the 2012 presidential election, 85.7 percent of the Muslims polled voted for Obama and 4.4 percent voted for Romney[6] (CAIR, 2012).

Though its primary concern is antidefamation, CAIR soon took on a role as research institute on the topic of Islam in America. A study on Mosques in America (413 mosques were surveyed, 66 percent of the total identified by the surveyors) was conducted in conjunction with Hartford Seminary's Institute for Religious Research in 2000. The results of the survey, reported in April 2001, sought to shed light on the demographics of the Muslim American community, its growth, leadership trends, the participation of women, and the nature of activity particularly in the context of organized mosque settings. However, concerns have been raised regarding the methodology and subsequent conclusions of the survey. While the survey report claims that the responding mosques revealed characteristics that can be considered true of most of the 1206 identified ones (5 percent margin of error), some scholars such as Karen Leonard (2003a) have suggested that this survey favors particular ethnic groups and economic and educational brackets. The survey seems to have excluded mosques without stable phone numbers or addresses, thereby excluding a large number of less wealthy and urban communities, particularly indigenous African American congregations without the capability to become permanent by the survey's definition yet still maintaining a high number of members and regular Friday prayer services. The survey also excluded Muslim communities associated with universities and businesses that do not have regular Friday prayers, thereby failing to consider the beliefs, trends, and persuasions of a hugely influential portion of the Muslim American demographic. Tom Smith, a professor at the University of Chicago, has also criticized the integrity of CAIR's survey methodology, particularly in regard to its estimates of the Muslim population in America (Smith, 2002).

In 2011, CAIR conducted another survey and found that there has been a 74 percent increase in the number of mosques since the previous survey in 2000 (from 1209 mosques in 2000 to 2106 in 2011). The survey called into question the existing low estimates of Muslims in America, 1 to 2.4 million, and instead suggested that since 2.6 million Muslims attend the Eid Prayer, the Muslim population should be estimated at around 7 million. Additionally, the survey claims that "the vast majority of mosques are located in metropolitan areas, but the percentage of mosques in urban areas is decreasing and the percentage of mosques in suburban areas is increasing," with 28 percent of mosques now located in the suburbs, whereas in 2000 only 16 percent of mosques were in the suburbs (CAIR, 2011, pg. 4). In terms of ethnic makeup, "3 percent of mosques have only one ethnic group that attends that mosque," and new immigrants, such as Somalis, West Africans, and Iraqis, are a significant new minority among the South Asians, Arabs, and African Americans. Furthermore, the 2011 survey concludes that Muslim involvement in American society is endorsed by mosque leadership, with "over 98 percent of mosque leaders agree that Muslims should be involved in American institutions; and 91 percent agree that Muslims should be involved in politics" (CAIR, 2011, pg. 4).

After 9/11, CAIR's role as hate-crime and discrimination sentinel was both intensified and diversified. The organization published numerous reports on discrimination and civil liberties in the aftermath of the terrorist attacks.

Between 1994 and 2001, CAIR established 12 regional offices, whereas 19 were formed within the past five years between 2001 and 2006. CAIR was one of the first American Muslim organizations to condemn the terrorist attacks publicly. Within a few days, it had published full-page ads in major news media, including *The Washington Post*, a trend that was then imitated by other national and local organizations. Increased incidents of discrimination toward both Muslims and non-Muslims, who were mistaken as Muslims, lead to a growth in CAIR's workload and services outside of the Muslim community. CAIR determined that the most effective way to combat the public's lack of knowledge about Islam and the dearth of accurate information on Muslims in America was to adopt a policy and program of proactive education. This led to new research initiatives such as annual surveys intended to monitor public opinion about Muslims in America. Proactive educational initiatives were also reintroduced with a new vigor, an example being the Library Project. In efforts to stock libraries with balanced and accurate information about Islam and Muslims CAIR undertook a campaign to compile 18-item resource packages. These packages are sponsored by CAIR members and gifted to public libraries; 8000 of the 16,000 registered US public libraries have accepted them to date.

CAIR's leadership was initially dominated by Muslims with a Middle Eastern immigrant background, although it has become more diverse in the past ten years. The organization was co-founded by Omar Ahmad and Nihad Awad in 1994. Omar Ahmad led CAIR through its inaugural decade (1994–2005) and oversaw its development into the largest Muslim civil rights organization. He emigrated to the United States from Jordan and holds a B.S. and M.S. in computer engineering. Ahmad is regularly interviewed by major news media including *The Washington Post, The New York Times,* and *The Los Angeles Times,* and is a well-known community activist in the San Francisco Bay area. Nihad Awad, who was born in Jordan and became an American citizen after studying civil engineering at the University of Minnesota, is currently CAIR's national executive director. Awad has met with secretaries of state Madeline Albright, Colin Powell, and Condoleezza Rice to discuss the American Muslim community. Awad was also invited by the White House days after 9/11 to join President George W. Bush for a press conference to express solidarity between the American public and American Muslims. He has also been requested to testify before both houses of Congress on numerous occasions.

CAIR stands out among other American Muslim organizations in that its leadership reflects not only immigrant Islam but also its indigenous counterpart. Ibrahim Hooper, currently CAIR national communications director, was also active in the establishment and development of the organization in its earliest years. Hooper is a white American convert to Islam and was a news producer for an ABC affiliate in Minneapolis, Minnesota, prior to joining CAIR in 1994. Long-time board members include Ihsan Bagby, an African American born in Cleveland, Ohio, and educated at the University of Michigan. Mohamed Nimer, a leading expert on the American Muslim community, headed CAIR's research department from 1995 to 2007.

CAIR's membership body similarly reflects a diverse American Muslim community including both first- and second-generation American Muslims, indigenous Muslims, and converts. Members are, on average, highly educated, having at least attained an undergraduate degree, and span all ethnicities including South Asian, Arab, African American, and white converts. South Asians form the majority of the membership base, reflecting their position in the breakdown of the general American Muslim population. However, where in reality African Americans converts outnumber white American converts, there are more white American CAIR members and volunteers than African American. Both women and men are significantly represented both as members as well as local and national staff and executive officials. At CAIR's national office, more than 50 percent of the staff are women. Over half a million people subscribe to CAIR's main communication line, the CAIR-Net online list serve, which includes non-Americans as well as non-Muslims.

CAIR has come under fire since 9/11 for its alleged ties to Islamic extremist groups. In 2001, Rabih Haddad, a CAIR fundraiser, was deported for his involvement with the Global Relief Foundation, a group found to have financed Al-Qaeda, among other terrorist organizations. CAIR funding practices have come under scrutiny since 9/11, after which CAIR solicited donations on its website for a "NY/DC Emergency Relief Fund," the link for which redirected users to the donation pages of the Holy Land Foundation (HLF). In 2004, a federal judge found HLF guilty of aiding and abetting Hamas, and thus liable for a $156 million lawsuit involving the death of an American teenager (*BBC News*, 2004). Various important board members, including Ghassan Elashi (one of CAIR's founders), Bassem Khafagi (director of communications), and Randal Royer (CAIR's former civil rights coordinator), have been convicted on multiple counts of terrorist activities (*Washington Times*, 2004). Although many government officials (notably Steven Pomerantz, former chief of counterterrorism at the FBI) have implicated CAIR as an extremist group (*Washington Post*, 2003), CAIR itself has never been convicted of supporting terrorist activities or organizations.

In recent years, CAIR has also been criticized by some Muslims, such as legal scholar Khaled Abu El Fadl, for presenting an uncritical defense of Islam and failing to speak out aggressively enough against Muslims whose religious rhetoric and activities are oriented toward violence (Abou El Fadl, 2002). Statements made by many of CAIR's members have provoked similar censure. For example, CAIR founder Omar Ahmad, speaking before a crowd of Muslims in California in July 1998, proclaimed, "Islam isn't in America to be equal to any other faith, but to become dominant. The Koran is the highest authority in America, and Islam is the only accepted religion on earth" (Gardiner, 1998). CAIR has maintained that it has condemned terrorism and agents of terror and will continue to do so, reaffirming the "Not in the Name of Islam" petition in 2004.

Developing a stronger political influence within government agencies has also been one of the priorities of American Muslim leaders. In less than a decade, lobbying groups such as the American Muslim Alliance (formed in 1989), the AMC (American Muslim Council, 1990), and MPAC (Muslim Public Affairs Council, 1998) have multiplied. The AMC was founded by a network of intellectuals and militant Muslims from a variety of backgrounds, convinced of the need for political mobilization to end discrimination and hostility toward Islam. They made a name for themselves after lobbying in the White House and Congress to include the preservation of identity and the rights of the Muslim community within the terms of American pluralism. Their goal has been to set themselves up as an intermediary between the Muslim community and institutions of power. One of their primary demands has been for the political acknowledgment of equal status between Muslims and other religious communities, as well transforming the well-known description of society,

"Judeo-Christian," into "Judeo-Christian-Islamic"—in the understanding that the Muslim tradition holds dear the same values as do Judaism and Christianity.

The goal of these lobby groups has been to defend the interests of Muslim populations in the halls of government, as well as to protest US policy in the Middle East. They have also worked to mobilize the Muslim community through regular voter-awareness campaigns. For the 2000 Presidential elections, the various Muslim lobbies banded together in coalition under the name American Muslim Politics Council Coordination (AMPCC) in favor of the candidate George W. Bush.[7] Since then, they have been more cautious in the official endorsement of political figures.

POST 9/11 CHALLENGES

In the past two decades, these groups have made significant changes to their strategy and the content of their message. Throughout the 1970s and before the Gulf War of 1991 there was an internal conflict—not always visible to the outside observer—between the Society of the Muslim Brothers and the Wahhabi movement, which reflected broader tensions across the Muslim world. For Wahhabis, the internal structure of the Muslim community should take precedence over any kind of inclusion or participation in American society. Those associated with the ideology of the Muslim Brothers, on the other hand, felt that communication with the non-Muslim community was essential. After the first Gulf war, however, domestic issues and the image of American Islam as a minority religion became strategically important. From that moment on, the debate has been defined as a conflict between liberals/progressives and conservatives/fundamentalists. Such a debate has been intensified in the post 9/11 context.

The Progressive versus Conservative Divide

Progressive Muslims have espoused the cause of justice in political, economic, and social terms.[8] Gender equity has been a particular focus for progressive Muslims. Though Muslims at different historical periods have espoused similar agendas, the progressive Muslim movement has become particularly prominent in America in the last decade. Within a few years of the 9/11 attacks, a large number of Muslims have publicly identified—and been identified—as progressive Muslims. However, progressive Muslim ideas, individuals, and organizations have been relatively controversial in American Muslim communities.

The academic Fazlur Rahman (1919–1988) pioneered discussion of some progressive Muslim concerns even though he is not called a progressive himself. Other writers and scholars of the past and abroad have influenced this movement: for example, Ṭaha husayn (1889–1973), an Egyptian writer, espoused the cause of women's rights. Muhammad 'Abduh (1849–1905) an Egyptian jurist and reformist religious scholar (see *Salafiyya* Movement), Sir Syed Ahmed Khan (1817–1898), Muhammad Iqbal (1877–1983), and Jamal al-Din al-Afghani (1839–1897) belonged to the Salafist movement that advocated a return to the Qur'an and Sunna to revive Islamic thinking; they also promoted the women's cause. Some American Muslim academics currently working on progressive theological reinterpretation are Omid Safi (1970–present), Amina Wadud (1953–present), Abdulaziz Sachedina (1942–present), a religious studies professor who focuses on human rights and democracy, Khaled Abou El-Fadl (1973–present), Riffat Hassan, and Kecia Ali (1971–present).

Mailing lists such as the Network of Progressive Muslims and the Progressive Muslims Network had been discussing concepts central to progressive Muslim thought. But only in the past few years has the progressive Muslim movement developed to the point where it has issued the type of mission statement found in the book *Progressive Muslims* (2003), edited by Omid Safi.. The book includes articles by Muslim academics exploring various issues, notably gender justice and sexual orientation. An organization called the Progressive Muslim Union of North America (PMUNA) was established by Ahmed Nassef in 2004. Nassef is an Egyptian American public intellectual who studied Middle East Studies at UC Berkley and has frequently appeared on television. In 2003 Nassef created a website, Muslimwakeup.com, which quickly became representative of an important and somewhat neglected strand of American Muslim thought (see Internet). PMUNA organized meetings for progressive Muslims in a number of cities in the United States and abroad . As the website grew bolder, hackers warned the authors to stop attacking *hijab* and for Mohja Kahf (1967–present) to stop writing sexually explicit articles for the website. Kahf is an associate professor of comparative literature at Rutgers University who works on issues of gender and sexuality.

The authors of the website have been popular as well as controversial: on March 18, 2005, the PMU organized a Friday congregational prayer led by a woman, Amina Wadud, professor of Islamic studies at Virginia Commonwealth University. This event led to considerable fiery discussion in the community and deepened the lines drawn between "Progressive Muslims" and their opponents.

Progressive Muslim figures have represented Wahhabi and Wahhabi-influenced thought as literalistic, irrelevant to modern times, spiritually devoid, and lacking in adequate concerns for justice. The agenda of global and social justice has been central in progressive Muslim activities. This necessarily includes gender justice and involves issues that have been neglected or politicized because of Western imperialist involvement. Most statements of progressive Muslims appear to be distinct from those of "liberal" Muslims. They appear to generally accept central articles of faith and traditional Islamic methodology, but they are dissatisfied with traditional interpretations in a variety of areas.

There is considerable diversity among people who identify as "progressive." Some Muslims who would otherwise agree with "progressive" approaches have been unhappy with sexually explicit articles on the Muslim Wake Up website. Objections were raised regarding the choice of certain board members on PMUNA such as Seeme and Malik Hassan (a Pakistani husband-and-wife team and namesake for the University of Southern Colorado business school), who headed the organization "Muslims for Bush." The subsequent resignation of board members Muqtedar Khan, Omid Safi, Sarah Eltantawi, and Hussein Ibish in July and August 2005 raised questions that the PMU was not succeeding in its goal of being a "broad tent" for Progressive Muslims in general.

The fact that no categorical, or even commonly accepted, definitions of "progressive Islam" exist makes the issue of representation a complex one. The fight to define the legitimate Muslim community—whether this definition is based on ethnic, linguistic, or religious considerations—has been intensified by the post 9/11 political context and the interference of political authorities in search of the moderate and good Muslims.

The case of Sheik Kabbani is a perfect illustration of these internal conflicts and their political consequences. In the late 1990s, Kabbani, of the Nakshabendi brotherhood,[9] had achieved a certain visibility in some political circles as well as the White House. In a meeting with State Department representatives during Clinton's second term of office in January 1999, the Sheik categorized the majority of Islamic leaders in America as "fundamentalists." These words were widely reported in the media; the Sheik subsequently faced violent opposition and censorship from the American Islamic elite, self-appointed guardians of the orthodox definition of the Muslim community.

Broadly speaking, Muslim strategy in the American public sphere has generally taken the route of moral persuasion, by justifying Islam's place in American culture through an appeal to the shared values of monotheistic religions. In other words, Muslims want to show that they, too, subscribe to the fundamental values of American society: "Internally, the US is the most Islamic state that has been operational in the last 300 years," says Karen Leonard. "It is generally seeking to aspire to its ideals, and the growing cultural religious material health of American Muslims is the best testimony to my claim" (Leonard, 2003, p. 23). The period after 9/11 has been a crucial one for the public status of American Islam. Despite their vigorous public denunciation of the attacks, Muslim leaders came under fire for their inability to take a position on Islam other than a defensive or apologist one. Since the terrorist attacks, both official and popular interest has increasingly focused on religious or intellectual figures who "read" Islam from a legal or theological standpoint. Hamza Yusuf is one of those who owe their rise in the media and in political circles to their status as religious leader. Born in Washington State and raised in California, he converted to Islam at the age of 17, received his training in Islam in Algeria, Morocco, and Mauritania, and now runs the "Zaytuna Institute" in the San

Francisco Bay Area. His charismatic religious authority attracts crowds of young Muslims to each of his conferences. Since 9/11, he has been a frequent guest at the White House. One of his most striking arguments, post-9/11, has been the critique of the monopoly on discourse held by physicians, engineers, and other "men of science" who know little or nothing about either religion or Islam. He has repeatedly stated that Islam has, for the most part, been interpreted by inexperienced and ill-informed individuals and sees the terrorists who executed the attacks of 9/11 as enemies of Islam.

Contested Political Influence

Islam's entry into politics comes at the price of tensions and conflict with other religious lobby groups, Christian and Jews. Daniel Pipes—essayist, public intellectual involved in several think-tanks with ties to the government, and a self-declared enemy of Islam—is upfront about considering American Muslims to be second-class citizens. On October 10, 2001, he made the claim that 10 to 15 percent of all Muslims are potential killers. Through his Internet site, Campus Watch, he reports on universities and intellectuals who are too sympathetic, in his opinion, to Islam or the Palestinian cause. His Fall 2003 nomination to the head of the USIP (United States Institute for Peace) raised such opposition among Muslim organizations that state authorities shortened his term to eighteen months instead of allowing him to serve out the customary four years.

The case of Salam Al-Marayati further demonstrates how the conflict between Muslims and pro-Israeli organizations can reach the highest levels of government. President Clinton named Al-Marayati, the president of MPAC, to the National Commission on Terrorism in 1999. After several Zionist organizations launched a virulent campaign against his appointment, he was quickly removed from his post.

The Obama administration adopted a new strategy by including several Muslims in his government, such as Farah Pandit, the first ever special representative to Muslim communities for the US Department of State; Rashad Hussein, the State Department special envoy to the Organization of Islamic Cooperation (OIC) and envoy to the OIC; and Huma Abedin, deputy chief of staff to Secretary of State Hillary Clinton (Abedin is perhaps most famous for being the wife of the disgraced former congressman Anthony Weiner).

As a consequence of the Islamophobic climate, this presence of Muslims in the Obama administration has come under attack. In June 2012 Michelle Bachmann, house representative from Minnesota, stated that Huma Abedin is "a part of a conspiracy by the Muslim Brotherhood to infiltrate the top reaches of the US government." She and other colleges have sent letters to the departments of Homeland Security, Justice, and State asking that investigations be made regarding whether the US government is being infiltrated by Muslims extremists (Esposito, 2012).

Obama responded by declaring that Abedin has been "nothing less than extraordinary in representing our country and the democratic values that we hold dear," which he stated at a White House Iftar dinner on August 10, 2012. His comments further went on to describe the August 5, 2012, shootings at a Sikh temple in Wisconsin and added that an "attack on Americans of any faith is an attack on the freedom of all Americans…every American has the right to practice their faith both openly and freely, and as they choose." Furthermore, other republican senators, such as John McCain, have chastised Bachmann for her attack on Abedin, stating that Abedin "represents what is best about America: the daughter of immigrants, who has risen to the highest levels of our government on the basis of her substantial personal merit and her abiding commitment to the American ideals that she embodies so fully" (Ritz, 2012).

CONCLUSION

Hostility toward Islam seems to be based on two underlying assumptions. The first is that practicing Muslims are a danger for American society. However, most data, including a 2007 poll by the Pew Forum on Religion and Public Life, and a 2009 Gallup survey, suggest the opposite: that Islamic religiosity and cultural identification are not obstacles to loyalty to America but vehicles to civic engagement. Not surprisingly, these attitudes are consistent with those of practicing members of other religious groups. The second is that Islam is an alien religion, impossible to accommodate to American political values. Such a perception does not reflect the long-standing presence of Islam in American society that some historians can trace back to the slave trades.

Updating a national narrative is a huge political and symbolic task, something equivalent to the combined efforts that led to the integration of the African American past into the dominant American narrative. This could be accomplished by telling the stories of the estimated 10 percent of all African slaves brought to the United States who were Muslim or the presence of Islam within several ethnic and cultural communities or the hybridization of Islam in the American pop culture. Most Islamic organizations are still trapped in the racial divide and unable to move along this path yet.

NOTES

1. The organization changed its name to American Muslim Society (AMS) in 2003; see Appendix.
2. Please note that the information on ISNA and ICNA until 2006 comes from the entries authored by Ba-Yunus in the Encyclopedia of Islam in the United States that I published in 2007.

3. In 2007 federal chargers were brought against the Holy Land Foundation for funding terrorist organizations such as Hamas, and NAIT was named an unindicted co-conspirator.
4. The party dominated Pakistan political life during the period of General Zia's rule in 1977.
5. Information on CAIR until 2006 comes from the entry of the same name authored by Nada Unus in the Encyclopedia of Islam in the United States I published in 2007.
6. http://www.cair.com/ArticleDetails.aspx?ArticleID=26999.
7. The main reason for this support was ironically the promise of the Bush candidate to abolish the 1996 antiterrorism law of secret evidence.
8. Information on Progressive Muslims taken from the entry of the same name authored by Shabana Mir in the Encyclopedia of Islam in the United States, 2007.
9. The Nakshabendi brotherhood is a Sufi order that is widespread throughout most of Asia (including the Indian subcontinent), Turkey, and Bosnia. The order is characterized by political activism, simple worship practices, the rejection of song and dance, and a strict adherence to shari'a.

References

Abou El Fadl, K., *Dr. Abou El Fadl's Response to CAIR on July 20*. Available at: http://www.scholarofthehouse.org/drabelfadres.html. Accessed August 26, 2012.

Ahmad, Mumtaz, Zahid H. Bukhari, John L. Esposito, and Sulayman S. Nyang, *Muslims' Place in the American Public Square* (Walnut Creek, Calif.: Rowman & Littlefield Publishers, 2004).

Ali, Tahir and Lisette Poole, "2004 Election Sees Second American-Muslim Bloc Vote," *Washington Report on Middle East Affairs*. Available at: http://www.wrmea.com/component/content/article/271/8635-election-watch-2004-election-sees-second-american-muslim-bloc-vote.html. Accessed August 26, 2012.

Ayloush, Hussam, 2010. "The New York City Mosque: Hussam Ayloush of CAIR Argues for Building It," *The Washington Post* (August 16, 2010). Available at: http://www.washingtonpost.com/wp-dyn/content/discussion/2010/08/16/DI2010081603061.html. Accessed August 17, 2012.

Bagby, Ihsan, Bryan T. Froehle, and Paul M. Perl, "Faith Communities Today: The Mosque in America: A National Portrait," *Hartford Seminary's Hartford Institute for Religious Research* (April 2001). Available at: http://stu.academia.edu/BryanFroehle/Papers/600953/The_Mosque_In_America_a_National_Portrait_A_Report_From_the_Mosque_Study_Project. Accessed August 20, 2012.

BBC News, "Hamas Victim's Family Get $156m." *BBC News* (December 8, 2004). Available at: http://news.bbc.co.uk/go/pr/fr/-/1/hi/world/middle_east/4080499.stm. Accessed August 20, 2012.

Bowers, Herman Meredith, *A Phenomenological Study of the Islamic Society of North America* (Ann Arbor, Mich.: Bell & Howell Company, 1989.)

CAIR, *A Rush to Judgment: A Special Report on Anti-Muslim Stereotyping, Harassment and Hate Crimes Following the Bombing of Oklahoma City's Murrah Federal Building, April 19* (Washington, DC: CAIR, 1995).

CAIR, *The Usual Suspects: Media Coverage of the TWA Flight 800 Crash* (Washington, DC: CAIR, 1996).

CAIR, *American Muslims and the 2008 Election: A Post Election Survey Report*. Available at: http://www.cair.com/Portals/o/pdf/Post_2008_Election_American_Muslim_Poll. pdf. Accessed August 17, 2012.

CAIR, *The American Mosque*. Available at: http://faithcommunitiestoday.org/sites/faithcommunitiestoday.org/files/The%20American%20Mosque%202011%20web.pdf.   Accessed August 17, 2012.

CAIR, *National Board and Staff*. Available at: http://www.cair.com/AboutUs/ CAIRNationalBoardandStaff.aspx. Accessed August 17, 2012.

Cesari, Jocelyne, *When Islam and Democracy Meet: Muslims in Europe and in the United States* (New York: Palgrave Macmillan, 2004/2006).

Cesari, Jocelyne, *Encyclopedia of Islam in the United States* (Westport: Greenwood Press, 2007).

Cesari, Jocelyne, *Muslims in the West Post 9/11: Religion, Law and Politics* (London:, Routledge, 2010).

Cesari, Jocelyne, *Why the West Fears Islam, Exploration of Muslims in Liberal Democracies*, New York City:, Palgrave McMillan, 2013.

Chaudhry, Amara S., "Challenging Pennsylvania's Misguided 'Anti-Shariah' Bill," *The Legal Intelligencer*. Available at: http://pa.cair.com/media/challenging-pennsylvanias-misguided-anti-shariah-bill/. Accessed August 17, 2012.

Cohen, Roger, "Religion Does Its Worst," *The New York Times* (April 4, 2011). Available at: http:// www.nytimes.com/2011/04/05/opinion/05iht-edcohen05.html. Accessed January 31, 2012.

Editorial, "CAIR: No Room to Judge," *The Washington Post* (April 15, 2003).

Editorial, "CAIR and Terrorism," *The Washington Times* (July 24, 2004). Available at: http:// www.washingtontimes.com/functions/print.php?StoryID=20040723-082950-9083r. Accessed August 17, 2012.

Elliott, Andrea, "The Man Behind the Anti-Shariah Movement," *The New York Times* (July 30, 2011). Available at: http://www.nytimes.com/2011/07/31/us/31shariah.html?_r=1&ad xnnl=1&pagewanted=all&adxnnlx=1325142029-MnrhdJvFojgkqHiVpO2aJA.   Accessed January 31, 2012.

Esposito, John L., "'Bachmann affair' against Clinton aide Huma Abedin is a wake-up call," *Washington Post* (July 26, 2012). Available at: http://www.washingtonpost.com/blogs/ guest-voices/post/bachmann-affair-against-clinton-aide-huma-abedin-is-a-wake-up-call/2012/07/26/gJQAFHP4BX_blog.html. Accessed August 17, 2012.

Gardiner, Lisa, "American Muslim Leader Urges Faithful to Spread Word," *San Ramon Valley Herald* (July 4, 1998). Available at: http://www.anti-cair-net.org/AhmadStateScanned.pdf. Accessed August 20, 2012.

Goodstein, Laurie, "Drawing U.S. Crowd With Anti-Islam Message," *The New York Times* (March 7, 2011). Available at: http://www.nytimes.com/2011/03/08/us/08gabriel. html?pagewanted=all. Accessed January 31, 2012.

Goodstein, Laurie and Sheryl Gay Stolberg, "Domestic Terrorism Hearing Opens With Contrasting Views on Dangers," *The New York Times* (March 10, 2011). Available at: http:// www.nytimes.com/2011/03/11/us/politics/11king.html. Accessed January 31, 2012.

Haddad, Yvonne Yazbeck, *The Muslims of America* (New York: Oxford University Press, 1993).

Hanif, Ghulam M., "The Muslim Community in America: A Brief Profile," *Journal of Muslim Minority Affairs*, 23, 2 (2003): 303–311.

Hassan, Riffat, *Women's Rights and Islam: From the I.C.P.D. to Beijing* (Louisville: NISA Publications, 1995).

Huffington Post, "Juan Williams: Muslims on Planes Make Me 'Nervous,'" *Huffington Post* (October 19, 2010). Available at: http://www.huffingtonpost.com/2010/10/19/juan-williams-muslims-nervous_n_768719.html. Accessed January 31, 2012.

Huffington Post, "Poll: Majority Of GOP Believes Obama Sympathizes With Islamic Fundamentalism, Wants Worldwide Islamic Law," (August 20, 2010). Available at http://www.huffingtonpost.com/2010/08/30/obama-islamic-fundamentalist-gop-polled-majority-says_n_699883.html. Accessed January 31, 2012.

Hunt, Carol Anne, "Many Republican Voters Still Believe Obama Is Muslim," *Examiner* (July 29, 2012). Available at: http://www.examiner.com/article/many-republican-voters-still-believe-obama-is-muslim. Accessed July 30, 2012.

ISNA, "ISNA President: Imam Mohamed Magid Mohammed." Available at: http://www.isna.net/ISNAHQ/pages/Mohamed-Hagmagid-Ali.aspx. Accessed August 20, 2012.

ISNA, "Mission & Vision." Available at: http://www.isna.net/ISNAHQ/pages/Mission—Vision.aspx. Accessed August 21, 2012.

Leighton, Kyle, "Pew: Some Voters Still Believer Obama Is Muslim, Most Unconcerned with Candidates' Religions" (July 26, 2010). Available at: http://2012.talkingpointsmemo.com/2012/07/poll-pew-mormon-romney.php. Accessed July 27, 2012.

Leonard, Karen, "American Muslim Politics: Discourses and Practices," *Ethnicities* 3(2003a): 147–181.

Leonard, Karen, *Muslims in the United States: The State of Research* (New York: Russell Sage Foundation, 2003b).

Muslim Wakeup! (November 2006). www.muslimwakeup.com.

New York City Bar, *The Unconstitutionality of Oklahoma Referendum 755—The "Save Our State Amendment."* Available at: http://www.nycbar.org/pdf/report/uploads/20072027-UnconstitutionalityofOklahomaReferendum755.pdf. Accessed July 22, 2012.

Newport, Frank, "Many Americans Can't Name Obama's Religion," *Gallup* (June 22, 2010). Available: http://www.gallup.com/poll/155315/Many-Americans-Cant-Name-Obamas-Religion.aspx. Accessed July 30, 2012.

Nimer, Mohamed, *The North American Muslim Resource Guide* (New York: Routledge, 2002).

Pew, *Muslim Americans: No Signs of Growth in Alienation or Support for Extremism.* Available at: http://www.people-press.org/files/legacy-pdf/Muslim-American-Report.pdf.   Accessed August 17, 2012.

Pew, "Little Voter Discomfort with Romney's Mormon Religion," *Pew Forum* 26 (July 2-12, 2012). Available at: http://www.pewforum.org/Politics-and-Elections/Little-Voter-Discomfort-with-Romney%E2%80%99s-Mormon-Religion-1.aspx. Accessed July 30, 2012.

PR Newswire, *CAIR Asks NYPD to Probe Use of Anti-Muslim Training Film.* Available at: http://www.prnewswire.com/news-releases/cair-asks-nypd-to-probe-use-of-anti-muslim-training-film-114219909.html. Accessed August 17, 2012.

PR Newswire, *CAIR: Kansas Muslims to Urge Veto of Anti-Sharia Bill.* Available at: http://www.prnewswire.com/news-releases/cair-kansas-muslims-to-urge-veto-of-anti-sharia-bill-151936265.html. Accessed August 17, 2012.

Progressive Muslim Union (November 2006). www.pmuna.org.

Ritz, Erica, "American Patriot": Obama Praises Clinton Aide Huma Abedin During Ramadan Dinner," *The Blaze* (August 11, 2012). Available at: http://www.theblaze.com/stories/american-patriot-obama-praises-clinton-aide-huma-abedin-during-ramadan-dinner/. Accessed August 17, 2012.

Rose, Alexander, "How Did Muslims Vote in 2000?" *The Middle East Quarterly* 8 (2001): 13–27.

Sachedina, Abdulaziz, *The Islamic Roots of Democratic Pluralism* (New York: Oxford University Press, 2001).

Safi, Omid, ed., *Progressive Muslims: On Justice, Gender, and Pluralism* (Oxford: Oneworld Publications, 2003).

Saletan, William, *Muslims, Keep Out*. Available at: http://www.slate.com/articles/news_and_politics/frame_game/2010/08/muslims_keep_out.html. Accessed January 31, 2012.

Smith, Jane I., *Islam in America* (New York: Columbia University Press, 1999/2011).

Smith, Tom W., "Review: The Muslim Population of the United States: The Methodology of Estimates," *Public Opinion Quarterly* 66 (2002): 404–417.

Waller, Douglas, "An American Imam," *Time Magazine U.S.* (November 14, 2005). Available at: http://www.time.com/time/magazine/article/0,9171,1129587,00.html. Accessed August 20, 2012.

CHAPTER 5

··

AFRICAN AMERICAN MUSLIMS

··

CAROLYN MOXLEY ROUSE

ANYONE with a passing familiarity with the history of Islam in the United States is aware that some percentage of slaves captured in Africa were Muslims, that many African Americans converted to Islam in the twentieth century, and that since 1965 many black Muslims have immigrated to the United States (Abdullah 2010; Ahmed 2010; Clegg 1998; Curtis 2009; Dannin 2002; Jackson 2005; Lincoln 1961). In addition to these three major tributaries to the largest Muslim demographic in the United States, African American Muslims identify with a diversity of approaches to Islam, including Sunni, Shi'a, Sufi, Salafi, Ahmadiyya, Moorish Science Temple, Nation of Islam, the Five Percenters, and numerous minor sects (Leonard 2003, McCloud 1995, Turner 1997). Given these different histories and beliefs, it is no small task to confirm that a categorical group, loosely identified as "African American Muslims," exists.

The claim that African American Muslims have a unique history or perspective of the world implies that their experiences are different from those of African Americans who are not Muslim and Muslims who are not black.[1] It even presumes that the racial categories used in the present are stable or objective. Therefore it is important to acknowledge up front that the category "African American Muslims" is itself imprecise. Regardless of its inexactness, as a descriptor "African American Muslims" does reference a particular history with an identifiable epistemology, or approach to knowledge production, that might best be described as "African American Islam" (Curtis 2002, Jackson 2005, McCloud 1995). This chapter addresses the concerns of African American Muslims in an effort to reveal the import of Islam for black Americans. In order to do so, it is necessary first to acknowledge that race is a social construct and to discuss why the social construction of race is a central leitmotif of African American Islam (Karim 2009).

The imprecision of racial and ethnic categories is a theoretical concern not only of social scientists. The fight against misrecognition, the defining feature of racism, has been an enduring facet of African American Muslim history. Put simply, African American Muslims have fought to be recognized as Muslims, which has been made difficult because of racism. Given their concerns, *intersectionality* best describes not only a theoretical approach to understanding African American Islam but also the protective value of the faith for African Americans.

First elaborated by legal scholar and critical race theorist Kimberle Crenshaw, intersectionality is the idea that people have more than one socially relevant identity. For example, it makes white women's experiences with gender oppression different from that of black women's (Crenshaw 1989). Crenshaw writes extensively about the intersections of race and gender, but identity also includes heritage, regional cultures, beliefs, professions, wealth, education, and bodily forms, which provoke culturally patterned responses (height, beauty, disability, health, athleticism). Because Islam is a poorly understood minority religion in the United States, African American Muslims typically navigate their identities consciously, attuned to the fact that being different, they are often asked to explain their differences and rationalize their choices.

Interviewing African American Muslims in the 1990s and early 2000s, I initiated conversations about identity and found that some Muslims identified as "American," and others as "African American" (Rouse 2004). Some refused any identity other than "Muslim," and the diversity within the community did not end there. There were some who identified with feminism (men included) and others who refused to consider themselves feminists because, they argued, women's rights are inscribed in the Quran. In addition to the contested political identities, there were personal identities and histories that shaped how many black Muslims experienced themselves and their faith. For example, before the 1970s, most African American Muslims were converts; with each passing decade, however, more have been born into the faith. I found that those born into the faith were often as politically engaged as those who converted, but there was a greater separation between their religious beliefs and their political ideologies. Also, the numbers of first- and second-generation Muslims from Africa and the Caribbean changed not only the demographics of the community but also the discourses about race, citizenship, and faith (Jackson 2005, Nashashibi 2009). The extraordinary diversity within the community, if we can even call it a community, makes it impossible to claim that there was or is one African American Muslim history or consciousness.

For many, developing an identity involves a negotiation between a personal sense of self and a social set of constraints. This process is both dialectical and coercive, with racism shifting it, in varying degrees, toward the latter. Importantly, being black does not mean that one practices a particular type of Islam, as the demographic category "African American Muslim" implies. "African American Islam," in contrast, uncouples race from belief, shifts the focus from people to ideas, and highlights the relationship between African American social history and Islamic exegesis. Essentially it is impossible to contain the variety of beliefs and practices; these are so great that many African American Muslims do not recognize one another as coreligionists.

Given all the diversity and dissension, African American Islam is not reducible to a set of beliefs but rather is best described as the use of Islam as a mediating strategy for making sense of and challenging forms of social injustice peculiar to the United States. If we think of African American Islam as a reading of the faith that is sensitive to particular aspects of the faith, much like a lens that filters particular parts of the spectrum, then identification with African American Islam does not have to be tied to the race of the adherent (Khabeer 2011, Karim 2009). There are, for example, white, Latino, and South Asian Muslims who identify with African American Islam in the sense that their faith has been influenced by exegetical approaches to Islam traceable to African American Muslim leaders, scholars, and/or communities (Abdullah 2010, Bald 2009, Karim 2009, Taylor 2009).

While the imprecision of the descriptor "African American Muslim" is clear to most Muslims, abandoning it introduces another set of problems. As Crenshaw notes, "The embrace of identity politics...has been in tension with dominant conceptions of social justice" (Crenshaw 1991, 1242). This tension arises from the fact that many of the categories are themselves the product of prejudice and past domination and therefore come to denote racist or sexist sentiments. The desire to escape the negative subtexts that overwhelm the categories is the reason why the accepted term "Negro" was replaced with "black," which is now subordinate to the more respected "African American." Many Muslims would like to be identified by their faith rather than by mainstream American notions of race or gender. They recognize, however, that these identities have the potential to empower them: "the social power in delineating difference need not be the power of domination; it can instead be the source of social empowerment and reconstruction" (Crenshaw 1991, 1242).

Paradoxically, therefore, as African American Muslims have tried to distance themselves from a social category that constrains them, racial identification continues to be a necessary tool of empowerment. Malcolm X, or El-Hajj Malik El-Shabazz, as he was also known, dealt with this by forming two organizations: Muslim Mosque, Inc., a religious group, and the Organization of Afro-American Unity, a political group. Always attentive to the tensions between constraint and empowerment, the exegetical approach of African American Islam is deeply influenced by both the refusal to legitimate mainstream categories of difference while also embracing those categories as necessary for understanding the values of the faith and mobilizing around those values. As Sherman Jackson notes in *Islam and the Blackamerican*, "The Blackamerican...is not a biological reality; he is a socialhistorical one" (Jackson 2005, 14). What Jackson argues is that African American Muslims have used Islam to challenge race as an essential marker of difference at the same time that racial history in America has shaped the black American experience with Islam.

Rather than catalogue the history of various African American communities, which can be gleaned by reading the extant scholarship on Islam in America, the rest of this chapter is devoted to describing three core themes in African American Islam: struggles over citizenship, the political economy of gender, and struggles to develop an empowering postcolonial subjectivity (Ahmed 2010, Curtis 2006, Dannin 2002, Haddad, Smith, and Moore 2006, Jackson 2005, Karim 2009, Manning and Aidi 2009, Rouse 2004). There is no fixed set of doctrinal suppositions regarding any of these topics. Rather, these are issues of ongoing debate, compelled by the continuing challenges of institutional racism, American imperialism, and white supremacy.

Citizenship

The first well-publicized case of a black Muslim in the United States was the story of Abd Rahman Ibrahima. In the early nineteenth century, Ibrahima was discovered to have been a prince before he was captured in what is now Guinea and sold to a Mississippi slave owner in 1788. In the 1820s, a campaign was launched to free Ibrahima based on the idea that he had moral and intellectual capacities that exceeded those of black slaves and therefore deserved not citizenship but the freedom to return to his place of birth. By then Ibrahima had been a slave for almost four decades and was married with children and grandchildren. But the stipulation of his release was that he would have to purchase each family member's freedom (Terry Alford 1986).

The reclassification of Ibrahima as Arab, or closer to white than black, speaks to how *Negro* did not solely reference the color of a person's skin but also denoted *illiterate, heathen, stateless, lacking culture,* and *uneducable.* Ibrahima regained his status as a human being because he was a Muslim (religious) who could read Arabic (literate) and had been the intended head of an established political system (civilized). Of course all the slaves came from cultures with political and religious systems, but most African cultures were unintelligible to European Americans. Given their potential connection to the exotic Orient, Muslim slaves were often treated differently. Hisham Aidi and Manning Marable capture the significance of this reclassification in the opening chapter of their edited volume *Black Routes to Islam.* "Blacks were thus still seen as inferior, but those of alleged Moorish or Arab origins were seen as suited for higher positions where they could monitor the majority of blacks and enforce the rules of the slave society" (Marable and Aidi 2009, 6).

What Ibrahima's story points to is that there was no such thing as a black American citizen. In the nineteenth century the only people who had full citizenship were white men, and they justified their exclusive rights to democracy, law, and violence based on the notion that they had the capacity for reason and hard work and were chosen by God. Citizenship, therefore, was understood to be a privilege granted to those with the moral character to take advantage of and properly use the freedoms granted by the Constitution. By casting blacks as lazy, uncivilized, and uneducable, racism turned the term *black citizen* into a conceptual oxymoron. Even in political discourse in the early part of the twenty-first century, African Americans were often represented as preferring welfare to work, and disparities in rates of incarceration between blacks and whites were justified partly by perceptions that blacks did not have the capacity for self-control and lacked moral character. Oddly enough, even Barack Obama, the first African American president, was taunted throughout his time in office with accusations that he was not an American citizen.

One of the things that continues to make Islam attractive to African Americans has been the clearly marked route out of the conceptual binds that make their disfranchisement from rights of citizenship seem reasonable. Because the social disparities that result from this partial citizenship have touched almost all black Americans, either directly or indirectly, the citizenship question remains a defining issue in African American Islam. While conversations about race and citizenship have occurred within all branches of the faith, the Nation of Islam's challenge remains the most iconic example.

The Nation of Islam (NOI) was an unorthodox sect of Islam that began in Detroit in the 1930s and, by the 1940s, was led by Elijah Muhammad (Clegg 1998, Curtis 2006, Evanzz 1999). By the late 1970s, the number of black Sunni Muslims in America far exceeded the number of NOI members. Although membership in the NOI has continued to decline, its powerful challenge to white supremacy remains a critical part of African American Islam. Religion scholar Edward Curtis argues that regardless of its unique doctrine, the NOI's theology was always in dialogue with traditional Islam. Curtis notes, in *Black Muslim Religion in the Nation of Islam,* that "While most American Muslims... would never defend Elijah Muhammad's doctrinal teachings ... Many continue to be committed to what they see as the NOI's mission of black liberation—social, cultural, political, and economic" (Curtis 2006, 186).

The NOI's challenge to black disfranchisement can best be described as a set of discursive and performative practices. These practices include (1) writing black people back into the history of civilization; (2) rejecting their racial assignment, reclassifying themselves, and then asserting that they are equal in the eyes of God; and (3) performing moral character—dress and behavior codes were strictly enforced— as a demonstration that they deserved not only full citizenship but also the right of self-protection against state-sponsored or state-endorsed racial terrorism (Curtis 2006, Turner 1997).

The NOI offers the most striking example of how Islam has been used to assert the moral and spiritual authority of people of color, identified as Asiatics by the NOI, in order to claim rights of citizenship. But followers of other branches of Islam have also dealt with the citizenship dilemma using different approaches. Sunni Muslims, for example, identify strongly as American but use traditional Islamic and historical exegesis to challenge the notion that white Europeans and Americans have been the sole creators of great religious traditions that attempt to determine the dynamic relationship between humans and God(s) and significant cultural leaps forward. For those who practice more traditional forms of Islam, interpreting the Quran—the injunction to read is strong in Islam—requires engagement with an extraordinary period in African history where the spread of Islam was tied to well-worn trade routes extending across the Sahara and the Sahel and across bodies of water as far east as the Persian Gulf and as far west as the Strait of Gibraltar. It is common for African American Muslims to be familiar with the works of medieval Islamic philosophers, such as Abu Nasr al-Farabi (d. 950 CE), Abu Hamid al-Ghazali (d. 1111 CE), and Ibn Rushd (d. 1198 CE) (Jackson 2005, McCloud 1995). Early Islamic philosophers wrestled with questions about the balance between free will and religious authority; they make the European and American Enlightenment of the seventeenth and eighteenth centuries seem not so much a novel phenomenon as simply another iteration of a recurring problematic taken up in many parts of the world.

In other words, African American Sunni Muslims challenge their partial citizenship through an historical exegesis that does not directly challenge the black/citizen binary. Rather, African American Islam names a kind of transcendent citizenship where the rights embodied in American law and in Islam provide a sense of freedom to move and explore across geographic, cultural, and temporal borders. It is about transcending categorical ways of thinking through a rereading of history without dismissing the inalienable rights and duties granted by the American Constitution as well as by Islam.[2]

THE POLITICAL ECONOMY OF GENDER

Since the time of chattel slavery, black women's bodies have been treated and understood primarily as laboring bodies. During slavery, their economic productivity was calculated as the output of their physical labor along with the number of children they bore who survived childhood. In contrast, white women of means were expected to participate in leisure activities, including education, and to be supported financially by white men. Black women were never expected to lead fulfilling lives but rather to live lives marked by hard labor, endured along with the indignities that come with institutionalized racism. When the second-wave feminist movement blossomed in the 1960s, many black women identified with the call for women's equality. But when it came to new feminist understandings of family and marriage, most black women could not relate to the idea that opening the labor market to women was either revolutionary or liberating. From their perspective, the availability of paid labor was not the issue. Their fight was about the quality of that labor, the pay, and how to lessen the personal sacrifices that accompany work, marriage, and raising children.

Skepticism about the liberating power of paid labor is something black women of any faith, or none at all, have shared. Like other black women, African American Muslims recognized second-wave feminism as a movement for middle- and upper-middle-class white women who were denied access to elite institutions and whose power was curtailed based on cultural ideas about "the weaker sex." All African Americans, regardless of sex, experienced the same lack of access to elite institutions, good jobs, and power. And their disfranchisement went well beyond labor issues to include loans, land, health care, good basic education, and law.

Although the feminist movement of the 1960s and 1970s seemed tone deaf to the concerns of minorities and the poor, African American women were not antifeminist. Importantly, black women have rarely if ever embraced Islam in order to fulfill some 1950s American fantasy of women's domestic servitude. Rather, Islam offered new ways of imagining the balance between the rights and duties of men to women and of the community to the family (Karim 2009, McCloud 1995, Rouse 2004). The concerns of many black women were pragmatic: "How can I take a few years off work to raise my children? How do I educate them properly given our poorly funded schools? How do I find time to volunteer to help improve the lives of people in my community?"

Many Muslims appreciate the fact that the Quran and hadith include edicts and examples of ways to manage the inevitable financial and personal sacrifices that come with marriage and family. In Islam, for example, men are required to financially support their families but women are not forbidden from working (Wadud 1999). Khadijah, the Prophet Muhammad's first wife, was a successful businesswoman when she proposed marriage to the future prophet. Aisha, the Prophet Muhammad's youngest wife, helped religious leaders interpret the faith after her husband's death and is remembered for having led the Battle of the Camel. These women are role models, providing examples of how women's power and gender roles do not have to be mutually exclusive. It is common, therefore, to find extremely well educated, highly successful African American women who have embraced Islam.

Women also feel empowered through *ijtihad*, or the interpretation of Islamic law, to discover for themselves the proper roles of men and women. Describing the attractiveness of Islam for women, African Americans included, Haddad, Smith, and Moore write, "They see Islam as a dynamic and flexible system, rather than a static and rigid set of rules and regulations, and want to open up avenues of participation in which women as well as men are the public faces of Islam" (Haddad, Smith, and Moore 2006, 20). It is critical to note that the types of debates about how to successfully strike a balance between work and family, and how to do all this while also trying to make a marriage work, have come to define a more mature feminist movement in the United States in the twenty-first century. The difference for Muslim women is the use of authoritative religious texts and religious history as starting points for making peace with complicated personal and economic challenges.

POSTCOLONIAL SUBJECTIVITY

One of the most unfortunate affective responses to white supremacy has been the formation of black self-hatred. But this was to be expected, given that most public school children in the United States are taught that the only contribution that black people have made to western civilization has been their slave labor[3]; that black people have lower IQs and therefore do not deserve the same rights of citizenship[4]; that the racial disparities in incarceration, health, and educational achievement are the result of black family and cultural dysfunction[5]; and that these conclusions are built on hard scientific and social scientific evidence. Where do African Americans begin to overcome the emotional wounds caused by this relentless negation? What evidence should they employ to counter the "facts"?

Most African American Muslims have found that their faith legitimates their value as human beings through religious doctrine about human goodness. An example of this is the Quranic ayah or verse, "O Mankind! We created you from a single (pair), of a male and a female, and made you into Nations and tribes, that ye may know each other (Not that ye may despise each other). Verily, the most honoured of you is (he who is) the most Righteous of you" (49: 13). This ayah celebrates men and women of different races and ethnicities as equal in the eyes of God; for African American Muslims this ayah has been contrasted with the biblical story of Ham, which has been used by white supremacist to justify racism. For many African Americans Muslims, the choice of faith is understood as a choice between the Quran, interpreted as affirming racial and gender equality, or the Bible, which has been used to legitimate racial hierarchies. African American Muslims accept that Jesus was a Prophet; this is an orthodox belief within Islam. Like other Muslims, however, they believe that the Prophet Muhammad completed God's message or sealed the prophecy.

But disrupting racialist ontologies only mark the beginning of the battle over self-hatred. The social scientific data have never been good for black Americans. In the early twenty-first century, the wealth of whites was almost twenty times that of blacks. Public education in the United States had become more, not less, segregated; even today, in most integrated schools, white students populate the advanced placement classes while the black and Latino students populate the special education classes. Disparities in health, education, wealth, employment, and incarceration speak of institutionalized patterns of discrimination, and public discussion of civil rights resides in social scientific euphemisms (culture, dysfunction, disorganized, at risk) and deceptive science (IQ, race, genes).

Islam for many African Americans has offered protection against this misrecognition through identification with historical touchstones, beliefs, and practices that differ from those of mainstream America. For example, the explanation for US exceptionalism can easily switch from being a story about freedom and laissez-faire economics to a story about how the economy was built on the backs of slaves, leased convicts, oppressed workers, and imperialist pursuits abroad. From the perspective of African American Muslims, the celebration of selective histories and epistemologies has provided legitimacy for the structures that reproduce racial inequalities. Even for African American Muslims who strongly identify with their country, Islamic history and exegesis offers a critical lens for assessing how Eurocentrism and white supremacy are embedded in everything from education to geopolitics. Although it is virtually impossible to avoid oppressive discourses and structures, African American Islam protects against the sense that one must prove oneself worthy.

New Discourses

Religions are never static but instead adapt to ever-changing cultural and political contexts. African American Islam is no different. Changes in the demographics of Muslim groups in the United States, engagements across Muslim communities in the United States and internationally, new political realities from 9/11 to the Arab Spring, and new representations in the media are changing how Islam is received and understood by Muslims and non-Muslims. African American Islam continues to be relevant because it has never been about a static set of beliefs or practices. Rather, as a religious dialogue framed by American struggles with social justice, African American Islam is finding new relevance in a changing world.

Much to the disappointment of many in both communities, tension between immigrant and African American Muslims still exists and relates in no small part to how immigrants position themselves with respect to the privileges of whiteness (Grewal 2009). Many immigrants may resent American policy toward Muslim countries, but they believe that their moral character and work ethic grants them access to full citizenship. What the children of these immigrants are finding, however, is that social mobility is not easy and that such things as skin color or foreignness still matter.

Given the experiences of youth, scholars of Islam in the United States are finding it harder and harder to draw borders around a group of people identified as "African American Muslims" (Manning 2009). America's cultural melting pot is producing syncretic engagements with the faith, which are reshaping African American Islam. The hybridity found in Muslim American hip-hop, dress, language play, religious practices, food, and identity speak to a future where social justice discourses remain central to African American Islam but race is displaced. As Hisham Aidi argues, "The attraction for African American, Latino, Arab, south Asian, and West Indian youth to Islam, and movements that espouse different brands of political Islam, is evidence of Western states' failure to integrate minority and immigrant communities and deliver basic life necessities and social welfare benefits" (Aidi 2009, 294).

It is important to clarify that the attractiveness of Islam for African Americans is not merely as a political counter discourse. There is great pleasure in practicing the faith that goes beyond the political-religious exegesis and accompanying sense of racial empowerment. The daily meditations, the beauty of Islamic scripture, the comfort provided by rituals, and the reminders of God's compassion and forgiveness are just a few examples. Nevertheless, the work of contemporary scholars demonstrates that African American Islam has been taken up by young Muslims—both immigrants and natives—eager to fight for social justice. This suggests that rather than characterizing African American Islam as a poor reading of religious orthodoxy, it should be thought of as an exegetical frame, highly attuned to the particulars of life in America, that speaks to many American Muslims regardless of which branch of Islam they identify with. Given its ability to absorb new social realities, the most exciting site for the study of African American Islam is in creative production: hip-hop, media, social media, art, fashion, literature, and theater. Through artistic expression, African American and American Muslims reveal how they negotiate their identities at the level of the day to day, what they hope for the future, and what role Islam plays in helping to make sense of it all.

Conclusion

African American Muslims feel that their faith liberates them from culturally patterned ways of thinking about race and, particularly for the women, about gender. "African American" is an over-determined category in the sense that it evokes a set of histories and concerns that are not or are no longer the concerns of many African American Muslims. Any history of African American Muslims must therefore be attentive to how the demographic category itself is and is not relevant. African American Muslims are often more concerned with the correct interpretation and practice of the faith than with the politics of race and gender in America. As a result, their identities do not fit easily into mainstream categories marking difference.

That said, for any American the development of a political and ethical consciousness requires coming to terms with African American social history. The centrality of African American history—particularly with respect to debates about individuals' rights and their duties to the state as well as what is meant by "freedom"—is unquestionable. Studying the emergence of ethical discourses like that occurring in African American Islam is critical to understanding the rise of progressivism in the United States. Since slavery, black Americans have been terrorized, denied basic human rights, and told that they deserve this because they are inferior. Despite all the abuse, African American religions have not responded with counterterrorist tactics. What African American religions such as Islam have given America are religious, political, and ethnical discourses that attempt to balance the inevitable conflicts between the constitutional objectives of justice, equality, and freedom (Wilmore 1984). The freedom of white men should not come at the expense of racial minorities and women; extrapolating from this, the freedom of a corporation should not come at the expense of the health of a community. African American Islam imagines what individuals, families, communities, and government need to do in order to strike a balance between all three objectives. African American Muslims may disagree on what is required to strike that balance, but all agree that the conversation must continue.

NOTES

1. It is necessary to use the word *black* because Moroccans and Egyptians, for example, are technically African American.
2. Anthropologist Zareena Grewal's analysis of the suspension of the African American Muslim basketball player Mahmoud Abdul-Rauf for not standing during the national anthem vividly captures this ethic (Grewal 2009).
3. Examples are included in *The Lies My Teacher Told Me: Everything Your American History Textbook Got Wrong*, by James W. Loewen. Also, the exclusion of marginalized subjects from mainstream US history inspired Howard Zinn to write *The People's History of the United States*. The 2011 Arizona legislative ban of ethnic studies, primarily Mexican American Studies, and the censoring of minority struggles against the US government in American textbooks, continue to disempower students of color.
4. Charles Murray's *The Bell Curve*, Philippe Ruston's *Race, Evolution and Behavior*, and the works of Henry Edward Garrett and Jared Taylor are just a few examples.
5. The articles and books that argue, on the basis of the "culture of poverty" theory, that poor people are poor because of their behavior and choices rather than structural inequalities are too numerous to list.

REFERENCES

The Holy Qur'an, edited by The Presidency of Islamic Researches, IFTA. (Al-Madinah Al-Munawarah, Saudi Arabia: King Fahd Holy Qur'an Printing Complex, 1405 AH).

Abdullah, Zain, *Black Mecca: The African Muslims of Harlem* (New York: Oxford University Press, 2010).

Adid, Rashad, *Elijah Muhammad and the Ideological Foundation of the Nation of Islam* (Newport, VA: U.B. and U.S. Communication Systems, 1993).

Ahmed, Akbar, *Journey into America: The Challenge of Islam* (Washington, DC: Brookings Institute, 2010).

Aidi, Hishaam D. "Jihadis in the Hood: Race, Urban Islam, and the War on Terror," in *Black Routes to Islam*, edited by Manning Marable and Hishaam D. Aidi (New York: Palgrave Macmillan, 2009): 283–298.

Alford, Terry, *Prince among Slaves: The True Story of an African Prince Sold into Slavery in the American South* (New York: Oxford University Press, 1986).

Bald, Vivek, "Overlapping Diasporas, Multiracial Lives: South Asian Muslims in the U.S. Communities of Color, 1880–1970," in *Black Routes to Islam*, edited by Manning Marable and Hishaam D. Aidi (New York: Palgrave Macmillan, 2009): 227–248.

Clegg, Claude Andrew, *An Original Man: The Life and Times of Elijah Muhammad* (New York: St. Martin's Griffin, 1998).

Crenshaw, Kimberle, "Demarginalizing the Intersection of Race and Sex: A Black Feminist Critique of Discrimination Doctrine, Feminist Theory and Antiracist Politics." *University of Chicago Legal Forum* (1989): 139–168.

——, "Mapping the Margins: Intersectionality, Identity Politics, and Violence Against Women of Color." In *Stanford Law Review*, 43, no. 6 (1991): 1241–1299.

Curtis, Edward E., *Islam in Black America: Identity, Liberation, and Difference in African-American Islamic Thought* (Albany: State University of New York, 2002).

——, *Black Muslim Religion in the Nation of Islam: 1960–1975* (Chapel Hill: University of North Carolina Press, 2006).

——, *Muslims in America: A Short History* (New York: Oxford University Press, 2009).

Dannin, Robert, *Black Pilgrimage to Islam* (New York: Oxford University Press, 2002).

Evanzz, Karl, *The Messenger: The Rise and Fall of Elijah Muhammad* (New York: Pantheon Books, 1999).

Grewal, Zareena, "Lights, Camera, Suspension: Freezing the Frame on the Mahmoud Abdul-Rauf-Anthem Controversy," in *Black Routes to Islam*, edited by Manning Marable and Hishaam D. Aidi (New York: Palgrave Macmillan, 2009); 191–205.

Haddad, Yvonne Yazbeck, *The Muslims of America* (Oxford, UK: Oxford University Press, 1991).

——, Jane I. Smith, and Kathleen M. Moore, *Muslim Women in America: The Challenge of Islamic Identity Today* (New York: Oxford University Press, 2006).

Jackson, Sherman A., *Islam and the Blackamerican: Looking Towards the Third Resurrection* (New York: Oxford University Press, 2005).

Karim, Jamillah, *American Muslim Women: Negotiating Race, Class and Gender within the Ummah* (New York: New York University Press, 2009).

Khabeer, Suad Abdul, "Hip Hop Is Islam: Race, Self-Making and Young Muslims in Chicago" Dissertation, Princeton University: (2011)

Leonard, Karen Isaksen, *Muslims in the United States: The State of Research* (New York: Russell Sage Foundation, 2003).

Lincoln, C. Eric, *The Black Muslims in America* (Boston: Beacon Press, 1961).

Marable, Manning, and Hishaam D. Aidi, *Black Routes to Islam* (New York: Palgrave Macmillan, 2009).

Marable, Manning, *Malcolm X: A Life of Reinvention* (New York: Viking Press, 2011).

Marsh, Clifton, *From Black Muslims to Muslims: The Resurrection, Transformation, and Change of the Lost-found Nation of Islam in American, 1930–1995* (Lanham, MD: Scarecrow Press, 1996).

McCloud, Aminah Beverly, *African American Islam* (New York: Routledge, 1995).

Muhammad, Elijah, *Message to the Blackman in America* (Chicago: Muhammad's Mosque of Islam No. 2, 1965).

Nashashibi, Rami, "The Blackstone Legacy: Islam and the Rise of Ghetto Cosmopolitanism," in *Black Routes to Islam*, edited by Manning Marable and Hishaam D. Aidi, 271–282 (New York: Palgrave Macmillan, 2009).

New Muslim Cool, Directed by Jennifer Maytorena Taylor. 2009.

Rouse, Carolyn, *Engaged Surrender: African American Women and Islam.* (Berkeley: University of California Press, 2004).

——. "Shopping with Sister Zubayda: African American Sunni Muslim Rituals of Consumption and Belonging," in *Women and Religion in the African Diaspora: Knowledge, Power, and Performance*, edited by R. Marie Griffith and Barbara Dianne Savage (Baltimore, MD: Johns Hopkins University Press, 2006).

Turner, Richard Brent, *Islam in the African American Experience* (Bloomington: Indiana University Press, 1997).

Wadud, Amina, *Qur'an and Woman: Rereading the Sacred Text from a Woman's Perspective* (New York: Oxford University Press, 1999).

Wilmore, Gayraud S., *Black Religion and Black Radicalism: An Interpretation of the Religious History of Afro-American People* (New York: Orbis Books), 1984.

CHAPTER 6

THE TWELVER SHI'IS IN AMERICA

LIYAKAT TAKIM

THE MANY FACES OF AMERICAN SHI'ISM

The term Shi'a refers to the partisans of 'Ali, the cousin and son-in-law of the Prophet Muhammad. After the Prophet died in 632 CE, the early Shi'is claimed that 'Ali, the cousin and son-in law of the Prophet, was the only legitimate successor to the Prophet Muhammad. They also believed that only family members of the Prophet, the *ahl al-bayt*, were qualified to lead the Muslim community after him. These leaders were called imams and all of them were descendants of the Prophet from the line of 'Ali and Fatima, the daughter of the Prophet. The Shi'is believed that the rights of 'Ali and the family of the Prophet were usurped by the companions of Muhammad. This meant that, from the very beginning, Shi'ism arose and grew as a dissenting group in opposition to the Muslim majority.

When 'Ali assumed power as the fourth Caliph of the Muslim community in 656 CE, Shi'ism emerged as a recognized religious movement in Islam. However, the massacre of Husayn, the son of 'Ali, and his forces at Karbala during his uprising against the Caliph Yazid in 681 proved to be a highly significant milestone in Shi'i history. It affirmed the conviction that injustices were being perpetrated against the progeny of the Prophet. From this disastrous occurrence there grew in the community a passion for grieving and martyrdom, specifically in commemoration of the cruel death of the grandson of Prophet Muhammad.

Shi'i theology and jurisprudence took definitive shape during the eras of the fifth and sixth imams, Muhammad al-Baqir, who died in the 730s, and Ja'far al-Sadiq, who died in 765. The latter was largely responsible for the construction of a Shi'i legal edifice and the formulation of the Shi'i doctrine of the imamate. The true imam, al-Sadiq stated, had to be divinely determined. The imam was also believed to be infallible and was empowered to provide authoritative interpretation of Islamic revelation. Designation by God and infallibility were complemented by the Imam's possession of special knowledge that was either transmitted from the Prophet or derived from inherited scrolls. It was this notion of the divinely inspired and charismatic leadership of the imams that distinguished and continues to distinguish Shi'ism from the majority Sunnis.

Four major Shi'i groups, the Twelver Shi'is, the Nizari, the Bohra Isma'ilis, and the Zaydis compose the American Muslim Shi'i population.

The Nizari Isma'ilis

After the death of Ja'far al-Sadiq, the sixth Shi'i Imam, one Shi'i faction proclaimed his son Isma'il, instead of Musa, as his successor. Thereby they became known as the Isma'ilis. After Isma'il's death, they went underground and reappeared in tenth-century Egypt to establish the Fatimid dynasty. In 1094 the Isma'ilis were divided into the Musta'li (now called Bohra) and Nizari Isma'ilis. The latter espouse esoteric doctrines and accept the Agha Khan as their spiritual leader.

Most of the early Nizari Isma'ilis migrated to North America in the mid-1960s and settled in Canada. This steady growth continued until the early 1970s, when political changes in many Asian and African countries led to the arrival of a larger number of Isma'ilis in America. Wherever the followers of the Agha Khan have settled, they have evolved a well-defined institutional framework through which they have made progress in the educational, health, housing, and economic spheres.

Under the leadership of the Aga Khan III (d. 1957), the Nizari Isma'ilis consolidated their identity and have engaged in educational and socioeconomic reforms that made the community self-sufficient. The unquestioning devotion of the Isma'ilis to the Aga Khan, in addition to the restructured hierarchical communal organization with the Aga Khan as the supreme authority, facilitated the implementation of religious, social, and economic reforms.

The fact that the Aga Khan is a spiritual leader who is believed to have access to esoteric understanding of texts means that he possesses the authority to interpret religious texts and laws in keeping with the times. Based on the *farman* (religious edicts) issued by the Aga Khan, Isma'ilis have their own genre of prayers and supplications as well as their own special religious taxes, and they have established congregational places (*jamaat khanas*).[1]

Bohra Isma'ilis

In 1094, when the eighth Fatimid caliph al-Mustansir died, there was a dispute regarding his successor. The Bohra Isma'ilis upheld the imamate of al-Musta'li (1094–1101) to succeed his father al-Mustansir in Egypt. The name Bohra denotes "trader, merchant." Most Bohras are now of Hindu origin, their ancestors having been converted by Isma'ili missionaries. In 1588, the Bohras chose Dawud b. Qutb Shah (d. 1612) as their leader; however, their Yemeni brethren supported the claims of Sulayman b. Hasan (d. 1597) who claimed to be the rightful successor based on a mandate from his predecessor, Dawud b. Ajab. Aliya Bohras proclaim 'Ali b. Ibrahim (d. 1637) as their twenty-ninth leader, having seceded from the Dawudis in 1625.

Most Bohras are Dawudis, whose headquarters are in Surat, India. A key feature of the Bohra community is that they form themselves into guilds and restrict their activities to commerce, do not intermarry even with other Muslims, and take little part in public affairs. Two proselytes (da'is) have led the Bohra community in the twentieth century. The fifty-first da'i, Tahir Sayf al-Din (1915–1965), was an erudite scholar, social activist, and man of great vision. During his period of fifty years he modernized the mission's organization and promoted welfare and education in the community.

Bohras reside in India, Pakistan, the Middle East, East Africa, and the West. The Bohra community in America is relatively small (about 25,000). Most have migrated since the 1970s and settled in different American cities, especially in Chicago, New York, and Detroit. The first Dawudi Bohra mosque was built in 1982 in Detroit. Even in America, Bohras observe strict dress codes for men and women, prefer to speak in Gujarati, and submit to the amil, a personal delegate sent from Mumbai to guide them.[2]

Zaydism in America

The Zaydis are named after Zayd ibn 'Ali (d. 740), a half-brother of the son of Husayn b. 'Ali. Zayd was killed in Kufa in 740, having rebelled against the Umayyad caliphate. Unlike other Shi'is, he is reported to have accepted the leadership of Abu Bakr, the first Caliph. Zayd qualified this by saying that Abu Bakr's was the leadership of the inferior (mafdul) since 'Ali was superior to the first two caliphs. Zaydis also came to assert that a true imam must be politically active, which often meant that he should "rise up" to establish his own rule. Unlike other Shi'i Imams, Zaydi Imams are not believed to have any superhuman powers. The only dynastic rule established by Zaydis is that of the Qasimi Imams in Yemen (1598–1851).[3] Today most Zaydis live in Yemen.

As with other Shi'i immigrants, Zaydis started coming to America in the 1930s. Larger groups of Zaydis began migrating from Yemen after the relaxation of immigration laws in 1965. Many Yemenis live in poor conditions, as they have limited education and vocational skills.[4] Most Zaydis established themselves in Dearborn, Michigan, where they have had their own mosque since the 1930s.[5] Of all the Shi'i groups, the Zaydis are the closest to Sunnis in their ritual practices and acceptance of the leadership of the first two caliphs.

The remainder of this chapter focuses on the largest group of Shi'is, known as the Twelvers.

TWELVER SHI'ISM IN AMERICA

Voluntary migration to America by members of the Muslim community is said to have begun between 1875 and 1912.[6] Among those who came in the 1880s were Shi'is from what was then called Greater Syria, many of whom settled in Michigan.[7] Between 1900 and 1914 several hundred settlers from diverse religious backgrounds migrated from the Middle East,[8] many of them Lebanese Shi'is who settled in Detroit to work at the Ford Motor Company. Migration by members of the Lebanese community increased further between 1918 and 1922. By the 1940s, about 200 Sunni and Shi'i families had settled in Detroit,[9] and by the 1950s many Shi'i families were dispersed in different parts of America.

It is estimated that about 200 Shi'i families settled in Michigan City, Indiana, in the 1920s. There is evidence that this group formed the first American Muslim society (called "al-Badr al-Munir") in 1914.[10] A booklet published by the Islamic Center of Michigan City states that the center was first organized on April 26, 1914, under the name of The Bader Elmoneer Society of Michigan City, Indiana. In the early 1920s, the Bader Elmoneer Society purchased land and erected one of the first mosques in America in 1924.

Soon, a larger community of Shi'is started to crystallize in America as other Shi'is arrived from areas such as India and Iran. The influx of Lebanese migrants led to the establishment of Shi'i institutions and centers of worship, the most sizable being in Detroit. In the mid-1940s Shi'is in Detroit rented a hall to mark religious and social events. The Hashimite club, as it was then called, served the Shi'i community until the early 1960s, when a permanent mosque was built. The first Shi'i mosque in Detroit was the Islamic Center of America, which opened its doors in Dearborn, Michigan, in 1963. Later on, in 2005, the center was relocated to Ford Road, where a magnificent multipurpose building was erected. With a population of about 35,000 Lebanese migrants, Dearborn now has one of the largest Shi'i communities in America.

The early Shi'a immigrants, most of whom were Lebanese, were quite liberal in their lifestyles and often assimilated themselves to mainstream white American culture. Unlike more conservative Shi'is, they did not mark important dates in the Shi'a calendar, like 'Ashura, which marks the time when Husayn, the grandson of the Prophet Muhammad, was killed in Karbala.

Some among the early wave of Muslim immigrants to enter America from the Middle East were Shi'is who settled in Quincy, Massachusetts. Political turmoil in the Middle East and forced conscription in the Ottoman army were important factors that led to their migration. By the beginning of the twentieth century, Shi'is had established themselves in major American cities from Cedar Rapids, Iowa, to New York City. The size and composition of the Shi'i community in America was to change drastically in 1965, when President Lyndon Johnson signed an immigration act repealing the quotas based on national diversity in the United States. Henceforth, immigration was no longer contingent on a person's national or ethnic origin, allowing Shi'is from different parts of the world to come to America.

The predominance of mainly Lebanese Shi'is in the early part of the twentieth century can be contrasted with the present American Shi'i community, which is composed of highly diverse ethnic and cultural groups. Originally from Iran, Iraq, Lebanon, the Indian subcontinent, the Gulf States, East Africa, and parts of North Africa, most contemporary Shi'is have come since the 1970s. In addition, a growing number of African Americans are converting to Shi'ism, after having initially converted to Sunnism or to the Nation of Islam.

Various factors have precipitated the proliferation of Shi'ism in America: the revolution in Islamic Iran,[11] the civil war in Lebanon, the civil strife and breakup of Pakistan, the exodus of East African Asians during the regime of Idi Amin in Uganda,[12] the Russian invasion and ensuing civil wars in Afghanistan, and the sociopolitical conditions in Iraq. During the Gulf War, many Iraqi soldiers escaped to Saudi Arabia from Kuwait. After spending some time in camps in Saudi Arabia, they sought and were granted asylum in America. Today, Iraqi refugees, who are predominantly Shi'is, are located in different parts of America.

THE ETHNIC FACTOR IN AMERICAN SHI'ISM

Increased immigration from various parts of the world has resulted in the Shi'i community in America becoming more fragmented, as bonds of common faith have been replaced by ties to common origins, ethnicity, and culture. As the Shi'i community has become more diverse, it has also fractured along ethnic and cultural lines. Major cities like New York, Los Angeles, Houston, Detroit, and Chicago are characterized by disparate Shi'i centers established along ethnic lines.

Many centers hold programs in languages and with customs that reflect their countries of origins (Urdu, Persian, or Arabic). The linguistic and cultural bias of these programs means that Shi'i communities often experience Islam in a culturally conditioned form, marginalizing them from other Shiʿi communities. It is only in smaller communities in America that multiethnic centers are to be found. It should be noted that the Shiʿi community has a higher percentage of immigrants than its Sunni counterpart. This is because of the lack of indigenous Shiʿis and because most converts accept Sunni rather than Shiʿi Islam. In the American Shiʿi community, tensions are felt more within the immigrant community itself than between immigrants and converts.[13]

Most Shiʿi immigrants try to impose the homeland culture by determining how the mosques are run as well as acceptable dress, language, and behavior. Newer immigrants also tend to have their own predispositions on issues such as gender integration, political activism in a non-Muslim country, engagement with different ethnic groups, interfaith dialogue, joint activities with Sunnis, and so on. More recent Shiʿi immigrants, who tend to emphasize the public expression of their religious beliefs and practices, are less likely to assimilate into mainstream American culture.

It is important to emphasize that the ethnic factor is more accentuated in Shiʿism than in Sunnism. This is because the Shiʿi notion of sanctity and holiness is markedly different from that of other Muslims. Sunni religious events generally are confined to daily or weekly prayers and annual events in which Muslims from different ethnic backgrounds congregate. The Shiʿis, on the other hand, have their own calendar of days wherein venerated Imams and holidays are clearly marked as distinct from profane time. Besides holding daily, Friday, and ʿeid prayers, Shiʿi communities across America hold functions to commemorate the martyrdom of Imam Husayn (d. 681). They also mark the birth and death anniversaries of other Imams and events like ʿeid al-ghadir, when the Prophet is reported to have designated ʿAli b. Abi Talib (d. 661) as his successor. Among other important holidays is the day of Arbaʿin, commemorating the fortieth day after the death of Husayn.

Especially after the events of September 11, 2001, many Shiʿi immigrants have felt ostracized and alienated from American society. The experience of marginalization creates binary and essentialist categories in relation to the dominant culture. The formation of ethnic-based organizations helps to offset the isolation and threat that many migrants have felt since 9/11. Relating to the culture of origin and ethnic solidarity helps Shiʿis sustain their self-identity under difficult and at times hostile circumstances.

Nationalism and American Shiʿism

Shiʿis from Iraq initially came to the United States as students. Many chose not to return home because of the adverse political conditions in Iraq. Other Iraqis sought asylum in America in the 1970s, after the establishment of Saddam Hussein's regime.

Dispersed in different parts of the country, these Iraqis are well educated, highly skilled, and affluent. Another group of Iraqi refugees comprises those who either escaped from the country or were captured by the allied forces during the Gulf War. Most of these form an unskilled labor force; they work in factories and perform other types of manual labor. The recently arrived Iraqi refugees renew ties with the homeland, in the process importing their own distinctive cultural accretions. Their religious fervor is not always shared by those Iraqis who migrated to America earlier. Many of these Iraqis live in areas like Lincoln, Nebraska; Dearborn, Michigan, and Nashville, Tennessee.

Iranians form the largest Shiʻi group in America. The number of Iranians migrating to America increased dramatically during the last three decades. Most of these Iranians came to America after the Iranian revolution in 1979 and settled in California, which is reported to have about 400,000 Iranians.[14]

The Iranian Shiʻi community in America can be divided into three distinct groups. The first group comprises professionals who left their native land fearing the policies of and reprisals from the new regime after the revolution in 1979. Having been influenced by the Shah's "white revolution" and modernization policies that introduced western norms and culture to Iran, many of these Iranians adopted a secular lifestyle and have little religious affiliation. In contrast are fellow Iranians who also came to America after the revolution but fully support the revolution and share its ideals. Many of them are students at various universities who promote the ideology of the current Iranian regime in Islamic centers. Much hostility is evident between the diverse Iranian groups. The third group of Iranians comprises those immigrants who are alarmed at the dissolution of religious values, especially among their younger generation, but who are not affiliated with the regime in Iran. To make sure that their youth receive proper religious instruction, they organize events like Sunday classes, weekly lectures, and Qurʾanic classes in their homes.

Lebanese Shiʻis, as mentioned, were the first to come to the United States. Thus they have adapted most to American culture. Members of the Lebanese community are increasingly playing more active roles in American civil life. They tend to adopt a less legalistic approach to Islam, as they have been more exposed to western lifestyles and they originate from a more pluralistic background. Many members of the Lebanese community live in Dearborn.

South Asian Shiʻis are composed of migrants from Pakistan and India and a lesser number from Bangladesh. In America, they tend to experience Islam mainly through the prism of "imported Islam" and are highly resistant to change. In their centers, Islam is mediated in a culturally conditioned form. Instead of conducting services determined exclusively by Islamic provenance, ethnic and cultural factors have become more pronounced. South Asian Shiʻis live in major cities like New York, Washington, Chicago, and Los Angeles.

The majority of the Khoja Shiʻis migrated to the West in the 1970s and 1980s as a result of adverse social, economic, and educational policies in East Africa. Increased emigration by the Khoja community was also precipitated by the expulsion of Ugandan Asians by Idi Amin in 1972. The Khojas are dispersed in different parts of America.

SUFI SHIʿIS

Among the Shiʿi population in America are various Sufi Shiʿi groups, the majority of whom have been active since the 1970s. Sufi movements in the Shiʿi community are not widespread or diverse; most of them are established within the Iranian community in California. Many Iranians prefer the esoteric dimension of Islam to the practices of more strict Iranian mosques, some of which, as already noted, subscribe to the ideology of the Iranian regime or emphasize a legalistic interpretation of Shiʿi Islam. There are at least three Sufi meeting places in Los Angeles.[15] Sufi Shiʿi orders include the Nimatullahi, the Nimatullahi-Gunabadi, the Uwaysi order, and the International Association of Sufism.

WOMEN AND AMERICAN SHIʿISM

In many Shiʿi centers, particular elements of culture brought by immigrants may be at odds with American cultural expectations. Women, for example, may be partitioned off in separate rooms where they can neither interact with a speaker nor contribute to the events. Their participation is restricted to serving meals. Most centers do not have a women's committee; even if they do, women are not represented on the boards or executive councils. Women rarely participate or have a say in the running of center activities.

Increasingly, American Shiʿi women have rejected an imported culture that has long subjugated or alienated them. They are engaged in redefining their role within the community. Centers are becoming aware of the need to give women more "space," such as opportunities to participate in the running of the centers. In some centers in Dearborn, women are seated in the same room as men and are able to fully interact in the proceedings. At one such center women recite supplications in front of men, an occurrence that would not be accepted in other traditional centers. Centers with close ties to homeland cultures tend to exclude female participation in events where males are present, whereas those with fewer cultural attachments encourage women to participate in the various genres of programs offered.

According to a recent survey, American women who convert to Shiʿism often feel marginalized in the community. Most of them describe a moderate to severe sense of exclusion from the Shiʿi community for racial, cultural, and linguistic reasons.[16]

Respondents who have participated in both the Shi'i and Sunni religious communities feel much more welcomed and accepted among Sunnis, who also provide material support to new converts, such as religious books and transportation to the mosque. In contrast, the survey shows that converts complain of racism in the Shi'i community and liken Shi'i mosques to "cultural clubs" rather than houses of worship.

Several women in the survey report that the most profound effect of their conversion on their identity is a greater sense of marginalization. In particular, African American women speak of the pressure of adjusting to a quadruple minority status, as a minority (black) within a minority (convert) within a minority (Shi'i) within a minority (Muslim) in North America. This multilayered minority status is specifically identified as a major stress factor. The few convert women who report taking significant leadership roles in the Shi'i community, such as being a member of a mosque board or engaging in frequent public speaking, seem more conscious of their position as women than as converts, and they describe taking leadership roles as an "uphill battle" because of their gender.

RELIGIOUS LEADERSHIP IN THE SHI'I COMMUNITY

Shi'i leadership is predicated on a highly stratified hierarchical system called the *marji' al-taqlid*, or *marji'iyya*. The term refers to the most learned juridical authority in the Shi'i community, whose rulings on Islamic law are followed by those who acknowledge him as their source of reference or marji'. The followers base their religious practices on his judicial opinions. The marji' has the authority to issue religious edicts, thereby empowering him to influence the religious and social lives of his followers all over the world.

The process of following the juridical edicts of the most learned jurist (*a'lim*) is called taqlid (literally imitation or emulation).[17] In Shi'i jurisprudence, the term taqlid denotes a commitment to accept and act in accordance with the rulings of the shari'a as deduced by a qualified and pious jurist. Taqlid also suggests that ordinary Shi'is adopt the rulings of a jurist without having to investigate the reasons that led the jurist to make his decisions. Stated differently, taqlid generates confidence in the believers that their religious practices, which are based on the juridical pronouncements of the *maraji'* (pl. of marji'), approximating the will of God.

The taqlid factor has required American Shi'is to be allied with the maraji' rather than to any foreign government. It has also acted as a catalyst for unity in the Shi'i community in America by fostering ties among different Shi'is who have often been divided by cultural, ethnic, and linguistic considerations. The maraji', who reside in the Middle East, have recognized the need to foster closer ties with their followers in the West. Besides establishing religious centers and internet sites in the West, they have tried to be more accessible to their followers in America by sending emissaries to visit them. New situations and contingencies have prompted them to delve into the sources and to use methodological devices in Islamic legal theory to enable them to deduce fresh juridical rulings.

A number of marajiʿ are seen as sources of reference. These include figures like Ayatullahs ʿAli Seestani, Hussein Waheed Khorasani, Lutfallah Safi Gulpaygani, Nasir Makarim Shirazi, ʿAli Khameneʾi, and Mohammed Hussein Fadlallah. Shiʿis living in the West have posed a wide range of questions to the marajiʿ, from the permissibility of taking mortgages to praying and fasting in areas where the sun does not set in summer. They have also broached sensitive issues such as examining and touching the reproductive organs of the opposite gender, looking at photographs of naked persons for studying physiology and anatomy, taking the pulse and other vital signs of patients of the opposite gender, and so on. The marajiʿ in the Shiʿi theological centers of Qum and Najaf have responded by composing a distinct genre of juridical texts called the *mustahdathat* (lit. "new matters or occurrences"). The literature is a collection of the marajiʿ's responses to questions posed by their followers, especially those living in the West.[18]

The appointment by the marajiʿ of financial and religious deputies to act as their representatives has enabled community members to provide facilities for religious education for the Shiʿi community in America and has generated the confidence to engage in major projects such as the construction of mosques, Islamic centers, and institutions considered necessary for the continued religious and spiritual well-being of the community. For example, in 1989 Ayatollah al-Khuʾi offered several million dollars to the Islamic Center of America, the Jamiʾ, to build an Islamic school in Detroit. The school was to be under the jurisdiction of the New York–based al-Khoei Foundation.[19]

Apart from the marajiʿ, authority in the American Shiʿi community is also wielded by the religious scholars, the ulama. Most Shiʿi ulamamigrated to America since the 1980s and originate from the Middle East or South Asia. Dearborn, with its large concentration of Lebanese and Iraqis, has the largest number of Shiʿi scholars of any US city. At present the Shiʿi community in North America comprises about 150 religious scholars. The majority of these scholars are affiliated with Shiʿi centers and perform basic religious functions like leading prayers, delivering sermons, and performing funerals and marriages. Differences between the ulama have arisen, as some support the Iranian ideology of *wilaya al-faqih* (authority of the jurist) whereas others follow the line of Ayatullah Seestani, who does not subscribe to that ideology. The taqlid factor, as outlined previously, has also led to division within the leadership of the American Shiʿi community.

In an effort to unite the diverse ethnic groups that make up the American Shiʿi community, an indigenous council of Shiʿi ulama was formed in 1993. Composed of scholars in North America, the Council of Shiʿa Muslim Scholars in North America meets annually to discuss issues germane to the community. Among the stated aims of the council is to support the Shi'i community of North America by strengthening unity and cooperation among the *ulama*.

Although it has been in existence since 1993, the Council has failed to formulate any definitive direction for the Shi'i community. It has not been able to bridge the chasm that has divided different ethnic groups within the community. Few ulama in the West are both conversant enough with issues relating to the local community and sufficiently instructed in the Islamic tradition to articulate a proper solution to the challenges faced by community members. Frequently these scholars are not able to converse in English, and the contents of their sermons are deemed by many to be irrelevant to the challenges of living in contemporary America.

While the traditional ulama have generally been unsuccessful in addressing issues posed by the younger generation, Muslim intellectuals and leaders who have become a significant part of the American academic scene have often been able to provide an interpretation of Islam relevant to life in America as well as to the modern world. Shi'i scholars like Mahmoud Ayoub, Abdulaziz Sachedina, and Seyyid Hossein Nasr have been able to capture the imagination of many Shi'is. In recent years, statements made by these scholars as a result of their academic research have differed from views enunciated by the ulama, thus challenging the authority of the latter to be the sole interpreters of Shi'i teachings. In particular, there is much debate in the Shi'i community on topics like religious pluralism, apostasy, slavery, the testimony and inheritance rights of women, and the correct mode of dressing for women. The views of Shi'i scholars trained in both the traditional centers of Islamic learning and in the universities differ appreciably from those propounded by the ulama.

OUTREACH PROGRAMS

Because most Shi'i centers have been established since the 1980s, few centers or mosques have reached out to non-Muslims or engaged in interfaith dialogue in a substantive way. Instead, these centers have used their limited financial resources to establish and consolidate their religious institutions and engage in communal activities rather than to proselytize or help improve the image of Islam outside the community.

Most Shi'i institutes in America lack the financial support that is available to Sunnis, for example, through the Saudi-backed Muslim World League. Lack of diplomatic relations between America and Iran, the only Shi'i country, has meant the latter has not been able not furnish the institutional infrastructure or financial support necessary to furnish Shi'i outreach work in America. Shi'i proselytization activities have been limited to a few poorly funded organizations that are not properly structured for extensive *da'wa* (lit. "invitation"). It is correct to state that Shi'i centers of worship are introverted rather than outward-directed. The activities of most centers are aimed at providing basic religious services like facilitating prayers, conducting marriages and funerals, and counseling members of the community.

Other factors also challenge the Shiʿi community's capacity to reach out to non-Muslims. The arrival of newer migrants has impinged on the American Shiʿi community, as it experiences Islam mainly through the phenomenon of "imported Islam." Generally the more recent immigrants' major concern is to preserve the traditional understanding of Islam rather than to reach out to potential converts or engage in dialogue with non-Muslims.

However, some Shiʿi institutes have tried to approach non-Muslims. An early Shiʿi institute was the Tahrike Tarsile Qurʾan (TTQ). Established in New York in 1978, TTQ has the specific aim of publishing copies of the Qurʾan, which are distributed to different parts of the world as well as to American prisons. Another important Shiʿi institute is the Khoei Foundation in New York, which caters to both the Shiʿi and non-Shiʿi community. In 1997, the foundation became the fourth Muslim organization—and the only Shiʿi Muslim organization—to hold General Consultative Status in the United Nations, where it currently promotes work on human and minority rights.

The Islamic Information Center (IIC), a grassroots organization, was established in 2003 in order to negate stereotypical images about Islam and the Muslim community. IIC is also engaged in interfaith dialogue, publishing articles and interviews on Islam as well as a bimonthly newsletter addressing issues that pertain to Islam and the Muslim world. Through educational and interfaith programs, IIC seeks to promote understanding and trust among people of all faiths and cultures.

Established since in 1987, the Qurʾan Account Inc. was initially called the Islamic School System, led by a retired pediatrician from Iraq. Its outreach focus has been primarily on correctional facilities. Since the institute's inception, it has converted over 6,000 people to Shiʿism. The institute sends out copies of the Qurʾan and other religious books and has published a quarterly *Bulletin of Affiliation*.

The Muslim Congress was established in 2005. Its primary goal is to provide educational services that will directly benefit members of the Shiʿi community. It has established a state-of-the-art website to serves as a focal point for all its activities. While still in an embryonic stage, the congress has promised to provide community services such as family counseling, matrimonial services, career/business guidance, online discussion forums, and so on.[20]

UNIVERSAL MUSLIM ASSOCIATION OF AMERICA

The most important American Shiʿi national institution and the first multiethnic Shiʿi movement, is the Universal Muslim Association of America (UMAA). In 2002, leaders of the organization felt that the Shi'i community needed an organization that could represent, speak on behalf of, and unite the Shi'is. As a result, UMAA proclaimed its distinct identity as a Shi'i Muslim national organization of North America. Its first convention was held in 2003. Among its main objectives is to facilitate discussion on social, political, and economic issues affecting the Muslim community. It seeks to encourage Muslims to vote and participate in the political process, to coordinate with the media, to educate the public on issues relating to Islam, and to provide a common platform and forum for Muslim youths.

UMAA also seeks to promote an accurate portrayal of Islam and to encourage both inter- and intrafaith dialogue. It provides a forum to foster effective grassroots participation by Muslims in the United States and to network with other organizations.[21] UMAA also aims to train Shi'i imams to serve the community in America.

The Black-Shi'ism Phenomenon in America

A relatively new phenomenon in America is the conversion of members of the black community to Islam, most of whom embrace Sunni rather than Shi'i Islam. This is primarily because Sunnis have more resources, reach out to Americans more, and have organized movements for da'wa purposes, especially within the African American community.

The experience of African American Shi'is is very different from that of their Sunni counterparts. For most other Muslims, the awareness of black Americans of Islam and their conversion to proto-Islamic movements as well as to Sunni Islam preceded the immigrant community. It was only in the 1950s and 1960s, when more immigrants arrived, that black Americans lost their interpretive voice. Black Shi'is, on the other hand, did not experience an existence independent from that of immigrants, and neither did they enjoy the kind of communal conversion that black Sunnis witnessed in transitioning from the Nation of Islam to traditional Sunnism. The immigrant Shi'i community, therefore, did not have a viable black community to contend with. Instead, it had to deal with earlier Shi'i settlers, many of whom had assimilated into mainstream American culture. Consequently tensions within American Shi'ism arose between different immigrant communities rather than between the black and immigrant communities.

Unlike its Sunni counterpart, Shi'ism came to black America through the immigrant community rather than through pseudo-Islamic movements. The views, outlook, and perceptions of black Shi'is were informed by the lens that immigrant Shi'is brought to America. This made black Shi'ism largely dependent on and vulnerable to the interpretations of immigrant Shi'ism.

Dependency on the immigrant community was accentuated by the fact that black Shi'is did not possess the resources to build their own institutions or centers. To date, only a very few black Shi'i mosques exist in America. The fact that they emerged only after the Iranian revolution, when many Shi'is migrated in America, meant that black Shi'is largely capitulated to rather than challenged the immigrant expression of Shi'i Islam. Black Shi'ism is a relatively new phenomenon; indeed, the number of black Shi'is does not exceed a few thousand. Lack of independent financial resources as well as of charismatic leaders who could articulate a vision for or initiate a movement within the black community has made black Shi'is dependent on immigrant Shi'is.

While all black Muslims have had to endure the stigmas of color and religion, black Shi'is have had to endure the additional stigma of being a minority within Islam. This is because transition to Shi'i Islam was deemed as an aberration by many in the black community. By the 1980s, when black Shi'ism made its appearance on the American religious landscape, the Wahhabis had already been actively promoting their ideology in American mosques, campuses, and prisons. Basing their views on a very parochial and literalist understanding of Islam, the Wahhabis had pronounced Shi'ism to be a heretical sect. By converting to Shi'ism, black Shi'is became alienated not only from their families and friends but also from the African American Muslim community, which felt betrayed by the black Shi'is.

Why do some African Americans find Shi'ism appealing? Since Shi'ism has been a minority religion in much of the Islamic world, concepts of resistance and opposition to tyranny and fighting for a just cause are deeply ingrained within it. Shi'ism also posits role models from which black Shi'is can derive inspiration in their quest for socioeconomic justice. Shi'i Imams, especially 'Ali and Husayn, have become role models owing to their opposition to tyranny and injustice. Such notions resonate strongly with black Americans, who have suffered from racism, unemployment, and discrimination in white America. Iran provided the contemporary paradigm of release from bondage and subjugation to white America.[22]

9/11 AND ITS IMPACT ON THE AMERICAN SHI'I COMMUNITY

The terrorist attacks of September 11, 2001, revived prejudices against Islam as a religion that promotes the killing of innocent people and of Muslims as an inherently militant and irrational people. The media have represented the "absent Muslim other" and sought to create stereotypical representations of Islam and Muslims that have been impossible to ignore. The American global "war on terror" and the invasion of

Iraq have invigorated stereotypes and suspicions against Muslims, especially those of Middle Eastern origin.

After 9/11, the US government implemented a wide range of domestic legislative, administrative, and judicial measures in the name of national security and the war on terror. Most of them were designed and have been carried out by the executive branch of government, with little a priori public discussion or debate. These measures included mass arrests, secret and indefinite detentions, prolonged detention of "material witnesses," closed hearings and the use of secret evidence, FBI home and work visits, wiretapping, seizures of property, removals of aliens with technical visa violations, and mandatory special registration.

Since 9/11 American Shi'is have been held responsible for the terrorist attacks even though none of the terrorists were Shi'is. Shi'is feel that they have been found guilty by religious association, drawn into a discourse on terrorism, and associated with a group (al-Qa'ida) that would, ironically, exterminate them if it could. Shi'is in different parts of the world were among the first to condemn the acts of 9/11 and show sympathy with its victims. Shi'is in Iran gathered on the night of 9/11 to hold a candlelight vigil and protest the attacks.[23] The maraji' have also unequivocally condemned acts of terror and the killing of innocent civilians, as have Grand Ayatullah of Iraq 'Ali Seestani and other Shi'i religious leaders across the world.

Especially since 2006, Shi'i organizations have been targeted by the government. After the war between Israel and Hizbollah in 2006, the American government declared Hizbollah a terrorist organization, a move that led to raids by the FBI of several Shi'i nonprofit organizations. Such raids have been carried out in Detroit, where there is some sympathy for Hizbollah. In recent years, owing to political upheavals in the Middle East, members of the Iranian, Iraqi, Pakistani, Lebanese, and Afghani communities in America have come under close scrutiny

It is nonetheless also true that the image of Shi'ism in America has improved somewhat since 9/11 and the American invasion of Iraq in 2003. Most of the resistance in Iraq, including acts of terrorism, has been perpetrated by Sunni al-Qa'ida-inspired insurgents. Shi'i resistance has been restricted to Muqtada al-Sadr's al-Mahdi army. Other Shi'i leaders, including Ayatullah Seestani, have neither supported this movement nor called for armed resistance to the American invasion. The Shi'i community has become more credible in the eyes of many Americans, as it is seen as representing a more moderate school. Ayatullah Seestani's role in brokering peace between Muqtada al-Sadr and the American forces in Iraq in 2004 and his nonviolent stance have all nurtured the view of Shi'ism as being a moderate influence.

Increased government surveillance and other measures have forced Shi'is in the United States to abandon their traditional ambivalent stance toward political engagement. They have realized that it is only by participation in the American civic and political orders that Shi'is can enjoy protection against the danger that some government agencies may violate their civil liberties.

Shi'is have also come to the realization that civic engagement may be the most powerful way to fulfill their political aspirations in America. Vital issues such as civil rights, immigration, foreign policy, education, and social and economic justice can be positively affected by political lobbying. They have become aware that political power can only be enhanced by engagement between American Shi'is and the political system.

POLITICAL AWARENESS WITHIN THE AMERICAN MUSLIM COMMUNITY

Until the 1990s, the Shi'i community was either politically inactive or relied on Sunni institutions to represent it. Lack of Shi'i involvement in the American political process can be attributed to the relatively young age of the centers. Shi'is have used their limited financial resources to build and consolidate their centers rather than to engage in political activity or make financial contributions to political campaigns. Shi'i political inactivity can also be explained by the fact that until 2002, the Shi'is had not formed institutions like the Council of Islamic American Relations (CAIR) or the American Muslim Council (AMC), which could enhance the community's political aspirations.

It was in the late 1990s that Shi'is became aware that Sunni organizations had influenced how Islam in America was presented and perceived. Increased tensions between America and Iran after the Iranian revolution and between Israel and Hizbollah made the need for Shi'i self-representation in American public space more imperative. Furthermore, the enhanced Sunni-Shi'i tensions in the 1980s (due to the Wahhabi infiltration in America) made the Shi'is aware that they could not depend on Sunni institutions to represent them or speak on their behalf.

Since it is one of the largest and the oldest of the Shi'i groups, the Detroit Shi'i community has played a more active civic and political role than all other Shi'i communities across America. Increasing political activism in the Detroit community is apparent from the fact that many community members are politically engaged with Arab organizations. The Arab American Political Committee (APAC) in Detroit has lobbied for certain political issues. Although many APAC members are Shi'is, they prefer to identify themselves with an Arab rather than an Islamic political entity. In all probability this is to avoid stereotypical images associated with Islamic organizations.

As the second generation of Shi'is has come to see America as their permanent home, it has appropriated distinctly American values and outlook. Shi'is all over America have opted for voluntary social activism and identification with American culture, developing a sense of patriotism leading to a greater politicization of the community and a sense of American national consciousness. This is their way of countering marginality, Islamophobia, and social exclusion.

CONCLUSION

American Shi'ism is interwoven with different cultures. Like other religious communities, its structures and rituals are impacted by the cultural markings of its members. The community is constituted in an environment in which its members form a conglomerate of disparate ethnic groups. This confluence of Shi'is sharing common space has proved to be problematic as Shi'is face the challenge of reconstituting themselves into more Islamic and less ethnically stylized institutions.

In many ways, Shi'is are involved in a paradigm shift, from being Shi'is in America to becoming American Shi'is. This silent revolution indicates that they are transitioning from being "the other" within the "Muslim other" to becoming a more visible and vocal minority group in America.

NOTES

1. See Liyakat Takim, "Khojas," in *Encyclopedia of Indian Religions*, Springer, 2013.
2. See Liyakat Takim, "Shi'a American Muslims" in *Encyclopedia of Muslim-American History*, edited by I. Curtis, 2010.
3. http://www.patheos.com/Library/Shia-Islam/Historical-Development/Schisms-Sects.html
4. Linda Walbridge, *Without Forgetting the Imam: Lebanese Shi'ism in an American Community* (Detroit: Wayne State University Press, 1997), 18.
5. Ibid., 44.
6. Yvonne Haddad, ed., *The Muslims of America* (New York: Oxford University Press, 1991): 11. Larry Poston, *Islamic Da'wah in the West*, (New York: Oxford University Press, 1992): 27; Yvonne Haddad and Adair Lummis, *Islamic Values in the United States: A Comparative Study* (New York: Oxford University Press, 1987): 13–15. The first identifiable Muslim in America is said to have been Estevan, a black Muslim guide and interpreter who came to Florida from Spain in 1527 with the Panfilo de Narvaez expedition. Richard B. Turner, *Islam in the African-American Experience* (Indianapolis: Indiana University Press, 1997): 11.
7. Yvonne Haddad and Jane Smith, *Mission to America: Five Islamic Sectarian Communities in North America* (Gainesville: University Press of Florida, 1993): 19. This was confirmed to me in an interview that I conducted with an informant in Dearborn, Michigan in 1996. She was sixty-seven years old and her mother was born in Michigan at the turn of the century.
8. Linda Walbridge, *Without Forgetting the Imam: Lebanese Shi'ism in an American Community* (Detroit: Wayne State University Press, 1997): 18.
9. Ibid., 42. Some Lebanese migrants settled in Alberta, Canada, in the early part of this century. Coming from La-la in the Baka Valley, Ali Hamilton took up fur trade and settled in Lac La Biche, north of Edmonton. He also served as President of Lac La Biche Chamber of Commerce. See *al-Ilmu Noorun* (Edmonton, Alberta, June 1995): 4. Subsequently, other Lebanese migrants settled in Lac La Biche.
10. See Liyakat Takim, *Shi'ism in America* (New York: New York University Press, 2009): 50.

11. According to some estimates, there are approximately a million Iranians in America, most of whom are Shi'is, although a considerable number follow the Baha'i faith. See Jane Smith, *Islam in America* (New York: Columbia University Press, 1999): 53.

12. Most of these Asians are Khojas, a term that refers to an Indian caste which initially converted from Hinduism to Nizari Isma'ilism. Today, there are Isma'ili, Sunni and Twelver Shi'i Khojas living in parts of India, East Africa, and the West.

13. See Liyakat Takim, *Shi'ism in America*, chapter 2.

14. Ibid., 27.

15. Ron Kelley, "Muslim in Los Angeles," in Yvonne Haddad and Jane Smith eds., *Muslim Communities in North America* (Albany: State University of New York Press, 1994): 160.

16. Liyakat Takim and Amina Inloes, "Giving Voice to the Voiceless: Female Converts to Shi'ism in the United States and Canada," *Studies in Religion* (forthcoming in 2014).

17. The need to follow the most learned jurist was first stated by al-Sharif al-Murtada (d. 1044). See 'Ali b. al-Husayn al-Murtada, *al-Dhari'a ila Usul al-Shari'a*, 2nd ed., vol. 2 (Tehran: Daneshghah Tehran, 1983), 2:317.

18. For details, see Liyakat Takim, *Shi'ism in America*, chapter 4.

19. Linda Walbridge, *Without Forgetting the Imam*, 64.

20. For more details on these and other institutions, see Liyakat Takim, *Shi'ism in America*, chapter 5.

21. See the constitution of UMAA.

22. See also Liyakat Takim, "Preserving or Extending Boundaries? The Black Shi'is of America," *The Journal of Muslim Minority Affairs* 30, 2 (2010): 237–249.

23. Vali Nasr, *The Shia Revival: How Conflicts Within Islam Will Shape the Future* (New York: Norton, 2006): 251.

REFERENCES

Abdo, Geneive, *Mecca and Main Street: Muslim Life in America after 9/11* (New York: Oxford University Press, 2006).

Abu-Laban, Sharon McIrvin, "Family and Religion Among Muslim Immigrants and Their Descendants," in *Muslim Families in North America*, edited by E. Waugh, S. M. Abu-Laban, and R. Qureshi (Edmonton: University of Alberta Press, 1991).

Bukhari, Zahid, *Muslims' Place in the American Public Square: Hope, Fears, and Aspirations*, edited by Zahid H. Bukhari, Sulayman S. Nyang, Mumtaz Ahmad, and John L. Esposito (Walnut Creek, MD: AltaMira Press, 2004).

Current Legal Issues According to the Edicts of Ayatullah al-Sayyid 'Ali al-Seestani (London: Imam 'Ali Foundation, 1997).

Haddad, Yvonne, ed., *Muslims in the West: From Sojourners to Citizens* (New York: Oxford University Press, 2002).

——, *The Muslims of America* (New York: Oxford University Press, 1991).

——, and Jane I. Smith, eds., *Muslim Minorities in the West: Visible and Invisible* (Walnut Creek, MD: AltaMira Press, 2002).

——, and Jane Smith, eds., *Muslim Communities in North America.* (Albany: State University of New York Press, 1994).

Al-Hakim, 'Abdul Hadi, *A Code of Practice for Muslims in the West in Accordance with the Edicts of Ayatullah al-Udhma as-Sayyid Ali al-Husaini as-Seestani*, Translated by Sayyid Muhammad Rizvi (London: Imam 'Ali Foundation, 1999).

——, *Jurisprudence Made Easy: According to the Edicts of His Eminence Grand Ayatullah as-Sayyid Ali al-Hussaini as-Seestani*, Translated by Najim al-Khafaji (London: Imam Ali Foundation, 1998).

Hejazi, Sayyed Mohammed, and A. Hashim, eds. *Ahlul Bayt Assembly of America: Abstract of Proceedings Convention of 1996* (Beltsville, MD: International Graphics, 1997).

Al-Husayni, al-Sayyid Husayn. *Ahkam al-Mughtaribin* (Tehran: Markaz al-Taba'a wa'l Nashr Lil-Majma' al-'Alami li ahl al-Bayt, 1999).

Kelley, Ron, "Muslim in Los Angeles," in *Muslim Communities in North America*, edited by Yvonne Haddad and Jane Smith (Albany: State University of New York Press, 1994).

Poston, Larry, *Islamic Da'wah in the West: Muslim Missionary Activity and the Dynamics of Conversion to Islam* (New York: Oxford University Press, 1992).

Sabagh, George, and Bozorgmehr Mehdi, "Secular Immigrants: Religiosity and Ethnicity Among Iranian Muslims in Los Angeles," in *Muslim Communities in North America*, edited by Yvonne Haddad and Jane Smith (Albany: State University of New York Press, 1994).

Smith, Jane I. *Islam in America* (New York: Columbia University Press, 1991/2009).

Takim, Liyakat, "Foreign Influences on American Shi'ism," *The Muslim World*, 90 (2000): 459–477.

——, "To Vote or not to Vote: The Politicization of American Islam," in *Politics and Religion in France and the United States*, edited by John Kelsay, Alec Hargreaves, and Sumner B. Twiss (Lexington, KY: Lexington Publishers, 2007).

——, "Shi'i Institutes in North America," in *Ahlul Bayt Assembly of America: Abstract of Proceedings Convention of 1996*, edited by Sayyed M. Hejazi and A. Hashim (Beltsville, MD: International Graphics, 1997).

——, *Shi'ism in America* (New York: New York University Press, 2009).

——, with Amina Inloes, coauthor, "Giving Voice to the Voiceless: Female Converts to Shi'ism in the United States and Canada," *Studies in Religion* (forthcoming in 2014).

——, "Preserving or Extending Boundaries? The Black Shi'is of America," *The Journal of Muslim Minority Affairs* 30, 2 (2010): 237–249.

——, "Reinterpretation or Reformation: Shi'i Law in the West," *Journal of Shi'a Islamic Studies* 3, 2 (2010): 141–165.

——, "A Minority with Diversity: The Shi'i Community in America," *The Journal of Islamic Law and Culture* 10, 3 (2008): 326–341.

——, *Encyclopedia of Muslim-American History*, edited by I Curtis (Facts on File, 2010) S.v. "Shi'a American Muslims."

——, *Encyclopedia of Islam in America*, edited by Jocelyne Cesari (Westport, CT: Greenwood Press, 2007). S. v. "Shi'a Communities."

Walbridge, Linda, *Without Forgetting the Imam: Lebanese Shi'ism in an American Community* (Detroit: Wayne State University Press, 1997).

——, *The Most Learned of the Shi'a: The Institution of the Marja' Taqlid* (New York: Oxford University Press, 2001).

——, "The Shi'a Mosques and Their Congregations in Dearborn," in *Muslim Communities in North America*, edited by Yvonne Haddad and Jane Smith (Albany: State University of New York Press, 1994).

CHAPTER 7

....

SUFI MOVEMENTS
IN AMERICA

....

MARCIA HERMANSEN

INTRODUCTION: WHAT IS SUFISM?

....

Sufism, known as *tasawwuf* in Arabic, is the mystical interpretation and practice of the Islamic religion. Sufis believe that their orientation derives from the Qur'an and the experience of the Prophet Muhammad and is at the heart or center of Islam. Sufism is not a separate Islamic sect, so that there are both Sunni and Shi'i Sufis. Institutional practices and identifications, however, make it possible to discuss distinct Sufi orders or movements that display their own sociological or intellectual influences and with which individual Muslims and even some non-Muslims may identify and affiliate.

Some early Sufis trace the emergence of Sufism to the circle around the Prophet known as the People of the Bench, who espoused asceticism and were attracted to devotional practices.[1] During the early centuries of Islam, some exceptional pious individuals pursued a lifestyle that ultimately developed into a broader social, spiritual, and intellectual movement. By the tenth century (third Islamic century) Sufis were developing their own technical vocabulary and theories of pursuing a spiritual itinerary that progressed through effervescent psychological states to more permanent acquisitions of virtues, such as love of God, trust in God, and so on.

Institutionally, Sufism became organized around master-disciple relationships and initiatory incorporation of disciples (*murids*) into established Orders (*tariqa*, pl. *turuq*). Some Sufis retired to live communally in centers or lodges known as *khanqahs, zawiyas, tekkes*, or *ribats*.

As Islam expanded eastward, Sufism, being engaged with material culture and emotive and embodied ritual and expression, proved adaptable and responsive to local practices, traditions, and cultures in Central, South, and Southeast Asia as well as Africa. The diffusion and popularity of Sufism has been associated with the appeal of the use of mystical poetry in the vernacular, pilgrimages to Sufi shrines, and belief in immanent spiritual and intercessory powers, which drew popular followings in diverse local contexts.

Classical Sufism was grounded in Islamic law (*shariʿa*) but conceived of itself as an inner pursuit going beyond externals while adhering to the pillars of the faith. In many cultures Sufism became the dominant premodern practice of Islam among the general population, particularly in the realm of popular local expressions such as art, music, and poetry. In the holistic world view of traditional philosophy, the symbolic correspondences of patterns in this world to signs of a higher reality, coupled with the concept that the divine is immanent and can be accessed in the here and now, sustained an integrated set of norms that suited the Sufi outlook. At a more mundane level, the networks provided by Sufi orders—especially in urban environments and among social affinity groups such as soldiers, tribes, or youth subcultures—provided systems of patronage and support that connected individuals and provided them material and social well-being. With the onset of modernity, Muslim reformists often critiqued certain Sufi practices as excessive or were downright hostile to Sufism. Some of these criticisms—for example, of superstitious behaviors or tomb worship—had already been made by premodern figures such as Ibn Taymiyya (d. 1328), who sought to eliminate heretical innovation (*bidʿa*) from the religion. Since Sufism is not explicitly mentioned in the Qur'an or enshrined in the shariʿa but rather is based on esoteric mystical interpretations, it was liable to be categorized as non-Islamic by religious puritans and literalists. Later developments in Sufism, such as devotion to a spiritual guide (*murshid* or *pir*) and the veneration of pious Sufi "saints" (*awliya*), were deemed heretical by such purists and reformers. In particular, the Arabian Wahhabi movement of the eighteenth century opposed Sufism. Sufis were also viewed with distaste and suspicion by both Muslim modernists and Islamists who felt that credulity, passivity, and superstition had permeated Muslim societies because of Sufism and therefore made them susceptible to European domination and colonialism.

Yet Sufi fighters from such orders as the Qadiriya in West Africa and the Sanusiya in North Africa often spearheaded resistance movements to colonialism. Sufi traditions of social service to the masses engendered loyalty to a group, while popular preaching influenced the styles and projects of the founders of twentieth-century Islamist movements such as Hasan al-Banna (d. 1949) and Abu al-Aʿla Mawdudi (d. 1978). Today, debates and contestations between Sufis and anti-Sufi Muslims arise on a regular basis. In some instances Muslim extremists have targeted Sufi shrines for bomb attacks and wholesale demolition. Imagining the future of Sufism, scholars have observed its adaptations to new urban environments, embrace of technologies such as the internet and social media, and appeal to new generations increasingly oriented to personal psychological fulfillment and individualistic interpretations of religious practice and experience.[2]

THE HISTORY OF SUFISM IN
NORTH AMERICA

The earliest yet elusive traces of Sufism in North America could be certain practices among slaves of Muslim background who were forcibly brought to the New World and may have chanted Sufi litanies on prayer beads. Some scholars have sought for vestigial Sufi-inspired practices remaining among descendants of such West Africa slaves along the Georgia coast.[3]

In 1893, Mohammed Alexander Russell Webb (d. 1916), Islam's early American missionary, appeared at Chicago's Columbia Exposition, where, as part of the Parliament of the World's Religions, he extolled Islam's virtues as a rational and scientific religion. While not explicitly Sufi, Webb observed that Islam contained spiritual esoteric religious dimensions in addition to practical exoteric religious elements.[4]

More substantial Muslim immigration to the United States began after World War I and consisted of persons from South Asia or the Arab World who had been displaced by colonial policies such as land reforms, general poverty, or conflict in the aftermath of the breakup of the Ottoman Empire. It has been noted that such immigrants thought of themselves as sojourners and rarely established mosques or other permanent institutions.[5] Therefore organized Sufi activity is not documented and one can only extrapolate on the basis of the cultures from which these immigrants came that some must have been Sufis.

The first intentional transmission of Sufism to the West, including the United States, is attributed to Hazrat Inayat Khan (1882–1927), an Indian classical musician and Sufi who first arrived in New York on a performance tour in 1910 and married an American. While he primarily resided in Europe, Khan returned to the United States for a short period in the 1920s. Eventually, a group of followers successfully established his teachings as the Sufi Order of the West, which combined Khan's training in the India-based Chishti Sufi Order with motifs and practices drawn from other religions as well as metaphysical strands from theosophy, esotericism, and religious eclecticism that were popular among a privileged class of spiritual seekers during that era.

The development of Sufi institutions and movements in the United States remained limited, however, until after World War II. Perhaps the earliest Islamic Sufi institution was a Bektashi Sufi Lodge, established in 1953 by Albanian immigrants in Michigan.[6]

The countercultural movements of the 1960s and concomitant interest in eastern spirituality sparked renewed interest in Inayat Khan's teachings. His son, Vilayat Khan (1916–2004), revived the movement in the late 1960s under the original name, Sufi Order in the West, or the Message in our Time. He too married an American and lectured frequently in the United States. In 1975 Vilayat Khan established a permanent center known as the Abode of the Message in New Lebanon, New York. His organization later adopted the name Sufi Order International, perhaps reflecting the transnational currents of the time. This also signaled a rapprochement across three branches of what is sometimes termed the "Inayati" movement, consisting of the lineages of Vilayat Khan, Samuel Lewis (see below), and a third branch known as the Sufi Movement, which has been more influential in Europe, Canada, and Australia. Inayat Khan's grandson, Zia Inayat Khan (b. 1972), was invested with the succession of the Sufi Order International in 2000 and since then has been conducting teachings internationally while based at the Abode of the Message.

Several distinct types of Sufi movements could be found in late-twentieth-century America. Scholars differ on how to best categorize the differences among them. I have suggested a garden metaphor of "perennials," "hybrids," and "transplants" in an attempt to capture the distinctive approaches to Islamic identity across them.[7] Others have more bluntly and normatively designated American Sufi movements as "Islamic," quasi-Islamic, or non-Islamic.[8]

UNIVERSAL SUFISM

Some American Sufi movements, universalistic in outlook, invoked Sufism along with other aspects of Muslim tradition but did not demand that their adherents formally convert to Islam. Gisela Webb notes that these "universal" groups were the earliest to emerge as a sort of "first wave" of American Sufism.[9] Included here are the Sufi Order International, the Sufi Ruhaniat International, and the Dances of Universal Peace Movement (Samuel Lewis). Some scholars characterize these groups as "New Age." More recently (since about 2002) the Golden Sufi Center, under Llewelyn Vaughan-Lee's leadership, has been espousing Sufism primarily in this eclectic and therapeutic mode,[10] indicating that while waning in influence, universalizing Sufi movements still hold some appeal for Americans.

Among the earlier movements of this type are the Inayati forms founded by Samuel Lewis (d. 1970), a San Francisco–based student of Inayat Khan who also followed Zen and yogic paths and teachers. His "Sufism" was transmitted to a smaller circle of disciples in San Francisco during the 1960s.[11] In particular, Lewis developed practices of "spiritual" movement and "Sufi dancing" utilizing circle and round dances in group settings accompanied by the chanting of litanies drawn from various religious traditions, including the Islamic profession of faith. The disciples that Lewis passed on to Vilayat Khan infused the latter's group with new leadership and energy in the early 1970s. Other disciples of "Sufi Sam" chose to remain within a distinct group called the Sufi Islamia Ruhaniat Society. In 2002 this group changed its name to Sufi Ruhaniat International. Another legacy of Samuel Lewis is the international movement practicing the "Dances of Universal Peace," developed by Lewis out of principles of bodywork and movement combined with the chanting of sacred phrases from the world's spiritual traditions.

A second type of "universalizing" influence on North American Sufism, more gnostic and intellectual in character, was perennialism or traditionalism, as espoused by Frithjof Schuon (d. 1998), a Swiss esotericist in the lineage of Rene Guenon (d. 1951). Schuon was an independent scholar of comparative religion who late in life settled in Bloomington, Indiana. Schuon initiated and headed a branch of the Shadhili Sufi tariqa called the Maryamiyya. His followers included a number of academics and his successor as leader of the Maryamiyya is the noted Iranian-American professor Seyyed Hossein Nasr. In addition to intellectual influences from classical Sufi figures such as Ibn Arabi (d. 1240) and al-Shadhili (d. 1258), the teachings of this order recognized a shared core of authentic tradition at the heart of all major religions in a concept known as the "transcendent unity of religion."[12] The intellectual traditionalism of Nasr is continued through his students, many of whom are professors of Islam, such as Joseph Lumbard, Walid al-Ansari, and Ibrahim Kalin.[13]

Yet another type of universalistic Sufism, more prominent in Britain but having some penetration in the United States, follows the wisdom traditions of G. I. Gurdjieff (d. 1949) and claims origins in Central Asian Naqshbandism. This type was most popularly articulated beginning in the 1970s by the literary figure Idries Shah (d. 1996) and his brother Omar Ali Shah (d. 2005). They claimed to be Sufis in the Naqshbandi lineage, but in reality for them Sufism was a wisdom tradition of awakening to the Real, only incidentally associated with Islam.

A further strand of universal "wisdom" Sufism termed Malamati has links to Turkish Naqshbandism in particular, to Hasan Şuşud, and to Shah movements as well as other wisdom Sufi traditions. A current American representative of this branch, Yannis Tasoullis, holds that Gurdjieff, Bennett, Idries Shah, and their followers promoted a form of occult elitism that emphasizes a hidden hierarchy in Sufism composed of superhuman beings who operate beyond or outside normative Sufism and Islam. Perhaps we may see a return to Islamic Sufism in his claim that "the true Sufism of the Khwajagan emphasized the nothingness of human beings next to God."[14]

During the late twentieth century both public and academic discussions of Sufi movements were concerned with the negotiation of Muslim and non-Muslim or New Age affiliations on the part of those who claimed to be Sufis—could a Sufi be a non-Muslim, for example? The growing immigrant Muslim community in the United States has had relatively little interaction with non-Muslim Sufi movements, yet some contacts occurred among the various types of Sufi groups who might participate on an equal footing at conferences such as the annual meeting of the International Association of Sufism.

ISLAMIC SUFI MOVEMENTS IN AMERICA: ADAPTATION AND AUTHENTICITY

The Immigration Reform Act of 1965 opened the door to an influx of much larger numbers of immigrants from Muslim societies, which gradually began to affect the presence and character of Sufi activities in America. Beginning in the late 1970s and early 1980s "Islamic" Sufism was brought by visiting and immigrant Sufi leaders trained in the Muslim world. Prominent among such orders were the Helveti-Jerrahis led by Shaykh Mozaffer Ozak (d. 1985) from Istanbul and the Naqshbandi-Haqqanis led by Cypriot Shaykh Nazim and Shaykh Hisham Kabbani, his Lebanese son-in-law.

The core of each of these Sufi movements was Islamic, although individual members and even subbranches continued to maintain eclectic or New Age beliefs and practices. During the 1980s and 1990s, these were the most vibrant and expanding Sufi groups in the United States, along with the Philadelphia-based followers of Sinhalese Guru Bawa (d. 1984), whose followers likewise included both shari'a-oriented and mystically eclectic elements.[15]

With the turn of the twenty-first century, the growth edge of Sufism in America was driven by new demographics. The spiritual seekers of the 1960s were graying, and the number of eclectic New Age Sufis was dwindling. At the same time immigration from the Muslim world continued to increase, such that most immigrant Muslims currently in the United States have arrived since 1980. Many children of the earlier immigrant waves began to take an interest in "authentic" Islam as opposed to "movement" or political Islam. For this audience Sufi teachers who could speak in an American idiom while presenting Islamic credentials had the greatest appeal. Within the context of national Muslim organizations such as the Islamic Society of North America (ISNA), specific Sufi tariqa allegiance was downplayed in favor of Islamic spiritual cultivation stressing concepts such as *ihsan* (righteousness) or purification of the *nafs* (soul). Groups like Zaytuna, led by American convert Hamza Yusuf Hanson (b. 1958), which represent traditional Islamic knowledge as a form of authentic Muslim identity, have been able to appeal to mainstream American Muslims as well as those more Sufi-inclined who yearned for "authentic" Islamic spirituality. Unlike some of the earlier movements brought by immigrant shaykhs, this form of Islamic Sufism does not inculcate specific cultural forms of dress or behavior associated with specific Muslim cultures.

Hamza Yusuf Hanson and Nuh Ha Mim Keller (b. 1954)—each of whom has contributed translations and commentary on the Islamic classics as well as having a media presence of web and audio lecture archives—began to acquire larger followings among Sufi-inclined American Muslim youth.[16]

Shaykh Nuh Ha Mim Keller is an American Shadhili shaykh in the sublineage of the 'Alawiyya, the Hashimiyya-Darqawiyya. Keller is a direct disciple and representative of the late Syrian shaykh 'Abd al-Rahman al-Shaghouri (d. 2004).[17] After briefly studying at the University of Chicago, Keller became a long-time resident of Amman, Jordan. He visits the United States regularly, where he holds sessions for his American disciples. Many young American Muslims travel to Amman to immerse themselves in the Sufi teachings of this order, pledging to conform to strict regulations such as abjuring the consumption of coffee or reading of newspapers. Keller is an example of the first generation of American convert Sufis who studied Islamic and Arabic sources extensively and have their own followings of shari'a-oriented Muslims.

Another group of Muslim Americans, mainly youth of South Asian background, follows Shaykh Zulfiqar Ahmad, a Pakistani-based Naqshbandi, who is represented by several American deputies, such as Shaykh Husayn Sattar in Chicago.[18] Such Sufi movements are linked with larger, non-Sufi constituencies within the American Muslim community. For example, Hamza Yusuf is a popular feature of most ISNA conferences, while Shaykh Zulfiqar's followers are often networked in South Asian Deobandi circles. Punctilious observance of Islamic law is promoted by such groups, including strict gender segregation with encouragement of women to adopt full face-veiling (niqab). The "knowledge" that they impart includes mastery of the details and discourse of Islamic jurisprudence (fiqh) and classical Islamic thought, along with Sufi training.

Another Sufi lineage with a strong emphasis on Islamic practice is that of the Ba Alawiyya through Habib Ahmad Mashhur al-Haddad and other ulama from Hadramaut, Yemen. A number of figures such as Hamza Yusuf, Umar Faruq Abdullah, and Briton Timothy (Abd al-Hakim) Winter have been associated with this influence.

Thus, on the whole, Sufism in America since the millennium has become increasingly Islamic in orientation and hence less likely to impact broader American culture than previous forms. This style, in turn, is influencing the broader tenor of Islam in America through increasing penetration into Muslim youth cultures. For example, the trend in many campus Muslim Student Associations seems to be increasingly devotional rather than Islamist. Terms such as spirituality and peace, combined with an emphasis on mercy, kindness, adab (proper Islamic behavior), and service, have supplanted political and Islamic identity discourse.

It is important to note that among the early generations of South Asian Muslim immigrants, many may be involved in "post-tariqa" Sufi movements such as Barelvi, Deobandi, Minhaj al-Qur'an, or Tablighi Jamaat organizations.[19] Each of these South Asian interpretive trends and affiliations had its origin in Sufism but moved away from the initiatory and transformational practices of the Sufi orders in the late nineteenth and twentieth centuries. Still, a persistence of quasi-Sufi elements is relevant in understanding the place of Sufism in the broader context of the Muslim community in the United States. In particular, South Asian Barelvi immigrant Muslims have at times interacted with members of Sufi tariqas in the United States. Examples are the Naqshbandiyya Islamic Educational Foundation (Chicago/Arizona) and the Islamic Studies and Research Association (ISRA) of North Carolina. ISRA originated in a "think tank" established in 1987 by South Asian Muslim professionals. Since 1998 the group has gathered Sufi scholars across ethnicities and tariqas every year in North Carolina for a Milad (celebration of the Prophet's birthday) conference. Milad celebrations, stigmatized and condemned by Salafi- and Islamist-controlled mosques, are now performed in American public spaces such as banquet halls, university auditoriums, and street processions.

Another case of post-tariqa Sufi movements becoming active in the United States since 2000 are branches of the Turkish Nur Cemaat—movements inspired by Said Nursi (d. 1961) and Fethullah Gülen (b. ca. 1941). These Turkish influences have developed a stronger presence since the late 1990s, corresponding to the rise of Turkey as an economic power, the immigration of Gülen to Pennsylvania, and the increasing activities of the Hizmet (Gülen) movement in establishing schools, participating in interfaith activities, networking, and organizing public performances of the Whirling Dervishes in a number of American states.[20]

Another feature of Sufism in the United States is the continued proliferation of local or "transplanted" Sufi activities wherever there are concentrations of Sufi-inclined Muslim immigrants—for example, among South Asians in Chicago and New York and Afghans in Washington, D.C., or San Francisco. Both travel and immigration have led to small groups or individuals becoming attached to Sufi teachers and orders from the Muslim world. Some less well known Sufi teachers have settled in America, while shaykhs who remain in the Muslim world have attracted American followers who have traveled and met them abroad. Examples are the Balkan 'Alami (Halveti/Rifa'is) in Waterport, New York, established by Shaykh Asaf in 1978,[21] and affiliates of the Moroccan Qadiri Boutchichiyya Order, led by Sidi Hamza, that have emerged more recently in several American cities.

SHIʿA SUFIS

Sufism is practiced in both the Shiʿi and Sunni branches of Islam, and a number of Shiʿi orders, including the Nimatullahi and the Oveyssi-Shahmaghsoudi, have developed followings drawn from both the Iranian émigré and American communities. Saleheddin Ali Nader Angha, the son of Shah Maghsoud Angha (d. 1980), heads an organization known as the Maktab Tarighat Oveyssi (MTO), or the Shahmaghsoudi School of Islamic Sufism, which claimed over thirty centers in North America in 2013. In some cities MTO groups have constructed impressive mosques and centers. Women have had a high degree of leadership within this movement, running a number of the local centers, giving lessons, writing books, and teaching Sufi practices.

Yet another branch of this order, the Uwaysi branch of the Kubrawiyya, is led by Nahid Angha and Ali Kianfar, the daughter and son-in-law of Shah Maghsoud. They established an International Association of Sufism in the 1990s, train a relatively small number of students, and sponsor annual Sufi conferences that attract teachers and students across a broad spectrum of Sufi movements, both local and international.

The Nimatullahi Order under the direction of Dr. Jawad Nurbakhsh (d. 2005) established centers in a number of American cities in the mid- to late 1970s, attracting both Iranian émigrés and Americans. The degree of shari'a observance within this group is left to the individual's own judgment. Alireza Nurbakhsh, the son of Dr. Nurbakhsh, who lives in London, continues to visit the fifteen or so centers in the United States and Canada. Since the 1979 Revolution, the discourse of the order has increasingly emphasized Persian identity and Iran as the source of Sufism; this has been less resonant for some western adherents of the movement.[22]

AFRICAN AMERICANS AND SUFISM

Early-twentieth-century African American proto-Islamic movements such as the Ahmadiyya and the Moorish Science Temple were sympathetic to mystical and occult strands within Islam, including some Sufi influences. Thus far, Islamic Sufism has had a proportionately smaller impact among African American Muslims, although some interest has been sparked by the activities of the Tijaniyya and the Muridiyya, both Africa-based orders.

The spread of Tijani teachings in the United States was largely due to the efforts of Senegalese Shaykh Hassan Cisse (d. 2008), a grandson of Ibrahim Niasse (d. 1975), the founder of the twentieth-century Tijani revival in Africa. Cisse studied at Northwestern University in Illinois and became active in the African American community beginning in 1976. Exchanges between the United States and Africa occurred when American Tijanis affiliated with the African American Islamic Institute sent their children to the order's Qur'anic school in Medina Baye, Kaolack, Senegal. Many later returned to teach the Qur'an in America. There is a Tijani presence in New York, Illinois, Michigan, Georgia, South Carolina, Ohio, Florida, Texas, and Washington, D.C. Ahmad Tijani, a Tijani shaykh from Gambia, based in Chicago, served as spiritual adviser to Louis Farrakhan and the Nation of Islam.

The Muridiyya is the other African Sufi tariqa influential in the United States, in particular in New York City, owing to the large presence of Senegalese immigrants there. It was only in 1984–1985 that the United States became an important destination for Murid migrants, some of whom came initially to trade in African crafts. Subsequent numbers became traders and street vendors of various inexpensive goods and trinkets. Of over 10,000 Senegalese in New York, about 80 percent are Murid affiliates, and a vibrant subculture has developed.[23] From concentrations in "Little Senegal" in Harlem, Murid affiliates join in study and fellowship circles called *dahiras* and operate within a vibrant transnational economy. An Ahmadu Bamba parade, held in honor of the order's founder (d. 1927), was established as an annual celebration beginning in 1989.

Some Murid shaykhs and a few other Senegalese Sufis—including Shaykh Abdoulaye Dièye (d. 2002) and Shaykh Harun Rashid Faye, who has established a center in Moncks Corner, South Carolina—have attracted American followers beyond the African diaspora and African American communities.

SUFI RITUAL AND PRACTICE

Adaptations of Sufi rituals and institutions to the American context include a falling away of some aspects of "popular" Islamic religious practice, such as the visitation of the shrines (mazars) of departed saints (awliya); they also have a more accommodating attitude to the presence and participation of females. In a few cases traditional Sufi rituals of pilgrimage to the gravesites or shrines of departed Sufis have been transplanted to the American context as part of the first generation of leadership. Murshid Samuel Lewis (New Mexico), Guru Bawa (Pennsylvania), Shah Maghsoud (Novato, California), and Baba Rexheb (Taylor, Michigan) have been memorialized by tombs planted in American soil.

The constituencies and membership of these various American Sufi movements have varied, since they represent diverse religious and social orientations. In the 1970s and 1980s the Sufi Order in the West and the Idries Shah Movement had a broader impact on mainstream American popular culture owing to their publishing activities and outreach to other communities through transpersonal psychology, holistic health, and Sufi dancing. Members did not have to make radical lifestyle or social adjustments and have tended to be white middle- and upper-class spiritual seekers. While some thousands of individuals are claimed to have taken initiation with Pir Vilayat Khan, many more Americans had contact with Sufi teachings through attending Sufi seminars and reading publications.

We may posit two levels of involvement in Sufi movements. One is based on face-to-face sustained contacts of disciples with a teacher, which, as Mark Sedgwick notes, usually are limited to several hundred members at most.[24] The other is Sufi movements that aspire to greater outreach and prominence, promoting themselves through conferences, publications, websites, and social media. Often they have secondary layers of deputies or local center leaders who may act as representatives of the primary teacher, initiating and spiritually mentoring disciples and organizing and presiding over Sufi meetings and rituals.

In larger Sufi movements the dispersal of charisma and limiting of personal contact with teachers encourages the construction of systematic models of transformation that can be applied irrespective of the status of the local leaders. This becomes evident as such networks are maintained through print publications and internet sites rather than personal contact.

"American" Elements of Sufism

Catherine Albanese, a leading scholar of American religion, indicates a number of features that are typical of American religiosity, including what she calls a therapeutic emphasis.[25] This category of religious response is pertinent to our discussion of Sufi orders, along with individualism, a need for fast results, and gender dynamics as well as promotion and advertising.

Americans are said to be the most religious people among the western industrialized nations on the basis of their responses to survey questions about belief in God or having personal religious experiences. Religion in America is characterized as being individualistic rather than institutional and shaped by a voluntarism that privileges individual choices of loyalty and allegiance. American civic values that translate into religious attitudes are love of liberty, democratic equality, and the separation of church and state. Resonant with the spirit of liberty and voluntarism is individualism, so that religion becomes a choice, a personal therapy, something attained by "design," which may be encountered and selected on the basis of promotion, leading to its association with consumption, commodification, and advertising.

While many of these tendencies are evident in the earlier forms of universalizing Sufism, they are less obvious in more recent "Islamic authenticity" style Sufism. This is intuitive, since "Islamic" Sufism makes fewer concessions to mainstream American culture and may in fact incorporate elements of resistance to the mainstream.

In terms of the therapeutic elements, admirers and practitioners of Sufism in the West have found it compatible with elements of modern psychological theory, especially the therapeutic orientations of "third wave" or "humanistic" therapies. For example, Robert (Ragip) Frager, a shaykh in the American branch of the Turkish Helveti-Jerrahi Sufi Order, is an American transpersonal psychologist and head of a degree-granting institute of transpersonal psychology in Redwood, California. The closest approach to Sufism in western systems, according to Frager, is "[t]ranspersonal psychology [which] deals with ego-transcending consciousness of the secret soul and the secret of secret souls."[26]

Within this typically American "therapeutic" approach to religion, some have recognized a parallelism between the Sufi shaykh and the western psychotherapist. Psychologists and psychiatrists in modern western secular culture in some cases have adapted the prerogatives of traditional healers and teachers. American Sufis often choose to contribute to this therapeutic aspect personally by being or becoming therapists or, institutionally, by sponsoring conferences and forming organizations for "Sufi psychology."[27]

The psychological systems most often adopted by American Sufis are Jungian psychology (Khan, Vaughan-Lee) and various transpersonal psychologies (e.g., Ken Wilber, Robert Ornstein). All have in common the idea that human beings must find a way to be in touch with and live in harmony/union with some transcendent or transpersonal source of meaning and orientation. The more explicitly spiritual psychologies that see this transpersonal reality as divine are probably the closest parallels to mystical philosophy in various traditional forms of spirituality, including Sufism.

One American Shadhili Sufi group, led by "Sidi" Shaykh Muhammad al-Jamal of Palestine, has developed a focus on Sufi healing, taught at the University of Spiritual Healing and Sufism near Sacramento, California, under Dr. Robert Ibrahim Jaffe, the Shaykh's representative. In 1994 Shaykh Jamal made his first visit to America, and he has continued to come each year to give seminars and teachings at centers across the United States, often staying for several months. The group's website claims a presence in some eighteen American cities; the healing links include "energy work," "herbs," and "cupping."[28]

Perhaps owing to its emergence in the Bay area, the Sufi Ruhaniat International developed systems of eclectic body work, dance, channeling, and so on as part of Sufi teachings, including special spiritual walks and breathing techniques. The Sufi Order International, established in 1925 by Inayat Khan, also has a subbranch known as the Healing Order. Current activities include healing services, retreats, and distance healing utilizing spiritual energies.

Another trend in American Sufism is that of promotion and advertising. Sufi movements in the United States want to be visible to prospective recruits and therefore employ vehicles such as lectures, seminars, and conferences. Unlike more aggressive new religious movements, such as the Hare Krishnas, they do not proselytize in airports and other public spaces; rather, they hope to attract those who are already seeking by posting announcements of lectures on university bulletin boards, sending out invitations to conferences through established mailing lists, and so on.

Perennialist or "traditionalist" Sufism as presented in the writings of Frithjof Schuon, Seyyed Hossein Nasr, and Huston Smith have reached a broad cultural audience through media such as documentary films, television interviews, and academic publishing activities. The impact of these traditionalist Sufi movements has primarily been through ideas rather than through participation in organized movements or public seminars and performances.

Great interest in the poetry of Jalaluddin Rumi in translations by Coleman Barks, an American poet himself associated with the Guru Bawa Sufi group, has also contributed to the popularization of Sufism in America.[29] Television and audio presentations of Rumi's work have been promoted by celebrities such as the singer Madonna and Deepak Chopra, the guru of holistic health.

American Sufi influence on poetry and the arts includes the original English mystical poetry of Daniel Abd al-Hayy Moore and the calligraphy of traditionally trained Muhammad Zakariyya, the artist responsible for the design of the annual Ramadan Eid stamp issued by the US Postal Service.

An interest in world music in western societies has included the popularity of Sufi forms such as Indian Qawwalis, Moroccan Gnawi, and elements of Sufi chanting and dhikrs such as the turning ceremony of the Mevlevi Whirling Dervishes.[30]

AMERICAN SUFI WOMEN

Contemporary American expectations of gender interactions and female leadership have at times challenged traditional Islamic norms in some Sufi groups. Inayat Khan married Ora Ray Baker (d. 1949), an American woman, and gave other women, including the American Murshida Rabia Martin (d. 1945), the highest levels of initiation and leadership in his organization. In the case of American Sufi women in the hybrid orders, traditional practices of gender segregation and other restrictions on female participation have provoked some discomfort. This has led to a subversive quality in certain American women's reflections on Sufism, in which they challenge normative Islamic concepts and cultural expectations regarding maleness and femininity and gender-specific roles. A symbolic masculinization has been adopted by some female American Sufis, including symbols of affiliation and authority that had been traditionally unique to men, such as wearing special caps or robes.

Some female participants in western Sufi movements have worked to negotiate their understandings of gender roles so as to reflect both traditional authenticity and gender justice. Female members of western Sufi movements have taken positions about gender along a continuum ranging from subversion and activism (Rabia Terri Harris, Laleh Bakhtiar) directed to challenging and reforming traditional Muslim practices to advocating "gender complementarity" as part of the divine cosmic order (Sachiko Murata)[31] to a discourse of female compliance and docility drawing on conservative American perspectives.[32]

Women Sufi teachers are somewhat rare outside of the Inayati movements; they include Shaykha Fariha, who leads one branch of the Jerrahis in New York City, Shaykha Maryam Kabir Faye,[33] Nahid Angha, and a Pakistani shaykha, Baji Tayyibah, based in Philadelphia.[34]

CONCLUSION: THE RELATIONSHIP BETWEEN CURRENTS IN THE AMERICAN MUSLIM COMMUNITY AND AMERICAN SUFI ORDERS

On the whole, the appeal of New Age or universal Sufism has waned since the 1970s, as is the case with most of the groups that attracted the "generation of seekers." Earlier American Sufi groups that remain, such as the Sufi Order, are increasingly limited in scope, and the membership is graying. A diffuse type of "cosmopolitan" Sufism may be represented by Imam Feisal Abdul Rauf, founder of the Cordoba Foundation. Rauf has authored works on Islam[35] and served as Imam of Shaykha Fariha's "Sufi" mosque (Masjid al-Farah) in New York City.[36] Rauf was initially positioned as a moderate Muslim through his interfaith work and books such as *What's Right with Islam Is What's Right with America*, which explained the confluence of Islamic and American democratic values.[37] Rauf's plan for an Islamic community center in Lower Manhattan achieved notoriety because of Islamophobic reactions to a "Ground Zero" mosque in 2010. He and Daisy Khan, his wife, established the American Sufi Muslim Association in 1997, which later became known as the American Society for Muslim Advancement.

As an example of a hybrid order, the Naqshbandi-Haqqani were studied as a "transnational"order. Researchers came to the conclusion that this Sufi movement was not being spread because of flows of people or "migration" but rather through networks connecting local concentrations. Shaykh Hisham Kabbani failed to gain access to major Muslim organizations in the 1990s, and after declaring that 90 percent of United States mosques were controlled by extremists, was ostracized by mainstream Muslims. He became for a time a "model moderate" Muslim, promoted by Daniel Pipes and conservative talk show hosts. His order, now based in Fenton, Michigan, continues to promote itself through dynamic websites, publications, and the cultivation of links to Washington, D.C. In general, the days of the hybrid orders under shaykhs with large followings seem to be waning, since the early cohort of immigrants has been passing away since the turn of the millennium, and the charismatic style of leadership of shaykhs such as Mozaffer Ozak has not been transferred or routinized by successors.

The current growth edge in American Sufism is "Islamic authenticity Sufism," primarily attracting the children of Muslim immigrants who are in their twenties and thirties. The engagement of these groups with mainstream Islam and broader American culture and institutions varies. Traditionalist but integrated in broader Muslim and non-Muslim American outreach, discourse, and institutions are Sufis promoting education, such as the Zaytuna project of Hamza Yusuf and the now defunct Nawawi Foundation under Umar Faruq Abdullah. For example, Zaytuna is a new college established near San Francisco, oriented to the Islamic sciences, that has been welcomed by the Muslim community and the American media as an important and innovative project. Sociologically, I would characterize the groups around Hamza Yusuf and Abdullah as more world-affirming and appealing to both mature and youth audiences. They have been received positively by groups such as the Islamic Society of North America and within the American media, which generally portrays them as moderating influences.

Other forms of "authenticity Sufism," such as Nuh Keller and Shaykh Zulfiqar's movements, are more world-rejecting and isolationist, with less outreach and publicity outside the confines of the group and less need to accommodate to American institutions and their legal and public frameworks. Yet even in the case of these groups, education can become a bridge to inclusion. For example, the Qasid Center for Arabic language study in Amman, closely linked to Keller's group, has achieved acceptance and recognition as a place to study Arabic in spheres much broader than American Sufi or even Muslim networks. US government programs such as Fulbright approve grantees studying there, despite the gender segregation and conservative atmosphere.

Overall, the character of Sufism in the United States is becoming more formally "Islamic," with the greater number of younger affiliates being involved with shari'a-oriented tariqas. A "bridge" generation of Sufi converts who formulated an intellectually cogent and culturally appealing and sophisticated presentation of Sufism was instrumental in this transition.

Major Islamic organizations, in particular the Islamic Society of North America, were initially inhospitable to any form of Sufism but over time have become comfortable and even supportive of moral and psychological edification in Islamic terms that was traditionally the purview of Sufi theorists such as Abu Hamid al-Ghazali (d. 1111). The title of Sherman Jackson's recent translation of the Shadhili text *Sufism for non-Sufis* is suggestive of the role of this integrative Sufism in the Muslim mainstream.[38]

NOTES

1. Abu Bakr Al-Kalabadhi, *The Doctrine of the Sufis*, trans. A. J. Arberry (Cambridge, UK: Cambridge University Press, 1935): 5.
2. See the chapters in *Sufism and the "Modern" in Islam*, edited by Martin van Bruinessen and Julia Day Howell (London: I. B. Taurus, 2007).
3. See Sylviane A. Diouf's essay "The First Stirrings of Islam in America" in this volume.
4. Umar Faruq Abdallah, *A Muslim in Victorian America: The Life of Alexander Russell Webb* (New York: Oxford University Press, 2006).
5. Yvonne Y. Haddad, "A Century of Islam in America," in *Hamdard Islamicus* XX1 (4, 1997).
6. Cemal Bayraktari, "The First American Bektaşi tekke," *Turkish Studies Association Bulletin* 9, no. 1 (1985): 21–24.
7. Marcia Hermansen, "In the Garden of American Sufi Movements: Hybrids and Perennials," in *New Trends and Developments in the World of Islam*, edited by Peter Clarke (London: Luzac Oriental Press, 1997): 155–178.
8. Alan Godlas, "Sufism, the West, and Modernity," available at http://islam.uga.edu/ sufismwest.html (Accessed March 19, 2013.)
9. Gisela Webb, "Third-Wave Sufism in America and the Bawa Muhaiyaddeen Fellowship," in *Sufism in the West*, edited by Jamal Malik and John Hinnells (London: Routledge, 2006): 92.
10. Llewelyn Vaughan Lee's books, DVDs, and information about the golden Sufi Center may be found at http://www.goldensufi.org/book_desc_fragments.html (Accessed March 19, 2013.)
11. Mansur Johnson, *Murshid: A Personal Memoir of Life with American Sufi Samuel L. Lewis* (Seattle, WA: Peaceworks, 2006).
12. For an extensive study of the history and teachings of Schuon and his successors, see Mark Sedgwick, *Against the Modern World* (New York: Oxford University Press, 2006).
13. Nasr lists his students in *In Search of the Sacred: A Conversation with Seyyed Hossein Nasr on His Life and Thought* (Santa Barbara, CA: ABC-CLIO, 2010): 74.

14. Yannis Tousullis, *Sufism and the Way of Blame: The Hidden Sources of a Sacred Psychology* (Wheaton, IL: Quest Books, 2011).

15. The Bawa Muhaiyaddeen Fellowship has been studied more extensively and ethnographically than most American Sufi movements. For example, see Gisela Webb, "Third-Wave Sufism in America and the Bawa Muhaiyaddeen Fellowship," in *Sufism in the West*, edited by Jamal Malik and John Hinnells (London: Routledge, 2006):, 86–102, and Frank Korom, "Charisma and Community: A Brief History of the Bawa Muhaiyaddeen Fellowship," *The Sri Lankan Journal of the Humanities* 37, nos. 1–2 (2011): 19–33.

16. For more information on Keller, see Marcia Hermansen, "The 'Other' Shadhilis of the West," in *The Shadhiliyya*, edited by Eric Geoffroy (Paris: Maisonneuve et Larose, 2005): 481–499; or Keller's autobiography, *Sea without Shore: a Manual of the Sufi Path* (Beltsville, MD: Amana Publications, 2011).

17. This Sufi teacher is apparently shared by Zaytuna leader Zaid Shakir.

18. Sacred Learning, "Shaykh Husain Abdul Sattar," available at http://www.sacredlearning.org/shaykh-husain-abdul-sattar/ (Accessed March 19, 2013.)

19. I define "post-tariqa" movements as ones with a Sufi background or that espouse some aspects of Sufism but that no longer require formal ceremonies of initiation (*bay'a*) or use the names of existing Sufi tariqas.

20. Hakan Yavuz, *Toward an Islamic Enlightenment: The Gülen Movement* (New York: Oxford University Press, 2013).

21. Julianne Hazen, "Beyond Whirling and Weeping," *Polyvocia: SOAS Journal for Graduate Research* 3 (2011): 1–32, available at http://www.soas.ac.uk/research/rsa/journalofgraduateresearch/edition-3/file67221.pdf (Accessed March 19, 2013.)

22. Leonard Lewisohn, "Persian Sufism in the Contemporary West: Reflections on the Ni'matu'llahi Diaspora," in *Sufism in the West*, edited by Jamal Malik and John Hinnells (London: Routledge, 2006): 49–70.

23. Cheikh Anta Babou, "Brotherhood Solidarity, Education and Migration: The Role of the Dahiras among the Murid Muslim Community of New York," *African Affairs* 101 (2002): 151–170.

24. Mark Sedgwick, "The Reception of Sufi and neo-Sufi Literature," in *Sufis in Western Society: Global Networking and Locality*, edited by Markus Dressler, Ron Geaves, and Gritt Klinkhammer (London: Routledge, 2009): 180–197.

25. Catherine Albanese, *A Republic of Mind & Spirit: A Cultural History of American Metaphysical Religion* (New Haven, CT: Yale University Press, 2007)

26. Robert (Ragip) Frager, *Heart, Self, and Soul: The Sufi Psychology of Growth, Balance, and Harmony* (Wheaton, IL: Quest Books, 1999).

27. Marcia Hermansen, "What's American about American Sufi Movements?" in *Sufism in Europe and North America*, edited by David Westerlund (London: Routledge, 2004): 36–62.

28. Cupping (Ar. *Hijama*) is a traditional practice recommended in the hadith where blood is drawn by vacuum from a small skin incision.

29. Coleman Barks, *The Essential Rumi* (San Francisco, CA: HarperOne, 1995) and many other collections of translated poetry.

30. Carl W. Ernst, *Sufism: An Introduction to the Mystical Tradition of Islam* (Boston: Shambala, 2011): 185–198, has a broad discussion of Sufi music and aspects popular in America.

31. An overview of positions taken by American Sufi women is Marcia Hermansen, *"Neither of the East nor of the West: Sufi Women in America,"* in Portraits of Women in Islam, edited by Susan Sanders (Chicago: St. Xavier University, 2009) 37–55.

32. According to a blog post by a former member of the group, female members in Jordan were encouraged to use texts such as *Fascinating Womanhood* by Helen Andelin and *The Surrendered Wife* by Laura Doyle, available at http://iseekrefuge.wordpress.com/tag/nuh-ha-mim-keller/ (Accessed April 14, 2013.)
33. Maryam Kabeer Faye, *Journey through Ten Thousand Veils: The Alchemy of Transformation on the Sufi Path* (Somerset, NJ: Tughra Books, 2008).
34. Marcia Hermansen, "South Asian Sufism in the United States," in *South Asian Sufis: Devotion, Devotion, and Destiny*, edited by Charles Ramsey (New York: Continuum, 2012): 247–268.
35. Rauf's most Sufi-oriented book is *Islam: A Search for Meaning* (Costa Mesa, CA: Mazda Publishers, 1996), but it has no particular tariqa identification.
36. Rosemary Hicks, "Translating Culture, Transcending Difference? Cosmopolitan Consciousness and Sufi Sensibilities in New York City after 2001," *Journal of Islamic Law and Culture* 10, no. 3 (2008): 281–306.
37. Feisal Abdul Rauf, *What's Right with Islam Is What's Right with America* (San Francisco: HarperOne, 2005).
38. Sherman A. Jackson, *Sufism for non-Sufis: Ibn 'Ata' Allah al-Sakandari's Taj al-'Arus* (New York: Oxford University Press, 2012).

BIBLIOGRAPHY

Abdallah, Umar Faruq, *A Muslim in Victorian America: The Life of Alexander Russell Webb* (New York: Oxford University Press, 2006).

Albanese, Catherine, *A Republic of Mind & Spirit: A Cultural History of American Metaphysical Religion* (New Haven, CT: Yale University Press, 2007).

Babou, Cheikh Anta, "Brotherhood Solidarity, Education and Migration: The Role of the Dahiras among the Murid Muslim Community of New York." *African Affairs* 101 (2002): 151–170.

Bayraktari, Cemal, "The first American Bektaşi tekke." *Turkish Studies Association Bulletin* 9, no. 1 (1985): 21–24.

Faye, Maryam Kabeer, *Journey through Ten Thousand Veils: The Alchemy of Transformation on the Sufi Path* (Somerset, NJ: Tughra Books, 2008).

Frager, Robert (Ragip), *Heart, Self, and Soul: The Sufi Psychology of Growth, Balance, and Harmony* (Wheaton, IL: Quest Books, 1999).

Godlas, Alan, "Sufism, the West, and Modernity." Available at http://islam.uga.edu/sufismwest.html (Accessed March 19, 2013.)

Hazen, Julianne, "Beyond Whirling and Weeping." *Polyvocia: SOAS Journal for Graduate Research* 3 (2011): 1–32. Available at http://www.soas.ac.uk/research/rsa/journalofgraduateresearch/edition-3/file67221.pdf (Accessed March 19, 2013.)

Hermansen, Marcia, "In the Garden of American Sufi Movements: Hybrids and Perennials," in *New Trends and Developments in the World of Islam*, edited by Peter Clarke (London: Luzac Oriental Press, 1997): 155–178.

——, "What's American about American Sufi Movements?" In *Sufism in Europe and North America*, edited by David Westerlund (London: Routledge, 2004): 36–62.

——, "South Asian Sufism in the United States," in *South Asian Sufis: Devotion, Devotion, and Destiny*, edited by Charles Ramsey (New York: Continuum, 2012): 247–268.

Hicks, Rosemary, "Translating Culture, Transcending Difference? Cosmopolitan Consciousness and Sufi Sensibilities in New York City after 2001," *Journal of Islamic Law and Culture* 10, no. 3 (2008): 281–306.

Jackson, Sherman A., *Sufism for Non-Sufis: Ibn 'Ata' Allah al-Sakandari's Taj al-'Arus* (New York: Oxford University Press, 2012).

Johnson, Mansur, *Murshid: a personal memoir of life with American Sufi Samuel L. Lewis* (Seattle, WA: Peaceworks, 2006).

Korom, Frank, "Charisma and Community: A Brief History of the Bawa Muhaiyaddeen Fellowship," *The Sri Lankan Journal of the Humanities* 37, nos. 1–2 (2011): 19–33.

Lewisohn, Leonard, "Persian Sufism in the Contemporary West: Reflections on the Ni'matu'llahi Diaspora," in *Sufism in the West*, edited by Jamal Malik and John Hinnells (London: Routledge, 2006): 49–70.

Nasr, Seyyed Hossein, In *Search of the Sacred: A Conversation with Seyyed Hossein Nasr on His Life and Thought* (Santa Barbara, CA: ABC-CLIO, 2010).

Rauf, Feisal Abdul. *Islam: A Search for Meaning* (Costa Mesa, CA: Mazda Publishers, 1996).

——, *What's Right with Islam Is What's Right with America* (San Francisco: HarperOne), 2005.

Sacred Learning, "Shaykh Husain Abdul Sattar," available at http://www.sacredlearning.org/shaykh-husain-abdul-sattar/ (accessed March 19, 2013.)

Sedgwick, Mark, *Against the Modern World* (New York: Oxford University Press, 2006).

——, "The reception of Sufi and neo-Sufi Literature," in *Sufis in Western Society: Global Networking and Locality*, edited by Markus Dressler, Ron Geaves, and Gritt Klinkhammer (London: Routledge, 2009): 180–197.

Tousullis, Yannis, *Sufism and the Way of Blame: The Hidden Sources of a Sacred Psychology* (Wheaton, IL: Quest Books, 2011).

Vaughan-Lee, Llewelyn, Various. Available at http://www.goldensufi.org/book_desc_fragments.html (accessed March 19, 2013.)

Webb, Gisela. "Third-Wave Sufism in America and the Bawa Muhaiyaddeen Fellowship," in *Sufism in the West*, edited by Jamal Malik and John Hinnells (London: Routledge, 2006): 86–102.

Yavuz, M. Hakan. *Toward an Islamic Enlightenment: The Gülen Movement* (New York: Oxford University Press, 2013).

CHAPTER 8

MUSLIM MINORITY GROUPS IN AMERICAN ISLAM

YVONNE Y. HADDAD AND

JANE I. SMITH

FOR virtually all American Muslims issues of leadership are of key importance, as they have been throughout the history of Islam. Two of the four non-Sunni groups selected here as illustrative of Muslim minority groups in America have long histories, while two are more recently conceived and developed. All have grown according to their individual understanding of who possesses the qualities necessary for viable leadership, whether inherited or proved. They have been selected for attention not necessarily because of size or influence, but rather because they provide different examples of the many ways in which American Islam is heterogeneous, multi-textured, and often linked to international communities and cultures.

NIZARI ISMAʿILIS

Elsewhere in this volume a chapter has been devoted to a study of Twelver Shiʿites. There the complex history of Shiʿism is summarized and the reader is invited to review that history as a prelude to the current study of the Ismaʿilis, sometimes referred to as the Seveners because of their adherence to the seventh Shiʿi Imam or leader and failure to recognize the subsequent leaders accepted by the Twelvers. Ismaʿilis today comprise the second largest branch of Shiʿa Islam after the Twelvers. The two groups differ in having followed different Imams or spiritual leaders after the death of the 6th Imam in 765 CE.

The Isma'ilis developed from being an obscure sect to one of great political, eco-nomic, and cultural power and prestige. In 969 they founded the Fatimid Dynasty in Egypt. From the tenth to the twelfth centuries they were the largest branch of Shi'ism, whose empire included North Africa and the Middle East. The movement split in 1094, and those identified as Nizaris at first found their home primarily in Iran. As the presence of Isma'ilis in the Middle East declined, they became a growing pres-ence in India and Pakistan and more recently in Africa, Europe, and North America.[1] The Isma'ili population increased in the United States, as is true of many South and Southeast Asian groups, after the 1965 change in immigration policies. The largest Isma'ili presence in the United States includes both the Nizaris, on whom this article focuses, and the Tayyibi or Dawoodi Bohras.[2] Nizari Isma'ilis around the world num-ber some 15 million.

Nizaris follow the leadership and the divine authority of the Agha Khan, their living Imam descended from the Prophet Muhammad through the line of 'Ali, the Prophet's cousin and son-in-law and Fatima, his daughter. In 1957, at the age of twenty, the current and forty-ninth Imam Karim Aga Khan IV succeeded his grandfather Sir Sultan Muhammad Shah Aga Khan III. As Imam he is considered to be infallible and immune from sin, the *hujjah* or proof of God on earth, with the authority to provide guidance on all religious matters for the Nizari Isma'ili community. Karim Aga Khan is also a highly successful businessman as well as a breeder of racehorses. His current net worth places him among the richest of the world's royal figures. A significant part of his income comes from contributions of believers around the world. Minimum tithing is expected to be 12.5% of earnings. These funds are used for the pursuit of Isma'ili goals, currently identified as the elimination of poverty, improving the status of women, promoting art and architecture, helping the environment, and numerous other causes, all pursued under the auspices of the Agha Khan Development Network. Some $100 million is distributed annually on nonprofit activities over the world. "By guiding Isma'ilis how to balance the spiritual and the material in an Islamic ethi-cal context," says a report coming out of the work of the large Nizari community in Houston, "the Imam mediates for Ismailis not only the intersection of the pragmatic and the spiritual, but also local moral worlds and universal Islamic ethics."[3]

Of particular interest to the current Aga Khan is modern educational reform; he urges his followers to be well educated in order to meet the meritocratic world of the twenty-first century.[4] He is also deeply concerned with the education and equaliza-tion of women and with issues of gender. A number of the Aga Khan's main structural subbranches devote their work to improving the status of women around the world. Issues of feminism and human rights are part of the continuing discourse of Isma'ili meetings.[5] In the United States annual conferences on women's issues are held, such as the 2009 Women's Conference in Long Beach, California, helping empower women to take charge of their lives and embrace change.

The Aga Khan encourages women to wear western dress and to become active in the community. Temporary marriage (*mut'a*), allowed by many Shi'ites, is unacceptable for Nizaris, as is polygyny and child marriage. Rather than following the South Asian custom whereby the father often signs his daughter's wedding contract, Nizari women must be present and speak for their willingness for the marriage to take place. Both parties have legal representatives. Marriage is not simply a family affair, it is a contractual arrangement between a woman and a man with the woman in full consent. Unilateral divorce by the husband is forbidden, and widows are allowed to remarry.[6]

Like his grandfather, Agha Khan IV has committed himself to modernization and promotion of a better understanding of Islamic civilization. He maintains the system of communal administration his grandfather developed and has extended it to the United States and Canada.[7] The largest Isma'ili communities in the west are in London, Toronto, and Vancouver, and in numerous American cities in Texas, California, Virginia, Georgia, New York, New Mexico, Alabama, Massachusetts, Illinois, Florida, Colorado, and Washington State. In 1986 the Imam promulgated a universal document called "The Constitution of the Shia Imami Ismaili Muslims," affirming fundamental Islamic beliefs and the guidance of the Imam in both spiritual and material affairs. An elaborate system of guidance through national councils has been set forth, with ultimate authority always vested in the Imam.

In 1977 the Aga Khan Program for Islamic Architecture was established to educate architects, planners, and teachers. Based at Harvard University and the Massachusetts Institute of Technology, the program is designed to help meet the building and design needs of contemporary Muslim communities as well as to develop increased cross-cultural interest in Islamic arts and culture. The Aga Khan Award for Architecture honors significant architectural initiatives primarily in the Islamic world but also elsewhere. In 1999 the trust established a chair for the Aga Khan Professorship of Landscape Architecture and Urbanism in Islamic Studies at the Graduate School of Design at Harvard.[8]

Nizaris generally are less concerned with the rituals of Islamic worship than with inner spiritual teachings, not observing either the month of fasting or the time of pilgrimage. Voluntary congregational worship is held twice a day, before sunrise and while the sun is setting, in meetinghouses called *jamaat khanas* (which non-Muslims may not enter). As do all Muslims before prayer, they perform ablutions and greet each other before entering the worship space. Unlike the practice of most other Muslims is the singing of hymns and providing of food offerings. Prayers include recitation of several Qur'an verses and asking the blessing of God on the Prophet and 'Ali and the Prophet's family and on the current Imam of the community.[9] Eid al-Adha, one of the two major holy days of Islam, is observed by many Nizaris as an opportunity to build bridges with the communities in which they live as they exchange information about each other's beliefs and practices. Nizaris celebrate Navroz (the Persian New Year), the birthday of Aga Khan IV, and the day he gained the Imamate.[10]

Through the leadership of Aga Khan IV, American Nizari Isma'ilis have been active in social services on a number of different fronts. Service to humanity is a deeply held Nizari goal, which they see as rooted in the Islamic tradition. The basis for this kind of work is Qur'an 2:177, which says that true piety is giving of one's own substance to the needy. The Nizari I-CERV initiative has been created to address issues of the environment, including projects intended to address poverty and hunger, renovate schools, clean parks and plant trees, visit the elderly, tutor children, provide disaster relief, and many other causes. The watchword for member participation is *volunteerism*. In Atlanta they have supported a free dental clinic using volunteers to serve underadvantaged communities. In Southern California they have developed a health advocacy program for poor and marginalized South Asians. New York City hosts several Nizari-sponsored food banks and other social services.

One of the most widely publicized Nizari projects in the United States is the Chicago-based Interfaith Youth Core, a nonprofit organization that unites young people of different religions to perform community service and explore their common values. The Aga Khan has been especially concerned with the education and training of youth, considering it a crucial aspect of global community-building.[11] The Core was organized by American Isma'ili Eboo Patel, who is a member of President Obama's inaugural Advisory Council on Faith-Based Neighborhood Partnerships. Patel details his own story, and that of his community, in his 2007 autobiography *Acts of Faith*.[12] He sees himself to be solidly within the Muslim tradition in his affirmation of the importance of a theology of pluralism in promoting better interfaith understanding. He is engaged, as are many Muslims, in trying to affirm a more open Islam to counter the images of intolerance fostered by events of 9/11 and after. His 2012 *Sacred Ground. Pluralism, Prejudice, and the Promise of America*[13] addresses issues of animosity against Muslims in the United States since 9/11, arguing that forces of pluralism repeatedly defeat forces of prejudice.

Another Nizari Isma'ili noted for his reflections on the pluralistic nature of Islam is Harvard professor Ali Asani, who adumbrates his views in his 2002 "On Pluralism, Intolerance, and the Qur'an."[14] Asani affirms the pluralistic nature of Islam, giving examples of tolerance in the history of Islam, the Qur'an's insistence on both universality and plurality, and the scriptural insistence that there is no compulsion in religion. His special contribution is his move to expand the term *People of the Book* to include other religious groups such as those encountered by Muslims in the early days of the spread of Islam (including Zoroastrians, Hindus, and Buddhists). Not all Muslims would feel comfortable about stretching the concept of People of the Book in this way, he admits, but in Asani's understanding "the fact remains that these types of interpretations were made possible by the pluralistic nature of the Qur'anic worldview."[15]

THE DRUZE IN THE UNITED STATES

The Druze constitute a religious and political community of approximately a million adherents, the majority of whom now live primarily in southern Syria, in the central

Lebanese mountains, and in Israel. Today an estimated 25,000 to 30,000 people of Druze heritage live in the United States.[16] Although much of their history is shrouded in mystery, we know that they originated when a group broke away from Isma'ili Shi'ism in Egypt. One of their founders, al-Hakim bi-Amr Allah (996–1021), claimed in 1017 that he was the fulfillment of the prophecy of the coming of the messiah. Traditional Druze belief affirms al-Hakim's claim to divinity, although some of his followers in the United States explain that he believed rather that he was experiencing the phenomenon of God in man (*nasut wa-lahut*, man and divinity).

A few years after his startling declaration, al-Hakim went to the desert to meditate and was never seen again. His followers faced extreme persecution in the succeeding years, causing the faith to go underground.[17] Another of the founders, Muhammad ibn Isma'il al-Darazi, began proselytizing members of the sect in Syria, who thereby became known as the *duruz* or Druze. Many of the esoteric beliefs of the Druze are kept secret from those who are not formally initiated into the faith. Primarily for political reasons in the Middle East, it has often been dangerous to identify as a Druze, and some members of the Druze religion keep their faith in secret. Even today in the United States, it is not always easy to obtain information about the community, which has become well organized but remains extremely private. In 1043 the faith was officially closed to new converts.[18]

The Druze have always referred to themselves as *muwahhidun*, those who declare God's oneness, and the religion accordingly is called the *din al-tawhid*. (Today there is a movement toward what is called the Tawhid faith among American Druze.) The spiritual hierarchy of the community gradually formed into a division of two classes. First are the *'uqqal*, knowers, who are chosen as the most learned and pious of the Druze and are then initiated into the doctrines of the religion. Traditionally they demonstrate their status by wearing white turbans. 'Uqqal are expected to lead impeccable moral lives. The rest of the Druze are the uninitiated majority known as the *juhhal* or the "ignorant" ones. They hold the same general theology and follow the same tenets of the religion as the 'uqqal. The Druze Research and Publications Institute USA was established in New York City as a not-for-profit institute in 1998 with the goal of conducting research on Druze people and theology around the world. According to its Vision statement: "The Druze Religion is the gift of God through Hakim Bi Amr Allah... The Druze theology is the last beacon of hope for the human salvation."[19]

At the head of the 'uqqal is the Shaykh al-'Aql, who is believed to determine God's will for his people and has the ability and the authority to control and govern the affairs of the world, including those who live in North America. The primary duty of the Shaykh al-'Aql is to instruct the laity in the basics of the faith, although at a rather general level of understanding. He is, in fact, precluded from revealing the more esoteric secrets to which he is privy. The current Shaykh al-'Aql lives in Lebanon. The Shaykh's personal representatives in the United States and Canada are known as the Mashaykhat al-'Aql, who meet with the initiated of the community in gatherings known as *khalwas* and with the unitiated in gatherings called *majalis*. They are able to perform marriages in the United States but not to rule on divorces (which are handled by Druze courts in Lebanon).

As expressed by members of the Druze community today, the religion is simple, not involving rituals, and focusing on the human search for a realization of the presence of God, who is Absolute Reality. There are seven commandments in the Druze religion that are similar to the five pillars or duties of Islam. Sometimes they are understood somewhat exoterically, particularly in the West. While they appear parallel to those of normative Islam, in the Druze religion they are different in meaning and interpretation. For many American Druze, the commandments are understood as guidelines rather than requirements. "The primary focus is to maintain a strong spiritual connection with God," says one Druze member, "instead of intermittent ritualistic practices."[20] Among the commandments is speaking the truth, defending each other, renouncing anything that negates God's oneness, recognizing al-Hakim as an incarnation of God, and submitting to the will of God. There is no proselytizing into the faith, as Druze believe that their number is fixed and will always remain constant.[21]

The religion is considered distinct from the Isma'ili as well as from other Muslim belief and practice. Some question whether or not the Druze are really Muslim, a call which must be made by individuals who claim this identity for themselves. Generally the belief system is not based on the primacy of the Qur'an and the Prophet or the dictates of the shari'a. Most Druze consider themselves fully assimilated in American society and do not necessarily identify as Muslims. Some, however, do consider themselves continuous with the faith of Islam while also feeling independent of it. One Druze spokesperson put it this way: "We Druze are Islamic but not Muslim."[22] One element of Druze belief that is not acceptable to mainline Muslims is the transmigration of souls. Druze believe that repeated lifetimes give each soul time to more fully comprehend God's oneness and to achieve unity with God.[23] Given the relative religious freedom of America, Druze feel able to express a rather ambivalent attitude toward what is generally referred to as "normative" Islam. Today, especially in the United States, there is a growing concern to share the teachings of the Druze religion so as to preserve them for future generations.[24] Parents are aware of the importance of the Tawhid faith as a safeguard against complete assimilation into secular American society as well as the threat of proselytizing by members of other faiths.[25]

Like the Nizaris, Druze women are well educated and in general considered to have equal rights with men; this helps Druze women to acculturate more easily to American society. Nonetheless, Druze women in America have been challenged in finding a balance between their own traditions and those of the United States. Traditional Shi'i practices such as the triple divorce (*talaq*), mut'a marriages, and polygamy are not lawful. Also common to both communities is the practice of paying dues, something that they have always had as part of their practice. Unlike the Nizaris, however, the Druze had never, before coming West, experienced the kind of congregational worship that is common to most religious groups in the United States. Traditionally the community had not worshipped together, music was not used, and only initiated members were allowed to lead the worship. As the community has become more acclimated to the West, changes have occurred. Services are regularly held in some Druze communities, often with music and often led by people without 'uqqal member status.[26] Annual conventions of the Druze Society usually include a congregational service of devotions.

Along with groups of Christians, the Druze were the first religious communities of Lebanon to begin the mass migration that characterized the late nineteenth century.[27] The first Druze immigrant to the United States was Malhim Salloum Aboulhosn. His arrival in 1881 was followed quickly by that of others, initially single men coming alone and sometimes intermarrying with American Christian women.[28]

The Druze community in the United States began to organize in 1908 in Seattle, Washington. The aim of the new Druze organization was to help the families of the community to draw closer to each other in order to sustain their identity, faith, and culture. It was called Albakourat al-Durzeyat ("the first fruit of the Druze"). In 1947 they adopted the name American Druze Society (ADS), and in 1962 they drafted a constitution and bylaws. They incorporated in 1971 and obtained tax-exempt status. Over the years the organization grew into many chapters. The largest and most active of these organizations is in Eagle Rock, California, which established the first Druze Cultural Center in the United States. Druze see the center as a symbol of unity, pride, and determination, as it is used for a variety of social, cultural, and religious functions including weddings, birthdays, graduations, and young adult social nights.[29] Chapters are also found in states including Arizona, Massachusetts, Florida, North Carolina, Connecticut, Texas, Georgia, Illinois, Michigan, Ohio, Pennsylvania, North Carolina, Washington, and Virginia as well as in Washington, DC.

The ADS has functioned to some degree as a means of helping the uninitiated members feel a more active part of the Druze community and not secondhand citizens to the elders, who have guarded the teachings so adamantly. One means was the creation of a biannual magazine called *Our Heritage*, which had the purpose of educating members of the community about the tradition and what it means to be Druze, especially in America. Teachings that heretofore had been hidden were now made accessible. Articles deal with the history of the community, their distinctive religious beliefs, Druze founders and heroes, and other subjects contributing to a sense of ethos and identity. Scholarly publications about the Druze began to appear, and newsletters with articles about Druze communities in different parts of the United States began to be published at various times throughout the year. Acculturation and education of second- and third-generation Druze immigrants has made it difficult to maintain the tight-knit, secretive structure that has historically characterized the Druze. Oral transmission in many cases has given way to written and standardized texts, which have then led to attempts to eliminate the category of juhhal, since no one can anymore claim to be "ignorant."[30]

A number of specific issues face the Druze community in America. Among them is the concern to determine whether to continue its policy of keeping much of their beliefs and practices secretive, and if so, in what form. Some members favor a much more open policy, while others fear that revealing its long-held secrets will lead to a weakening and final dissolution of the community. Another issue is that of acculturation itself. While wanting to establish themselves firmly as a part of American culture, Druze still understand the necessity of maintaining a relationship with the central authority in Lebanon. Essential in the eyes of some but not all American Druze is maintaining facility in the Arabic language. Feeling their identity with Lebanon and the Arab Middle East, some have stood against the Zionist lobby and have tried to influence American policy in the region. Social welfare organizations have been established in support of Druze communities abroad. Insofar as the Druze have not constituted a visible independent religious community until quite recently, Druze have no houses of worship, such as majalis or khalwat. The first Druze majlis was built in 1993 as part of the ADS in California.

In the 1970s books about the Druze began to appear in the United States, and the demand for information, especially on the part of the youth, has grown. Religious curricula tailored specifically to American Druze youth are now being produced by the ADS. Following the strong commitment of the Druze community to whatever nation they inhabit, Druze youth today increasingly try to participate in the public and political life of the United States. Most youth are college graduates and are known to be high achievers. Lebanese custom still prevails in many Druze families, and the great majority still expects their children to marry within the faith. The ADS has become very active in helping to develop means for young men and women to meet and socialize. Youth are playing important roles in fostering the community's commitment to interfaith engagement.

THE AHMADIYYA

The Ahmadi community in the United States is a branch of an international organization. Ahmadis, who may number some 10 million in all, are found primarily in Pakistan and the subcontinent but also in Indonesia, and East and West Africa as well as in lesser numbers in many of the countries of the Middle East. They are best known for their educational and missionizing efforts, especially for leadership in translating and making available the Qur'an in a great variety of languages. The worldwide Ahmadi Muslim community continues to grow, both through *bai'ats* ("conversions") and by immigration. While the community has experienced gradual growth in the United States, the largest increases are in West Africa and the Indian subcontinent. The United States currently has a population of about 15,000 Ahmadis.

Mirza Ghulam Ahmad, founder of the Ahmadiyya movement, was born in 1835 in Qadian, a village in the Punjab (hence the name Qadiani was given to the movement). Ahmad, who from an early age displayed a propensity for religious study, maintained in 1876 that he received revelations from God. These revelations continued throughout his life, increasing in frequency and duration. His study went beyond Islam to the major faiths of the world, after which he concluded that indeed Islam was the most worthy and true of them all. However, he felt that the faith was full of superstition and ignorance and deeply in need of reform and revival. Thus Ahmad saw his own role to be that of the renewer of the faith, expected in Islamic tradition to appear once in each century.[31]

This path led Ahmad to claim in 1889 that he was the long-expected Mahdi of Islam, as predicted by the Prophet Muhammad. Followers have taken pains to explain that he did not consider himself to be one of the prophets, the long line of whom ended with Muhammad, the "seal of the prophets." Mirza Ghulam saw his role as subordinate to the Prophet Muhammad but nonetheless the fulfillment of the second coming of the Messiah (see Qur'an 61:6). The Ahmadiyya Muslim Community United States website says: "We are Muslims who believe in the Messiah, Mirza Ghulam Ahmad Qadiani." In 1896 Ahmad gave a speech at a conference of religions in Lahore entitled "A Grand Piece of News for Seekers after Truth." The news was that God had illumined his heart, and that he was devoting himself to the transformation of the world and to exposing the untruth of false religions. He wrote over eighty books, one of the most cherished by his followers being the four-volume *Truths of the Ahmadiyya*.

Three distinct beliefs characterize Ahmadi theology. Along with their conviction that the figurative readvent of Jesus, Son of Mary, has already taken place in the person of Mirza Ghulam Ahmad, the Promised Messiah, Qadianis also believe that Jesus did not ascend into heaven but died a natural death (Sunnis affirm his ascension). The affirmation that Prophet Muhammad was the seal of the Prophets means that he was the authenticator and not just last in a line.[32] They also, like the Qur'anists described below, believe that too much emphasis has been put on the traditions of the Prophet as authoritative rather than relying on the Qur'an alone.

Mirza Ghulam Ahmad's intent was to rid Islam of the corruptions, harmful beliefs, and and wrongful practices that he believed prevailed at his time. When he died in 1908, leadership began to pass through others known as khalifas ("caliphs") in succession. Each khalifa holds his position for life. At one point the group split over ideology into the "Lahore Jamaat" and the "Qadiani Jamaat." Both groups now have representation in the United States, although it is the latter who, since the 1920s, have been more actively engaged in the propagation of the faith. Ahmadis consider themselves to be not only Muslims but to be the truest representatives of Islam. After years of persecution by the Sunni Muslim community in India, in 1901, under the second Khalifa, the Qadianis separated themselves from Sunni Islam. In 1920 they sent their first missionary, Mufti Muhammad Sadiq, to preach to the people of the United States.

"The Ahmadiyya was unquestionably one of the most significant movements in the history of Islam in the United States in the twentieth century," writes historian Richard Brent Turner, "providing as it did the *first multi-racial* model for American Islam."[33] While both blacks and whites in America heard the message of Islam through the Ahmadis and many converted, the movement was particularly attractive to African Americans. Ahmadis established mosques and reading rooms, translated the Qur'an into English, and countered what they saw as the distortions of Islam by the media. They also served as a kind of link, or bridge, between immigrant Muslims from very diverse countries of origin and the black American community, whose knowledge of Islam in the early part of the twentieth century rarely went beyond the very heterodox teachings of groups such as the Moorish Science Temple.

Mufti Muhammad Sadiq was a learned and well-respected representative of his faith, a philologist and expert in Arabic and Hebrew.[34] He also had a deep spiritual commitment, and came to his task with ardor. He began preaching in New York, but soon moved the headquarters of the Ahmadiyya mission to Chicago (he later went to Detroit but was forced back to Chicago when some Sunni Muslims accused him of preaching an unorthodox form of Islam). From the beginning Sadiq was committed to bringing together people of all races and ethnic groups under the banner of Islam. One of the major accomplishments of the newly established Ahmadi community was the publication of the quarterly journal *The Moslem Sunrise*, the first English-language Muslim newspaper in the United States.[35] The title (and the picture on each cover) symbolized the rise of Islam in the West. It also accords with a Muslim tradition saying that in the last days the sun will rise in the west, along with the coming of the Messiah. Ahmadis interpret this as a symbol for the conversion of westerners to Islam and particularly to the Ahmadiyya movement.[36] The fact that many of Ghulam Ahmad's revelations apparently came to him in English was taken as supporting the task of missionizing the English-speaking world. Because authentic knowledge about Islam was not easily available at this time, the Ahmadis were successful in winning a considerable number of converts.[37]

Sadiq became increasingly aware of the racism of mainstream Christianity and of the United States, having expected to find America a land of freedom and equality. His preaching began to take on the tone of harsh critique of American racism. He preached, of course, that Islam was the solution to the problem of American racism.[38] He thus began to concentrate his conversion efforts on African Americans, who formed the majority of those interested in becoming Ahmadis. Many of the converts were the black residents of Chicago and Detroit, with activity also in St. Louis and Gary, Indiana. After converting, several African Americans themselves became missionaries for the movement. Adoption of new Islamic style dress and Arabic names enhanced the conversion experience—veils, long dresses, robes, turbans, and skull-caps became common.[39]

Sadiq was succeeded by a series of missionaries sent to the United States, one of the most popular of whom was Mutiur Rahman Bengalee. He too preached Islam as the solution to many of the problems of the West, including both racism and religious prejudice. "The contribution of Islam in this respect is unparalleled," he said. "I claim... the superiority of Islam."[40] The arrival of the Ahmadis in the United States coincided with the height of the search by African Americans for a new identity in the American context. The Ahmadiyya movement became directly related to the followers of Marcus Garvey and the Universal Negro Improvement Association. The Ahmadis preached the basic doctrines of Islam, especially emphasizing the oneness of God, yet they were different from the Sunni Muslims in their inclusiveness and essentially heterodox approach to Islam. They preached against the racism of the United States yet were different from the black nationalist movements in their multiracial mix. Ahmadis advocated racial equality, pan-Islamism, and Indian nationalism. They succeeded in providing what Richard Brent Turner calls "the first model of multi-racial community experience for African-American Muslims."[41]

By 1940 major structural changes occurred in the Ahmadi community in the United States, which then had some 5,000 to 10,000 members. The community was divided into "circles," located in four major cities, with annual conventions held for members to discuss mutual concerns. By 1948 national secretaries were appointed to supervise matters of education, social outreach, and propagation of the faith. The community was also divided into five associations according to the age and gender of the members, each association having a particular contribution to the overall community. In 1950 the headquarters were moved to Washington D.C, where meetings were held in the American Fazl Mosque. Ahmadi headquarters are now located in Silver Spring, Maryland.

The Ahmadis were unquestionably the most influential group in African American Islam until the rise of the Nation of Islam. In the black community they particularly appealed to jazz musicians, who used the vehicle of music to propagate the Ahmadi faith. Some of the earnings from jazz concerts were used to bring Ahmadi teachers from Pakistan. Ahmadi Islam seems to have served as a very positive force for African Americans in the middle decades of the twentieth century, helping them to abstain from debilitating habits such as drugs and alcohol. Musical achievement for many partnered with efforts to be more spiritual as well as more physically healthy. In Dayton, Ohio, an Ahmadi mosque was built in 1955, the first mosque erected in the United States by black converts to Islam. By the later 1950s, however, it was clear that the Ahmadis were unable to attain their original goal of helping create a real multiracial society. Even their efforts to attract African Americans waned in the face of the rising popularity of the Nation of Islam, and some felt that as blacks they would never be allowed to reach the upper ranks of leadership in the Ahmadiyya movement. This split in the community was augmented in the 1960s with the change in immigration laws and the sharp influx of Asians, including Pakistani Muslims, into America. Trying to maintain a middle ground between black nationalist politics on the one hand and Pakistani politics on the other, the Ahmadiyya continued to model the possibility of a multiracial community in the United States, but they lost much of the strength of their hold on African Americans. Ahmadi African American mosques are usually found in the inner city, although immigrants prefer to live in the suburbs and prefer to have their mosques closer to home.

Today most Ahmadi religious leaders receive their initial training at the Ahmadi headquarters in Pakistan. They train to be teachers and missionaries, looking always at ways to promote service as a major goal of the community. From their inception, proselytizing has been a majority activity of the Ahmadis. They have done it through preaching, through the dissemination of printed materials, through the *Moslem Sunrise* as well as by various other means. Increasingly they are being drawn into interfaith dialogue and encounter and are serious about trying to promote peaceful relations among the different religions both in America and overseas. Such encounters, however, are still used to propagate their version of Islam, to counter Islamophobia, and often to voice their political opinions relating both to American affairs and those in the Middle East and South Asia. The Ahmadiyya Muslim Community United States webpage states: "Our members actively counter the voice of extremism in Islam and advocate interfaith dialogue and non-violence."

One of the major goals of the community is education for both youth and adults. Sunday schools and summer schools provide instruction in the elementals of the faith. Curricula usually include Qur'an studies, hadith, elementary law, history of Islam, a study of Mirza Ghulam's writings, history of the Ahmadiyya, comparative and religious studies, and sometimes instruction in Arabic and/or Urdu language. Increasingly electronic education is being used for instructional purposes. Education for women is considered very important, and women have always played an important role in the American mission. Special organizations have been set up for both younger and older female members of the Ahmadi community, and they have their own journals such as *Ayesha, Lajna News* and *Nasraat News*. Women have often played important roles in reaching out to non-Muslims and introducing them to the faith. They also observe the Ahmadi emphasis on modesty and chastity. The rules of purdah involve both dressing modestly (including wearing a head scarf, face veil or *niqab*, and long dress) and being subject to gender segregation. Some women find wearing the veil to be liberating while others struggle with it.

Young Ahmadis are strongly encouraged to be chaste, moral, and modest by abstaining from drink, mind-altering substances, gambling, or dating. Instead they are expected to spend time with their families, play sports, volunteer for assistance in worthy causes, and the like. Girls may join age-related auxiliaries designed to provide help to the community, those from ages seven to fifteen becoming "female helpers of the community" and those from fifteen to twenty-five becoming members of the Association of Maidservants of Allah. Younger boys join the Association of Ahmadi Boys and young men become part of the *Majlis Khuddam-ul-Ahmadiyya*, or Servants of the Community. Through these organizations young Ahmadis have an opportunity to share common concerns and issues with peers as well as to strengthen their bonds to the larger community of Ahmadiyya.

For many years the Ahmadi community in the United States has been dedicated to interfaith relations and fostering religious harmony among communities of faith. Ahmadis are active in outreach efforts, serving the needs of the wider population; they hold regular blood drives at their mosques, run soup kitchens, adopt highways, serve as chaplains for jail ministries, and donate food and clothing in times of need. In 2011 they launched Humanity First International's United States chapter, dedicated to disaster relief and charitable development. Ahmadis have participated in more than twenty disaster relief activities through Humanity First, including Hurricane Sandy. Much of the social services that Ahmadi Muslims offer is done in collaboration with churches and synagogues.[42]

In general Ahmadis adhere in both letter and spirit to the Five Pillars of Islam and hold to the six generally understood articles of faith.[43] They follow the injunction to pray five times a day and are expected to read daily from the Qur'an. The Ahmadi community has mosques throughout the United States, with new ones being constructed in many of the major cities. They gather on Fridays for prayers and hold general meetings at other weekend times. Currently they have seventy-one chapters in thirty states.

The Ahmadi community today is subject to critique from a number of directions. One, as we have seen, can arise from tension between African Americans and immigrants. Relations are complicated by class, cultural, and racial differences as well as from disappointment on the part of some African Americans that the Ahmadis have not been successful in combating American racism and, now, American prejudice against Muslims. There are differences between immigrant Pakistanis and African Americans. The former tend to be more conservative and most comfortable within their prescribed family roles, while the latter often assume leadership more easily and are active in the governance of the mosques. However, with the increased immigration of Pakistani Muslims, African American men and women are less prominent in the movement than used to be the case.[44] Another contentious issue can arise if non-Ahmadi Pakistani immigrants strongly object to the Ahmadi representation of Islam and the association in the United States of the Ahmadi interpretation with Pakistan. Pakistanis who cannot practice their Ahmadi faith in Pakistan can do so publicly in the United States but may run into conflict with other Pakistani immigrants who are not Ahmadi.

Although Ahmadis consider themselves largely indistinguishable from the Sunni Muslim body, Sunnis are highly critical of Ahmadi doctrines to the point where in 1974 they were officially declared by Zulfiqar Ali Bhutto in Pakistan to be "non-Muslims." In 1989 Benazir Bhutto, then prime minister of Pakistan, stated that her government would grant no concessions to the Qadianis, who were considered to be "non-Muslims." Nawaz Sharif, chief minister of the Punjab, said that the Qadianis are declared infidels in the constitution of Pakistan and forbidden to hold conferences anywhere in that country.[45] In the May 2013 presidential elections in Pakistan, Ahmadis were allowed to vote only if they registered as non-Muslims! Sunni Muslim leaders in the Arab world have been in agreement with the exclusion of Ahmadis from the Ummah or community of Muslims. Even in the United States, the Council of Masaajid of North America has warned Muslims about the teachings and heterodoxy of the Ahmadiyya, which Ahmadi leaders have interpreted as repression of basic human rights and freedom of expression.[46]

THE QUR'ANISTS

Who are the Qur'anists and what do they share in terms of a specific understanding of Islam? It is inappropriate to refer to them as any kind of sectarian movement, as they specifically deny being either a sect or a movement. To talk about the Qur'anists is to describe not an identifiable group—as has been the case with the Isma'ilis, the Druze, and the Ahmadiyya—but adherents of an interpretation, a way of understanding the Qur'an and therefore Islam itself. Qur'anism is a contemporary response with deep roots in interpretations long established in Islamic history. Qur'anists may also be referred to simply as Reformists or Progressive Muslims as well as Quraniyoon (those who ascribe to the Qur'an alone). It is clear from the Qur'anist website, entitled Ahl AlQuran. International Qur'anic Center,[47] that progressive Muslims do not share the beliefs of Islamic sectarians, by which they mean Sunnis, Shi'is, Isma'ilis, Ahl-i-Hadith, and Salafis.

One "school" of the Qur'anists is a direct descendant of a contemporary American Muslim movement called United Submitters International (USI).[48] USI's leader, an Egyptian named Rashad Khalifa, was assassinated on January 31, 1990, in the Tucson, Arizona, mosque where he served as imam. The apparent reasons for Khalifa's murder, although nothing was ever specifically clarified, had to do not with the interpretations that he shared with today's Qur'anists but with particular doctrines that many have considered beyond the pale of true Islam. Those claims had to do with exegesis of the Qur'an, with eschatology, and with his own understanding of himself as God's messenger. What he did share with the Qur'anists was his denunciation of those Muslims who follow the hadith and the sunna and consider them equally authoritative with the Qur'an.

Khalifa was a scientist with a doctorate in biochemistry. He brought his scientific background to the analysis of the Qur'an. His doctrine of the "miraculousness" of the Qur'an was based on his conviction that the number nineteen was the organizing principle of the entire scripture.[49] So orderly is its structure, with nineteen appearing in a variety of ways, that only God and not any human being could have constructed it. And it is only in this modern age, with the help of the computer, he argued, that we could penetrate into this amazing complexity. Khalifa began to be known worldwide with the publication of his first book entitled *Miracle of the Qur'an: Significance of the Mysterious Alphabets*,[50] and was even better known for his 1981 *The Computer*

Speaks: God's Message to the World. With the help of science, he says, we have indisputable proof for the existence of God, God's message to humankind, and (spectacularly) evidence of the exact year when the world will end.

While Khalifa's claims about the use of nineteen as a tool of scriptural analysis, his predictions concerning the end of world, and his understanding of himself as "the promised one, the expected Savior, the long-awaited Benefactor"[51] may have contributed to the motives of his slayer, they do not carry over as part of the theological approach of those who today call themselves Qur'anists. It was Khalifa's conviction of the divine nature of the Qur'an, and its message to humanity, compelling him to believe that only the Qur'an should be the source of faith and action, that provides the theological heritage of these interpreters.

In Khalifa's 1982 book *Qur'an, Hadith, and Islam*,[52] he presents his attack on the sunna and hadith (i.e., the cherished sayings and deeds of the Prophet Muhammad). Hadith and sunna, he said, are equal to 100 percent conjecture. He wrote articles with such titles as "You Shall Not Idolize Muhammad," and "Muhammad Does Not Know the Future." He said that the belief that Muhammad will serve as an intercessor with God at the last day, a cherished hope of many Muslims, is nothing but myth. Or even worse, it amounts to deification of Muhammad, the worst sin in the litany of Muslim theological errors. Muslims who look to the sunnah and the hadith for truth, therefore, are nothing but disbelievers (*kafirs*). Perhaps the most shocking of Khalifa's denunciation of those who revere the hadith and sunna is identifying them as partisans of Satan, insofar as Satan is the inventor of these misleading sources of information and thereby his "trap" for human beings. The only mission of the Prophet was "to deliver the Qur'an, the whole Qur'an, and nothing but Qur'an,"[53] he said, and to adopt the inventions of hadith and sunnah are to be in complete defiance of God and the Prophet. Therefore much of the structure of religious and family law, shari'a, based on the hadith, should not be binding on Muslims. The implications for contemporary reform of Islam no doubt contributed not only to Khalifa's appeal but to his ultimate condemnation.

United Submitters International (or sometimes just called Submitters) is now seen as a branch of the Qur'anists. It is described on its website as a moderate reformist religious community. Khalifa's claim to be a messenger of God is considered by most Muslims to be heretical, but his emphasis on submission to God and recognition that "Islam as the world knows it today has been corrupted beyond recognition by adherence to hadith and sunnah"[54] is the shared baseline for Qur'anist interpretation. Like many reform movements in the history of Islam, Qur'anists consider themselves to be just Muslims, thereby refuting any kind of group identity or sectarianism. Many reject organized religion as a whole, specifically the Islam that places so much emphasis on the traditions of the Prophet and the injunctions and expectations derived from them. The movement is thus implicitly condemning schools of thought such as Wahhabism or Salafism, which enjoy such popularity today.

Qur'anism is a universal movement, with some of its most articulate exponents now living in the West. One of the recognized Qur'anist leaders is Ahmed Subhy Mansour, an Egyptian-born activist who presents himself as a scholar of Islamic history, culture, theology, and politics. When the Qur'anist trend appeared in Egypt, it was met with positive responses from a number of Egyptian and Muslim intellectuals because of its rejection of fanatic and extremist Islam. Mansour argued that both Sunnism and Shi'ism are sects that have deviated from the original form of Islam, primarily because of their reliance on hadith as authoritative for doctrine and practice. Mansour now lives as a political refugee in the United States, after having been discharged from teaching at al-Azhar University (1985), arrested (1988), and serving time in prison for his liberal social, political, and religious views, including his advocacy of religious harmony and tolerance among Egyptian Muslims, Christians, and Jews. He was granted political asylum in the United States in 2002.

Today Mansour continues to be a leading spokesperson for Qur'anist understanding. He has absorbed Khalifa's followers who read his website and support his views on Qur'an and tradition. He and his sons now live in exile in northern Virginia. Their primary mode of communication is an internet site run in both Arabic and English. Mansour is the founder of the International Qur'anic Center (IQC), which is dedicated to supporting his understanding of moderate Islam. His teachings have put him in the same kind of danger that Khalifa faced. Considered by many to be an apostate, he has faced dozens of death threats, put in the form of *fatwas* or legal rulings, from other Muslim clerics.[55] The website for the IQC makes clear Mansour's understanding that there are two kinds of Islam: The first, and clearly the one he advocates, understands the Qur'an according to its own terminology and language. The second version, and that to which the Qur'anists are so opposed, uses methodology based on many sources other than the Qur'an, including traditions of the Prophet, narrated causes of revelation, and interpretations of ancient jurists and exegetes.

Qur'anists differ from other Islamic reformers in their method of addressing questions of religion. Not tied to reliance on the hadith but looking only to the Qur'an means that they can be more flexible in their interpretations.[56] One of the primary watchwords for Qur'anists is *tolerance*. They advocate openness and tolerance, and above all not condemning others as unbelievers (*kafirs*) as they suggest characterizes many who hold to the use of traditions and other non-Qur'anic sources. It is always more important to honor true knowledge than one's own opinion and to study one's own religion in depth before undertaking the study of another. "It is those who do not know their own religion, much less that of others, who condemn the religion of others," says the IQC website. Ultimately it is God, not human beings, who will be the judge. Qur'anist Muslims thus celebrate diversity as part of God's creation, based in Qur'an 5:48, which recognizes the long heritage of different prophets and messengers. The idea of tolerance is also extended to an understanding of women, who must be granted the same degree of dignity as men. Qur'anists strongly critique those who honor certain Islamic traditions establishing male superiority. Such interpretations, they say, are based on the cultural needs of patriarchal societies rather than on the word of God. No believer can be superior to another, male or female.

In practice as well as in doctrine, Qur'anism differs from majority Sunni belief. Some pray five times a day, some three, and some only two on the understanding that the Qur'an specifically mentions only two prayers. Not all Qur'anists think that attending Friday prayer is obligatory. They also do not accept the classical division of the Qur'an into verses revealed to the Prophet in Mecca and others revealed in Medina. As has been indicated, they consider the traditions of the Prophet (*ahadith*) to be unreliable as sources of religious direction. They also differ with many traditional Sunnis in that they consider music in general to be permissible, going so far as to say that the very act of prohibition of music is in itself not permissible (*haram*).

Another of the important leaders of American Qur'anism is Edip Yuksel, who immigrated from Turkey to the United States in 1989, where he became a prominent member of Rashad Khalifa's United Submitters International. A traditional Sunni by background, Yuksel has come to believe that the Qur'an is the only legitimate source of religious guidance in Islam. Among his teachings is what is called "theistic evolution," an alternative to the traditional Islamic belief in creationism. Like Rashad Khalifa and Subhy Mansour, Yuksel has received many death threats; even his traditionalist father has declared his son an apostate. Yuksel maintains two websites to sponsor his ideas and is the author of many books on the Qur'an and Islam. With colleagues Layth Saleh al-Shaiban and Martha Schulte-Nafeh, in 2007 he published *Qur'an: A Reformist Translation.*[57] This version of the Qur'an provides accompanying narrative that shows that the holy book is a continuation of God's revelation through Abraham and other prophets. It is intended to contain a message of peace and justice and to inspire conversation among both Muslims and non-Muslims.

Qur'anism in one way repeats and restates many of the basic elements of Islamic reform through the ages. In another way it is modern, innovative, and designed to promote a tolerant and inclusive version of Islam. "Postmodern Qur'anism, which is my term for Qur'anism in an internet age," says Farouk Peru, "has unlimited potential to change the face of Islam for better as well as to offer humanity solutions to its current problems."[58] There is little question that it is also disliked and scorned by many traditional Muslims. It remains to be seen whether its advocates face the threat of physical danger as has been the case for reformers in many religious traditions throughout the ages.

NOTES

1. Farhad Daftary, *A Short History of the Ismailis: Traditions of a Muslim Community* (Princeton, NJ: Markus Weiner, 1998): chapter 1.
2. Bohras currently have 39 centers in the United States.
3. "Embodying Ethics, Performing Pluralism: Volunteerism Among Ismailis in Houston, TX" (2003). Online.

4. Ibid, p. 503.
5. Jonah Steinberg, *Isma'ili Modern: Globalization and Identity in a Muslim Community* (Chapel Hill: University of North Carolina Press, 2011): 68–69.
6. Karen Isaksen Leonard, *Muslim in the United States. The State of Research.* New York: Russell Sage Foundation, 2003): 38, 68.
7. Farhad Daftary, *The Isma'ilis, Their History and Doctrines.* (Cambridge, UK: Cambridge University Press): 497.
8. See Aga Khan Trust for Culture webpage online.
9. Edward E. Curtis IV, *Muslim in America. A Short History.* (New York: Oxford University Press, 2009): 110–11.
10. Karen Isaksen Leonard, op. cit., p. 85.
11. Ibid, p. 159.
12. Patel, *Acts of Faith. The Story of an American Muslim* (Boston: Beacon, 2007).
13. Boston: Beacon Press, 2012.
14. *The American Scholar* 7/1 (2002): 52–60.
15. Asani, "On Pluralism, Intolerance and the Qur'an," *The American Scholar* 7, 1 (2002): 57.
16. Personal communication by the authors with Dima Suki, member of the Board of Trustees of the American Druze Society (of America), April 2013.
17. Rebecca Erickson, "The Druze." *Encyclopedia of New Religious Movements* (New York: Routledge, 2000): 1–2.
18. Ibid., p. 2
19. "A Word About Our Vision." Druze Research and Publications Institute USA. Online.
20. Dima Suki, personal communication.
21. "Druze." Countries and Their Cultures. Online, p. 3.
22. Abdallah E. Najjar (prominent Druze leader), interview with the authors, June 23, 1990.
23. Ibid., p. 3
24. For a fuller treatment of the Druze in America, see Yvonne Y. Haddad and Jane I. Smith, *Mission to America. Five Islamic Communities in North America.* (Gainesville: University Press of Florida, 2003): 34–48.
25. Dima Suki, personal communication.
26. Ibid., p. 108.
27. Fuad I. Khuri, *Being a Druze* (London: Druze Heritage Foundation, 2004): 86.
28. Leonard, *Muslims*, p. 39.
29. "American Druze Society Southern California Chapter." Online.
30. Haddad and Smith, *Mission to America*, 35–38, 47.
31. See Yvonne Y. Haddad and Jane I. Smith, *Mission to America. Five Islamic Sectarian Communities in North America* (Gainesville: University Press of Florida, 1993): 51–54.
32. Personal conversation with al-Ballegh Naseem Mahdi, Ahmadi missionary in Washington, DC, April 10, 2013.
33. Richard Brent Turner, *Islam in the African-American Experience.* (Bloomington: Indiana University Press): 109–110.
34. Ibid., p. 118.
35. Leonard, p. 7.
36. Muhammad Zafrulla Khan, *Ahmadiyyat. The Renaissance of Islam* (London: Tabshir Publications, 1978): 75.
37. Zafar Ishaq Ansari, "Islam among African Americans: An Overview." In *Muslims' Place in the American Public Square*, Z. Bukhari et al., eds. (Walnut Creek, CA: Altamira, 2004): 232.

38. See Charles S. Braden, "Islam in America," in *International Review of Missions* 48 (1959): 313.
39. Turner, 126.
40. M. R. Bengalee, "Religious Prejudice—Can It Be Overcome? *Muslim Sunrise* 56/3 (1990): 18, 21.
41. Turner, 130.
42. Zafar Ansari interview.
43. The five commonly accepted articles of faith are faith in God, the reality of angels, God's messengers, the Holy Books, and the Day of Resurrection. The sixth, accepted by some groups besides the Ahmadis, is faith in God's *qadr* or the divine will.
44. Leonard, 40.
45. "Politicians Radicalize Pakistan," presented by the Department of Public Affairs of the Ahmadiyya Muslim Community USA. Online.
46. Mubasher Ahmad, 1991, personal communication with the authors.
47. http://www.ahl-alquran.com/
48. See Haddad and Smith, pp. 137–168.
49. See his 1981 volume *The Computer Speaks: God's Message to the World.* (Tucson AZ: Renaissance Productions).
50. St. Louis, Islamic Productions International, 1982.
51. Haddad and Smith, p. 151.
52. Tucson AZ: Islamic Productions International, 1982.
53. Rashad Khalifa, *Qur'an: Visual Presentations of the Miracle* INFO, p. 4
54. United Submitters International, Wikipedia, online.
55. "Ahmed Subhy Mansour," Wikipedia, online.
56. See Gabriel Said Reynolds, *The Emergence of Islam* (Minneapolis: Fortress Press, 2012): 208.
57. Rainbow Press.
58. Farouk A. Peru, "An Analysis of Quranist Fundamentalism. Online.

BIBLIOGRAPHY

Abu-Izzeddin, Nejla M. *The Druzes: A New Study of Their History, Faith and Society.* (Leiden: E. J. Brill, 1984).
Asani, Ali, "On Pluralism, Intolerance and the Qur'an." *The American Scholar* 7,1 (2002): 52–60.
Ansari, Zafar Ishaq, "Islam among African Americans: An Overview," in Z. Bukhari, et al. (eds.), *Muslims' Place in the American Public Square* (Walnut Creek, CA: Altamira, 2004): 222–267.
Betts, Robert Brenton. *The Druze* (New Haven, CT: Yale University Press, 1988).
Daftari, Farhad, *A Short History of the Isma'ilis: Traditions of a Muslim Community* (Princeton, NJ: Markar Weiner Publishers, 1998).
——, *The Isma'ilis: Their History and Doctrines* (Cambridge, UK: Cambridge University Press, 1990).
Dana, Nissim. *The Druze: A Religious Community in Transition* (Jerusalem: Turtledove Publications, 1980).
——, *The Druze in the Middle East: Their Faith, Leadership, Identity and Status.* (Brighton, UK: Sussex Academic Press, 1998).

Erickson, Rebecca. "The Druze," in *Encyclopedia of New Religious Movements*, ed. Peter B. Clarke (New York: Routledge, 2000): 1–5.

Haddad, Yvonne Y., and Jane I. Smith, *Mission to America. Five Islamic Communities in North America* (Gainesville: University of Florida Presses, 2003).

Khan, Muhammad Zafrullah, *Ahmadiyyat: The Renaissance of Islam* (London: Tabshir Publications, 1978).

Khuri, Fuad I., *Being a Druze* (London: Druze Heritage Foundation, 2004).

Leonard, Karen Isaksen, *Muslims in the United States: The State of Research* (New York: Russell Sage Foundation, 2003).

Musa, Aisha Y., *Hadith as Scripture: Discussions on the Authority of Prophetic Traditions in Islam*. New York: Palgrave Macmillan, 2008.

Obeid, Anis, *The Druze & Their Faith in Tahwid* (New York: Syracuse University Press, 2006).

Patel, Eboo, *Acts of Faith. The Story of an American Muslim* (Boston: Beacon, 2007).

——, *Sacred Ground. Pluralism, Prejudice, and the Promise of America*. (Boston: Beacon, 2012).

Reynolds, Gabriel Said, *The Emergence of Islam: Classical Traditions in Contemporary Perspective* (Minneapolis: Fortress, 2012).

Salibi, Kamal, *The Druze. Realities and Perceptions* (London: Druze Heritage Foundation, 2005).

Steinberg, Jonah, *Isma'ili Modern: Globalization and Identity in a Muslim Community* (Chapel Hill: University of North Carolina, 2011).

Trost, Theodore Louis, *The African Diaspora and the Study of Religion* (London: Palgrave/Macmillan, 2007).

Turner, Richard Brent, *Islam in the African American* Experience. (Bloomington: Indiana University Press, 2003).

Walbridge, Linda, and Fatimah Haneef, "Inter-ethnic Relations Within the Ahmadiyya Muslim Community in the United States," in *The Expanding Landscape: South Asians and the Diaspora*, ed. Carla Petievich (Delhi: Manohar, 1999).

PART II

INSTITUTIONALIZATION OF ISLAM IN NORTH AMERICA

CHAPTER 9

....

PRACTICING ISLAM
IN THE UNITED
STATES

....

MUZAMMIL H. SIDDIQI

MUSLIMS across America base their religious practices on the same requirements gleaned from scripture and tradition. Although they represent many different races and cultures and even many different interpretations of Islam, they follow the same basic expectations in terms of prayer, fasting, almsgiving, and other prescribed acts of worship. On a typical Friday shortly after noon, some worshippers may enter a storefront building, converted to serve as a place of gathering, where the carpets are threadbare and the space is cramped. Others, with access to more plush facilities, enjoy worship in purpose-built mosques with large prayer halls and thick carpets ready for prayer and prostration. Whether they formally observe it or not, all Muslims understand that prayer to God is a daily obligation, and congregational prayer on Friday is one of the several expectations of all Muslims. For some, the details by which they implement these expectations reflect the cultures from which they have originated, while others are focused on understanding how traditional practices of the faith can find their expression in the new culture of America.

Such efforts represent nothing new for Muslims, whose practices always have differed slightly in different places according to the conditions of time and place. Islam, which means active surrender and submission to God (Allah), emphasizes both beliefs and practices based on the two primary sources of Islam: the Qur'an and Sunna. The Qur'an is the word of God as revealed to the Prophet Muhammad. The Sunna is the Prophet Muhammad's words, deeds, and approvals as recorded by his followers in the collections of books of Hadith. Muslim theologians and jurists elaborated and continue to elaborate the Qur'an and Hadith through various exegetical methods.[1]

Although there is a variety of interpretation in theology and many schools of jurisprudence, the main features of Islamic beliefs in particular and Islamic practices in general are constant and remain the same across the many cultures and traditions that represent American Islam.[2]

According to Islamic Shari'a (law), practices of faith or obligations in Islam are of two kinds: those related to God, or acts of worship (*'ibadat*), and those that involve dealing with other beings (*mu'amalat*). The prescribed acts of worship are summarized by the Five Pillars of Islam. These are (1) declaration of faith, (2) ritual prayers, (3) charity or almsgiving, (4) fasting, and (5) pilgrimage.[3] Dealings with others are both personal and social; they include such things as laws and rules related to food, clothing, family life, business, and so on. The scope of relations is vast and covers every aspect of life. Even with this division, all of these responsibilities are considered in general to be acts of worship, particularly as they affect Muslims in general and the Muslims of America in particular.

In Islam the concept of worship is very broad, covering every aspect of life. Thus worship is not just prayers and rituals; it is the whole of life. The particular acts of worship are designed to keep a person aware of his or her role as God's servant. Acts of worship are both individual and communal.[4]

DECLARATION OF FAITH (*SHAHADA*)

The Shahada is the first and most essential act of worship. It consists of the testimonial that says "I bear witness that there is no god but God (Allah) and I bear witness that Muhammad is the Messenger of God." The Shahada is required when any person converts to Islam and it affirms his or her joining of the *Ummah* or Muslim community. The testimonial is repeated daily as part of the personal prayer. At birth the Shahada is whispered into both ears of the infant as a reminder of a primordial covenant to worship God alone. It is also whispered into the ears of a dying person as a reminder of allegiance as he or she meets the Almighty. Shi'ites sometimes add to the Shahada a special prayer in praise of 'Ali. Observant Muslims begin the day by saying the Shahada and end it with that declaration before going to sleep. Five times throughout the day these words are heard in the Muslim community in the call to congregational prayer (*adhan*), and they are reiterated in the five daily prayers.

PRAYER (*SALAT*)

Prayer occupies a very important place in Islam. There are two types of prayers: those that are obligatory and those that are highly recommended. Formal obligatory prayers with prescribed forms and times are known as *salat* (pl. *salawat*), and informal prayers without any prescribed forms or times are called *du'a* (pl. *du'at*)

Formal Prayers

Five daily prayers are obligatory upon every adult sane Muslim, male or female. For the Muslim, prayer is not just a mental or spiritual attitude or even a way of expressing thanks to God. It involves the response of the whole body: standing, bowing, sitting, and performing prostrations. It is for that reason that mosques do not have pews or chairs. Children from the age of seven are encouraged to pray; from the age of ten they are urged to pray; from the age of puberty formal prayer becomes obligatory. Women are not to perform salat during their menses and postchildbirth bleeding. The requirements for the traveler are less stringent: those who are sick or under hardship can pray shorter prayers or combine some prayers. Before the ritual prayer can be carried out, certain prerequisites must be observed:

- *Cleanliness.* This entails the cleanliness of the body, clothes and the place of prayer. There are elaborate rules of personal hygiene in Islam. After sexual intercourse both males and females, and women at the end of their menstrual cycle, are required to bathe before they can pray. Ablution (*wudu*) is required after "minor pollution" (i.e., after using the toilet or passing wind or bleeding from a wound). The ablution consists of washing both hands including the elbows, rinsing the mouth and nose, washing the whole face, wiping over the head with a wet hand and then washing both feet including the ankles. Washing is done three times for every part of the body to make sure it is clean. Wiping over the socks if they are worn after ablution is permissible for one full day or three days for travelers. It is also permissible to wipe over a bandage if one cannot remove it because of medical advice. In case of scarcity of water, it is sufficient to wash only once. In case water is not available or one is not able to use water due to sickness, a symbolic dry ablution (*tayammum*) is allowed.
- *Proper dress*: For Salat one must wear appropriate and clean clothes. Women must cover their heads. Men are also encouraged to cover their heads, although it is not mandatory.
- *Direction* (*qiblah*): For Salat it is necessary to locate and face the direction of Makkah. In the United States many devices such as wristwatches, Qibla applications on mobile phones, and other electronic means have made the task of facing towards Mecca easy.
- *Times*: All Sunni Muslims agree that there are five obligatory prayers, but they have slight differences in the timings of these prayers. The Qur'an has given only general guidelines about the times of the prayers, with the details taken from the Sunna: Morning Prayer (*fajr*), to be performed anytime from the breaking of morning twilight or dawn (about one hour and half before sunrise) until sunrise; Noon Prayer (*zuhr*), any time after midday until early afternoon; Late Afternoon Prayer ('*asr*), any time after the end of Zuhr until the sun sets; Evening Prayer (*maghrib*), soon after sunset until the disappearance of red twilight; Night Prayer ('*isha*), after the onset of darkness until the middle of the night.

– Every salat requires concentration of the mind plus certain verbal recitations and physical movements. In salat one tries one's best to emulate the practice of the Prophet. Salat is performed in Arabic and recitations are done from memory without holding or looking into any book of prayer or the Qur'an.

Each prayer cycle consists of one bowing, hence each cycle is known as *rak'a*. Each prayer has units of two, three or four rak'as. The physical positions of salat are:

– *Standing*: Salat begins with the standing position facing the direction of Makkah. With open palms, men raise their hands to their earlobes and women to their shoulders and say, "*Allah Akbar* (God is great)." Then they fold their hands over their stomachs or chests (with slight variations among the various schools of Islamic law. The Malikis among the Sunnis and the Shi'is leave their hands hanging to their sides. A short prayer of glorification is then recited followed by the Opening Surah (*al-Fatihah*) of the Qur'an and another Surah (chapter) or a few verses of a Surah. In the United States Muslims sometimes have found it hard to perform prayers in the workplace, and then they may combine the noon and afternoon prayers. Students in schools often are given permission to pray at the appropriate times. Some Muslim students are even collaborating with Christians students in organizing prayer clubs in the after school hours.
– *Bowing*: After the standing position one inclines forward holding the knees and bowing the head down. In this position one recites at least three times: "Glory be to my Lord, the Great." Then standing straight one says, "God hears those who praise Him. Our Lord, for you is the Praise."
– *Prostration*: Each cycle of prayer consists of two prostrations. After bowing one stands straight and then prostrates placing knees, then palms and then the tip of the nose and forehead touching the ground. In this position one says at least three times, "Glory be to my Lord, the most High." Then one sits up straight for a while and then goes again into the second prostration repeating the same words of glorification. After that one stands up repeating the same prayers in each position except reciting a different passage of the Qur'an.
– *Sitting (Julus)*: After every two rak'as one sits with folded legs and recites some specified prayers. The prayer ends with a final sitting position. After reciting some special prayers one ends the salat with the words "Peace and God's mercy be with you," turning the head on the right side and then on the left side. The basic structure of formal prayer (salat) is always the same with variation only in the recitations from the Qur'an.

Salat is performed both individually and collectively. It is required for men to offer the five daily salat in congregation as often as possible. Wherever there are two or more Muslims they can hold the congregational prayer. In most mosques women can join the congregational prayers and pray with men, but separately. Often this means in separate prayer lines, usually at the rear of the worship space. In other mosques women may come through a separate entrance and worship on the second level on a kind of balcony from which they observe the imam and the male worshippers. In very conservative mosques women pray in a room separate from the main prayer hall. Congregational prayers can also be held at home with family members.

Salat prayers are held in congregation five times in the Muslim places of worship, known as mosques (*masjid*, meaning the place of *sajda*, plural *masajid*) The Prophet said, "The whole earth is made as *masjid* for me." This means that one can pray at any clean, respectable place. However, mosques are built (or adapted, in the case of converted buildings) for prayer and they hold a central and significant place in Islamic life. The congregational prayers require the following elements:

- *Call to prayer* (*adhan*): The person who calls for prayer (*mu'adhin*) says with a loud and melodious voice: "God is great" (four times), "I bear witness that there is no god but God" (two times), "I bear witness that Muhammad is Messenger of God" (two times), "come to prayer" (two times), "come to salvation" (two times), "God is great" (two times), "there is no god but God" (once). In the morning (*fajr*) prayer, after "come to salvation," is added, "Prayer is better than sleep," (twice). When the congregational prayer begins, the same words are again said but with the additional statement, "Prayer has begun (lit. has risen up)."
- *Leader of the Prayer* (*imam*): The congregational prayers are led by a prayer leader. In mixed congregations of men and women the imam is always a male; women can lead the prayers of women only. Several years ago a woman did lead congregational prayers for a mixed male and female congregation in New York, but the practice failed to appeal to most Muslims even in the United States. According to some authorities, a learned woman can also lead the prayer at her home with her family. Some mosques have full-time imams, although most mosques in America cannot afford this luxury. Any person known for his knowledge, piety and maturity can lead the prayer. People stand behind the *imam* in lines while facing the direction of Makkah.

Friday (*Jumu'ah*) prayer is a weekly congregational prayer. It takes place at noon in place of the of daily noon *Zuhr* prayer. While three or more Muslims can hold the Friday congregational prayer, the importance of sharing this prayer with larger groups is emphasized. Friday prayer is preceded by a short sermon (*khutba*) on religious, moral and social issues of concern to the congregation. Until recently the custom in the United States has been that sermons were given in the language best representing the culture of the majority of those in attendance. Increasingly American mosques are realizing the importance of giving the sermon in English so that all congregants, especially the younger generation, can understand it.

Special prayers are also required for festivals (*eids*). The two major festivals of Islam are *Eid al-Fitr* (at the end of the month of fasting, Ramadan) and *Eid al-Adha*

(the feast of sacrifice at the time of pilgrimage). Both festivals begin with large congregational prayers followed by a short sermon and greetings. Muslims of a town or
locality are urged to share these prayers together as much as possible.

Special funeral (*janaza*) prayers are held at the time of death. Muslims bury their
dead after washing the body of the deceased and then hold a congregational prayer.
The body is placed in front of the imam, with the whole congregation praying in the
standing position behind him. Very specific laws regulate the burial of the deceased,
difficult to carry out in most American cemeteries. Occasionally a section of a cem-
etery will now be dedicated to the burial of Muslims, allowing them to observe the
practices specified in Islamic law.

Night prayers (*tarawih*) are special prayers said during the month of Ramadan.
After breaking the fast, Muslim gather together and pray the *'isha* (night prayer), then
hold long prayers (composed of twenty or eight *rak'as*). The imam recites one part of
the Qur'an every night and thus completes all the thirty parts during the Ramadan
night prayers.

Congregational prayers may also be said for collective thanks, repentance, or sor-
row; at the time of sun or moon eclipses; during times of war or disaster; or for rain at
the time of drought. Some individuals also observe additional highly recommended
salat after midnight (*tahajjud*) and in the midday (*duha*) or anytime they enter the
mosque and whenever they choose to pray.

Du'a—Informal Prayers

These are prayers without any specified form or time. *Du'a* means calling upon God
or supplication. It can be done at any time with or without ablution, in any language
and in any position: standing, sitting, or lying in bed.

There are hundreds of du'as of the Prophet reported in the books of hadith and
other manuals of prayers. These prayers reflect the Prophet's deep devotion, humility and gratitude to God. Some of these prayers are general and some are for special
occasions such as getting up from sleep in the morning, at the start and end of a
meal, beginning a journey or riding a vehicle, beginning important work, visiting a
sick person, hearing a good or sad news, congratulating a person or ending the day
and retiring to bed. Muslims generally memorize the Prophet's prayers and recite
them exactly in his words, but sometimes translations in local languages are also
used. The special prayers (du'as) of some pious persons, Sufi saints, and others are
repeated in many different languages, some in prose and some in poetry. Beside
these informal prayers, Muslims have a very rich tradition of *dhikr* (remembering
God with devotion and praise), often associated with the Sufi tradition but not
limited to Sufis.

American Muslims observe their prayers in a variety of ways. There are many who very carefully observe the five daily prayers at the specified time. However, a very small number of Muslims actually perform their daily congregational prayers at the mosque, mainly because of work schedules but also because there are not enough mosques that are easily accessible. Because of the various reasons that Muslims may not be able to pray at prescribed times, many are forced to combine two prayers into one.

Prayer, and the preparation for it, is often more complicated in the United States than in Muslim majority cultures. Making ablution (*wudu*), for example, especially washing the feet in public places, can be problematic for some people. The accommodation of wiping over the socks rather than removing them can make the ablution requirement easier to meet. Working men and women sometimes find it difficult to have their noon and afternoon prayers in their workplaces. Some delay their prayers until they return home, while others try to find discreet ways to fulfill this obligation in their places of work. Employers who fail to provide breaks or facilities for their Muslim workers who want to pray may find themselves the subject of a lawsuit brought by civil rights organizations such as the Council on American Islamic Relations.

Fewer than a quarter of Muslims in America actually attend the Friday congregational prayers at a mosque or observe it in their office complexes, at school or on college campuses. The number of mosques holding Friday services, however, is on the rise. A 2011 survey of mosques reports that 11 percent of the mosques in America are now holding Friday congregational prayers two or three times each day, with a short break between, because they cannot accommodate all the worshippers at one time.

Many mosques in America have a large number of women attending the Friday congregational prayers, and some women also attend the daily prayers. Women are also actively involved in the administration of some mosques, often serving on boards. This trend is slowly spreading and is generally accepted and supported, though with some resistance on the part of a small group of more traditional or conservative Muslims.[5]

In some place in the United States controversy has arisen when neighbors have complained that the call to prayer is disturbingly loud. For that reason most mosques in America do not use external loudspeakers for the call of prayer so as to avoid any inconvenience to their non-Muslim neighbors. While the call to worship in Muslim countries is traditionally made outdoors from the top of the minaret, in the United States it is often made from inside the mosque, especially in the early mornings and at night. Because mosques are few and most of them are too small to accommodate all the worshippers, traffic and parking may also cause problems. Worshippers may have difficulty gaining access to the mosque, and in some areas neighbors have complained about excessive noise and traffic congestion. Slowly new and larger purpose-built mosques are being constructed, although some are facing resistance from the local populations.

CHARITY OR ALMSGIVING (*ZAKAT*)

The third in the list of religious obligations on Muslims is that of charity toward the poor and needy. Like prayers, there are two types of charity in Islam: (1) that which is formal and compulsory, known as Zakat, and (2) that which is informal and recommended, known as Sadaqat.

Zakat is obligatory on every Muslim, male or female, who owns a certain amount of wealth beyond his or her personal needs for one year. This amount, known as *nisab*, varies for different categories of wealth. The nisab for gold, silver, cash, stocks, bonds, and so on is eighty-five grams of gold or the equivalent market value. The ratio of zakat for Sunnis is 2.5 percent on the total cash after deducting personal expenses. Shi'ites have a different calculation. Residential home, transportation vehicles, clothes, household items, and so on are exempt from zakat. Livestock and poultry for domestic use and for agricultural work are exempt from zakat, but it is levied on animals for commercial purposes. On agricultural products the zakat is due at the time of harvest.

The Qur'an (9:60) specifies eight categories of recipients for zakat: the poor, the needy, zakat workers, those whose hearts are to be reconciled (new Muslims in need), those in bondage (slaves or captives), the debt-ridden, the wayfarers (the stranded or those traveling who lack resources), and those in the way of God (to support and defend Islam and Muslims). The basic rule in zakat expenditure, according to the Prophet, is that it is taken from the rich and given to the poor. Zakat funds are generally given to the needy and are not used for public projects, such as building of mosques and schools. Some jurists now allow the use of zakat funds for public projects in poor areas and where Muslims live as minorities and have no other public or governmental support available for their institutions.

There is also a special zakat, known as *zakat al-fitr*, given at the end of the month of Ramadan. Zakat al-fitr is about two kilograms of wheat, rice, or barley or its cash value to be given by the head of the household on behalf of every member of the family including newborn babies. Zakat al-fitr is given at the end of the festival of Ramadan to the poor and needy in the community to support them and their families.

In the United States zakat is often understood as a way to provide service other than financial to members of the Muslim community. This service may be done individually or through organizations and Islamic centers. Young people especially are working in hospitals, retirement homes, soup kitchens or other places in which their services can be used. Youth report that they feel good to be contributing to those with particular needs.

Sadaqat refers to general charity without any specific amount, ratio or time. Islam encourages Muslims to help those who are in need all the time. Some scholars say that the best charity is to prefer the needs of others over one's own needs; next comes the charity in which one shares what one has with others who are in need; and next comes the charity in which one gives what is beyond one's own need. Muslims give charity to help the poor and needy as a token of gratitude to God and sometimes as repentance offerings for the expiation of sins and errors.

American Muslims on the whole are very generous and charitable. They help the poor and needy in their own communities. They have also established many charitable relief organizations that collect millions for the aid of victims of natural and human-made disasters all over the world. Many charities provide assistance to people of all faiths and of no faith. Besides taking care of their places of worship and schools for their children, they often fund free clinics in their communities. Major US cities and towns where Muslims live sponsor monthly and sometimes weekly fundraising programs, bake sales, and appeals for funds. In addition to serving local needs, immigrant Muslims often feel a special obligation to help their relatives in their native lands.

FASTING (*SAUM*, PL. *SIYAM*)

In Islam fasting entails abstaining from food, drink, and sexual activity from dawn (1 ½ hours before sunrise) to dusk. Like prayers and charity, Islam also requires obligatory fasting and optional fasting.

Obligatory fasting in Ramadan: The ninth month of the lunar calendar is known as Ramadan. It marks the month in which the first revelation of the Qur'an came in 610 CE to Prophet Muhammad while he was in the Cave of Hira in Makkah. The revelation of the Qur'an then continued for about twenty-two years until the Prophet's last year of life in 632. Fasting is done in gratitude for the Qur'an as well as for self-discipline and to help the poor and needy.

Fasting during Ramadan is obligatory on every Muslim male or female who has reached the age of puberty. Those who are sick or traveling are allowed not to fast if they find it difficult to fulfill this duty. Women are not allowed to fast during their menses. The travelers, the sick, and women who miss their fasts due to their monthly period all have to make up the missed fast at a time when they are ready. Those who are terminally ill and not able to fast at all are supposed to give to the poor and needy one day's meal or its value for each fast missed. Children usually start fasting from the age of eight or ten, but it is not obligatory for them until they reach puberty. American women sometimes have to work with their children's teachers to explain why the children are not eating lunch as is generally expected.

On the day of fasting Muslims rise early in the morning about an hour before dawn (or 1 ½ hours before sunrise). They take an early morning meal (*sahur*). At the time of dawn they begin their fast. Although one is obliged to abstain from eating during the fast as well as from drinking and sexual activity, fasting is not only abstention from material things. It also requires moral discipline and a proper spiritual attitude.

One is supposed to spend more time in prayers, devotion, reading of the Qur'an, and dhikr (remembrance of God) as well as deeds of charity. Ramadan is the month of great spiritual and moral revival and rejuvenation. At dusk Muslims break their fast, an activity known as *iftar*. At this time Muslims usually take one or two dates, following the custom of the Prophet, or they take water or some juices or soft drinks. Each ethnic and national community has its own traditional Ramadan foods. It is a custom to invite family members and friends for iftar. People distribute food among the poor and needy during Ramadan. After iftar people offer the evening prayer (*maghrib*).

Shortly after evening prayer, dinner is taken and then Muslims rush to the night prayer (*'isha*). During Ramadan the night prayer is followed by a special prayer known as *tarawih*, as mentioned previously. At the end of Ramadan is the festival known as Eid al-fitr. The day begins with a prayer (the *Eid* prayer) and is then followed by day-long and in some places three-day-long festivities.

Voluntary fasting: Muslims also fast other days during the year, but these are optional fasts and are not observed by everyone. In the first month of the Islamic calendar (*Muharram*) Sunnis usually observe the fasts on the ninth and tenth days of the month, known as *Ashura*. The Prophet observed this fast when he learned upon arrival in Madinah that Jewish people fasted on the tenth day of Muharram in commemoration of Passover. Prophet Muhammad did that out of respect for Prophet Moses and in gratitude to God's favor to Moses and his followers on that day. Fasting on every Monday and Thursday of the week is also observed by some pious Muslims. Some fast for three days (the thirteenth, fourteenth, and fifteenth days) of every lunar month. There are also personal fasts for penitence, thanks, and vows. All fasts are similar in structure and are observed from dawn to dusk with abstentions. People generally avoid fasting on Friday as it is a kind of weekly festival, and it is forbidden to fast on the two main festival days of Eid al-fitr and Eid al-adha.

Many but not all Muslims in America observe the fast in the month of Ramadan. Some may observe it in modified ways, while others profess that they would like to fast but that the circumstances of their jobs do not easily allow it. During the month of Ramadan mosques and Islamic centers have bigger gatherings than usual for daily and Friday prayers and also tarawih prayers. Many Islamic centers hold community iftars and provide free meals to everyone. Interfaith iftars are also becoming quite common where Muslims invite their non-Muslim friends as well as interfaith leaders and local officials. Chapters of the Muslim Student Association on a number of college campuses encourage iftars to which they invite Christian and Jewish students or those of other religious traditions or no tradition. The White House, the State Department, Muslim embassies, as well as some state and city officials also invite Muslims and interfaith leaders for iftar during Ramadan. Breaking the fast has traditionally been a family activity, shared by relatives from all generations. In the United States it is often the case that nuclear Muslim families do not have relatives nearby with whom to share the occasion. Meals offered by local mosques provide a new kind of "family" for many Muslims in America.

In recent years the American media have become increasingly aware of the Muslim observance of the fast during this special month of the year. Many articles have appeared in local newspapers with photos featuring shoes left outside a mosque door during Ramadan worship or community groups invited to share the iftar. Rather than writing about "Islamic extremism," increasingly the press is taking the opportunity to cover special Ramadan events in mosques, universities, and other settings. Muslims themselves are taking advantage of the burgeoning new means of online communication to talk about how to observe Ramadan in the context of America, including ways of sharing this important time with non-Muslims.

The issue of when and how to observe the exact beginning and end of the month of Ramadan is still not settled among the Muslims of America. Traditionally, the month starts and ends with the actual sighting of the new crescent. In many Muslim countries there are official religious bodies that make this announcement, but in the United States there is no single religious body that makes that determination for all American Muslims. Some Islamic centers determine the beginning and ending of the month of Ramadan on the basis of the local US sighting of the crescent; some follow Saudi Arabia (due to the respect of the two sacred cities of Makkah and Madinah), and some follow scientific calculations. For many Muslims waiting until the last minute to determine the beginning of the fast of Ramadan and the 'Eid festival at its end has been causing great difficulties. Some communities have to wait until midnight to find out whether or not the crescent has been sighted. Often the sighting reports are conflicting. At the time of the 'Eid festival it is even more difficult as Muslims are not able to inform their employers, and students their school authorities, when they will need to be absent. Some former and present Muslim jurists have considered it permissible to use scientific calculations to determine the lunar months. They emphasize that the objective of the Shari'a is to make sure that the new lunar month has begun. In the past it was possible only by means of sighting, but now more accurate scientific methods are available and most American Muslims feel that they should be used. The Fiqh Council of North America, after long discussions and deliberations on various juristic positions, accepted the validity of the scientific calculation method. It has published a long-term Islamic lunar calendar and it announces the dates of Ramadan and 'Eid well in advance for the Muslims of America. Many communities are slowly accepting this method, but it continues to excite controversy, humorously called the issue of "moon fighting" rather than "moon sighting."

PILGRIMAGE (*HAJJ*)

For Muslims the pilgrimage means more than just a visit to a holy place; it is an act of worship. Each prayer cycle consists of one bowing, hence each cycle is known as *rak'a*. Each prayer has units of two, three or four *rak'as*. Hajj is obligatory at least once in his or her lifetime on every Muslim, male or female, who is adult and capable (physically and financially) of undertaking the journey. Technically only the visit to Makkah and its surroundings during the first ten days, and specially the ninth day of the twelfth month *Dhul Hijjah* ("month of Hajj") is called Hajj. A ceremonial visit to Makkah at any other time of the year is called *'Umrah*. Visits to Madinah (Prophet Muhammad's mosque and tomb) or Jerusalem (al-Quds) are called Ziyarah. Such visits also are emphasized, but they are not called Hajj and are not obligatory.

Hajj is a very important annual event bringing together millions of Muslims from all over the world. It takes about five days, beginning on the eighth day and concluding on the twelfth day of the pilgrimage month. Pilgrims generally start coming to Makkah a few days or weeks earlier to get ready for the ceremonies of Hajj. Males who enter the city of Makkah for the pilgrimage (either Hajj or 'Umrah) must wear two white unstitched sheets of cloth called *ihram*, one for the lower body and other for the upper body. The head is not covered and only slippers or low-cut shoes are worn on the feet, without socks. Women must wear simple dresses. All pilgrims announce their intention to do the Hajj before they arrive at the boundaries of *miqat*, which refers to the five towns or points at different sides (from 50 to about 450 kilometers in distance) from Makkah, which were marked by the Prophet. Today pilgrims may enter from many different places; each point is connected to the others by virtual lines drawn by Islamic scholars. Thus anyone who crosses this pentagon shape must be in ihram whether coming by land or air.

Many rituals (*manasik*) combine the Hajj experience, each with some historical or symbolic meaning. The basic philosophy of Hajj is to connect the pilgrims vertically to God and to the long cherished memory of God's prophets and blessed people, and horizontally to the other believers who gather there. Hajj is a great occasion of the gathering of Muslims from around the world representing all walks of life. After settling in their hotels or any other place they plan to stay, pilgrims go to the Grand Mosque of Makkah. It is called the Noble Sanctuary (*al-Haram al-Sharif*) and is built in the shape of a circle around the *Ka'bah* (the house of worship believed to have been built by the Prophet Abraham). It is a huge mosque and can accommodate over two million people in its three floors and courtyards. The pilgrims first go to the Ka'bah and circle around it seven times, the circumambulation referred to as *tawaf*. Each circle begins from the corner of the Ka'bah, where one kisses, touches, or points to the Black Stone (al-Hajar al-Aswad). The larger the crowd, the wider the circle becomes; thus it can take anywhere from fifteen minutes to two hours to complete a tawaf. During tawaf people walk together while saying prayers in low voices and asking for God's blessings. At the end of tawaf, people go to the place where Abraham stood in prayer. They try to find a spot as close to that area as possible and offer a short prayer.

After tawaf, pilgrims drink water from the well of Zamzam, built over the spot where Hagar, Abraham's second wife, pleaded with God to provide water for her son Ishmael and herself. According to Islamic belief, God miraculously caused water to burst forth. The well of Zamzam still serves millions of pilgrims with its blessed water. During their stay in Makkah pilgrims drink as much of this water as they can and some even bring it home. Pilgrims returning to America after the Hajj may be seen carrying plastic bottles of Zamzam water off the plane.

The next step on the pilgrimage at Makkah is to go to the hills of Safa and Marwah. These hills are now within the boundaries of the Grand Mosque of Makkah. Tradition says that Hagar ran between these two hills (about a kilometer apart) searching and praying for water. Each pilgrim commemorates this event by running between these two hills in remembrance of the mother of Ishmael. This is called 'sa'y' or walking fast between Safa and Marwah. Sa'y also has seven trips starting from Safa to Marwah and then from Marwah to Safa. The seventh walk ends at Marwah, where the pilgrim stands and makes a special du'a (personal prayer) for himself or herself and others in the family. After this those who came early to Makkah take off their ihrams and put on their regular clothes. Before leaving the state of ihram, however, men must trim or shave the hair of their heads. Women cut only a small portion from the end of a hair plait.

On the eighth day of the twelfth month, the actual Hajj ceremonies begin. This is the first day of Hajj. From Makkah the pilgrims depart to Mina and spend the day there. The second day (ninth of the month) is the main day of the Hajj. The pilgrims leave from Mina to 'Arafah, where they spend the whole day until sunset in prayers and devotion. After sunset they leave for Muzdalifah, where they spend the night before returning the next morning to Mina. Thus Mina, Arafah, and Muzdalifah are three important sites of Hajj, some three or four miles distant from each other. In earlier days the trip used to take hours because of the huge crowds, but now the three sites are connected by a fast monorail which has served to reduce the traffic. These trains transport hundreds of thousands of pilgrims to the sites of Hajj within a relatively short time.

On the third day of the Hajj (the tenth day of the month), the pilgrims return to Mina, where they stay until the fifth day. During their stay they go to three sites, known as Jamarat, where they observe Abraham's temptation by the devil to disobey God and spare the life of his son. Every pilgrim reminds himself or herself of the devil's temptation in their own lives by casting seven small stones or pebbles as Abraham did. Because of the millions of pilgrims merging from every direction to go to Jamarat within a short time, this part of the Hajj has been very hazardous and accidents have happened in the past. Now the government of Saudi Arabia has constructed four levels of Jamarat. Crowds coming from various directions in Mina can walk or use the many escalators and elevators provided to reach the Jamarat. The area also has been widened to spread out the crowds. Muslims note that the scene of human waves coming to Jamarat and reenacting the spirit of Abraham provides Muslims with a most moving and unforgettable Hajj experience.

Umra or optional visit to Makkah: Visiting Makkah's holy environs at any time other than when one is participating in the Hajj is called 'Umrah. This visit used to be limited primarily to local people or those from neighboring towns and lands because travel to Makkah from longer distances was so difficult. Now, with the ease of travel, many people from all over the world make 'Umrah throughout the year. In 2012 Saudi authorities reported about 6 million 'Umrah visitors. Tour groups come at different times and spend some days in Makkah and Madinah for both worship and recreation. 'Umrah in the month of Ramadan has become most popular. A shorter version of the Hajj, it consists only of circling around the Ka'bah and walking between the hills of Safa and Marwah in the state of ihram. Makkah has become a modern city with many hotels and furnished apartments. Malls and international food courts catering to foreign visitors by providing international cuisines are a big attraction, especially appealing to Muslims who come from all over for spiritual renewal as well as vacation.

American Muslims and Hajj: Hajj and 'Umrah are both very popular among American Muslims, young and old, men and women. It is also relatively easy financially for American Muslims to undertake this journey. There are many tour groups that organize Hajj and 'Umrah visits, especially during summer and winter holidays, offering a wide range of accommodations. Some people also stop for Hajj or 'Umrah while on their way to visit their relatives in the Middle East or the Indo-Pakistan subcontinent. In recent years a significant number of books and films have been produced describing the experience of the Hajj and its component elements. Michael Wolfe's *The Hadj: An American's Pilgrimage to Mecca*,[6] for example, goes through each stage of the pilgrimage so that the reader is able to share in the actual experience. This book is on the recommended reading list for American Muslims going on the Hajj for the first time and for those who are interested in descriptions of this important "pillar" among the obligations of being a Muslim. More educational material about the Hajj is available for Muslims and non-Muslims in the West, and the media are becoming more aware of the importance of highlighting this experience for the general edification of the American public.[7]

Not all Muslims observe all of these five pillars or obligations of Islam, and some choose to follow selected ones. More conservative Muslim believers may be critical of those who do not follow the practices rigorously, but at the same time Muslims in America understand that there is great variety in adherence and practice. Traditionally men have been expected to follow them more rigorously than women, but in the United States women increasingly are developing ways in which they can participate in all five. These pillars continue to be held as the standard of belief and practice and constitute the goals that believing Muslims everywhere hope to attain.

Notes

1. See George F. Hourani, "Ethical Presuppositions of the Qur'an," in Mona Siddiqui, ed., *Islamic Thought, Law and Ethics* (London: Sage Publications, 2010): 351–376.
2. See, e.g., Colin Turner, *Islam: The Basics* (New York: Routledge, 2001): 98–139.

3. Many basic books on Islam include attention to these requirements, e.g., John Esposito, *The Straight Path* (Rijadh: International Publishing House, 2010).
4. For a particularly sensitive treatment of the topic, see Timothy J. Gianotti, *Light of a Blessed Tree: Islamic Belief, Practice, and History* (Eugene OR: Wipf & Stock, 2011): 51–66.
5. See Jane I. Smith, *Islam in America*, 2nd edition. (New York: Columbia University Press): 135–38.
6. New York: Grove/Atlantic, 1998.
7. Many texts on Islam provide excellent descriptions of the pilgrimage experience. See, in particular, John Renard, *In the Footsteps of Muhammad. Understanding the Islamic Experience*. (New York: Paulist Press, 1992).

Bibliography

Cook, Miriam, and Bruce B. Lawrence, eds., *Muslim Networks: From Hajj to Hip Hop* (Chapel Hill: University of North Carolina Press, 2005).

Curtis, Edward E. IV, *The Columbia Sourcebook of Muslims in the United States* (New York: Columbia University Press, 2008).

Denny, Frederick M., *An Introduction to Islam* (New York: Macmillan, 1994).

Esposito, John, *Islam. The Straight Path* (Ridayh: International Publishing House, 2010).

Gionotto, Timothy J., "Islamic Path of Sacred Action (Obligatory Religious Practices)," in *In the Light of a Blessed Tree. Illuminations of Islamic Belief, Practice and History* (Eugene OR: Wifp & Stock, 2011): 51–66.

Grieve, Paul, "The Practice of Islam," in *A Brief Guide to Islam* (New York: Carroll and Graf, 2006): 205–265.

Haddad, Yvonne Y., Jane I. Smith, and Kathleen Moore, *Muslim Women in America: The Challenge of Islamic Identity Today* (New York: Oxford University Press, 2006).

Hassaballa, Hesham A., and Kabir Helminski, "The Five Pillars," in *The Beliefnet Guide to Islam* (New York: Doubleday, 2006): 31–51.

Norcliffe, David, "The Five Pillars of Islam," in *Islam: Faith and Practice* (Portland OR: Sussex Academic Press, 1999): 128–141.

Renard, John, "Hajj: Signs Among Believers and Return to the Center on the Main Road (Shari'ah)," in *In the Footsteps of Muhammad. Understanding the Islamic Experience* (New York: Paulist Press, 1992): 49–82.

Siddiqui, Mona, ed., *Islam*: Vol. II, *Islamic Thought, Law, and Ethics*. (London: Sage Publications, 2010).

Smith, Jane I., *Muslims, Christians, and the Challenge of Interfaith Dialogue* (New York: Oxford University Press, 2007).

Turner, Colin, *Islam: The Basics* (New York: Routledge, 2011): 98–139.

Wolfe, Thomas, *The Hadj: An American's Pilgrimage to Mecca* (NY: Grove/Atlantic, 1998).

CHAPTER 10

SHARI'A AND FIQH IN THE UNITED STATES

ASMA AFSARUDDIN

THE Arabic term *shari'a* literally means "the way," or, more expansively, "the way or path to the watering hole (or spring)." In theological and juridical spheres, the term is understood to refer to divinely revealed law. More accurately, shari'a refers to a wide-ranging moral and behavioral code and broad ethical principles that may be interpreted to yield specific legal rulings (Kamali 2008; Hallaq 2009).[1] The process of interpretation of the shari'a through human reasoning and effort is called *fiqh*. Fiqh in its original, basic signification, means understanding and discernment; the one who seeks to understand and discern is a *faqih* (pl. *fuqaha*). In the legal domain, fiqh thus came to mean jurisprudence or the science or study of the law (in this case the shari'a), while a faqih is a jurist who interprets and implements the shari'a. The choice of terminology is revealing of both the ontological connection between shari'a and fiqh and the conceptual differences between them.

According to the distinguished legal historian Khaled Abou El Fadl, "The Sharī'ah is God's Will in an ideal and abstract fashion, but the *fiqh* is the product of the human attempt to understand God's Will." In this sense, the *sharī'ah* is always fair, just and equitable, but the *fiqh* is only an attempt at reaching "the ideals and purposes of shari'a (*maqasid al-Shari'a*)" (Abou El Fadl 2001).[2] Shari'a as God's will is thus perfect and unchanging and ultimately unrealizable to the fullest. Fiqh, as the product of human reasoning, is consequently contingent and fallible and represents at any given time an imperfect attempt by humans to translate God's will as befitting specific historical and sociopolitical circumstances.

Shari'a in its metaphysical and theological dimensions may be usefully compared to the concept of natural law as articulated by Aquinas, Grotius, Pufendorf, and others in the western Christian tradition. According to this concept, natural law emanates from God and is naturally knowable by human beings and naturally authoritative over them. Nature as the product of God's creative power was regarded by a number of Muslim jurists as the link between the divine will and human reason. Nature is created by God and reflects His goodness. This natural predisposition toward the good is encompassed by the Islamic concept of *fitra*, which fundamentally applies to human beings and all creation. Nature is therefore a legitimate object of rational inquiry—that is to say, of fiqh, so that humans may thereby discern the good that must be pursued for normative and empirical reasons (Emon 2010).[3]

The distinction between *shariʿa* and *fiqh* was usually upheld by premodern jurists at least conceptually, but there was a certain amount of conflation between the two terms as well. This was primarily due to the development of the legal concept of *ijmaʿ* or "juridical consensus," which conferred a degree of infallibility on humanly derived legal rulings (*ahkam*) when widely accepted by scholars. However, the legal culture of premodern Islamic societies was never monolithic, and the internal pluralism of Islamic legal thought manifested itself in a multiplicity of legal schools (*madhahib*) in the early period. In the course of the fifth through eleventh centuries, four schools of Sunni law became predominant; these survive today. It is also during this period that the four sources of Sunni jurisprudence (*usul al-fiqh*) became stabilized: Qur'an, *sunna* (the sayings and practices of the Prophet Muhammad), *qiyas* (analogical reasoning), and *ijmaʿ* (consensus). The predominant Shiʿi school of law (the Jaʿfari *madhab*) substituted *ʿaql* for ijmaʿ as one of the sources of fiqh. In terms of actual legal rulings, there are often very few differences between Sunni and Shiʿi schools of law.

As the legal schools matured and a stable corpus of juridical literature emerged in this period, independent legal reasoning (*ijtihad*) sometimes took a back seat to following an established legal precedent (*taqlid*). The former, however, never died out: the doors of ijtihad were never closed, as has been dramatically stated in some modern sources; this erroneous view has been cogently refuted by Hallaq (1986).[4] Traditional fiqh activity continued well into the early modern period but almost always within the parameters of the elaborate legal edifice painstakingly constructed by the classical jurists and their immediate successors.

In the course of the thirteenth through nineteenth centuries, encroaching western colonialism had considerable influence on transforming Muslim perceptions of Islamic law, and the consequences of this are still with us today. Between 1839 and 1876, the sultans of the Ottoman Empire instituted a series of legal reforms known collectively as the *Tanzimat*, which drew its inspiration from French civil law. These reforms ended in the codification of a part of the shariʿa-based Ottoman law; the resulting civil code, known as the *mecelle*, did not include family law. These events in the Ottoman Empire set the ball rolling for subsequent legal reform to be attempted elsewhere in Egypt, Tunisia, India, and Iran, and in some cases these attempts were successful. Attempts were made to restrict the power of government, to end polygamy, and to enhance the legal rights of women in a number of Muslim-majority societies. With the large-scale adoption of European civil and public legal codes in many Muslim-majority societies under the impetus of western colonial occupation, Islamic law has become restricted to essentially personal status or family law, governing issues such as marriage, divorce, inheritance, maintenance, paternity, and the custody of children. With a few notable exceptions, such as Saudi Arabia and Iran, this remains the prevailing situation in the overwhelming majority of Muslim countries today (Esposito 2001).[5]

MUSLIMS IN THE UNITED STATES

As a religious minority in the United States, Muslims struggle for recognition of their beliefs and practices within the religious mosaic of contemporary America. While Muslim presence in American goes back to the eighteenth century, large-scale emigration by Muslims to the United States did not start until the mid-twentieth century. The American Muslim community—estimated, according to various sources, to be between 3 to 8 million strong—is one of the most diverse communities in the United States. About half of American Muslims are immigrants from Asia and the Middle East, Africa, and Europe, while the other half are indigenous African Americans, European Americans, Latinos, and Native Americans as well as second- and third-generation children of immigrant parents. Before September 11, 2001, American Muslims were a largely prosperous, well-educated, but relatively invisible community, but all this changed after that fateful day. Now, American Muslims and their faith are very much in the public eye and are often subject to negative publicity. Post 9/11, in the media and the public sphere, the term *shari'a* has been much bandied about in connection with American Muslims, often with the intent of generating fear of a repressive Islamic theocracy that might be imposed on an unsuspecting American public. Highly charged rhetoric emanating from right-wing groups has referred to a "creeping shari'a," implying that it is a kind of contagion that will cripple American society. These developments have caused American Muslims to feel, on the one hand, reluctant to talk about their religion and defensive in referring to the importance of religious law in their lives. On the other hand, they have instigated an internal conversation in the American Muslim community, particularly among Muslim scholars and organizations, about defining shari'a and its place within the American legal and social systems. The aim is to clarify points of convergence with predominant American religious, ethical, and political values, particularly in the context of a democratic and civil polity.

In the rest of this chapter, some of these conversations occurring among American Muslim scholars and thinkers on the role of shari'a in the modern world and particularly in the United States are discussed, followed by a focus on the Fiqh Council of North America, widely perceived as the primary Islamic organization that adjudicates legal matters pertaining to the situation of Muslim citizens in the United States. The activities of two other American Muslim organizations—Karamah and the Shura Council of the Women's Initiative for Spirituality and Equality—will also be discussed in the context of women's juridical and interpretive activity within the United States.

Debates about the Nature of Shariʿa in the Modern Period

The distinction between shariʿa and fiqh provides the point of departure for modern and modernist reconceptualization of Islamic law and reintepretation of its sources, as it did for the early modernists of the eighteenth and nineteenth centuries in Egypt, Turkey, and elsewhere. Thus Muhammad ʿAbduh (d. 1902), the famous rector of al-Azhar University and prominent Egyptian intellectual of the late eighteenth century, distinguished between the noncontingent and contingent aspects of Islamic law to pave the way for legal reform in Muslim-majority societies. The noncontingent aspects referred to matters of worship (ʿibadat) grounded firmly in revelation and therefore invariable, while the contingent aspects referred to worldly transactions (muʿamalat), which by their very nature are open to multiple interpretations and in themselves are fallible and negotiable (Hourani, 1983).[6] While worldly transactions are to be governed by broad essential principles derived from the shariʿa—mercy, justice, and equity, for example—their specific applications, which are part of fiqh, are always contingent on time and locale. This is a basic distinction that has been eagerly embraced by contemporary Muslim reformers, both in the Islamic heartlands and in the West, since it makes much of what is traditionally deemed to be Islamic law subject to legitimate reinterpretation and reform in the context of modernity.

As mentioned earlier, the purview of Islamic law in most Muslim societies is now restricted to family or personal law; this is similarly the situation in the United States, where Muslims are governed in their public lives by secular federal and state law. Issues concerning marriage and occasionally divorce are typically decided on the basis of traditional Islamic law as interpreted by imams (prayer leaders) of local mosques and/or community leaders and scholars. Sometimes Muslim attorneys and social workers act as mediators in cases of domestic conflict. The internal plurality of the American Muslim community makes the situation more complex, as Islamic law can be both an asset and a liability. Given the wide range of ethnic and cultural backgrounds of the immigrant and indigenous Muslim communities, one finds a broad spectrum of views among American Muslims on issues of marriage, divorce, polygyny, gender roles, and so on. Ikhtilaf (difference in legal opinion) has always been a characteristic and generally positive feature of classical Islamic law, underscoring as it does that there are many ways of realizing the basic objectives (maqasid) of the law. But at the same time, because there is no centralized religious hierarchy, particularly in Sunni Islam, the very diffusiveness of juridical authority can make for a proliferation of legal opinions, which can prove bewildering for the lay person. The lack of a clearly recognized credentialing system has often compounded the problem. Not all imams, for example, are equally grounded in Islamic texts and trained in the necessary Islamic sciences. Immigrant imams often tend to transmit cultural assumptions and mores imported from their indigenous societies as legally sanctioned precepts within Islam.

In recent decades, the situation has begun to change, as Muslim organizations dedicated to ameliorating this situation have emerged. We now turn our attention to three of the most prominent among them.

THE FIQH COUNCIL OF NORTH AMERICA

The Fiqh Council evolved out of the Religious Affairs Committee of the then Muslim Students Association of the United States and Canada in the early 1960s. When the Islamic Society of North American (ISNA) was founded in 1980, the Religious Affairs Committee was renamed the Fiqh Committee of the Islamic Society of North America. In 1986 the Fiqh Council became the Fiqh Council of North America (FCNA) to better reflect the needs and complexity of the growing American Muslim community. The Council remains an affiliate of ISNA to this day. According to its brochure, "the qualified members of FCNA conduct juristic research that focuses on resolving the ever-increasing modern jurisprudential issues in accordance with the pristine objectives of Islamic law and the general welfare of the entire community."[7]

The FCNA's executive council includes prominent religious leaders and scholars in North America. Its primary objectives, as outlined in its bylaws, are as follows:

1. To consider, from a shari'a perspective, and offer advice on specific undertakings, transactions, contracts, projects, or proposals, guaranteeing thereby that the dealings of American Muslims fall within the parameters of what is permitted by the shari'a.
2. To consider issues of relevance to the community and give, from a shari'a perspective, advice and guidelines for policy, procedure, and practice. Such advice may take the form of position papers, *fatawa*, research papers, sample forms for legal agreements, or whatever else is deemed effective.
3. To consult, on issues requiring specialized knowledge and experience, with professionals or subject specialists.
4. To establish and maintain working relationships with shari'a experts worldwide, including muftis, university professors, researchers, shari'a court justices, and members of national and international fiqh councils and academies.
5. To assist local and national organizations in the resolution of conflicts.
6. To advise in the appointment of arbiters, and review arbitration proceedings and decisions for their consistency with Islamic legal principles.
7. To commission research on relevant Islamic legal issues.
8. To maintain and develop a comprehensive shari'a library.

9. To anticipate and serve the particular needs of minority groups within the community; youth, women, prisoners, recent converts, etc.
10. To develop a fiqh for Muslims living in non-Muslim societies.

Decisions made during the process of *istifta* (meaning seeking a *fatwa* or "legal opinion") are the result of collective deliberations by the members of the council. Individual members have the right to write dissenting opinions. The *mustafti* or "petitioner" has the right to accept or not whichever opinion is more acceptable to him or her; a fatwa by definition is not binding on the one who seeks it. In recent years, the council has dealt with questions submitted not only by individual Muslims but also by local and national Muslim organizations, by Muslim and non-Muslim trial lawyers, immigration lawyers, the US Departments of Justice and Defense, and journalists seeking answers to questions on a broad array of issues, such as cloning and Middle Eastern political culture.

In terms of methodology, the FCNA bases its decisions on the two fundamental sources of Islam: the Qur'an and the reliable Sunna of the Prophet Muhammad. It employs the principles of the classical *usul al-fiqh* ("principles of jurisprudence") and takes into consideration the opinions of premodern Muslim jurists in relevant situations. The council considers all the schools of law to be equally authoritative and equally available as intellectual resources in the process of interpretation of foundational texts in the contemporary period.

The fact that American Muslims reside as religious minorities in a non-Muslim society governed by secular laws presents particular challenges for the application of some aspects of Islamic law in the North American environment. The council seeks to adjudicate matters pertaining to American Muslims, for many of which there are no legal precedents, by taking into consideration the higher purposes or the maqasid of the shari'a and deliberating on their application in a non-Muslim environment. Traditional fiqh is predicated on Muslims being the majority and governed by a Muslim state that promises to uphold the shari'a. Because these conditions cannot be met in non-Muslim-majority societies, it is now essential to revisit the process of determining fiqh appropriate to the new context. The minority status of Muslims in the United States has led to the formulation of a "jurisprudence of minorities" (*fiqh al-aqalliyat*) that takes into consideration their particular circumstances. This jurisprudence is not only based on the traditional usul al-fiqh but also makes liberal use of juridical principles such as the common good, objectives of the law, convenience, common practice, necessity, and prevention of harm. These principles, sparingly used in the past, are currently invoked to respond to a whole spectrum of issues having to do with dress, food, marriage, divorce, sexual segregation or the lack thereof, and relations with non-Muslims. These considerations often lead to new, sometimes divergent, interpretations. Practices such as military service and political participation in a non-Muslim polity are still subject to debate among Muslims in general, including American Muslims. Those in favor of Muslims discharging all their duties as citizens of a modern secular polity often cite the juridical principle of *maslaha* (commonweal/public interest) and the objectives of the shari'a to create a religiously based mandate for active Muslim citizenship in non-Muslim polities.

A formal fatwa issued by the FCNA, titled "On Being Faithful Muslims and Loyal Americans," explicitly points to the convergences between Islamic and American public values that create the basis for full Muslim participation in American civic and political practices. The fatwa begins as follows:

> Like other faith communities in the US and elsewhere, we see no inherent conflict between the normative values of Islam and the US Constitution and Bill of Rights. Contrary to erroneous perceptions and Islamophobic propaganda of political extremists from various backgrounds, the true and authentic teachings of Islam promote the sanctity of human life, dignity of all humans, and respect of human, civil and political rights. Islamic teachings uphold religious freedom and adherence to the same universal moral values, which are accepted by the majority of people of all backgrounds and upon which the US Constitution was established and according to which the Bill of Rights was enunciated.[8]

It then goes on to assert the compatibility of American secular law and democratic institutions with the principles and objectives of the shari'a as follows:

> The Shari'a, contrary to misrepresentations, is a comprehensive and broad guidance for all aspects of a Muslim's life—spiritual, moral, social and legal. Secular legal systems in Western democracies generally share the same supreme objectives, and are generally compatible with Islamic Shari'a. Likewise, the core modern democratic systems are compatible with the Islamic principles of Shura mutual consultation and co-determination of all social affairs at all levels and in all spheres, family, community, society, state and globally.[9]

These fatwas stress the compatibility of basic Islamic juridical principles and practices and the objectives of Islamic law with those of secular American law, creating a legal and moral rationale for American Muslims to be loyal to their country and fostering an ethic of committed citizenship. Such legal opinions override the traditional juridical hesitancy to acknowledge and endorse the permanent minority status of a Muslim in a majoritarian non-Muslim society. A powerful counterargument to this classical legal perspective is frequently made. This argument posits that since Muslims are relatively free to practice their religion in the United States, the usual proscription against taking up residence in a predominantly non-Muslim nation is no longer necessary because the original *ratio legis* (*'illa*)—that Muslims are thereby prevented from observing their religious duties—lapses.

The Council is often expected to speak in one voice on behalf of American Muslims as a collectivity. This is particularly true in regard to concerns of national security, in which American Muslims become implicated by the actions of overseas militants from Muslim-majority countries. To commemorate the first anniversary of the 9/11 attacks, the FCNA issued a strongly worded statement on August 29, 2002, the first part of which stated:

> The Fiqh [juristic] Council of North America reiterates its earlier, repeated, unequivocal and unqualified condemnation of the destruction and violence committed against innocent men and women on September 11, 2001. This condemnation is deeply rooted in true Islamic values based on the Qur'anic instructions which consider the unjust killing of a single person equivalent to the killing of all humanity (Quran, 5:32). It also forbids destruction and mischief on earth (Quran, 28:77, 83). This violence is contrary to the authentic universal core message of peace, love, tolerance and mutual cooperation taught by Islam and all of God's Prophets.... The Council supports bringing the perpetrators of this violence to justice before a competent court of law and in accordance with due process of law.[10]

The council issued another trenchant denunciation of terrorism in the aftermath of the London bombings on July 7, 2005. The edict affirmed that:

> Islam strictly condemns religious extremism and the use of violence against innocent lives. There is no justification in Islam for extremism or terrorism. Targeting civilians' life and property through suicide bombings or any other method of attack is haram or forbidden—and those who commit these barbaric acts are criminals, not "martyrs."[11]

The fatwa went on to assert that Muslims are forbidden to associate with any individual or group involved in terrorism or violence, and that Muslims have a "civic and religious duty to cooperate with law enforcement authorities to protect the lives of all civilians."[12] These legal opinions expressing solidarity with fellow citizens not on the basis of shared religion but on the basis of shared values and the notion of the common good emanate from *fiqh al-aqalliyat* reasoning, which is fundamentally concerned with creating moral relationships between Muslim and non-Muslim citizens in non-Muslim-majority societies.

KARAMAH: MUSLIM WOMEN LAWYERS FOR HUMAN RIGHTS

Karama is another US-based nonprofit organization, albeit less well known than the FCNA. It is concerned with the legal rights of American Muslims and particularly of Muslim women. *Karamah* in Arabic means "dignity," and refers to Qur'an verse 17:70, which reads: "We have given dignity to the Children of Adam." The organization was founded in 1991 by Azizah al-Hibri, a law professor and scholar of Islam at the University of Richmond in Washington, D.C. The organization's mission statement emphasizes that:

> Through education, legal outreach, and advocacy, Karamah contributes to the understanding and promotion of human rights worldwide, particularly the rights of Muslim women under Islamic and civil law.... We believe that through education, women will be empowered to transform archaic, culture-based interpretations of women's status in Islam, to the betterment of themselves and their communities.[13]

Since 2003, Karamah has launched a program of intensive educational workshops in the United States and abroad that offer courses on the gender-equitable principles of Islamic law and help participants to acquire skills in leadership and conflict resolution. In addition to these educational programs, Karamah has also created a network of Muslim women jurists, lawyers, and community leaders who contribute to what the organization calls "equitable Islamic legal scholarship." The organization has established a solid reputation in the Washington D.C. area and is often consulted on legal matters pertaining to Islam by various branches of the US government and foreign governments as well as by academics, the media, and many human rights organizations.

As an organization fundamentally concerned with Muslim women's rights, Karamah has done pioneering work in the field of Islamic family law, especially in the context of American society. One of the issues with which it has been concerned is the Muslim marriage contract and some of its stipulations, for which there are no parallels in secular western law. Primary among these stipulations is the *mahr/sadaq*, which refers to the wife's bridal gift or dower paid by to her by the husband. Study and interpretation of mahr serves as an excellent example of new directions in legal ijtihad being undertaken by Muslim scholars in the American context.

The majority of classical Muslim jurists have regarded the dower as an automatic feature of the marriage contract. In the event that a dower is not stipulated, the wife is still entitled to a "proper dower," based on the assessment of her peers and her individual standing. Usually the dower is divided into a part immediately payable upon marriage (this can be a token amount) and a part deferred to a later specified date or more commonly payable on the termination of the marriage by death or divorce. Written marriage documents thus routinely include mention of the dower arrangements. In the United States, many mosques and imams include a fill-in-the-blank provision in standard marriage contracts. A survey of Muslim marriage litigation cases in the United States reveals that Muslims customarily include mahr/sadaq provisions in their marriage contracts, which tend to vary according to the financial status and personal preferences of the parties (Quraishi and Vogel 2009).[14]

The idea of particularizing one's Islamic marriage contract is gaining attention among American Muslims. Encouraged by Muslim women's organizations and activists that see the use of additional stipulations (such as the right to work outside the home or forbidding the husband from taking a second wife) as a tool for women's empowerment, more and more women are educating themselves about how to use the Muslim marriage contract. Far from considering it a new reformist feminist tool, many see the proactive use of the Islamic marriage contract as a way of protecting their basic Islamic rights.[15]

On account of the importance of this matter particularly for Muslim women, Karamah has undertaken the task of creating a model marriage contract, grounded in classical Islamic legal principles, to be used by Muslims worldwide. The potential of the Islamic marriage contract, which provides a perfectly legitimate albeit under-utilized jurisprudential tool to protect and improve the rights of married women, is being increasingly recognized and hailed as a contemporary tool to effect women's empowerment. Use of the contract stipulations of course presumes that the woman has the necessary education and awareness to resort to it. This is why Karamah, among other women's activist organizations, stresses the need for Muslim women to educate themselves concerning their rights within marriage and particularly in reference to the marriage contract, in whose stipulations they can play a key role in order to safeguard their shariʿa-based rights.

The Shura Council of the Women's Initiative for Spirituality and Equality

The activities of the WISE Shura Council, based within the organization American Society for Muslim Advancement (ASMA), are also worthy of note. The Shura Council is composed primarily of Muslim women scholars. Not necessarily trained as jurists or specialists in Islamic law but more broadly trained in Islamic studies, these scholars can read and interpret primary texts. The mission statement states that the Shura Council was established with the following aims in view:

> To serve as a global and inclusive council of Muslim women scholars, activists, and specialists that will: engage with issues of social injustice against Muslim women through critical review and interpretations of legal and religious texts and practices; disseminate these interpretations around the world and, in doing so, re-establish women's authority in religious discourse; as supported by the pluralism inherent in Islam, to enable women to make dignified and autonomous choices; develop a variety of training programs, both short-term intensive and long-term, in order to equip women with expertise in the Islamic legal and ethical traditions.[16]

Like those of the FCNA, members of the WISE Shura Council have issued legal edicts against terrorism and violence against women on the basis of shariʿa/fiqh reasoning and have affirmed their commitment to gender equality primarily on the basis of the Qur'an and reliable hadith. This has often entailed critiquing classical juridical and exegetical discourses on the topic. The WISE Shura Council uses bold and innovative legal reasoning within scriptural and classical shari'a parameters (emphasizing particularly the maqasid al-shari'a). It also bases its interpretations on historical research and social science data is particularly displayed in the position paper they produced seeking to establish the permissibility of adoption in Islamic law, further discussed below.

In its preamble, the position paper states the necessity of revisiting the classical juridical position on the legality of adoption and urges new ijtihad on the topic of adoption, given the urgent need worldwide to provide families for orphaned children. The paper then goes on to compare *kafalah*, a system of guardianship prevalent in Muslim-majority societies, which allows a child to be brought up by a family without the rights and responsibilities of a biological child—that is, without inheritance rights and transference of family name. Through a comprehensive and meticulous treatment of the two primary sources of fiqh—Qur'an and sunna—as well as appealing to the scholarly consensus on the objectives of the law, the council concluded that "instead of banning adoption, Islam has brought some ethical restrictions to the process, condemning dissimulation and foregrounding compassion, transparency, and justice in the treatment of orphaned children." The document argues that adoption of a child in countries where adoption is the law of the land can be justified under Islamic law, as long as certain ethical guidelines are followed, such as prevention of the usurpation of the property of the orphan child when applicable and suppression of information about the child's biological parents, practices specifically condemned in the Qur'an. Furthermore, the six objectives and fundamental principles of the shari'a—which emphasize the protection of life (*al-nafs*), mind (*al-'aql*), family (*al-nasl*), wealth (*al-mal*), dignity (*al-'ird*), and religion (*al-din*)— when applied to contemporary circumstances would support full adoption rights for children. Thus the first principle that upholds the protection and promotion of life can be particularly applicable to children who are growing up in institutions or on the street and who are therefore more vulnerable to physiological and psychological harm than children who are being reared in a stable family environment. Classical jurists have in fact maintained that taking in a foundling can literally mean saving a human life. Beyond protecting life in the physical sense, this principle also promotes quality of life and encourages self-realization—that is, the achievement of a human being's full potential in all areas of life.[17]

This innovative position paper, affirming the permissibility of adoption particularly in western countries where full adoption of children exists, has been disseminated in the United States and in Muslim-majority societies. It serves to establish a new precedent for women scholars of Islam exercising their right to ijtihad, particularly in matters deemed critical to women and the family.

CONCLUSION

It has been argued that western Muslim scholars are leading the way toward legal reform within Islam because they can work and disseminate their scholarship in relative safety (this is not to discount the severity of vilification directed at a number of American Muslim scholars who teach and write on the subject of Islamic law in the American academy and outside of it). All the organizations described here maintain close links with Muslim scholars and jurists in the Islamic heartlands, so that knowledge of their work does not remain circumscribed within American Muslim circles. Their efforts win both plaudits and criticism from overseas scholars. Karamah and WISE, working specifically on matters related to women's rights, have sometimes been criticized for being too "modernist" and influenced by western secular feminism. Other respondents, however, have embraced their activism and juridical interpretations as valid and responsible instances of ijtihad by learned scholars, both women and men. These consciously forged connections between American Muslim scholars and Muslim scholars in the heartlands allow for better awareness of each other's work and augur important synergies that may have far-reaching implications for Islamic law and its application in the twenty-first century.

NOTES

1. See generally Hashim Kamali, *Shari'ah Law: An Introduction* (Oxford UK: Oneworld Publications, 2008); Wael Hallaq, *Shari'a: Theory, Practice, Transformations* (Cambridge, UK: Cambridge University Press, 2009).
2. Khaled Abou El Fadl, *Speaking in God's Name: Islamic Law, Authority and Women* (Oxford, UK: Oneworld Publications, 2001): 32.
3. For a comprehensive study of natural law within Islam, see Anver Emon, Islamic Natural Law Theories (Oxford, UK: Oxford University Press, 2010)
4. Wael Hallaq, "Was the Gate of *Ijtihād* Closed?" *International Journal of Middle East Studies* 18 (1986): 427–454.
5. John Esposito, *Women in Muslim Family Law* (Syracuse, NY: Syracuse University Press, 2001)
6. Albert Hourani, *Arabic Thought in the Liberal Age, 1798–1939* (Cambridge, Eng.: Cambridge University Press, 1983), 145–150.
7. The online brochure is available at www.fiqhcouncil.org/sites/default/files/FCNABrochure.pdf. This statement occurs on p. 2. (Last accessed November 5, 2012.)
8. Available at http://fiqhcouncil.org/node10 (Last accessed on August 31, 2012.)
9. Ibid.
10. www.alhewar.org/SEPTEMBER11/statement_of_the_fiqh_council.htm (Last accessed on November 5, 2012.)
11. Available at http://fiqhcouncil.org/node40 (Last accessed on August 31, 2012.)
12. Ibid.

13. Available at http://karamah.org/about/vision-and-mission (Last accessed August 31, 2012.)
14. Asifa Quraishi and Frank Vogel. *The Islamic Marriage Contract: Case Studies in Islamic Family Law* (Cambridge, MA: Harvard Series in Islamic Law, 2009).
15. Asifa Quraishi and Najeeba Syeed Miller, "The Muslim Family in the USA: Law in Practice." in *Women's Rights and Islamic Family Law: Perspectives on Reform*, edited by Lynn Welchman (London: Zed Books, 2004).
16. Available at http://www.wisemuslimwomen.org/about/shuracouncil/#background (Last accessed on November 5, 2012.)
17. Position paper "Adoption and the Care of Orphan Children: Islam and the Best Interests of the Child"; available at http://www.wisemuslimwomen.org/images/activism/Adoption_(August_2011)_Final.pdf

REFERENCES

Abou El Fadl, Khaled, *Speaking in God's Name: Islamic Law, Authority and Women* (Oxford, UK: Oneworld Publications, 2001).
Emon, Anver M, *Islamic Natural Law Theories* (Oxford, UK: Oxford University Press, 2010).
Esposito, John, *Women in Muslim Family Law* (Syracuse, NY: Syracuse University Press, 2001).
Hallaq, Wael, "Was the Gate of *Ijtihād* Closed?" *International Journal of Middle East Studies* 18 (1986): 427–454.
——, *Sharī'a: Theory, Practice, Transformations* (Cambridge, UK: Cambridge University Press, 2009).
Kamali, Hashim, *Shari'ah Law: An Introduction* (Oxford UK: Oneworld Publications, 2008).
Quraishi, Asifa, and Frank Vogel. *The Islamic Marriage Contract: Case Studies in Islamic Family Law* (Cambridge, MA: Harvard Series in Islamic Law, 2009).
——and Najeeba Syeed Miller, "The Muslim Family in the USA: Law in Practice." in *Women's Rights and Islamic Family Law: Perspectives on Reform*, edited by Lynn Welchman (London: Zed Books, 2004).

CHAPTER 11

··

MUSLIM WOMEN IN THE UNITED STATES

··

KATHLEEN M. MOORE

STILL picking up the pieces from the aftermath of the strongest tornado on record to hit New York City,[1] the people of Brooklyn might not have anticipated the perfect storm that was about to descend on their borough's education system in the fall of 2007. A confluence of forces drastically aggravated an already troubled wellspring of post-9/11 anxieties. The Khalil Gibran International Academy, the city's first Arabic-English dual language school, opened with the ambitious goal of preparing its elementary school students to succeed in an increasingly global society by providing a multicultural curriculum and intensive language instruction. Yet in its first year, the academy encountered hardship and trials from which it would never fully recover. A high-profile "Stop the Madrassah" rally brought dozens of protesters to the steps of City Hall to voice objections to the curriculum and demand that the school be closed. At the center of the maelstrom was the academy's founding principal, Debbie Almontaser, an American Muslim woman of Yemeni background. Forced to resign only a few weeks before the academy opened, Almontaser was branded in the tabloids, on blogs, and on radio talk shows a "9/11 denier" and a "jihadist" who secretly planned to proselytize her students.[2] In spite of her hard-won reputation among New York City's interfaith stakeholders as a Muslim moderate, her opponents succeeded in a matter of days in recasting her image to that of a terrorist.[3]

Anti-Islamic populism, in the United States as well as much of Europe, has set the tone and shaped the narrative for a divisive national debate about the Muslim presence in the West, deploying certain tropes about Muslim women. In the first decade of the twenty-first century, popular media representations of Muslim women swathed in black from head to toe created the impression that being female and Muslim was a particularly somber affair, involving patriarchal oppression and conformity to type. Social understandings of Islam and women have been consumed by narrow,

reductionist views, propagated through a widening range of popular-oriented publications designed either to mitigate or intensify the fears that Muslims and their
religious devotion constitute a "fifth column" in American society.[4] Some of the same
backers of the Stop the Madrassah coalition also organized the Jihad Watch and the
Stop the Islamization of America (SIOA) groups of anti-Muslim activists who attempt
to vilify Islam through various means, including paid advertisements designed to
expose what they consider to be the greatest threats posed by Islam. In 2010, SIOA
paid for advertising on New York City cabs of an "honor killing awareness" campaign, contending that Muslim women who rejected Muslim values and became "too
Americanized" were at risk of extreme family and community condemnation, even
death.[5] These ads exploited one of the most overused themes in American politicized discourse about Islam by fixating on the Muslim woman[6] who must renounce
her religion, culture, and even family before being able to access the universal good
of gender equality and freedom. This narrative of victimhood portrays the western
woman as emancipated by comparison and thus able to offer rescue.[7]

Elaboration of the difference between Islam and the West often centers on the status of women. While questions of gender and women's status in Islam have a long and
complex history, they have taken on a particularly vociferous tone since the attacks
of September 11, 2001. Women have found themselves at the center of contestations
about their identities and their faith, both among Muslims and between Muslims and
non-Muslims. In the process, polarized debates have brought into the mainstream
the concept that the cruel oppression of women is the signature trademark of a radicalized Islam that seeks to impose its will on the world. For women and scholars of
Islam in North America, there is a hidden yet ever-present demand to "answer" the
negative public concern about women's status in Islam, an unarticulated expectation
that has shaped the field of North American Islamic studies. For more than a century,
western perceptions of Islam as necessarily inimical to women's rights has made the
status of women in Muslim societies into a pronounced litmus test of Muslims' ability
to "modernize" (Hammer, 2012: 5; Elouafi 2010). These gender issues are also of concern for the US government in its quest to ally with the "moderate" Muslim. While the
effects of this may be fairly obvious—generalizations about Islam and Muslim women
have been constructed, internalized, and deployed in American media, education,
and other public spheres—changes within and among American Muslim communities may be less so. The furor created by anti-Muslim activists and new media polemi-
cists who argue that Islam is not a religion but instead is an expansionist drive toward
global theocracy has successfully, if inadvertently, diverted attention from the steps
that have brought together strands of feminist thought and engaged Muslim gender
critique, which have led to the emergence of a range of Islamic feminisms.[8]

Many intellectuals, activists, and community members paved the way for these new
kinds of feminisms. Yet the formulation and negotiation of gender in intra-Muslim
debates and observances, not to mention their translation into action, have not been
adequately assessed as yet in the scholarship on North American Islam. Only recently

have scholars begun to consider the particular dynamics of interpretive activity, representation, and context. Discussions of gender in Islam have been given significance in contemporary Muslim thought, raising questions of authority, tradition, Islamic law, social organization, and justice, such that gender "has become part of mainstream discourses among Muslims worldwide rather than the concern of a few privileged or activist women" (Hammer, 2012: 11). The entrance of more women into the field of religious scholarship explains this turn to questions of gender and sexuality and has begun to change the way we understand the formation of Islamic knowledge. As one scholar suggests, "if you are a female Muslim academic writing on and talking about Islam, particularly in the West, sooner or later the conversation will inevitably turn to gender issues" (Afsaruddin 2010: 111). It is this input that has been responsible in recent years for reinstating women in dominant narratives. What once was presumed to be generically true of Muslim women until only recently—the lack of agency, free will, and voice in key events in Islamic history and intellectual heritage—has begun to be refuted by current scholarship.[9] Since at least the 1990s, what it means to be Muslim and female has become an increasingly popular subject for both academic and popular analyses.

The academic field of North American Islam has turned not only toward gender and sexuality as a focus of inquiry but has also taken a discursive turn in framing research on Islam and women, asking the question, "How are women located in terms of the dominant tropes?" The field is looking at notions of moral agency and gender construction in a way that enriches the analysis of the social production of conditions in "the diaspora," which means that a new generation of scholars has centered attention on how a feminist discourse has emerged as a set of practices, a disposition, and a specific cultural and social condition. Through this lens we begin to see how the various forms of self-understanding and religious practice are envisaged and develop in a diasporic context and how the reality of being an American Muslim woman is discursively constructed through what is attributed to it or how it is classified while also taking into consideration the localized dynamics and transnational ties and connections.

Much of the current discourse about gender and Islam is locked into a set of binary oppositions between the Muslim woman and the western woman, or Islam and the West, as if these were clear-cut and mutually exclusive categories. Recent scholarship has begun to soften up the polarity in various ways by looking at how Muslims engage resources that are local and from elsewhere to grapple with domestic challenges of life, collectively and singly. Generally these arguments are in agreement that what makes an identity, practice, or interpretation "Islamic" is not necessarily its congruence with some broadly accepted standard of orthodoxy or orthopraxy but its reference to the ongoing series of debates that constitute Islam as a living tradition. This raises interesting questions: What kind of public interventions do American Muslim women make in the contemporary American environment? How do they negotiate conflicting norms of gender and sexuality at a time of heightened security concerns?

Let's begin exploring these by looking at three important areas of American life for Muslim women that are often contested and defy the common stereotypes: contested discourses, women's public leadership, and the law.

CONTESTED DISCOURSES

Any exploration of gender practices needs to take account of the political and discursive constraints that have inflected popular and scholarly debates about feminism and Islam in the contemporary era. Current attitudes about whether Muslims or Islam ought to be conceived of as the central enemy in the global war on terror, or as the "bad other to liberalism and progress" (Calhoun, 2003: 531), have colored the larger climate in which conversations about and between Muslims take place. Formations of American Muslim solidarity (as fractious as they are[10]) around events like the Arab/Israeli wars, the Iranian Revolution, the Gulf War, 9/11, and, most recently, the "Arab Spring" have important social and religious implications that have put women in a treacherous position. That is, American Muslim women all too often are caught between the proverbial "rock and a hard place" created on the one hand by the (external) homogenizing tendencies of anti-Islamic populism—speaking in a pernicious manner about Muslims and Islam—and on the other the (internal) traditionalism found within dominant constructs of "the Muslim community" in which gender practices become essential in defining the (presumed) incompatibility between American and Muslim culture. The intense post-9/11 scrutiny of Muslims left little room for internal conflict and dissent about core issues of social existence and community cohesion; even in inward-focused discussions, self-censorship is not an unfamiliar resolution to the dilemma many women face.

Yet the reductive representations of Muslim women throughout US society—in the media, education, government, and popular culture—have inspired a great deal of discussion, since 9/11 in particular, among Muslims—mosqued and unmosqued alike—about Islamic perspectives on family and marriage, gender relations, and women's rights and responsibilities. As has happened in many faith communities under stress,[11] young Muslims faced with these images in their daily lives have turned to Islamic teachings to learn Islamic perspectives, equipping themselves to respond to ambiguities and critics within broader society. Muslim campus organizations have stocked their tables with pamphlets about women in Islam, and conferences, attended by Muslims and non-Muslims alike, have had many panels on gender issues. Men and women have taken questions about Islam and women to heart and have defined it as their religious duty to counter negative information in their public work and offer a gender-egalitarian rendition of Islam.

In arenas of debate and celebration, American Muslim women—whether religiously observant, secularist, or somewhere in between—have reflected on the circumstances for Muslim women in the United States. Ideas and practices fashioned from Islamic materials have probed far deeper into cultural tropes than ever before, and different kinds of arguments, both by and about Muslim women, have become a part of the contestations over the presence of Islam in the United States. For instance, many organizations have taken up the topic of Islamic models for womanhood from viewpoints that range from conservative to progressive. Others, which have made cultural literacy their primary mission, actively encourage Muslim women to build relationships with non-Muslims in order to counter prejudice and discrimination (see e.g., Islamic Networks Group at http://www.ing.org/index.php).

In the 1950s, when books about Muslims in America began to appear, Muslims were advised to adopt a traditional view of women's roles; in subsequent decades, American Muslim leaders who favored a more traditional model of Islamic life continued to teach and preach the importance of conforming to traditional values, including the exclusion of Muslim women from community affairs (Haddad, Smith, and Moore, 2006: 147–148). Some, including Lamya al-Faruqi—a specialist in Islamic art who was murdered along with her husband, Temple University professor Ismail al-Faruqi in 1986—have provided an overview from a conservative understanding of the role of women. The Faruqis argued that the goals of feminism are specific to western culture, are hostile to religion, and thus are not relevant for Muslim women (Haddad, Smith, and Moore, 2006: 149). However, at the opposite end of the spectrum a small but growing number of Muslim women have represented a more nuanced understanding of Islam. These women saw themselves as Muslims who may or may not observe all of the ritual requirements of the faith and researched and wrote about women's issues in Islam in a way that was not conditioned by the doctrinal or methodological requirements formulated by medieval jurists. Included among these women is Riffat Hassan, an early prominent female Muslim academic in the United States who interpreted the Qur'an as a text affirming the equality of men and women. Hassan wrote several articles and chapters in the 1970s, 1980s, and 1990s on the liberation that could be achieved through a feminist theology and the formulation of a Muslim feminist hermeneutics. Like feminists in the Muslim world, such as Fatima Mernissi, Hassan insisted that the position of women in society was determined by social causes and not religion. Like Mernissi, she saw Islamization to be taking hold overseas and, in response, wrote on the traditions in order to bring about social change from within. Such women influenced a later generation of scholars who became convinced that it is crucial for women to participate in the creation of Islamic knowledge. Their questions were far-reaching in their implications regarding wider forms of inquiry and contesting the dominant discourses about male control over the making of meaning and women's status in Islam.

In the first decades of the twenty-first century, research on American Muslim women's agency, theory, practices and methods of Islamic interpretation began to make rapid strides. Beginning with ethnographic work on the experiences and viewpoints of first-generation women—those who were directly involved in adapting to significant change and forming new identities—this genre related the stories of American Muslim women who either were immigrants coping with assimilation or were new converts to Islam (e.g., Anway, 1996; Van Nieuwkerk, 2006). This was soon followed by works that documented an array of voices by a generation of American Muslim women under age 40 who have never lived without Islam but have been raised outside of Muslim majority countries. For these women neither Islam nor western models of feminism are alien influences (e.g., Abdul-Ghafur, 2005; Hasan, 2002; Ebrahimji and Suratwala, 2011; Webb, 2000). The next step of this scholarship illuminated the various ways in which female authority is currently being reconstituted and the productive tensions between embodying patriarchal norms and subverting them (e.g., Ahmed, 2011; Badran, 2009; Hammer, 2012). This trajectory has added richness and different perspectives to the literature on American Muslim women, since the focus is on women not merely as transmitters but as *producers* of Islamic knowledge. Some of these women scholar/activists have argued that the Qur'an and Islamic jurisprudence can both liberate and empower women (e.g., Wadud, 2006; Ali, 2006; Hidayatullah, 2009; Ali, Hammer and Silvers, 2012).

The Qur'an, for many of these women, is not seen as an inflexible and unchanging source of patriarchy but as open to different interpretations that address the exigencies of changing times and circumstances. By recovering the past, they are keen to point out that one perception of womanhood should not be privileged above others. This type of discourse, called progressive reformism, is familiar to students of modern Islamic history. It calls for a reformulation of Islamic practice and belief based on a reengagement with the primary sources of Islam (Barzegar, 2011: 534). The product of decades of work by reformers throughout the Islamic world, the core message of this approach is that men and women should be able to read Islamic texts independently, freeing themselves from conventional interpretive authorities in order to comprehend and transform significant parts of the tradition to fit their circumstances. In the United States, gender equality and sexual ethics are common themes of this trend. In 2005, the mixed-gender Friday congregational prayer led by Amina Wadud represents reformist thought and brought the discourse to the public's attention (Hammer, 2012: 13–35; Barzegar, 2011: 535). What makes this trend characteristically *reformist* is precisely its alienation from imposing structures and institutions of the North American Muslim communities, such as mosques, Islamic centers, religious schools, or conventional Muslim-American organizations, which typically generate and dominate the conversation of "organized" Islam. Instead, the progressive reformists' dialogue is maintained in newly formed, sometimes alternative community organizations, advocacy groups, and cyberspace networks, often housed in North American and European universities and nurtured by significant transnational connections (Barzegar, 2011: 536.).[12] Whether it is in attempts to reengage with scriptural sources, to rethink and perform Islamic rituals such as congregational prayer, or to claim religious and communal authority, the reformists are in constant conversation with their immediate surroundings and interlocutors. Thus

American Muslim men and women who pursue a focus on gender issues in the conceptualization of faith do so within a complicated matrix of influences and must address not only the ways in which women have been represented in the media but also the intra-Muslim debates simultaneously shaped by transnational projects and networks and negotiated through the particular histories, circumstances, and intellectual trends of American society. What they hold in common is the conviction that Islam is eternally valid at all moments in history but that it contains an inherent flexibility that allows it to change (Haddad, Smith, and Moore, 2006: 154).

It is not surprising that for many Muslims in the United States who consider themselves to be more traditional in their interpretation of Islam, the discourse of progressive reformism is viewed with suspicion. The concern is that Muslim scholars, in criticizing Islamic traditions, may be reinforcing the growing anti-Islamic attitudes of the American public. These scholars are accused of, and rejected for, adopting western discourses and modes of critique. When Muslim feminists say they are not questioning the validity of the Qur'an but only the exclusively male interpretation of it, they engender misgivings from those who believe that their intentions are destroying community consensus. Yet the efforts toward a "gender jihad" are designed to open discourse as well as practice about the possibility of individual interpretation, creating an attractive alternative to the specter of dogmatic traditionalism with its patriarchal overtones on the one hand and the unwanted secular aspects of feminism on the other.

WOMEN'S LEADERSHIP

Organizational Leadership

Another noticeable change after 9/11 is the pronounced appearance of Muslim women in the American public square. Impelled by increased surveillance and the potential for backlash, men began to keep a low profile, thus creating the opportunity for women to move to the forefront and assume responsibilities for administering important Islamic institutions (Haddad, 2011: 89–90). Women have become spokespersons for their communities, raised funds for victims of 9/11, and marched in protest over deportations and surveillance authorized under the USA Patriot Act and anti-Muslim discrimination. They have written op-ed pieces and have become media professionals, pursued careers in human and civil rights, and established advocacy groups to fight for Muslims' rights. In 2001, for the first time in its history, the Islamic Society of North America (ISNA) elected a woman, Ingrid Mattson, to serve as vice president, and later president (2006–2010) of the organization, bringing her into the ranks of national leadership. To these examples others could be added.

Yet like many other American women, Muslim women continue to encounter the "glass ceiling," or the unseen yet unbreakable barrier that keeps them from reaching upper-level positions in the Muslim public sphere. In a word, in the world of American Muslim advocacy and service organizations, the organizational structure is gendered. A Gallup poll conducted in 2009 shows that American Muslim women are among the most highly educated female religious groups in the United States (second only to Jewish women) and are as likely as American Muslim men to say that they hold a professional job (Gallup International, 2009: 56). Yet surprisingly few women have served as top executives of national American Muslim organizations.[13] Notable exceptions include the aforementioned Dr. Ingrid Mattson, and also Dr. Azizah al-Hibri, the founding executive director of Karamah: Muslim Women Lawyers for Human Rights, and Farhana Khera, the founding executive director of Muslim Advocates, two smaller American Muslim advocacy organizations that are staffed almost entirely by women. In contrast, two Arab American organizations—the American-Arab Anti-Discrimination Committee (ADC) and the Arab American Institute (AAI)—have had a long history of women's involvement in their hierarchies. These two organizations focus on defending Arab Americans from discrimination and bias, including but not limited to Arab Muslims. The ADC's national board of directors has included women since its beginning in 1980. The AAI's president (it has had only one) is male, but the executive director, Maya Berry, is a woman who grew up in Dearborn, Michigan. Its affiliate organization, the AAI Foundation, has been presided over by a woman since its inception in 1996. Other prominent women in the history of the ADC include former president Hala Maksoud (1996–2000) and the former ADC communications director Laila al-Qatami, who was often the public face of ADC in international and national media. Controversy over the ADC's handling of sexual harassment allegations involving the ADC Michigan director led some to protest the national organization's "failure to act" for over a decade while women complained of repeated violations (Hicks 2013: 1). Yet, in spite of the fallout from this incident, there is little evidence to suggest that gender is a particularly significant impediment at either ADC or AAI. But for two of the largest Muslim American organizations—the Council on American Islamic Relations (CAIR) and the Muslim Public Affairs Council (MPAC)—the picture is more complex. Women have never occupied the executive leadership at the national level of either of these organizations, although in the case of MPAC, Edina Lekovic recently became the director of policy and programming (she was formerly the communications director), and a handful of other positions (e.g., development coordinator, youth leadership coordinator) have been held by women in this decade. As of this writing, CAIR, on the other hand, lists no women on its website among its "key staff" and only one woman on its national board of directors; very few women have ever served in these capacities since CAIR's founding in 1994. The situation is different, though, at CAIR's chapter offices, where women serve in a range of capacities. One scholar notes that in his interviews with current and former employees of CAIR, he found that the role of women in the organization generally was described as "controversial" or "in flux," and there seemed to be ongoing tensions about the role of women outside the home and appropriate contact between women and men (Love, 2011: 96–97). An American Muslim female law professor observes that the "legacy groups"—those founded before 9/11—remain dominated by men, which has meant that many of the Muslim women entering the legal profession post-9/11 "decide their efforts and skills are most productively spent starting new organizations where they can focus on substantive work rather than fight internal gender battles" (Choo, 2013).

Muslim women in America, however, are actively engaged in public affairs. Many organizations, organized and staffed by American Muslim women at local, state, and national levels, provide social services, including financial aid for education, referrals for domestic violence services, and shelter services for the homeless, such as the Muslim Women's Resource Center, started in 2001 by executive director Sima Quraishi (http://www.mwrcnfp.org/), and the American Muslim Women's Association (Arizona) (http://www.amwaaz.org/). Others are primarily advocacy or activist organizations, such as Karamah, the Muslim Women's League (http://www.mwlusa.org), and the Women's Islamic Initiative in Spirituality and Equality (WISE) (http://www.wisemuslimwomen.org/activism/). These organizations have provided an arena in which to discuss the interpretation of scripture and tradition, to confront prejudice, and to raise awareness. There are too many to list here. However, Table 11.1 is a chart with a selection of the 501(c)(3) nonprofit organizations that have been founded by and for Muslim women in the United States.

Many women's biographies could be added here. An example is Shareefa Alkhateeb (1946–2004) and the Peaceful Families Project (PFP), a nonprofit organization she

Table 11.1 Nonprofit Organizations by and for American Muslim Women

Name	Date Founded
The Sisters' Wing of the Islamic Circle of North America (ICNA)	1978
International League of Muslim Women	1984
Muslim Women United (Richmond, Virginia)	1989
Muslim Women's League	1992
Women in Islam	1992
Rahima Foundation	1993
Karamah: Muslim Women Lawyers for Human Rights	1993
Peaceful Families Project	2000
Muslim Women Resource Center (Illinois)	2001
Muslim Advocates	2005
Women's Islamic Initiative in Spirituality and Equality (WISE)	2006

founded in 2000, which itself evolved out of an earlier organization led by Alkhateeb, the North American Council of Muslim Women (NACMW). In its first four years PFP provided workshops across the country that raised awareness of domestic violence issues, developing victim resources in many Muslim communities, and cultural sensitivity training modules for non-Muslim service providers and professionals working with a Muslim clientele. Its stated goal is "to promote attitudes and beliefs that emphasize justice, freedom from oppression, and family harmony." A catalyst for the growth of domestic violence services at the grassroots level, PFP's activities sometimes result in the creation of new organizations that are independent of mosque leadership, as well as service groups under the auspices of local mosques and Islamic centers. In a speech she delivered before a gathering of imams and community leaders on Christmas Eve 2001, Alkhateeb related how, when many Muslims hear a battered wife complain, they resort to a hadith about concealing the faults of a Muslim and another about keeping private the intimate things of the household. Entitled "Who Has the Right to Save Muslim Women from Abuse?" the speech relies on references to the life of the Prophet Muhammad and the Qur'an to suggest a model for marital counseling. Alkhateeb lays the blame on the Muslim community for keeping quiet in the face of growing signs of domestic violence; she says that the Qur'an (Q4:148) empowers the community to speak out about all forms of injustice, including spousal abuse. In conclusion she says,

> The Imam or community leader or friend is not a traitor to the Muslim community by helping the family—that person is helping to save the family from extinction and disgrace and is helping to reestablish a peaceful family that can raise children who are happy and consequently will want to be Muslim and to remain connected to the peaceful Muslim community. Who has the right to save battered Muslim women? The answer is: everyone in the Muslim community.
>
> (Alkhateeb 2002: 20)

Mosque Participation

While more leadership roles in organizational life have been claimed by Muslim women, female participation in American mosques remains relatively low. It still is the case that mosques are often filled with men on Fridays; Ihsan Bagby reports that fully three-quarters of attendees at Friday Jumu'ah prayers in mosques across the United States are male, while female attendance had risen to only 18 percent by 2011, slightly higher than the 15 percent observed in 2000 (Bagby 2012: 5). This disparity both reflects and contributes to the marginalization of women's roles in the mosque. Moreover, many mosques continue to separate women from the main prayer area by means of a physical barrier such as a divider or a separate room. In 1994 just over half of the mosques in the United States maintained sex-segregated prayer spaces, but by the year 2000 two-thirds of them did so, a figure that had not budged by 2011 (Bagby, 2013: 8). This trend commands attention. Women make up roughly half of the American Muslim population; therefore their presence, contributions, and frequent absence from certain parts of communal worship, organizational leadership, and historical narratives must be clarified in current accounts of American Muslim life.

However, others have considered American mosques to be places where women's participation in community affairs grew. Abdo Elkholy, a sociologist who studied Muslims in Detroit and Toledo in the 1950s, argues that mosques were affirming spaces where women often ran Sunday schools, organized community fundraisers, saw to the administrative needs of the imams, ran youth clubs, organized holiday celebrations, and made purchasing decisions. But the expanded roles of women often came into conflict with new imams and midcentury newcomers, who were likely to judge mosques not by the standards then widely accepted in the United States, where there was a general pattern of increased women's participation in immigrant congregations (Christian, Jewish, and Muslim). Instead, they tended to judge mosques according to the standards of their homelands, where women's participation in mosques was minimal. However, the newly arrived immigrants of the mid-twentieth century gradually adjusted to American Muslim norms, and women attend congregational prayers and serve on governing boards in small but increasing numbers while also influencing the activities of the mosques that are responsible for the maintenance of religious organizations (Howell, 2013: 123). Imam (prayer leader) training in the United States is still relatively rare, although a few institutions (e.g., Hartford Seminary) have created imam and chaplain training programs, "primarily to train prison and military chaplains according to government standards" (Hammer, 2012: 133). Chaplains have been trained not only for prison and military service but also for hospitals, universities, and colleges (Haddad, Smith, and Moore, 2006: 133–136). Women have been enrolled in these programs and their very presence problematizes the position that leadership tasks and areas should be distinguished by gender.

ONLINE ACTIVISM

A direct engagement with international (and secular) conceptions of women's rights is evident on irreconcilably different discursive levels, and deserves attention because "very rarely do we encounter empowering images of American Muslim women" (Abdul-Ghafur, 2005: 3). On the pervasive platform of social media, tirades about Islam and women are increasingly common. Early in 2013, Amina Tyler, a nineteen-year-old Tunisian woman, posted on Facebook a topless photo of herself with the words, in Arabic, "my body is mine, not somebody's honor" scrawled across her bare chest. In Tunisia, where Islamist conservatives have gained ground since the revolution ousted President Zine al-Abadine ben Ali, a Salafi cleric who heads the government's commission on vice condemned Tyler's action as obscene and called for her death by stoning. In response, a Ukranian-based feminist movement, called Femen, upon whose Facebook page Tyler had posted her photo, called for an international "topless jihad day" in front of Tunisian embassies and mosques across Europe and elsewhere on April 4. Later another photo appeared on Femen's Facebook page, of a topless woman protesting in front of a mosque in San Francisco, with the following caption, which can be read as demeaning to Arabs and Muslims: "Today is Amina Topless Jihad Day. I was at the Islamic Mosque in San Francisco. Some Arab guy tried to grab my sign and pushed me in a violent way. My friend stopped him. MY BODY IS MY TEMPLE." Femen leader Inna Shvechenko called this protest tactic the "naked shock troops of feminism," while thousands of exasperated Muslim women uploaded their own photos on the Facebook page "Muslim Women Against Femen," with comments declaring that they could fight for themselves, whether behind the hijab or not. These latter women mounted a counterprotest, Muslimah Pride Day, to represent their own voices on social media, including Facebook and Twitter, to contest the way they were portrayed by Femen and others in the West as helpless and in need of rescue by means of the circulation of offensive and essentializing stereotypes. However, Shevchenko was not convinced, and on *Huffington Post UK* she wrote, "They write on their posters they don't need liberation, but in their eyes it's written 'help me'" (cited in Alpert, 2013).

One finds here the discursive construction of oppressed Muslim women ensconced in this drama of patriarchy and western imperialism. The Muslim woman is perceived as passively indoctrinated (read nonliberated) and, although patriarchy is not specific to Islam, the script of religious oppression and necessary escape for women in search of liberation and self-fulfillment is built around the uncritically liberal position that Islam is irretrievably patriarchal. Yet on the other hand, Muslim women are engaged in grassroots organizing and activism that contests not only internal barriers to women's full participation but also outside forces that exploit the conditions of Muslim women as a justification for western imperialism. Behind this dichotomy of patriarchy/imperialism lies a long history of oversimplified portrayals of Muslim women, which have been used in European and American relations with the Islamic world to justify the superiority of western values and technology and the colonizing mission of Christianity to rescue oppressed and vulnerable women. For many Americans, the overarching symbol of victory in the war against the Taliban and al-Qaeda was to be the image of the Muslim woman throwing off her burqa. In the narratives of anti-Muslim activists in some corners of the United States, the elaboration of differences between the sexes simply reinforces the "clash of civilizations" approach to explain why Islam is inferior, while the question of gender equality in secular American society remains unexamined.

AMERICAN MUSLIM WOMEN IN THE LAW

Muslims in the United States are confronted with the dominant paradigm in liberal democratic theory, based on modern rationality and the privatization of religious practice. This means that family law, including the personal status of women, is viewed officially as an aspect of private religion and is constitutive, categorically, of the (monolithic) Muslim way of life. So, for instance, when women seek to dress in accordance with what they interpret to be Islamic prescriptions about modesty and solidarity, they find themselves caught between prevailing standards that require greater conformity with a secular vision of womanhood and their personal convictions. The phenomenon of wearing hijab in America is problematic not for its numbers but for what it symbolizes. Most Muslim women, in the United States and elsewhere, do not wear hijab, but in the American context the matter has become one of liberty *for* public displays of religiosity and faith, in spite of the small numbers of women concerned.

Contests such as these are nowhere more apparent than in American courts of law. There are divergent views among Muslims about whether Islam requires women to dress in a particular way, and those views are especially pronounced in a religiously diverse and publicly secular culture such as the dominant society in the United States. Many issues about dress codes and similar bans on wearing the hijab in public have been tested in the courts. As indicated above, women in headscarves have become focal points for anti-Muslim sentiments ranging from hate crimes to pushback and discrimination in employment, education, and transportation. We can see the contestation in a landmark ruling which favored Bilan Nur, for example, who sued her employer, Alamo Rent-A-Car, because, while she had been permitted to do so prior to 2001, she was denied permission to cover her head during the month of Ramadan after the 9/11 attacks. The appellate court's ruling in Ms. Nur's favor set an important precedent for working women who dress for religious reasons. Another highly publicized trial is the case of Sultaana Freeman, the Florida resident who wished to have a driver's license not including her photo. One had been granted to her before 2001, but the Florida Department of Motor Vehicles suspended that license and required Ms. Freeman to replace it with a license having a photograph showing her face. The trial court ruled in favor of the state on the basis that while Freeman "most likely poses no threat to national security, there likely are people who would be willing to use a ruling permitting the wearing of a fullface cloak in a driver's license photo by pretending to ascribe to religious beliefs in order to carry out activities that would threaten lives."[14] The state's national security concerns outweighed the individual woman's interest in religious liberty, a ruling that was upheld on appeal.

How personal and professional lives intersect continues to be a complicated area. While religious liberty is a fundamental principle of the US Constitution, the very expression of religious belief evokes consternation when it overlaps with the work environment. When an employee is censored in her religious expression at work, she may bring a lawsuit against her employer for an infringement of her First Amendment rights or for discrimination on the basis of religion, which is prohibited under civil rights laws. Charges of employment discrimination were brought against a large clothing retailer, Abercrombie & Fitch, in one case in which a Muslim woman was fired for wearing the hijab after working for four months in a San Francisco Bay area store, and in another case in which an additional Bay-area store of the company failed to hire a Muslim woman because she wore the hijab to her interview. In Oklahoma in 2011, a jury awarded $20,000 in compensatory damages to a Muslim woman who had not been hired to work at an Abercrombie Kids store because she wore the hijab. The woman had been told that the headscarf violated Abercrombie's trademarked "Look" policy, and the deputy director of the American Civil Liberties Union in Oklahoma said that "Certainly, a headscarf is part and parcel of the Islamic experience."[15] As of this writing, the jury award was still on appeal.

Questions of marriage, divorce, and child custody also bring prescriptions of Islamic law into the courts. Not all stipulations of the religious law are observed or upheld. For instance the traditional stipulation that allows Muslim men to marry up to four wives at one time is not upheld under civil law in the United States because it would contravene the laws of the states. However other regulations, such as those dealing with the payment of a marriage dower (*mahr*), are upheld in American courts of law at times when court officials have struck a balance between the fundamental rights of all and the diverse traditions and religious beliefs of the litigants. Some American Muslim attorneys, such as Azizah al-Hibri, try to help Muslim women understand and protect their rights under Islamic law through careful wording of their marriage contracts. Women's rights in marriage are underutilized, al-Hibri states, and the right to insert conditions into the marriage contract (*nikah*) and modify conventional marital relations are chief among these. Efforts to review and revise guidance on marriage and other social issues for Muslims living in the United States include those of the Fiqh Council of North America.[16]

Studies have shown that the use of Islamic marriage and divorce processes are widespread in the United States, and that for the vast majority of American Muslims there is no incompatibility between using informal Islamic processes and formal state procedures combined to solemnize lawful marriages and divorcing. One important consideration is whether an American court of law should substitute the *mahr* provision of the Islamic marriage contract for the usual provisions of alimony and child support or for the equitable division of marital property called for under state law. A brief discussion of the *mahr* provision in American state courts is provided elsewhere (Haddad, Smith, and Moore, 2006: 113–119), and Julie MacFarlane has provided a book-length treatment of marital conflict in Muslim households in North America and of Islamic marriage and divorce, including the roles of imams and other community leaders in attempting reconciliation and the voices of divorced men and women (2012). MacFarlane gives us personal narratives of women whose sense of religious obligation leads them to accept their imam's efforts to attempt marital counseling, even when they know their marriages are over and they want both a legal and religious divorce. For example, despite feeling that her marriage was over, Sana succumbed to her imam's pressures to attempt reconciliation with her husband. "I was patient, I accepted the process...even though I was frustrated and I knew I wanted a divorce right away," she said (cited in MacFarlane, 2012: 95). After three months, the imam gave the couple permission to divorce. In another instance, a combination of religious principles and personal circumstances influenced the decision to divorce. Kareema had been married for twenty years and had four children. Yet for the last ten years, her husband had lived in the United Arab Emirates, leaving Kareema alone with her children and eventually failing to send her financial support. Despite several efforts to convince her husband over the phone and to pray to God for guidance, Kareema could not get her husband to reconcile, and she asked him, "How can I give you all your rights as your wife, when I'm not taking any of my own rights that Islam gave me?" (MacFarlane, 2012: 99). Seeing no alternative, she asked her imam to contact her husband overseas to request a religious divorce.

The reasons these women give for wanting a divorce in many ways reflect the broader social changes found in American society that affect gender roles and expectations. The economic and social roles of women both within and outside the family sometimes result in marital conflict because of sharp differences over perceived responsibilities and authority within the family and community. Conflicts tend to become worse when there is strong contrast between the expectations and values of the young couple and those of their parents or in-laws (MacFarlane, 2012: 102). Divorces also result when there are different approaches taken by the husband and wife in their religious practices such as prayer and fasting. And finally, domestic violence has been recognized as a serious social problem and a cause of divorce in Muslim families; in roughly one-quarter of Muslim divorces, abuse has played a central role in the breakdown of the marriage (MacFarlane, 2012: 103; Alkhateeb and Abugideiri, 2007).

Today there are many American Muslim women who are lawyers and law professors. Some have rejected the idea that oppression and violence are innate to Islam and have argued that patriarchal tribal and cultural practices, over time, have seeped into Islamic traditions. Certain women maintain that by looking at the scriptural sources with fresh eyes, a new jurisprudence can be developed from a women's and human rights' perspective. The conviction that seems to be shared by nearly all Muslim female lawyers educated in the United States in recent years is the emphasis on independent interpretation, freed from the hold of religious institutions and authorities. Amina Saeed, for example, the cofounder and director of the Muslim Bar Association of Chicago, says her university studies showed her that, "I did not have to blindly accept what I was told about Islam, be it by my parents or a world-renowned scholar." Moreover, learning about the great female leaders in

Islam's history inspired her. "Why should I achieve anything less?" (cited in Choo 2013). In the post-9/11 environment, young Muslim women began to consider pursuing careers in law. Farhana Khera, founder and president of Muslim Advocates, had been a counsel to the US Senate Judiciary Committee before establishing her organization in 2005. Amina Saeed was a thirty-year-old appellate attorney in Chicago; she lost her cousin in the 9/11 attack on the Twin Towers when she was chosen to become the first female director of the Council of Islamic Organizations of Greater Chicago, a federation of more than fifty mosques, schools, and community service groups. And in the San Francisco area, Shirin Sinnar was one of a small number of Muslim law students who joined with a single lawyer to form the Bay Area Association of Muslim Lawyers. Women attorneys have been at the forefront of advocating for Muslims rights in the United States and are challenging stereotypes about women's status in Islam.

Civil cases that affect women in the workplace, in education, the military, transportation, and in marriage and divorce cases, among others, are important because of the cultural generalization that Islam is irremediably patriarchal. There is a religiously driven racial discrimination that has developed particularly in the context of the war on terror, which has no end in sight. The Equal Employment Opportunity Commission reports that more than 20 percent of work-based claims of religious discrimination were against Muslims in 2011, a figure that is on the rise. No single narrative can capture the varied American Muslim female experience with the law. Instead, we see that women are the legal subject at times—for example, in discrimination cases or marital conflict—and at other times are the active agents in using the law to advocate for their rights.

Conclusion

From the preceding we can see that American Muslim women are engaged in producing a viable habitat and ethos; prepared to take on the burdens of place, identity, and history; and ready to work within the locational possibilities and limitations, found and made, that shape human lives. Within a deeply divided American society beset with security anxieties, the experiences and standpoints of American Muslim women may provide us a view of how power operates and how constructive thought and action begin to emerge from current trends. These women are self-critically cognizant of being part of and specifically located within a social world that both constrains and enables practices, where knowing and acting always generate consequences. Living their faith in a situation of minority status makes Muslim women conscious of the meaning and challenges of adhering to their religion.

NOTES

1. C. Moynihan. "Two weeks later, evidence and memories of the tornado remain vivid." *New York Times*, August 23, 2007 (1923–Current File). Available at: http://search.proquest. com/docview/848085632?accountid=14522 (Retrieved May 24, 2013.)

2. Andrea Elliott, "Battle in Brooklyn: A Principal's Rise and Fall; Critics Cost Muslim Educator Her Dream School." *New York Times*, April 28, 2008, p. A1. Available at: http:// www.nytimes.com/2008/04/28/nyregion/28school.html?ei=5070&en=eb31e0ad46ef2 191&ex=1210046400&emc=eta1&pagewanted&_r=0 (Accessed April 25, 2013.). Also, Pamela Geller, cofounder of the "Stop the Madrassah" and the subsequent "Stop the Islamization of America" campaigns, levied personal attacks against Almontaser, calling her "jihad loving" and "a documented Islamist...in the guise of a multicultural educator." Cited in the Anti-Defamation League, "Backgrounder: Stop Islamization of America," September 19, 2012. Available at: http://archive.adl.org/main_Extremism/pamela-geller-s top-islamization-of-america.htm?Multi_page_sections=sHeading_2 (Accessed April 25, 2013.)

3. In March 2010, the Equal Employment Opportunity Commission (EEOC) released a determination letter stating that Almontaser had been discriminated against on the basis of her race, religion, and national origin and that in forcing her resignation, the US Department of Education had "succumbed to the very bias the creation of the school intended to dispel and a small segment of the public succeeded in imposing its prejudices on D.O.E. as an employer" (see Almontaser 2011, p. 52). However, Almontaser was never reinstated to the position and the academy eventually closed in 2011. A lawyer for the Stop the Madrassa Coalition, David Yerushalmi—the same lawyer responsible for drafting the model shari'a ban legislation that swept through the country—said dismissively about the EEOC's determination letter: "I think the EEOC is constitutionally constructed to find discrimination in a high-profile case" (cited in Elliott, "Bias Is Found in City's Ouster of a Principal," *New York Times*, March 13, 2010, p. A1. Available at: http://search.proquest. com.proxy.library.ucsb.edu:2048/nytimes/docview/434331407/13E8F3A1B231617358E/8?a ccountid=14522 (Accessed on April 25, 2013.)

4. Publications mitigating the myth include such titles as John L. Esposito's *The Future of Islam* (New York: Oxford University Press, 2010) and *Unholy War: Terror in the Name of Islam* (New York: Oxford University Press, 2003); publications intensifying the myth include such titles as Daniel Pipes's *Militant Islam Reaches America* (New York: Norton, 2003) and Martin Peretz's "Entry-Level: When America-Haters Become Americans," *New Republic*, October 15. 2001, in which he writes that America houses people who wish to kill us and they are disproportionately located in certain religious and ethnic communities. Available at: http://infoweb.newsbank.com.proxy.library.ucsb.edu:2048/ iw-search/we/InfoWeb?p_product=AWNB&p_theme=aggregated5&p_action=doc&p_ docid=1392530F4A218180&p_docnum=4&p_queryname=2) (Accessed May 13, 2013.)

5. In an interview with World News Daily (WND), a conservative website, SIOA's cofounder Geller said, "Our ad campaigns directed threatened girls to go to LeaveIslamSafely.com, and some Islamic supremacist taxi drivers defaced our signs by cutting out the word 'Leave,' so that the ad read, 'Islamsafely.com.' But not to worry, we bought the URL for that, too." Cited at the Anti-Defamation League, "Backgrounder: Stop Islamization of America," September 19, 2012. Available at: http://archive.adl.org/main_Extremism/pamela-geller-

stop-islamization-of-america.htm?Multi_page_sections=sHeading_2 (Accessed April 25, 2013.)
6. Miriam cooke highlights how inseparable religion and gender have become in European and American discourses about Islam, such that "Muslim" and "woman" have melded as one. In her words the term *muslimwoman* is a label that "reduces all diversity to a single image" and contributes not only to the visibility of Muslim women but to the creation of a "visually enforced collective identity," one that serves as a stereotypical ascription (of patriarchy) and a model of self-identification (cooke, 2007: 140).
7. This in spite of the fact that the Centers for Disease Control estimates that nearly 1,300 deaths occur in the United States each year due to domestic violence, and more than half a million intimate-partner–related injuries require medical attention annually. See National Center for Injury Prevention and Control. "Costs of Intimate Partner Violence Against Women in the United States" (Atlanta, GA: Centers for Disease Control and Prevention, 2003). Available at: http://www.cdc.gov/violenceprevention/pdf/ipvbook-a.pdf (Accessed May 31, 2013.) Second, the appearance of the "honor killing campaign" is a clear indication that the Stop the Islamization of America campaign is greatly influenced by its counterpart, Stop Islamization of Europe (SIOE). In some European countries, questions of honor killings and forced marriages are more common in public debates than we find in the United States.
8. I use the plural form of the word *feminisms* to recognize the multitude of practices and reflections that claim this appellation, including the political and personal work of those activists who do not base their ideals or personal conduct on normative Islam but believe that, in order for social change to take hold and have wide acceptance among Muslims, they must convincingly be presented as compatible with Islam. A voice is "feminist" when it disrupts an ideology of control and symbolic or social structures that marginalize women. With respect to Islamic feminist scholarly analysis, the rich array of arguments and approaches can be characterized broadly as historiographies that develop a body of historical work on the subject of women's movements (e.g., Ahmed 1992; Sonbol 1996) and exegetal studies that reason from within the Islamic scholarly traditions and utilize, challenge, and reinterpret the normative doctrines and juridical sciences (e.g., Wadud 2006; Ali 2006; Ali, Hammer and Silvers 2012). Other scholars use the term *Islamic feminisms*, in the plural, too. Useful overviews of the arguments for and against the use of the term *feminist* can be found in Hammer, 2012: 57–61.
9. While the range of scholarship is too large and varied to list comprehensively here, examples that have excavated a past populated by learned and gifted women who shaped the trajectory of early Islamic history include Asma Sayeed's book *Women and the Transmission of Religious Knowledge in Islam* (Cambridge, UK: Cambridge University Press, 2013); the book of Asma Afsaruddin et al. *Hermeneutics and Honor: Negotiating Female "Public" Space in Islamic/ate Societies* (Cambridge, MA: Harvard University Press, 1999); Leila Ahmed's book *Women and Gender in Islam* (New Haven, CT: Yale University Press, 1992); and Asma Barlas's book *"Believing" Women in Islam: Unreading Patriarchal Interpretations of the Quran* (Austin, TX: University of Texas Press, 2002).
10. Scholars of African American Islam like Sherman Jackson and Aminah Beverly McCloud have indicated the important fracture lines between African American Muslim interests and the interests of immigrant Muslims and their progeny, which deny a strong foundation for a comprehensive solidarity among American Muslims.

Liyakat al-Takim makes a similar point about the Shiʻi-Sunni divisions within important Islamic organizations like the Muslim Student Association (see "A Minority with
Diversity: The Shiʻi Community in America." *The Journal of Islamic Law and Culture*,
10.3 [2008]: 326–341).

11. Many have compared the situation of Arabs and Muslims after 9/11 and their integration into the American mainstream with that of other ostracized religious groups such
as Mormons, Jews, and Catholics. One might consider in particular how religious
minorities reacted to being stigmatized, with Catholics learning their traditions more
thoroughly and emphasizing the importance of sacraments and liturgy in the face of
Protestant opposition and mob violence. Sheikh Hamza Yusuf Hanson, founder of
the Zaytuna Institute (accredited as a college in 2009), wrote an editorial tracing his
ancestry to his great great grandfather Micheal O'Hanson, who arrived from Ireland
in the 1840s. Yusuf proclaims Muslims to be the "new Irish" and urges them to follow
the example of earlier ethnic and religious communities who have become a part of the
American mosaic (see "Amid Mosque Dispute, Muslims Can Look to Irish-Catholics for
Hope," *Christian Science Monitor*, September 16, 2010. Available at: http://www.csmon-
itor.com/Commentary/Opinion/2010/0916/Amid-mosque-dispute-Muslims-can-l
ook-to-Irish-Catholics-for-hope [Accessed September 3, 2010.]). However, Yvonne
Haddad writes that "in the aftermath of 9/11, a more productive comparison might be
the experience of the Germans during World War I, the Japanese during World War II,
and the communists during the Cold War. The measures adopted by the Bush administration were reminiscent of those taken during critical moments in American history that made it necessary to suspend American legal protection and constitutional
guarantees for all citizens and to scrutinize persons identified as a potential threat to
the nation" (Haddad 2011: 78).

12. Examples include Abdullahi an-Naʻim at Emory School of Law and his 2008 Muslim heretics conference (cited in Barzegar, 2011); www.musawah.org (for equality in the Muslim
family); and www.karamah.org (Muslim Women Lawyers for Human Rights).

13. This is not unprecedented. In American civil rights history, when women were shut out
of formal leadership positions in churches and advocacy organizations, they would provide "bridge leadership" whereby women would do grassroots work that would allow large
organizations to bridge geographic gaps or bridge between public and private spheres in
ways that were necessary for the survival of the protest movement. One scholar says that
although African American women often provided new ideas and initiated activism in the
civil rights movement, they would often "recede into the background," excluded from the
privileges and notoriety associated with formal leadership (See Robnett, 1997: 218, n. 31).
However, most American Muslim organizations emerged after the 1960s, presumably
positioned to benefit from the successes of the civil rights movement and second-wave
feminism. Also, American Muslim women are unique in the levels of education and
income they have attained, which is something their counterparts in the earlier civil rights
movement could not claim.

14. Cited in Kathleen M. Moore, *The Unfamiliar Abode: Islamic Law in the United States and
Britain* (New York, NY: Oxford University Press, 2010): 134.

15. *Time Magazine*. Available at http://www.time.com/time/business/article/0,8599, 1925607,
00.html (Accessed June 30, 2013.)

16. To view opinions of the Fiqh Council of North America, see http://www.fiqhcouncil.org
(Accessed June 30, 2013.)

REFERENCES

Abdul-Ghafur, Saleemah, ed. *Living Islam Out Loud: American Muslim Women Speak* (Boston: Beacon Press, 2005).

Ahmed, Leila. *Women and Gender in Islam: Historical Roots of a Modern Debate* (New Haven, CT: Yale University Press, 1992).

Ahmed, Leila. *A Quiet Revolution: The Veil's Resurgence from the Middle East to America* (New Haven, CT: Yale University Press, 2011).

Ali, Kecia. *Sexual Ethics and Islam: Feminist Reflections on Qur'an, Hadith, and Jurisprudence* (Oxford, UK: Oneworld Publications, 2006).

Ali, Kecia, Juliane Hammer, and Laury Silvers. *A Jihad for Justice: Honoring the Work and Life of Amina Wadud*. Available at: http://www.bu.edu/religion/files/2010/03/A-Jihad-for-Just ice-for-Amina-Wadud-2012-1.pdf (Accessed May 13, 2013.)

Alkhateeb, Maha B., and Salma Elkadi Abugideiri, eds. *Change from Within: Diverse Perspectives on Domestic Violence in Muslim Communities* (Great Falls, VA: Peaceful Families Project, 2007). Available at: www.peacefulfamilies.org

Alkhateeb, Shareefa. 2002. "Who Has the Right to Save Muslim Women from Abuse?" *Journal of Religion and Abuse* 4, 1 (2002): 17–20.

Almontaser, Debbie. "Khalil Gibran International Academy: Racism and a Campaign of Resistance." *Monthly Review: An Independent Socialist Magazine* [serial online]. 63.4 (September 2011): 46–57. Available at: http://web.ebscohost.com.proxy.library.ucsb. edu:2048/ehost/pdfviewer/pdfviewer?vid=3&sid=92a43a2a-d6b7-47df-b574-1fc1a708e1 ac%40sessionmgr13&hid=25 (Accessed April 26, 2013.)

Alpert, Emily.. "Muslim Women Fire Back at the 'Topless Jihad,'" *Los Angeles Times*, April 13, 2013. Available at: http://articles.latimes.com/2013/apr/13/world/la-fg-wn-muslim-topless-protest-femen-20130412 (Accessed May 4, 2013.)

Afsaruddin, Asma. "Literature, Scholarship, and Piety: Negotiating Gender and Authority in the Medieval Muslim World." *Religion and Literature* 42.1–2 (Spring/Summer 2010): 111–131.

Anway, Carole L. *Daughters of Another Path: Experiences of American Women Choosing Islam* (Lee's Summit, MO: Yawna Publications, 1996).

Badran, Margot. *Feminism in Islam: Secular and Religious Convergences* (Oxford, UK: OneWorld Publications, 2009).

Bagby, Ihsan, "The American Mosque: Activities, Administration, and Vitality of the American Mosque." *U.S. Mosque Survey 2011*. Report No. 2 (2012).

Bagby, Ihsan, "Women and the American Mosque." *U.S. Mosque Survey 2011*. Report No. 3 (2013).

Barzegar, Abbas. "Discourse, Identity, and Community: Problems and Prospects in the Study of Islam in America." *The Muslim World* 101.3 (July 2011): 511–538.

Calhoun, Craig. "'Belonging' in the Cosmopolitan Imaginary." *Ethnicities* 3.4 (2003): 531–553.

Choo, Kristin. "Muslim Women Lawyers Aim to Reconcile Traditional Beliefs with Secular Society." *ABA Journal* (February 1, 2013). Available at: http://www.abajournal.com/maga zine/article/walking_the_tightrope_muslim_women/#correction (Accessed June 30, 2013.)

cooke, miriam. "The Muslimwoman." *Contemporary Islam* 1.2 (2007): 139–154.

Ebrahimji, Maria M., and Zahra T. Suratwala, eds. *I Speak for Myself: American Women on Being Muslim* (Ashland, OR: White Cloud Press, 2011).

Elliott, Andrea. "Her Dream, Branded as a Threat." *New York Times*, April 28, 2008, p. A1. Available at: http://search.proquest.com/docview/433821708?accountid=14522 (Accessed April 25, 2013.)

Elliott, Andrea,. "Bias is Found in City's Ouster of a Principal," *New York Times*, March 13, 2010, p. A1. Available at: http://search.proquest.com.proxy.library.ucsb.edu:2048/nytimes/docview/434331407/13E8F3A1B231617358E/8?accountid=14522 (Accessed April 25, 2013.)

Elouafi, Amy Aisen. "The Colour Of Orientalism: Race And Narratives of Discovery in Tunisia." *Ethnic and Racial Studies* 33.2 (2010): 253–271.

Gallup International/Muslim West Facts Project. "The Muslim Americans: A National Portrait," 2009. Available at: http://www.gallup.com/strategicconsulting/153572/REPORT-Muslim-Americans-National-Portrait.aspx (Accessed September 30, 2010.)

Haddad, Yvonne Yazbeck. *Becoming American? The Forging of Arab and Muslim Identity in Pluralist America* (Waco, TX: Baylor University Press, 2011).

Haddad, Yvonne Yazbeck, Jane I. Smith, and Kathleen M. Moore. *Muslim Women in America: the Challenge of Islamic Identity Today* (New York: Oxford University Press, 2006).

Hammer, Juliane. *American Muslim Women, Religious Authority, and Activism: More than a Prayer* (Austin, TX: University of Texas Press, 2010).

Hasan, Asma. *American Muslims: The New Generation* (New York: Continuum Publishers, 2002).

Hicks, Mark, "Michigan American-Arab Group Postpones Banquest Over Sex Harassment Case." *The Detroit News* December 12, 2013: 1. Available at http://www.detroitnews.com/article/20131212/METRO01/312120116/Michigan-American-Arab-group-postpones-banquet-over-sex-harassment-accusations (Accessed January 4, 2014.)

Hidayatullah, Aysha Anjum. "Women Trustees of Allah: Methods, Limits, and Possibilities of 'Feminist Theology' in Islam." Ph.D. thesis (Santa Barbara: Department of Religious Studies, University of California, 2009).

Howell, Sally. "Laying the Groundwork for American Muslim Histories: 1865–1965." In Omid Safi and Juliane Hammer, eds., *Cambridge Companion to American Islam* (New York: Cambridge University Press, 2013): 98–131.

Love, Erik. "Confronting Islamophobia: Civil Rights Advocacy in the United States." PhD dissertation (Santa Barbara: University of California, 2011).

MacFarlane, Julie. *Islamic Divorce in North America: A Shari'a Path in a Secular Society* (New York: Oxford University Press, 2012).

Robnett, Belinda. *How Long? How Long? African American Women in the Struggle for Civil Rights* (New York: Oxford University Press, 1997).

Sonbol, Amira, ed. *Women, the Family and Divorce Laws in Islamic History* (Syracuse, NY: Syracuse University Press, 1996).

Van Nieuwkerk, Karin. *Women Embracing Islam: Gender and Conversion in the West* (Austin, TX: University of Texas Press, 2006).

Wadud, Amina. *Inside the Gender Jihad: Women's Reform in Islam* (Oxford, UK: Oneworld Publications, 2006).

Webb, Gisela, ed. *Windows of Faith: Muslim Women Scholar. Activists in North America* (Syracuse, NY: Syracuse University Press, 2000).

CHAPTER 12

MARRIAGE IN AMERICAN MUSLIM COMMUNITIES

JULIANE HAMMER

"Whoever marries has achieved one half of the Religion. Thereafter let him fear Allah regarding the other half."

(Prophetic Hadith)

THE first part of the preceding statement, alluded to in the title of this essay as well, is an oft-quoted saying of the Prophet Muhammad. Regardless of its authenticity, it is notable just how often it appears in American Muslim conversations and discourses on marriage and the family. Evidently marriage is an important topic for American Muslims, and there are many good reasons for its endurance as such since the early twentieth century, albeit in different forms and venues. At the outset, it is important to point out that although some research has been conducted on the topic, empirical data is typically limited to small samples with all the particularity that entails, which has led me to combine them in my analysis with discourses in various forms. I argue then that an analysis of the ways in which American Muslims discuss and negotiate marriage—in magazines, books, on websites, in online forums and elsewhere—are all indicators of prevailing practices and, simultaneously, markers of the perpetual negotiation of ideals and realities. In other words, discourses on marriage and family in Muslim communities can tell us both how Muslims want this part of their religion to look and how it actually does look. In what follows I argue that marriage and family in discourse as well as in practice are mutually shaped and informed by developments and discourses in the larger American society as well as by the extensive transnational ties and practices of American Muslims. These developments include feminist critique of patriarchal family structures, fundamental changes in marriage attitudes and practices, the continued negotiation of marriage as a religious as well as state-regulated practice, and changing attitudes to sexuality, women's bodies, and gender roles in American society as well as in Muslim communities.

This chapter cannot possibly do justice to the history of marriage and family discourses and practices among American Muslims or to their diversity in contemporary communities. In light of this fact, I present three brief episodes in the lives of three American Muslim women—fictional composites of accounts told to me, published in various venues, and/or presented in scholarly works.[1]

These episodes are interwoven with my analysis of American Muslim approaches and attitudes to marriage and family. Each takes personal specifics to illustrate broader arguments and thus paints a particular picture in order to cautiously generalize from there. Choosing to tell the stories of three women is certainly women-centric, which is primarily a function of the women-centeredness of much of the existing research on marriage, family, and heterosexuality. Ironically though, most of the normative discourses on Islamic marriage come from male scholars and community leaders. And more ironic still, most research of other aspects of American Muslims' experiences, institutions, attitudes, and activities have focused on men, while women appear most prominently in discussions of gender, marriage, and family. Perhaps over time this imbalance will shift to incorporate more prominently men's experiences and perspectives into our picture of marriage gender, and family, while women will receive more inclusive treatment of the many other aspects of their lives and experiences.

A review of scholarly sources on marriage and family in American Muslim communities reveals that before there was literature/research on American Muslim women, there were studies of Muslim family values and structures as well as some on marriage patterns and generational interactions.[2] In part, the shift from a focus on family to a focus on women, which happened in the mid-1990s, can be attributed to the influence of feminist theory and scholarship. A renewed interest in and focus on marriage and family in Muslim communities in the 2000s may, on the other hand, be described as a backlash against the perceived attack of secular feminist theory on marriage as a cornerstone of religious, here especially Islamic, foundations of family and community. It may also have been a response to increased scrutiny and surveillance of Muslim communities after September 11, 2001, by law enforcement and the American public, which in turn led to increased concern for the very foundations of communities and their building units—Muslim families.

In what follows I focus on how American Muslims create their families, how they negotiate ideals and realities in their family life, and what happens when families "fail." I will thus discuss spouse selection and dating, domestic harmony, and divorce. This is not to imply that the majority of Muslim marriages end up in divorce but rather that the issue of divorce is especially useful in outlining the boundaries of Muslim marriage ideals and the anxieties of Muslim communities over the preservation of Muslim families.

FINDING THE RIGHT SPOUSE AND THE
QUESTION OF DATING

*O mankind! Be conscious of your Sustainer, who has created you out of one living
entity, and out of it created its mate, and out of the two spread abroad a multitude of
men and women.* (Q 4:1)[3]

Rabia is twenty-three years old and a first-year master's student in psychology. She
is the daughter of Pakistani immigrants and grew up in California. Since Rabia finished college last year, her mother and other older female relatives have become more
insistent in talking about marriage. They have offered information about young men
in the community and keep pointing out that she may soon be too old to find a suitable spouse. But Rabia has also talked at length with her friends about marrying for
love. How would her parents react if she approached them with news of a potential
spouse from outside the community, someone she met in school?

Some version of this story happens in the United States every other day. As young
American Muslims come of age, the question of how (not if) to build their own
families becomes more important. American Muslims are very well educated and,
like many of their non-Muslim peers, have tended to defer marriage to after they
complete their education. This, in turn, increases the average marriage age, which is
typically not a problem for men but can become one for women. Muslim women are
as educated as their male peers and many are also successful and established professionals. These achievements often clash with the gender expectations of both their
parents' generation and their potential spouses. While young educated men might be
looking for a wives who will take care of the home and children, women expect to be
able to continue their professional lives and have higher expectations of their future
spouses in terms of sharing in household and family duties. There are of course also
plenty of young Muslim women whose life aspiration is focused on the role of wife
and mother, which we should not see as less relevant or valuable.

Where would Rabia meet her prospective spouse? While the answer to this question varies tremendously from community to community, several possibilities
emerge. In some communities, especially among immigrants from Muslim-majority
countries, it was historically very common for female relatives or even professional
matchmakers to play an important role in this process. The involvement of the family in such an important life decision offered support for the potential spouses and
distributed responsibility for the decision beyond the couple. Families who rely on
matchmaking consider questions such as the economic and educational compatibility of the spouses and the reputation of the respective families; very often, they
expect young Muslims to marry from within their ethnic or even local communities.
Alternatively, spouses from the country of origin could also be considered a viable
option for the preservation of cultural and ethnic bonds and life patterns. Discussions

about arranged marriage abound and range from outright rejection of the practice as old-fashioned and obsolete to a newfound sense of appreciation for the ways in which the practice safeguards the individuals involved and preserves the dignity of potential spouses.

An alternative to matchmaking with the help of the family is meeting a prospective spouse in a school or work setting or within the framework of other life activities. Such meetings occur all the time, especially for Muslims in more urban settings, where larger numbers of other Muslims may be found in the same environments. Colleges and universities, companies and nonprofit organizations, hospitals and law firms, as well as Muslim students' associations and other venues for activism are all places where Muslim women and men can have opportunities to interact with other Muslims, thus being able to observe them in nonmatrimonial environments. For some young Muslims, this opportunity is provided in mosques and Muslim community settings as well. It is in such alternative settings that young American Muslims are more likely to consider marriage to someone from outside their ethnic communities.

The debate about "cultural" compatibility is often one that pitches parents against children. The younger generation has turned to arguments about religiosity and religious practices in order to counter their parents' concerns about the preservation of cultural traditions in the next generation. Language preservation still plays an important role in these arguments. Compatibility in terms of level of religious commitment has always been a consideration, either by way of expecting harmony from similar commitments or in the form of expecting one spouse to be a positive influence in helping the other to become more "practicing" or knowledgeable about Islam. However, in more recent iterations of this conversation, young American Muslims seeking to select spouses increasingly turn to religious arguments that override concerns for ethnic and cultural similarity.

Zareena Grewal has shown in a particular setting how young Muslims negotiate questions of race and religious practice within their mosques, communities, and families. Grewal asserts that

> Many young Muslim Americans in these communities identify themselves as "Muslim." They employ Islam to subvert certain racial values and what they perceive as the restrictive expectations of their "cultural parents," demonstrating how culture and religion can come to operate in a discursive opposition. As they test the boundaries of what constitutes an eligible spouse, they draw on sources that their parents recognize as authoritative in part because Islam serves as a common moral ground between generations that came of age in different cultures, creating a space for negotiating conflicting visions.[4]

The negotiation of racial categories discussed in Grewal's work also points to a particularly American dimension of this debate. Prevailing attitudes to skin color are here debated against the backdrop of racial boundaries and constructions in the United States and, equally importantly, in response to the presence of a significant

African American Muslim community. The distinction between racial boundaries and culture is demonstrated in an especially poignant chapter of Zain Abdullah's *Black Mecca*, a study that analyzes the experiences of West African Muslim immigrants in Harlem. Here the issue of intermarriage between African and African American Muslims is not primarily framed in racial terms but rather as a question of cultural compatibility. Abdullah reports cases of intermarriage and describes how potential spouses negotiate differing expectations about work outside the home, homemaking, and—on several occasions—also polygyny. He finds that sometimes African Muslim men and women turn to African American Muslims as potential spouses in order to negotiate differing as well as rapidly changing expectations about gender roles.[5]

Beyond family and other forms of direct encounters for the purpose of finding a spouse, American Muslims have also turned to matrimonial ads and more recently to websites in order to connect with other Muslims. Many Muslim matrimonial sites are international, thus reflecting the transnational ties and connections of American Muslim communities. Some specialize in connecting Muslims of similar ethnic backgrounds, while others emphasize religious commonality over such boundaries. Matrimonial ads and sites expand the circle of available mates but also carry all the risks inherent in virtual self-representation and meeting people in cyberspace.[6]

If Rabia were a recent convert to Islam, her situation would be significantly different from that of a South Asian, Arab, or other American Muslim who was born into the faith. Rather than her parents being the conversation partners (or adversaries) in the negotiation of prospective spouses, the community she had become part of would likely be involved in the conversation. Single converts are often strongly encouraged to find suitable spouses as soon as possible—both in order to channel their sexuality and in reference to the hadith, mentioned at the beginning of this chapter. Of course the regulation of sexuality extends to normative Islamic practice regardless of whether one is a convert or was born a Muslim. In Islam sex is considered to be lawful only within marriage; thus both premarital and extramarital sexual acts are deemed legally prohibited. The prohibition of premarital sex explains both the pressure and expectation to marry young—taking care of developing sexual needs as soon as possible—and impacts the boundaries and guidelines for premarital encounters between potential spouses.

If Rabia had found a man she was interested in, chances are they would meet before agreeing to marry. Even arranged marriage seldom means that future spouses do not meet extensively in person and have opportunities to discuss their expectations, interests, and backgrounds. More traditional families would insist on chaperoned meetings or conversations in public spaces in order to minimize the possibility of sexual encounters. Of course American Muslims have at their disposal all the technological means of communication that the twenty-first century has to offer, so virtual face-to face encounters, phone conversations, text messages, emails, and chats are possible and taken advantage of.

And whether Muslims like to acknowledge it or not, there are members of their community who engage in premarital sex, with or without the prospect of eventual marriage. Such encounters, which happen more frequently than the parent generation would like to admit, put women at higher risk, both because of the possibility of pregnancy (a visible sign of the purported transgression) and because a loss of reputation has much more severe consequences for women than for men in Muslim communities. Because Muslim communities are hesitant to acknowledge that premarital sex, dating, as well as casual sexual relations happen among American Muslims, they are often at a loss to know how to address issues arising from such changing relationships and encounters—including but not limited to dating violence, sexually transmitted diseases, sex education, and not least the possibility of lesbian, gay, bisexual, transgender, or questioning (LGBTQ) relationships and families.[7]

Once potential spouses had had a chance to get to know each other, they would take formal steps toward marriage. Depending on family, community, and individual, they would announce their engagement, sign a marriage contract, agree on a dowry (symbolic or otherwise), and then make preparations for the wedding, all of which serves as a formal announcement of their marriage to the community. While many American Muslims have separate Islamic and civil marriage ceremonies, thus getting married both according to Islamic and state law, others combine the two by employing an imam who is also a certified civil celebrant. Of course Rabia could also have met a young man several times and then decided that he was not a prospect. It is here that the involvement of family and friends can be a face-saving measure for negotiating rejection.

The last decade has seen an increasingly vocal campaign led by American Muslim organizations and community leaders to require premarital counseling as a precondition for performing marriages in mosques. The campaigners argue that such counseling, ranging from one to several meetings with an imam or community leader, will disclose mutual expectations, allow for candid discussion of potential conflict, and provide the future spouses with "Islamic" guidelines for their marriage. Mohamed Magid, the imam of ADAMS in Northern Virginia, has developed a questionnaire for both potential spouses, which they have to fill out and then discuss with him.[8] Other similar lists of questions are circulated and discussed in communities. The questions recognize changing and potentially other contentious attitudes to issues such as housework, professional development, further education, expectations of the extended family, friendships outside marriage, and a long list of other questions, many of them related to gender roles and expectations. The questions are an indicator of both changing attitudes and the challenges of negotiating such changes in real time.

Another community campaign, supported by some community leaders as well as by women's organizations and lawyers, pertains to the legal possibilities and potential of an Islamic marriage contract. Advocates encourage women in particular to formulate a contract as part of their negotiations of the conditions of marriage. In Islamic law, women have the right to incorporate conditions for where to live, the possibility of further education or professional advancement, number of children, and also divorce into a binding contract that can mitigate the heavily patriarchal provisions of Islamic marriage and divorce law. The advocacy on this issue focuses, on the one hand, on informing Muslim communities, especially women, of this right, while also, on the other, trying to ensure that such a contract would hold up in American courts.[9] This issue is especially important in the case of divorce as we will see below.

Of course not all American Muslims are young when they marry, especially when they remarry. Converts of all ages, even beyond childbearing age, are encouraged to marry and generally do so in practice. Divorce is discussed in greater detail below, but suffice it to say here that, while there is stigma attached to divorce in some communities, remarriage after a divorce is common in others. The stigma is greater for women than for men, especially in immigrant communities. However, especially in African American Muslim communities, remarriage is common for both men and women.[10] Men of immigrant background usually find it much less difficult to remarry than women do. The process one has to go through for finding a "new" spouse would be similar in most other ways.

DOMESTIC HARMONY: AMERICAN MUSLIM FAMILIES BETWEEN IDEAL AND REALITY

And among His Signs is this, that He created for you mates from among yourselves, that ye may dwell in tranquility with them, and he put love and mercy between you: verily in that are Signs for those who reflect. (Q 30:21)[11]

Salma has been married for twenty-five years. She is a nurse and has recently started working again after raising her three children and seeing the last one off to college. The children are doing well in school, with the older two in college, but they do not pray regularly and Salma suspects that one of her sons is dating a young woman who is not Muslim. Her husband is a successful engineer who owns his business. The couple are involved in the mosque community and her husband has been on the board of the mosque for several years. After her father-in-law passed away last month, her husband asked Salma to let her mother-in-law move in with them.

The family life described in the preceding Qur'anic passage constructs an ideal— which is often repeated in American Muslim discourses on marriage and family. It focuses on three key terms: *sakinah* (tranquility), *mawaddah* (love), and *rahmah* (mercy). The discussion of these Qur'anic terms is combined with a part of another oft-quoted verse of the Qur'an: 4:34, the first portion of which reads: "[husbands] are protectors and maintainers of their [wives] because Allah has given the one more [strength] than the other, and because they support them from their means. Therefore the righteous women are devoutly obedient." (Q 4:34)[12]. Qur'an 4:34 has engendered a spirited and vast debate about meaning, interpretation, and the authority to derive meaning from the Qur'an, with participants ranging from traditional (and male) religious scholars to American Muslim feminist interpreters. While this debate can only be pointed toward in this context, it is important to mention it as it provides a glimpse of the issues at stake in discussing scriptural interpretation and the construction of ideals and norms for Muslim family life. The verse seems to point toward a hierarchical construction of Muslim families in which the husband is the financial maintainer of the wife and children while the wife accepts him as her maintainer and protector and acts accordingly. Both translation of key terms and context for interpretation are at stake here. In its practical application the verse has been called upon to construct such a hierarchical family, which will be one of tranquility, love, and mercy (Q 30:21) if both spouses accept their ordained roles. It has also been debated and its meaning contextualized to support women as heads of families and breadwinners and to challenge gender hierarchies based on understandings rooted in seventh-century Arabia, when the Qur'an was revealed to the Prophet Muhammad.[13]

But let us return to Salma. Her experience of marriage and family has not been without challenges, but overall it has not been terrible either. Her husband is also of Egyptian background and the two initially met at a community wedding. It took some time to negotiate the details of their life together, from cooking food that he liked in a particular way to agreeing to stop working until her children had grown. Having three children within five years quickly changed the dynamics of their relationship and family life. They had always been financially stable, so there was no worry there. Salma felt responsible for her children's religious education; it was she who took them to Arabic and Qur'an lessons on Sundays and who woke them up for dawn prayers while they lived at home. Once they grew older, they no longer wanted to come to the mosque. Salma is concerned but has heard from a friend that her oldest son is active in the Muslim Students Association, so he at least has found an alternative community. That her younger son, who is only twenty-two, may be dating, as she suspects, concerns her more. What if he engages in a forbidden relationship and it does not lead to marriage? Living with her mother-in-law after all these years will be a challenge, but Salma feels obliged to offer care and support for this elderly family member. There will be fights and disagreements, much as there were when she first got married.

Many of the issues negotiated and discussed before marriage will find their way into the negotiations of marital life as well. The possibility and acceptance of working women, further education, distribution of marital assets, home life, and number of children rank among the top concerns for American Muslim families. Those are, of course, not specific to Muslim families but appear in discussions of family life and dynamics in the larger American society as well. In some Muslim families, these negotiations are intertwined with religious discourses, while in others they take place in decidedly secular form. It is important to stress, then, that Muslims as members of society and as human beings are not solely defined by the Qur'an or religious discourses but rather are shaped by social, cultural, economic, and political factors (just like everyone else) and that they have choices in regard to the significance of religious practice and reflection as factors shaping their lives.

Salma discusses her concerns about the children with her husband and she is grateful that he does not blame her for their lack of religious commitment. He is hopeful that they might change their attitudes, as their oldest son already seems to have done. Both parents are proud of their children's education achievements, and it looks like their daughter is on her way to becoming a medical doctor. For guidance on how to deal with her mother-in-law, Salma turns to the imam of her mosque. He has been in the community for a long time, but Salma is concerned whether he will keep their conversations confidential, especially from her husband. The imam points to passages in the Qur'an and the practice of the Prophet Muhammad for guidance. He also advises Salma to be patient and respect her elders.

Marital counseling (for individuals and couples) has become an important aspect of the work of religious and community leaders in the American Muslim context. As Muslim communities have become American religious congregations, carrying out functions far beyond daily and Friday congregational prayers, so the demands on the leaders of such congregations have grown. Many of the imams of American mosques have no or very little training in the counseling of married couples, families, or otherwise. They thus find themselves in situations they do not have the tools to address adequately. They do, however, actively participate in the construction and dissemination of Islamic marriage ideals and norms, against which American Muslims will measure their own families and marriages.

American Muslims also turn to more distant sources of religious authority: online information, weekend courses, and lectures, conferences, and conventions. There is a long list of available literature on Muslim marriage, the example of the Prophet Muhammad, and ideal wives and husbands. AlMaghrib, Zaytuna Institute, and Seekers' Guidance are several of the organizations that supply Muslims with courses, lectures, and materials elaborating on legal and practical elements of Muslim marriages. Annual conventions like those of the Islamic Society of North America regularly feature, and have done so for decades, panels and speakers on issues of marriage and family. Muslims who seek information, guidance, and knowledge online frequently ask questions related to marital life, acceptable sexual practices, and the challenges of raising Muslim children in a non-Muslim environment. And not least, conventions also serve as acceptable spaces for matrimonial activities.

The emphasis on tranquility, love, and mercy between spouses is a helpful example for the construction of an Islamic ideal that can be seen as genuinely Islamic while also drawing on American popular culture and societal dynamics: the majority of Muslims might not have married someone they first fell in love with (this question is debated), but love, developed through life together, is a key ingredient for a successful marriage. Far from an emphasis on the contractual nature of Islamic marriage, there should be love and mercy between spouses, which in turn will lead to a tranquil, peaceful family life. The family is then presented as the cornerstone of a healthy and prosperous Muslim community in America, which makes family problems a community concern.

Of course not all American Muslim families are economically as stable as Salma's. Economic instability and poverty, while more common in some communities than others, produce and/or exacerbate existing relationship problems and allow less control over potential solutions. There are also concerns about privacy and community interference in family affairs. Abstaining from interfering in family issues can mask problems that are more adequately described as abuse, while interference of the extended family and community are also often blamed as exacerbating factors for increasing family problems.

And last, the question of care for Salma's mother-in-law reflects a growing issue for the American Muslim community as it literally ages—as traditional extended family structures that took care of aging family members are being replaced by geographically mobile smaller family units, American Muslims have to develop solutions for the care of the elderly. Community discussions have for the most part not moved beyond pointing out the problem, and no practical communal solutions have been found. This situation adds to the burden of female community members, who are obliged to take on the care of elderly family members beyond their own familial and professional obligations.

WHEN MARRIAGES END: DIVORCE IN DISCOURSE AND PRACTICE

If ye fear a breach between them twain, appoint two arbiters, one from his family and the other from hers, if they wish for peace, Allah will cause their reconciliation. (Q 4:35)[14] Thus when they fulfill their term appointed either take them back on equitable terms or part with them on equitable terms. (Q 65:2)[15]

Khadijah has been married for ten years. The couple have a daughter who will be six in a few months. The marriage was never free of problems, but as of late Khadijah has had several arguments and discussions with her husband that have tipped the scales for her. Khadijah wants to go back to school and get a master's degree in counseling, but her husband has told her that he will not allow her to enroll in any courses. He is worried that she might spend too much time away from home and from him. He would prefer to see her have another child soon. The family's financial situation is complicated, as Khadijah's husband was laid off a year ago and he has not yet found a new full-time job. He refuses to go to family counseling, even in the mosque, and accuses Khadijah of ruining his reputation by discussing their marital problems with her family and girlfriends. She is seriously considering a divorce.

What happens when a marriage does not work out? In the words of Mohamed Magid, already mentioned, "there is this thing called divorce in Islam,"[16] and it exists so that married couples who have irreconcilable differences can find a way out of unacceptable marital situations. The Qur'anic excerpts given here indicate both encouragement for arbitration (of family members) in cases of familial conflict, and point to the required procedures for an Islamic divorce. In fact, the Qur'an contains a surprising number of verses addressing the dynamics and requirements for how to achieve a divorce. Examples include a large section of Surah 2 of the Qur'an (verses 224 to 237) and an entire chapter of the Qur'an (65) titled "Divorce."

Despite the existence of these passages and the development of detailed legal prescriptions and conditions for divorce, which acknowledge both that some marital bonds cannot be salvaged and that conflicts need to be addressed in a peaceful and measured manner, divorce is a difficult topic for American Muslims. On the discursive level, Muslim community activists and scholars have to acknowledge that the traditional application of Islamic law regarding marriage and divorce favors the interests of men by allowing them unilateral divorce without the involvement of a jurist or judge. Women have some recourse to initiating a particular kind of divorce called *khul'*, which requires forfeiting their maintenance and deferred dower. However, Muslim couples are also in a complicated legal limbo resulting from the simultaneous investment in Islamic and American state laws. While American Muslim scholars and religious leaders can act as agents of the state for performing weddings, no such state authority is invested in them for divorce proceedings. American Muslims, like everyone else, have to turn to the American legal system to go through state-regulated divorce proceeding. The same imams who perform Islamic wedding ceremonies often do not have the Islamic legal/jurisprudential qualifications to grant American Muslim women a divorce. This can create an Islamic legal limbo and significant hardship, especially to women and especially in cases in which the husband refuses an Islamic divorce. The Islamic marriage contract reenters the picture here, as only a marriage contract that is legally enforceable in the American legal system can be applied in the case of a divorce.

Moreover, divorce is perceived as undesirable by many American Muslims and thus carries, again especially for women, significant social stigma, which acts as a deterrent for initiating or even contemplating divorce. This reluctance to dissolve unhappy and dysfunctional marriages is often linked, in communal debates of the topic, to particular cultural attitudes. It is potentially dangerous, in my view, to attach cultural characteristics to a particular group of American Muslims as if they were in and of themselves a homogenous group, as each ethnic and other subgroup of

American Muslims contains significant variation and diversity. As will become clear below, the discursive investment in cultural particularities and challenges to that investment are an important feature of American Muslim community discourse on religion and culture. The social stigma already mentioned for women more often than men means social isolation and, maybe more importantly, severe limitations on remarriage. Women thus have to contemplate whether they are prepared to spend the rest of their lives without a partner—a prospect that is discussed as terrifying both in terms of emotional and sexual companionship and economic stability. An important role in negotiating the possibility of divorce is played by the extended family, both in the United States and abroad, and by the community to which a Muslim woman or man belongs.

In a sociological study of American Muslim divorce experiences conducted by Julie MacFarlane and published in 2012, the researcher was particularly interested in the ways in which American Muslims negotiate the tension between American legal tradition and their various commitments to Islamic law with regard to marriage and divorce. The study states that divorce rates have risen in American Muslim communities, more than in Muslim majority countries, while communities and individuals have had to negotiate changing attitudes as well as circumstances. MacFarlane writes:

> This four-year empirical study has encouraged individuals and groups to discuss marital conflict openly and frankly. The goal was to explore what they understand as their Islamic obligations in marriage, the challenges they face in their married lives, and under what circumstances they might consider divorce—including their decision-making process, where they turn for help, and what rituals of closure and divorce outcomes are important to them.[17]

MacFarlane also touches upon the negotiation of religion and culture and asserts that

> Muslim couples face many of the same challenges as non-Muslim couples as they adapt to changing societal values and norms, including gender roles within marriage, attitudes towards the participation of women in work and education, the role of the extended family, and attitudes towards divorce. At the same time, contemporary Islamic family identity is emerging from a range of traditions and practices which are rooted in cultural values as well as religious principles.[18]

One reason for divorce among American Muslims (not unlike American society at large) is the experience of domestic violence in Muslim families. This is a large topic deserving its own degree of attention and research. Suffice it to say here that American Muslim efforts against domestic violence uphold the purposes and principles of the Islamic marriage ideal already discussed, rejecting any religious support for any form of abuse in Muslim families. Religious leaders involved in efforts to curtail domestic violence continually point to the possibility of divorce to end a domestic abuse situation, and community advocates have invested much effort in educating their communities on Islamic marriage ideals and the ways in which domestic abuse violates these principles.

The perceived (and possibly real) increase of divorce rates in Muslim communities has prompted not only interest in and debate over the causes of that growth but, importantly, has generated a lively and engaged discussion of marriage and family issues more broadly. American Muslims have found themselves negotiating their ideas and practices regarding marriage and family vis-à-vis an equally fast-changing American society that is also in the process of debating and changing marriage ideals and practices. Concerns over the nature of marriage, regulation of gay marriage on the state and federal level, growing divorce rates, and domestic violence are all issues of concern for many Americans. American Muslims as members of American society as well as transnational Muslim communities and networks carry out their conversations on this topic between and occasionally beyond these poles of their collective existence.

CONCLUSION

In 1996, Yvonne Haddad and Jane Smith, the editors of this volume, wrote about the negotiation of "Islamic values" in American Muslim communities:

> The importance of the family, of the respective roles of women and men in society, of socializing children in order that they might avoid the problems of western society, of finding appropriate ways to care for the elderly—all of these issues necessitate formulating responses to the pressures of American society that neither compromise the ideals of Islam nor to take refuge in what some consider an unwieldy and unrealistically conservative dogmatism.[19]

This paradigm creates a number of powerful yet constructed juxtapositions that, as I argue, are continuously negotiated among American Muslims. Discussions of marriage and family norms and practices are one fertile ground for this negotiation. The juxtaposition explored in the quotation above is that between American or "western" society or culture and the culture(s) that American Muslims come from or to which they feel attached. As immigrant Muslims and their descendants have until recently been studied separately from African American and other American-born Muslims, it was quite common both in scholarly literature and community discourse to find the construction and subsequent juxtaposition of American and Pakistani/ south Asian/Arab/Iranian (or other) culture with a monolithic American culture. American Muslims negotiated these two poles as part of determining and continually reinventing their hyphenated or otherwise complex and differentiated identities. Haddad and Smith argue that Islam has shaped Arab (and by extension other Muslim) cultures,[20] thus influencing even those Americans of immigrant and

Muslim background who do not practice their religion. More recent developments in American Muslim communities have complicated this assertion and have resulted in the development of a juxtaposition between "authentic" Islam and culture. While the American-vs.-Muslim culture dichotomy stays in place, this new negotiation allows American Muslims of different background to make claims to Islamic ideals, an authentic Islamic tradition, sacred texts, and the authority to interpret them, which in turn allows them to question and challenge cultural practices as either un-Islamic or irrelevant for their authenticated Islamic lives. We saw this dynamic at work in the study by Zareena Grewal, cited above.

The focus on developing normative marriage and family values and ideals drawing directly on sacred sources and the legitimacy of certain interpreters and interpretations allows especially younger Muslims to define and adjust their religious as well as marriage and family practices to an ever-changing environment. It is common to hear members of the American Muslim community argue that this American Islam is not simply an American cultural expression of the diversity of Muslim practices and Islamic norms but rather an ideal Islam free of what they perceive as cultural constraints. This argument strengthens the normative power of religious interpretations but also often devalues diverging cultural practices and differing interpretations wholesale. Questions of courtship, matrimony, family values, sexuality, divorce, and associated issues have been and continue to be a fertile ground for this broader negotiation of American Muslim ideals, practices, and lives.

NOTES

1. A number of memoirs and collections of personal narratives, especially of American Muslim women, have been published since 2004. Many of them include reflections and stories about marriage and family. See Saleemah Abdul-Ghafur (ed.), *Living Islam Out Loud: American Muslim Women Speak* (Boston: Beacon Press, 2005); Asra Nomani, *Standing Alone: An American Woman's Struggle for the Soul of Islam* (Sand Francisco: Harper, 2005); Sumbul Ali-Karamali, *The Muslim Next Door* (Ashland, OR: White Cloud Press, 2008); Maria Ebrahimji and Zahra Suratwala (eds.), *I Speak for Myself: American Women on Being Muslim* (Ashland, OR: White Cloud Press, 2011); Ayesha Mattu and Nura Maznai (eds.), *Love, Inshallah: The Secret Love Lives of American Muslim Women* (Berkeley, CA: Soft Skull Press, 2012). Strikingly, there is currently only one collection of similar narratives by American Muslim men: Wajahat Ali and Zahra Suratwala (eds.), *All-American: 45 American Men on Being Muslim* (Ashland, OR: White Cloud Press, 2012), which contains no reflections on marriage and family. Two of the forty-five chapters address issues of sexuality: one by an openly gay imam (Daayiee Abdullah, 40–45) and another by a transgender man (Tynan Power, 86–90).

2. See Earle Waugh, Sharon Abu-Laban, and Regula Qureshi (eds.), *Muslim Families in North America* (Edmonton: University of Alberta Press, 1991); Barbara Aswad and Barbara Bilge (eds.), *Family & Gender among American Muslims: Issues Facing Middle Eastern Immigrants and Their Descendants* (Philadelphia: Temple University Press, 1996).

Works on (and later also by) American Muslim women are too numerous to list here. For examples see Carolyn Rouse, *Engaged Surrender: African American Women and Islam* (Berkeley: University of California Press, 2004); and Yvonne Haddad, Jane Smith, and Kathleen Moore, *Muslim Women in America: The Challenge of Islamic Identity Today* (New York: Oxford University Press, 2006).

3. Translation by Muhammad Asad, *The Message of the Qur'an* (Gibraltar: Dar al-Andalus, 1980):, 100.

4. Zareena Grewal, "Marriage in Colour: Race, Religion and Spouse Selection in Four American Mosques," *Ethnic and Racial Studies* 32:2 (February 2009): 323–345; 341–342. For a somewhat earlier study of souse selection and marriage practices in American Muslim communities, see Denise al-Johar, "Muslim Marriages in America: Reflecting New identities," *Muslim World* 95:4 (October 2005): 557–574.

5. Zain Abdullah, *Black Mecca: The African Muslims of Harlem* (Oxford, UK: Oxford University Press, 2010): 199–230.

6. Examples from a large number of available sites include http://www.muslimmatrimony. com/, http://www.icmarriage.com/, http://nikah.com/, http://www.muslimwedding. org/. These sites function very similarly to dating portals with many of them requiring a subscription or sign-up, allowing Muslims to post and browse profiles by search criteria.

7. Many American Muslims have negative views of homosexuality or any other form of sexual identity outside heteronormative marital relations. There is a growing literature on Islam and homosexuality. See for example, Scott Kugle, "Sexuality, Diversity and Ethics in the Agenda of Progressive Muslims," in Omid Safi (ed.), *Progressive Muslims* (Oxford, UK: Oneworld, 2003): 190–235; Scott Kugle, *Homosexuality in Islam: Critical Reflections on Gay, Lesbian, and Transgender Muslims* (Oxford, UK: Oneworld, 2010). However, in community discourse, the issue is either ignored or discussed in mostly negative terms. Like the avoidance of discussions about premarital and extramarital sex, the discomfort with discussing lesbian, gay, bisexual, transgender, or questioning (LGBTQ) issues makes it impossible to discuss dating and relationship violence and gendered power dynamics.

8. See http://www.adamscenter.org/services/marriage for several forms including the pre-marital counseling form. Mohamed Magid is the imam of All Dulles American Muslims (ADAMS), a mosque and community center in Herndon, Virginia. He was elected president of the Islamic Society of North America in 2010.

9. See Asifa Qureishi and Frank Vogel (eds.), *The Islamic Marriage Contract: Case Studies in Islamic Family Law* (Cambridge, MA: Harvard University Press, 2008); Azizah al-Hibri, "The Nature of the Islamic Marriage: Sacramental, Covenantal, or Contractual?" in *Covenant Marriage in Comparative Perspective*, edited by John Witte and Eliza Ellison (Grand Rapids, MI: Eerdmans, 2005), 182–216.

10. See Carolyn Rouse, *Engaged Surrender: African American Women and Islam* (Berkeley: University of California Press, 2004), especially chapter 7, "Performing Gender."

11. Translation by Abdullah Yusuf Ali, *The Meaning of the Holy Qur'an* (Beltsville, MD: Amana Publications, 2001): 1012–1013.

12. Translation by Abdullah Yusuf Ali, *The Meaning of the Holy Qur'an* (Beltsville, MD: Amana Publications, 2001): 195.

13. For examples of different voices in this debate, see Amina Wadud, *Inside the Gender Jihad* (Oxford, UK: Oneworld, 2005); Azizah al-Hibri, "An Introduction to Muslim

Women's Rights," in *Windows of Faith*, edited by Gisela Webb (Syracuse, NY: Syracuse University Press, 2000): 51–71; Zainab Alwani and Salma Abugideiri, *What Islam Says about Domestic Violence* (Herndon, VA: FAITH, 2003). Every translation of the Qur'an into English demonstrates the struggle of the translator as interpreter with the meanings of this verse as well.

14. Translation by Abdullah Yusuf Ali, *The Meaning of the Holy Qur'an* (Beltsville, MD: Amana Publications, 2001): 196.
15. Translation by Abdullah Yusuf Ali, *The Meaning of the Holy Qur'an* (Beltsville, MD: Amana Publications, 2001): 1484.
16. Interview with author, Herndon, May 14, 2011.
17. Julie MacFarlane, "Understanding Trends in American Muslim Divorce and Marriage," (Washington, DC: Institute for Social Policy and Understanding, May 2012): 5. Available at   http://www.ispu.org/pdfs/ISPU%20Report_Marriage%20II_Macfarlane_WEB.pdf MacFarlane subsequently published a longer book version of her findings and analysis. See *Islamic Divorce in North America: A Shari'ah Path in a Secular Society* (Oxford, UK: Oxford University Press, 2012). It is significant that the study was supported by the Institute for Social Policy and Understanding (ISPU), an American Muslim research organization founded and supported by community members. ISPU support is one indicator of the interest and concern of American Muslim communities in issues of marriage and divorce. ISPU has also supported my own research regarding American Muslim efforts against domestic violence, presumably out of the same concern.
18. MacFarlane, "Understanding Trends."
19. Yvonne Haddad and Jane Smith, "Islamic Values among American Muslims," in *Family & Gender among American Muslims*, edited by Barbara Aswad and Barbara Bilge (Philadelphia: Temple University Press, 1996): 19–40.
20. Haddad and Smith, "Islamic Values," p. 20.

References

Abdul-Ghafur, Saleemah (ed.), *Living Islam Out Loud: American Muslim Women Speak* (Boston: Beacon Press, 2005).
Abdullah, Zain, *Black Mecca: The African Muslims of Harlem* (Oxford, UK: Oxford University Press, 2010).
Al-Hibri, Azizah, "The Nature of the Islamic Marriage: Sacramental, Covenantal, or Contractual?" in *Covenant Marriage in Comparative Perspective*, edited by John Witte and Eliza Ellison (Grand Rapids, MI: Eerdmans:, 2005): 182–216.
Ali, Wajahat, and Zahra Suratwala (eds.), *All-American: 45 American Men on Being Muslim* (Ashland: White Cloud Press, 2012).
Ali-Karamali, Sumbul, *The Muslim Next Door* (Ashland, OR: White Cloud Press, 2008).
Al-Johar, Denise, "Muslim Marriages in America: Reflecting New identities," *Muslim World* 95:4 (October 2005): 557–574.
Aswad, Barbara, and Barbara Bilge (eds.), *Family & Gender among American Muslims: Issues Facing Middle Eastern Immigrants and Their Descendants* (Philadelphia: Temple University Press, 1996).
Ebrahimji, Maria, and Zahra Suratwala (eds.), *I Speak for Myself: American Women on Being Muslim* (Ashland, OR: White Cloud Press, 2011).

Grewal, Zareena, "Marriage in Colour: Race, Religion and Spouse Selection in Four American Mosques." *Ethnic and Racial Studies* 32:2 (February 2009): 323–345.

Haddad, Yvonne, Jane Smith, and Kathleen Moore (eds.), *Muslim Women in America: The Challenge of Islamic Identity Today* (New York: Oxford University Press, 2006).

Kugle, Scott, "Sexuality, Diversity and Ethics in the Agenda of Progressive Muslims," in *Progressive Muslims*, edited by Omid Safi (Oxford: Oneworld, 2003): 190–235.

Kugle, Scott, *Homosexuality in Islam: Critical reflections on Gay, Lesbian, and Transgender Muslims* (Oxford, UK: Oneworld, 2010).

MacFarlane, Julie, "Understanding Trends in American Muslim Divorce and Marriage" (Washington, DC: Institute for Social Policy and Understanding, May 2012): 5, available at http://www.ispu.org/pdfs/ISPU%20Report_Marriage%20II_Macfarlane_WEB.pdf

MacFarlane, Julie, *Islamic Divorce in North America: A Shari'ah Path in a Secular Society* (Oxford, UK: Oxford University Press, 2012).

Mattu, Ayesha, and Nura Maznai (eds.), *Love, Inshallah: The Secret Love Lives of American Muslim Women* (Berkeley, CA: Soft Skull Press, 2012).

Nomani, Asrai, *Standing Alone: An American Woman's Struggle for the Soul of Islam* (San Francisco: Harper, 2005).

Qureishi, Asifa, and Frank Vogel (eds.), *The Islamic Marriage Contract: Case Studies in Islamic Family Law* (Cambridge, UK: Harvard University Press, 2008).

Rouse, Carolyn, *Engaged Surrender: African American Women and Islam* (Berkeley, CA: University of California Press, 2004).

Waugh, Earle, Sharon Abu-Laban, and Regula Qureshi (eds.), *Muslim Families in North America* (Edmonton: University of Alberta Press, 1991).

CHAPTER 13

···

MOSQUES IN THE UNITED STATES

···

IHSAN BAGBY

THE word *mosque* (in Arabic, *masjid*) literally means a place of prostration; therefore it represents the Islamic house of worship. In the Muslim world, mosques are usually built and governed by the state or wealthy donors. Thus most mosques function not as "congregations" or community centers but simply as places of worship. Muslim theologians have made it clear that mosques belong only to God. Accordingly Muslims in the larger Muslim world are not considered members of a particular mosque. They are members of the *ummah* (worldwide community of Muslims) and thus pray in any mosque that is convenient.

Despite this, Muslims in America have always followed congregational patterns in their attachment to specific mosques. They have gathered in voluntary associations that govern themselves, and they have sponsored programs and activities that transform mosques into community centers that attempt to serve the needs of Muslims in relation to birth, marriage, death, and—most important—passing on the legacy of Islam to their children. Mosques in the United States thus have served as the primary vehicle for the collective expression of Islam in the American Muslim community; as such, they symbolize the commitment of Muslims to find a place in America for themselves as well as for Islam.

HISTORICAL OVERVIEW

···

The history of the American mosque can be divided into two eras: 1890–1964 and 1965–2013.

The First Era, 1890–1964

The first reference to a mosque in America appeared in 1893, when the first recorded American convert to Islam, Alexander Russell Webb (1846–1916), designated an area in his organization's headquarters as a mosque. Webb's organization, American Islamic Propaganda, rented two offices in Manhattan in 1893 and each office had a mosque. The mosques, however, were short-lived, as Webb moved in 1894 and disbanded his efforts in 1896.[1] Nonetheless Webb's leadership set a pattern that has proved to be one of the unique aspects of mosques in the United States. American converts have continued to play a major role in shaping the history and development of mosques in this country.

The history of the American mosque is linked in part to the influx of Muslim immigrants. The turn of the twentieth century witnessed the first wave of Muslim immigrants from Europe and the Middle East—almost all young, uneducated single males seeking economic opportunity and ready to return home after making good. They first established coffee houses, ethnic clubs, charitable associations, and burial associations, fulfilling their religious impulses in a more ad hoc fashion by praying in apartments and rented halls. As long as these migrant laborers intended to return home, there was no need for a permanent house of worship. However, when they began to consider staying in America, they married and started families. Immediately the challenge arose—most strongly felt by the wives—of how to transfer the legacy of Islam to their children. Added to this mix was the catalyst of a few religiously motivated individuals who longed to see Muslims practice their religion fully in America. The result, starting in the 1920s, was the establishment of mosques, which were the manifestation of the commitment of Muslims to plant the tree of Islam in America.

The first purpose-built mosque was established in Highland Park, Michigan, in 1921 by a highly diverse coalition of Muslim immigrants drawn to the promise of employment at the new Ford factory. However, internal disputes sapped enthusiasm and soon led to the demise of the plan in 1922. The oldest existing purpose-built mosque in America is in Cedar Rapids, Iowa, where Lebanese immigrants finished construction in 1934. The first Muslim immigrants in the Cedar Rapids area were Lebanese Muslim men who started to arrive around 1885. By 1914, some forty-five Muslims worked as peddlers and shop owners. Almost all single men, they looked to Lebanon for wives. By 1920, Muslims were renting halls to use for various social and religious activities and for the religious education of their young children. In 1925 they formed an organization called the Rose of Fraternity Lodge, which was a combination ethnic club and religious organization. When the idea of building a mosque emerged, the wives took the lead in raising money and pushing the effort. Ground was broken in 1930 and the mosque was finished in 1934, having been delayed by the Depression. It looked like a prairie school house with a dome over the entrance. On one side of the entrance was an English plaque that read "Moslem Temple," demonstrating their desire to avoid a foreign word (*mosque*) in favor of a more familiar word (*temple*). On the other side of the entrance was an Arabic plaque reading "*al-Nadi al-Islami*" (Islamic Club), which, because it was intended to house activities other than prayer, signaled their reluctance to call their building a mosque.[2]

While American mosques were always community centers, the early immigrants were not sure that it was right for a mosque to house social activities; thus they called their new building both a temple and a social hall. In the 1950s Muslims started using the term *Islamic Center* to signal that the building housed more than just a prayer area. The American mosque has functioned in a similar fashion throughout its history: It has served as the locus of worship services, a wide range of educational and social activities, and as a platform for dialogue with the wider American community. However pre-1965 mosques differed in some respects from mosques of the later period in that builders of the pre-1965 mosques were much more willing to step outside the Islamic tradition. In contrast, those constructing post-1965 mosques have been more conservative because of their desire to adhere to the Islamic tradition.

These differences can be understood simply as a result of the very different eras in which Muslims lived. In early-twentieth-century America the pressure of Americanization meant that immigrants were expected to assimilate. The push for assimilation was exacerbated by public prejudice against Muslims as well as other nonwhite peoples. The Muslim world was also different. Before World War II, Muslims lived under European colonial rule, and Islam, being blamed for the backwardness of the Muslim world, was on the defensive. As a result the Muslims who came to America were less confident in their religion and more willing to accept the ways of their adopted country. They were also reluctant to enforce traditional standards out of fear that Muslims, especially the youth, would reject the mosque as out of step with American society. Compounding their lack of confidence was the fact that they were lacking in education both about the West and about Islam.

Observers of the pre-1965 Islamic institutions have noted the lack of adherence to Islamic culture in that early period. Around 1948 the newly arrived Albanian Imam Vehbi Ismail, having found some men in his new congregation drinking alcohol in the hall, contemplated leaving America.[3] In his research on Detroit and Toledo mosques, conducted in 1959, Elkholy reported that only 30 percent of the Muslims in his study fasted for as many as seven days in the month of Ramadan.[4]

Although the mosque was the community's religious center, religious activities in the period before 1964 were limited. Before World War II only a few mosques regularly held the Friday prayers, and even after World War II attendance at mosque services was sparse. Undoubtedly the small number of Muslims in this early period contributed to the low attendance. In the early 1960s, only twelve people regularly attended Friday prayers at the Dearborn mosque.[5] No mosque during that period held all the five daily prayers in congregation. 'Eid prayers attracted the largest number of attendees, but often the 'Eid prayers were observed on the weekend if 'Eid fell on a weekday. In the Shi'ite mosques, celebrations for 'Ashura and the birthdays of the imams did not appear until trained imams started to arrive in the 1950s.

Deeply concerned about losing their younger members, mosques had youth groups and sponsored youth activities. Sunday school for children was a major activity, as it is today. In Detroit in the late 1950s, Sunday school attendance at the Shi'te Hashimite Hall was an impressive 160, and in Toledo it was 150. Music and American-style dancing were often part of the activities—although there was some grumbling about the twist, the new dancing rage of the 1960s.[6]

Social events drew the largest numbers to the mosque. Community dinners (often monthly) and especially marriage feasts were a relished time for the community to come together to socialize and celebrate their Islamic identity. Belly dancing was not uncommon at such events. Many women's auxiliaries thrived during this earlier period, and they served a vital role in the mosque as the backbone of the support for Sunday schools, social events, and fund raising. Women's attendance at Friday prayers, however, was low, and few women served on mosque boards.

Mosques in this period also served a clear civic function as their leaders consciously recognized that mosques could help make their members better citizens. Politicians and church groups were hosted at the mosques.

From the very beginning, African American Muslims have been an essential part of the story of Islam in America. African Americans saw in Islam an alternative identity to the racist stereotypes projected by white America, a spiritual and moral alternative to the hedonism and materialism of "street" culture, and a vehicle for uplifting African American people. African American Muslims typically established mosques as an expression of their new religious identity; their mosques were unique in their concern for and engagement in issues of social justice related to black people and in their missionary activities to bring other African Americans to the more wholesome life of Islam.

African American mosques, which embraced a mainstream or Sunni understanding of Islam, emerged for the first time in the 1930s. The first African American mosque was the First Cleveland Mosque, founded by Imam Wali Akram (1904–1994) in 1937. Wali Akram converted to Islam in 1924 through the efforts of the Ahmadiyyah—a heterodox Muslim movement from India. In 1937 he left the Ahmadiyyah mosque in Cleveland owing to a dispute over South Asian dominance and culture (in particular the seclusion of women) and founded a new mosque. Akram took pride in establishing for the first time regular Friday prayers.

Many other African American Muslims came out of the Moorish Science Temple, a proto-Islamic movement that mixed Islam with black nationalism, masonry, and theosophical/new thought philosophy. After the death of Noble Drew Ali (1886–1929), the Moorish Science Temple's founder, many followers sought out or stumbled upon mainstream Islam. In the 1940s there were almost as many African American mosques as immigrant mosques.

Also emerging out of the Moorish Science Temple was the Nation of Islam, which was the most successful "Muslim" organization in this early period. Founded in 1930 by Fard Muhammad (b. 1893), an apparent Muslim from the East, the Nation of Islam evolved under Fard's successor Elijah Muhammad (1897–1975) into a highly heterodox version of Islam that did not include the requirements of daily prayer, Friday prayer, or 'Eid prayer. Elijah Muhammad called his houses of worship temples rather than mosques. In the late 1950s, under the leadership of Malcolm X, the number of temples started to increase. In 1971, as he moved to identify more with mainstream Islam, Elijah Muhammad changed the name of each Nation of Islam house of worship from *temple* to *mosque*. By 1975, when Elijah Muhammad died, there were about seventy-five such mosques.

The Second Era, 1965–2012

The second era in the history of the American Muslim community, during which the Muslim population began to grow significantly, witnessed a dramatic increase in the number of mosques. The expansion of the Muslim community started in the late 1960s with the arrival of Muslim students and immigrants from the Muslim world and was enhanced by the large number of African American converts, spurred largely by the black power movement and the success of the Nation of Islam. The Muslims—both immigrant and African American—of this second era were also quite different: They were more self-confident in their desire to practice and not compromise their Islamic tradition, more resistant to assimilation, and more critical of American culture and politics. As a result, mosques were more insular and isolated in the early decades of this era. As these immigrants and converts aged, however, they moderated, becoming more flexible in Islamic practice and more outward looking in their relationship with society.

Many mosques were started around universities, where they began as Muslim student associations and then evolved into mosques as the Muslim nonstudent population increased. In cities, earlier immigrant mosques were overwhelmed by new arrivals who were both more educated and more conservative. In Chicago in 1954, for example, Palestinian peddlers and shopkeepers founded the Mosque Foundation with the dream of building a mosque. They purchased land in a Chicago suburb but continued to hold Friday prayers in rented storefronts. When the more conservative new Arab immigrants arrived in the 1970s, they joined with the earlier Palestinians to build a mosque, and by 1981 a modest one was opened. Soon afterward, however, cultural differences such as those having to do with the role of women arose—women were strongly encouraged to cover and males and females sat separately at mosque events—causing the original founders to leave the mosque. When the doors opened, only about 75 Muslims attended Friday prayers, while by the 1990s some 800 were attending.[7]

From the 1960s through the 1980s, student and immigrant mosques were focused primarily on building an infrastructure, setting prayer times, and developing Sunday school and Islamic studies classes. The 1990s, however, marked a time when mosques were called to be more outwardly focused on interfaith community service and local politics. Slowly a consensus developed that mosques and the American Muslim community should be a part of the fabric of America. The jolt of 9/11 and the emergence of shrill anti-Muslim rhetoric sealed the argument that mosques cannot afford to be isolated from American society.

African American Mosques Post-1965

The most remarkable story for African Americans was the transformation of the Nation of Islam into a mainstream Muslim group. When Elijah Muhammad passed away in 1975, the consensus successor was his seventh-born child, W. Deen Mohammed (at that time Wallace Muhammad), who wasted little time in ordering, for instance, the chairs to be removed from the main meeting room of all mosques and rugs installed so that Muslim prayers following the established traditions could be held. The hierarchal, regimented nature of the organization was also altered, and by 2003 W. Deen Mohammed actually disbanded the national organization, making each mosque independent. The mosques of the former Nation of Islam are now an integral part of the American Muslim community.

A number of African Americans converted to mainstream Islam starting in the 1960s, often inspired by black power and black nationalist movements. These new African American converts were energized by the vision of resisting American racism and white cultural hegemony by embracing Islam as an alternative way of life. Although they were introduced to Islam either through earlier African American or immigrant mosques, they usually ended up establishing their own mosques. While in the early years these mosques served as headquarters and hangouts for members, most established the five daily prayers as one of their commitments to living Islam completely. Their practice of Islam was more conservative than that in the earlier African American mosques. Thus a similar dynamic existed in both the African American Muslim community and the immigrant community, where a newer generation sharply criticized an earlier generation for being lax in their practice of Islam.

Mosques in the Contemporary Period

Growth of Mosques

The number of mosques in America has grown exponentially since the 1960s. Piecing together historical records and mosque studies plus figures from the 2011 US Mosque Study that asked when a particular mosque was founded, a reasonable picture can be drawn of the growth of mosques in America. The first spurt of growth came in the 1930s, when mosques went from five in number to forty. Growth slowed through the 1940s and 1950s and then accelerated starting in the 1960s. The greatest growth in the actual number of mosques came in the first decade of the new millennium, when from 2001 to 2011 a total of 897 new mosques were counted. In 2011 a total of 2,106 mosques were reported—a 252 percent increase from 1984.[8] Mosques are now found throughout urban America. The driving force behind the increased number of mosques has been the dramatic increase in the number of Muslim immigrants, the greater wealth of such immigrants, and to a lesser extent the increase in the number of converts to Islam.

The 2011 US Mosque Study shows that 90 percent of all existing mosques were founded since 1960 and 54 percent were established after 1990. Mosques in America, therefore, are remarkably young as institutions and still very much in their formative stage of development.

Mosque Participants

The great diversity of the American Muslim community is evidenced by the fact that 97 percent of all mosques report that they have more than one ethnic/national group in attendance at Friday prayers. Such diversity is partly due to the theology, which teaches that mosques are for all Muslims; therefore Muslims pray where it is convenient. This means that on Friday they pray near their work. At the same time, three fourths of mosques are largely attended by one ethnic group—typically either South

Table 13.1 Number of Mosques in the United States

Year	Number	New Mosques	Percentage of Mosques Started	Increase
1930	5			
1940	40	35	700%	
1950	75	35	88%	
1960	120	45	60%	
1970	290	170	142%	
1984	598	298	106%	
1994	962	364	61%	
2000	1,209	247	26%	
2011	2,106	897	74%	

Source: Chart compiled from a variety of sources, including Y.Y. Haddad and Adair Lummis, *Islamic Values in the United States* (NY: OUP 1987, p.3); Ihsan Bagby, *The American Mosque: A National Portrait* (Washington DC: Council on American-Islamic Relations, 2001, p. 3; Ihsan Bagby, *The American Mosque 2001: Report No. 1 from the US Mosque Study of 2001* (Washington DC: Council on American-Islamic Relations, 2011, p. 5).

Asian, Arab, or African American. Relations between mosques—especially African American and other immigrant mosques—were nonexistent or strained through the 1980s. In the last few decades relations have improved significantly, coinciding with the increased diversity in Friday attendance.

Most mosques are of moderate size—the median attendance at Friday prayers is 173. However attendance has grown steadily over the decades: two thirds (65 percent) of mosques in 2011 reported an increase of over 10 percent in attendance over the past five years. Only 6 percent experienced a decline.

Mosque Activities

The weekly Friday prayer is undoubtedly the most important activity at a mosque. The ritual of Friday prayer in American mosques is virtually the same as that found in mosques throughout the Muslim world. One clear sign, however, of the acculturation of American mosques is the fact that in 70 percent of American mosques the sermon (*khutbah*) is given only in English. This is a marked increase from the year 2000, when 53 percent of mosques used only English.

Another difference in the pre-1960 mosque and the present-day mosque is the performance of daily prayer. Before 1960 few if any mosques held all five of the daily prayers, but by 2011 approximately 60 percent of all mosques prayed all five prayers in congregation. Only 9 percent of mosques do not hold any of the five daily prayers.

Overall, however, the main mosque activities have not changed much over the decades. The weekend school for children is still among the highest priorities for mosques. In 2011 over three fourths of all mosques reported that they conduct a weekend school, with an average attendance of 107 children. Almost all mosques have some type of monthly or weekly community social gathering (93 percent) and some type of religious studies class (83 percent). A wide variety of other activities are held in mosques, including women's activities/programs (71 percent), youth activities/ programs (65 percent), Qur'an memorization classes (50 percent), and parenting/ marriage enrichment (32 percent). The mosque has remained a nexus of activities in addition to being a place of prayer.

Interface with the Wider Community

The American mosque has always served as a vehicle for interfacing with the wider community, and this tradition has even deepened since 2000. A remarkable 63 percent of all mosques in 2011 reported hosting an open house for their non-Muslims neighbors in the preceding twelve months. Most mosque leaders acknowledge that 9/11 awakened them to the necessity of reaching out to the wider community. Another indicator of this trend is that over 79 percent of mosques in 2011 were involved in some form of interfaith activity, an increase from 66 percent in 2000.

Another aspect of congregational life that has received greater attention in the past few decades is community service programs aimed at Muslims and non-Muslims. While African American mosques have been involved in these types of programs for many years, most immigrant mosques are in the process of developing them for the first time. As an example, 45 percent of mosques indicated that they organized a health fair, health clinic, or health education program in the past year. Almost half of all mosques (47 percent) are involved in social issue advocacy or community service programs such as anticrime, affordable housing, community gardening, and other projects.

Another type of activity that again demonstrates the greater external focus of mosques is voter registration. In 2011 almost half (48 percent) of mosques had a voter registration drive at the mosque, either organized by themselves or by another group that came to the mosque.

Mosque Structures

The overall youth of the American mosque is reflected in the fact that most mosques (56 percent) are still converted structures, including houses, storefronts, former churches, and commercial properties. Only 30 percent of mosques were specifically purpose-built. Although this percentage is relatively small, it is a dramatic increase from past decades. In 2011 the actual number of purpose-built mosques was approximately 632; this figure represents a substantial increase from 2000, when 314 purpose-built mosques existed (26 percent of all mosques). Therefore from 2000 to 2011 there was a 101 percent increase in the number of purpose-built mosques. The first decade of the new millennium represented a remarkable building boom for mosques. Most likely this boom is indicative of the growing financial resources of the Muslim community, as Muslim immigrants have become more prosperous over the decades.

Most mosque communities have two primary concerns in considering the construction of a mosque: keeping the price tag as low as possible and including some traditional design elements such as domes, arches, and minarets. The lack of funds is largely due to the desire of mosque leaders to avoid Islamically prohibited, interest-bearing bank loans; thus they finance their projects entirely from donations. Through the 1980s many mosques went to the oil-rich Gulf countries to raise funds from charities and merchants, but the First Gulf War (1990–1991) and then 9/11 in 2001 ended overseas fund raising. Now funds are raised locally. Limited budgets mean that most purpose-built mosques in America are not lavishly designed. Nevertheless, mosque leaders desire a design that proclaims their identity as Muslims, although typically they do not have a strong preference for any one traditional style of architecture (i.e., Mamluk, Ottoman, or other). The result is that the design of most purpose-built mosques in America is a transplanted traditional one that mixes styles, usually with a nod to some modern elements. Mosques are thus not replicas of those in the home countries of their attendees so much as eclectic reinterpretations of traditional designs.

Mosque Finances

The developing nature of mosques is also indicated in the fact that the median mosque income is only $70,000, an extremely modest figure. Approximately 61 percent of all mosques have a budget below $100,000. Although attendance may be robust for Friday prayers, these numbers do not translate into donations to mosques. The absence of a tradition in the Muslim world of giving to mosques and of mosque membership has undoubtedly made it more difficult for American mosques to raise funds. Low budgets translate into few paid staff. Only 44 percent of all mosques have a full-time paid imam. Half of all mosques have no full-time paid staff. Mosques are run largely by volunteers.

Issues of Integration

American mosques have been likened to conservative fortresses blocking the integration of members into American society; mosques have been labeled bastions and incubators for radical Islam. These accusations and suspicions have surrounded mosques since 9/11, leading to increased mosque vandalism and community resistance to new mosque construction. However, all recent studies indicate that mosques are aiding in the integration of Muslims in American society. The study of American Muslims conducted in 2011 by Karam Dana and colleagues concluded that "88 percent of those who are very involved in their mosque agree that mosques help integrate as opposed to only 12 percent who think they contribute to isolation."[9] In this study 95 percent of those with the highest level of religiosity agreed that Islamic teachings are compatible with Muslim political participation in the American public square.[10] In the US Mosque Study 2011, some 91 percent of mosque leaders agreed that Muslims should be involved in the American political process, and 98 percent agreed that Muslims should be involved in civic institutions. Gallup's survey found that "Muslim Americans who attend religious services at least once a week have higher levels of civic engagement."[11]

The civic activities of mosques—such as interfaith community service and voter registration—are another demonstration of the American mosque's embrace of civic engagement. While mosques in the 1960s through the 1980s might have been more internally focused and more isolated from American society, it is clear that American mosques now are serving as a vehicle for greater civic involvement.

Women

In comparison with mosques overseas, where women generally are excluded from participating, women in American mosques are increasingly present and involved, although they remain largely marginalized. Throughout the history of mosques in America, women have been most active in organizing and running weekend activities such as Sunday schools and social activities, but they have never attended Friday prayers in significant numbers and they have rarely served on mosque boards. In 2011 women accounted for only 18 percent of attendees at Friday prayers, and this figure has largely remained stable over the past few decades.

Another indicator of the marginalization of women in the mosque is that two thirds of mosques in the 2011 Mosque Study report women praying behind a barrier or in another room. In the 2007 Pew study, 48 percent of all Muslim men and 45 percent of all Muslim women agreed that women should pray separately behind a curtain or in another area.[12] Many Muslim women argue that they prefer a private area that they can control. Their biggest complaint is that the private area is too often dirty and small or removed from sight of the imam. Nevertheless, according to the Pew study, an equal number of Muslim men and women feel that women should not have to pray in a separate area, and there is growing pressure on mosques to accommodate this desire.

A major improvement for women has occurred in the percentage of mosques that allow women to serve on mosque boards. From 2000 to 2011 the number of mosques that allowed such a practice went from 69 percent to 87 percent. The actual percentage of mosques who actually have women on their boards—as opposed to just allowing them to serve—has also significantly increased, from 50 percent in 2000 to 59 percent in 2011. It is expected that as women become more active in mosque governance, mosques will become more sensitive to women's perspectives.

Approaches to Islam

More than half of mosque leaders (55 percent) indicate that they follow a relatively flexible approach to Islam in that they adhere to the authority of the textual sources (Qu'ran and Sunnah) but prefer interpretations that take into account modern circumstances and the overall purposes of the texts. Mosques with such leaders are the most supportive of civic engagement and are more accommodating to women in that most have women on their mosque boards and allow women to pray without a curtain separating them from the men. Shi'ite mosques, which constitute approximately 7 percent of all mosques in America, display the same characteristics of flexibility.

The mosques that follow one of the traditional legal schools (*madhahib*) and the salafi way, which is akin to Wahhabi thought, are less likely to support political involvement or to accommodate women. Many of these mosques are more comfortable in remaining isolated from American society and attempting to re-create an interpretation of Islam from overseas. However, they are small in number: Mosques that follow a *madhhab* are only 7 percent of all mosques, and salafi mosques are 1 percent.

Approximately 30 percent of all mosques are situated between these two poles. They do not follow a *madhhab* or the salafi way, but they continue to look to the past and its great scholars for guidance. These mosques tend to be very open to civic engagement but more conservative when it comes to accommodating women. No mosque in America has adopted an approach of so-called liberal or secular Islam, which in some cases endorses women leading prayers or the practice of homosexuality.

NOTES

1. Umar F. Abd-Allah, *A Muslim in Victorian America: The Life of Alexander Russell Webb* (New York: Oxford University Press, 2006), 165.
2. Philip Harsham, "Islam in Iowa," *Saudi Aramco World* (November/December 1976) and "The Mother Mosque of America," retrieved June 3, 2012 from http//mothermosque.org/page.php?2.
3. Sally F. Howell, "Inventing the American Mosque: Early Muslims and Their Institutions in Detroit, 1910–1980," (Doctoral dissertation, University of Michigan, 2009): 186.
4. Abdo A. Elkholy, *The Arab Moslems in the United States: Religion and Assimilation* (New Haven, CT: College and University Press, 1966): 117.
5. Atif Amin Wasfi, "Dearborn Arab-Moslem Community: A Study of Acculturation," (Doctoral dissertation, Michigan State University, 1964): 132.
6. Op cit., 153.
7. Noreen Ahmed-Ullah, Kim Barker, Laurie Cohen, Stephen Franklin, and Sam Roe, "Hard-Liners Won Battle for Bridgeview Mosque," *Chicago Tribune*, February 8, 2004, accessed November 14, 2012. Available at: www.chicagotribune.com/news/local/chi-0402080265feb08,0,3486861.story
8. All statistics on mosques in this section are taken from Ihsan Bagby, *The American Mosque 2011: Report Number 1 from the US Mosque Study 2011*, (Washington, DC; Council on American-Islamic Relations, 2011) and *The American Mosque 2011: Report Number 2 from the US Mosque Study 2011*, (Plainfield, IN: Islamic Society of North America, 2011).
9. Karam Dana, Matt A. Barreto, and Kassra A. R. Oskooii, "Mosques as American Institutions: Mosque Attendance, Religiosity and Integration into the Political System among American Muslims," *Religions* (2011, 2, 504–524): 514.
10. Dana et al: 515.
11. Abu Dhabi Gallup Center, *Muslim Americans: Faith, Freedom, and the Future*, (Author, August 2011): 6
12. Pew Research Center, *Muslim Americans: Middle Class and Most Mainstream*, (Washington, DC: Author, 2007): 26.

CHAPTER 14

DEVELOPMENTS IN ISLAMIC EDUCATION IN THE UNITED STATES

SUSAN L. DOUGLASS

MUSLIMS in North America are following a path consistent with their predecessors in Islamic history in upholding the transmission of knowledge of Islam and learning in general. This applies to educating the next generation as a collective and individual responsibility as well as looking outward to the communities in which they live. This path involves a spectrum of activities from homeschooling within the family to various levels of organized educational instruction in mosques and Islamic centers to schools of specialized and general education.

Contemporary needs and opportunities, however, have taken this community into territory beyond the educational efforts of its predecessors. Writing and publishing in print and electronically, creating new types of media, and participating in the flourishing of academic publishing and university centers of Islamic and area studies, foundations, and other public institutions in North America has resulted in an outpouring of projects, books, films, and commentary. This chapter provides an overview of institutions, trends, and types of educational endeavors. While touching on some recent history and background, it focuses mainly on the current status of education related to Islam and Muslims in North America at the beginning of the second decade of the twenty-first century.

From what we know about the earliest Muslims who arrived in America as slaves from West Africa, they lacked the opportunity to transmit their beliefs and practices to their offspring except informally. Among the sparse evidence of transmission are documents written in Arabic, such as the manuscript of Omar Ibn Said transcribing Qur'an verses apparently from memory.[1] Oral evidence such as the survival of some version of ritual practice reminiscent of Islam in the Sea Islands and the cadences of Qur'anic recitation and the call to prayer in blues music attests to continuity in the face of the most difficult circumstances.[2] Research into survivals of indigenous African religions in the New World indicates practices and expressions but little systematic transmission.

Evidence from later Muslim immigrants who came voluntarily, such as those who founded the earliest mosques in the United States, indicates that Muslims were interested in preserving their rituals by establishing institutions. Transmission from parents or knowledgeable members of the community to children is a mode of cultural survival common to migrants living in a culturally alien society. While informal transmission is hard to detect in the historical record, we can be confident that it preceded the establishment of formal institutions. The following section describes formal schooling efforts of various types in the Muslim community.

ISLAMIC SCHOOLING

Weekend Schools

Mosques (in Arabic, *masjid*, pl. *masajid*, or place of bowing in prayer) are the primary Islamic institutions; their educational function dates to the 6th century CE under Prophet Muhammad. The community met in the mosque to pray and to hear Muhammad teach men and women, young and old. After Muhammad's death, the mosque continued and expanded as a place where adults and children learned to recite the Qur'an and study its meaning, and to perform Islamic rituals and life practices. Wherever Islam spread by migration or conversion, mosques have continued to serve as centers of education. Scholars taught in mosques until specialized institutions assumed these functions. Colleges, or madrassas (literally, places of instruction), developed by the 10th century and carried out both general and religious education. Schools for basic literacy skills emerged both in the mosques and in other settings, such as the *khuttab* schools for primary education in cities and villages across Muslim lands.[3] These educational traditions moved and changed with time and the spread of Islam and were carried over into the American landscape in substance if not always in form.

Muslim immigrants to North America in the nineteenth century were few in number. Education of the young would have taken place in homes and small community settings, and mosques and *musallas* (informal places of prayer) served the education of the young in more or less organized fashion. Muslim immigration remained at a trickle until the change in immigration law in 1965. The new immigrants began to establish ties and grow families in the 1970s and 1980s, setting up places of prayer and educational institutions in their communities. Thus education became more systematic. It took the community a decade or more to purchase a building and even longer for a purpose-built mosque. Educational programs for adults and children were often scheduled for weekends. Muslims in towns, suburbs, and cities prayed and held classes in church basements, storefronts, repurposed vacant churches, commercial buildings, and single-family homes, loaned or purchased for the purpose.

Until the 1990s, there were few data on American mosques. National surveys led by Ihsan Bagby in 1994, 2001, and 2011 provide direct and indirect data on weekend schools. The 1994 study counted 962 mosques, and by 2001, the number of mosques in America (1,209) represented a 25 percent increase. By 2011, that number had increased by 75 percent for a total of 2,106 mosques. The 1994 and 2001 studies contains detailed information about weekend schools for adults and children. Based on telephone and written surveys from a sample of mosques, the study found that weekend, weeknight, or summer school programs were common in mosques: 71 percent had a regular weekend school, with 49 percent only for children and teens, and 46 percent had schools for both adults and children.[4] The 2009 study estimated that 29,500 adults and 79,600 children and teens attended weekend school. The 2011 study did not gather such data, but it is likely that weekend schools increased with the rise in mosque attendance. The 2001 study records increases in average Friday prayer attendance from 150 (1994) to 292 (2001) to 353 (2011). A proportionate increase would mean that weekend school attendance would approach 200,000 adults and children today.[5]

The curriculum of Islamic weekend schools consists of basic teaching about obligatory worship such as the Five Pillars, the practices and values that undergird them, Qur'an recitation and memorization, and Arabic instruction. Narratives from the lives of prophets and Islamic history are also featured. Some weekend schools teach an additional language, such as Urdu or Farsi. Instructional materials for weekend schools drove early publishing efforts in Islamic education. Since the 1980s, Muslim institutions such as the Islamic Society of North America and its education offices and the International Institute of Islamic Thought, as well as other international organizations, have concerned themselves with improving weekend school instruction.

Educational efforts have frequently run into difficulties. For example, Khan et al. describe a disconnect between teachers and students in weekend Islamic schools "due to a combination of factors, including a curriculum that does not relate to the students, outdated teaching strategies, and communication barriers between students and teachers"; they recommend including American Muslim history to make the curriculum more relevant.[6] A recent issue of *Islamic Horizons* magazine focusing on education includes an article about the efforts of the Iqra International Educational Foundation to publish standardized tests that seek a common denominator among multiple publishers' textbooks, and another article by Hamed Ghazali, chairman of the Muslim American Society Council of Islamic Schools, advocating data-driven assessment of learning in weekend and full-time schools.[7] Islamic weekend schools generally have too little time to teach subjects in depth, have difficulty commanding the attention of students, are taught by dedicated but often poorly trained and under-compensated teachers, and are unevenly administered. The fact that many women teach in weekend schools, however, may serve to preserve some of the feminine legacy of storytelling known to earlier generations of Muslims but often displaced by institutional learning in modern states.[8] Weekend schools are an experience shared by many if not a majority of Muslim youth in the past few decades and represent a vital link to religious knowledge, cultural heritage, and socialization into the community. Some recent fiction written by American Muslims serves to illustrate aspects of the weekend school experience.[9]

Sister Clara Muhammad Schools

The Clara Muhammad Schools, founded in Detroit in 1932, were the first formal schools developed in North America. The Nation of Islam movement established by Elijah Muhammad, an amalgam of religious ideas from Christianity, Islam, and black nationalism, attracted a large following among African Americans in the United States. Clara Muhammad, the wife of founder Elijah Muhammad and mother of Warith Deen Mohammed, established a home school for her children and others in the community as an alternative to public schooling. The primary and secondary school was called the University of Islam (UOI) for its universal curriculum. The UOI moved to a theater building in Detroit as enrollment increased. Curriculum supported the vision that Muslim children acquire the values and knowledge system of the Nation of Islam, with the goal to " 'know self,' 'love self,' and 'do for self.' "[10] The NOI strove to provide a school in every NOI temple, and by the mid-1960s, the UOI became an educational model for black nationalist schools as well. By 1975, according to Rashid and Muhammad, there were 41 University of Islam schools. Smaller schools offered primary education only, while large schools in Chicago, New York City, Atlanta, and Washington, D.C., boasted well-equipped buildings with certified teachers, secondary programs, and bus fleets. The curriculum supported the NOI ideology and historical narrative, its economic and community development goals, and skill in academic subjects.

In 1975, after Malcolm X left the NOI and following Elijah Muhammad's death, W. D. Mohammad led the NOI and the schools away from the original belief system promoted by Elijah Muhammad and toward mainstream Islam.[11] This transition was difficult and resulted in some fragmentation of the educational system. The schools were then renamed after founder Clara Muhammad, mother of Warith al-Din Mohammad, who assumed the leadership of the movement.

The transition from NOI to Sunni Islam had serious economic consequences, which affected the school system. Some schools closed and others reduced their programs. Educators from the community built upon the strengths of the system to shift the educational focus while maintaining academic strengths and infrastructure. The newly named American Muslim Mission held several conferences on the Sister Clara Muhammad Schools in 1982, with a focus on resolving leadership issues and curriculum development. In 1991, the Muslim Teachers' College was established with the intention of eventually offering degrees.

The Council of Islamic Schools in North America (CISNA) was founded by the Islamic Society of North America in 1991. Its purpose was to assist existing schools, of which Clara Muhammad Schools were the largest segment. These institution-building efforts bore fruit at the level of linking various communities and individual efforts among educators. While they did not realize many of their major goals in centralizing curriculum development and training, they did represent an important milestone in bringing indigenous American Muslims and immigrants together in the work of educating the young and did result in cross-fertilizing numerous curriculum and training projects.[12]

The number of Clara Muhammad Schools today is uncertain. From a high of 41 schools in the 1970s it declined to about 30 in the early 1990s and has fallen to approximately 20 today. They are affiliated with the Mohammed Schools Consortium of the United States and Bermuda, which lists twenty-four schools, both full-time and weekend.[13] The very successful full-time Mohammed Schools of Atlanta celebrated its 40th year as "the only private African-American Muslim school accredited by the Georgia Accrediting Commission (GAC), The Commission on International and Trans-Regional Accreditation (CITA), and Southern Association of Colleges and Schools (SACS)."[14]

Full-Time Islamic Schools

Establishment of full-time Muslim or Islamic schools in the United States parallels the recent history of mosque growth, but with considerable lag time and reduced numbers. While there may have been scattered alternative schools for Muslims outside the Clara Muhammad network before the 1980s, they were isolated or very small-scale efforts in homes. Among the earliest full-time schools established in the immigrant community in the 1980s were the Islamic School of Seattle (1980); Orange Crescent School, in Garden Grove, California (1983); Al-Ghazaly School, in Jersey City, New Jersey (1984); New Horizon School, in Pasadena, California (1984); Muslim Community School, in Potomac, Maryland (1985); and Islamic Saudi Academy, in Virginia (1985). The Saudi school operated under Saudi Embassy control and was more of an expatriate school, although community members were among its students and staff. A second wave of schools was established in the next decade, including the Universal School, in Chicago (1991); Universal Academy, in Florida (1992); and Darul Arqam Schools network of Greater Houston (1992).

The first attempt to survey Islamic full-time schools was published in 1989 by ISNA, identifying about fifty schools. Before the Internet became widely available, there was no central organization of schools, making it difficult to disseminate curriculum materials among the schools, and even more difficult to survey their historical development. Some were associated with mosques, while others were independent. Few had purpose-built structures. In the 1994 study, 17 percent of all mosques indicated that they had a full-time school.[15] The 2011 study found that about one in five mosques had a full-time Islamic school. Information was incomplete, leading some researchers to speculate that as many as 400 Islamic schools existed.

The most systematic survey of schools was undertaken by Karen Keyworth, founding director of the Islamic Schools League of America (ISLA), beginning with its online registration in 2004, which yielded detailed data on 106 schools and on 32 schools that joined ISLA. A 2011 report yielded a figure of 235 schools as the "definitive number of Islamic schools in the United States," with an estimated number of students between 26,000 and 35,500.[16] Keyworth states that at most 3.5 percent attend full-time Islamic schools, while about 10 percent of American children are in private schools overall, including some Muslims.[17,18]

Keyworth's study is the most reliable and rich source of data on the schools, using a thorough, multilayered methodology, including self-registration, membership, mailings and telephone interviews, and consulting local mosques and list serve educators. ISLA deserves credit for dogged persistence with meager support, collecting data from 1998 to 2004 and establishing a system to maintain and update its information. ISLA's Islamic Educators' Communication Network, a list serve with about 450 members, created the ability to find schools as well as to communicate with educators to discuss common problems.

Elementary classes can enroll up to 25 or more students with one teacher each, plus a few Arabic and Islamic studies teachers who serve more than one class. Many parents are eager to start children in an Islamic school, and a school of a hundred or so can function with fewer than a dozen teachers. Only the teacher of a self-contained classroom needs to be trained and/or certified in all subjects. For middle and high school, the triangle is inverted. Subject area specialists in math, science, social science/history, and English are needed in addition to those teaching Arabic and Islamic studies, and the curriculum is now more demanding in terms of content knowledge. While the cost of faculty and facilities rises exponentially, there seem to be fewer parents willing to risk their students' precollege careers despite the fact that these are the most vulnerable years for social development.

Keyworth's report identified trends, challenges, and priorities for the schools.[19] The schools are generally small and often operate in buildings that are than ten years or more old. Slightly less than half of the schools are newer, usually housed in mosques or purpose-built structures. The majority of schools report written building plans, and many Islamic centers have plans to build schools. Some communities construct multipurpose buildings with classrooms before building a mosque. Very few schools have all their teachers certified, with exceptions for Arabic and Islamic teachers. Only a few schools report no certified teachers, although half employ uncertified Arabic and/or Islamic studies teachers. It should be noted, however, that while public schools hire mostly certified teachers, private schools regularly hire as many as 48 percent uncertified teachers.[20] Almost half of Islamic schools hire some non-Muslim teachers owing to the shortage of certified Muslim educators. Only about a quarter say that they would hire only Muslim faculty.[21] Their reluctance relates to the vision that Islamic schools integrate Islamic values and knowledge across the curriculum. Many Islamic schools are now accredited, and many more seek accreditation as a milestone of official approval that makes them much more attractive to donors and parents.

Keyworth's study reveals that only 21 percent of the schools are governed by a mosque, despite a widespread assumption to the contrary. While some schools began as mosque weekend education programs, they later constituted themselves as independent full-time schools.

HOMESCHOOLING

Homeschooling was the first type of Islamic education in America, and every Muslim household homeschools informally. Homeschooling was institutionalized by Clara Muhammad. In the contemporary Muslim community, a growing number of parents school their children at home, following in the footsteps of other American homeschool pioneers.

In the early 1990s, Massachusetts homeschooling parent Cynthia Sulaiman founded the Muslim Home School Network and Resource, including a list serve, information for Muslim families on legal issues, and networking with other homeschool organizations. She provided one of the first online efforts to link Muslim parents with the educational resources that were being published. Priscilla Martinez documented the rationales and varieties of what she sees as the fast-growing practice of homeschooling. No reliable figures exist, but homeschoolers have a presence in many mosques, as they participate in Qur'an recitation programs, scouting, teaching cooperatives and course offerings, and in mainstream organizations for homeschoolers.[22] Muslim homeschooling curricula vary widely, as Martinez notes, from "unschooling" models[23] of discovery learning to commercially available prepackaged texts and workbook programs, to classical education as laid out by Jessie Wise and Susan Wise Bauer in *The Well-Trained Mind*.[24] Zaytuna Institute assembled a liberal arts program for Muslim homeschoolers called Kinza Academy, which maintains a website, offers webinars, and includes Islamic studies and Arabic programs.[25]

Ikhlas Homeschool also offers a curriculum and support on its website and has published its journal, the *Muslim Home School in America*, since 2007.[26] Experience with Muslim homeschooling parents reveals a spectrum of schooling from providing the basics in a close-to-home environment to what parents jokingly call "car school-ing," because they take their children's learning experience to parks, science centers, astronomy clubs, museums, theaters, and enrichment programs. Some homeschool parent groups have spawned brick-and-mortar schools.

INSTITUTES OF HIGHER LEARNING

Before discussing Islamic institutions of higher learning, it is important to note the rise in programs of religious studies, Islamic studies, and area studies in North American universities. Two 2009 studies on the study of Islam in universities by Charles Kurzman and Carl Ernst and an edited volume published by the International Institute of Islamic Thought chart the remarkable growth of the field in the western academy in the past century.[27] Many Muslim professors teach in these institutions, and many Muslim students have received degrees from them. American universities have influenced the plan to found distinctly Islamic institutions of higher learning with the goal of acquiring accreditation to grant course credit and ultimately degrees. Many Muslim faculty have received degrees from western universities or served as faculty in them. Others obtained training from traditional Islamic institutions or universities in Muslim majority countries.

The American Islamic College (AIC) in Chicago was the first such attempt, founded in 1981 and occupying its own building in 1983. The AIC was accredited to grant asso-ciate of arts and bachelor of arts degrees in 1991, but it states on its website that "this authority was later removed by the IBHE [Illinois Board of Higher Education] due to the administration's inability to meet IBHE criteria." It has since been reorganized and is applying to restore its degree-granting status.[28]

The Graduate School of Islamic and Social Sciences (GSISS) was founded in the 1990s by the International Institute of Islamic Thought. It was the first training insti-tution for US military chaplains, a status that was rescinded in the wake of September 11, 2001; its training mandate was given to Hartford Seminary. GSISS has been granted a religious exemption from the State Council of Higher Education for Virginia and operates mainly as a theological seminary, holding adult education and certificate courses and establishing the Cordoba School of Professional Studies.[29]

Zaytuna College was founded in 2009 as a residential college of liberal arts and Islamic studies; in 2012 it purchased a permanent campus in California. It was founded in 2009 by Imam Zaid Shakir, Shaykh Hamza Yusuf, and Dr. Hatem Bazian "to restore broad-based and pluralistic scholarship to its proper place as a central priority of Muslims."[30] A pilot seminary program at Zaytuna Institute began in 2004. The institute graduated five students in 2008 and intends to seek accreditation as a four-year college. Zaytuna's reputation and philosophy were built on the strength of its core faculty, who are prominent speakers and authors, and on their programs for training young Muslims.

Other Islamic colleges founded in the past decade or so grant bachelor's and master's degrees and certificates in subjects such as Arabic and the Qur'an as on-site and online courses. None of these colleges is yet accredited by the appropriate regional and national agencies, so students take their chances on employment. The Islamic University of Minnesota opened in 2007, offering degrees but lacking accreditation. The Islamic University of North America in Houston opened in 2008 and offers seminars and certificates. Islamic American University, a project of the Muslim American Society, offers online and on-site study. Online programs include American Open University (AOU) established in 1995, offering Islamic studies in Arabic or English through distance learning. AOU is affiliated with California University in Pennsylvania, where students can enroll in degree programs and transfer credit. The Islamic Online University, founded in 2007 by Dr. Bilal Philips, has the goal of offering courses tuition free. Over 13,000 students enrolled in 2009, representing at least ten countries.[31]

As a young community with both continental and global reach, American Muslims are steadily moving through the stages of institution building. Surely the most difficult stage is higher education, but the fledgling institutions listed, along with informal programs in the United States as well as overseas institutions, indicate both the need and desire to connect with the heritage of Islamic learning.[32] Some of these programs seek to shore up learning according to particular sects or tendencies, while others provide connections to traditional learning and Arabic language mastery. Most significantly, several of these institutions demonstrate "forward thinking" rather than "backward looking" philosophies, expressing the mission to combine the best of traditional learning and innovative thinking in a globalized world with its broad challenges.

PRODUCTION OF EDUCATIONAL MATERIALS

The problem of educational media has been daunting in every setting. Islamic studies and Arabic language textbooks written overseas—albeit by governments that portray themselves as modern, secularizing nations—soon proved unsatisfactory for American pupils. Arabic language books, though relatively neutral in teaching modern standard Arabic, did not teach non-Arabic speaking American children effectively, including immigrants. Stories of the Prophets, instruction in Islamic practices, aids to reading the Qur'an, and literature that mirrored the experience of Muslim American children simply did not exist. Immigrant parents imported copies of children's books and a few vendors began assembling catalogues, but the unmet need was for material produced in North America for the homegrown audience. Books from the Islamic Foundation in Leicester, UK, were among early offerings in English.

Late-twentieth-century Islamic education gained impetus with the South Asian immigrants to the United States after 1947, who arrived with a long tradition of publishing in English. Beginning in the late 1960s, pioneers Abidullah and Tasneemah Ghazi began writing weekend school textbooks on a typewriter while teaching Muslim children in Cambridge, Massachusetts. They published the first textbooks in 1976 and established Iqra' International Education Foundation in 1983. This foundation now publishes 150 different textbooks for an estimated 600 weekend and 250 full-time schools.[33] Iqra's catalogue includes textbooks as well as children's books, history, Islamic studies, and other products.

Kazi Publications in Chicago, founded in 1972, is best known for adult books. Sound Vision, established in 1988, was an early developer of educational media for adults and children, including video, music, audio, and books. Sound Vision's puppet show *Adams World* was the equivalent of *Sesame Street* for Muslim children, teaching about prayer and boosting self-esteem with humor and knowledge. Several publishers started to provide teaching aids for weekend schools, such as Noorart, founded in 1997 as an online catalogue offering a wide range of domestic and foreign educational products.

Astrolabe, Inc., was launched by Suhaib al-Barzinji in the mid-1990s with the animated film *Al-Fatih*; it then produced and distributed *Muslim Scouts* and other media. Unity Productions Foundation, founded in 1999 by Alex Kronemer and Michael Wolfe, has produced nine documentary films, beginning with *Muhammad: Legacy of a Prophet*, and has successfully built an interfaith community outreach program. It offers a variety of educational materials and has received significant donations, prestigious awards, and grants.

Several educational organizations engaged the issue of effective approaches to Islamic studies curricula for American children. The International Institute of Islamic Thought (IIIT) commissioned a social studies series to supplement the standard textbook that most Muslim schools use.[34] The IIIT also published the graded eighteen-book American Family Series by Uthman Hutchinson.[35] Prolific Muslim children's authors and educators include Noora Durkee, Yahya Emmerich, Rukhsana Khan, and Freda Shamma, whose dozens of titles were published in the decade since 1990 and are distributed widely through online catalogues and conventions.

Islam in the Public School Curriculum

Teaching about Islam, like other world religions, has had a place in state and district social studies curricula and textbooks for over twenty years. World religions content appears in world history and geography courses for grades 5 through 7 and/or in high

school world religions electives. Coverage of world religions has increased gradually since the 1980s, and current middle and high school history textbooks provide
a chapter or a unit on each world religion. The template for world religions in most
standards includes their origins and basic beliefs, their rise and spread as organized
religions, including political and territorial expansion, and the civilizations and cultures associated with them.[36]

Since the 1970s, consensus has emerged that a discussion of religion in history
textbooks is a valuable topic for American public schools, as documented by the
First Amendment Center (FAC), the organization largely responsible for its success.[37]
The FAC guidelines for teaching about religion prescribe a neutral but nonsecular
approach, emphasizing the *academic* rather *devotional* approach, *awareness* rather
than forced *acceptance, study about* rather than *practice of religion in the classroom,*
exposure rather than *imposition, education* rather than *promotion or denigration,*
informing about rather than *seeking conformance.*[38] This consensus grew out of the
work of theologians, Supreme Court cases, and activists among educational, legal,
civic, and religious groups. Its core achievement was to develop constitutional guidelines for teaching about religion, to disseminate them, and to take steps toward educational implementation in textbooks and teacher training.

Achieving coverage of world religions that is accurate and balanced in comparison
with traditional coverage of European Christianity has been a struggle. Textbooks
in the 1980s were rife with factual errors and significant omissions. Errors in the
description of Islam were the account of its origins, description of its beliefs and
practices, and the lack of accurate historical information on its spread, often with
contradictions and outdated scholarship.[39] In the era of standards and FAC guidelines, textbook publishers have proved willing to listen to academic reviewers, and
coverage has improved.[40] Structural issues include inadequate definitions of complex
concepts like jihad and shari'a, failure to describe important institutions, to show
change over time, or to explain geographic diversity. Contemporary expressions of
religion are inadequately presented within the tradition/modernity dichotomy for all
world religions, including Christianity.[41]

In the wake of the September 11 attacks and the rise of Islamophobia, there have
been attempts to undermine improvements in the coverage of Islam in the textbooks
through smear campaigns, accusing the textbook publishers of bowing to pressure,
and trying to enlist school board and state adoption committees as allies in spreading
fear that the coverage of Islam is too positive. The object has been to enlist political
and education officials by pitting Islam against Christianity as competitors in the
education system in order to pressure publishers into showing Islam as a dangerous
religion with few redeeming qualities in its fourteen centuries of history and culture.[42]

The key to continued improvement in coverage of Islam and other world religions,
including Christianity, is to follow the same principles and methods that brought
improvement during the decade of the 1990s. That means continuing to work with
world historians and scholars of religious studies to base textbook coverage and

teaching in K–12 education on sound scholarship and balanced geographic and chronological coverage.[43] This work requires attention to the way world history and geography courses are structured; it must seek to improve teachers' access to sound scholarship through publications and educational outreach and to encourage the teaching of historical thinking skills. It is a vital civic enterprise that involves the application of rigorous but creative academic standards, constitutionally appropriate education about all world religions, and global world history education based on ongoing interdisciplinary international scholarship.

NOTES

1. For example, see *Documenting the American South*, "North American Slave Narratives," University Library, University of North Carolina, Chapel Hill, 2004, n.d. Available at http://docsouth.unc.edu/neh and the Library of Congress
2. Sylviane A Diouf, *Servants of Allah: African Muslims Enslaved in the Americas* (New York: New York University Press, 1998).
3. Mehdi Khan Nakosteen, *History of Islamic Origins of Western Education* (Boulder: University of Colorado Press, 1964): 41–57.
4. Ihsan Bagby, Paul M. Perl, and Bryan T. Froehle, *The Mosque in America: A National Portrait A Report from the Mosque Study Project* (Washington, DC: Council on American-Islamic Relations, April 26, 2001): 13.
5. Ihsan Bagby, *The American Mosque 2011, Report Number 1 from the US Mosque Study 2011: Basic Characteristics of the American Mosque, Attitudes of Mosque Leaders*, (January 2012): 4–5, 7. Available at http://faithcommunitiestoday.org/muslim-faith-group
6. Shaza Khan, Wajahat Husain, and Sehar Masood, "Situating Weekend Islamic Schools in the American Muslim Context," A paper delivered at the ISNA Education Forum, March 10, 2005 Available at http://www.docstoc.com/docs/26374575/Situating-Weekend-Islamic-Schools
7. Samana Khan, "Standardizing Islamic Studies," and Hamed Ghazali, "Education Forum Focus: Examining Data for Tailored Results," *Islamic Horizons*, 41, 2 (2012): 36–37, 55.
8. This interesting concept is developed in C. M. Naim, "A Hyper-Masculinized Islam?" *Outlook India*, January 16, 2004. Available at http://www.columbia.edu/itc/mealac/pritchett/oolitlinks/naim/txt_naim_hypermasc.html
9. Two examples are Mohja Kahf, *The Girl in the Tangerine Scarf: a Novel* (New York: Carroll & Graf, 2006) and Eboo Patel, *Acts of Faith: The Story of an American Muslim, the Struggle for the Soul of a Generation* (Boston: Beacon Press, 2007).
10. Rashid, Hakim M., and Zakiyyah Muhammad. "The Sister Clara Muhammad Schools: Pioneers in the Development of Islamic Education in America." *The Journal of Negro Education* 61, 2 (April 1, 1992): 179.
11. "America's Other Muslims: *The Wilson Quarterly* (1976), 29, 4 (Autumn, 2005): 16–27. Available at http://www.jstor.org.mutex.gmu.edu/stable/40261485
12. Rashid and Muhammad, op. cit., p. 184.
13. "Mohammed Schools Consortium of U.S. & Bermuda," n.d. Available at http://mohammedschools.tripod.com/id4.html. Cities listed with full-time schools are Detroit; Atlanta; Corona; New York; Baltimore; Oakland; Los Angeles; Washington, DC (this school has

been reported as closed at this writing); Brooklyn; New Medina, MS; Philadelphia; Little Rock; Milwaukee; Stockton, CA; Dallas; and St. Louis. Hartford, Memphis, Richmond, and Kansas City list weekend schools in the consortium. South Carolina, Tennessee, South Florida and Bermuda list schools but not cities as belonging to the consortium, and the website heading states that the list of schools is not exhaustive.

14. "Mohammed Schools of Atlanta," n.d. Available at http://mohammedschools.org/
15. Bagby, op. cit. (2011), 35.
16. Karen Keyworth, *ISPU Report: Islamic Schools of the United States: Data-Based Profiles* (2011 Institute for Social Policy and Understanding, 2011), Available at http://ispu.org/GetReports/35/2099/Publications.aspx (p. 13.)
17. Ibid., p. 15.
18. Ibid., p. 15.
19. The economic recession in 2008–2009, and the aftermath of September 11, 2001, dealt a double financial blow to Muslim institutions. Contraction in the economy that led to reduced donations and shrinking investments was compounded by fear of giving to Muslim charities and organizations in the wake of US government prosecution of numerous charities and the hurdles placed in front of them by the Department of the Treasury, which were so severe as to raise objections by other US charities. See "Council on Foundations Calls on Treasury to Withdraw Anti-Terrorism Financing Guidelines | PND | Foundation Center," n.d. Available at http://foundationcenter.org/pnd/news/story.jhtml?id=164900006 and "Introduction to Treasury's Updated Anti-Terrorist Financing Guidelines Also see http://www.treasury.gov/resource-center/terrorist-illicit-finance/Pages/protecting-charities-intro.aspx
20. Ibid, p. 17.
21. Ibid., pp. 17–18.
22. For a thorough exposition of the variety and motives of Muslim homeschoolers, see Priscilla Martinez, "Muslim Homeschooling," in *Educating the Muslims of America*, edited by Yvonne Haddad, Farid Senzai, and Jane I. Smith (Oxford and New York: Oxford University Press, 2009): 109–121.
23. Unschooling, a term dating to the 1970s, is reflected in the writings of John Holt, John Taylor Gatto, and others, rejecting the model of compulsory schooling and emphasizing cultivation of the natural impulse of children to learn.
24. Ibid, pp. 111–113.
25. "Kinza Academy: Homeschooling, Traditional Education, Hamza Yusuf," n.d. Available at http://www.kinzaacademy.com/
26. "Muslim Homeschool Resources | Ikhlas Homeschool," n.d. Available at http://www.freewebs.com/ikhlashomeschool/allabouthomeschool.htm
27. Charles Kurzman and Carl W. Ernst, "Islamic Studies in U.S. Universities," Social Sciences Research Council workshop, "The Production of Knowledge on World Regions: The Middle East" (The University of North Carolina at Chapel Hill, September 30, 2009). Available at http://www.unc.edu/~cernst/pdf/Kurzman_Ernst_Islamic_Studies.pdf and Nyang et al., *The State of Islam in American Universities* (Herndon, VA: International Institute of Islamic Thought, 2009).
28. "Islamic American University, Home," n.d. Available at http://www.islamicau.org/static/Default.aspx
29. "Cordoba University," n.d. Available at http://www.siss.edu/
30. "Zaytuna College, Home," n.d. Available at http://www.zaytunacollege.org

31. Websites of these institutions and programs are listed here: American Islamic College, n.d. Available at http://www.aicusa.edu/ American Open University, Home, n.d. Available at http://www.aou.edu/english/index.php Islamic American University, Home, n.d. Available at http://www.islamicau.org/static/Default.aspx Islamic Online University, n.d. Available at http://islamiconlineuniversity.com/about-us.phpIslamic University of Minnesota, n.d. Available at http://www.iumn.net/English/eHome.aspx Islamic University of North America, Home, n.d. Available at http://www.mishkahuniversity.com/houston/Home.php;

32. Nadia Inji Khan, "Guide Us to the Straight Way: A Look at the Makers of 'Religiously Literate' Young Muslim Americans," in Haddad, Senzai, and Smith, eds., op. cit., pp. 123–153.

33. Leena Saleh, "The Ghazis of Education," *Islamic Horizons*, 41, 2 (March/April 2012): 36–37.

34. S. L. Douglass, Social Studies Teaching Unit Series. *I Am a Muslim: A Modern Storybook*, 1994; *Eid Mubarak! Islamic Celebration Around the World, 1995; Muslims in Our Community and Around the World*, 1994; *Cities Then and Now*, 1996; *Where In the World Do Muslims Live?*, 1996; *Traders and Explorers in Wooden Ships*, 1995; *Islam and Muslim Civilization*, 1995. Published jointly by the International Institute of Islamic Thought and Kendall/Hunt Publishing Co.

35. Uthman Hutchinson, *American Family Series* (Brentwood, MD: Amana Publications, 1997) "Uthman Hutchinson's American Family Series," n.d. Available at http://www.islamicbookstore.com/children-uthman-hutchinson-s-american-family-series.html

36. Susan Douglass, *Teaching about Religion in National and State Social Studies Standards* (Council on Islamic Education and First Amendment Center, 2000), passim; Susan L. Douglass and Ross E. Dunn, "Interpreting Islam in American Schools," in Hastings Donnan, ed., *Interpreting Islam* (London: Sage Publications, 2002) and Susan Douglass, "God Spoke: Guidelines and Coverage of Abrahamic Religions in World History Textbooks," *Religion & Education*, 25,1–2 (Winter 1998): 45–58.

37. Charles Haynes, and Oliver S. Thomas, *Finding Common Ground: A First Amendment Guide to Religion and Public Education* (Nashville, TN: Freedom Forum First Amendment Center at Vanderbilt University, 1998–2001).

38. Charles Haynes, *A Teacher's Guide to Religion in the Public Schools* (First Amendment Center, 1999), Available at http://www.religionpublicschools.com/teachersguide.pdf.

39. Dunn and Douglass, "Interpreting Islam in American Schools," in Hastings Donnan, ed. *Interpreting Islam*, London: Sage Publications: 2001, pp. 76–98. [Reprinted in *The Annals of the American Academy of Political and Social Science*, 588 (July 2003)], and Douglass, "God Spoke: Guidelines and Coverage of Abrahamic Religions in World History Textbooks." *Religion and Education* 25, vols. 1&2 (Winter 1998): 45–58.

40. See, for example, publications and assessments on textbook reviews by the Council on Islamic Education scholars, now the Institute on Religion and Civic Values, at "Assessments, Institute on Religion & Civic Values," n.d. Available at http://ircv.org/category/assessments/.

41. S. L. Douglass, "Teaching about Religion, Islam, and the World in Public and Private School Curricula," in Haddad, Senzai, and Smith, eds. *Educating the Muslims of America* (New York: Oxford University Press, 2009), pp. 92–100.

42. For example, *Education Week* has covered this issue over several years, as in "Report Says Textbook Handling of Islam 'Indoctrinates' Students—Curriculum Matters—Education

Week.," Available at http://blogs.edweek.org/edweek/curriculum/2012/03/report_says_textbook_treatment.html.

43. See, for example the AAR website's expanded guidelines and teaching resources for middle and high school at, "American Academy of Religion," n.d. Available at http://www.aarweb.org/Public_Affairs/Religion_in_the_Schools/default.asp

BIBLIOGRAPHY

American Academy of Religion, "American Academy of Religion," n.d. Available at http://www.aarweb.org/publications/e-publications and http://www.aarweb.org/sites/default/files/pdfs/Publications/epublications/AARK-12CurriculumGuidelines.pdf

American Broadcasting Corporation, "Page 2: Muslim Home Schooling on the Rise—ABC News," n.d. Available at http://abcnews.go.com/Health/story?id=117997&page=2#.UBMMcqOEEUM

American Islamic College, "American Islamic College," n.d. Available at http://www.aicusa.edu/

American Open University, "American Open University—Home," n.d. Available at http://www.aou.edu

American Textbook Council, "American Textbook Council—Publications & Reports," n.d. Available at http://www.historytextbooks.org/reports.htm

An-Na'im, Abdullahi Ahmed, "Religion and Culture: Meeting the Challenge of Pluralism, a Ford Foundation Project," n.d. Information at http://www.tc.columbia.edu/academics/index.htm?facid=lfc12

Bagby, Ihsan, Masjid Study Project, n.d. Available at http://higginsctc.org/terrorism/Masjid_Study_Project_2000_Report.pdf

——, "The American Mosque 2011," n.d. Available at http://faithcommunitiestoday.org/2011-mosque-report-ihsan-bagby

Bergen, Peter, and Swati Pandey, "The Madrassa Myth—New York Times, June 14, 2005," n.d. Available at http://www.nytimes.com/2005/06/14/opinion/14bergen.html?_r=0

Council on Foundations. "Council on Foundations Calls on Treasury to Withdraw Anti-Terrorism Financing Guidelines | PND | Foundation Center," n.d. Available at http://foundationcenter.org/pnd/news/story.jhtml?id=164900006.

Douglass, Susan L., "Guidelines and Coverage of Abrahamic Religions in World History Textbooks." *Religion and Education* 25, 1&2 (Winter 1998): 45–58.

——, *Teaching About Religion in National and State Standards Documents* (Nashville, TN: Council on Islamic Education and the First Amendment Center, 2000).

——, *Social Studies Teaching Unit Series*, 7 volumes (Herndon, VA: International Institute of Islamic Thought and Kendall/Hunt Publishing, 1994–1996).

Dunn, Ross E., and S. Douglass, "Interpreting Islam in American Schools," in *Interpreting Islam*, ed. Hastings Donnan (London: Sage Publications, 2001): 76–98. [Reprinted in *The Annals of the American Academy of Political and Social Science*, 588 (July 2003)].

Graduate School of Islamic and Social Sciences, "Cordoba University," Available at http://www.cordobauniversity.org/gsiss/index.asp

Haddad, Yvonne Yazbeck, Farid Senzai, and Jane I. Smith, eds., *Educating the Muslims of America* (Oxford, UK, and New York: Oxford University Press, 2009).

Haynes, Charles C., *A Teacher's Guide to Religion in the Public Schools* (Nashville, TN: First Amendment Center, 1999). Available at http://www.freedomforum.org/publications/first/teachersguide/teachersguide.pdf

———, and Oliver S. Thomas, *Finding Common Ground: A First Amendment Guide to Religion and Public Education* (Nashville, TN: Freedom Forum First Amendment Center at Vanderbilt University, 1998–2001).

Horan, Deborah, "Put off by Public Schools, More Muslims Home-Teach," *Chicago Tribune* 12/16/2002, Available at http://articles.chicagotribune.com/2002-12-16/news/0212160217_1_home-school-muslims-pupils

Ikhlas Homeschool, "Muslim Homeschool Resources/Ikhlas Homeschool," n.d. Available at http://www.freewebs.com/ikhlashomeschool/

Institute for Social Policy and Understanding, *Islamic Education in America*, n.d. Available at http://www.ispu.org/GetReports/35/1897/Publications.aspx

Institute for Religion and Civic Values, "Assessments | Institute on Religion & Civic Values," n.d. Available at http://ircv.org/category/assessments/

Institute for Social Policy and Understanding, "Georgetown Report," n.d. Available at http://www.ispu.org/pdfs/georgetown%20report%20(si).pdf

———, *Educating the Muslims of America*, n.d. Available at http://www.ispu.org/content/Educating_the_Muslims_of_America

Islamic American University, "Islamic American University, Home," n.d. Available at http://www.islamicau.org/static/Home/tabid/36/Default.aspx

Islamic Online University, "Islamic Online University," n.d. Available at http://islamiconlineuniversity.com/about-us.php

Islamic Schools League of North America, "Islamic Schools as Change Agents," n.d. Available at http://www.theisla.org/filemgmt_data/files/IslamicSchoolsAsChangeAgents.pdf

Islamic University of Minnesota, "Islamic University of Minnesota," n.d. Available at http://www.iumn.net/

Islamic University of North America, "Islamic University of North America,Home," n.d. Available at http://www.mishkahuniversity.com/

Kahf, Mohja, *The Girl in the Tangerine Scarf: A Novel* (New York: Carroll & Graf, 2006).

Keyworth, Karen, ISPU Report "Islamic Schools of the United States: Data-Based Profiles," (Clinton, MI: Institute for Social Policy and Understanding, 2011). Available at http://www.ispu.org/pdfs/609_ISPU%20Report_Islamic%20Schools_Keyworth_WEB.pdf

———, *ISPU Report on Islamic Schools*, (Clinton, MI: Institute for Social Policy and Understanding, n.d.). Available at http://www.ispu.org/GetReports/35/2099/Publications.aspx or http://www.ispu.org/pdfs/609_ISPU%20Report_Islamic%20Schools_Keyworth_WEB.pdf

Kurzman, Charles, and Carl W. Ernst, "Islamic Studies in U.S. Universities," paper for Social Sciences Research Council Workshop in *The Production of Knowledge on World Regions: The Middle East*, Conference Proceedings, Chapel Hill, NC: University of North Carolina at Chapel Hill, September 30, 2009. Available at http://www.unc.edu/~cernst/pdf/Kurzman_Ernst_Islamic_Studies.pdf

Mohammed Schools Consortium of U.S. and Bermuda, "Mohammed Schools Consortium of U.S. & Bermuda, n.d. Available at http://mohammedschools.tripod.com/id4.html

Mohammed Schools of Atlanta, "Mohammed Schools of Atlanta," n.d. Available at http://mohammedschools.org/

Nakosteen, Mehdi Khan, *History of Islamic Origins of Western Education*. (Boulder: University of Colorado Press, 1964).

Nyang, Sulayman S., Mumtaz Ahmad, and Zahid H. Bukhari, *The State of Islamic Studies in American Universities* (Herndon, VA: International Institute of Islamic Thought, 2009). Available at http://iiit.org/iiitftp/PDF's/Islamic-Studies.pdf

Patel, Eboo, *Acts of Faith: The Story of an American Muslim, the Struggle for the Soul of a Generation* (Boston: Beacon Press, 2007).

Pew Forum on Religion & Public Life, "Mapping the Global Muslim Population," n.d. Available at http://www.pewforum.org/2009/10/07/mapping-the-global-muslim-population/

Public Broadcasting Service, "Interviews—Vali Nasr | PBS—Saudi Time Bomb? | FRONTLINE | PBS," n.d. Available at http://www.pbs.org/wgbh/pages/frontline/shows/saudi/interviews/nasr.html

Rashid, Hakim M., and Zakiyyah Muhammad, "The Sister Clara Muhammad Schools: Pioneers in the Development of Islamic Education in America." *The Journal of Negro Education* 61, 2 (April 1, 1992): 178–185.

Robelen, Erik, "Curriculum Matters: Report Says Textbook Handling of Islam 'Indoctrinates' Students," *Education Week*, March 27, 2012, n.d. Available at http://blogs.edweek.org/edweek/curriculum/2012/03/report_says_textbook_treatment.html

Shaza Khan, Wajahat Hussein, and Sehar Mahmoud, "Situating Weekend Islamic Schools" (Chicago: ISNA Education Forum, 2005), n.d. Available at http://www.docstoc.com/docs/26374575/Situating-Weekend-Islamic-Schools

Skerry, Peter, "America's Other Muslims," *The Wilson Quarterly* (1976): 29, 4 (Autumn 2005), 16–27. Available at http://www.wilsonquarterly.com/essays/americas-other-muslims

Sulaiman, Cynthia, "Outside, In: From Public School to Home-school," n.d. Available at http://www.muslimhomeschool.net/hsa/outsidein.html

U.S. Treasury Department, "Introduction to Treasury's Updated Anti-Terrorist Financing Guidelines," n.d. Available at http://www.treasury.gov/resource-center/terrorist-illicit-finance/Pages/protecting-charities-intro.aspx

Weekend Learning, "Weekend Learning: Publisher of Islamic Textbooks," n.d. Available at http://www.weekendlearning.com/

Zaytuna College, "Zaytuna College | Home," n.d. Available at http://www.zaytunacollege.org/

Zaytuna Institute, "Kinza Academy: Homeschooling, Traditional Education, Hamza Yusuf," n.d. Available at http://www.kinzaacademy.com/

CHAPTER 15

AMERICAN MUSLIM YOUTH MOVEMENTS

RABIA KAMAL

INTRODUCTION

A central concern for religiously observant Muslim parents living in the United States is the Islamic education of their children. Many Muslim parents strive to inculcate a strong religious identity in their children in the face of a largely secular or Judeo-Christian American society. Early Muslim immigrants to America often dealt with this "threat" of assimilation by circumscribing their children's exposure to mainstream society, limiting after-school activities or interactions with people beyond the familial or community setting. This protective attitude has shifted over time, particularly with the growing establishment of Muslim organizations and groups catering to Muslim youth across the country. Second- and third- generation Muslim American parents, as well as new immigrants to the United States, now find a number of alternative platforms that allow their children to develop a strong Muslim identity outside of the home, including Islamic center youth groups and organizations such as the Muslim Student Association and its affiliates.

Organizations catering to Muslim youth in the United States have proliferated in the last several decades, offering a wide range of services and activities to an increasingly diverse number of Muslim Americans. While Muslim "youth movements" in the United States continue to grow in range and size, this chapter specifically focuses on major established Muslim organizations that serve youth in America and the kinds of resources and services they provide.

Early Muslim Organizations in America

While many scholars writing on Islam in America note that Muslims established their first major national organizations in the 1950s (see, for example, Younis 1995), such claims fail to consider the history of black Islam in the United States. The earliest Muslim organizations were in fact established by African American Muslims, who trace their history back to the transatlantic slave trade in nineteenth-century America. The first of such national organizations emerged in the 1930s with the founding of the Nation of Islam (Curtis 2002). While there is much scholarly work on the nation and its various offshoots, there is limited information available about early youth movements within the African American Muslim community. Thus this chapter's focus is limited to youth-oriented organizations started by Muslims of immigrant background in the United States.

The growth of immigrant Islam in America associated with institution building occurred chiefly through post-1965 immigrants, with Muslims from South Asia arriving and becoming a major constituent group. Many scholars (such as Leonard 2004) have noted that the passing of the 1965 US Immigration and Nationality Act[1] vastly increased the number of immigrants from South Asia and the number of Muslims overall, reflecting a preference for well-educated professionals. Thus the South Asian Muslims who migrated after that time period differed greatly from previous Arab Muslim immigrants in terms of socioeconomic status, national diversity, institution building, and political ambitions in American society. These South Asian Muslim professionals actively began establishing local and communal Muslim institutions, building mosques, taking up positions of leadership within Muslim communities, and dominating the political representation of Muslims at the national level. The nature of these Muslim institutions and organizations reflected and shaped notions of "mainstream Islam" in America. While earlier organizations founded by Arab Muslim immigrants often revolved around issues outside the United States linked primarily to politics and Arab pan-nationalism in the Middle East, these newly established institutions abandoned the stance that assumed only temporary residence in the United States (Leonard 2005, 10). Such organizations included the Muslim Student Association on American university campuses (Safi 1999), national organizations such as the Islamic Society of North America (ISNA), and Islamic schools and centers (Haddad, Senzai, and Smith 2009, 6–7). The Muslim Student Association would become one of the key Muslim organizations in shaping the future of Islam in America.

The Muslim Students
Association: Background and History

Established in 1963 on the Urbana campus of the University of Illinois, the Muslim Student Association (MSA) became one of the earliest unifying forums for Muslim students in the United States. This organization was seminal in shaping the future of Islam in the country for a number of reasons. First, it was one of the sole public platforms to bring together young Muslims regardless of their ethnic background. While early members tended to be predominantly South Asian or Arab men, the MSA was influential in establishing itself as the first organization of Muslims in America "regardless of their ethnicity," as is stated in an early brochure (Ghamari-Tabrizi 2004, 70). This explicit statement was important in distinguishing the MSA from other early immigrant Islamic institutions, such as mosques or community centers, which were often ethnically homogenous and segregated (Haddad and Esposito 1998).

Second, as a space for young student activists, the organization as well as the kinds of identities it facilitated evolved over time, mobilizing and connecting young Muslims.

Early goals reflected in MSA periodicals, such as *MSA News* and *Islamic Horizons*, focused on the preservation of an Islamic identity vis-à-vis strong ties to Muslim homelands (Schumann 2007). Such publications also emphasized political solidarity with the Islamic world and an outward-looking focus for most Muslim students. In addition, during the early years of its formation, MSA activities and publications were largely oriented toward support and religious education for Muslim students without much engagement with the larger American society.

This pattern shifted, however, in the late 1970s and early 1980s, as many Muslim immigrant families decided to settle permanently in the United States. This was reflected in changing understandings of MSA student *da'wah*, which is often equated with the Christian concept of "mission." Da'wah, according to many Muslims however, is not so much about proselytizing as it is the practice of making God's work known and providing information about Islam, and can take many forms (Poston 1992). Writing about shifts in da'wah trends in MSAs, Schumann notes that "during the 1980s and up until today, there was and still is a broad consensus among authors that *da'wah* activity must aim at energizing and organizing their own community first. Yet, young activists and recent converts particularly wanted to step ahead and reach out to non-Muslim Americans by applying new methodologies" (2007, 21). Such shifts in approach to da'wah reflected a change in young Muslim attitudes toward their host country, demonstrating the hope of becoming part of rather than separate from the larger American society.

The MSA thus turned out to be one of the most important organizations for Muslims in the United States. The evolution of Muslim student activism in relation to religious and national identity through this organization foreshadowed and influenced the direction of the larger Muslim community. In addition, the MSA eventually gave birth to several other Muslim national organizations with a strong youth base (Haddad and Smith 1994, 234).

THE MSA TODAY

Since the 1970s, the growth of the MSA on school and college campuses across the United States has been exceptional. One study cites that by early 1990, "the MSA had already established 310 student chapters with more than 45,000 members."[2] The MSA of the United States and Canada, or MSA National, is the national umbrella organization that holds annual conferences and facilitates the establishment of local MSA chapters. On its website, it is represented as "a non-profit organization that strives to facilitate networking, educating, and empowering the students of today to be citizens of tomorrow's community."[3] To this end, MSA National hosts a number of annual regional conferences, the key ones drawing thousands of students to attend lectures, network, and build a sense of Muslim American community.

MSA National further develops manuals, guides, and online tools and resources to facilitate information sharing and unite students across different platforms. It provides training services to MSA executives through classes, online manuals, and leadership conferences. In order to promote more effective networking, the regions of the United States are divided into five zones, and zonal representatives from each area work toward networking between local MSAs. MSA National maintains a speakers' bureau and has established a number of task forces to tackle specific issues such as community service, political action, media and communications, da'wah, and technology.

While MSA National has developed an elaborate organizational structure, local MSA chapters on university campuses and in high schools tend to work independently of MSA National and are not required to be affiliated (Mir 2006). In high schools, MSAs often serve to provide peer support and guidance for students in both religious and academic matters (Zine 2001). While such chapters are important for Muslim high school students, MSAs on college campuses represent, mobilize, educate, and connect Muslims in unprecedented ways.

MSAs can now be found on university campuses across the United States. In contrast to earlier times, members are now frequently American-born Muslims who are more interested in learning how to integrate and institutionalize Islam into American society and culture (Abdo 2006; Leonard 2004, 2005). College MSAs promote "a self-definition [that] involves initially and fundamentally [an] Islamic identity" (Abdo 2006: 194) of its members as well as an appropriate Islamic lifestyle for Muslim college students. Students of Muslim background coming to a college or university for the first time will often choose to affiliate with either an "ethnocultural" campus group *or* a religious one. As one study notes, the result on many campuses is a binary scene, divided between "hard-core" or conservative Muslims and "cultural" or liberal Muslims (Horr and Saeed 2008). This division often occurs because many students may view MSAs as too strict or exclusive in terms of member beliefs and approaches to religious identity. A "conservative" approach to religion is often seen as associated with an isolationist tendency on campus, protecting Muslim students from American college social norms such as drinking, dating, having sex, and doing drugs. Writing about prevalent trends in MSAs across American campuses, anthropologist Shabana Mir notes:

> Muslim students often construct MSA spaces as the public official face of Islam. "Gatekeepers" (MSA student officers) practice "strategic essentialism"...and employ stricter "Islamic" gendered practices than most Muslims practice in their personal lives. Constructing nonsexualized spaces that are markedly different from majority culture serves both inter- and intracommunity purposes: representing Muslims on campus recognizably as Muslims, and providing leadership, community, and religious frameworks to Muslims.

(Mir 2009a, 245)

Thus, inclusivity, gender mingling, and the "constant tension between becoming a mainstream student organization versus appealing to students who have a more conservative or stricter interpretation of Islam" (Horr and Saeed 2008) are all difficult topics as Muslim students wrestle with "the yawning gap between American college traditions and those of Islam" (MacFarquhar 2008).

Despite such struggles, many college MSAs continue to be active in providing services and doing campus outreach. Basic services for Muslim students include providing a space for daily prayers, holding Friday congregational prayers, hosting religious lectures, fostering Islamic study circles, and doing da'wah. Da'wah activities often involve handing out educational pamphlets on Islam, providing copies of the Qur'an, and promoting major MSA campus events. Key MSA campus events throughout the year include Islam Awareness Week and the Ramadan Fast-a-Thon. Started in the 1990s, Islam Awareness Week has become a national program held in the spring semester of each academic year. During this week, "events are held by the MSA to encourage awareness of Islam, dispel misconceptions, reach out to the larger campus community, and encourage less active Muslims to participate in an MSA event."[4] Depending on the size and member activism of campus MSAs, Islam Awareness Week events can include everything from "food tasting" of cuisine from Muslim countries around the world, documentary screenings, and guest lectures to political forums, interfaith services, and art exhibitions.

During the month of Ramadan, many MSA chapters organize Fast-a-Thons to educate people of other faiths about Islam, raise funds for charity, and build a sense of community during that holy month. Muslim students encourage their non-Muslim peers to fast for one day and get local business to sponsor the event, donating money to a local food bank, shelter, or for a specific cause.[5] Ramadan is also a time when MSAs hold daily *iftars*, bringing together a diverse array of Muslim students to break their fast together.

Finally, many large MSAs across the United States have initiated programs that seek to foster dialogue and understanding through Muslim student activism and community service. Drawing on the notion of "da'wah by example," members of the MSA are reminded that they are representatives of Islam within the campus and larger community and are encouraged to engage in service projects that shed light on Islamic values of charity and helping those in need. Such community service activities include working in soup kitchens, volunteering at nursing homes, doing environmental cleanups, and holding charity toy drives. Such activities not only foster a sense of solidarity between Muslim students but also serve to challenge negative stereotypes of Islam through action and interaction with non-Muslims in different spaces.

CHANGES IN THE MSA AFTER 9/11

While the term *conservative* has often been used to characterize the MSA as a whole, recent shifts on major urban campuses, particularly after the events of 9/11, have served to challenge the status quo. The post-9/11 backlash in the United States has put the spotlight on Muslim communities across the country, and student associations on campus have been targeted by both governmental and nongovernmental surveillance. As a response to such discrimination, some MSAs have withdrawn further into an isolationist and defensive position. However, many MSAs, particularly those in major cosmopolitan centers, have increased their activism and outreach in order to challenge negative depictions of Islam in the mainstream media. Muslim student outreach has extended beyond typical da'wah or past programmatic efforts, often involving new kinds of alliance building and "mobilizing middle-class Muslim values in American civil society in ways that normalize the difference of being Muslim in an Islamophobic environment" (Laird and Cadge 2010, 227). For example, Muslim youth have begun to actively mobilize the social and cultural capital of their faith-based organization to engage in new and different kinds of interfaith collaboration with religious groups on and off campus. Building interfaith alliances in an effort to counteract their publicly stigmatized identity, members of the MSA who believe in the importance of religious identity and pluralism have begun to connect with other young people of faith. Both Catholics and Jews in America have shared a history of coming to the United States as immigrants or children of immigrants. These communities have also faced discrimination based on their religious and ethnoracial differences from a mainstream understanding of America as a white Anglo-Saxon

Protestant nation.[6] Building on these relationships has become a major way in which Muslim students assert spatial and symbolic belonging in the post-9/11 context.

Other kinds of activities involve engaging with media in new and active ways, thereby finding a more diverse group of spokespeople to represent Islam to the American public. New leaders have emerged to either join or represent campus MSAs, challenging stereotypes both within and outside the Muslim American community that posit MSAs as spaces solely for "conservative" Muslims or certain ethnic groups. MSA students and leaders often have been interviewed in the post-9/11 context, on news channels such as CNN as well as on popular entertainment programs such as *The Daily Show with Jon Stewart*. Many have done their best to challenge the idea that Muslims do not belong in this country or are somehow un-American. Furthermore, in an attempt to diversify means of communication and educational materials, MSAs have encouraged the frequency and breadth of content in Muslim campus publications and have increasingly turned to the internet and social media to make their voices heard.

While MSAs across the United States have sought to hold and participate in events that go beyond the typical religious endeavors of most MSAs post-9/11, this does not mean that such groups are going through a period of "secularization." On the contrary, just as members of various MSAs are focusing on exerting an "American" identity in the face of marginalization, they simultaneously are careful to maintain an overt religious sensibility. It is important to note, however, that in the post-9/11 context MSAs have become important spaces where both the meaning of "Americanness" and the range of Islamic sensibilities are constantly being negotiated and expanded.

OTHER YOUTH-BASED ORGANIZATIONS

A number of other Muslim organizations that cater to youth in America have been established over time, either independently or as offshoots of the MSA. One such offshoot, the Islamic Society of North America (ISNA), is considered the largest Muslim organization in North America. Founded by South Asian immigrant Muslim professionals, ISNA directs a wide array of educational, religious, and social welfare activities (Williams 1998, 185). The organization's goals include "being an exemplary and unifying Islamic organization in North America that contributes to the betterment of the Muslim community and society at large" and providing a common platform for presenting Islam in America.[7]

ISNA's Youth Programming and Services Department (YPSD), after a period of inactivity, experienced a revival in 2007 by joining forces with the Muslim Youth of North America (MYNA). The latter organization is described as a "self-managed program of the Islamic Society of North America... a charitable organization whose constituents and leaders alike are all between the ages of 12 and 18."[8] Founded in 1985, the organization's website describes the complicated position of Muslim American youth in society today:

> The youth of today are now, more than ever, often regarded as the source of society's challenges and deficits. Underage drinking, drugs and violence are only a few examples of what have become synonymous with the word "youth." On the top of such a negative perception of this vibrant segment of our society, American Muslim youth have to cope with other stereotypes such as terrorism and "un-Americanism." Muslim youth often find themselves in unfriendly environments within their own communities, where activities and programs are not relevant to their needs, where their opinion doesn't count, and where their voice is seldom heard.[9]

In the face of such challenges, YPSD and MYNA have collaborated to provide Muslim American youth with the platform to organize, express themselves, connect and support one another, and spearhead their own organization with the guidance of advisors. In 2007–2008, ISNA, YPSD, and MYNA National organized more than thirty camps, conferences, seminars, and leadership retreats for young Muslims across the nation. These programs have served more than 3,500 youth from around the United States and Canada, and the organization's website claims "a 300 percent growth per year in its operations over that period."[10]

In addition to these activities, YPSD and MYNA offer academic scholarships, parenting workshops, and training programs that utilize multimedia to engage Muslim youth, offering comprehensive youth development models rooted in religious and civil ideas. Youth-related issues are addressed through online publications and social media such as podcasts, which deal with topics ranging from religious education and "giving back" to one's community to identity struggles and communicating with parents.

Another well-known Muslim American organization with an active youth program is the Islamic Circle of North America (ICNA), established in 1968. Within the Muslim American community, the organization is said to focus heavily on countering the ethnicization that divides Muslim communities in the country by "bringing together much more ethnically diverse groups of Muslims for common action and mutual strengthening" (Denny 1995, 335). ICNA's youth efforts are divided into two different age groups, with the Muslim Children of North America focusing on youth between the ages of seven and thirteen and Young Muslims (YM) targeting teens and those in their early twenties. The foundation of YM's activities is the NeighborNet, a weekly study circle that gathers to share religious knowledge, offer advice, and provide spiritual empowerment. Compared with other Muslim American organizations, ICNA and YM are known to put heavy emphasis on religious education, creating Islamic media for youth featuring series such as *Adam's World, Muslim Scouts,* and *Salam's Journey.* These programs feature *Sesame Street*–like characters—"with a bit of Disney, PBS, and Oprah all rolled into one"[11] —with the aim of introducing children to Islamic morals, values, and culture in a manner that is both entertaining and educational. Other youth-oriented initiatives include hosting Muslim Family Days, Muslim Sports Days, the YM Quiz Competition, and the annual ICNA youth conference. The latter conference involves a weekend of interactive workshops and lectures that focus on youth-related issues such as finding appropriate role models, dealing with Islamophobia on campus, and addressing drug and alcohol problems. Such conferences also include basketball and ping-pong tournaments, Qu'ran competitions, and Spanish sessions for young Muslims.

Other Muslim organizations catering to youth, while promoting religious education as well as service and outreach, often put an emphasis on one or the other in their programming. The Muslim American Society (MAS), for example, expresses a distinctly outward-looking approach to youth development in its organizational mission. Established in 1993, MAS has evolved into a nationally recognized "grass-roots movement" that focuses on promoting "active involvement in communities across the United States by providing opportunities for community service, interfaith initiatives, youth programs, and civic engagement."[12] It is interesting to note that on MAS's website, the organizational vision is simply articulated as the endeavor to create "a virtuous and just American society," without specific mention of Islam. While imparting Islamic knowledge is part of MAS's youth agenda, the emphasis on bringing about positive change in American society through service, equality, and justice clearly distinguishes this organization from the youth chapters of both ISNA and ICNA.

Ongoing Evolution and Development of Muslim Youth Movements

It is evident that the post-9/11 context fostered a sense of self-reflection for Muslim American organizational leaders in terms of their goals and visions. Members of youth based organizations realized that the monopoly of leadership in Muslim organizations in the last several decades, comprising mostly South Asian Muslim male professionals, needed to be challenged or at least supplemented with fresh voices and faces. Many young Muslims leaders realized that they needed to step up to their responsibility to "represent American Islam" in more balanced and nuanced ways in order to counter mainstream media stereotypes in post-9/11 America. Aside from new kinds of representation, youth organizations have also begun to increasingly emphasize the social responsibility of Muslim Americans to domestic and local causes. In addition, many young Muslim Americans for the first time have begun to address ongoing forms of racial exclusion and ethnic segregation that have marked Muslim American worship and identity in previous generations.

A particularly poignant example of the new kinds of Muslim youth-based organizations that have emerged to the forefront is the Inner-City Muslim Action Network (IMAN), based in Chicago. Unlike most Muslim organizations that cater to youth through focusing on religious education or networking within particular circles of the Muslim American community, IMAN is a community-based nonprofit organization that works for social justice, delivers a range of direct services, and cultivates the arts in urban communities. Its focus on responding to "the pervasive symptoms of inner-city poverty and abandonment"[13] through community service and social justice distinguishes the way in which IMAN imparts "education" to its young Muslim members. Rather than holding religious study circles, members of IMAN tackle problems faced by more marginalized urban communities, including issues of limited access to resources, low levels of positive adult involvement, drugs, gangs, and violence. IMAN's youth forums not only bring together young Muslims from across different racial and ethnic backgrounds but also emphasize collaboration across *class*-based communities. IMAN's organizers emphasize art and cultural expression as an integral aspect of its programming, spearheading such initiatives as the Community Café and Taking' It to the Streets. IMAN's Community Café is one of the few Muslim-led efforts in the United States that provides a space for "socially conscious people to collectively celebrate and engage in diverse and creative artistic expression," utilizing "the arts as a tool for cross-cultural communication, civic engagement and social change."[14] IMAN's leaders take advantage of online blogs and multimedia to create educational material and document young Muslims' activities, highlighting such new social endeavors as free health clinics, rehabilitation, and a holistic approach to health and well-being.

Another organization that has taken steps towards youth leadership development in the Muslim American community is the Muslim Public Affairs Council (MPAC), which hosts annual Young Leaders National Summits in Silicon Valley, Washington D.C., New York City, and Los Angeles. MPAC's summit is designed to provide a platform for emerging Muslim American leaders to enhance civic participation and redefine the Muslim image in the fields of media, technology, and government. Young Muslims are exposed to influential individuals in the government, policymakers, new networks, and leadership development to help shape themselves into future leaders who can address local issues, national problems, and public opinion. MPAC also hosts internship programs for youth and has initiated NewGround, a Muslim-Jewish partnership for change. Such interfaith collaboration aimed at promoting religious pluralism among youth is at the forefront of another organization, the Interfaith Youth Core (IFYC), started by Muslim American Eboo Patel. Based in Chicago, IFYC aims to counter the "divisive public conversation about religion" (Patel 2007) in the United States by emphasizing cooperation and cultivating interfaith leadership on college campuses across America. The IFYC campus campaign encourages students of different faiths to collaborate on service projects, discuss social issues, and do outreach, using religion as a bridge rather than a barrier. While not specifically a "Muslim" organization, IFYC has been highly successful in encouraging Muslim youth to expand out of their inner-city circles and engage in proactive change.

Finally, it is important to mention the proliferation of Muslim American youth movements in recent times that transcend traditional organizational structures. The growing popularity of new forms of social media applications such as Twitter, Facebook, blogs, and YouTube, as well the increasing ways in which identity formation and social relations are being facilitated by virtual mediums, have shifted the space and scope of such movements. Increasingly, young Muslim Americans are using the power of social media and the internet to learn about Islam, engage in multiple forms of identity claims making, and organize socially and politically. For example, a recent online campaign called MyJihad seeks to correct misunderstandings about the meaning of *jihad*, or "struggling in the way of God," and about Islam in the United States. The campaign aims to showcase Muslim voices, lives, and ideas through various mediums in order to counter stereotypes, and asks young participants to join the Facebook page, "tweet your jihad," sponsor public ads on buses and trains, and host events at one's school, church, or synagogue in order to educate people about the meaning of jihad. The website for the campaign calls for young Muslim Americans to engage in jihad against urban and inner-city problems, poverty, domestic violence, misunderstanding, and the faith divide and displays a photo gallery of public ads featuring such submissions as "Our jihad is to be united in diversity," and "My jihad is to create films that open hearts and minds and revel our shared humanity."[15] Such hybrid mediated environments informed by the interrelationship between cyberspace and "the socialized scapes of community networks" (El-Nawawy and Khamis 2009), creating new conditions in which young Muslim Americans engage in reconstructing Muslim youth norms, challenge traditional power structures, and shape new identities in contemporary America.

NOTES

1. The Immigration and Nationality Act of 1965 abolished the national origins quota system that had been American immigration policy since the 1920s, replacing it with a preference system that focused on immigrants' skills and family relationships with citizens or US residents (see Ludden 2006).
2. *Arabia: The Islamic World Review*, May (1983): 63.
3. http://msanational.org/about-us/
4. *MSA National Chapter Starter Guide 2008.*
5. *MSA National Chapter Starter Guide 2008.*
6. See, for example, Brodkin 1998; Ignatiev 1995; Marty 1970.
7. See http://www.isna.net/ISNAHQ/pages/About-Us.aspx
8. http://www.isna.net/Youth/pages/Multi-Media.aspx
9. http://www.isna.net/Youth/pages/Muslim-Youth-of-North-America.aspx
10. http://www.isna.net/youth/youth.aspx

11. http://soundvision.com/Info/adam/
12. http://www.muslimamericansociety.org/main/content/about-us
13. http://www.imancentral.org/about/
14. http://www.imancentral.org/arts-culture/community-cafe/
15. http://myjihad.org/photo-gallery/user-submitted-ads/

REFERENCES

Abdo, Geneive, *Mecca and Main Street: Muslim Life in America After 9/11* (New York: Oxford University Press, 2006).

Ahmed, Akbar, *Journey Into America: The Challenge of Islam* (Washington, DC: Brookings Institution Press, 2010).

Akou, Heather Marie, "Interpreting Islam through the Internet: making sense of hijab," *Contemporary Islam* 4, no. 3 (2010): 331–346.

Bayoumi, Moustafa, *How Does It Feel to Be a Problem?: Being Young and Arab in America* (New York: Penguin Press, 2008).

Brodkin, Karen, *How Jews Became White Folks and What That Says About Race in America* (New Brunswick, NJ: Rutgers University Press, 1998).

Bunt, Gary R., *Islam in the Digital Age: E-Jihad, Online Fatwas and Cyber Islamic Environments* (London: Pluto Press, 2003).

Cainkar, Louise, "Islamic Revival Among Second-Generation Arab Muslims in Chicago: The American Experience and Globalization Intersect," *Bulletin of the Royal Institute for Inter-Faith Studies* 6 (2004): 99–120.

Curtis, Edward E., *Islam in Black America: Identity, Liberation, and Difference in African American Islamic Thought* (Albany: State University of New York Press, 2002).

——, *Muslims in America: A Short History* (New York: Oxford University Press, 2009).

Denny, Frederick, "The *Umma* in North America: Muslims 'Melting Pot' or Ethnic 'Mosaic'?" In *Christian-Muslim Encounters*, edited by Yvonne Y. Haddad and Wadi Z. Haddad. (Gainesville: University Press of Florida, 1995): 342–357.

El Horr, Jane, and Sana Saeed, "Campus Radicals: A New Muslim Student Group Tries to Rouse the Moderates." *The Wall Street Journal* (June 20, 2008). Available at http://online.wsj.com/article/SB121391832473590285.html

El-Nawawy, Mohammed, and Sahar Khamis, *Islam Dot Com: Contemporary Islamic Discourses in Cyberspace* (New York: Palgrave Macmillan, 2009).

Ewing, Katherine P., *Being and Belonging: Muslims in the US since 9/11* (New York: Russell Sage Foundation, 2008).

Ghamari-Tabrizi, Behrooz, "Loving America and Longing for Home: Isma'il al-Faruqi and the Emergence of the Muslim Diaspora in North America," *International Migration* 42, no. 2 (2004): 61–84.

Haddad, Yvonne Y., and Jane I. Smith, *Muslim Communities in North America* (Albany: State University of New York Press, 1994).

——, and John I. Esposito, *Islam, Gender and Social Change* (New York: Oxford University Press, 1998).

——, *Not Quite American? The Shaping of Arab and Muslim Identity in the United States* (Waco, TX: Baylor University Press, 2004).

——, Farid Senzai, and Jane I. Smith, *Educating the Muslims of America*. New York: Oxford University Press, 2009.

Hefner, Robert W., and Muhammad Qasim Zaman, *Schooling Islam: The Culture and Politics of Modern Muslim Education* (Princeton, NJ: Princeton University Press, 2006).

Ignatiev, Noel, *How the Irish Became White* (New York: Routledge, 1995).

Jackson, Sherman, *Islam and the Blackamerican: Looking Towards the Third Resurrection* (New York: Oxford University Press, 2005).

Karim, Jamillah, "Between Immigrant Islam and Black Liberation: Young Muslims Inherit Global Muslim and African American Legacies," *The Muslim World* 95, no. 4 (2005): 497–513.

Laird, Lance D., and Wendy Cadge, "Negotiating Ambivalence: The Social Power of Muslim Community-Based Health Organizations in America," *PoLAR* 33, no. 2 (2010): 225–244.

Leonard, Karen I. "*American Muslims: South Asian Contributions to the Mix*" (Stanford, CA: Stanford University, October 9, 2004). Available at http://francestanford.stanford.edu/sites/francestanford.stanford.edu/files/Leonard.pdf

——, "American Muslims and Authority: Competing Discourses in a Non-Muslim State," *Journal of American Ethnic History* 25, no. 1 (2005): 5–30.

Ludden, Jennifer, "1965 Immigration Law Changed Face of America," *NPR* (May 9, 2006). Available at http://www.npr.org/templates/story/story.php?storyId=5391395.

MacFarquhar, Neil. "For Muslim Students, a Debate on Inclusion," *New York Times* (February 21, 2008). Available at http://www.nytimes.com/2008/02/21/education/21muslim.html?pagewanted=all

Maria, Sunaina, "Youth Culture, Citizenship and Globalization: South Asian Muslim Youth in the United States after September 11th," *Comparative Studies of South Asia, Africa and the Middle East* 24, no. 1 (2004): 219–231.

——, *Missing: Youth, Citizenship, and Empire after 9/11*. (Durham, NC: Duke University Press, 2009).

Marty, Martin E., *Righteous Empire: The Protestant Experience in America* (New York: Dial Press, 1970).

Metcalf, Barbara D., *Making Muslim Space in North America and Europe* (Berkeley: University of California Press, 1996).

Mir, Shabana, "Constructing Third Spaces: American Muslim Undergraduate Women's Hybrid Identity Construction" Ph.D. dissertation, Indiana University:, 2006.

——, "'Where You Stand on Dating Defines You:' American Muslim Women Students and Cross-Gender Interaction on Campus," *American Journal of Islamic Social Sciences* 24, no. 3 (2007): 69–91.

——, "Not Too 'College-Like,' Not Too Normal: American Muslim Undergraduate Women's Gendered Discourses," *Anthropology & Education Quarterly* 40, no.3 (2009a): 237–256.

——, "'I Didn't Want to Have That Outcast Belief about Alcohol': Muslim Women Encounter Drinking Cultures on Campus," in *Educating the Muslims of America*, edited by Yvonne Y. Haddad, Farid Senzai, and Jane I. Smith (Oxford, UK: Oxford University Press, 2009b): 209–230.

——, "'Just to Make Sure People Know I Was Born Here': Muslim Women Constructing American Selves," *Discourse* 32 no. 4 (2011):547–563.

"MSA and Family Builds in the U.S.," *Arabia: The Islamic World Review* (1983): 63.

Nyang, Sulayman S., *Islam in the United States of America* (Chicago: ABC International, Inc., 1999).

Patel, Eboo, *Acts of Faith: The Story of an American Muslim, the Struggle for the Soul of a Generation*. (Boston: Beacon Press, 2007).

Peek, Lori, "Reactions and Response: Muslim Students' Experiences on New York City Campuses Post 9/11," *Journal of Muslim Minority Affairs* 23 (2003):273–285.

Poston, Larry, *Islamic Da'wah in the West: Muslim Missionary Activity and the Dynamics of Conversion to Islam* (New York: Oxford University Press, 1992).

Safi, Loui M., "The Transforming Experience of American Muslims: Islamic Education and Political Maturation," in *Muslims and Islamization in North America: Problems and Prospects*, edited by Amber Haque (Beltsville, MD: Amana Press, 1999): 33–48.

Schmidt, Garbi, "Dialectics of Authenticity: Examples of Ethnification of Islam Among Young Muslims in Sweden and the United States," *The Muslim World* 92 (2002): 1–17.

Schumann, Christoph, "A Muslim 'Diaspora' in the United States?" *The Muslim World* 97 (2007): 11–32.

Sirin, Selcuk R., and Michelle Fine, *Muslim American Youth: Understanding Hyphenated Identities Through Multiple Methods* (New York: New York University Press, 2008).

Williams, Raymond B., "Asian Indian and Pakistani Religions in the United States," *Annals of the American Academy of Political and Social Science* 558 (1998): 178–195.

Younis, Adele L., *The Coming of Arabic-Speaking People of the United States* (New York: Center for Migration Studies, 1995).

Zine, Jasmin, Muslim Youth in Canadian Schools: Education and the Politics of Religious Identity, *Anthropology & Education Quarterly* 32 (2001):399–423.

CHAPTER 16

DA'WA IN THE UNITED STATES

KATHLEEN M. MOORE

INTRODUCTION

The meaning of the word *da'wa* is often translated as "missionizing," "proselytizing," "bearing witness," and "propagation of the faith." It has been used to refer to evangelical work, encouraging people to embrace Islam as the true religion, but it also has other meanings. From its earliest days in Islamic history, *da'wa* has often been viewed as a means to inspire fellow Muslims in their struggle to lead more pious lives. In the late nineteenth-century era of colonialism and the formation of the modern nation-state, reaching the non-Muslim other was not so much the aim of *da'wa* activity as was exhorting Muslims to "wake up" and rise to challenges presented by modernity—specifically, Western imperialism and the spread of a secular worldview. In more recent times, *da'wa* has served the purposes both of spreading the message to nonbelievers *and* reinforcing the imperative for greater piety on the part of Muslims.

A number of Muslim activist intellectuals present distinctive examples of these twin purposes at work within their specific settings and their modern world experience. But while intellectuals may have laid claim to critique and guide society in particular times and places, in *da'wa* activity they are certainly not alone. Also important are the everyday actions of ordinary people and organizations that carry out the lay passions and extol the virtues of Islam that are most useable to them and their agendas. All things considered, *da'wa* is a term that signifies a wide range of arguments that are sometimes at odds with each other because they are designed to accomplish different aims: to exhort and guide Muslims to practice what is considered to be proper behavior; to justify the existence of millions of Muslims in non-Muslim pluralistic societies (which a few have called *dar al-da'wa*, the place where Islam is to be propagated); and to address misinformation about Islam (or "mislam") spread in the name of cultural warfare.

In this essay I follow three strands of thought about *da'wa*: the semantic meaning; the emphasis on education and solidarity during the late colonial era; and the shift in emphasis to meet the need to propagate the faith in the contemporary United States. What, for Muslims, is the imperative to propagate one's faith? What are some of its basic principles? What form(s) does *da'wa* take? To answer these questions, we need to look at text-based interpretations and at explanations that arise from context.

DA'WA IN ISLAMIC TEACHING

The semantic field around the word *da'wa* gives us some insight into what the Qur'an teaches about the duty to propagate the faith. The root of the word *da'wa* means "to call, to summon, to appeal (or pray) to, and to invite."

The sense in which propagation of the faith is an act of *calling* or summons operates at a few levels. One level has to do with the Qur'anic teaching that testimony to the existence of the one God is paramount. Testimony, or *shahada*, is one of the five pillars of Islam, the first of the five crucial elements of what it means to live in "submission" to God (the literal meaning of the Arabic word *islam*). Apart from the solemn obligation to testify in the form of the *shahada*—*la ilaha ila Allah* (there is no god but God) *wa Muhammad rusul Allah* (and Muhammad is God's messenger)—how does one confess one's faith? The Qur'an (16:125) reads, "Invite [all] to the way of your Lord, with wisdom and beautiful preaching, and argue with them in ways that are best and most gracious."[1] As significant as is the *shahada* as a confession, it is understood as only a minimum requirement designed to prime the pump for a lifetime of what is known as *da'wa*, a calling to witness according to one's ability and knowledge. Many commentaries cite this Qur'anic injunction to encourage Muslims toward moral eloquence and sincerity in calling people to follow in the way of God (*fi sabil Allah*).

The sense in which *da'wa* is an *appeal* has to do with the Qur'anic concept of the single act of prayer. In certain places the word "*da'wa*" is associated with intercessory prayer: "When My servants ask thee about Me, I am indeed close by and answer the prayer of everyone when they pray to Me" (Q2:186). Here the term means a supplication to God, an individual's invocation of God for a special purpose. The Qur'an is filled with warnings against trying to call on a god other than the One God, and a primary message is that it is futile to appeal to false gods either in this life or the next. Only the One True God grants the appeal of his servants. In the same way, each of God's servants must recognize that God's *da'wa*—his summons—requires their faithful response. Thus, there is a double meaning—God both summons the faithful through his *da'wa* and God alone answers the *da'wa* of the faithful. This is reflected in the Qur'an (13:14): "To Him the prayer of truth [*da'watul haqq*] and all those they pray to, other than Him, answer them not at all, no more than if they stretched their hands out for water, which reaches them not, for the prayer of the unbelievers is futile." From this we can see that the basic meaning of the word "*da'wa*" as appeal or supplication is closely connected to the concept of monotheism (*tawhid*)—there is only One God to whom the faithful are to pray and who can answer prayers.

Aside from the duty to pray to the One God, Muslims are obligated to respond to the *da'wa* (the call) of the *agent* of the call, the *da'i*—the one who makes the call or invites. Muhammad is said to be *da'i Allah* in the Qur'an: "Prophet, we have sent you as a witness, as a bearer of good news and warning; as one who calls people to God by His leave, as a light-giving lamp" (Q33:45–46); and "Our People, respond to the one who calls you to God. Believe in Him: he will forgive you your sins and protect you from the painful torment. Those who fail to respond to God's call cannot escape God's power anywhere on earth, nor will they have any protector against Him; such people clearly have gone far astray" (Q46:31–32). Muhammad summons on God's behalf. Other prophets were also *da'is* in their own time, each called in some particular way to his own people. Like the prophets before him, Muhammad issued his own call summoning people to the straight path (e.g., Q23:73). In this way, the Qur'anic concept of *da'wa* includes the obligation to follow Muhammad's guidance (*sunna* or "lived example") on the straight path and is more than the simple confession of belief in the One God. The *da'wa* becomes the call to the straight path.

The sense of *da'wa* as an *invitation* leads us to a very important concept: the community of believers (*ummah*). The significance of the response to the invitation by the community cannot be underestimated. The community is directed to respond by "enjoining what is right and forbidding what is wrong" (Q3:104). In this sense, the *da'i* invites the entire community, and the community of believers in turn calls upon society at large to promote justice (*'adl*) and fight oppression (*zulm*). Thus, the obligation to call others to "do the right thing" can rather easily be understood as the believing community's response to the Prophet's call and, correspondingly, that community's duty to invite nonbelievers to follow in the way of God (*fi sabil Allah*, Q2:261) and accept the message of Islam. Not only the prophets but the community of believers itself is constituted as a *da'i*, one who summons or invites others to the faith. This has the dual effect of making a more just society and deepening the community of believers' acknowledgment of God and his Prophet.

The Qur'anic exhortation cited at the beginning of this section, "Invite [all] to the way of your Lord, with wisdom and beautiful preaching, and argue with them in ways that are best and most gracious" (Q16:125), is addressed to Muhammad and can be read narrowly to apply to his discourses against his opponents.[2] However, in modern Islamic apologetics it has been relied on most frequently as the Qur'anic injunction for *da'wa* in general. It has become one of the most cited verses in support of the external mission of Islam and has encouraged the view that the propagation of one's faith is best pursued through patient argumentation, as opposed to forced conversion through military conquest. It is often coupled with the Qur'anic injunction that there is "no coercion in religion" (Q.2:256) to support the notion of consent. Compulsion, force, bribery, threat, and exploitation are inconsistent with the sense of invitation, which in most modern usage must include the element of free will.

DA'WA ACTIVITY, COLONIALISM, AND MUSLIM SOLIDARITY

The doctrine of *da'wa* was given modern form beginning in the nineteenth century by Muslim intellectuals in various parts of the colonized Islamic world. The emphasis was on bringing Muslims to a better understanding of the moral imperative to rejuvenate Muslims and Islam in order to face the challenges of modernity. We should keep in mind that vigorous Christian missionary work accompanied European colonial government and was viewed by many Muslims as a political and cultural challenge. In India, for instance, Sir Sayyid Ahmad Khan (1817-1898) sought to convert his fellow Muslims to a modernist understanding of their religion. His concerns about the future of India were provoked by a sense of shortcoming compared with Western Europe's (specifically Britain's) military, scientific, and technological advancements. While the Hindus were readily adopting the new language, administrative science, and intellectual milieu of Britain's colonial rulers, Khan felt that the Muslims of India were sinking into cultural isolation. Preferring to have their sons study Arabic and Persian in traditional schools, the Muslim elites of India discouraged contacts with the British and strongly eschewed the introduction of new elements (e.g., modern science and technological education) in their lives. As a result, the social status and material fortune of the Muslims steadily declined. Khan chastised the religious leaders (*ulama*) and schools (*madrasas*) for failing to prepare the Muslims of India to face the new sociopolitical demands of the modern era.[3]

This trend toward cultural isolation was reversed in large part due to the effort of Sir Sayyid Ahmad Khan, who in 1875 founded the Muhammadan Anglo-Oriental College at Aligarh (renamed the Aligarh Muslim University in 1920), offering an education in science and rationalism that shaped graduates who then went out to the various regions of India to persuade other Muslims of the merits of this approach. In the belief that modern education was the key through which the Muslim decline could be redressed, the college at Aligarh emerged as an important center of Islamic modernism with which a number of important intellectuals were associated.[4] Khan's ideas on education challenged conservative ways of thinking and acting to cultivate the exercise of critical rationality, presenting the case for a shift away from the undisputed power of the *ulama*. This marked the emergence of a new class of modern Muslim intellectuals who, aided by the technological and educational advancements of the late 19th century (primarily the establishment of modern educational institutions and the new print media), claimed the right to interpret Islam for themselves and speak for the Muslim community.[5]

The *da'wa* that Khan presented to his contemporaries was to modernize their outlook on religion and science. Muslim civilization(s) would be restored to former greatness by shunning customs that had resulted in the denigration of Islam, customs that in India were influenced by contact with Hindus and by accretions that had entered into Islam through the efforts of Muslim jurists, commentators, and Sufis. Only that part of Islam that Muslims consider to be divinely revealed (i.e., the Qur'an and a few authenticated Hadith) need be studied in light of science and reason. Khan, in effect, was conjuring the Muslim community into a nation by using the tool of *da'wa* to call upon Muslims to modernize their understanding of the material and the sacred worlds and (re)create solidarity in an age when ideas of nationalist self-determination and secularism had become a major influence. Khan argued that the traditional *ulama* and the jurists (*fuqaha*) had distracted believers from using their own intellects and hearts to discern the true meaning of Islam. He called upon the modern Muslim intelligentsia to provide a reinterpretation of Islam and its institutions in light of present-day exigencies, an interpretation that would free Muslims from the tyranny of the past and provide a message of empowerment for the colonized Muslim. At the same time, he also encouraged the adoption of Western sociopolitical ideas and institutions of government and argued that the science of political economy, having been perfected by Europe, should be adapted for the benefit of the Muslim community. Strongly attached to Islam, Khan looked to Islamic revelation as an important source to help face the challenges of his times. He should also be understood, however, as being in very positive dialogue with Western political thought.

This approach maintains that human beings are endowed with adequate cognition and free will to pursue their own spiritual destiny through the study of the revealed message of God, that religious interpretation was no longer the exclusive purview of scholars and theologians. Each individual is called to respond to the invitation (*da'wa*) and has the capacity as a rational being to do so within his or her specific cultural heritage. Like Khan, Egypt's Muslim reformer Rashid Rida (d. 1935), reflecting the rationalist theology of his teacher, Muhammad Abduh (d. 1905), argued that the purpose of revelation is to elucidate what is already known through the human intellect. Prophets come to confirm and clarify what is intuitive (e.g., the existence of God), and so there is an essential unity in the beliefs of "the people of divine religions (*ahl al-adyan al ilahiya*)" who have been exposed to divine guidance as well as having an innate disposition to believe in God and do good works.[6] Of lasting impact were these reformers' efforts to strengthen Islamic awareness and solidarity in the face of modernity. Thus, *da'wa* increasingly came to be framed in terms of education (*tarbiya*).

For these Muslim reformers, then, the need to spread the faith stressed the importance of *da'wa* yet interpreted this as the imperative to bring Muslims back into the fold of a desirable theology (*kalam*) as much as, if not more than, the need to teach non-Muslims about Islamic principles and creeds. The technological, educational, and institutional changes wrought by the West, Christian missionaries, and the scholarship on Islam written by Western orientalists all made a lasting impact on the understanding of *da'wa*. As of the 1930s, *da'wa* increasingly became an endeavor to reform the individual, rather than the public institutions of society. Society was to be "Islamized" from below, and this vision can be attributed mainly to Egyptian Hassan al-Banna (d. 1949), the founder of Egypt's Muslim Brotherhood (*Ikhwan*), and South Asian Abul Ala' al-Mawdudi (1903–1979), the founder of Jama'at-i Islami,[7] who both left a powerful legacy among later generations of Islamists.[8] For these thinkers, the educational and devotional aspects of *da'wa* require that Muslims more fully and self-consciously reappropriate their Islamic identity. They spoke of *da'wa* as the teaching that will bring deficient Muslims back to the "true Islam."

In contrast to the modernists, Islamists present a contemporary response to what has been called the "westoxification" of the Muslim world (i.e., the pollution of Islamic cultures with Western influences), attempting a reassertion of Islamic values and institutions in the face of Western economic, political, and cultural dominance around the world. This strand of thought increasingly rejects Western scholarship as a cultural attack on Islam and critiques those reformers who adopted or used Western sociopolitical ideas and institutions in their home countries. Islamists are highly critical of Western models of economic and political development as inappropriate transplants from another time and culture, and in their place advocate continuity with older forms of Islamic knowledge, law, and government. Generally Islamists today advocate a literalist interpretation of Islam as the solution for all political wrongs and moral shortcomings. From this perspective, *da'wa* is addressed to *all* people in order to educate others about the message of Islam. For this generation of Islamists, it has become obvious that the whole world is suffering, and the solution is to be found in the embrace of what is perceived as "the true Islam" practiced by *al-salaf al-salih*, or the first generation of Muslims of the Islamic era (i.e., the seventh and eighth centuries C.E.). Sayyid Qutb (1906–1966), for instance, maintained that Islam is the perfect social order that achieved its moral excellence for a unique (although brief) period of time—when the community at Medina lived under God's guidance—before impurities and the evil forces of worldly materialism crept in. The significance of this historical period is that it can be created again; Islam's idealized state will be reestablished for the entire world to see and be persuaded by its superior values and principles.[9] Al-Mawdudi argued that performing *da'wa* was the most important duty entrusted to Muslims. This meant witnessing not only through the spoken and written word but by example, illustrating the message of Islam by living it openly in a way that will entice others to examine the merits of the message. He succinctly summarized the core principle of his teachings on *da'wa*: "[t]he only objective behind raising you as a distinct Ummah (community), titled Muslim, as enunciated by the Holy Qur'an, is that you should leave no stone unturned in making out the truthfulness of the Faith before the whole of Mankind."[10]

But at what level is *da'wa* to be addressed? The modernist reformers' liberal interpretation generally accepted western ideas and institutions but gave them an Islamic justification, whereas the advocates of overtly Islamist agendas favored the opposite end on the continuum of attitudes and proposals regarding this-worldly engagement and the role of Islam in public life. This has had implications for *da'wa* activity whether it has been appreciated for its educational, devotional, or political ends. Under the diasporic conditions in which Muslims are living in (sometimes emphatically) non-Muslim societies, *da'wa* has become a refashioned conceptual tool that helps us understand what Tariq Ramadan has called the "new presence" of Muslims in Europe and North America. Specifically, immigration and conversion in "the West" during the twentieth century produced strong Muslim constituencies in many countries where Islam became the second or third most popular religion, after Christianity.

In terms of their numbers and permanent settlement, Muslims in non-Muslim societies are experiencing completely new circumstances. They reflect on their texts in this new context, ask questions, and experiment on educational, theological, social, political, and cultural levels. Recognizing that we live in a time of "deep intellectual ferment and transformation," Ramadan evaluates and defines the conceptual space of "the Western abode" to be not *dar al-harb* (the abode of war) but rather *dar al-shahada* (the abode of testimony), a space of responsibility in which the possibility of permanent involvement—to achieve more just conditions—exists.[11] *Dar al-shahada* is any environment that guarantees freedom of conscience and worship to Muslims, allows them to fulfill their religious obligations, protects their physical integrity, and is not in fact a hostile space.[12] In somewhat different fashion, Faisal al Mawlawi calls the West the *dar al-da'wa*, the abode of invitation, the space in which the Islamic message needs to be spread. Regardless which appellation one prefers, the very process of reworking categories of fiqh classifications as *this* but not *that* always problematizes the area around the category. With the abode of invitation (*dar al-da'wa*) we get not only its opposite—rejection—but endless debates around what is invited, who is invited, what and who is rejected, and where one ends and the other begins. All of this suggests that despite the pitfalls represented by dichotomized thinking about "Islam and the West" or "the West and the rest," a place like the United States still appears to be an abode where Muslims can live securely with certain fundamental rights guaranteed. We are left with the question, then, for those who locate themselves within this abode: Has the work of *da'wa* been refashioned in truly significant ways?

PROPAGATION OF ISLAM IN AMERICA

Considerable Muslim proselytizing took place in the United States during the twentieth century, much of it among, though by no means confined to, African Americans.[13]

In fact, conversion has been a significant part of the African American Muslim experience for more than 100 years, making Islam a noteworthy American religious tradition. However in spite of this reality the word "*da'wa*" is rarely mentioned in the literature and discourse by and about Muslims in the United States.[14] This might be because *da'wa* activity, in Muslim majority countries, has been aimed at convincing already existing Muslims to embrace a politicized Islam rather than reaching out to non-Muslims in order to gain new proselytes. Or it might be because more expansive (i.e., not literal) interpretations of *da'wa* as "propagating the faith" have emphasized outreach and education rather than proselytization, supporting the creation of Muslim organizations and Islamic centers that offer public seminars, talks, and opportunities for interfaith dialogue. Or perhaps *da'wa* is understated because it is represented less by institutional efforts than by individuals striving to assume moral responsibility for their own condition.

In this section I explore four aspects of contemporary *da'wa* in the United States. The first is a brief look at the historical role of *da'wa* in the formation of a few key African American Muslim communities. The second aspect is found in the commitment to education represented by the ideas of Palestinian-American thinker Isma'il al-Faruqi. I then discuss the recent *da'wa* manuals written by and for American Muslims, concerned with the scriptural and the pragmatic implications and requirements of the faith in their everyday lives. Finally, I look at the way in which conversion narratives give us insight into what triggers conversion and what else besides conversion might be counted as *da'wa*.

How Islam came to America is covered elsewhere in this volume. A brief summary is needed here, however, in order to illustrate the place of *da'wa* in that process. Muslims in America are a very diverse group that came from many different places at different times. The historical record indicates that the first known Muslims in what is now the United States came as chattel slaves during the period of the Middle Passage.[15] However, under the conditions of slavery, it was not possible for slaves to maintain their original Islamic practices and the traces of Islam in early America have all but disappeared. Today, as a result, many African American Muslims came to Islam through the conversion process largely through the Muslim organizations established well after the post–Civil War Reconstruction period in the United States. One of the first of these organizations was the Moorish Science Temple of America founded by Noble Drew Ali in the early 1900s. Another was established in the 1930s as the Lost-Found Nation of Islam, better known as the Nation of Islam or NOI, under the leadership of Elijah Muhammad. This organization's mission was to restore African Americans to their original religion, language, and culture through Islam. Aided by his young minister, Malcolm X—possibly the NOI's most famous convert— Elijah Muhammad during the 1950s and 1960s brought the NOI to national attention as a militant Islamic black nationalist group. *Da'wa* meant "fishing for converts"[16] in the NOI's vocabulary, which is what members were strongly encouraged to do especially among young people and the incarcerated.

The Ahmadiyya Movement, founded in the Punjab region of India in the late 19th century, also encouraged African Americans to protest their second-class citizenship in the United States by converting to Islam. During the 1920s, an Indian immigrant by the name of Muhammad Sadiq established himself in Detroit and Chicago as an Ahmadiyya missionary. In short order he tapped into the popularity of the pan-Africanist movement of Marcus Garvey, lecturing at United Negro Improvement Association (UNIA) meetings and gaining converts to Islam in the process. Sadiq's message compared Islam to Christianity and attempted to demonstrate Islam's superior claim to rationality, universalism, and progress. Moreover, it described Islam as the proper religion for Africans and argued that racial inequality in America could be traced to the corrupting influence of Christianity, which debases people of color. In this manner, Sadiq's *da'wa* activity was moderately successful. Although he did not limit his proselytizing to the African American community, Sadiq frequently encouraged Garveyites and their sympathizers to link their black nationalism with Islam, hoping to create a sense of group solidarity in the midst of racial oppression. In 1923, he wrote in the pages of the journal he started, called *The Moslem Sunrise*:

> My dear American Negro...the Christian profiteers brought you out of your native lands of Africa and in Christianizing you made you forsake the religion and language of your forefathers—which were Islam and Arabic...Christianity cannot bring real brotherhood to the nations. Now leave it alone. And join Islam, the real faith of Universal Brotherhood, which at once does away with all distinctions of race, color, and creed.[17]

By the 1940s the Ahmadis claimed between 5,000 and 10,000 American converts, half of them African American.[18] However, a rift developed between the national leadership of the movement—almost entirely South Asian—and African American local leaders. This split is especially noteworthy in the cases of Cleveland, Ohio, and Pittsburgh, Pennsylvania, where two of the earliest and best known black "Sunni" mosques were built by those former members who rejected the Ahmadiyya Movement's centralized authority—the First Cleveland mosque (1936) and the First Muslim Mosque of Pittsburgh (1945).[19]

This is only a snapshot of *da'wa* activity in the first half of the twentieth century, and like all photographic representations it has a perspective that puts some features into sharper focus than others. However, it shows at least something about the unique development of Islamic *da'wa* in the United States and the macro questions of religious interpretation, race, and identity. In large part, the appeal of the message was about universal brotherhood, critique of the status quo, and a resistance to racial hierarchy. Importantly, it also shows that face-to-face (also known as "door-to-door") proselytizing afforded the opportunity to make strong social connections and to customize meaningful linkages between the personal life experiences of the "missionized" and the content of the message. All three organizations I have mentioned—the Moorish Science Temple, the NOI, and the Ahmadiyyas—continue to operate in the United

States though each has experienced extensive change and limited influence. Once reliant on interpersonal networks to strengthen their organizations, these groups and others like them in recent years have had to face very different challenges from those of the first half of the twentieth century. Not the least of these are the ubiquitous technology of the Internet and the greatly increased range of Islamic sects, orientations, perspectives, practices, and materials newly available in the United States as a result of changes in immigration. Given that each of these groups articulates a theology and practices rituals that other Muslim groups find problematic, their efforts at proselytizing have been countered by other Muslims who want to neutralize their message, which is considered to deviate from so-called normative Islam in important ways.

The recent large-scale immigration of Muslims to the United States has dramatically altered the demographics of the Muslim American population. Among other things, it has resulted in unprecedented growth in the number of mosques and Islamic schools, organizations, and publishing houses in the United States. This growth in organizational life led to changes in the conceptualization and practice of *da'wa* in the United States. Forms of *da'wa* were developed in the second half of the twentieth century that had broader segments of the American audience in mind. First, modeling an exemplary lifestyle became a popular method for propagating the faith. Like Mawdudi's idea of *da'wa* by example, this strategy is to live in such a way that others will be attracted to the Islamic message and may be persuaded by example to embrace Islam In this way, the everyday performance of Islamic values is favored over the concept of preaching/teaching by word. This method also tends to be more conservative and status-quo-oriented than the messaging of the past (e.g., that Christianity is racially oppressive). Second, the concept of *da'wa* broadened to include an emphasis on education of both the so-called nominal Muslim and the non-Muslim American. In important ways this resembles the point made by Muslim reformers of the nineteenth/twentieth century, that education (*tarbiya*) empowers the individual Muslim to perform *da'wa*. This approach has followed two trajectories at once, exhorting the Muslim constituency to equip themselves with better Islamic knowledge, and addressing people of other faiths.

Isma'il Raji al-Faruqi (1921-1986), founder of the International Institute of Islamic Thought (IIIT) and professor at Temple University from the late 1960s until his death in 1986, was very influential in defining a successful da'wa strategy that saw as necessary both the call for greater ecumenism and coexistence with other faiths, and the imperative to lead Muslims (and others) to a better understanding of Islam. In direct contrast to the work of his precursors in the United States, Faruqi's approach was to engage in dialogue with other faiths in a manner that did not deliberately "score points" for Islam at the expense of other religions. Instead he emphasized the notion of *din al-fitrah*, the natural religion, arguing that Islam is innate and that God has endowed humanity with an intuitive faculty to recognize God's presence in the natural world. Da'wa in this understanding is an invitation to return or "revert" to one's natural state of being in relationship with the divine, shedding all indoctrinations of history; thus the role of the *da'i* is that of a "midwife" inspiring the one who is called to rediscover what God has already put within his or her conscience. Moreover, *din al-fitrah* is said to be at the base of all historical religious experience. Adherents of all (monotheistic) religions are equal members of a universal brotherhood. The essence—theocentrism—is knowable and is revealed in the Qur'an for all to know, although the basic message can also be found in the revelations given to other prophets.[20] This becomes the basis for interfaith dialogue. Faruqi advocated Islamic *da'wa* as a means to enable the individual to assume his or her birthright, to become the vicegerent (*khalifah*) of God in order to refashion the world in accord with God's will. The emphasis is placed on the moral obligation to inform and educate according to one's abilities without concern for the result, which is to be determined by God, for "God guides whomever he will to the straight path." In the end both the convert and the long-time Muslim are charged with the responsibility to deepen their knowledge for the sake of improving the culture and circumstances of the United States.[21]

In terms of the need to enlighten the nominal Muslim, Faruqi wrote that "the Islamic vision provides the immigrant the criterion with which to understand, judge, and seek to transform the unfortunate realities of North America." This particular directive increasingly can be found in literature aimed at a Muslim audience post-9/11. It implies an obligation to transform not only their own lives but the society, and so *da'wa* is more about social activism than it is about directly gaining new converts. Recently, *da'wa* has also been used to encourage Muslim Americans to redress the widespread negative images of Islam ("Mislam") in American institutions, media and culture by learning more Islamic knowledge themselves in order to properly educate the American public (more on this below). This approach means counteracting stereotypes about Islam and Muslims stemming from the non-Muslim environment.

The shift in meaning of *da'wa* as education (*tarbiya*) so the Muslim can contribute to the advancement of society has not entirely left the concept of missionary work out of the picture. At the same time there has been an increase in the output of what I will call "*da'wa* manuals," written in English, to encourage Muslims to engage in *da'wa* activity. One can find on the Internet a burgeoning cottage industry of manuals and training videos with respect to proselytizing. Media technology has facilitated this process and the new media have shaped current *da'wa* trends in myriad ways. A new spin on old methods has merged the traditional rationale for propagating the faith and renewing Muslims' religious commitment with the new digital media and the Internet in ways that are mindful of changes in context. To get the flavor of this one need go no farther than the Texas Dawah Convention.[22] In addition, satellite television has added a "visual *da'wa*" dimension known around the world as Islamic televangelism. Moreover, contemporary *da'wa* materials addressing a western audience mark an important break with methods used around the world. On the international scene, so-called bricks and mortar institutions—academies in Saudi Arabia, Pakistan, and other Muslim countries—offer programs for the education and training of imams, community leaders and other professionals, which continue to draw on historical understandings of *da'wa* as being tied to a particular path to God. For instance, in Pakistan the International Islamic University houses a *da'wa* academy that has developed an integrated approach for national and international propagation of Islam. Most of the students are trained to be imams in mosques rather than scholars, and beyond the traditional curriculum the *da'wa* academy runs international educational (*tarbiya*) training camps largely for young people from different parts of Asia and Africa but also increasingly for Muslims who are experiencing religious pluralism. The general aims are to cultivate a *salafi* orientation, to re-Islamize the *ummah*, and to integrate various ethnic, social, and sectarian groups under the aegis of a central authority in charge of Islamic renewal, which can be seen in the academy's journal, *Da'wah Highlights*.[23]But because of significant language and culture gaps most of these graduates are not successful in the American context. Preferred are the seminars, conferences, and training courses for Muslims offered in American institutions well-versed in the vicissitudes of life in pluralistic settings. While most curriculum include very little if anything specifically called "*da'wa*," they all teach theology, jurisprudence, literature, Arabic language, etc., for the purpose of increasing Islamic literacy. The goal is to acquire and circulate knowledge and illustrate Islamic virtues to the wider Muslim community and to the non-Muslim public sphere, seeking to raise the general level of discourse. Many publish literature, audiovisual materials, computer software, and other aides to communicate the message. All utilize the Internet to advertise their materials.[24]While a portion of the messaging reflects an exclusivist viewpoint and extols the superiority of Islam as a religion and way of life, the vast majority of these materials adapt to pluralism by expressing respect for what is sacred to others and for religious freedom.

Some websites specifically offer *da'wa* manuals in skills training. One such source posts articles and lectures in English with such titles as the "ABCs of da'wah," "the Prophet's Da'wah Methodology," and "What Are YOU Doing for the Da'wah?"[25] This source offers video and lesson plans on proper presentation and communication, as well as research and statistics to equip the *da'i* with the necessary prerequisites to offer guidance to seekers. There is even a section on how to conduct *da'wa* in the age of the iPhone with the message that Muslims have a lot of work to do in order to counter the disinformation about Islam spread by anti-Islamic websites, rants on YouTube, and powerful bloggers.

In the early years of this century WhyIslam.com, the media project of the Islamic Circle of North America (ICNA), was launched as a *da'wa* activity. ICNA thought this essential because, according to its website, "given the prevalent misinformation, misunderstanding, and stereotypes coupled with our duty to spread truth about Islam and our community," new methods of *da'wa* were needed. Advertising through signs on city buses, billboards, transit stations, shopping centers and so on, the advocacy organization's main goal has been to reach the general public in order to clarify misconceptions. The ad copy prominently displays a 24-hour hotline with a toll-free telephone number with "live operators" to answer questions about Islam and Muslims.[26]

As Muslims have become more visible in the American society, the fears and contempt for them, which used to be expressed less openly, are now easily found on cable news talk shows, media campaigns, and other locations. Mitt Romney's aide declared that the presidential candidate opposed the construction of the Park 51 (also given the misnomer the "Ground Zero mosque") Islamic community center because it had the potential for becoming an extremist headquarters for "global recruiting and propaganda."[27] In 2011, US congressman Peter King (R-NY), chair of the House Homeland Security Committee, held a highly publicized hearing to determine whether American Muslims are law-abiding people and whether they ignored the radicals among them. Without giving any evidence, King once declared that as many as 80 percent of mosques in America are run by extremists.[28] Thus, Muslims have raised *da'wa* to a new level in order to respond to the fear and address several stereotypes that link Islam to terrorism and extremism.

Many organizations, such as Sound Vision, an online purveyor of Islamic educational materials, have incorporated *da'wa* into interfaith relations. Sound Vision offers many products to introduce Islam to a Western audience. Its founder, Abdul Malik Mujahid—Chicago-area imam, executive producer of Chicago's Radioislam. com, host of a daily one-hour radio talk show, and current chair of the council of the World Parliament of Religions—has been recognized globally as a leader in promoting interfaith dialogue. Imam Mujahid encourages his fellow Muslims to take a gradual approach to *da'wa*. After several years of *da'wa* efforts in the United States, Muslims have made few inroads because, he argues, Americans are immune to religious messaging. Because of their preference for talking about immediate subjects such as sports, the weather and celebrities, Americans by and large are not responsive to questions of a deeper nature. Nevertheless, Mujahid continues, Americans are equally committed to fair play, and when one gives them something to read things begin to happen. Americans, he writes, are tolerant in the sense that while they may dislike a particular group—an often-cited example is communists—they will staunchly defend the right to have books expressing the group's viewpoint on the public library's shelves. Thus, solid American commitments to fair play and to the right to free thought and expression create an appropriate milieu for *da'wa* work, and the challenge is to adjust older *da'wa* strategies to the Western environment of secularism and pluralistic values.[29] In a related vein, the Islamic Society of North America (ISNA), one of the largest and oldest umbrella organizations for Muslims in the United States, has established an office for interfaith and community alliances, which functions as an informational bureau to offer a positive image of Islam and Muslims and to engage in joint projects with other mainstream religious organizations. An example is the "standing shoulder to shoulder" campaign, which aligns the United Church of Christ and others to stand with American Muslims and uphold American values.[30] The stated rationale for this initiative is to break down barriers and dispel misunderstanding.

The book *How to Tell Others About Islam*, written by the Muslim American convert Yahiya Emerick, is a manual for *da'wa* training. Because Islam has no ordained clergy or a category of professional missionaries, Emerick argues, it is incumbent upon all believers to summon others to the right path. One means suggested to do this is a *dars* or a study circle. Emerick's book contains advice about best practices, when and where to perform *da'wa*, the ethics of calling people to Islam, the challenges of reaching Hispanic and Asian communities, and the challenges presented by popular culture, the military, gender-consciousness, etc. It also provides doctrinal justification for the performance of *da'wa* and suggests the *da'i* not rely on pamphlets or literature to do the job. Emerick believes the "old fashioned" method of personal contact or face-to-face proselytizing is most effective.[31]

Activities associated with *da'wa* in the United States, then, can be summarized in the following ways. First, there is missionary work, calling non-Muslims to embrace Islam, which Faruqi and others have referred to not as conversion but as *reverting* to the natural religion. Second is exhortation directed at already existing Muslims to guide them to a more righteous path. And third is the circulation of Islamic knowledge, which results in a more just society. Given this range it is problematic to consider conversion to be the only appropriate measure of the impact of *da'wa* because it applies only to missionary work. It leaves out the effect of propagandizing Muslims and the spread of Islamic knowledge. Nevertheless, the conversion process is typically the one location to which researchers look to see whether *da'wa* is effective. Recent years have seen an increase in conversion studies done in the humanities and social sciences, showing that conversion language speaks of new forms of relatedness, of possessing a newly inscribed "communal self defined through the gaze of others."[32] Moreover, the conversion occurs primarily because it corresponds with the convert's preexisting feelings about truth and meaning.[33]

In many Muslim conversion narratives a common theme emerges: conversion (often referred to as *reversion*) is a gradual awareness of converts that their ideas and beliefs had always been "Islamic" though they had realized it only recently. These are narratives of recognition; for instance, "I was a Muslim and just wasn't aware of it" or "So it was almost natural to become a Muslim, it was always what made sense anyway."[34] According to most accounts, there was no dramatic turning point and, although other Muslims are an important source of inspiration, many converts relate that they were convinced by reading books, especially the Qur'an. Notably, however, many converts say that they began to learn more about the religion only after they had embraced Islam; for instance, "The next morning, I started looking into Islam." Thus, there is only scant evidence in the narratives to suggest that direct proselytizing resulted in conversion. Rather, it is typical that the new convert knew someone—a brother-in-law, a friend, a spouse—who attracted him or her to investigate the religion. Establishing close social ties with a Muslim is often the precursor to becoming a Muslim.

Trends in Latino Muslim conversion offer insights into this debate. Some Latinos convert to Islam as a way of connecting with an uprooted past in Spain. Others use Islam as a means to distance themselves from the scandals and bloody history of the Roman Catholic Church. Still others are finding their way to Islam through marriage and other family connections. As Islam continues to make inroads into the Latino community, it is clear that there is also a prison connection. While conversion among the incarcerated was brought to the public's attention many years ago with the "reversion" to Islam of several African Americans in prison resulting many constitutional court battles in the 1960s and 1970s,[35] in this century an increasing number of prison converts has been Latino. According to one analyst, the spread of "Prislam" groups connects religious ideology with Latino gang values, presenting what may be the most likely domestic security threat and source of extremism among American Muslims.[36]

Conclusion

Da'wa in the United States, where Muslims live as a minority faith, is a constant (if sometimes understated) factor motivating the welfare of the community. The obligation to summon the faithful is translated into the need for better education and more accurate information. Those who were born Muslim need education to become both more "pious" and better able to interact successfully with majority society. New converts are attracted by the living example of Islamic values embodied by Muslims in their midst; once their curiosity is stirred, they tend to seek out more information for themselves. And finally, the "mislam" proliferating in post-9/11 America is viewed as an urgent call to Muslims since it can only be counteracted by the clear and convincing presentation by Muslims of reliable information about Islam. Da'wa activity is seen as an integral part of something much larger: the efforts of ordinary Muslims to spread information about their faith.

Notes

1. This and all Qur'anic passages are from the translation by M.A.S. Abdel Haleem, accessed at Oxford Islamic Studies Online.
2. Another interpretation of this verse reads, "Prophet, call [people] to the way of your Lord with wisdom and good teaching. Argue with them in the most courteous way, for your Lord knows best who has strayed from His way and who is rightly guided." For this interpretation and a similar discussion, see Paul E. Walker, Reinhard Schulze, and Muhammad Khalid Masud, "Da'wah," The Oxford Encyclopedia of the Islamic World, accessible at Oxford Islamic Studies Online. Available at: http://www.oxfordislamicstudies.com.proxy.library.ucsb.edu:2048/article/opr/t236/e0182?_hi=4&_pos=3#match. Accessed July 30, 2012.

3. See Iqbal Singh Sevea, *The Political Philosophy of Muhammad Iqbal: Islam and Nationalism in Late Colonial India* (New York: Cambridge University Press, 2012): 7.

4. Ibid., p. 8.

5. Ibid., p. 12.

6. See Abdulaziz Sachedina, *Islam and the Challenge of Human Rights* (New York: Oxford University Press, 2009): 204.

7. See Jamaat-I Islami (Islamic Political Party) is the Indo-Pakistani party founded in 1941 that represented Mawdudi's intellectual contribution, defining the nation as the *ummah*, or religious community, as the core of the Islamic state.

8. Islamist is a term used increasingly in the late twentieth century to designate those who advocate the slogan, "Islam is the solution (*Al-Islam huwa al-hal*)," associated with the idea that the Islamic *shari'a* provides guidance for all aspects of human life. In general they advocate for the creation of an Islamic state and are opposed to 'secularism' understood as a system of government and society that is based on Western-derived ideas and practices.

9. See Yvonne Y. Haddad, *Contemporary Islam and the Challenge of History* (Albany, N.Y.: SUNY Press, 1982): 92–3.

10. See Maulana Abul Mawdudi, *The Evidence of Truth* (Lahore, Pakistan: Islamic Publications, Ltd., 1967): 3–4.

11. See Tariq Ramadan, *Western Muslims and the Future of Islam* (New York and Oxford: Oxford University Press, 2004): 104.

12. Ibid., p. 70.

13. Islam has become modestly popular among Hispanics in the United States. In 1997 the Latino American Dawah Organization was founded to disseminate information about the history of Islam in Latin America and Spain, and to promote Islam among Hispanics in the United States. See www.latinodawah.org.

14. Noteworthy studies include Larry Poston, *Da'wah in the West: Muslim Missionary Activity and the Dynamics of Conversion to Islam* (1992), and Isma'il Raji al-Faruqi, "On the Nature of Islamic Da'wah," in *Christian Mission and Islamic Da'wah: Proceedings of the Chambesy Dialogue* (1985). See also Joseph Henry Smith, *The Practice of Dawah Activity in the North America and the Attraction of Islam*, a Ph.D. dissertation written at Fuller Theological Seminary (1994/5).

15. See Sylvaine Diouf, *Servants of Allah: African Muslims Enslaved in the Americas* (New York: New York University Press, 1998): 140.

16. See Manning Marable, *Malcolm X: A Life of Reinvention* (New York: Basic Books, 2011): 102.

17. Ibid., p. 83.

18. Ibid., p. 84.

19. Ibid., p. 213.

20. This is what Faruqi called "Islamicity." See Isma'il R. al-Faruqi, "Towards a Historiography of a Pre-Hijrah Islam," *Islamic Studies* 1, 2 (June 1962): 65–87.

21. From al-Faruqi, "On the Nature of Islamic Dawah," especially pp. 47–40.

22. Information is available at http://goingtotdc.com/. Accessed January 11, 2013.

23. See David A. Kerr, "Islamic Da'wa and Christian Mission: Towards a Comparative Analysis," in *International Review of Mission*, 89, 353 (2009): 150–72; see p. 159. See also Jamal Malik, "Islamic Mission and Call: the Case of the International Islamic Univeristy, Islamabad," in *Islam and Christian-Muslim Relations*, 9, 1 (1998): 31–47.

24. For instance, see Sheikh Kamal al-Mekki, and his online seminar called "Shahadah: Fiqh al-Dawa." Available at: http://forums.almaghrib.org/showthread.php?t=43376. Accessed

September 27, 2012. See also the Soundvision Foundation, a nonprofit founded by Abdul Malik Mujahid of Chicago, at http://www.soundvision.com/Info/education/pubschool/edu.dawapublic.asp. Accessed September 27, 2012, for "dawa in public schools," extensive advice on strategies for Muslim students to spread the message.

25. See www.dawahskills.com, accessed on August 28, 2012. See also www.themodernreligion.com, accessed September 5, 2012, which provides information on what it means to convert with such subheadings as "Islam is for those who think," "Islam is your birthright," and an explanation that every person is born a Muslim because we are all created by God.

26. Accessed on December 12, 2012, at www.whyislam.org. For another example of *da'wa* as corrective of misinformation, see The Deen Show at www.thedeenshow.com.

27. Boston Globe editorial, "Romney's Cave-in on Mosque Violates His Own Principles," August 25, 2011, last accessed on January 13, 2013, at http://www.boston.com/bostonglobe/editorial_opinion/editorials/articles/2010/08/25/romneys_cave_in_on_mosque_violates_his_own_principles/.

28. For discussion, see Kathleen M. Moore, "Muslim Advocacy in America," in Jeffrey Kenney and Ebrahim Moosa, eds., *Islam in the Modern World* (New York: Routledge, 2013).

29. See Abdul Malik Mujahid, "A Case for Indirect Methods of Da'wa: In Light of American Reading Habits and Tolerance," last accessed January 13, 2013, at http://www.dawanet.com/research/indirect.asp.

30. Last accessed on January 13, 2013, at http://www.shouldertoshouldercampaign.org/.

31. See Emerick, *How to Tell Others About Islam*, 3rd ed. (Long Island, N.Y.: International Books & Tapes Supply, 1996).

32. See Andrew Buckser and Stephen Glazier, eds., *The Anthropology of Religious Conversion* (Lanham, Md.: Rowman & Littlefield, 2003): 2.

33. See Rebecca Sachs Norris, "Converting to 'What' Embodied Culture and the Adoption of New Beliefs," in Buckser and Glazier, eds., *Anthropology of Religious Conversion* (Lanham, Md.: Rowman & Littlefield, 2003):171.

34. For conversion narratives, see Carol L. Anway, *Daughters of Another Path: Experiences of American Women Choosing Islam* (Lee's Summit, Missouri: Yawna Publications, 1996); Anna Mansson McGinty, *Becoming Muslim: Western Women's Conversion to Islam* (New York: Palgrave Macmillan, 2006); Karin Van Nieuwkerk, "Islam is your Birthright': Conversion, Reversion, and Alternation: the Case of New Muslimas in the West," in Jan N. Bremmer, Wout J. van Bekkum and Arie L. Molendijk, eds., *Cultures of Conversions* (Lueven, Paris, and Dudley, Mass.: Peeters Press, 2006): 151–64. See also this website soliciting conversion narratives for a book, Latino Muslims: Our Journey to Islam, at www.latinomuslim.com.

35. See Kathleen M. Moore, *Al-Mughtaribun: American Law and the Transformation of Muslim Life* (Albany, NY: SUNY Press, 1995).

36. See SpearIt, "Islam, Prisons and Latinos," an article for Institute for Social Policy and Understanding, February 2, 2012, last accessed January 13, 2013, at http://www.ispu.org/GetArticles/48/2557/Publications.aspx.

References

Buckser, Andrew and Stephen Glazier, eds., *The Anthropology of Religious Conversion* (Lanham, Md.: Rowman & Littlefield, 2003).

Diouf, Sylvaine, *Servants of Allah: African Muslims Enslaved in the Americas* (New York: New York University Press, 1998).

Emerick, Yahiya, *How to Tell Others About Islam*, *3rd edition* (Long Island, NY: International Books & Tapes Supply, 1996.)

Faruqi, al-, Ismaʿil Raji, "On the Nature of Islamic Daʿwah," in *Christian Mission and Islamic Daʿwah: Proceedings of the Chambese Dialogue Consultation* (Leceister, UK: The Islamic Foundation, 1982) pp. 33–51.

Faruqi, al-, Ismaʿil Raji, "Towards a Historiography of a Pre-Hijrah Islam," *Islamic Studies*, 1, 2 (June 1962), 65–87.

Haddad, Yvonne Yazbeck, *Contemporary Islam and the Challenge of History* (Albany, N.Y.: SUNY Press, 1982).

Kerr, David A., "Islamic Daʿwah and Christian Mission: A Comparative Analysis," *International Review of Mission*, 89, 353 (2009), 150–172.

Malik, Hafeez, "Sir Sayyid Ahmad Khan's Doctrines of Muslim Nationalism and National Progress," *Modern Asian Studies*, 2, 3 (1968), 221–224.

Marable, Manning. *Malcolm X: A Life of Reinvention* (New York: Basic Books, 2011).

Masud, Muhammad Khalid. "Dawah: Modern Usage" in Oxford Islamic Studies online, retrieved September 12, 2012, at http://www.oxfordislamicstudies.com.proxy.library.ucsb.edu:2048/article/opr/t236MIW/e0182#e0182-s0003.

Mawdudi, al-, Abul ʿAla. *The Evidence of Truth*. (Lahore, Pakistan: Islamic Publications, Ltd., 1967).

McGinty, Anna Mansson. *Becoming Muslim: Western Women's Conversions to Islam*. (New York: Palgrave Macmillan, 2006).

Moore, Kathleen M. "Muslim Advocacy in America," in Jeffrey Kenney and Ebrahim Moosa, editors, *Islam in the Modern World*, (New York: Routledge Publishers, 2013).

Mujahid, Abdul Malik. "A Case for Indirect Daʿwa: In Light of American Reading Habits and Tolerance. Last Accessed January 13, 2013 at http://www.dawanet.com/research/indirect.asp

Poston, Larry. *Islamic Daʿwah in the West: Muslim Missionary Activity and the Dynamics of Conversion to Islam*. (New York: Oxford University Press, 1992).

Ramadan, Tariq. *Western Muslims and the Future of Islam*. (New York and Oxford: Oxford University Press, 2004).

Sachedina, Abdulaziz. *Islam and the Challenge of Human Rights*. (New York: Oxford University Press, 2009).

Sachs Norris, Rebecca, "Converting to What" Embodied Culture and the Adoption of New Beliefs," in A. Buckser and S. Glazier, eds, *The Anthropology of Religious Conversion*, pp. 171–182. (Lanham, Maryland: Rowman & Littlefield, 2003).

Sevea, Iqbal Singh, *The Political Philosophy of Muhammad Iqbal: Islam and Nationalism in Late Colonial India* (New York: Cambridge University Press, 2012.)

Van Nieuwkirk, Karin. "Islam Is Your Birthright: Conversion, Reversion, and Alternation: The Case of New Muslimas in the West," in Jan N. Bremmer, Wout J. van Bekkum, and Arie L. Molendijk, eds., *Cultures of Conversions* (Leuven, Paris, and Dudley, Mass:.: Peeters Press, 2006) pp. 151–164.

CHAPTER 17

ISLAM IN AMERICAN PRISONS

SUSAN VAN BAALEN

A number of commentators and even government agencies confuse "conversion" with "radicalization," implying that prisoners who take up purist strains of Islam are all at risk of becoming terrorists. In reality, the two are not always connected. While prison conversions to Islam are frequent and significant percentages of converts and "born-again Muslims" are attracted by the purity and rigor of the Salafist tradition, no serious researcher claims that this automatically translates into support for terrorism.[1]

Confusion exists concerning exactly who the Muslims in prison are, particularly as society attempts to assess the national security threat Muslims might pose. The general public typically imagines that twenty-first-century incarcerated American Muslims are either Islamist immigrants or "Black Muslims." They envision a cabal of immigrant Muslims guilty of acts of violent jihad against the United States, or they imagine uneducated, angry, and antagonistic black gang members. However, this is simply not the case. The vast majority of Muslims prisoners are converts and followers of the late Warith Deen Mohammed, who first established a place for black Americans within global Islam after his 1979 break with the Nation of Islam.

In the attempt to clarify the historical evolution of Islam in prisons in the context of a fuller understanding of American Islam, this chapter analyzes six topics: (1) Muslims in US prisons, (2) conversions to Islam, (3) program accommodations, (4) religious service providers, (5) extremist threats, and (6) aftercare in a divided community.

Muslims in US Prisons

Multiple expressions of Islamic beliefs and practices have existed in US prisons since the early 1960s. The current situation has evolved from the interplay of three distinct religious groups asserting a Muslim identity: (1) global Islam, (2) the Nation of Islam ("the Nation"), and (3) the Moorish Science Temple of America (MSTofA). Those who followed Warith Deen Mohammed embraced global Islam. Their expression of Islam is uniquely western because of language and cultural differences. However, they have become strict adherents to the global beliefs and practices of Islam and assert a distinctive Muslim identity.

The lack of information among prison officials about Islam in general, and more specifically the differences between the Muslim-based religious movements, has led to the tendency to accommodate all Black Muslims as a unit. Currently, the term *Muslim* belongs to those who embraced a uniquely black American expression of Sunni Islam under the leadership of Imam Warith Deen Mohammed in the last decades of the twentieth century.

The expression of Islam in American prisons emerged from black American culture and experience as well as the black American prisoners' need for a collective identity that is both distinct and positive. There are a very small number of Middle Eastern, Caucasian, and North African prisoners within the population of incarcerated Muslims, but they are overshadowed by the number and the influence of the black American Muslims who embrace global Islam and have dominated Muslim leadership roles in the prisons since the 1980s. Attempts to bring the ethnic groups together have been largely ineffective because of cultural and ethnic differences. Consequently those who are not black or of black African descent tend to play a peripheral role. Most even prefer to perform their religious duties privately rather than pray behind an American black prayer leader.

The movement toward Islam in prisons began in the 1950s. For more than twenty-five years, prison officials were insufficiently educated about the differences that existed among the three groups. Consequently those who expressed any affiliation with Islam were accommodated under the rubric of one religious group identified as Black Muslims. It was not until the early 1980s that the prison followers of global Islam, under the leadership of Warith Deen Mohammed, successfully asserted their distinctiveness, rejecting the Moors and the Nation as pseudomovements.

The other two groups in the prison system belong either to the Nation of Islam, followers of Louis Farrakhan, or to the MSTofA, who follow the teachings of Noble Drew Ali. For a quarter of a century (1950–1975), incarcerated members of the MSTofA and the Nation shared the moniker "Black Muslims," although the term correctly belongs only to the Nation. Standing on a common African heritage and the strength of the mid-twentieth-century civil rights movement, significant numbers of urban black Americans asserted their black Muslim identity, particularly after the charismatic rhetoric of Malcolm X popularized Islam as an African-based religion attractive to black American youth. As members of the MSTofA or the Nation of Islam, young black men claimed an inherent sense of dignity and purpose not generally afforded to black Americans of that era. In reality only their shared African heritage bound these religious movements to global Islam.

Prison records for the 150-year period before 1950 provide scant evidence of Muslims in US prisons. In the "Annual Report to the Warden" at the US Penitentiary in Atlanta on July 1, 1922, Chaplain Joseph A. Sewell identified three "Mohammedans" among the 2,334 prisoners.[2] Shortly thereafter California prison records confirm that Wallace D. Fard, the Nation of Islam founder, was incarcerated in California in 1926. At the time Fard was classified as a New Zealand–born Caucasian with no apparent religious affiliation.[3] His establishment of the Nation occurred only after he was released from San Quentin in 1929. The earliest documentation of incarcerated Muslim groups occurred during the World War II era, when Fard's successor, Elijah Muhammad, and a band of his followers were imprisoned because of their refusal to register for the draft, a refusal grounded in the tenets of the Nation.[4]

The MSTofA and the Nation were two of many social movements founded by black men who sought to distance themselves from the image of common sharecropper descendants of slaves. The goals and values of these organizations appealed to poor urban black men who had migrated north in search of employment. The very rapid growth of these movements in prisons occurred during the 1960s, as leaders borrowed from the culture, language, rituals, and practices of Islam to give sacred meaning to their search for dignity as men and women of God.

This rise in visibility was due in large part to one former prisoner, Malcolm X (also known as Malcolm Little), who had been incarcerated in Massachusetts prisons from 1946 to 1952. A lapsed Christian before his incarceration, Malcolm had, by 1948, become a devoted disciple of Elijah Muhammad, having experienced a miraculous vision of Wallace D. Fard.[5] Malcolm's wholehearted embrace of the Nation marks the onset of a pattern of black Christian conversions to Islam in US prisons— a pattern that continues today. After Malcolm's release from prison, he became the national spokesperson for the Nation. The organization then grew exponentially, inspired by his rhetorical eloquence and his faithfulness to the message of Elijah Muhammad.

The years between 1955 and 2000 were characterized by growth and divisiveness for Muslims in prison. The earliest documented groups of Black Muslims were incarcerated in San Quentin (1955), The Washington, D.C., Lorton Reformatory, (1957), and The New Jersey and District of Columbia Penitentiaries (1959). There were marked divisions among the various religious movements asserting Islamic roots, yet these same factions were united against "the Man" in their struggle to overcome religious and racial discrimination. The struggle in the 1960s for equal access to religious leaders and sacred writings, halal foods, and religious apparel—as well as opportunities for congregate worship and study—stands in stark contrast to the well-established twenty-first-century religious accommodations accorded to both global Islam and other Muslim movements.

The accommodations granted to new religions in prisons today grew out of the civil rights struggles and litigation by imprisoned Black Muslims during the 1960s and 1970s. Like most US institutions of the mid-twentieth century, prisons were oriented toward Christianity. By 1957, however, members of the Nation had begun to litigate in federal courts to secure the right of non-Christians to equal religious opportunities. Suspicious activities and litigation by the Black Muslims resulted in harsh punishments for their prison leaders, who sometimes spent months or even years in solitary confinement.[6] Black Muslims were typically associated with gang activity, and the fact that they challenged the religious status quo was viewed as a serious threat to the security of prison systems. Clair Cripe, then general counsel for the Bureau of Prisons, described the changing landscape of religion and correctional law in 1976:

> This interest [Black Muslim] mushroomed into broader reviews of all prison activi-
> ties, into the effectiveness of confinement in the criminal justice scheme of things,
> and into prison as a component of sentencing. Not all would agree, but I think there is
> considerable validity to the proposal that Black Muslim litigation was the fuse of this
> explosion...and...the religious cases brought by Black Muslims in the early 1960s
> brought about a Correctional Law revolution.[7]

History may ultimately judge this struggle for the religious rights of non-Christian prisoners to be among the greatest legacies of the Nation of Islam. In 1979, as the shift from black Muslim to global Islam was occurring, Norman A. Carlson, director of the Federal Bureau of Prisons, dispelled the long-held perception that incarcerated Muslims were a security threat when he described the Muslims as "very quiet, well-disciplined followers of the true Muslim religion." He continued: "[they] are no longer a threat to prison discipline because they are no longer taught racial hatred. Many of the fears and trepidations were unfounded."[8] By this time many incarcerated Black Muslims had already begun to migrate toward global Islam, following the example of their own leaders, Malcolm X and Imam Warith Deen Mohammed. Only a small number of members of the Nation and even smaller numbers of immigrant jihadists are incarcerated in twenty-first-century prisons.

Global Islam, 1980–2000

The majority of Muslims in twenty-first-century prisons identify themselves as Sunni Muslims and full participants in the global community of Islam.[9] As the population of incarcerated adherents to global Islam has grown, other black Muslim groups have dwindled to only a remnant of their mid-twentieth-century membership. Black Muslim movements continue to flourish only in correctional institutions in

California, along the Atlantic coast, and in midwestern urban centers. Sunni pre-dominance is due to three factors: (1) the influence of Malcolm X's conversion to Islam, (2) the prison *da'wa*, was designed too teach Muslims about their faith and/or to invite non-Muslims to learn about Islam,work of the Dar-ul-Islam movement in the 1960s and 1970s, and (3) the leadership of Warith Deen Mohammed, who lever-aged a unique place for disadvantaged black Americans within global Islam.

By the early 1960s both Malcolm X and Warith Deen Mohammed had begun to express reservations about the teachings of the Honorable Elijah Muhammad (HEM), particularly with respect to contradictions between his teachings and the word of God revealed in the Qur'an. It became increasingly clear to these men that the "preachments" of HEM vilifying white Americans as devils were not consistent with the teaching of Islam and that his teachings in general were not grounded in the Qur'an. While each struggled with the tensions between the two expressions of Islam in the United States, neither had the courage to effect change among the masses until their respective Hajj experiences transformed their own lives. Informed by these experiences, both Malcolm and Warith Deen now envisioned an Islam that was larger than any one race or culture. They found this in Sunni Islam. This in 1965 at the hands of three members of the Nation of Islam who were fiercely loyal to the leadership of the Honorable Elijah Muhammad. The charismatic Malcolm's conver-sion to global Islam was a serious threat to the credibility and continued growth of the Nation of Islam. In reality, Malcolm's death only delayed the inevitable migra-tion of members of the Nation to global Islam.. It was more than a decade later, after the death of HEM, that Warith Deen was able to invite tens of thousands of black American Muslims to join him in embracing the beliefs and practices of global Islam. Among those thousands were incarcerated men and women throughout the country.

Along a parallel track in the early 1960s a group of black American men and women embraced Dar-ul-Islam (1962–1983), a new fundamentalist Islamic movement based in New York City. Its uniqueness rested with the group itself. Leaning heavily on Pakistani leaders of the Tablighi Jamaat movement, three converts to global Islam established the Dar-ul-Islam, a black American movement committed to a lifestyle patterned on the life of the Prophet Muhammad. The Dar, as it was called, was equally committed to restoration of the place of black Americans through participation in the Civil Rights Movement. The commitment to da'wa was central to the Dar's mis-sion, because the future of a strong black American presence within global Islam depended on serious, devout, and pure black American Muslim converts. The da'wa committee was headed by Yahya Abdul Kareen, one of the founders, who brought to New York State prisons the strict interpretation of Islam called Salafism. It is more than likely that this is where the strong "Salafish" ideology in American prisons origi-nated, but there is no documentation to support this theory.

The contribution of other Islamic movements to the culture of Islam in the pris-ons has been minimal. The numbers of Shias, Sufis, or other groups constitute such a small percentage of the Muslim prison population that their influence is negligible.

In only a very few state systems have Shias successfully litigated and won the right to have separate worship and study opportunities. Unyielding sectarianism—meaning the refusal of incarcerated American Muslims to accept pluralism within Islam—separates American black Sunnis from immigrant Muslims. Recent African American converts often embrace global Islam because they see it as a liberator from racism and discrimination. Distinct and ideologically distant from the American Sunnis are small ethnic clusters of Asian or North African prisoners who tend to adhere to the practices of Sunnis, Shias, or Sufis, also mixing in elements of their respective cultures. Immigrant Muslims are for the most part invisible unless they are of African descent. Middle Eastern and central Asian Muslim prisoners often opt not to practice their religion publicly, refusing to pray behind a black American inmate leader whom they regard as less than Islamic or, more accurately, as a member of an American cult unrelated to global Islam. Pulitzer Prize–winning journalist Andrea Elliott concluded that "At the heart of the conflict is a question of leadership. Much to the ire of African-Americans, many immigrants see themselves as the rightful leaders of the faith in America by virtue of their Islamic schooling and fluency in Arabic, the original language of the Koran"[10] Only the puritanical views of Wahhabism and Salafism seem to unite subgroups of both immigrant and black American converts.

CONVERSIONS TO ISLAM

The US penal system was established in the nineteenth century in Philadelphia. Prison was a place where criminals could be isolated from society for a time in order to atone for their sins and recommit to living within the Christian norms of the fledgling country. This system was influenced by the Quaker belief that the solitude and deprivation of incarceration would restore them to grace. It was shaped by Calvinists to bring about penitence and true regret for one's sins. This theological underpinning left no place for non-Christians, nor did the policymakers ever imagine that any individuals other than Christians might be incarcerated in the penal system.

Since conversions to Islam began in the late 1950s, correctional officials have viewed the phenomenon with suspicion, because such conversions shattered the US penal system's bedrock of Christian penitence. In addition, Middle Eastern beliefs and practices generally remain quite unfamiliar to prison officials. The prevailing perception has been that Islam is embraced by many men of color who are more commonly affiliated with gangs than with religious programs, leading to the assumption that the religion is merely a cover for gang activities. Unfortunately this assumption has some truth to it, as the new Muslim converts have struggled to find religious and social cohesion. The phenomenon of conversion raises such questions as why black men identify so closely with Islam during incarceration and why they persevere in their search for meaning within Islam when they apparently cannot find it in the faith in which they were raised.

Prisons are daunting places, particularly for young men who have lived exclusively among other black people, having little knowledge of the Caucasian communities surrounding their disadvantaged neighborhoods. In prison they find themselves in a predominantly white world peopled by mostly black men. That is, the system itself is white in its orientation and cultural mores. Propriety is determined by standards that differ from those established in black urban communities. Values, language, mannerisms, food, music—all are white—but the prisoners living in this subculture are mostly people of color. Because congregating by race is not authorized in prisons, men and women often choose to identify with a religion in which most of the adherents are of their race. Islam thus offers a venue where black prisoners can spend time in their own cultural comfort zone, a mindset in which they can feel safe from the predators and gangs who flourish in this alienating environment. Such identification is essentially what brings people, particularly young men, to prison Islam.

What keeps them there is another matter. With their preference for Islam comes the opportunity to congregate with other black people each week. More important is the fact that study and practice of the religion often brings with it a previously unknown heightened sense of dignity and discipline. A common thread within prison Islam is the discipline that is derived from fidelity to ritual prayer, a halal diet, and the annual fast. Many whose initiation into Islam came through the Nation gradually move from the less complicated fast and prayer of the Nation to global Islam, where they submit to Allah before witnesses and observe the rigors of the fast of Ramadan and the five daily ritual prayers. Such disciplines seem to enhance a sense of dignity and self-worth. Additionally, the Qur'anic prescriptions of modesty, hygiene, and community give new meaning to their lives—a meaning they *intend* to hold on to forever. Men who can barely read English delve into Arabic study with far greater fervor than they gave to their Sunday school lessons. Embracing Islam in community with others seems to bestow feelings of self-dignity. Now, together, they are using the same energies they formerly used to create havoc in urban streets to find the God who offers them inner peace, dignity, and a sense of meaning.

The analysis of prison conversions to Islam would be incomplete without noting the constancy of the Muslim population in prisons over a thirty-year period. This is particularly important in view of the rhetoric employed by twenty-first-century politicians and journalists portraying prisons as hotbeds of terrorism in which vast numbers of black Americans are being led unwittingly into Muslim extremism. This is the reality: Twenty-first-century prisons have not witnessed unprecedented growth in the Muslim population. There has not been a significant growth in the *percentage* of incarcerated Muslims. It is true that the number of prisoners has increased exponentially since passage of the Comprehensive Crime Control Act of 1984. Nevertheless, the percentage of prisoners who express a religious preference for Islam has remained constant for more than thirty years. In 1979, the chaplain director of the Bureau of

Prisons reported that 6 percent of 25,000 prisoners were Muslims, and Muslim prison programs existed in twenty-four of thirty-eight federal prisons.[11] Thirty years later, the computer-generated record of prisoners' religious preference indicated 5.7 percent of 195,300 prisoners identify as Muslim.[12] Journalists and anti-Muslim groups have forged an image of American prisons as hotbeds of terrorism wherein vast numbers of black Americans are being led unwittingly into Muslim extremism. Extremist views have emerged from prison Islam, but rarely are these views that foment acts of violence or terrorism.

Religious Programs in Prisons

Religious programs in prison are under the jurisdiction of the *Standards for Adult Correctional Institutions* prepared by the American Correctional Association. Muslim programs vary from system to system and security level to security level, but established industry standards for religious services underpin a relatively standard program for incarcerated Muslims. The standard program for adherents of global Islam is grounded in the beliefs and pillars of Islam revealed in the Qur'an and developed in the Sunnah. Only the *jumaah* (Friday) observance and Ramadan procedures require special accommodation, while the profession of faith, daily prayers, and almsgiving do not.

Jumaah

The authorized weekly congregate prayer includes the *wudu* purification ritual; the *adhan* (call to prayer), which is typically chanted *inside* the chapel area; and afternoon prayer and *khutab*, or brief sermons.

Congregate prayer is scheduled as close to the prescribed time as the security and order of the institution permits. The ritual purification begins after lunch, when prisoners bathe or perform wudu; it ensures that their attire is appropriately clean and modest. By the time the muezzin intones the adhan, prisoners have already transformed the multipurpose area into a sacred space. Images are removed, stained glass windows are covered, and a large clean carpet is laid for those who will prostrate themselves in prayer.

The Jumaah ritual is the same as that performed by millions of Muslims congregating on Fridays throughout the world. Some prisons have a chaplain or volunteer to serve as the imam (prayer leader) and the *khateeb* (preacher), although most prisons do not employ a prayer leader from the community. In the absence of a community imam, a devout and knowledgeable prisoner leads the prayer and delivers the *khutba*. While this is standard practice in many US prisons, some systems never authorize congregate services without the presence of a community leader. In such cases congregate services are infrequent, necessitating the performance of ritual prayers privately or with one or two others. Prisoners in special confinement units for disciplinary, safety, or security reasons do not participate in congregate prayer, although they may be granted access to a soft-cover translation of the Qur'an for private prayer, study, and reflection.

Until the twenty-first century, full-time Muslim chaplains, especially immigrants, experienced a great deal of resistance from black American Muslims because the long-standing absence of Muslim chaplains had given the Muslim prisoners the unprecedented opportunity to plan and lead their own worship and study. This level of authority and prestige was threatened by the presence of an imam from the outside community. In subtle ways, Muslim prisoners often refused to allow the full-time chaplain to lead Jumaah prayer and preach the khutbah, and newly employed Muslim chaplains tacitly accepted the situation. After September 11, 2001, however, full-time Muslim chaplains became perhaps the most sought-after religious staff members in any prison. The presence and influence of a Muslim chaplain contributes significantly to the overall Muslim program and to staff understanding and respect for Muslim beliefs and practices. Muslim chaplains act as advocates to ensure that the religious rights of the Muslims are protected. They protect against unnecessary cancellation of scheduled Muslim prayer and study sessions, instruct staff on the proper respect and handling of sacred books, make sure that administrators and kitchen staff understand and respect the dietary laws, and coordinate special observances for Ramadan, Eid feasts, and other special occasions. They instruct new Muslims in a balanced understanding of the Qur'an, the Hadith, and Shari'a; provide counseling and support for prisoners in segregation or seclusion; and assist and advise Muslim prisoners who are seriously ill or dying to ensure that Muslim rituals are performed at the time of death if this is the wish of the Muslim prisoner, since often the family of the prisoner is not aware of the prisoner's preference for Islam.

Ramadan

The Ramadan observance incorporates fasting, the *Iftar* community meal, and the study of one thirtieth of the Qur'an each day. The orderly running of the institution is challenged by the Ramadan observance because meals and prayer times have to be coordinated without interrupting the routine of prisoners who are *not* participating in the rituals. Observances are typically accommodated with appropriate reverence and respect, although there are recorded instances of irreverence or disrespect shown by staff members who doubt inmates' sincerity. Ritual breaking of the fast is universal, but procedures for doing so vary significantly. Unavoidable are the inflexible security regulations that require prisoners to be secured in their cells during the customary overnight hours.

Certain particulars of the fasting process require special accommodations in the prison:

- Bagged breakfasts for the following day are distributed at the Iftar meal each night.
- "Wake up" methods are devised in order to facilitate predawn morning prayer and breakfast.
- The evening prayer, Iftar meal, and Qur'anic study pose significant challenges when Ramadan occurs during the summer. Long daylight hours require prisoners to break their fast after they would ordinarily be locked in their cells for the night.
- The Eid celebration typically includes one day free from work and a halal ceremonial meal.

Halal Diets

A major equity issue in most systems is the denial of a halal (Islamically acceptable) regimen, even though kosher meals have been provided in prisons since the 1970s. Because the right to a prescribed religious diet was established for Jewish prisoners, Muslims doubled their efforts to win the legal right to a similar accommodation. A half-hearted attempt to provide such an accommodation for Muslims was initiated in the federal prisons in 1983, with the twelve-year rollout of a systemwide religious diet program aptly named the Common Fare Program.[13] Before that time the only dietary accommodation accorded to Muslims had been the provision of a pork-free protein substitute (usually peanut butter or cheese) whenever pork was served.

The Common Fare Program initiated by the federal system and adopted by many states provides certified kosher fare for prisoners requesting a religious diet. Though similar, kosher fare differs somewhat from the halal prescription of the Qur'an. Muslim prisoners may opt to participate in the Common Fare Program, or they may choose a more flexible vegetarian option, of either a meat or a vegetarian entree at any given meal. Neither, however, is an equitable resolution to the reasonable request for halal meat and food free from pork. Until the federal courts order a distinct halal regimen for Muslim prisoners, it is unlikely that anything more than the common fare will be provided, because the existing program operates with a minimum of problems. Expanding the dietary accommodation for Muslims instead of providing a common fare for all religious diets would establish a precedent for a number of distinct religious diets. Although common fare and the vegetarian option ensure a sufficient intake of protein and calories, the regimen is specifically an accommodation designed for kosher-observant Jewish prisoners. Yet significantly more Muslims than Jews participate in the religious diet program. Confusion about religious dietary requirements and the suspicion of some prison staff about the sincerity of Muslim requests serve to postpone a decision to provide a separate halal diet for Muslims.

Religious Services Providers

Providers of religious services for incarcerated Muslims fall into three categories: full-time chaplains, contract imams, and volunteer imams. Each fills a specific role based on religious credentials and security clearance levels.

The most highly valued of the providers are the full-time Muslim chaplains. Prisons fortunate enough to employ a full-time Muslim chaplain usually have a greater number of Muslims in residence than those without a Muslim chaplain. Full-time chaplains often also accommodate the spiritual and religious requests of non-Muslim prisoners. While they do not perform services or rituals for Christians, Jews, or other faith groups, they do accommodate their religious requests by helping to secure faith-specific, credentialed individuals to provide services for their respective faith groups.

Contract and volunteer imams are not required to meet the same level of academic and security requirements as full-time chaplains because their services are provided *only* to those of the Muslim faith. As part-time religious service providers, they are not obliged to manage the complexities of universal accommodation or to supervise prisoners. They do not have access to prisoners except those who voluntarily attend their sessions. Ordinarily the imams' need and desire to pray with their own communities of faith restricts their availability to lead Friday prayers in prisons. The window of time prescribed for the ritual does not allow the contract chaplain to lead Jumaah prayer in both places.

Instead, the contractor or volunteer is often an instructor for the study of Arabic or Qur'anic studies. If contract chaplains are not available on a regular basis, an effort is made by the prisons and the faith community to ensure the presence of a community leader during Ramadan or for Eid celebrations. Contractors generally serve as subject-matter experts or provide expertise to non-Muslim chaplains responsible for the accommodation of Muslim religious requests.

Employment and Training

Graduate-level seminary study is not a customary part of an imam's preparation for spiritual leadership. Pioneer Muslim chaplains were employed in the early 1980s without benefit of professional preparation for specialized ministry. Some had received Saudi-financed scholarships for study in the Middle East; others were prepared for ministry in secular or Christian schools whose curriculum included Islamic studies.

By the mid-1990s chaplain candidates were ordinarily expected to present credentials verifying a graduate-level education paralleling Christian seminary curricula.

After the attacks of 9/11 cast a wide net of suspicion around American Muslims, procedures for hiring religious services providers and the roles of each were carefully examined. Suspicion of religious service providers was heightened by the remarks of a New York contract chaplain who outspokenly defended the 9/11 actions of Al Qaeda to prisoners in state and federal prisons.[14] Consequently a US senator from New York, reeling from the losses in his own state at the hands of terrorists, initiated an investigation of the Bureau of Prisons' Muslim Religious Services Providers.[15] The investigation examined policies, procedures, and roles of Muslim religious service providers. The inspector general recommended additional preemployment security reviews, including a clearance regarding applicants' foreign travel and formal education in Middle Eastern madrassas or Islamic schools. Concerned that programs might be influenced by Salafist extremism, investigators scrutinized the ideology of specific endorsing agencies and US chaplaincy training programs designed to prepare chaplains for military and correctional chaplaincy positions. The uneven investigation targeted programs that had enjoyed a long-standing professional relationship with the federal prison system. Suspicions generated from federal law enforcement raids and unsubstantiated claims of material support for terrorist organizations necessitated curtailment of the federal system's participation in these chaplaincy training programs.

To overcome this setback, the US Muslim community rose to the twenty-first century demand for prison chaplains by initiating seminary-like graduate theology programs in various regions of the country. Professional preparation for ministry evolved as both corrections officials and Muslim scholars acknowledged the critical demand for American Muslim chaplains who have a thorough understanding of the tenets of Islam and also understand and choose ministry in a pluralistic environment. A trailblazer in this endeavor was the Duncan Black Macdonald Center Chaplain Training Program at Hartford Seminary, and by 2012 institutions of higher education in Chicago, Los Angeles, and Virginia had expanded nationwide availability for institutional chaplaincy training by introducing comparable Islamic courses of study.

THREATS OF EXTREMISM

It is not extremism but the threat of extremism that dictates constant vigilance on the part of prison officials, particularly within high-security prisons. Tensions within Islamic programs exist because of differing interpretations of the Qur'an and the Hadith among diverse movements. While most incarcerated Muslims identify as Sunni, the prison bars have not kept out community tensions that persist among movements such as Salafism and Islamism. Each movement brings to the prison its own mission and approach to Islam. The correctional environment heightens sectarianism by placing limits on practices viewed as extreme by US and state governments. Perceived prison extremism fueled by the media after 9/11 resulted in adaptations to the Muslim program. For example, many Islamists assert that all of the obligatory daily prayers must be prayed in a congregate setting, but prisoners may not be authorized to congregate for prayer except on Fridays.[16] Similarly, if there is a large Muslim prison population, not all Muslims are authorized to congregate for prayer at the same time. Instead, the community is divided into more manageable units that congregate one group at a time. This is similar to the practice of community mosques, where the number of worshipers necessitates the scheduling of two *Jumaah* prayer sessions or the opening of a separate overflow room. Many prison converts, however, possibly correctly believe that the practice is driven by security considerations.

Congregate worship, study, and fellowship are subject to live audio and video monitoring. Many prisons require that sermons and teachings be delivered in English. Prisoners are permitted to pray formulaic prayers in Arabic, but sermons and teachings must be in English to protect against message-encoding and radicalization through the use of a language unfamiliar to supervisory staff. The use of English is considered both reasonable and practical in prisons because more than 90 percent of the worshipers have English as a first language, and their mastery of Arabic is limited at best. Those who do not speak English typically share no other common language except Arabic, and some may know Arabic only as written text. Prisoners often learn to read and pronounce Arabic religious words and phrases long before they understand the meaning and syntax, because greater emphasis often is placed on proper pronunciation and rubrics in prayer than on understanding the words.

Da'wa (call to Islam) is difficult in post–9/11 correctional settings. Prisoners may unwittingly hand on to one another a slanted interpretation of the tenets of Islam. The need for sound religious instruction is great among converts, who are drawn to Islam as much for Islam's social and cultural proprieties as for its religious beliefs and practices. Ideally, this aspect of religious formation would be provided by well-balanced instructors from the community. However, groups such as the Salafists, whose mission includes a strong outreach component, are often overrepresented among the prison da'wa missionaries. This fosters tensions between the First Amendment guarantee of religious freedom and prison regulations prohibiting proselytizing. After 9/11, prison da'wa was curtailed because of the potential threat of da'wa-based extremism.

After 9/11, government officials and journalists seized the opportunity to challenge the legitimacy of Muslim chaplains and programs, alleging that prisons were hotbeds of terrorism. Hasty assumptions and suspicions frequently shape references to prison Islam. FBI officials alleged that the government lacked adequate controls to prevent radicalization. John Pistole, then deputy director of the FBI, testified before the Senate Judiciary Committee, Subcommittee on Terrorism, Technology, and Homeland Security on October 14, 2003:

Prisons are becoming fertile grounds for terrorism, due to the combination of the spread of Islam and the poor social and economic circumstances facing most inmates once out of prison....In the last three decades, Islam has become one of the largest protective groups within the prison system. In addition to the issue of national security, the state of U.S. prisons creates a profound problem regarding the proliferation of Islam.[17]

At a Congressional hearing nine years later, Congressman Peter King, Chairman of the House Committee on Homeland Security, stated: "A number of cases since 9/11 have involved terrorists who converted to Islam or were radicalized to Islamism in American prisons, then subsequently attempted to launch terror strikes here in the US upon their release from custody." During the same June 2012 hearing, King claimed "dozens of ex-cons who became radicalized Muslims inside US prisons had gone to Yemen to join an al-Qaida group run by a fellow American, Anwar al-Awlaki, believed to be a senior talent recruiter and motivator of al-Qaida.[18]

Empirical studies, however, have not supported the assertions of the intelligence community that US prisons are fertile grounds for terrorism.[19] Of the 7 million adults under supervision in the United States in 2004, only one black American prison convert was convicted for involvement in a terrorist plot. The alleged gravity of the problem must be questioned in light of these data—one in 7 million hardly suggests a hotbed of terrorism.[20]

AFTERCARE IN A DIVIDED COMMUNITY

Religious, racial, and ethnic differences among immigrant Muslims create divisions within the communities to which Muslim converts return after incarceration. How future generations of Muslims prisoners will approach Islam depends largely on the quality of training and support they receive from the community beyond prisons. Some 1,600 men and women return to the community from state and federal prisons each day. Perhaps one tenth of those released on any given day are black American Muslim converts. They approach their adopted communities without an awareness of the divisions. The task of leaders of mosques and Islamic centers is to prepare their brothers and sisters to receive the converts in a way that reinforces their peaceful and balanced commitment to submit to God within Islam. Otherwise the men and women returning from incarceration, when they enter a mosque, will face disillusionment and confusion, expecting to be greeted with open arms into a community that is de jure defined by its oneness but de facto defined by the culture and ethnicity of its members. Although they are united with all Muslims in beliefs and practices, Black American Muslims are estranged culturally. Opportunities for incarcerated Muslim converts to grow into mature and committed Muslims rest with the openness of the broader Muslim community to accept them as equal coreligionists. Incarcerated men and women often return to their communities with a renewed focus on God as their source of strength for change. For Muslim returnees, hopes for success in their personal journey to wholeness can be easily shattered by an attitude of benign neglect from the community of believers.

Conclusion

At a Tenth Anniversary Commemoration of 9/11, John L. Esposito suggested the need for a new American Muslim metanarrative: "a data-driven narrative informed by facts, not fiction."[21] Any new narrative must include information about Islam in prisons. It must address the fact that more than 90 percent of incarcerated Muslims are African American converts to Sunni Islam—individuals in search of a new path. They seek a straight path that will give them hope for a new beginning and the opportunity to grow spiritually. The narrative must articulate the strength and dignity that grows from religious kinship and the hope this offers to those whose previous experiences of kinship have been grounded in gang affiliations or dysfunctional families.

NOTES

1. Peter R. Neumann. *Prisons and Terrorism: Radicalisation and Deradicalisation in 15 Countries.* Report prepared by the International Centre for the Study of Radicalisation and Political Violence. Available at: http://www.icsr.info/publications/papers/1277699166,2010 (Accessed January 20, 2011.) Sociologist Bert Useem was the US subject matter expert for this study.
2. "Annual Report of the Warden," US Penitentiary, Atlanta, Georgia, 1922, 34.
3. FBI Investigative Report 100-43165-15, March 25, 1965, 15–17 (unclassified, 1980).
4. Elijah Muhammad, *Message to the Blackman in America* (Chicago: Muhammad's Temple No. 2, 1965), 164.
5. Alex Haley (ed.), *The Autobiography of Malcolm X: As Told to Alex Haley* (New York: Grove Press, 1965), 192.
6. Walter Craven, "The Muslim Menace," *The Annual Congress of Corrections* (1961), 1–3.
7. Clair Cripe, "Religious Freedom in Institutions," in *Proceedings of the 106th Annual Congress of Corrections of the American Correctional Association,* 1977, 19, 25.
8. Associated Press, "Catholic Works for Muslim Rights," *Salem Oregon Capitol Journal* November 16, 1979.
9. Imam Dr. Salahuddin M. Muhammad, *Bridging the Divide Between Immigrant and African-American Muslims by Utilizing the Concept of Tawheed as the Catalyst.* The book was published in (Wilmington, IN: Xlibris Corporation, 2011), p. 11.
10. Andrea Elliott, "Between Black and Immigrant Muslims, an Uneasy Alliance," *New York Times,* March 11, 2007.
11. Associated Press, "Catholic Works for Muslim Rights." Associated Press, "Catholic Works for Muslim Rights," *Salem Oregon Capitol Journal* November 16, 1979.

12. U.S. Department of Justice, Federal Bureau of Prisons, Religious Preference Profile, February 6, 2008.
13. Bureau of Prisons Operations Memorandum 253–283 (5360), November 4, 1983. The Common Fare Pilot Program was gradually expanded to all institutions in 1995.
14. Paul M. Barrett, "How a Muslim Chaplain Spread Extremism to an Inmate Flock: Radical New York Imam Chose Clerics for Prisons," *Wall Street Journal*, February 5, 2003.
15. U. S. Department of Justice, Office of the Inspector General, "A Review of the Federal Bureau of Prisons' Selection of Muslim Religious Services Providers, Washington DC: April 2004.
16. There is currently a federal religious freedom lawsuit, brought by "American Taliban" John Walker Lindh, alleging that under terms of the Religious Freedom Restoration Act, this restriction places a substantial burden on his free exercise of religion. This promises to be a landmark decision that will shape the future of incarcerated Muslims' accommodation nationwide.
17. Congress, Senate, Judiciary Committee, John Pistole, Testimony before the Senate Judiciary Committee, Subcommittee on Terrorism, Technology and Homeland Security, 107th Congress.
18. Peter King, "Opening Statement, "Prisons and Terrorism Hearing" House Committee on Homeland Security, June 15, 2012.
19. Mark S. Hamm, *Terrorist Recruitment in American Correctional Institutions: An Exploratory Study of Non-Traditional Faith Groups Final Report.* (Washington, DC: National Institute of Justice, 2007): 10; Neumann, *Prisons and Terrorism.* Available at http://www.icsr.info/publications/papers/1277699166. Stephanie C. Boddie and Cary Funk, *Religion in Prisons: A 50- State Survey of Prison Chaplains* (Washington, DC: Pew Forum on Religion and Public Life, 2012) 57–59.
20. Mark S. Hamm, *Terrorist Recruitment in American Correctional Institutions*, 10.
21. John L. Esposito, "Welcome and Intro," Remarks given at the opening of the Colloquium: Religion and the American Muslim Community Post 9/11, Georgetown University, September 8, 2011.

REFERENCES

Ali, the Noble Prophet Drew, The Holy Koran of the Moorish Science Temple of America, n.d.
Ali, Kamal Hassan, *Dar-ul-Islam: Principle, Praxis, Movement* (New York: Dar-ul-Islam History Project, 2009).
Ammar, N. H., R. R. Weaver, and S. Saxon, "Muslims in Prison: A Case Study from Ohio State Prisons," (2004): 414–428.
Andrade, Sheikh Mahmoud, *The Dar ul Islam Movement: An American Odyssey* (Create Space, 2010).
Austin, James, "Prisons and Fear of Terrorism," *Criminology and Public Policy 7*, no. 1 (February 2008): 143–152.
Beckford, James A., Daniele Joly, and Farhad Khosrokhavar, *Muslims in Prison: Challenge and Change in Britain and France* (New York: Palgrave Macmillan, 2005).
Bennett, James V., *Federal Prisons Fiscal Year 1960: A Report of the Work of the Federal Bureau of Prisons.* (El Reno, OK: United States Reformatory, 1961).
Boddie, Stephanie C., and Cary Funk, *Religion in Prisons: A 50- State Survey of Prison Chaplains* (Washington DC: Pew Forum on Religion and Public Life, 2012).

Butler, K., "Muslims Are No Longer an Unknown Quantity," *Corrections Magazine* 4 (1978): 55–63.

Caldwell, Wallace F., "Black Muslims Behind Bars," *Research Studies* 34 (December 1966), 185–204.

Ciluffo, Frank, *Out of the Shadows: Getting Ahead of Prison Radicalization.* (Washington, DC: GW-HSPI/UVA CIAG, 2006). Available at www.investigativeproject.org/documents/testimony/345.pdf

Clear, Todd, and M. T. Sumter, "Prisoners, Prison, and Rehabilitation: Religion and Adjustment to Prison." *Journal of Offender Rehabilitation* 35(2002), 127–160.

Clemmer, Donald, and John M. Wilson, "The Muslims in Prison," *Proceedings of the Ninetieth Annual Congress of Corrections of the American Correctional Association*, Denver, Colorado, August 28–September 2, 1960. (New York: 1961): 147–155.

Craven, Walter E., "The Muslim Menace," *Proceedings of the Ninetieth Annual Congress of Corrections of the American Correctional Association*, Denver, Colorado, August 28–September 2, 1960. (New York: 1961)

Cripe, Clair, "Religious Freedom in Institutions," *Proceedings of the 106th Annual Congress of Corrections of the American Correctional Association*, Denver, Colorado, August 22–26, 1976. (College Park, MD:, 1977): 19–25.

Cripe, Clair, and Michael Pearlman, *Legal Aspects of Corrections Management*, 2nd ed. (Boston: Jones and Bartlett, 2005).

Danner, Harry R., "The Reasons for Religious Involvement in the Correctional Environment," *Journal of Offender Rehabilitation* 35 (2002), 35–58.

Dix-Richardson, F., and B. Close, "Intersections of Race, Religion and Inmate Culture: The Historical Development of Islam in American Corrections," *Journal of Offender Rehabilitation* 35(2002), 87–107.

Essien-Udom, E. U., *Black Nationalism: A Search for Identity in America* (Chicago: University of Chicago Press, 1962).

Hamidullah, Matthew B., ed., *"A Report with Recommendations on Religious Ministry in the Federal Bureau of Prisons,"* African American Work Group Report. (Washington, DC: U.S. Department of Justice, Bureau of Prisons, 1992).

Hamm, Mark S., *"Terrorist Recruitment in American Correctional Institutions: An Exploratory Study of Non-Traditional Faith Groups, Final Report"* (Washington DC: National Institute of Justice, 2007).

Hannah, Greg, Lindsay Clutterbuck, and Jennifer Rubin, *Radicalization or Rehabilitation: Understanding the Challenge of Extremist and Radicalized Prisoners.* (Santa Monica, CA: Rand Corporation, 2008).

Hill, Gary, "The Religious Rights, Duties and Customs of Muslim Inmates," *Corrections Compendium* 27, no. 1 (November 2002), 3–8.

King, Anthony E. O., "An Afrocentric Cultural Awareness Program for Incarcerated African-American Males," *Journal of Multicultural Social Work* 3, no. 4 (1994), 17–28.

Kusha, Hamid Reza, *Islam in American Prisons: Black Muslims' Challenge to American Penology* (Burlington, VT: Ashgate, 2009).

Lassiter, J. E., "African Culture and Personality: Bad Social Science, Effective Social Activism, or a Call to Reinvent Ethnology?" *African Studies Quarterly: The Online Journal of African Studies* 3, no. 2, (1999). Available at http://web.africa.ufl.edu/asq/v3/v3i2a1.html

Marable, Manning, *Malcolm X: A Life of Reinvention* (New York: Viking Press, 2011).

Marranci, Gabriele, *Faith, Ideology and Fear: Muslim Identities Within and Beyond Prison* (New York: Continuum 2009).

McCloud, Aminah, and F. Thaufeer al Deen, *A Question of Faith for Muslim Inmates* (Chicago: Kazi Publications, 1999).

Meijer, Roel, ed., *Global Salafism: Islam's New Religious Movement* (New York: Columbia University Press, 2009).

Muhammad, Elijah, *Message to the Blackman in America* (Chicago: Muhammad's Temple No. 2, 1965).

Nance, Susan, "Mystery of the Moorish Science Temple: Southern Blacks and American Alternative Spirituality in 1920s Chicago," *Religion and Culture: A Journal of Interpretation* 12, no. 2 (summer, 2002), 123–166.

Noble, Roosevelt L., *Black Rage in the American Prison System* (New York: LFB Scholarly Publishing, 2006).

O'Connor, Thomas, and M. Perreyclear, "Prison Religion in Action and Its Influence on Reoffender Rehabilitation," *Journal of Offender Rehabilitation* 35 (2002), 11–34.

"Prisons: Prisoners—Inmate Subcultures and Informal Organizations." Available at http://law.jrank.org/pages/1796 (Accessed March 9, 2011).

Rideau, Wilbert, and B. Snider, "Religion in Prison: A Look at the Pulpit behind Bars," *Angolite* (Angola Prison Magazine) (January-February, 1981), 31–56.

Ripley, Amanda, "The Case of the Dirty Bomber" *Time Magazine* (June 16, 2003). Available at www.time.com/time/nation/article/0,8599,262917,00.html (Accessed January 9, 2011.)

Sheehy, Donald F., "The Black Muslims and Religious Freedom in Prison," *Proceedings of the 93rd Annual Congress of Corrections of the American Correctional Association*, Denver, Colorado, August 25–29, 1963. (Washington, DC:, 1964): 63–78.

Thomas, James, and Barbara H. Zartow, "Conning or Conversion? The Role of Religion in Prison Coping," *The Prison Journal* 86, no. 2 (June 2006) 242–259.

Thompson, D., "FBI to Do Prisoner Threat Assessment." Available at www.usatoday.com/news/washington/2005-08-30-fbi-terrorism_x.html (Accessed September 9, 2005.)

U.S. Congress, Senate Committee on Homeland Security and Governmental Affairs. Prison Radicalization: Are Terrorist Cells Forming in US Cell Blocks? (September 19, 2006).

U.S. Department of Justice, Office of the Inspector General, A Review of the Federal Bureau of Prisons' Selection of Muslim Religious Service Providers (April 2004).

U.S. Department of Justice, Office of Legal Policy, Prison Gangs: *Their Extent, Nature and Impact on Prisons* (South Salem, NY: Criminal Justice Institute, 1985).

Useem, Bert, "Jihadists Recruiting Behind Bars." Available at www.weeklystandard.com/print/Content/Public/Articles/000/000/015/491gncur.asp (Accessed September 17, 2008.)

——, and Obie Clayton, "Radicalization of United States Prisoners," *Criminology and Public Policy*, 8, no. 3 (August 2009) 561–592.

Vidino, Lorenzo, *The New Muslim Brotherhood in the West*. (New York: Columbia University Press, 2010).

Waller, J. Michael, "Prisons as Terrorist Breeding Grounds," in *The Making of a Terrorist: Recruitment, Training and Root Causes*, edited by James J. F. Forest (Westport, CN: Praeger, 2005).

CHAPTER 18

VOLUNTEERISM AMONG AMERICAN IMMIGRANT MUSLIMS

ALTAF HUSAIN

INTRODUCTION

The focus of this chapter is the volunteerism of Muslim immigrants and their descendants as reflected in their individual and collective behaviors as well as through the organizations that serve as the sites of those behaviors. The scope is limited to immigrants who arrived into the United States in the last half of the twentieth century and who self-identify as Muslims. Owing to Islam's emphasis on serving others, Muslims might be expected to be inherently predisposed to involvement in volunteer efforts. Because of a combination of factors explored in this chapter, however, it appears that the resulting volunteerism has been uneven in spirit and action.

The chapter begins with a brief explication of the religious inspiration to volunteer, followed by a glimpse of volunteerism as it has been practiced by immigrants generally. Next, voluntary individual and collective behaviors among the early Muslim immigrants are chronicled, especially during the initial periods of arrival and adjustment, which resulted in inwardly focused volunteer efforts. The next section demonstrates that a shift in the mindset from being Muslims living in America to participating fully in American society as Muslims of America turned the focus of volunteerism in an outward direction, with a substantial growth in the number of Islamic institutions and ultimately a fostering of a spirit of volunteerism among subsequent generations. The chapter concludes with a robust discussion of the challenges and trends facing the Muslim American community in the area of volunteerism.

RELIGIOUS INSPIRATION: WHY VOLUNTEER?

It is important at the outset to note that because this chapter addresses volunteerism specifically among Muslims in America, a slight enhancement is being made to the typical definition of volunteerism. At least three elements usually are included in definitions of volunteerism: (1) actions or activities that are undertaken willingly; (2) no financial compensation for the action or activities; and (3) the action or activities benefit other people. While these three elements are applicable to the Muslim context, serving others is not seen as an end in itself. Although the actor does not receive financial compensation, he or she may be motivated to serve by a desire for spiritual benefit. Service as a means of drawing closer to Allah is among the values of Islam that inspire believers to expend their time, energy, talents, and wealth in charitable endeavors (Hamid, 1989).

The various Qur'anic injunctions to believe and engage in righteous conduct along with the exhortations and role modeling of the Prophet Muhammad to serve others form a guide for voluntary behavior. Having faith in Allah is a starting point, to be juxtaposed with righteous conduct benefiting the various systems comprised by one's life: family, relatives, neighbors, and society at large (Nasr, 2002). Individual acts of volunteerism are to be undergirded by an intention to serve, seeking no reward or recognition. From an early age children are reminded to engage in acts of kindness and generosity because the teachings emphasize that even if no other person is watching or knows about those acts, the angels are watching, recording, and reporting them to Allah. Prophetic teachings exemplify a concern for all of God's creation, not just for Muslims. The beneficiaries of volunteerism fall broadly into several categories: (1) immediate family and relatives, (2) other Muslims, (3) others of diverse ethnic or religious backgrounds outside the Muslim community, and (4) God's creation from among the animal and plant kingdoms (Hamid, 1989).

Implicit in the code to guide voluntary behavior is an emphasis on humility. Sometimes even family members or friends may be pleasantly surprised to find out after a person's death that he or she had volunteered on the committee of a local masjid or social service agency. Similarly, it is also not acceptable for a person to volunteer and in the process of doing so, either insult or remind the beneficiaries of his or her benevolence (Nasr, 2002). Finally, a distinction is made between the charity one gives voluntarily in the form of financial contributions and the actual service in terms of effort one provides to others willingly and without compensation. This chapter focuses on the latter. This connection between religion and volunteerism, while it can be extended to other faiths, is especially salient for Muslim immigrants because those who arrived in the 1960s were "more likely to have witnessed the rise of normative (reform) Islam within their ancestral countries, a move which re-emphasized visible behavioral codes" (Abu-Laban, 1991, 22).

VOLUNTEERISM AMONG IMMIGRANTS

The very process of adjusting to new lands engenders among some immigrants a simultaneous desire to ensure family well-being while also assisting others from among the cohort of new arrivals. Faced with anxiety and uncertainty of what the new lands might offer them, immigrants often turned to religion, sometimes with greater affinity than they had in their native lands. For those who were already religious and considered religion as a way of life, their migration served to further strengthen their faith (Handlin, 2002). Even for those who were not very religious, the migration process often was found to foster in their hearts a yearning for religious rituals and celebrations, which filled a nostalgic rather than a spiritual void.

Over time, however, the immigrants developed a sense of grounding and took on voluntary responsibility not only for attending but also for helping organize those rituals and celebrations (Herberg, 1983). Inspired as well by religious teachings to care for the poor among the newcomers, immigrants engaged in voluntary activities ranging from the preparation and serving of food to helping orient them to the new society, for example by teaching them English.

Unlike wholesale migrations of particular racial or ethnic groups to predominantly homogenous populations, as in Europe, immigrants to the United States discovered tremendous racial, ethnic, linguistic, socioeconomic, and religious diversity (Herberg, 1983). Social cohesion became a concern on at least two levels: one constituted the immigrants as a group and the other the established population of Americans and immigrants of various racial and ethnic backgrounds who shared a common faith (Peek, 2005). Coming together to worship a common god allowed the immigrants to transcend racial and ethnic differences, replacing heretofore national and ethnic bonds with faith bonds (Herberg, 1983). Also, whereas the earliest Christian immigrants found at least a modicum of an existing religious community, as discussed in the next section, the early Muslim immigrants had to piece together faith communities at the local level, one worshipper at a time. To be sure, Muslim immigration to the United States is not a new or even recent phenomenon. Studies of the Muslim presence and the development of Muslim communities have divided up the discussion according to the time period during which the Muslims arrived. I prefer to use Abu-Laban's (1991) categorization of the arrival of Muslim immigrants: (1) pioneers—those arriving during the late nineteenth century and up through World War II; (2) transitional—those arriving after World War II and through 1967; and (3) differentiated—those arriving during the period 1968 to the present (year in which Abu-Laban's work was published), or 1991. The first two categories are beyond the scope of this discussion on volunteerism. The focus is on a modified differentiated category—that is, those Muslim immigrants who arrived from the early 1960s on.

1960s—Early 1980s: Volunteerism Postarrival and During Adjustment

Throughout the history of immigrant arrival in the United States, volunteerism has been the backbone of efforts to help fellow immigrants to adjust to the new society (Handlin, 2002; Herberg, 1983), and the patterns of Muslim migration and adjustment to the United States are no exception (Elkholy, 1966). However, not unlike earlier cohorts of immigrants, most of the early Muslim immigrants treated their stay in the United States as temporary (Nyang, 1999). Indeed, owing to the visa preferences instituted after the 1965 immigration reforms, the early Muslim community was made up mostly of graduate students and some professionals, so the hub of the community was often the local college or university. The students aspired to complete their higher education and the professionals perhaps aspired to accrue both work experience and financial savings. Both groups planned to return to their homelands. Even until the late 1970s and early 1980s, as evidenced in newsletters and themes and program sessions of annual conferences, it appeared as though Muslim immigrants continued to believe in the myth of return to their homelands (Haddad, 1991). The "return" mindset clearly influenced the spirit of volunteerism that emerged among the early immigrants—that is, a sense of taking care of our own until we return home. The community generally continued to be quite insular, living *in* America but not yet *of* America.

While it is not impossible that some of these immigrants participated in voluntary activities in mainstream society, there are at least two reasons why it is unlikely that they did so. First, like most immigrants, in the years following their arrival they had little spare time between work and family obligations to devote to voluntary activities outside of their community (Schmidt, 2004). Second, given the state of development of social services and nongovernmental organizations in the respective countries from which they hailed, they would not have been exposed to formal volunteer opportunities. Whether because of less spare time or the generally inward-looking attitude, the modest individual voluntary efforts to serve were more than likely directed at Muslims within one's local community.

Early accounts of such volunteerism range from the social to the spiritual domains. Within the social domain, the self-identifying Muslim immigrants literally were perhaps the only five or ten or at most twenty families in a particular locale. Transcending national and ethnic bonds, their voluntary activities ranged from hosting new arrivals within their homes to assisting them to find their own housing, orienting especially newly married couples to the community to sharing in after-school child care, providing informal advice and counseling, to just listening or providing a shoulder on which to lean or cry. Within the spiritual domain, the voluntary activities ranged from finding places to establish the Friday prayers, cooking for the collective meals signifying the end of a day of fasting in Ramadan, and arranging for the two 'eid prayers annually as well as the funeral prayer and burial for those who died in the new land.

MSA: Built and Sustained Through Volunteerism

No discussion about volunteerism among Muslims can be complete without an appreciation for and understanding of the phenomenal demonstration of service and sacrifice that occurred on college and university campuses since the early 1960s and continues to occur among members of the Muslim Students Association (MSA) chapters. As described above, a sizable proportion of the cohort of Muslim immigrants who entered the United States in the late 1950s and early 1960s were students. Some among these students were from educated families and had experience with organizing and leading extracurricular activities. Others were experienced in managing volunteers by virtue of membership or leadership positions they held in religious groups and student movements in their countries of origin. Upon arriving on college campuses, these students in particular sought one another out and formed Muslim student organizations mostly as forums in which to gather with other Muslim students and as a means of both promoting and protecting their Muslim identities (Nyang, 1999). With modest means and relying totally on one another's goodwill, the voluntary leaders and members of these organizations made them a hub of programs and activities addressing topics ranging from international affairs to religious affairs to social affairs (Ghayur, 1981). By 1962, there was a loose network of such organizations named variedly as Muslim Students Associations, Muslim Students Unions, and Islamic Societies. On January 1, 1963 members from this patchwork of chapter-level organizations gathered and agreed to coordinate their efforts through a continentwide organization, calling it the Muslim Students Association of the United States and Canada (commonly referred to as the MSA National) (Ba-Yunus and Kone, 2006).

In the early days of MSA National, the executive committee and members of other committees spent their own time and money to start building a field structure and ultimately setting up an office. Founders such as Ahmed Sakr have publicly recalled the early period, explaining how he and other graduate students would literally spend nights conducting scientific experiments in their respective university research laboratories and then rest their eyes momentarily in the labs before starting off again the next morning to donate their time to manage the affairs of MSA National. Other pioneers have related stories of riding the Greyhound bus from coast to coast, stopping at cities where they had received news of new Muslim student arrivals, informing them about the work of MSA National and inviting them to start their own campus MSA chapter. And yet others used funds from meager student assistantships to subsidize the purchase of literature about Islam for dissemination to Muslim students as well as people of other faiths. Through perseverance and determination, those initial voluntary efforts paved the way for the founding of printing and publishing houses such as International Graphics and Amana Publishing. Before long, thanks to the growing numbers of students as well as the growing demands on the organization to serve the needs of those students, contributions were solicited from the governments of oil-producing countries. Although those funds supported the core staff and office of the continentwide organization until the early 1990s, the bulk of the work was always carried out by volunteers. By 2013, when MSA National commemorated the fiftieth anniversary of its founding, it was clear that the spirit of service and sacrifice of the pioneer students built the organization, and the continued voluntary contributions of subsequent generations of students have sustained it.

THE MUSLIMS OF AMERICA

Sometime in the late 1970s and early 1980s there appears to have been a conscious shift among the voluntary national leadership and even individual families with regard to the return mindset. Perhaps owing to a lack of change in the political or economic conditions of their respective countries of origin, such as perpetual authoritarian regimes or minimal prospects for career advancement, a shift occurred from living and working as Muslims *in* America to settling permanently as the Muslims *of* America (Haddad, 1991; Poston, 1992). As noted earlier, MSA National was a major hub of voluntary activity both on individual campuses and nationally. By the late 1970s, the leadership of the MSA had set into motion plans to form a new organization reflective of the transition of its membership from students to members of the American society, aptly naming it the Islamic Society of North America (ISNA) (Salem, 2013). To the extent that such a shift impacted the long-term organizational planning and forward-thinking attitudes of the national leaders, it was also reflected at the local level with the emergence of well-organized communities in college towns and major cities throughout the United States, such as Boston and New York in the northeast; Washington D.C., Atlanta, and Miami in the southeast; Chicago, Detroit, and Milwaukee in the northern Midwest; Dallas, Houston, and Tulsa in the southern Midwest; and Sacramento and Los Angeles on the West Coast. A key indicator of the shift in mindset is that as the Muslim population in the United States continued to steadily increase, the number of masjids and Islamic centers being built, presumably a sign of settling down, also increased in the late 1970s (Bagby, 2009). This is an especially significant milestone in the discussion on volunteerism for at least two reasons. First, these immigrants had little if any experience in financing the building of such facilities because in most countries with majority Muslim populations, such matters are managed by the governments' religious affairs departments and financed mostly through established endowments. The purchase of existing structures or the building of new masjids in the United States has been and continues to be financed almost entirely through donations from the congregation members (Bagby, Perl, and Froehle, 2001). Second, with regard to the administration and management of these newly established American houses of worship, the immigrants adopted wholesale the structures governing typical American nonprofit organizations, complete with a constitution and bylaws and a board of directors. Until the late 1980s and early 1990s these facilities were staffed by congregation members who assumed voluntary roles as varied as serving as imam or as administrators or board members. In comparatively larger communities, organizations such as the Muslim World League provided a few trained Imams and underwrote entirely or heavily subsidized their salaries. Over time, owing to the increasing financial capacity of the congregation members, their desire to have a professional operations structure and the availability of trained, indigenous imams, volunteer opportunities at the masjids have been more often than not limited to serving on the board of directors or on any of the specialized committees.

In addition to the building of masjids and Islamic centers, another indication of the shift in mindset is the investment of time, energy, and personal finances during the 1990s to create specialized nonprofit organizations whose activities ranged from the dissemination of the message of Islam to the provision of basic social services domestically and relief and development initiatives internationally (Smith, 1999). Despite some among the immigrants assuming positions such as president or executive director or any other staff title, much of the human and financial resources necessary to operate these organizations was contributed voluntarily by the founders and their families. A downfall of such an approach was that some of these organizations did not last longer than the lifespans of the founders and benefactors. (Smith, 1999). Those organizations, which had a national focus or a fairly timeless mission, adopted a nonsectarian philosophy, developed and maintained a sufficiently strong operational structure, and achieved financial self-sufficiency; they remained relevant and continued to flourish. Examples of national organizations include the continent-wide MSA, the Islamic Circle of North America (ICNA), the Islamic Society of North America (ISNA), the Muslim American Society (MAS), the Muslim Public Affairs Council (MPAC), and the Council on American Islamic Relations (CAIR). Examples of local and specialized organizations include ACCESS

in Dearborn, Michigan, founded to provide orientation and assistance to the growing Arab immigrant population in 1971 with Hajjah Aliyah Hassan as the first volunteer director (ACCESS, n.d.); the Indian Muslim Relief Committee, founded in
1981 to give opportunities for Muslims to contribute towards antipoverty efforts
in India; UMMA Community Clinic founded in 1992 (discussed further, below);
ICNA Relief, founded in 1994 to address hunger prevention, establish women's shelters, provide counseling and other family services, and disaster relief, all inside the
United States; Muslim Community Center for Human Services (MCCHS), founded
in 1995, in Tarrant County, Texas, providing medical and social services; and the
Inner-City Muslim Action Network (IMAN) (discussed further, below).

Volunteerism among the Children of Immigrants

A common phenomenon to almost all immigrant groups is that their children often
outpace them in the process of adjusting to a new country. Even if volunteering was
not a formal part of their parents' upbringing, children of immigrants are more likely
to be socialized with both the religious settings and through their school experiences to value service and sacrifice (Ecklund and Park, 2007). The focus of American
Muslims was on volunteer opportunities to promote and sustain religious and social
life. However, as indicated earlier, for various reasons, the early Muslim immigrants
did not extend the reach of their voluntary activities beyond their immediate communities. Schmidt (2002) asserts with regards to volunteerism among the children
of Muslim immigrants that "whereas their parents struggled to learn the English language, to find jobs, to establish the first Muslim organizations and institutions, and
to own the first shops to buy halal meat, their children no longer have to deal with
such concerns."

Owing to the steadily increasing population and the complexity of the issues being
faced by families and communities, most of the energies of those who were inclined
to volunteer were spent attending to the immediate challenges in their lives and
within the local and national Muslim communities and organizations. The impact of
the extrafamilial time commitments on the children of these immigrants was varied.
On the one hand, some of the children stayed close to their parents and volunteered
alongside them, assisting as much as possible; even if they did not assist, they were at
least being socialized into the spirit of giving of time, energy, and wealth to serve others or to work for a cause. When they came of age, some of them had been influenced
so positively that they either continued to volunteer on their own, or as discussed
later in this section, started their own projects intending to serve both Muslims and
people of other faiths. On the other hand, the multiple demands of the community

and organizations meant that some parents, fathers especially, were left with little quality time to spend with their own spouses and children. Such absences from the family often caused the children of those parents to become resentful of the activities or organizations which demanded so much of their parents' time and energy. They treated their parents' volunteerism as competing with them for quality time. Especially detrimental were those voluntary activities which ended up impacting the mood and demeanor of their parents when they brought home problems being experienced in the course of their volunteering. The resentment in some cases was so strong that it resulted in an aversion on the children's part to anything in the volunteerism domain.

Nonetheless, volunteerism among the second, third, and now fourth generation of Muslim immigrants is on the rise and has inspired noteworthy contributions toward the improvement of the quality of life for Muslims and people of other or no faiths. Young people compelled to address complex social issues such as homelessness, hunger, poverty, lack of affordable health care, and education, for example, are harnessing the triple power of their religious teachings, their educational and professional background and preparation, and their genuine good will to serve the vulnerable and at-risk populations. In the final section below, some of the challenges confronting their volunteerism are addressed. In the meantime, two noteworthy examples from among many are included here because they were both organizations founded by Muslim American college students of diverse racial, ethnic, and socioeconomic backgrounds and their mission was to improve the quality of life of people of diverse sociodemographic characteristics. Emphasizing the religious inspiration for their work, the acronyms of these two organizations reference two concepts central to Islamic teachings, Umma and iman, i.e.—that is, community and faith.

UMMA—University Muslim Medical Association Community Clinic

Even from among the earliest arrivals of Muslim students in the 1950s, a choice destination for higher education has been the campus of the University of California at Los Angeles (UCLA). Tracing the development of the Muslim community in Southern California, it becomes evident that the shift in mindset mentioned earlier occurred in this region perhaps even earlier than in other parts of the United States (Kelley, 1994). Progressive thinkers such as Maher and Hassan Hathout and Ahmad Sakr, as well as Muzzammil Siddiqi, found no contradiction between being Muslim and being American and through their writings and lectures engendered in the youth of that region a love for service and sacrifice. When race riots erupted in Los Angeles during 1992, second- and third-generation Muslim American medical students from UCLA and Charles Drew University opened a part-time free clinic as a program of their University Muslim Medical Association (UMMA). In a comparative study of

Muslim youth in Sweden and the United States, Schmidt (2002) cites the UMMA among others as an exemplar of the projects and organizations developed by socially conscious Muslim students.

The riots, which brought to the surface underlying tensions between the predominantly African American residents of South Central Los Angeles and the increasing population of Latino and Asian immigrants, left over 2,000 mostly poor and uninsured individuals injured (Bergesen and Herman, 1998). Volunteering their own time, eliciting strong support from the local residents and elected officials, collecting donated medical equipment, and recruiting volunteer physicians and medical students in training from among the Muslims and other faiths, the founders of the UMMA Community Clinic ensured that the most vulnerable and at-risk populations received quality healthcare (Laird and Cadge, 2009). Two significant milestones in the history of the UMMA clinic, under the leadership of CEO Yasser Aman, are its recognition in Congress by the Honorable Maxine Waters in 2006 and its designation by the US government as a Federally Qualified Health Center in 2008. Congratulating the UMMA Clinic on its tenth anniversary, Congresswoman Waters noted that "it was the first charitable medical facility in the United States founded by Muslim Americans" (Congressional Record, 2006). Citing the intense anti-Islamic bigotry which has surfaced during the twenty-first century, she noted that "the UMMA Clinic allows Muslims to put their faith into action through service, selflessness and compassion" (Congressional Record, 2006).

IMAN—Inner-City Muslim Action Network

Not unlike residents of South Central Los Angeles during the 1990s, residents of Chicago's South Side also lived in neighborhoods characterized by poverty and a lack of access to quality food, housing, health care, and jobs. Muslim American students in Chicago-based universities felt compelled to sacrifice their time to develop initiatives to address some of these issues. The Inner-City Muslim Action Network (IMAN) was formed in 1995 and incorporated in 1997 to address poverty and abandonment while seeking "to create a community organization driven by the spiritual ideals of community service, social justice and human compassion". (IMAN, n.d.). Schmidt (2004) dedicates much of a chapter in her book *Islam in Urban America: Sunni Muslims in Chicago* to IMAN in the context of describing the social consciousness among Muslim American college students in that city. IMAN is led by founder-executive director Rami Nashashibi, a soft-spoken, charismatic scholar-activist (with a PhD in sociology from the University of Chicago) of Palestinian-American descent who has inspired volunteerism among several generations of college students in Chicago and around the United States. IMAN does have paid staff, however, most of whom are health and human services professionals They provide services to populations ranging from those reentering society after completing prison sentences to those battling neighborhood grocers who carry substandard food items to those who are uninsured or underinsured and in need of health care. Significant among IMAN's achievements are truly unique and innovative projects such as Green Reentry, "a project that seeks to convert foreclosed and vandalized properties in the Chicago Lawn neighborhood into vibrant, environmentally sound (green) transition housing for formerly incarcerated individuals reentering society" (IMAN, n.d.) and the tremendous support IMAN elicits from interfaith partners within the Chicago area. Much like the previous example of the UMMA Community Clinic, IMAN volunteers are also representative of diverse sociodemographic groups, and they combine the spirit of Islamic teachings of service and sacrifice with best practices from American volunteerism (Laird and Cadge, 2010).

CHALLENGES AND TRENDS

The centrality of values such as service and sacrifice in the lives of the early Muslim immigrants and their children is evident as described above. However, receiving much less attention in public discourse and scholarship are the challenges past and present that persist and often dissuade or restrict broad participation in voluntary activities. The discussion does not offer a critique of specific individual efforts or organizations. Rather, the intention is to identify past and present challenges as well as trends for readers interested in analyzing volunteerism among Muslims. Among the most salient challenges are a persisting ad hoc approach to volunteerism, the meaningful and sustainable participation of women and youth, and the potential of intense government scrutiny of Muslim voluntary activities and nonprofit organizations, thus dampening the spirits of sacrifice and service among forthcoming generations.

Ad hoc Approach to Volunteerism

Religious inspiration to serve others and to sacrifice one's time, energy, and wealth constitutes the backbone of volunteerism for Muslims generally and, as described above, for Muslim Americans in particular. Here religion itself is understood as "an underlying system of sacred values and cultural directives that orient the believers in a fundamental manner" (Waugh, 1991, 70). The focus on religion as a system is critically important; any attempt at practicing that religion should, optimally, occur in a systematic, goal-oriented manner. In looking at the issue of volunteerism among the early Muslim immigrants and even among their descendants, it appears that an ad hoc approach has been used with regard to the recruiting and ongoing participation of volunteers and the planning and implementation of voluntary activities.

Whether because of a sense of humility in not wanting their volunteerism to be noticed, recorded, or praised or perhaps owing to the return mindset, each endeavor that required volunteers was treated uniquely and not connected in any way with a larger effort to institutionalize volunteerism per se. It was not uncommon, then, that pitfalls and mistakes from previous volunteer efforts were repeated and best practices could not emerge. Following the formation of the continentwide MSA, there was a concerted focus on leadership development and management training, but only a minority of the students benefitted. Owing to the transient population of students at the local chapter levels, there has yet to develop a systematic approach to ensure that trained and experienced leadership is in place as former leaders and volunteers graduate, transfer, or begin graduate education at other institutions of higher learning.[1] Even masjids, relief agencies, and other nonprofit organizations continue to be impacted adversely because of shortsighted, ad hoc approaches to volunteering. Despite the fact that all of these types of organizations require a steady flow of volunteers, there is such a persistent lack of sophistication that it is almost impossible to find a "volunteer coordinator" within the structure of most of these organizations.

Meaningful and Sustainable Participation by Women and Youth

Owing partly to the ad hoc approach to volunteerism described above, until the mid-1990s there had also not been much thought given to broadening the volunteer base to include women and youth. The assertion here is not that women did not comprise the volunteer base during the period from the 1960s to the 1980s; rather, the focus is on discerning the difference between their heretofore marginal and sporadic involvement and the more meaningful and sustained participation characterizing the post-1990s period. One possible explanation is that during the 1960s and 1970s most of the organizational volunteer work was taken up by the men, although the community-based volunteer work did involve women in activities such as organizing bake sales, bazaars, and almost everything food-related (Haddad and Smith, 1994). Either out of convenience, an individual-level insecurity, or a particular religious interpretation that called for limiting the involvement of women to the domestic sphere, men turned to other men to find volunteers. As the success of the often informal community-based volunteer work by women became sustained and more formal organizational structures were developed in the masjids, women no longer wanted to be relegated to involvement through just the "women's affairs committee."

An almost two-decade-long insistence on broadening the female participation by notable women such as Sharifa Al-Khateeb led to a shift in the dominant thinking among the men. Al-Khateeb had witnessed at first hand the evolution of the Muslim community from her involvement in the MSA in the late 1960s, and she remained outspoken both about the equitable treatment of women and also the full participation of women in matters concerning the development and implementation plans impacting organizations or the community at large. By the early 1990s, Al-Khateeb and colleagues felt sufficiently empowered to found the North American Council of Muslim Women (NACMW). Webb (2000) and Bullock (2005) feature other women pioneers in their own voices, with Webb suggesting the category of *scholar-activists* and including a comprehensive list (now dated) of organizations for Muslim women's advocacy, higher education, and rights. There are examples especially of college-age and young professional Muslim women making significant contributions to the Muslim community and society at large through their assumption, appointment, or selection into roles of growing responsibility (Ba-Yunus and Kone, 2006; Karim, 2008). Indeed the continued meaningful and sustained participation in volunteerism of women opened doors for the participation of youth generally.

As they began to pursue higher education, women's involvement in local MSA chapters also increased. By the mid-1990s even the national MSA had a young female vice-president—although she was appointed to fill the vacancy created by the resignation of a male vice-president. During this period other national organizations had women serving as members of their boards of trustees or directors, although this was more the exception than the rule. In the summer of 2004, the first non-gender-specific organization to elect a woman as its national president was MSA National. Following that milestone, ISNA elected its first female president.

The meaningful and sustained participation of youth, males and females, in volunteerism became a reality as a critical mass of second- and third-generation Muslim Americans came of age in the early 1990s. During their middle and high school years, they were moved by a combination of religious inspiration and youthful idealism to address various domestic and international causes. Although they participated in and became leaders of their school-based volunteer committees or organizations, these youth often met with frustration as they attempted to extend their volunteerism to their local masjids and Muslim communities (Wormser, 2002). Some of the *uncles,* as the men in leadership of local organizations came to be known with a somewhat derogatory connotation, were neither prepared nor had the imagination to allow for the seamless involvement of these youth. I, along with other youth, have had the experience of being assigned such menial tasks as stuffing envelopes for a fundraising campaign without ever having been involved in or consulted about the spirit or the content of the actual fundraising materials to ensure that the latter were visually appealing and without spelling or grammatical errors. The challenge remained and to some degree still remains to develop some sense of clarity or understanding about how to give progressively more meaningful and challenging tasks to the youth to complete and how to involve youth in the overall planning and direction of specific projects. Women and youth are no longer passive bystanders but rather are at the forefront of creating opportunities for their own meaningful voluntary participation in addressing some of the complex and persistent social challenges in the United States and around the world.

Impact of Government Scrutiny and Suspicion of the Muslim Community

A final noteworthy challenge is the potential dampening of the spirits of service and sacrifice among forthcoming generations of Muslims in response to the intense governmental scrutiny and suspicion of the Muslim community following the terrorist attacks of September 11, 2001. Siddiqui (2010) discusses the impact of government raids on Muslim American nonprofit organizations based on allegations that those organizations supported terrorism. Media reports of those raids, along with unsupported statements by elected officials at both the national and local levels, further exacerbated the situation for Muslims who wanted only to exercise their religious obligations to donate for charitable causes or to volunteer their time to support those organizations. The relentless pursuit by government agencies of the alleged support of terrorism by these organizations intimidated potential donors and volunteers, especially parents and older adults. Some parents cautioned their children lest the latter become entangled in the possible allegations being raised by the government against the nonprofit organizations. Even immigrant youth at first experienced distress, viewing themselves as victims of both the war on terror and the war on immigration (Maira, 2004). However, second- and third-generation Muslim youth remained steady and empowered the community by shifting the discourse from a victim mentality to one of constructive civic engagement, rooted in the belief that Muslim Americans constituted a positive force in society. Youth inspired by this discourse have improved in their own knowledge of constitutional guarantees and rights as citizens and, as noted below, they have begun to foster a unique culture of volunteerism. Despite the best efforts of these youth to serve, continued unwarranted government scrutiny and surveillance of the community will pose a challenge to the volunteer recruitment efforts of these nonprofit organizations.

CULTURE OF VOLUNTEERISM

As the Muslim American population continues to increase, it is reassuring that the spirit of service and sacrifice that characterized the post-1960s immigrants is being sustained and manifesting itself through the goodwill of subsequent generations as well as the increasing numbers of nonprofit organizations. Despite the challenges highlighted above, there is a clear trend of an emerging culture of volunteerism, one that reflects a unique combination of the highest ideals of Islam and the values that undergird American volunteerism. Among the many indicators of this culture of volunteerism, three are noteworthy: (1) the selflessness, dedication, and sophistication of the volunteers themselves; (2) the use of technology and social networking to expand the reach of volunteerism, analyze the voluntary activity, and ascertain best practices; and (3) the contributions of Muslim Americans to mainstream society.

First, there has been concerted effort expended by the local and national leadership to convey the teachings of the religion insofar as they concern ideals such as selflessness, compassion, mercy, kindness, and generosity. With the increasing likelihood of multiple generations of families living either together or in close proximity to one another, children especially are being socialized into voluntary behaviors by observing and even participating willingly in service of the local masjid, Islamic school, or relief agency or working in nonsectarian locations such as soup kitchens, homeless shelters, or some such nonprofit organizations. Volunteer recruitment is more likely to be systematic, with a description of the task at hand and an enumeration of the necessary time commitment. At the completion of voluntary activities, feedback about the volunteering experience is being sought, along with core organizers actually planning "volunteer appreciation" events.

Second, just as technology and social networking have impacted almost every walk of life, the voluntary sector has also been affected, especially among Muslim Americans. Whereas the early Muslim immigrants relied mostly on telephone and handwritten letters and printed materials to inform people, if at all, about opportunities to serve others, innovations in technology have exponentially increased both the efficiency and to some degree the effectiveness of organized voluntary activities. The technology and the social networking applications through which socially conscious ideas, for example, can be turned into flyers with visually appealing graphics or into video clips which can then, with a single click, be shared with tens of thousands of potential volunteers, have been embraced by Muslim Americans of all demographics. Unlike the ad hoc nature of the planning and implementation of the past decades or even the limited involvement of women and youth, all of which impacted the overall sense of accomplishment among Muslim American volunteers, the trend is towards an enhanced experience for organizers and volunteers. Knowing almost exactly the number of individuals who are available to volunteer, or the particular time blocks during which each of them can come and go, or the skill sets which each has to offer, or the real-time communication of changes in location or start and end times or even postponements or cancellations due to inclement weather, are efficiencies which have the potential to raise substantially the level of satisfaction which Muslim Americans can experience in the process of volunteering.

Third, during the years following the September 2001 terrorist attacks, as media coverage of the Muslim community increased, there were and continue to be human interest stories highlighting the contributions of ordinary Muslim Americans to mainstream society (Patel, 2007). Although this trend began during the late 1990s, it was not so much as a reaction than a proactive desire to contribute to society, Muslim Americans of all ages and racial and ethnic backgrounds are increasingly found among the list of volunteers for national organizations such as Habitat for Humanity or for political campaigns or environmental protection campaigns or for local efforts such as the Parent Teacher Associations of public and Islamic schools. A unique phenomenon has occurred, prompting even those individuals to volunteer for service who may not have primarily identified with their religion but felt compelled to act in the face of the misinformation being disseminated about Islam. Volunteering is seen by many as a way to show through deeds that theirs is a faith with universal values such as compassion and kindness (Laird and Cadge, 2009). In addition to joining existing volunteer efforts, Muslim Americans are also at the forefront of new initiatives. Examples of post-2001 initiatives created by Muslims include Fast-a-thon and Project Downtown, for example, which attempt to alleviate the hardships experienced by the poor and homeless. The Fast-a-thon was conceived on the campus of the University of Tennessee at Knoxville during the winter following the 2001 terrorist attacks (Conwill and Jooma, 2008) and has continued on many college campuses. Muslim students invite people of other faiths to fast for a day under the sponsorship of individuals and businesses and then donate the money raised through those sponsorships to local organizations operating homeless shelters, domestic abuse safe havens, and soup kitchens, for example.

Final Thoughts

During the late twentieth and early twenty-first centuries, Muslim immigrants and their descendants have emerged on the volunteer scene, giving generously of their time, energy, wealth and talent to serve Muslims and people of various other backgrounds. Inspired by a combination of religious teachings, personal motivation, and institutionalized American volunteerism, their voluntary behaviors have evolved from being mostly inwardly focused, concerned about other Muslims in the United States and around the world, to being both inwardly and outwardly focused. Community and organizational development initiatives have been mostly volunteer-driven, and there remain very real challenges to ensure the meaningful and sustained participation of women and youth in those initiatives. As illustrated in this chapter, a hopeful trend can be discerned based on a culture of volunteerism that is taking hold among the descendants of those post-1960s immigrants.

Note

1. In 2003, MSA National initiated COMPASS, a state- of-the-art management training program designed to train graduates to become trainers themselves.

References

Abu-Laban, Sharon McIrvin. Family and religion among Muslim immigrants and their descendants. In *Muslim families in North America*, eds. Earle Howard Waugh, Sharon McIrvin Abu-Laban, and Regula B. Qureshi (Edmonton, Alberta: University of Alberta Press, 1991): 6–31.

ACCESS. A brief history. Available at: http://www.accesscommunity.org/site/PageServer?pagename=ACCESS_History2 (Accessed June 6, 2013.)

Bagby, Ihsan. The American Mosque in transition: Assimilation, acculturation and isolation. *Journal of Ethnic and Migration Studies* 35.3 (2009): 473–490.

Bagby, Ihsan Abdul-Wajid, Paul M. Perl, and Bryan Froehle. *The mosque in America, a national portrait: A report from the Mosque Study Project* (Washington, DC: Council on American-Islamic Relations, 2001).

Ba-Yunus, Ilyas, and Kassim Kone. *Muslims in the United States* (Westport, CT: Greenwood Publishing Group, 2006).

Bergesen, Albert, and Max Herman. Immigration, race, and riot: The 1992 Los Angeles uprising. *American Sociological Review* (1998): 39–54.

Bullock, Katherine. *Muslim women activists in North America: Speaking for ourselves* (Austin: University of Texas Press, 2005).

Congressional Record. Maxine Waters. Available at: http://www.gpo.gov/fdsys/pkg/CREC-2006-07-26/pdf/CREC-2006-07-26-pt1-PgH5940-4.pdf (Accessed June 6, 2013.)

Conwill, W. L., & Jooma, K. (2008). Thwarting ethnoviolence against Muslim women: performing identity in social action. *Journal for Social Action in Counseling and Psychology*, 1(2), 31-47.

Ecklund, Elaine Howard, and Jerry Z. Park. Religious diversity and community volunteerism among Asian Americans. *Journal for the Scientific Study of Religion* 46.2 (2007): 233–244.

Elkholy, Abdo A. *The Arab Moslems in the United States: religion and assimilation* (New Haven, CT: College & University Press, 1966).

Ghayur, M. Arif. Muslims in the United States: Settlers and visitors. *The Annals of the American Academy of Political and Social Science* 454.1 (1981): 150–163.

Haddad, Yvonne Yazbeck, ed. *The Muslims of America* (New York: Oxford University Press, 1991).

Haddad, Yvonne Yazbeck, and Adair T. Lummis. *Islamic values in the United States: A comparative study* (New York: Oxford University Press, 1987).

Haddad, Yvonne Yazbeck, and Jane Idleman Smith, eds. *Muslim Communities in North America* (New York: State University of New York Press, 1994).

Hamid, Abdulwahid. *Islam the Natural Way* (London: Muslim Education and Literary Services, 1989).

Handlin, Oscar. *The uprooted: The epic story of the great migrations that made the American people* (Philadelphia: University of Pennsylvania Press, 2002).

Herberg, Will. *Protestant, Catholic and Jew: An essay in American religious sociology* (Chicago: University of Chicago Press, 1983).

IMAN—Inner-city Muslim Action Network. About us. Accessed May 15, 2013. http://www.imancentral.org/about/

Karim, Jamillah. *American Muslim women: Negotiating race, class, and gender within the Ummah* (New York: New York University Press, 2008).

Kelley, Ron. Muslims in Los Angeles. In *Muslim Communities in North America*, eds. Yvonne Yazbeck Haddad and Jane Idleman Smith (New York: State University of New York Press, 1994): 135–168.

Laird, Lance D., and Wendy Cadge. Constructing American Muslim identity: Tales of two clinics in Southern California. *The Muslim World* 99.2 (2009): 270–293.

Laird, Lance D., and Wendy Cadge. Negotiating ambivalence: The social power of Muslim community—based health organizations in America. *PoLAR: Political and Legal Anthropology Review* 33.2 (2010): 225–244.

Maira, Sunaina. Youth culture, citizenship and globalization: South Asian Muslim youth in the United States after September 11th. *Comparative Studies of South Asia, Africa and the Middle East* 24.1 (2004): 219–231.

Nasr, Seyyed Hossein. *The heart of Islam: Enduring values for humanity* (New York: HarperCollins, 2002).

Nyang, S. S. (1999). *Islam in the United States of America*. (Chicago, IL: Kazi Publications Incorporated).

Patel, Eboo. *Acts of faith: The story of an American Muslim, the struggle for the soul of a generation* (Beacon Press, 2007).

Peek, Lori. Becoming Muslim: The development of a religious identity. *Sociology of Religion* 66.3 (2005): 215–242.

Poston, Larry. *Islamic Da'wah in the West: Muslim missionary activity and the dynamics of conversion to Islam* (New York: Oxford University Press, 1992).

Salem, Jackleen M. Muslim society: Life and integration in the United States, pre- and post-9/11. In *Immigrants in American history: Arrival, adaptation, and integration*, ed. Elliott Robert Barkan, 1809–1824 (Santa Barbara, CA: ABC-CLIO, 2013).

Schmidt, Garbi. Dialectics of authenticity: Examples of ethnification of Islam among young Muslims in Sweden and the United States. *The Muslim World* 92.1–2 (2002): 1–17.

Schmidt, Garbi. *Islam in urban America: Sunni Muslims in Chicago* (Philadelphia: Temple University Press, 2004).

Siddiqui, Shariq. Giving in the way of God: Muslim philanthropy in the United States. In *Religious giving: For love of God*, ed. David H. Smith (Bloomington, IN: Indiana University Press, 2010): 28–48.

Smith, Jane Idleman. *Islam in America* (New York: Columbia University Press, 1999).

UMMA—University Muslim Medical Association Community Clinic. History. Available at: http://www.ummaclinic.org/who-we-are/history (Accessed May 15, 2013.)

Webb, Gisela. *Windows of faith: Muslim women scholar-activists of North America* (Syracuse, NY: Syracuse University Press, 2000).

Wormser, Richard. *American Islam: Growing up Muslim in America* (New York: Walker Books for Young Readers, 2002).

PART III

INTEGRATION AND ASSIMILATION OF MUSLIMS

CHAPTER 19

MUSLIM AMERICANS AND THE POLITICAL SYSTEM

ABDULKADER H. SINNO

INTRODUCTION

Muslim Americans have become the improbable targets and tools of the discourses of some politicians in the search for votes, right-wing newspapers seeking enlarged readerships, and conservative activists advocating for their causes. These discourses have often taken bizarre twists, such as the surprisingly successful attempt during the 2007 Democratic primaries by a right-wing organization to depict (the Christian) candidate Obama as a Muslim who attended a "Madrasa" as a child. While the hoax was soon exposed by CNN, many mainstream media outlets (e.g., Fox News) uncritically adopted the story and about a sixth of the American public apparently continues to believe that President Obama is a Muslim.[1]

Such puzzling political behavior indicates that there is still much to be learned about the politics of American Muslims, which I understand to mean both their instrumentalization for political purposes by others and their own political activism and engagement. Some topics for research in the first area include understanding how Muslim minorities are instrumentalized in politics, the political spaces they are allowed to occupy or that their members attempt to fill, the attitudes of the US public toward Muslims generally and Muslim candidates in particular, and the role of media outlets and religious institutions in shaping politically relevant public opinion of

Muslims. On the minority's side, it is interesting to explore the evolution of the views, well-being, activism, and voting behavior of members of Muslim American groups, the political dynamics affecting their political representation and integration, and the quality and quantity of Muslim political representation. I describe below the state of the art in researching the policy-relevant and theoretically interesting aspects of the politics of American Muslims, identify lacunae in academic knowledge, and suggest methodological approaches to fill them.

ATTITUDES TOWARD MUSLIM MINORITIES AND THEIR POLITICAL INSTRUMENTALIZATION

The American public has negative attitudes toward Islam, Muslims in general, and Muslims living among them (Nisbet et al. 2011; Wike and Grim 2010). Dislike of Muslims is largely correlated with feelings of fear and threat, among other factors (Benson, Merolla, and Geer 2011; Nisbet et al. 2011). These are feelings that can be, and are being, effectively used to achieve political goals such as restricting the civil rights and liberties of Muslim minorities and undermining Muslim candidates and other public figures.[2] Fear is also leveraged to promote policies that have little to do with Muslims. One example is the "Victory Mosque" campaign to paint the desire of moderate Muslims to build a house of worship in Manhattan as an act of support for al-Qaeda's attack. It dominated the discourse of Republican politicians only in the months leading to the 2010 elections, well after the mosque project became public, and disappeared from the airwaves almost immediately after the Republican electoral victory even though there were no changes in the plans to build it. It is assumed that the reason Republican politicians and right-wing media used the Park 51 mosque so vociferously during the campaign is that they knew from long-existing studies that voters tend to vote more for Republicans when concerned about matters of security and threat. They therefore heightened feelings of threat by raising the specter of a Muslim "victory mosque" by fallaciously analogizing it to historical mosques in Istanbul and Muslim Spain.[3]

Another example is provided by Congressman Todd Tiahrt (R. Kansas) who introduced the No Welfare for Terrorists Act (H.R. 2338) in 2009 and published an emotional commentary in *The Washington Times* accusing US President Barack Obama and the Democrats of wanting to release terrorist detainees incarcerated in Guantanamo Bay and to provide them with welfare benefits.[4] Of course, this was never the content or intent of proposals by the Obama administration. The intention was to repatriate detainees in Guantanamo who were found innocent of ties to terrorism, as many were, to their own countries and, if not possible, to other countries willing to host them while holding others in high security prisons on American soil. Although Tiahrt's bill was co-sponsored by twelve other Republicans, it never made it past the House Committee on Oversight and Government Reform. The highly improbable association between the foreign Muslim detainees in Guantanamo and welfare services was simply a rhetorical tool that the congressman used to attack what he considered to be the left and its support for redistributive programs.

The instrumentalization and "othering" of American Muslims in the discourses of influential politicians, Evangelical churches, and media outlets suggest several lines of research. The first deals with the public attitudes that allow such strategies to be effective. It is not clear what makes Americans support extreme measures such as depriving American citizens of constitutional rights just because they are Muslims, as 44 percent did in 2004 according to a survey commissioned by Nisbet and Shanahan (2004).[5] While demographic correlates are important and useful, we still do not know what sways a member of the public to adopt such views and what sources of information influence her most.[6] Well-crafted experimental designs would allow the quantification of influences on different types of individuals from various media (religious, partisan, and news) and persons of authority such as Evangelical preachers and different types of politicians.[7]

One way to explore how the use of electoral strategies that capitalize on negative attitudes toward Muslims increases Islamophobia within the public is to prepare a series of national surveys that anticipate their use. The researcher would conduct a base survey of attitudes toward Muslims early in the electoral cycle before parties and candidates attack the minority and repeat the survey soon after the attacks and in the wake of the election campaign. This approach would allow the measurement of both their immediate and residual long term effects. If such electoral strategies are used on a regional basis, then the surveys will consist of a natural experiment that can isolate the effect of the use of these strategies from other factors that may also increase hostility toward Muslims such as wars involving US troops in the Middle East.

Another track that would dialogue with the experimental approach by informing its design would be to conduct both qualitative and quantitative content analyses of the media, religious and political discourses that target or instrumentalize Muslims. Such studies provide valuable clues about the purpose of such discourses by measuring their frequency and timing and reveal the full panoply of rhetorical strategies used to galvanize target audiences across media, periods and types of elections. Experimental designs also allow for testing the effect of different types of anti-Muslim discourses by varying the content of frames used in political messages.

A third track would be to analyze the dynamics of groupthink on Muslim issues. When the bizarre attacks on then candidate Obama took place, only two public figures in the United States asked rhetorically, "So what if he were a Muslim?"—a CNN journalist and retired General Collin Powell.[8] Very rarely does anyone other than Muslim organizations respond to the many attacks on the minority and Muslim organizations receive little media coverage. Such groupthink, from across the aisle, where even unreasonable assumptions go unchallenged, is frequent in human history. The case of American Muslims provides a particularly interesting opportunity to research its cultural, financial, political, power, religious, and ideological mechanisms.

IMPACT OF "OTHERING" ON MUSLIM WELL-BEING, MOBILIZATION, ATTITUDES, AND VOTING BEHAVIOR

The instrumentalization of American Muslims for political gain involves the promotion of negative depictions and the assumption that they are, at the least, threatening and implacable nemeses. These stereotypes have receptive audiences within the public and the fact that they are aired unchallenged, as they often are, by individuals in positions of power and prominence makes them legitimate to adopt, act on, and enforce. The increasing acceptance of these depictions likely encourages discrimination against individuals with an apparent connection to Islam in areas such as education, the job market, housing, services, and political recruitment. It most likely also encourages hate crimes, social hostility, damage to relationships, and stress to physical and mental health. This impact on American Muslim lives, welfare, and well-being is underresearched and deserves to be quantified for both academic and policy reasons.

American Muslim individuals respond emotionally and strategically to political instrumentalization and marginalization, and their social repercussions. Some ways, such as the shift of the bulk of support from the Republican Party to the Democratic Party between the 2000 and 2004 elections are well documented (Barreto and Bozonelos 2009). Others, such as the propensity of members of the minority to mobilize and the methods of political action its members choose, deserve more scholarly attention. The correlates of such personal decisions are complex and can vary from complete disengagement to civic engagement and even militancy outside the scope of the political system. For Muslims who decide to engage in political activism, we still do not know what motivates the adoption of a specific approach, such as choosing between joining Muslim organizations, ethnic associations or broad civil rights groups; voting for and otherwise supporting marginal parties or established ones; and the type and purpose of alliances with which Muslims are comfortable on both the individual and organizational levels.[9] Most importantly, we do not know what guides these decisions and how to explain variation across organizations, demographic groups and individuals. These research questions are not only useful to increase our understanding of Muslim minorities but also in general to better theorize the effect of duress on the political choices individuals make to balance between retrenchment and engagement (type of organization); principles and pragmatism (type of party); group interest and personal interests (wealthy Muslims who would have voted Republican if it were not for the party's hostility toward the faith); domestic and international concerns (e.g., alliances with Jewish or Hindu groups within the country when these are possible); and theological imperatives and pragmatic priorities (alliances with gay groups because of common minority interests where these are possible).

Qualitative field work will continue to be necessary and valuable to identify different patterns within and across communities and to understand what quantitative studies cannot reveal: strategic choices, the effect of socialization, local contingencies, and whatever the quantitative analyst does not know of and therefore cannot theorize.[10] Sociologists and anthropologists in particular have been doing informative ethnographic and other field work on the political and civic activism of American Muslims and its institutional contexts. In the United States, a critical mass of such scholarship focuses on a few geographic areas where the Muslim population (and Arab one with which it overlaps) has a substantial presence—Greater Detroit, Los Angeles, the Bay Area, Chicago, and New York.[11] These studies produce a complex image of a group of people with a generally consolidating sense of Muslim identity,[12] who are defining what this identity means in many ways, who are quickly making the intellectual and organizational transitions from immigrants (or marginalized minority in the case of African American Muslims) to engaged American citizens, and who are figuring out how to deal with the hostility targeting them. Some, such as the more established Muslims of Michigan and the wealthy ones in the liberal Bay Area and Florida, do better than others in their civic and political engagement (Senzai 2012).

Still, the acceleration of Muslim American organization in the United States since 9/11 on both local and national levels has been quite impressive, even if its effectiveness has been tempered by general public and political hostility. American Muslim political expression also has taken many forms, including engagement with broader civil rights organizations, bringing out the Muslim vote (Senzai 2012), lobbying, and even comedy and popular culture (Bilici 2012). Evidence of increased mobilization among Muslim Americans includes the growth of Muslim organizations focusing on civil rights (e.g., Council on American-Islamic Relations [CAIR]) and political activism (e.g., Muslim Public Affairs Council [MPAC], American Muslim Alliance [AMA], and local ones), higher levels of political visibility, lobbying, outreach programs, and increased turnout rates of Muslim voters (Ayers and Hofstetter 2008, Jalalzai 2009, Peña 2007, Terry 2006).

While Muslim organizations such as MPAC and the AMA most likely exaggerate the importance of the "Muslim block vote" and its decisiveness in swing states, their efforts to mobilize Muslims through email lists and publications may contribute to the development of a Muslim American political identity and drive in part the increase and direction of the votes of Muslim Americans. The American Muslim Task Force on Civil Rights and Elections, an umbrella organization, endorsed John Kerry in 2004 in an election that witnessed a large increase in the number of Muslim

American voters over the previous election and a dramatic shift of the Muslim vote from the Republican Party to the Democratic Party. Major Muslim organizations and nearly nine in ten Muslim-Americans also supported Barack Obama in 2008.

While the agreement between Muslim voters and their organizations is obvious, it is not clear to what degree these organizations helped shape voters' preferences—they may have voted as they did anyway. While slowly improving, voter turnout rates for Muslim-Americans remain below those of the American public in 2011—66 percent said they were certain they were registered to vote, compared with 79 percent among the general public (Pew 2011). It would therefore be interesting to research the degree to which infringements on civil rights and other policy issues that interest Muslim Americans drive some of them to vote and others to withdraw. Because researchers can only study what they observe, and they can observe the activities of Muslim organizations that want to increase the visibility of Muslim Americans better than the activities of those that do not want to do so in a hostile environment, they may want to devise a research design that remedies this selection bias in assessing the mobilization efforts of the complete universe of Muslim organizations. The visibility dilemma (Cainkar 2002, Haddad and Smith 2002) exists because the visibility of Muslims encourages transgressions on their rights in a context of excessive securitization and hostility. Yet, Muslims need to become more visible to assert and protect their rights.

Rapid changes also open up new research agendas. They include comparative studies of the effect of local political institutions on Muslim activism; the effect of generational change and gender on civic and political activism; the effect of religiosity, ethnicity and sect on political engagement; the ability of Muslims to engage in alliances with other political interest groups; the effect of Muslims' engagement on non-Muslims' attitudes toward them; and the role of transnational, trans-group and trans-regional learning on the activism of the minority.

Quantitative data of good quality on the political attitudes of American Muslims are limited because it is costly to conduct surveys of small and diffuse populations and because of the high likelihood that members of a generally mistreated population would refuse to self-identify as such to a pollster on the phone. It takes roughly 60,000 calls, for example, to connect with a sample of some 1000 Muslims who are reasonably representative of the US Muslim population.[13] So far, only organizations with tremendous resources such as the Pew Foundation and Gallup have conducted such surveys of rigorously-selected representative samples. It is even costlier to conduct experiments embedded in surveys on national samples because of the large number of questions they normally involve and because large polling organizations favor simpler queries that can be reported in a more straightforward way to a broad audience.

There are several ways to reduce the high cost of such surveys, all of which have substantial downsides.[14] One method is to focus on a subpopulation with a high concentration of Muslims, as was done in the 2003 Detroit Arab American Study (DAAS).[15] The obvious downside to this approach is that the Muslims of Detroit or New York may not be representative of all American Muslims. A way to reduce this disadvantage at an increased cost is to sample the largest three or four areas of higher concentration, but this is problematic in the case of this specific minority because of how diffuse it is. Another approach is to define the population of interest as that of mosque-visiting practicing Muslims who could be easily surveyed at their places of worship, but this is only suitable to a subset of research questions that may interest social scientists. An example is a 2007–2008 mosque-based survey of Muslims in ten cities done by Matt Barreto and Karam Dana.[16] One method to avoid is to survey mosque members and leaders in the hope of learning about the broader Muslim population, the way Bagby et al. (2001) did, because community leaders tend to grossly overstate membership and the self-selected respondents to such surveys sometimes have personality traits that make them unrepresentative of the general Muslim population.

As of now, high-quality survey datasets on American Muslims are produced by Gallup and the Pew Foundation.[17] The Gallup datasets are very costly for social scientists to acquire but those done by Pew are made available on the organization's website after an embargo period..[18]

The findings from these surveys are too complex to adequately summarize here, but they reveal impressive socioeconomic integration, fulfillment, and economic attainment among American Muslims, particularly among immigrants and their descendants. American Muslims either exceed or equal other Americans in educational and professional accomplishment; have high levels of trust in government and American society; generally disagree with the use of violence against civilians; feature similar levels of political engagement between Muslim men and women (Read 2007); have a generally strong sense of identification with the country, readiness to adopt American culture and to become part of the mainstream; perceive harmony between their faith and national identity; and accept differences (except for sexual orientation, tolerance increased in this area). Surveys also reveal a positive correlation between religiosity and mosque attendance, on the one hand, and levels of civic engagement on the other. American Muslims are more concerned with domestic affairs, particularly the economy, than foreign policy but have views on US involvement in the Middle East that are markedly different from those of other Americans: they do not support the wars in Afghanistan and Iraq, do not believe in the sincerity of the "war against terror", and most continue to believe that Israel and Palestine can coexist and that a solution to the conflict is possible.

MUSLIM MINORITY POLITICAL REPRESENTATION

Muslim minority representation to elected and appointed office is important because it encourages institutional and legislative solutions to problems that could otherwise fester and because it reduces groupthink toward this politically marginalized minority within legislative bodies. Of course, this is only possible if elected officials choose, or are permitted, to represent minority interests along with those of their party or district.[19] Other advantages include increasing the sense of belonging to the country within the Muslim minority at large and acceptance of it by the general public.

Muslims are generally underrepresented in elected and appointed office in the United States. In some areas, like Metro Detroit, they are underrepresented in elected office but much less so in appointed positions (Sinno and Tatari 2011). At this writing, there are two Muslims in Congress (Keith Ellison and André Carson, both in the House) and a smattering of members of state legislatures (less than 10 of 7382 state legislators in 2010) and members of city councils. Interestingly, almost all Muslim candidates on the state and federal levels have been attacked by opponents or supporters of their opponents based on their religious identity at one point or another. Muslims are also underrepresented among congressional staffers, even though their numbers have increased considerably in the last few years (few dozen of some 9000 staffers at any one time in the last five years).

The reasons for underrepresentation differ from one context to another. Factors behind variation among districts include differences in electoral systems on the local level, district size and Muslim minority concentration within districts, party dynamics and recruitment, the availability of mentorship by established politicians or of family ties that introduce Muslim converts to politics, levels of organization and understanding of political institutions, the degree of fragmentation within the Muslim community, the quality of relations with non-Muslim elected officials, turnout rates, intersectionality in the identity of the candidate, and hostility within parties or publics (Sinno 2009).

In addition to understanding the correlates of rates of representation, researchers may be interested in understanding whether and why elected officials behave as representatives of a minority as well as representatives of their district or party, the component of the minority identity they identify with (Islam, sect, ethnicity, age group or gender), and how effective they are in their advocacy on behalf of the Muslim minority.

One of the major hurdles facing Muslim candidates for elected office in the United States is that some voters would not vote for them because they are Muslim. A small number of articles have been published to quantify voters' anti-Muslim bias and identify its correlates but they leave room for further innovation and refinement. Most are based on data from a Pew Research Center survey that asks American respondents whether they are more or less likely, or just as likely, to vote for a candidate for the presidency if the candidate has specific traits. Of the twenty-three traits that respondents were prompted about, being Muslim tied with being homosexual as the third-worse one (46 percent of public less likely to vote for candidate, 1 to 2 percent more likely to vote for her). The only candidate traits that are less attractive to American voters are "never held elected office" (56 percent less likely, 7 percent more likely) and "doesn't believe in God" (63 percent less likely, 3 percent more likely) (Republicans Lag in Engagement and Enthusiasm for Candidates 2007, pp. 12–13).

Another way to gauge bias is to conduct a simple experiment embedded in a survey where respondents are asked about whether they would support a candidate described in a vignette. The experimental treatment consists of varying the candidate's identity in the vignette for different representative subsets of the sample. Comparing the means for the different groups of respondents with the baseline group (no specified identity) allows the quantification of bias against candidates with specified identities.[20]

Even though a very high proportion of voters are ready to divulge their anti-Muslim bias to a stranger, it could be that others dissimulate similar attitudes to avoid appearing bigoted. The best method currently available to gauge sincere preferences is the list experiment developed by Ted Carmines and Paul Sniderman (1999) to study attitudes toward blacks. The experimental treatment consists of asking respondents in different representative samples to answer how many items on a list make them uncomfortable or they would refuse to do, while giving each group of respondents other than the baseline group an additional list item that is the focus of the research project. Respondents can answer in ways that may be racist or bigoted without worrying about being identified as such because it is impossible for the researcher to discern on an individual basis (absent ceiling effects) which specific items on the list the respondent dislikes. Calculating mean differences among groups produces a more accurate estimate of bias than a straightforward survey question but does not permit the multivariate analysis of the individual correlates of bias the way survey questions do. Benson et al. (2011) conducted such an experiment in 2008 and found that 58 percent of their sample of the American public would answer "I could not support a qualified Muslim for President" if they were not concerned about being recognized as biased, a 12 percent increase over the albeit differently worded question in the Pew survey. Carmines, Easter, and Sinno (2012) used data from a similar experiment from 2008 as well and found that the probability that a randomly picked American voter would disclose that it bothers her that "a Muslim be elected as president" is 70 percent when she feels that her privacy is protected, as opposed to 49 percent when a statistical model of voters' attitudes the authors developed is applied to the data from the Pew survey. We still do not know how attitudes change if respondents are prompted about types of elected office other than the presidency, whether intersectionality matters, whether attitudes toward hypothetical versus real candidates differ, and of course how these attitudes will change over time.

It is also still not completely clear exactly what motivates voters to be wary of Muslim candidates. One way to research motivation is to use attribution in an experimental setup (Braman and Sinno 2009). Respondents, for example, are asked to read a vignette about candidates defending controversial positions, with half the respondents reading a version of the vignette in which the candidate is described as Muslim and the other half a version where the candidate's faith cannot be recognized.

Respondents are then asked a list of theoretically-motivated questions about why they feel the candidate behaved this way. Comparing the answers of the two groups reveals how respondents believe the motivations of Muslim candidates differ from those of non-Muslim ones and, consequently, why they may be less comfortable with Muslims in elected office.

The net effect of bias on representation is also difficult to measure by holding all other factors constant. There are currently two ways of measuring the effect of bias on representation, both with considerable disadvantages. The first is to simply count the number of representatives from the minority and to compare their ratio within the elected body with the proportion of the minority population within the district (Sinno 2009). This approach is vulnerable to measurement errors such as the mis-identification of legislators who do not advertise their faith because they fear being penalized by the electorate, dependence on inaccurate demographic statistics because the US Census does not ask about religion, and the fact that it is only meaningful in the presence of rarely available data on citizenship rates. Even more problematically, it does not identify where bias resides (parties or electorate) or isolate its effect from other possible explanations such as minority political culture. A second and much more sophisticated approach, best applied by Rafaela Dancygier (2011) in a study of British local elections, consists of using a differences-in-differences statistical set-up to measure the effect of bias in elections when natural experiments such as changes in election rules take place. The biggest limitations of this approach are the scarcity of the data necessary to implement it in a convincing way and the rarity of the requi-site natural experiments. Most changes in local election systems in the United States took place in the South when whites feared increased black representation because of demographic changes. They are much rarer today.

Much of what is important and interesting about Muslim (and other) minority representation can only be learned from long stints of field research. These include, for example, the dynamics of recruitment, selection, discrimination, and mentor-ship within parties; the roles elected officials of Muslim background choose, or are allowed, to play in regard to minority rights advocacy; the way they connect with minority and majority constituencies; and the strategies Muslim candidates adopt to reduce their identity-based disadvantages.[21] Often these matters are much more complicated than the researcher anticipates and require elaborate qualitative research designs that join the rigor of the social sciences with the flair of good jour-nalism. Other areas include the roles of both Muslim organizations (CAIR, MPAC, ISNA) and anti-Muslim ones (pro-Israel groups such as AIPAC and Evangelical organizations) in affecting attitudes against Muslim candidates and elected officials.

Minority political representation is most visible in elected office, but it also plays an important role within party institutions and bureaucracies where the presence of minority appointees can reduce institutional biases and discrimination and partly remedy underrepresentation in elected office (Sinno and Tatari 2011). Research in this area is almost nonexistent because the complexity and opacity of institutions such as parties and bureaucracies sometimes deter research when easier publications can be produced at the early stages of growth in an emergent field. Still, this is an important area of research because political parties and bureaucratic institutions have much power to discriminate, help, empower, and redistribute and they affect the lives and livelihoods of minorities, including American Muslims, and the quality of social relations in society.

CONCLUSION

Although the amount of research on the politics of American Muslims—as agents, tools, and targets—is increasing, it has yet to reflect the importance of the topic in the politics of the United States. The recent development of advanced statistical, survey, content analysis, and experimental methods, along with ways to integrate them synergistically, now allows the exploration of attitudes and political behavior toward vulnerable and marginalized minorities, and, within them, in ways that were not available before. Muslims today happen to be among the most targeted of minorities in the United States (along with gays and somewhat less than Mormons) where this research infrastructure can be best deployed and informed by qualitative research facilitated by easy access to the minority. This convergence of methodological developments, availability of research infrastructure, access, and contentious politics provides an opportunity not only to learn more about the dynamics of the politics of American Muslims, but also more generally about human political behavior in the context of fear, hate, tokenization, and discrimination. It may also help produce better policies and outcomes for American society by exposing the sources of Islamophobia, reduce harm against members of a marginalized minority, and limit the potential for radicalization among its aggrieved members.

NOTES

1. "CNN debunks false report about Obama," available online at http://articles.cnn.com/2007-01-22/politics/obama.madrassa_1_islamic-school-madrassa-muslim-school?_s=PM:POLITICS. For numbers of Americans who falsely believe that Obama is a Muslim, see the report from the Pew Research Center for the People & the Press, "Growing Number of Americans Say Obama Is a Muslim," available online at http://pewresearch.org/pubs/1701/poll-obama-muslim-christian-church-out-of-politics-political-leaders-religious.
2. Such strategies sometimes fail when targeted constituencies are not amenable to them. This was the case when the opponent of Keith Ellison, the first Muslim to be elected to Congress, mocked his Muslim background and analogized him to Hitler in the very liberal Fifth District of Minnesota. Ellison won by a landslide (Sinno 2009).
3. See in particular the campaign advertisement of Renee Ellmers (featured in an AC360 segment on CNN, available online at http://www.youtube.com/watch?v=SfAqarG8l6w)

and the speeches on the issue made by Newt Gingrich (example available online at http://
www.youtube.com/watch?v=cmtk30-sTaY). The two politicians' claim are fallacious on
whether the Park 51 mosque is comparable to mosques built by conquering empires centuries earlier (the Sufi leader of the Park 51 mosque does not share Usama bin Laden's
understanding of the faith; the mosque was to be built two blocks away from the destroyed
World Trade Center buildings, not supplant them; and Muslims have not conquered
New York), the symbolism of Cordoba (a space for coexistence, not a symbol of victory),
and by failing to realize that supplanting houses of worships with others used to be done
by conquering empires of all faiths, not just Muslims, in the middle ages and is now a
defunct practice. Work by Elisabeth Ivarsflaten (2008) provides an interesting argument
for the European context that may hold traction in the United States as well—populist
parties promote xenophobia (particularly Islamophobia) so they can get votes from both
ends of the economic policy continuum.

4. Todd Tiahrt, "No Welfare for These Enemies; Any Release of Detainees with Benefits
   Must Be Resisted," *Washington Times* (May 15, 2009): Friday, p. A19.

5. A 2011 survey by Nisbet et al. (2011) also finds the percentage of Americans who agree
   that "profiling individuals as potential terrorists based solely on being Muslim is wrong"
   at 63%; disagreement with "Muslims in the United States should register their whereabouts with the U.S. government" and "law enforcement agencies should closely monitor
   all Islamic mosques for terrorism" at 52% and 41% of respondents, respectively; and that
   opposition to a nationwide ban on mosque construction in the United States is at 57%.

6. We know for example that the older, more conservative, less educated, Protestants (particularly Evangelicals), Catholics, and Republicans are more likely to support such measures
   (Nisbet, Ostman, and Shanahan 2009; Jamal 2009).

7. For a nonexperimental analysis of the role of Christian and Conservative media in the
   U.S., see Nisbet, Ostman, and Shanahan (2009).

8. The relevant clip from Collin Powell's interview with NBC's *Meet the Press* is online at
   http://www.youtube.com/watch?v=dYELqbZAQ4M.

9. Some of the studies on Muslim mobilization include Jamal (2005) and Ayers and Hofstetter
   (2008).

10. For an example of the large-scale use of extended interviews and focus groups to study
    Muslim minorities in Europe, see the Open Societies Foundations' *A Home in Europe
    Project* (2011), accessible online at http://www.soros.org/initiatives/home.

11. See, notably, recent work by Baker et al. (2009), Abraham, Howell, and Shryock (2011),
    Bakalian and Bozogmehr (2009), and Bilici (2012).

12. See also Barreto and Bozonelos (2009) on the consolidation of Muslim identity.

13. For more on the challenges of sampling the Muslim American population and on tech-
    nical solutions, see the methodological sections of the important reports by the Pew
    Research Center for the People & the Press (2007, 2011). The Pew Foundation and Gallup
    have many advantages, including databases of respondents who previously self-identified
    as Muslims to re-contact, which are not available to most researchers and institutions.

14. Researchers generally contract out the fielding of surveys and experiments they design to
    professional survey organizations. The most frequently used ones are the Internet-based
    YouGov and Knowledge Networks. Some scholars, however, use more expensive *ad hoc*
    telephone-based polling centers at their universities or commission Gallup or Zogby
    International for their surveys. Several grant-funded organizations, such as Time-sharing
    Experiments for the Social Sciences (TESS), allow scholars to submit proposals in a

competitive process to include their survey or experimental questions in omnibus survey instruments.

15. The Detroit Arab American Study (DAAS) data are available online at http://www.icpsr.umich.edu/icpsrweb/ICPSR/studies/04413.

16. Information on Barreto and Dana's Muslim American Public Opinion Survey (MAPOS) is available at http://faculty.washington.edu/mbarreto/research/islam.html but the data are not shared.

17. The Pew Foundation conducted extensive surveys of Muslim Americans in 2007 ("Muslim Americans: Middle Class and Mostly Mainstream") dataset accessible online at http://www.people-press.org/2007/05/22/2007-muslim-american-survey/) and 2011 (Muslim Americans, online at http://www.people-press.org/2011/08/30/muslim-americans-no-signs-of-growth-in-alienation-or-support-for-extremism/). Gallup produced two reports on American Muslims based on data collected in 2008 and 2010 ("Muslim Americans: Faith, Freedom, and the Future" report online at http://www.gallup.com/se/148805/Muslim-Americans-Faith-Freedom-Future.aspx).

18. In addition, there are less rigorously-collected data available from countrywide or regional surveys. Georgetown University's Project MAPS, for example, produced two early surveys of Muslim American opinion (2000, 2004) that were executed by Zogby International and are available from UCONN's Roper Center's public opinion archive at http://webapps.ropercenter.uconn.edu.

19. There is a rich literature about the representation of other minorities to inform research on the dynamics of U.S. Muslim minority representation. Much of this literature is on U.S. "race" minorities. The literature on the representation of U.S. blacks and Latinos, and women generally are too large to describe here. The religious identity of candidates in the U.S. recently started to gain scholarly attention (Benson, Merolla, and Geer 2011; Campbell, Green, and Layman 2011). Research on the representation of women and gays also provides methodological tools, concepts, and perspectives to better understand some aspects of the representation of Muslims. For broad comparative (cross-national) collections that provide good introductions to recent developments in the field, see Benbassa (2011) and Bird, Saalfeld, and Wüst (2011).

20. See, for example, Brouard and Tiberj (2010) who conducted such an experiment in France.

21. For examples of involved qualitative and mixed-methods studies of Muslim minority representation from other national settings, see Eren Tatari (2010) on elected Muslim officials in London, Fatima Zibouh (2010) on Muslim elected officials in Brussels, Jytte Klausen (2005) on European Muslim elites, and Sinno and Tatari (2009) on elected officials at all levels in the United Kingdom. On the quality of representation, see Sinno (2011).

References

Abraham, Nabeel, Sally Howell, and Andrew Shryock, eds., *Target of Opportunity: Arab Detroit in the Terror Decade* (Detroit: Wayne State University Press, 2011).

Ayers, John W.., and C.. Richard Hofstetter, "American Muslim Political Participation Following 9/11: Religious Belief, Political Resources, Social Structures, and Political Awareness," *Politics and Religion* 1 (2008): 3–26.

Bagby, Ihsan; Paul M.. Perl, Brian T.. Froehle, *The Mosque in America: A National Portrait* (Washington, DC: Council on American-Islamic Relations, 2001).

Bakalian, Anny, and Mehdi Borzorgmehr, *Backlash 9/11: Middle Eastern and Muslim Americans Respond* (Berkeley: University of California Press, 2009).

Baker, Wayne, Sally Howell, Amaney Jamal, Ann Chih Lin, Andrew Shryock, Ron Stockton, and Mark Tessler, *Preliminary Findings from the Detroit Arab American Study* (Detroit: Detroit Arab American Study, 2004).

Barreto, Matt A., and Dino Bozonelos, "Democrat, Republican or None of the Above? The Role of Religiosity in Muslim American Party Identification," *Politics and Religion* 2 (2009): 1–31.

Bilici, Mucahit, *Finding Mecca in America: American Muslims and Cultural Citizenship* (Chicago: University of Chicago Press, 2012).

Benbassa, Esther, *Minorités Visibles en Politique* (Paris: CNRS Éditions, 2011).

Benson, Brett V.., Jennifer L.. Merolla, and John G.. Geer, "Two Steps Forward, One Step Back? Bias in the 2008 Presidential Election," *Electoral Studies* 30 (2011): 607–620.

Bird, Karen, Thomas Saalfeld, and Andreas M.. Wüst, *The Political Representation of Immigrants and Minorities: Voters, Parties and Parliaments in Liberal Democracies, Routledge/ECPR Studies in European Political Science* (New York: Routledge, 2011).

Braman, Eileen, and Abdulkader H.. Sinno, "An Experimental Investigation of Causal Attributions for the Political Behavior of Muslim Candidates: Can a Muslim Represent you?" *Politics and Religion* 2 (2009): 247–276.

Brouard, Sylvain, and Vincent Tiberj, "Yes They Can: An Experimental Approach to the Eligibility of Ethnic Minority Candidate in France," in Karen Bird, Thomas Saalfeld, and Andreas Wüst, eds., *The Political Representation of Immigrants and Minorities: Voters, Parties and Parliaments in Liberal Democracies* (Oxford: Routledge, 2010): 164–180.

Cainkar, Louise, "No Longer Invisible: Arab and Muslim Exclusion after September 11," *Middle East Report* 224 (2002): 22–29.

Cainkar, Louise, "American Muslims at the Dawn of the 21st Century: Hope and Pessimism in the Drive for Civic and Political Inclusion," in Jocelyne Cesari, ed., *Muslims in the West* (London/New York: Routledge, 2010): 176–197.

Campbell, David E.., John C.. Green, and Geoffrey C.. Layman, "The Party Faithful: Partisan Images, Candidate Religion, and the Electoral Impact of Party Identification," *American Journal of Political Science* 55 (2011): 42–58.

Carmines, Edward G.., Beth C.. Easter, and Abdulkader H.. Sinno, "The Changing Nature of Bias against Minority Candidates: Discrimination, Dissimulation and Compromise" (2012), unpublished manuscript.

Dancygier, Rafaela, "The Representation of Muslims in Local Legislatures: Election, Selection and the Role of Electoral Rules in English Cities" (2011), unpublished manuscript.

Erik C.. Nisbet, and James Shanahan, "Restrictions on Civil Liberties, Views of Islam, and Muslim Americans," in *MSRG Special Report* (Ithaca, N.Y.: Media and Society Research Group, Cornell University, 2004). Available online at http://www.yuricareport.com/Civil%20Rights/CornellMuslimReportCivilRights.pdf

Haddad, Yvonne Yazbeck, and Jane I. Smith, eds., *Muslim Minorities in the West: Visible and Invisible* (Oxford: Altamira Press, 2002).

Ivarsflaten, Elisabeth, "What Unites Right-Wing Populists in Western Europe? Re-Examining Grievance Mobilization Models in Seven Successful Cases," *Comparative Political Studies* 41 (2008): 3–23.

Jalalzai, Farida, "The Politics of Muslims in America," *Religion and Politics* 2 (2009): 163–199.

Jamal, Amaney, "The Political Participation and Engagement of Muslim Americans: Mosque Involvement and Group Consciousness," *American Politics Research* 33 (2005): 521–544.

Jamal, Amaney, "The Racialization of Muslim Americans," in Abdulkader H. Sinno, ed., *Muslims in Western Politics* (Bloomington, Ind:.: Indiana University Press, 2009).

Klausen, Jytte, "The Islamic Challenge: Politics and Religion in Western Europe (New York: Oxford University Press, 2005).

Nisbet, Erik C., Ronald Ostman, and James Shanahan, "Public Opinion toward Muslim Americans: Civil Liberties and the Role of Religiosity, Ideology, and Media Use," in Abdulkader H. Sinno, ed., *Muslims in Western Politics* (Bloomington, Ind:.: Indiana University Press, 2009).

Nisbet, Erik, Michelle Ortiz, Yasamin Miller, and Andrew Smith, "The 'Bin Laden' Effect: How American Public Opinion about Muslim Americans Shifted in the wake of Osama Bin Laden's Death." Available online at http://www.eriknisbet.com/files/binladen_report.pdf

Peña, Aisha, "Protecting Muslim Civil and Human Rights in America: The Role of Islamic, National, and International Organizations," *Journal of Muslim Minority Affairs* 27 (2007): 387–400.

Pew Research Center for the People & the Press, "Muslim Americans: Middle Class and Mostly Mainstream" (2007).

Pew Research Center for the People & the Press, "Republicans Lag in Engagement and Enthusiasm for Candidates" (2007).

Pew Research Center for the People & the Press, "Muslim Americans: No Signs of Growth in Alienation or Support for Extremism" (2011).

Read, Jen'nan Ghazal, "More of a Bridge than a Gap: Gender Differences in Arab-American Political Engagement," *Social Science Quarterly* 88 (2007): 1072–1091.

Senzai, Farid, "Engaging American Muslims: Political Trends and Attitudes," research report, Institute for Social Policy and Understanding. http://www.ispu.org/pdfs/ISPU%20Report_Political%20Participation_Senzai_WEB.pdf

Sinno, Abdulkader, "Muslim Representation in American Politics," in Abdulkader H. Sinno, ed., *Muslims in Western Politics* (Bloomington, Ind:.: Indiana University Press, 2009).

Sinno, Abdulkader, "Opportunités et Risques de la Représentation des Musulmans Occidentaux dans les Institutions élues," in Esther Benbassa, ed., *Minorités Visibles en Politique* (Paris: Éditions CNRS, 2011).

Sinno, Abdulkader, and Eren Tatari, "Muslims in UK Institutions," in Abdulkader H. Sinno, ed., *Muslims in Western Politics* (Bloomington, Ind:.: Indiana University Press, 2009).

Sinno, Abdulkader, and Eren Tatari, "Toward Electability: Public Office and the Arab Vote," in Sally Howell, Nabeel Abraham, and Andrew Shryock, eds., *Target of Opportunity: Arab Detroit in the Terror Decade* (Detroit: Wayne State University Press, 2011).

Sniderman, Paul M., and Edward G. Carmines, *Reaching beyond Race* (Cambridge, Mass:.: Harvard University Press, 1999).

Tatari, Eren, *A Contingency Theory of Descriptive Representation: Muslims in British Local Government*, Ph.D. dissertation, Indiana University: (2010).

Terry, Janice, "Arab-American Political Activism and Civil Liberties in the Post 9/11 Era," in Philippa Strum, ed., *American Arabs and Political Participation* (Washington, DC: Woodrow Wilson International Center for Scholars, 2006): 117–129.

Wike, R., and B. J. Grim, "Western Views Toward Muslims: Evidence from a 2006 Cross-National Survey," *International Journal of Public Opinion Research* 22 (2010): 4–25.

Zibouh, Fatima, *La Participation Politique des élus d'Origine Maghrébine* (Brussels: Academia-Bruylant, 2010)

CHAPTER 20

THE INTELLECTUAL CONTRIBUTIONS OF AMERICAN MUSLIM SCHOLARS

SARA J. CHEHAB AND

MARVIN R. WHITAKER, JR.

THIS chapter reviews the work of five American Muslim intellectuals and scholars: Taha Jabir Al-Alwani, Amina Wadud, Abdullahi Ahmed An-Na'im, Fazlur Rahman, and M. A. Muqtedar Khan. The main publications and contributions of these five scholars are discussed in an effort to see how their work informs, shapes, and influences the ongoing philosophical and theological debates on a variety of issues, most notably *ijtihad* and the "Islamization of knowledge" (al-Alwani), gender equality (Wadud), human rights (an-Na'im), democracy and reform (Rahman and Khan), and interfaith dialogue (Khan). Many Muslim, non-Muslim, American, and non-American scholars, activists, university professors, and political philosophers have contributed to the general study of Islam, shari`a, and to the topics mentioned above. With the exception of Fazlur Rahman, who wrote in the 1960s and 1970s, the thinkers whose work this chapter elucidates were published in the 1990s and 2000s.

Al-Alwani, Wadud, an-Na'im, Rahman, and Khan use different approaches and focus on different topics in their research. They constitute the focus of this chapter because of the variety of themes they cover in their scholarly work. Nonetheless certain common threads can be identified. First, all five scholars acknowledge that there is some kind of intellectual and philosophical crisis in Islamic thought and in the Muslim world, a crisis that is due partly to colonialism and oppression but more so to the inability of Muslim communities to use and reinterpret the Qur'an and other Islamic sources to fit contemporary times and conditions. Indeed, al-Alwani believes that the crisis is due primarily to Muslim communities and thinkers abandoning ijtihad as a tool for human progress. In addition, says Wadud, Muslims have relied on old and male-centered interpretations of the Qur'an that do not elevate women to the same standards as men, resulting in great inequalities between genders.

An-Na'im believes that Muslim societies adopted secular discourses and systems without integrating and developing the principles of shari'a to fit modern times, leading the Muslim world to use laws and institutions devoid of moral and ethical codes. For Rahman, that crisis stems from the lack of serious educational reform and the absence of spirituality in Muslim countries. Moreover, according to him, the fact that ordinary individuals are excluded from interpreting the Qur'an creates a crisis of thought where new ideas, such as democracy, are dismissed on the grounds that they are un-Islamic. The lack of thought and understanding given to Islamic democratic theory is a concern for both Rahman and Khan. The latter believes that the traditional epistemological models of Islamic thought are insufficient to understand and adapt to modernity and different cultures, a crisis most apparent in the Muslim countries of the developing world. Such inadequate understandings of the Muslim faith have produced a vicious cycle. According to Khan, flawed and literal interpretations have led to the growth of radical groups which, through their actions and beliefs, help generate Islamophobia (fear of Islam) in western societies, mainly the United States. Prejudice, in turn, fuels more radical behavior and so the vicious cycle continues, generating a crisis-laid reality for Muslims all around the world.

In the face of the multifaceted epistemological, intellectual, and philosophical crisis plaguing Muslim communities in different ways, these five scholars have offered sophisticated and scholarly solutions that they believe could improve the socioeconomic and political status of Muslim societies while developing and building on Islamic teachings. Although the scholars differ in the focus they take and the solutions they offer, a second commonality among them can be seen. They all agree that, no matter where reform starts, it cannot happen without going back to the Qur'an and incorporating Islamic teachings in the new understandings of democracy, human rights, interfaith living, gender equality, and education. More important, it cannot happen without a *continuous* and *progressive* exegesis of the Quran and an *uninterrupted* effort at ijtihad.

For al-Alwani, a constant re-interpretation of the sources using ijtihad is the only means through which reform, progress, and revival can be achieved. Taking into account history, or what he refers to as time and space, is essential to achieve a true understanding of the Qur'an. For Wadud, a feminist and hermeneutical exegesis of the Qur'an is the only way to end gender inequality and the subordination of women to men in Muslim societies. An-Na'im similarly believes that by adopting an evolutionary approach to shari'a, scholars can abandon teachings that no longer serve a purpose in modern times and embrace the ones that have not been interpreted yet. For Rahman, rereading the Qur'an in historical order, or the order in which the verses were revealed, and taking into account context and history are crucial steps to avoid misinformation and misleading interpretations. Finally, Khan also argues for a continued process of ijtihad and an ongoing use of the sacred text and teachings of the Prophet in an effort to find common ground across religions and integrate Islamic thought and principles into the modern application of democratic ideas.

The third and final similarity found in these five scholars' work is their inclusion of a wide range of individuals—whether trained legal scholars, researchers, community leaders, community members, and/or *ulama*—in the ijtihad and exegesis process with the ultimate goal of achieving reform, revival, and integration. They all acknowledge the importance of involving a wide array of people or agents without whom the intellectual and epistemological crisis cannot end. While this can be common sense to many, the scholars discussed in this chapter are adamant about considering women (for Wadud), regular Muslim individuals and community members (Rahman and Khan), and progressive ulama (al-Alwani and an-Na'im) to be effective agents of change and reform who can significantly contribute to the reinterpretation effort and to the well-being of Muslim societies around the world. With these trends, similarities, and differences in mind, the discussion below focuses on the intellectual contributions of each scholar in his or her respective area of expertise, and details how each of them both understands the crisis present in Islamic thought and practice and suggests ways with which to solve it.

Fazlur Rahman

Fazlur Rahman was a modernist Islamic reformer and a professor at both McGill University in Canada and the University of Chicago in the 1960s and 1970s. Rahman attended Oxford University and then started his career as a professor of Persian and Islamic philosophy at Durham University before moving to McGill University and then the University of Chicago in 1969. He died in 1988. Broadly speaking, his research focused on Islamic thought and philosophy.[1] Rahman also wrote on a variety of topics including health and medicine in the Islamic tradition,[2] Islamic revival and reform,[3] philosophy and science, and the value of spirituality.[4]

Rahman's view of Islamic reform favored democracy, which he sees as closely connected to educational reform. Muslims should have the ability to vote as members of a legislative assembly so that they can have the authority to enact Islamic laws. He claims that the function of the ulama is not only to make laws and legislate but also to provide religious guidance, leadership, and the preaching of Islamic ideas to the community.[5] His version of democratic reform involves legal and political as well as spiritual and moral reforms. His inclusion of the spiritual realm stems from his view that, even with great educational reforms and scientific and technological advancements, humankind is not happy because of the general lack of faith and the absence of moral values and spirituality.

One of Rahman's greatest contributions as an American Muslim intellectual was to argue in favor of a democratic understanding of Islam and a democratic system based on an Islamic discourse. He says that "those who. . . think that the legal interpretation of Islam cannot be left to the people" (assembly members), since they are generally "ignorant of Islam," and that it is the function of the *ulama* to enact Islam into law."[6] Rahman spent the greater part of his life arguing that the spirit of Islam is democratic and that therefore Muslims, through a legislative assembly and a representative body, should get to decide what constitutes the shari'a for themselves. Rahman's conception of the shari'a comes from an understanding that it is both evolving and able to adapt in its historical and sociohistorical context.[7] He argues that there is a way to intrepret the message of Islam contained in the Qur'an, and it can be done by studying the sacred text in "historical order" in an effort to understand its various ideas. If history and context are not taken into account in studying the Qur'an, one can easily be misled and misinformed.[8]

Rahman posits that individual Muslims without specialized legal training could come to correct interpretations of the shari`a; yet at the same time he does not abandon the ulama's role completely. In a way, he is arguing in favor of Muslims' empowerment when he asserts that any Muslim can have the ability to interpret shari`a. To that end, *the ulama* and the public can work together in deciding what should be the proper understanding of shari`a. The ulama's role is to persuade the public "through discussion and debate, for there is no other way in a democratic society."[9] Thus Islamic reform must retain a democratic essence with elected officials of the assembly guiding the process and maintaining a close link with those who elected them. At the same time, the ulama must not be taken as infallible and they should serve in an advisory role.[10]

Throughout his writings, Rahman emphasizes that no reform can start or be effective without educational reform, which he believes to be the primary and only approach to solving the plethora of problems that plague the Muslim world. For educational reform to take place and if societies want to enact laws and models of ethical behavior that reflect those of the Prophet, Rahman asserts that there must be a reconnection between the life of the mind and inner spirituality.[11] In addition, Rahman believes that Islamic intellectualism is "virtually dead" because the Islamic world has had to deal with western colonialism, which has led to the rise of more Islamic fundamentalist thought and practices.[12] Islamic fundamentalist movements, he says, are a reaction against both the western world (the colonizers) and early Islamic modernism.[13] To lessen the spread of fundamentalist ideas and encourage moderate Islamic reform, the creation of "an authentic Islamic political orientation" should be established, whose foundation would be a reformed educational system and the "Muslim Community itself through interpreting the *Shari`a* democratically."[14] There would be no Caliph acting as the chief executive officer or president executing the community's will. Rather, this function would now be given to "an elected president or prime minister who enjoys the Community's mandate for a defined and restricted period of time."[15] At the center of Rahman's thought for Islamic reform is an enhanced, democratic, and free community that interprets and accepts the shari`a and elects a representative assembly. Rahman's contribution to the concept of Islamic reform and perhaps his greatest scholarly achievement is his insistence that Muslim communities can enjoy democratic and egalitarian politics where all Muslims can contribute to the power structure of their society, which they can further help to constitute. This cannot be done, however, without reforming existing institutions and integrating comprehensive Islamic and shari`a-based discourse about democracy.

TAHA JABIR AL-ALWANI

Taha Jabir al-Alwani is an Islamic scholar who has served as president of the Graduate School of Islamic Social Sciences (GSISS), the International Institute of Islamic Thought (IIIT), and the Fiqh Council of North America. Al-Alwani's historical view of ijtihad is important because it serves as a blueprint of his thinking on the central role that ijtihad can play in modern times. As he puts it, "It is *only* through *ijtihad* that Muslims will be able to construct a new specific methodological infrastructure capable of addressing the crisis of Islamic thought and so, propose alternatives for the many problems of the contemporary world."[16] This is a strong statement and one worth investigating. Why *is ijtihad* the only way forward when addressing the ongoing crisis of Islamic thought? Al-Alwani answers that it was through ijtihad that Islamic civilization achieved its Golden Age, which helped to influence the European Renaissance and other religions, leading to great scientific advancements in Europe. European scholars and thinkers made use of much of the research and knowledge available in the universities of the Muslim world and Muslim Spain. Without this existing knowledge, they would not have been able to develop their own theories and inventions. Earlier in their history Muslim thinkers practiced ijtihad, which allowed for a constant generation of new ideas, theories, and knowledge.[17]

　　Al-Alwani argues that Muslim thinkers and scientists today should resort to the basic principles laid down by Islam and discussed by Muslim thinkers in order to "revitalize contemporary Islamic thought and sciences, in a renewed effort to organize contemporary life."[18] Indeed, the enemy of ijtihad which caused the decline of Islamic civilization, according to Al-Alwani, is taqlid (the blind imitation of religious leaders). He argues that, historically, the *ummah* (Muslim people as a whole) started to face an ongoing crisis after it stopped using ijtihad and replaced it with taqlid.[19] Ijtihad, therefore, becomes an absolute necessity and the key to reform, revival, freedom, and salvation.[20] It is "incumbent upon the *ulama* [Islamic legal scholars] to practice *ijtihad* and respond to the needs of [this] time."[21] To achieve genuine reform and progress, al-Alwani stresses the importance of thought and reason. He argues that "the human mind is the only instrument, a responsible and accountable one … [to] understand human nature and cosmic laws.… Moreover reason is a tool for understanding [revelation and the objective world] and thus for promoting civilizational progress."[22] To al-Alwani, the ulama, armed with their ability to reason, are the true agents of change.

In addition, al-Alwani emphasizes the importance of context and history when understanding the Qur'an and Islamic teachings. He argues that in order to incorporate ijtihad, Muslims must locate the meaning of the holy text within the "time-space factor." This means that Muslim scholars in particular must understand that "time constantly travels forward, making it impossible for situations or events to recur in exactly the same way."[23] For example, what was used as a proposal in Madinah by Imam Malik and his contemporaries 1,400 years ago would be impossible to impose on today's Muslims.[24] Considering the time-space factor means that one cannot take sayings of the Prophet literally as instructions for Muslims for today. Thus when the Prophet Muhammad ordered zakāt (to give charity to the poor) by giving up "a measure of dates, barley, corn or rice," some Muslims took it literally to mean that this was the only charitable giving they could or should provide.[25] Al-Alwani's form of ijtihad would allow zakāt to be interpreted practically rather than literally. This response to zakāt shows the necessity of using ijtihad to bring about commonsense solutions that are equally adaptable to contemporary times.[26] In addition, Al-Alwani argues for another common sense measure, that of using science (by way of the NASA scientists) to figure out when the moon appears at the beginning of Ramadan, rather than insisting that one must see the moon with the naked eye before one can break the fast for the day.[27] Both of these examples show the method of ijtihad in practice as opposed to literal interpretation of the sayings of the Prophet.

Al-Alwani's emphasis on the importance of ijtihad stems from his personal world view. He laments that the Muslim world is stuck in literal interpretations of Islam that promote neither progress nor development. To him, focusing on smaller elements of the faith such as what form the zakāt should come in or the actual sighting of the moon for Ramadan really do not matter as much as the fact that the Muslim world is failing to address "fundamental ethical, political and economic issues,"[28] such as hunger disease, war, and the absence of socioeconomic rights. According to Al-Alwani, it is this shortsighted theological understanding of Islam that is at the root of the political and economic problems that the Muslim world faces today. It is a crisis of thought that needs an Islamic reformation if things are to change for the better.

Al-Alwani promotes ijtihad in all human fields, including the economy. He posits that because ijtihad is not used, capital markets today are devoid of any ethics or religious consideration. The economic and intellectual heritage of the Muslim world could inform sound economic behavior, but it has not been given the opportunity to do so yet.[29] This absence of ijtihad in the economic and financial realms is another reason why economic problems plague the Muslim world. Commenting on neoliberalism as the main economic system used in the West, Al-Alwani argues that its philosophical grounding is based on psychological egoism and self-interest alone. Instead, he is in favor of markets based on Islamic economic principles:

> Islamic economics [however] recognizes that man's will is capable of moral heroism in positive mode.... Confident generosity is therefore the opposite of egoism, avarice and meanness; We do not love truth and the good just because we want to gain something.... Every action or desire is centered on God with Truth as the motivating cause.... Hence, neoclassical economics can be seen as a false religion based on the crucial error that the relative is absolute in the form of utility. It is a parody and inversion of revelation, and is diametrically opposed to Islamic economics.[30]

Finally, the last underpinning of Al-Alwani's thought is his promotion of what Ismail al-Faruqi calls the "Islamization of knowledge" which should not be limited to one field but rather be defined as a general search for truth in the sciences and philosophy while staying connected and *reconnected* to a search for the Divine Will as provided in the Islamic tradition. Al-Alwani's work pushes Muslims to practice, or repractice, ijtihad at all levels of human life and activity, including economics and science, in an effort to move past the current problems facing the Muslim world and achieve true reform and revival.

Amina Wadud

Amina Wadud is an American Muslim scholar whose pioneering work focuses on issues of gender inequality and women's rights within Islam. Wadud also gained some notoriety for leading a controversial mixed-gender Friday prayer (*salat*) on March 18, 2005, in New York City's Synod House of the Cathedral of Saint John the Divine to a congregation of 100 people, almost half of whom were men.[31] Many religious leaders criticized her decision to serve as the spiritual leader of a mixed-gender Friday prayer, arguing that it is improper for Muslim women to preach to male audiences.[32] Yet, Amina Wadud's bold move, intellectual contributions, Qur'anic analyses, and ongoing activism underscore her contention that through a progressive, continuous, and hermeneutical *tafsir* (exegesis) of the Qur'an, social injustice, gender inequality, patriarchy, discrimination, subordination, segregation, and prejudice do not have a place within the Muslim faith.

Wadud's seminal book, *Qur'an and Woman: Re-reading the Sacred Text from a Woman's Perspective* (1992), offers a feminist evaluation of the Qur'an in an attempt to reshape interpretations that have been offered by male Islamic scholars and thinkers. She is concerned with fundamental elements of tafsir (interpretation), mainly "*what* the Quran says, *how* it says it, what is said *about* the Quran, and *who* is doing the saying" italics in original.[33] Using a hermeneutical model, she outlines three main factors that influence the current understandings of the faith and argues that, by paying attention to context, grammar, and worldview (*weltanschauung*), flawed and hierarchical understandings of the roles and positions of women can be changed to reflect the true values of Islam. According to Wadud, these "extrahistorical and transcendental"[34] values are "justice among humankind, human dignity, equal rights before the law and Allah, mutual responsibility, and equitable relations between humans."[35]

The first factor that her book outlines is context. Wadud echoes al-Alwani's belief in the importance of context if one wishes to avoid narrow explanations and renditions. Thus if one is aware of the fact that a text was written in a specific place, at a specific time, and in a specific context, then one can escape from making generalizations about the text or the interpretation's message. Second, Wadud discusses the relevance of language and grammar in exegesis. She outlines the difficulty of conceptualizing Allah and his messages with limited linguistic abilities. Given the shortcomings of language and in this case, the gendered grammar of the Arabic, words take on specific genders, which literal interpretations then accept and perpetuate. To take Qur'anic interpretations as gender-specific is to risk accepting and justifying the superiority of one gender over another. Deconstructing the Arabic language and freeing it from its gendered grammar would help lead to impartial, fair, and just interpretations that can have universal meanings.

The third and final factor that Wadud looks at is world view. In *Qur'an and Woman* she argues that the way one conceives of the Qur'an influences one's interpretations. Hence, when one acknowledges that the Qur'an promotes and emphasizes the values of justice, equality, and dignity, any interpretation that hints at inequality between the genders, hierarchy, and patriarchy is not supported by the text itself. Given the sacred text's equitable nature, it does not delineate, assign, or distinguish different roles to be played by women and men and does not recognize a natural hierarchy between the genders. Any Qur'anic interpretation that favors the subordination of women would be false because it goes against the text itself.

Wadud continues her feminist exegesis by breaking down words, outlining grammatical and gender-specific terms, and studying contexts in three specific themes: the story of creation, the afterlife, and women's representation in the Qur'an. Wadud studies the terms used to describe the story of creation such as *min* (from), *nafs* (soul), and *zawj* (pair, spouse) and finds that the story is "not expressed in gender terms"[36] and that both woman and man are together the first "parents" to be created by Allah.[37] Then by examining the theme of the afterlife, Wadud emphasizes the limits posed by language in describing the experience of life after death. Here, she deconstructs the verse relating to faithful men being given *houri* (heavenly virgins) after they die and analyzes the social context of this particular revelation. She argues that this verse is not meant to give unfair rewards to men in the afterlife but that it was revealed in the way it was to convince certain political leaders to join Islam.[38]

Finally, regarding women's representation in the Qur'an, Wadud posits that the "Qur'an does not support a specific and stereotyped role for its characters, male and female"[39] and, again, that one should pay attention to context. Indeed, women-related examples given in the sacred text are not intended to be universal guidelines to be applied everywhere and to everyone, regardless of time and place, but they serve as context-based instances to explain universal and essential directives. The examples of roles played by certain women in the Qur'an should be understood in their specific social and cultural context or should be looked at as gender-neutral functions that could have been done by anyone else but that happened to be done by women.[40]

Wadud also sets out to deconstruct Verse 4:34 of the Qur'an, *Surat An-Nisa'* in an effort to dispel the male-based interpretations of the verse that have justified and favored women's subordination to men.[41] Wadud takes issue with the way the first part of the verse has been interpreted to mean that men are in control and in charge of women. The expression *qawwamun 'ala*, which was translated and interpreted to mean "in control," perpetuates the norm that women are inferior to men and justifies violence against women who transgress. By problematizing the expression *qawwamun 'ala*, Wadud favors translating the term to mean "guidance" instead of control.[42] Guidance is not limited to financial support but can include other areas of family life, such as parental support. Wadud wants to show that by adopting a more positive translation and explanation of a term, a more equitable translation of the verse can then be offered. Regarding the second part of the verse, Wadud finds issue with the way the verb *daraba* (to strike or hit) has been translated and used in the case of female disobedience and favors a nonviolent interpretation of daraba and a peaceful way to resolve marital disputes that does not include hitting or beating women.

In her 1995 article "Towards a Qur'anic Hermeneutics of Social Justice: Race, Class, and Gender," Wadud uses a hermeneutical approach to study what the Qur'an has to say about the role of women. Here again, she is critical of the fact that Qur'anic interpretations have been made by men and argues that the message of the Qur'an diverges from how Muslim societies have evolved. Thus, by using a methodology based on *tafsir al-Qur'an bi al-Qur'an* (interpreting the Qur'an through the Qur'an), Wadud looks at the sacred text from a female perspective.

Amina Wadud's scholarly work, textual exegesis, and activism provide a platform for reforming patriarchal and hierarchical interpretations and laws that have not benefited women in the past.[43] Through her hermeneutical study of the Qur'an and other works, she offers a solid critique of male-dominant structures and social inequalities as they have been perpetuated in Muslim societies. Wadud contributes to the global discourse on women's rights, gender equality, and social justice through a progressive re--exegesis of Islam. More importantly, she stresses the importance of considering gender in Islam as a "category of thought—not just a subject for discourse,"[44] that would give women the agency and ability to participate in the construction of their own spiritual, moral, social, economic, and political directives and postulates. To her, Muslim women should act as dynamic agents in offering new interpretations of Qur'anic verses.

ABDULLAHI AHMED AN-NAʿIM

Abdullahi Ahmed An-Naʿim is the Charles Howard Candler Professor of Law at Emory University School of Law, having received his Ph.D. in the study of law from the University of Edinburgh in Scotland. He is also a faculty affiliate at the Emory University Center for Ethics.[45] Al-Naʿim has served as director of the Religion and Human Rights Program at Emory and the executive director of the African bureau of Human Rights Watch. A strong advocate of Islamic reform,[46] he has argued in favor of the universality of human rights as an Islamic principle.[47] He has also advocated against seeing religion, secularism, and universal human rights as dichotomous or incompatible. An-Naʿim is a known scholar in the fields of international law, human rights, comparative law, and Islamic law and has written on constitutionalism in Islamic and African countries.[48] His current research projects include the study of American Muslims, the secular state, human rights, and universality and sovereignty.[49] In his 2008 volume, he further develops his theory of Islam and the secular state.[50] In all of his writings over the last twenty years he makes the case for global justice in the Islamic context.[51]

An-Naʿim was born in 1946 in Sudan. Many of his ideas were profoundly influenced by the Islamic reformer Mahmoud Mohamed Taha, the founder of the Republican Brotherhood, who at the age of seventy-six was arrested and executed by the Sudanese government for his religious views (in which he called for the end of shariʿa law). An-Naʿim involved himself in the public affairs of Sudan, and his experiences as a student and lawyer shaped his thinking. As a law student at the University of Khartoum in the late 1960s he attended many lectures given by Taha and joined him in his house for informal discussions. Taha's landmark book *The Second Message of Islam* so influenced al-Naʿim that by early 1968 he formally joined the Republican Brotherhood.[52] Taha and thirty other Republican leaders, including An-Naʿim, were interned without charge for about a year and a half. Taha was released briefly in late 1984 only to be arrested again and publicly executed in January 1985. As Naʿim relates it, he "took the lead in negotiating the release of as many as four hundred members" but he was "not able to secure the pardon of his teacher."[53]

Since that time An-Naʿim has stated that it is his prerogative and duty to develop the initial teachings of Taha, not merely to reform Islamic law but to transform how Muslims understand the basic foundations of the law. He argues for the reform methodology of Taha, which he describes as "the evolution of Islamic legislation, in essence a call for the establishment of a new principle of interpretation that would permit applying some verses of Qur'an and accompanying Sunna instead of others."[54] An-Naʿim goes on to argue that "if accepted and implemented by Muslims today, [this new principle] would succeed in breaking the deadlock between the objectives of reform and the limitations of the conception and techniques of historical Shariʿa."[55] To him, reinterpretations of Qur'anic verses can bring religion and reform together.

An-Na'im is against the type of secularism that regulates religion outside the discussion of political life, arguing that shari'a can be restored as a liberating influence in the lives of Muslims rather than an oppressive influence over them.[56] Further, he argues for the religious neutrality of the state as being a requirement for the future and for the ongoing development of shari'a law.[57] Al-Na'im gives both a pragmatic and a moral reason for including religion in public life. As he posits it, Islam and spirituality are valuable resources and underpinnings in how Muslims develop their identities. Thus it is not likely that Muslims would be in favor of a secular system and a public life devoid of religion and moral codes.

While Al-Na'im believes that many aspects of the Shari'a are unachievable, he does not believe that secularism holds the answer. Instead, he discusses the process of *naskh* (abrogation or repeal) of certain texts to produce a "coherent and comprehensive system of shari'a which is consistent with the totality of the Qur'an and Sunna."[58] Introducing what he calls the "the evolutionary approach" using naskh,[59] he explains that:

> "Evolutionary principle of interpretation is nothing more than reversing the process of *naskh* or abrogation so that those texts which were abrogated in the past can be enacted into law now, with the consequent abrogation of texts that used to be enacted as Shari'a. Verses that used to be enacted as Shari'a shall be *repealed*, and verses that used to be *repealed* shall be *enacted* as modern Islamic law.... I submit that a system of public law based on the Qur'an and Sunna, albeit "not necessarily the classical medieval Shari'a," would be the modern "Shari'a." [60]

Al-Na'im thinks that by relying on Taha's evolutionary principle of interpretation for *naskh*, Muslims can, for example, overrule a statute of the shari'a that was formulated in the 7th century and is no longer relevant to modern times. He argues that the purpose and development of shari'a is based on this process: shifting from a text that is no longer relevant or applicable to one whose purpose had been postponed and unused until the present day. The evolution of shari'a is necessary and does not mean that the ulama must change their opinions on certain matters. On the contrary, it is a mature process of using different texts at different times.[61] Inasmuch as criticism of the shari'a is considered by many Muslims to be heretical, An-Na'im argues that one must demonstrate that the laws emanating from shari'a are not really divine "in the sense of being the direct and invariable will of God."[62] Seen under this light, one can open up a space in talking to fellow Muslims and show that it is not "heresy" to develop and discuss Islamic laws.[63]

In addition to his views on shari'a, An-Na'im has written extensively on his conception of global justice and universal human rights, which he believes are compatible with Islam. An-Na'im argues that the United Nations' human rights discourse or platform is the "effective framework for global justice" and is "contingent on" whether such rights retain their universality. He argues that human rights are not merely rights of the citizens of a particular country but supersede that standard and become universal human rights for all people everywhere, regardless of country and place. To that end, An-Na'im posits that paying less attention to the importance and application of state sovereignty and citizenship rights and thinking in more regional and global terms can result in a general and universal application of human rights everywhere. An-Naim is aware of the peculiarities of cultures and societies and emphasizes the importance of economic, social, and cultural rights to be interpreted by each society on its own.

An-Na'im's view of the universality of human rights is directly related to his interpretation of Islam. He recounts the story of Prophet Muhammad having told his followers to "support the aggressor as well as the victim."[64] The Prophet's followers were confused as to how they should support an aggressor. The Prophet then responded by telling his followers to "drive the aggressor back from his aggression."[65] An-Na'im claims that we can "drive back the aggressor" by "collective action of the international community" through "lawful institutional mechanisms of justice and accountability... not by arbitrary self-help and vigilante justice."[66]

At first it may seem that implementing global justice within the idea of universality itself might go against cultural and religious differences. However, An-Naim believes that humans can develop a general consensus on the principles that they agree on universally. With that said, An-Naim believes that people "do not need to have the same reasons for sharing that view"[67] but that all people can agree to certain standards of behavior that are more similar than different. The more multilateral and globally inclusive the source of the norm is and the more consistently we apply the norms to ourselves, the more the other will be motivated to change the "offending practices" that go against universal human rights.[68] An-Na'im believes that focusing on Islamic reform using evolutionary and continuous interpretations of shari`a and Qur'an could transform the Islamic world without getting caught up in the debates regarding secularism versus religious fundamentalism.

M.A. MUQTEDAR KHAN

Four main themes emerge and intertwine in the scholarly and intellectual work of American Muslim scholar Muqtedar Khan: Islam and democracy, interfaith dialogue and Islamophobia in the United States, and American foreign policy in the Muslim world. An associate professor in the Department of Political Science at the University of Delaware since 2005 and director of its Islamic Studies program, Khan received his Ph.D. in international relations and islamic thought from Georgetown University in 2000. In addition to his extensive publications, Khan is a dynamic blogger,[69] a frequent radio and television commentator, and an engaged activist who has given numerous talks and lectures to Muslim, Christian, and Jewish audiences and communities all around the United States about interfaith dialogue, intercommunal living, and US foreign policy in the Middle East. Khan is generally recognized as an important contributor to the development of progressive and liberal understandings of Islamic thought and practice.

In his first book, *American Muslims: Bridging Faith and Freedom* (2002), Khan posits that Muslim Americans are in a perfect position to prove that Islam is not antiwestern or undemocratic. On the contrary, by participating in the US political system and being politically active, which Khan encourages, American Muslims can prove to themselves and the rest of the world that Islam is a moderate, equitable, and tolerant religion. Khan believes this to be an important task that should be fulfilled by American Muslims, who are well placed to influence the future and well-being of Muslim societies around the world.[70] To achieve that, Khan pushes for a reinterpretation and a progressive exegesis of the Qur'an and Sunna, for a continuous ijtihad, and for the development of a new discourse and a newly constructed Muslim identity, the "self." In this he is arguing against what he sees among fellow Muslims as rejection of western values simply on the basis that they are un-Islamic. It is the duty of American Muslims, because of the possibilities and freedom given to them by an open social and political system, to take charge of developing a good understanding of the West, of the "self," and of how Muslims can thrive and prosper within a western society.

Khan's arguments are echoed again in his article "American Muslims: In Search of a Third Way." In the wake of the 9/11 terrorist attacks, American Muslims found themselves having to defend their religion and assets against a prejudiced and strong public backlash. They were caught between an outright rejection of terrorism and the beliefs of Bin Laden's al Qaeda and a staunch opposition to the interventionist domestic (Patriot Act) and foreign policies of the George W. Bush administration, namely the 2001 Afghanistan War and the 2003 Iraq War. Khan argues that in the face of such pressure, the American Muslim community needs to find "a third way."[71] Even though he does not specify what the third way would actually be, Khan hints that the American Muslim community once again, with the help of academics and intellectuals, needs to redefine itself away from the "Islam versus the West" discourse and affirm its presence as a prosperous, educated, and engaged community.

Khan's emphasis on a continuous reinterpretation of the Qur'an within the American Muslim community assumes a more practical side when he encourages Muslims to stay engaged and patient in the face of controversial events and Islamophobia. In a conference presentation in 2006, Khan asserted that anti-American feelings in the Muslim world are a response to American foreign policy in the Middle East, mainly American support of Israel, the weak commitment of the United States to building a viable Palestinian state, and the two US wars on Afghanistan and Iraq in 2001 and 2003 respectively. Interestingly, he contrasts anti-Americanism, which he believes to be purely political and in reaction to certain policies and events, with Islamophobia in the United States, which he believes to be irrational and in reaction to Islam and Muslims in general. Khan posits that Islamophobic attitudes against American Muslims anger Muslims and push radicals and extremists to react violently, which in

turn, increases Islamophobia in the United States.[72] It is a vicious cycle that perpetuates negative opinions of Muslims and their beliefs.

Khan's second edited volume, *Islamic Democratic Discourse: Theory, Debates, and Philosophical Perspectives* (2006), analyzes the efforts of Muslim countries to reconcile Islamic thought with the practice of democracy, good self-governance, political
reform, and modernity.[73] The book discusses how, after gaining independence in the
twentieth century, former colonies in the Muslim world struggled to discover a stable
and thriving political model and found that traditional epistemological models of
Islamic thought were inadequate to build new social structures and to "comprehend
and negotiate the new realities of modernity."[74] This new shift is forcing Islamic thinkers and scholars to engage in new epistemological debates and to redefine what they
know in light of political instability, violence, and reform. The book brings together
various Muslim scholars and political philosophers with the aim of debating how
Islam can engage with various theories and aspects of democracy, both from a theoretical and empirical standpoint.[75]

All in all, the various contributions of the volume, under Khan's direction, present compelling arguments that reject the various criticisms that some Islamic thinkers have voiced about democracy and delve into studies of shari`a, legal practices,
early writings of Islamic scholars, classical Islamic sources, and present-day politics
in countries such as Malaysia and Turkey to try and find an acceptable governance
structure within the Islamic discourse. They all agree that it is indeed possible to
develop new democratic structures guided by Islamic principles and laws. They
also agree, perhaps influenced by Khan's own thinking and by the other scholars
mentioned in this chapter, that evolution in the way Muslim scholars think and a
progressive and continual exegesis of the Qur'an and other sources is crucial. New
interpretations and methods are "not a modification of the sources, but a transformation of the mind and eyes that read them, which are indeed naturally influenced
by the new social, political and scientific environment in which they live,"[76] even if
they lead to disagreements and divergent opinions about the best governance system
within an Islamic democratic discourse.

With that said, the authors believe that different communities and generations will
develop new ways of adapting Islamic law and practice to the peculiarities of their
own times as long as they remain morally and spiritually bound to the principles of
the Qur'an and Sunna. The authors also agree, in accordance with Khan's previous
assertions, that educated and well-trained scholars and intellectuals in each community should contribute to this debate in an effort to "determine what is best for individuals and for the community. . ., to enjoin good and proscribe evil."[77] Here again, the
burden is placed on the shoulders of scholars and intellectuals to drive discussions of
reform further.

One such debate is about interfaith dialogue and the place of shari`a in the US
legal system. Here too Khan's intellectual contributions and analyses influence his
commitment to enhancing intercommunal living in the United States. He merges

the various themes that shape his scholarly work (Islam and democracy, interfaith dialogue, and US foreign policy) in his recommendations. For instance, following remarks by Oklahoma and Tennessee politicians about banning shari`a law in US states in 2010, Khan recognized that such prejudiced rhetoric might stem from uninformed fatwas emerging from certain places in the Muslim world. Nonetheless, he made the argument that there are many similarities between the principles of shari`a and the Ten Commandments and that "Islamic *Sharia* is based on the same principles [as] Judeo-Christian values."[78] His novel approach to explaining Islamic law to non-Muslims argues that the fundamentals of shari`a are *tawhid* (oneness/monotheism) and *adl* (justice), fundamentals on which Christianity and Judaism are also built.

Additionally, by elaborating on the Bible's Ten Commandments as being the normative underpinnings of Judeo-Christian value systems and finding them in the Qur'an, Khan makes a good case for accepting shari`a as another set of principles that condition human behavior. He finds that the same commandments that inform Christian behavior are present in the Qur'an, albeit in different wording. For example, the first three commandments in the Bible taken together say: "I am your Lord, the one true God and you shall take no God before me. You shall not make idols or images of God and you shall not take the Lord's name in vain." Khan finds the same basic message in the Qur'an. "And your God is one god and he is most Compassionate and Merciful (Quran 2:163), Do not take other Gods other than Allah; Indeed idolatry is a great sin (Quran 31:13). Do not swear by Allah in vain (Quran 2:224)."[79] Other commandments in the Bible talk of honoring one's parents and forbid crimes such as stealing, killing, and committing adultery. They are revealed in the Qur'an as well, as "Quran forbids the taking of life except as justice for crimes (Qur'an 17:33), it forbids stealing and punishes it with amputation (Quran 5:38), and Islam forbids unlawful sexual intercourse as evil (Qur'an 17:32)."[80]

CONCLUSION

Taken together, the large body of work produced by Taha Jabir al-Alwani, Amina Wadud, Abdullahi Ahmed An-Na'im, Fazlur Rahman, and M. A. Muqtedar Khan provides a solid foundation for discussing and developing new understandings of legal reform, democracy, human rights, gender equality, interfaith dialogue and living, and modernity through the eyes of Islam. While these debates continue in American academic circles and beyond, it is important to note how these five scholars consider general topics from different approaches and how they recommend that other scholars think about them. They all acknowledge that a crisis of thought does indeed exist and was created owing the absence of ijtihad. Moreover, social, economic, and political problems plague the Muslim world and Muslim communities in the West, and these problems are partly engendered by taqlid and a reliance on old interpretations of the Qur'an. Through their extensive writings and community engagements, these scholars posit that reform, justice, and integration (in the case of Muslims living in non-Muslim countries) cannot and will not happen if Muslim scholars and intellectuals do not drive these debates forward, starting by progressive exegetical exercises and reopening the doors of ijtihad.

NOTES

1. Rahman, Fazlur, *Philosophy, Science and Other Essays* (Pakistan Philosophical Congress, Publication number 9, 1961), 9.
2. Rahman, Fazlur *Heath and Medicine in the Islamic Tradition*, (Crossroad Publishing, 1987).
3. Rahman, Fazlur, *Revival and Reform in Islam*, (Revival and Reform in Islam, 2000).
4. Rahman, *Philosophy, Science*.
5. Rahman, Fazlur. *Islam* (Chicago: University of Chicago Press, 1966), 261.
6. Ibid., 261.
7. Ibid., 260–261.
8. Ibid., 261.
9. Ibid., 262.
10. Ibid., 263.
11. Ibid.
12. Ibid. 264, 265.
13. Ibid., 265.
14. Ibid.
15. Ibid.
16. Taha Jabir Al-Alwani, *Ijtihad: Occasional Papers 4*, International Institute of Islamic Thought, p. 31, 1993. Emphasis added.
17. Ibid.
18. Ibid.
19. Ibid.
20. Ibid., 20.
21. Ibid., 21
22. Ibid, 22.
23. Ibid., 24–25.
24. Ibid., 25.
25. Ibid., 25–26.
26. Ibid., 26.
27. Ibid., 27.
28. Ibid, 28–29.
29. Taha Jabir Al-Alwani and Waleed Adel El-Ansary, *Linking Ethics and Economics: The Role of Ijtihad in the Regulation and Correction of Capital Markets* (Washington, DC: Center for Muslim-Christian Understanding: History and International Affairs, Georgetown University, 1999): 1.
30. Ibid, 70, 72–74.

31. Andrea Elliott, *"Woman Leads Muslim Prayer Service in New York,"* New York Times, March 19, 2005. Available at http://www.nytimes.com/2005/03/19/nyregion/19muslim. html?_r=0

32. "Woman Leads US Muslims to prayer," BBC News, March 18, 2005. Available at http:// news.bbc.co.uk/2/hi/americas/4361931.stm

33. Wadud, A., preface to the second edition of *Quran and Woman: Rereading the Sacred Text from a Woman's Perspective* (Oxford University Press: 1999).

34. Wadud, A. *Quran and Woman: Rereading the Sacred Text from a Woman's Perspective*, 1992: p. 29

35. Wadud, 1992: p. 63

36. Wadud, 1992: p. 20

37. Wadud, 1992: p. 16

38. Wadud, 1992: p. 55

39. Wadud, 1992: p. 29

40. Wadud, 1992: p. 29

41. Surat An-Nisa', or Verse 4:34 in the Quran, relates to marital issues between women and men.

42. Wadud, 1992: p. 71

43. "Interview: Amina Wadud," Frontline, March 2002. Retrieved from: www.pbs.org/wgbb/ pages/frontline/shows/muslims/interviews/wadud.html

44. Wadud, 1998, preface to the 2nd edition

45. Abdullahi Ahmed An-Na'im's Faculty Profile at Emory University http://www.law.emory. edu/faculty/faculty-profiles/abdullahi-ahmed-an-naim.html

46. Abdullahi Ahmed An-Na'im, *Toward an Islamic Reformation*, (Syracuse University Press, 1990).

47. Abdullahi Ahmed An-Na'im, "Islamic Foundations of Religious Human Rights," in *Human Rights and Religious Values*, (Martinus Nijhoff Publishers, 1996), 339.

48. Abdullahi Ahmed An-Na'im, *Human Rights Under African Constitutions*, (University of Pennsylvania Press, 2003), 1–28.

49. Abdullahi Ahmed An-Na'im's Faculty Profile at Emory University http://www.law.emory. edu/faculty/faculty-profiles/abdullahi-ahmed-an-naim.html

50. Abdullahi Ahmed An-Na'im, *Islam and the Secular State*, (Harvard University Press, 2008).

51. Abdullahi Ahmed An-Na'im, *Muslims and Global Justice*, (University of Pennsylvania Press, 2011).

52. An-Na'im, *Toward an Islamic* 1990, xi.

53. Ibid,, xi–xii.

54. Ibid.,34.

55. Ibid., 34–35.

56. Ibids, 290, 293.

57. Ibid.

58. Ibid., 49.

59. Ibids, 50–51.

60. Ibid, emphasis added.

61. Ibid., 60.

62. Ibid., 67–68.

63. Ibid

64. An-Na'im, *Muslims and Global Justice*, 13.
65. Ibid
66. Ibid
67. Ibids, 16.
68. Ibid.
69. In addition to his active use of social media platforms such as Facebook, Khan's personal websites are: www.ijtihad.org and www.glocaleye.org
70. Khan, M. A. Muqtedar, *"American Muslims: Bridging Faith and Freedom,"* Amana Publications, 2002
71. Khan, M.A. Muqtedar, "American Muslims: In Search of a Third Way," retrieved from: http://www.ijtihad.org/AM911.htm
72. Author notes, Newark, DE. Khan's remarks were part of a conference presentation he gave on the topic of "State of US-Islamic World Relations" on May 16, 2006 at the University of Delaware.
73. Khan, M. A. Muqtedar (ed.), *"Islamic Democratic Discourse: Theory, Debates, and Philosophical Perspectives,"* Lexington Books: Oxford, UK, 2006
74. Khan 2006, p. 11
75. Contributions to the book were made by scholars such as Asma Asfaruddin, Tariq Ramadan, March Lynch, Muqtedar Khan, and Abudlaziz Sachedina, to name but a few.
76. Tariq Ramadan, "Ijtihad and Maslaha: The Foundations of Governance," in *Islamic Democratic Discourse: Theory, Debates, and Philosophical Perspectives*, Khan, Muqtedar M.A. (ed), 2006
77. Tamara Sonn, "Elements of Government in Classical Islam," *Islamic Democratic Discourse: Theory, Debates, and Philosophical Perspectives*, Khan, Muqtedar M.A. (ed), 2006
78. Khan, M. A. Muqtedar, *"Sharia is based on Ten Commandments,"* The Washington Post, July 26, 2010, retrieved from: http://newsweek.washingtonpost.com/onfaith/panelists/muqtedar_khan/2010/07/islamic_shariah_is_based_on_the_ten_commandments.html
79. Ibid
80. Ibid

Bibliography

Al-Alwani, Taha Jabir. *Ijtihad: Occasional Papers 4*. International Institute of Islamic Thought, Herndon, VA: 1993.

——, *Occasional Papers 8: The Islamization of Knowledge: Yesterday and Today* (International Institute of Islamic Thought, 1995).

——, *Linking Ethics and Economics: The Role of Ijtihad in the Regulation and Correction of Capital Markets* (Wahsington, DC: Georgetown University, 1999).

An-Na'im, Abdullahi Ahmed, *Toward an Islamic Reformation*. (Syracuse, NY: Syracuse University Press, 1990).

——, *Human Rights and Religious Values*. With Gort, J.D, Jansen, H., & Vroom H.M. Grand Rapids, MI: William B. Eerdmans Publishing Company, 1995

——, Human Rights Under African Constitutions (Philadelphia: University of Pennsylvania Press, 2003).

——, *Islam and the Secular State* (Cambridge, MA: Harvard University Press, 2008).

——, *Muslims and Global Justice* (Philadelphia: University of Pennsylvania Press, 2011).

Elliott, Andrea, "Woman Leads Muslim Prayer Service in New York." *New York Times*, March 19, 2005. Available at http://www.nytimes.com/2005/03/19/nyregion/19muslim. html?_r=0

"Interview: Amina Wadud," *Frontline*, March 2002. Available at www.pbs.org/wgbb/pages/ frontline/shows/muslims/interviews/wadud.html

Khan, Muqtedar M. A., *American Muslims: Bridging Faith and Freedom.* (Amana Publications, Beltsville, MA: 2002).

——,*American Muslims: In Search of a Third Way.* 2002. Available at http://www.ijtihad.org/ AM911.htm

——, (ed.). *Islamic Democratic Discourse: Theory, Debates, and Philosophical Perspectives* (Oxford, UK: Lexington Books, 2006).

——, "Sharia Is based on Ten Commandments." *Washington Post*, July 26, 2010. Available at   http://newsweek.washingtonpost.com/onfaith/panelists/muqtedar_khan/2010/07/ islamic_shariah_is_based_on_the_ten_commandments.html

Rahman, Fazlur, *Health and Medicine in the Islamic Tradition* (New York, NY: Crossroad Publishing Company, 1987).

——, *Philosophy, Science, and Other Essays* (Pakistani Philosophical Congress, 1961): publication number 9.

——, *Islam* (Chicago: University of Chicago Press, 1966).

——, *Revival and Reform in Islam* (Oxford, UK: Oneworld. 2000).

Ramadan, Tariq, "Ijtihad and Maslaha: The Foundations of Governance," in *Islamic Democratic Discourse: Theory, Debates, and Philosophical Perspectives*, edited by Muqtedar M.A. Khan (Oxford, UK: Lexington Books, 2006).

Sonn, Tamara, "Elements of Government in Classical Islam," in *Islamic Democratic Discourse: Theory, Debates, and Philosophical Perspectives*, edited by Muqtedar M.A. Khan (Oxford, UK: Lexington Books, 2006).

Wadud, Amina, *Qur'an and Woman.* (Kuala Lumpur: Fajar Bakti 1992).

——, "Towards a Qur'anic Hermeneutics of Social Justice: Race, Class and Gender," *Journal of Law and Religion* 12, No. 1 (1995).

——, *Quran and Woman: Re-reading the Sacred Text from a Woman's Perspective* (Oxford, UK: Oxford University Press, 1999).

"Woman Leads US Muslims to prayer," *BBC News*, March 18, 2005. Available at http://news. bbc.co.uk/2/hi/americas/4361931.stm

CHAPTER 21

MUSLIM–CHRISTIAN RELATIONS IN THE UNITED STATES

PETER MAKARI

"Most people today see a heavy and dangerous storm of tensions between Christians and Muslims that is menacing the world.... But many of us sense a new wind of hope beginning to blow.

—Miroslav Volf[1]

"Christian leaders who don't understand or who even fear Islam would do well to engage local Muslim leaders...in an open and good-spirited dialogue."

—Imam Faisal Abdul Raouf[2]

PESSIMISM or optimism? Fear and mistrust, or engagement and commitment? In the United States today, it is possible—indeed accurate—to characterize Muslim–Christian relations with an array of descriptors, covering the full range of the spectrum of possibilities. By reading and watching media reports, one finds sufficient and significant episodes of conflict between members of the two faith communities to bode ominously for the future. Among those who are active practitioners of dialogue, however, there are many constructive efforts and initiatives that offer hope for improved understanding and effective community building. In a society as complex and diverse as the United States, it would be dangerous to attempt to understand Muslim–Christian relations as simply positive or negative or even to characterize trends in dialogue and relationships as polarized. In addition to domestic complexities, what happens in the United States does not necessarily stay here, and what happens beyond this country's borders can and does have a deep impact on interfaith relations in the United States. This chapter examines the current context of Muslim–Christian dialogue in the United States, suggesting the context for both tension and positive engagement. It explores the intersection of the US domestic context and the global context to demonstrate that each impacts the other in contexts of Muslim–Christian dialogue, and that events in either setting have significant influence on the other. Finally, the chapter provides examples of initiatives that offer hope for relations and dialogue between American Muslims and American Christians. Indeed, in spite of the hope and challenges, much is taking place that does not receive adequate attention.

"New Beginnings": President Obama's Speech

On June 4, 2009, President Barack Obama made a highly anticipated speech at Cairo University entitled, "Remarks on a New Beginning." The speech was significant for its setting in the heart of the Arab world, in a city deeply rooted historically as a center of Islamic learning. It was heard locally by Egyptians as well as globally—instantly—as it was broadcast live and available via the internet. The purported theme of the speech was to reboot relations between the United States and the Muslim world, as relations that had been fraught with an overriding tension in the wake of the attacks of September 11, 2001 and subsequent US military campaigns in Afghanistan and Iraq. The president seemed to want to extend a hand and offer a way forward that would generate goodwill instead of angst. President Obama began by stating,

> We meet at a time of great tension between the United States and Muslims around the world—tension rooted in historical forces that go beyond any current policy debate. The relationship between Islam and the West includes centuries of coexistence and cooperation, but also conflict and religious wars.… I've come here to Cairo to seek a new beginning between the United States and Muslims around the world, one based on mutual interest and mutual respect, and one based upon the truth that America and Islam are not exclusive and need not be in competition.[3]

The speech has been both lauded and criticized, but it continues to serve as a point of reference. Its significance cannot be minimized, no matter what one's perspective.

Especially relevant for this chapter's theme is that, first, President Obama continued to focus extensive portions of the speech on US policy in the Middle East, even more than on US-Muslim relations. Second, through the structure of the speech, the president perpetuated a dichotomy between the United States and Islam. This combination of representations results, on the one hand, in a perception that Islam and Muslims are to be associated with the Middle East, while only about 20 percent of the world's Muslims are Arab; on the other hand, there is the view that the United States and Islam are organically separate while in fact, with 7 to 8 million Muslims who are also American, the United States and Muslims are organically joined.

The former perception is problematic because the global demographic distribution of Muslims is antithetical to the stereotype that has linked Muslims and the Middle East. The president's presentation left non-Middle Eastern Muslims wondering where they fit in. In Africa, Asia, Europe, Latin America, and North America, Muslim presence, heritage, history, and legacy beg affirmation and appreciation. At the same time, in the Middle East, indigenous, non-Muslim populations seek recognition and affirmation. By conflating relations with Islam on the one hand and US foreign affairs (in this case, US Middle East policy) on the other, the president implied that Islam is both foreign and a category parallel to that of nations.

First, US citizenry includes Muslims as a religious community. While the Muslim population of the United States comprises a religious minority, it is made up of a mosaic of contemporary and not-so-recent immigrants from many countries, African American and white Americans, and recent converts and generationally rooted Muslims, reflecting the full diversity of the American populace. Second, Islam is a religious identity, not a national identity. The implied dichotomy of the United States and Islam is, in those senses, false and misleading, alienating, and inappropriate. The dichotomy sets Muslim Americans apart (explicitly challenging their "Americanness") from other Americans who have inflicted rhetorical and physical violence on Muslim Americans (and any other American "mistaken" for being Muslim). Those who hold antagonisms toward Muslims could find a degree of validation in the president's representation. Such a representation of a dichotomy between the United States and Islam is also dangerous because it conveys in a fairly explicit manner that Muslims and the United States are somehow separate. The most dangerous conclusion, implied as a (likely unintended) subtext in the president's speech, is that this "incompatibility" is due to the "Christian character" of the United States. Such an implication is harmful to the US Muslim community as well as to American Jews, Buddhists, Hindus, Sikhs, and members of other religious communities as well as those who do not affiliate with any religious group.

Soon after the speech, a regular meeting was convened of the National Muslim–Christian Initiative, a dialogue established in 2006–2007 between the National Council of Churches of Christ in the United States and its member churches, and major Muslim American organizations, including the Islamic Society of North America, the Islamic Circle of North America, and several others (see below). In discussing the Cairo speech, American Muslim participants responded by saying two things: first, none of what Obama said was new. Most Muslims in the United States and around the world knew and were sympathetic to much of what President Obama identified—that the history of Islam and the West is mixed in terms of positive and negative interaction; that Islam and America are not mutually exclusive in terms of culture, government, and borders; and that US policy history is littered with examples and episodes that are unpopular with Muslims (and others, to be sure); contradictory, sometimes exhibiting a double standard; and in need of change. All of these ideas and others were worthy of affirmation, although in this sense the speech did not break any new ground. Muslim members of the initiative also affirmed that President Obama's references to sacred texts were appropriate but were ones that people engaged in fostering good relations among faith communities would cite frequently. So, according to these American Muslims, the speech was nothing new.

At the same time, Muslim participants in the dialogue meeting stated that, while the content of the speech was perfectly consistent with the ideas of those who promote dialogue and a fairer and more just US foreign policy, the speech was a watershed— remarkable simply because the president of the United States took the responsibility to compose such a sensitive speech, demonstrating commitment to better relations and better policy. The speech synthesized an element of personal history, drawing on Obama's own heritage, rooted in both Christianity and Islam; it included scriptural references from all of the Abrahamic traditions and spoke about the difficulties of the status quo in the Arab-Israeli conflict. That a sitting president would say what Obama had, in such a widely anticipated—and advertised—speech, was significant for the American Muslim community represented at the meeting. For them, it was gratifying to hear such a change coming from the White House after a less than positive direction in recent years.[4]

Even though President Obama's speech may have reinforced some ideas that could have better been critiqued, the speech did point to some undeniable realities. It encapsulated many factors intertwined with Muslim–Christian relations in the United States today, including understandings of the place of Muslims in the United States and the intersection of domestic and international contexts. The global and domestic contexts are interrelated and cannot be so facilely bifurcated. In the next section, this chapter explores the inseparable relationship between them, especially that of the Middle East, and the impact on Muslim–Christian relations.

THE US-GLOBAL NEXUS AND AMERICAN MUSLIM–CHRISTIAN RELATIONS

Global events clearly have an impact on Muslim–Christian relations in the United States. The converse is also true, that US policy, as well as domestic rhetoric and actions involving American Muslims and Christians, affect relations between Muslims and Christians around the world. Such consequences are similar, but the dynamics are most often reversed: in the United States, the greater proportion of the population is Christian, with a small (less than 3 percent) Muslim population; in a number of other countries, the demographics are shifted, with a Muslim-majority population and (many times) a small Christian presence. (Of course there are examples where Muslim and Christian populations are lesser in number than other religious communities, as in India.) The imbalanced dynamic in such nations means that social and political interaction can often be heavily skewed to one community's advantage. Reaction and response to (most often) negative events or incidents are also manifested negatively, so such instances can become sources of fear and anxiety to the smaller community. As will be shown, it is in such situations that the presence of a wide diversity of viewpoints can not only help to diffuse a crisis but also provide avenues for debate and discussion as means of advancing more harmonious relations. In many such settings, mechanisms for dialogue already exist and are employed for this very purpose; in other instances, pathways to dialogue are opened by the presence of viewpoints that differ from hostile actions.

The Impact of the Global Context on US Muslim—Christian Relations

Contemporary and historical events both have demonstrable consequences on motivation and quality of Muslim—Christian relations in the United States. Space is not sufficient to analyze the events themselves; instead, this chapter focuses on the effects they can have on dialogue and relations. It is easy to identify examples of several categories from the global context that have had negative impact on the possibility of broader Muslim—Christian engagement in the United States or that have simply created hesitancy and/or fear of such engagement. The first category includes incitement—or the perception of hostility—of one religious community by another (even if the issues at stake are not religious). This category includes incidents such as the late Pope Benedict's speech at Regensburg and the Danish paper *Jyllands Posten* cartoon contest controversy. This type of incident has taken place in a Christian-majority context and has led to strong reactions locally and globally. A second category is that of violence attributed to people acting "in the name of their faith." This category would include, most prominently, incidents of suicide bombings (such as those that have taken place in Iraq, Afghanistan, Israel, and elsewhere); attacks on churches (in Iraq, Egypt, and Syria, for example), and acts of general violence (such as violent political demonstrations against a particular regime). These acts generally are reported from majority-Muslim countries and are either explicitly or implicitly linked to the "Muslim character" of those countries. (It is worth noting that violence by non-Muslims against Muslims in other parts of the world is very rarely reported in mainstream media outlets in the United States. An example of such violence is the recent attacks on Muslims in Myanmar by religious extremists.[5]) While studies and context show that such incidents are perpetrated for a variety of motivations, they are often reduced and simplified to "religious" motives.

A third category can be described as violations of human rights in Muslim-majority countries. This category might include the actions of dictatorial regimes that violate international standards and agreements on human rights, or systematic violence against women that may include human trafficking, female genital mutilation, and other such condemnable practices. Of course such actions are unique neither to Muslim-majority countries nor to the Muslim communities within Muslim-majority countries. But again, such realities are often overlooked. A fourth category includes hostility resulting from historical events and the communal memory that remains alive, such as the deadly impact of the Crusades on Muslims, perpetrated by Christians; and similarly the tragedy of the "deportations," population transfers, and deaths of Christians by Muslim Turks in 1915 and following, commonly known as the Armenian Genocide, but which was experienced by other Christian communities as well. It might also include the legacy of European colonialism on Arab and Muslim-majority countries, and the perception that the United States, as the lone remaining post–Cold War superpower, assumes a similar posture in its foreign policy.

All of these categories impact Muslim–Christian relations in the United States today to some degree. Some of them have provided fodder for, are an active part of, or are influenced by the attitude of Islamophobia, a response that singles out Muslims and Islam in a directed campaign to frame a

> world view . . . that sees Islam as at war with the West [and/or its ideals] and the West needing to be defended. . . . This network of hate is not a new presence in the United States. Indeed its ability to organize, coordinate, and disseminate its ideology through grassroots organizations increased dramatically over the past 10 years.[6]

The fear that has been created has both contributed to and been fed by segments of the American Christian community that do not actively engage in Muslim–Christian dialogue—and are often hostile to Muslims and Islam—either because they understand Islam simply not to be part of the Judeo-Christian tradition and therefore an incorrect expression of faith; because their goal in encountering Muslims would be to convert them to Christianity; or because of their understanding of Islam as antagonistic to their Christian understanding of God, a view that has been present in Christianity for centuries. Such views on global contexts, therefore, exacerbate tensions that already exist in the United States generally and among particular parts of the American Christian community in particular.

FROM THE UNITED STATES TO THE WORLD: THE "DAGGER" AND "BOOMERANG" EFFECTS

Policies and incidents that originate in the United States also have often interjected complicating dynamics into Muslim–Christians relations, not only in the United States but globally. This reality is due in part to the perception of the United States as a "Christian" nation and, by extension, the idea that government policies somehow represent a "Christian" approach. Two main categories of such events can be identified. The first is policies and governmental actions. In this category is a wide range of US Middle East policies, such as official support for Israel and a lack of substantive critique of the occupation of Palestinian lands, the imposition of sanctions on Iraq in the 1990s and the decision to invade and occupy in 2003, policies of rendition and torture, and the documented violation of human rights exposed in the Abu Ghraib prison (Iraq) and Guantanamo Bay (Cuba). It also includes congressional hearings on the "Radicalization of American Muslims," convened by Rep. Peter King (R-NY) in 2011, FBI surveillance of New York and Connecticut mosques and their members, and the feeling that "random" security checks by the Transportation Safety Administration since September 11, 2001, have disproportionately selected Muslims, Arab Americans, and Southeast Asians. A second such category includes incidents of incitement that problematize Muslim–Christian relations, such as Rev. Terry Jones and his declaration of an International Burn the Qur'an Day (Florida 2011); a Coptic American filmmaker who produced a YouTube video entitled "The Innocence of Muslims," and attacks on mosques and Islamic centers as hate crimes, especially following September 11.

Such categories of provocation have a twofold effect on Muslim–Christian relations. The first is a "dagger" effect, which impacts Muslim–Christian relations in majority-Muslim contexts. The incidents and acts cited above—by virtue of their focus on Muslims, the Muslim world, and the Middle East and the fact that they are immediately broadcast and followed throughout the world—all have caused active responses in many parts of the Muslim-majority world. In some cases, the responses have been violent. In addition, some of the violent responses have been directed at the local Christian community, with church burnings or threats to local Christians. For example, as a result of the Iraq invasion in 2003, the Christian community of Iraq, which numbered between 650,000 and 1 million before the war, suffered a highly disproportionate displacement—including both internally displaced persons in the protected regions of Iraq and the more than 2 million refugees who sought safety and security in neighboring countries such as Jordan, Lebanon, and Syria. Many Iraqi Christians experienced demands for payment in order to receive protection, others received death threats, and churches were physically damaged. Among some in the region, Middle Eastern Christians are seen as being connected to the policies of the western (read "Christian") nations and are treated as proxies in acts of response and revenge; they are "guilty by association." Here, the "dagger" represents the physical attacks on the Christian communities as a result of the US incidents. It also represents the wounds inflicted on more harmonious Muslim–Christian relations in the region, based on centuries of adjustment and learning, of coexistence and toleration, of tension and resolution of tension. Such relations are manifest in dialogues of life and of intellectual and theological engagement.

For US Muslim–Christian relations, such examples can have a "boomerang" effect. First, anytime the policy or actions of the US government targets a Middle Eastern or Muslim-majority country (such as Iraq, Iran, Afghanistan or Pakistan), or American Muslims (such as FBI surveillance or congressional hearings), the general level of suspicion with regard to the Muslim community is raised, having an adverse effect on the perceptions of Muslims in the United States. Second, the negative responses of people in other parts of the world to such policies and incidents, which are described above, are often covered in US news media in a religiously biased—and some would say racialized—way so as to portray Muslims (and often non-Muslim Arabs or Southeast Asians) negatively, which also impacts public perception of Muslims in the United States. As a result, American Muslims (and Arab- and Southeast Asian Americans who are Christian, Hindu, and Sikh) are also stigmatized and subjected to increased suspicion. The "boomerang" follows this trajectory: A policy or act originates in the United States, it engenders a public reaction in a Muslim-majority country, it impacts local interfaith relations in that context, and then it comes back to impact interfaith relations in the United States.

In each case—for global events and for actions that originate in the United States—Muslim–Christian relations are tested. Generally at least two outcomes are sure to happen. First, for those who have a proclivity to be suspicious and to point to the stereotypical image of the other, reactions are negative. Those reactions range from rhetorical attacks and hate speech to physical violence. Such reactions are sometimes initiated in the name of one's religion. Second, for those committed to fostering better relations, despite a context that is hostile, efforts are immediately made to protect, to defend, and to draw on existing relationships to deepen a sense of solidarity with those communities under attack. The issuance of statements by one community can help in mitigating such backlash. For example, when the United States decided to go to war against Iraq in 2003, many church denominations in the United States were opposed to war for a variety of reasons. When those public expressions of dissent from US policy are shared with Christian partners in the Middle East, Christian churches there are able to share them with Muslim leaders and with the general public to demonstrate that not all US Christians approve the policies of their government, implying that the policy is not reflective of the faith. One Christian leader in Lebanon told this author that such statements accomplish a great deal to help preserve Muslim–Christian relations in times of broader political conflict. Similarly, when violent actions are taken by Islamic groups or Muslim populations (such as the attack on 9/11 and the Boston Marathon attack in 2013), American Muslim organizations make public their condemnation of such actions, clearly stating their disapproval both from a Muslim point of view and from a human perspective. Sharing these statements among constituents and in the public domain can and does make a difference in many ways. First, it dispels common stereotypes that are simultaneously held among a somewhat uninformed populace that is generally a "receptive audience," and [that] are "air[ed] unchallenged…by individuals in positions of power and prominence mak[ing] them legitimate to adopt, act upon, and enforce."[7] Second, it demonstrates that opinions in any given community do not always reflect the voices amplified by the media, which then appear to be dominant, or in circles of policy. Third, it can encourage people to explore more deeply the beliefs and opinions of people in the other community, which often results in dialogue. A positive by-product of tragic events initiated in the name of religion has been the emergence of books and, more importantly, dialogue groups, to explore one another's beliefs more profoundly.

A COMMON WORD

A major invitation to Muslim–Christian dialogue was issued on October 13, 2007. Called *A Common Word Between Us and You*, the letter carries a clear invitation to the Christian world to renew efforts to build peaceful relations together, and is an example of how the global context can impact the US setting in a positive way. The document concludes by stating, "As Muslims, and in obedience to the Holy Qur'an, we ask Christians to come together with us on the common essentials of our two religions" and that

> this common ground be the basis of all future interfaith dialogue between us.…. If Muslims and Christians are not at peace, the world cannot be at peace…Our common future is at stake…Let us vie with each other only in righteousness and good works. Let us respect each other, be fair, just and kind to another and live in sincere peace, harmony and mutual good will.[8]

Two of its original 138 signatories are Mr. Muhammad al-Sammak and Shaikh Hani Fahs, both of whom are Lebanese Muslims, Sunni and Shi`ite leaders respectively. They are members of the Arab Group for Muslim–Christian Dialogue, a high-level organization that brings together Middle Eastern Muslim and Christian clergy, intellectuals, journalists, and other opinion-forming cadres. From Mr. Sammak's perspective, the need and timing of the letter were important because the gap between the Islamic world and the rest of the world is widening. This is dangerous, not only for Muslims but also for the peace of the world, particularly as Muslims reside in almost every part of the world. In addition, the image of Islam is often negative and distorted. Islamophobia is increasing, in large part due to the role of international media. Finally, poor relations are exacerbated by the fact that Islam is both misunderstood and misinterpreted. Actions toward Muslims are based on misconceptions, and reactions by Muslims are based on incorrect interpretations.[9] As a result of this set of problems and in the wake of the Pope's Regensburg speech in 2006, the Royal Al al-Bayt Institute for Islamic Thought in Amman, Jordan, held an international conference called Love in the Holy Qur'an. The *Common Word* letter grew out of that conference. Mr. Sammak described the purpose of the letter as having the following motivations:

1. To demonstrate the values of Islam, particularly love, not violence; moderation, not extremism; and trust and confidence in other faiths, not opposition or clash.
2. To correct the perception of Islam in the world by breaking the link between Islam and its political use; demonstrating Islamic values that are consistent with similar Christian values; extending a hand of dialogue and cooperation; and working toward creating a new world based on civilizational complementarity, and not a clash of civilizations.
3. To direct the message of the letter to two audiences: the Christian community worldwide, and the Muslim community itself. To accomplish this, the letter is addressed to the many Christian leaders named at its opening, and it is openly directed to the Muslim community worldwide, to put forth an interpretation of scripture that prescribes engagement and interaction with the religious other.[10]

Most historical dialogue initiatives, especially those of the past decades, have been Christian. Muslims have not been the initiators and have therefore felt somewhat less enthusiastic about dialogue. *A Common Word* is different because it is a Muslim initiative. This observation might best be understood as a caution to Christians not to appropriate the initiative or take it over but to be willing partners in this Muslim outreach. In the estimation of Dr. Tarek Mitri, this historical pattern has led to a degree of "dialogue fatigue" in both communities.[11] In the Christian community, such fatigue has resulted from taking initiatives without responsiveness which, Mitri explains, is partly due to a lack of participatory symmetry. On the Muslim side, in addition to the associations with colonialism and modernity, Mitri suggests that there has perhaps been an emphasis on the Vatican, because of its easily identifiable central structure, and less attention to Orthodox and Protestant Christians.

In the United States, *A Common Word*'s issuance resulted in initiatives in academic settings as well as in faith communities. The efforts at Georgetown and Yale Universities to study, discuss, and engage the document are quite well known. These institutions have been active settings of dialogue for this initiative and have held conferences and published books on the topic *A Common Word*.[12] Complementarily, the Christian communities in the United States have responded seriously and extensively to the invitation of *A Common Word*. In addition to the individual responses from various churches, such as the Christian Church (Disciples of Christ),[13] the Evangelical Lutheran Church in America,[14] the Presbyterian Church (USA),[15] and the United Church of Christ,[16] the National Council of Churches of Christ in the USA (NCC) sent an ecumenical response to the letter. In each of these responses, messages of welcoming dialogue and affirming the common basic theological underpinnings—love of God and love of neighbor—were present.

The National Council of Churches, which is made up of thirty-seven member communions—Orthodox and Protestant, Peace churches and historic African-American churches, among others—developed a document that elaborated a Christian theology of engagement.[17] It began by affirming the theme of hospitality and the ongoing relationships that the Christian and Muslim communities in the US have developed over the past three decades and asserted "that striving together as people who would seek to be peacemakers—as Christians and Muslims, and also in cooperation with people of other religious traditions—for fairness, justice and mutual goodwill is indeed necessary for the welfare of the world."[18] Wishing to engage the theological bases for dialogue and engagement, the NCC document articulated an authentically Christian perspective that recognized historical differences:

> There are differences as to how Muslims and Christians each understand the realities that make up the common ground upon which we stand. *Oneness* of God compels a discussion about how the revelation of God has been differently understood by the communities that call upon God's name. *Love* of God demands an exploration of how each community perceives a genuine response to God's love for the world. Even the word *neighbor* requires frank analysis: as historically played out, despite theological mandates to care for the other (as in the parable of the Good Samaritan, Luke 10:25–37), in both Muslim and Christian societies, the word "neighbor" has sometimes been limited to the designation of a member of one's own community. In various places and times, Christian minorities and Muslim minorities have both fared well and fared badly in the context of religious majorities of the other faith.… In both communities, there is a growing understanding of the "other" as "neighbor," and increasing clarity that equal status in society, based on human dignity and freedom of conscience, is the ideal that should be sought and legally established.[19]

Expressing the Christian understanding of the Trinity as a way to communicate the idea of community, the NCC's ecumenical response concludes with an expression of hope that, despite undeniable contextual and historical tensions, Muslims and Christians in the United States can live out the common message of peace:

> At the heart of "A Common Word," we hear a call for Christians to consider that Muslims are *with us*, and that this togetherness bears upon the state of the world.…

We lament on every occasion when violence is committed in the name of religion.... Our churches, in ecumenical solidarity through the National Council of the Churches of Christ in the USA, commit themselves to actively seek, together with you, ways to take up the challenge you have presented to us in "A Common Word": "Let us vie with each other only in righteousness and good works. Let us respect each other, be fair, just and kind to one another and live in sincere peace, harmony and mutual good-will." May we discern together, in the various places of our common life and work, how to give concrete expression to this commitment, *"not [only] in word or speech, but in truth and action" (1 John 3:18, NRSV)*. In this way, in all contexts and in all places, equality, fairness, justice, and peace may prevail.[20]

The invitation to dialogue and engagement of *A Common Word* was thus disseminated through its member communions, and became not only an encouraging motivation for dialogue by local churches but also an additional teaching resource in various Christian settings about the beliefs of Islam and Muslims' desire to develop and nurture closer relations with Christians. It is an example of institutional and public dialogue which has the effects of advancing substantive strands of theological and intellectual engagement, providing public documents as tools for learning, and encouraging local and regional settings to seek each other out to form and nurture relationships. It is also an example of positive engagement in the United States resulting from a global initiative.

Muslim–Christian Dialogue and Relations in the United States: Positive Engagement

The NCC's response to *A Common Word* noted thirty years of ecumenical Christian relations with US Muslims through the institution of the NCC, not to mention the active engagement of denominations and of local and regional Christians and Muslims. It would be accurate to identify three categories of Muslim–Christian engagement in the US context. The first is theological/intellectual dialogue. This type includes the theological exchanges that resulted from *A Common Word* through the NCC and directly by the denominations, as described above. This category includes as well the ongoing regional Muslim-Catholic dialogue, which has focused on various theological issues. This dialogue takes place in the Midwest, Mid-Atlantic, and West Coast regions of the nation, which began in 1996, 1998, and 1999 respectively. These dialogue meetings lead to plenaries that have dealt with issues such as revelation, marriage, and relational questions. They involve the US Conference of Catholic Bishops and the Islamic Society of North America, the Islamic Circle of North America, and the Islamic Shura Council of

Southern California.[21] The results of this relationship include published papers and online videos that offer voice to participants, sharing the content of the ongoing dialogues.

A second category of dialogue deals with issues of common concern as faith communities living in US society in the beginning of the twenty-first century. Especially in the post–September 11 context, national Christian and Muslim leaders have worked together to establish dialogues to explore together such issues, and to serve as a model of and resource for dialogue between Christians and Muslims nationwide. After organizing and preparation, a new National Muslim–Christian Initiative (NMCI) was established in 2007. The NMCI included representatives from several National Council of Churches member churches and a roughly equal number of representatives from US Muslim organizations, including the Islamic Society of North America and the Islamic Circle of North America. The NMCI identified four areas of work on which it would concentrate:

1. Encouraging the local settings of the respective constituencies to engage with each other in new and positive ways, to be accomplished in the short term by pairing churches and mosques to meet each other and discover in what ways active faith communities can develop modes of interaction and witness;
2. Educating each other about the respective faiths and communities, so that leadership of each is able to educate about the other with authenticity and credibility, especially given the great desire in NCC churches, especially since Sept. 11, to learn more about Islam and the Middle East;
3. Establishing a mechanism for public response when events unfold that beg public voice; and
4. Publicizing the work of the NMCI so that constituent members and the media will have access to positive interaction between the respective communities.[22]

These areas were identified together, which in itself represents a model of cooperation and interaction—something recognized by both Muslims and Christians as an urgent priority. In addition to the priorities, a mission statement of the NMCI was developed and was consistent with the message of A Common Word: "We, from various streams of Muslim and Christian communities, seek to enhance mutual understanding, respect, appreciation and support of what is sacred for each other through dialogue, education and sustained visible encounters that foster and nurture relationships."[23]

The mission statement encourages dialogue among national leaders as well as among local and regional institutions. It focuses on increased understanding which leads to exploration of the counterpart faith community's faith and practice. It also is a basis for engagement on issues of common concern. The NMCI met on a regular basis for four years. A period of relative dormancy followed, owing to a variety of factors, but efforts are being made to revitalize this forum of interaction. The emergence of a new initiative, called the Shoulder-to-Shoulder campaign, has been a focus of interfaith efforts and energy more recently and is discussed below.

The third category that can be identified is common activism and public witness. The efforts of national dialogue initiatives to promote increased encounter and more sustained engagement are certainly not undertaken without a knowledge and recognition of the context surrounding them. The US context of heightened misrepresentation, misunderstanding, and distrust of Islam and Muslims has already been discussed above. Documentation of a concerted network to promote Islamophobia,[24] cases of discrimination against Muslim employees,[25] corporate decisions to withdraw advertising from particular television shows,[26] the "International Burn the Qur'an Day," protests outside Islamic organizational fundraisers that have involved violence (rhetorical and in some cases physical),[27] and US congressional hearings on the "Radicalization of American Muslims" all contribute to an environment that has had both negative and positive outcomes. Some American Christians and churches have been visibly hostile to Islam and Muslims, while for many others such a context has provided an opportunity for increased engagement and for expressions of support and solidarity, including the passage of resolutions at national denominational general meetings. For example, in the summer of 2011, the United Church of Christ adopted a resolution at its biannual General Synod entitled, "On Actions of Hostility against Islam and the Muslim Community,"[28] which "denounce[d] actions against Islam or Muslims based on ignorance or fear" and encouraged dialogue. The Christian Church (Disciples of Christ) approved a resolution at its General Assembly in the same year entitled, "Addressing Anti-Muslim Action in the United States and Canada,"[29] which "condemns anti-Muslim speech and activity and calls upon the Church to promote respect, civility and love toward our Muslim neighbors" and encourages dialogue. Such resolutions reflect an explicit desire by members of such churches to speak out against actions hostile to members of another faith community and to work deliberately to foster better relations.

Beyond those of local churches and national denominations, ecumenical and interfaith initiatives have emerged to respond to such a context. Significant among them is the campaign called "Shoulder-to-Shoulder: Standing with American Muslims; Upholding American Values." Of the almost thirty predominately Jewish, Christian, and Muslim organizations comprising Shoulder-to-Shoulder's membership, twelve are Christian.[30] Founded in November 2010, the initiative declared itself "a national campaign of interfaith, faith-based and religious organizations dedicated to ending anti-Muslim sentiment." It is made up of "local, state and regional faith-based, interfaith and religious organizations that are dedicated to ending anti-Muslim sentiment."

Through this national network of organizations, Shoulder-to-Shoulder works to present a new story of interfaith engagement and solidarity that focuses on positive, normative relationships across faith lines; ensure that local organizations have access to quality resources and examples of effective work; provide local organizations with support in using quality resources; connect local organizations to one another for peer-to-peer resourcing across the country.

Shoulder-to-Shoulder has highlighted in national press conferences and events the work of the interfaith community, particularly of the Abrahamic faiths, to join together to oppose religious bigotry in the United States.[31] It has also submitted testimony to Congress in the context of the "Radicalization of American Muslims" and "Homegrown Terrorism" hearings.[32]

A final example of engagement on public and global issues is the joint work of churches and organizations from the faith communities to advocate for justice and peace in Palestine/Israel. This advocacy is accomplished together in many ways. One institutional vehicle is the National Interreligious Leadership Initiative (NILI), which was established in 2003, and brings together Jewish, Christian, and Muslim organizations to focus "on building support for strong US leadership for a two-state solution to the conflict that brings security and recognition to Israel and establishes a viable and independent state for the Palestinians—two states living side by side in peace and security—with peace agreements between Israel and all her Arab neighbors."[33] Such interaction, in the category of social witness, has become increasingly important in the context of an increasingly polarized United States.

All of these activities illustrate a range of positive interaction and dialogue between US Muslims and Christians: on theological and intellectual levels, on the level of social engagement as faith communities in the twenty-first-century United States, and on the level of joint action and advocacy on important social issues, including responding to attacks on one another and on issues of common concern, such as peace and justice in Palestine/Israel.

CONCLUSIONS

With the proliferation of national initiatives and the expansion of local and regional dialogue, one can conclude that, even in the midst of a rather challenging context, there are reasons for optimism in the realm of Muslim–Christian relations in the United States. This chapter has attempted to acknowledge that the state of Muslim–Christian relations in the United States can be seen both negatively and positively. Efforts to promote better relations between US Muslims and Christians have emerged based on theological rationales as well as the heightened context of hostility against Islam and the Muslim community in this country. Both have contributed to the levels of engagement at the national, regional, and local settings that are currently taking place. The chapter has also asserted the important relationship between the domestic and the international contexts and their impact on each other. Events in the global arena, particularly in the Middle East and Muslim-majority countries, impact the US context; similarly, what happens here in the United States impacts global Muslim–Christian relations. Finally, the chapter has described areas of positive engagement in the United States, primarily focusing on national initiatives. Such a focus should not be read to minimize the importance and widespread presence of regional and local, for they represent the grassroots and day-to-day interaction that constitutes a "dialogue of life"—encounters at school, work, and community activities—the interaction that takes place in public and private spaces. Such interaction is also on the rise and is documented extensively.[34]

Amir Hussain, in his book *Oil & Water*, states, "some Christians may have more in common theologically with some Muslims than with other Christians. The reverse is also true for Muslims who may find the behavior of their Christian neighbours to be more "muslim"....than some of their fellow Muslims."[35] It is through dialogue and discovery at a personal and direct level that each discovers the other's humanity, friendships are established, and relationships built. While there are formidable challenges to overcome, there are real opportunities and much commitment to building on what already exists to continue to expand upon decades of direct and indirect engagement, ultimately to work for peace and justice together.

NOTES

1. Miroslav Volf, "A Common Word for a Common Future," in *A Common Word: Muslims and Christians on Loving God and Neighbor*, ed. Miroslav Volf, Ghazi bin Muhammad, and Melissa Yarrington (Grand Rapids, MI: Eerdmans, 2010): 18.
2. Feisal Abdul Rauf, *What's Right with Islam Is What's Right with America* (New York: HarperOne, 2004): 266.
3. "Remarks on a New Beginning," by Barack Obama, delivered at Cairo University, June 4, 2009. Available at: http://www.whitehouse.gov/the_press_office/Remarks-by-the-President-at-Cairo-University-6-04-09/
4. From the author's notes of a meeting of the National Muslim-Christian Initiative, convened in Los Angeles, February 24, 2010.
5. "Deadly Clashes Erupt Again in Myanmar Targeting Muslims," *OIC Journal* 23 (January-March 2013): 4–5.
6. Wajahat Ali, Eli Clifton, Matthew Duss, Lee Fang, Scott Keyes, and Faiz Shakir, *Fear, Inc.: The Roots of the Islamophobia Network in America* (Washington, DC: Center for American Progress, 2011): 2. For a helpful discussion on the emergence and study of Islamophobia, see Erik Bleich, "Defining and Researching Islamophobia," in *The Review of Middle East Studies*, 46.2 (Winter 2012): 180–189.
7. Abdelkader H. Sinno, "The Politics of Western Muslims," *The Review of Middle East Studies*, 46.2 (Winter 2012): 219.
8. *A Common Word between Us and You.* Available at http://www.acommonword.com/the-acw-document/
9. Email correspondence between Mr. Sammak and the author, January 14, 2008.
10. Ibid.
11. The idea of "dialogue fatigue" was part of Dr. Tarek Mitri's remarks at a World Council of Churches meeting on *A Common Word* in Geneva, January 2008.

12. For example, see *A Common Word: Muslims and Christians on Loving God and Neighbor*, ed. Miroslav Volf, Ghazi bin Muhammad, and Melissa Yarrington (Grand Rapids, MI: Eerdmans, 2010).

13. See: http://www.acommonword.com/response-from-the-leaders-in-the-christian-church-disciples-of-christ/

14. See: http://www.acommonword.com/response-from-bishop-rev-mark-s-hanson/

15. See: http://eif-pcusa.org/InterfaithRelations/Muslimletter.html/

16. The United Church of Christ's positive response was a letter sent to signatories who are UCC dialogue partners. It was not a public letter.

17. The National Council of Churches of Christ response to *A Common Word* is available on its website: http://www.ncccusa.org/news/ecumenicalresponse.html

18. Ibid.

19. Ibid.

20. Ibid., in original.

21. See: http://www.usccb.org/beliefs-and-teachings/ecumenical-and-interreligious/interreligious/islam/

22. From the author's notes of February 2008 meeting of the NILI.

23. "National Muslim-Christian Initiative Meets in Los Angeles," March 2, 2010. Available at: http://globalministries.org/news/mee/national-muslim-christian-1.html.

24. See *Fear, Inc.*, referenced above.

25. See "Muslim Ex-Whole Food Employee Sues Company for Discrimination," Nov. 8, 2011. Available at: http://abcnews.go.com/US/muslim-foods-employee-sues-company-discrimination/story?id=14905251#.Ud2r2BXD_cs

26. See "NCC says Lowe's should resume advertising on TLC's "All American Muslim"," December 15, 2011. Available at: http://globalministries.org/news/mee/ncc-says-lowes-should-resume.html

27. See "ICNA Relief Thanks Community & Local Officials," February 15, 2011. Available at: http://www.icna.org/icna-relief-thanks-the-community-and-local-officials-for-their-support/

28. Text of resolution Available at: http://uccfiles.com/synod/resolutions/Resolution-On-Actions-of-Hostility-Against-Islam.pdf

29. Text of resolution Available at: http://www.disciples.org/Portals/0/PDF/ga/2011/Business/GA1116-AddressingAntiMuslimActionInTheUnitedStatesAndCanada.pdf

30. List of Shoulder-to-Shoulder's members available at: http://shouldertoshouldercampaign.org/members/

31. See, for example, "Shoulder-to-Shoulder Marks decade since Sept. 11, 2011," September 8, 2011. Available at: http://globalministries.org/news/mee/shoulder-to-shoulder-marks.html

32. "Shoulder to Shoulder coalition submits testimony to Congress," Dec. 12, 2011. Available at: http://globalministries.org/news/mee/shoulder-to-shoulder-1.html.

33. See: http://www.nili-mideastpeace.org/

34. See: http://www.pluralism.org/

35. Amir Hussain, *Oil & Water: Two Faiths: One God* (British Columbia: Wood Lake Publishing, 2006): 198.

CHAPTER 22

....

AMERICAN MUSLIMS IN THE AGE OF NEW MEDIA

....

NADIA KHAN

INTRODUCTION

....

Qasim Latif[1] was startled to see an FBI agent at his door. He was questioned about the heavily trafficked blogging community Latif had founded for young American Muslims to record their own narratives and thereby counter anti-Muslim sentiment. Before the agent's visit, Latif noticed that a Samir Khan had registered a new blog on his site called *InshaAllah Shaheed*.[2] The FBI had been tracking Khan, whose blog sympathized with the motives of jihadists. This led them to Latif, who defended his website's civic mission.

This anecdote encapsulates some anxieties surrounding American Muslims' use of the Internet. Intelligence agencies fear that terrorists recruit American Muslims online. Some Muslims fear that American Muslim bloggers can exacerbate a crisis of religious authority since they provide platforms for ordinary Muslims to broadcast self-taught religiolegal opinions. In contrast, proponents celebrate how the Internet empowers lay Muslims to challenge the American Muslim status quo.

Some Muslims do engage in clandestine activity, proselytize, and challenge the authority of traditional Muslim leadership online. However, a false dichotomy often arises: the American Muslim webscape is either portrayed as dystopic (for fomenting radicalization) or utopic (for empowering progressive Muslims). This binary misrepresents the multifaceted ways in which ordinary American Muslims behave online. This article explores the history of American Muslims' online activity. It investigates how American Muslim digital activists engage in a "double-critique" against those who foment anti-Muslim sentiment and against the actions of unscrupulous Muslim leaders and institutions.

HISTORY

Much of the content that American Muslims upload predates the Internet in cassette, radio, and print formats. In the 1960s and 1970s, just as the Internet was first conceived, changes in immigration laws allowed more Muslim students into America, including many computer scientists.[3] Although most lacked religious training, these professionals created the first Islam-related websites long before Muslim organizations' official websites appeared.[4] Early users uploaded Islamic print materials onto mailing lists, Telnet, file transfer protocols, Gopher, and Bulletin Board Systems—all precursors to the World Wide Web.[5] In the 1980s it became easier to work with Arabic and other Islamicate languages on computers, resulting in more digitization of religious texts.[6] These developments led to speculation that the Internet may one day replace the *ulema* with robotic muftis.[7]

When the World Wide Web debuted in the 1990s, it became easier for amateur Muslim web developers to express their religious enthusiasm online.[8] By 1995, major portals were launched, such as *IslamiCity* and the Islamic Society of North America's homepage.[9] Soon, seminarians from Al-Azhar and Qom began learning hypertext alongside classical texts[10] and digitizing classical works.[11] Their efforts competed with Salafists, some of whom became online celebrities for translating Arabic tracts into an English vernacular.[12]

In 1997, Islam Online went live, featuring the writings of Yusuf Qaradawi, a Qatar-based scholar. In the late 1990s, despite more Middle Eastern countries going online, the majority of Muslim Internet users lived in North America and Europe.[13] Near the decade's end, Muslim organizations like the *Muslim World League* and the *Organization of the Islamic Conference* still did not have websites, though many American mosque communities already had homepages.[14] ISNA sponsored conferences to discuss how to improve online representations of Islam and Muslims and to encourage networking among digital entrepreneurs.[15]

American Muslim businesses took advantage of e-commerce. Websites such as *Zabihah* provide ratings and locators for *halal* food, while other websites market fashionable modest clothing. Yet in 2000, despite the increasing number of American Muslim merchants advertising online, Gary Bunt observes that when searching "Islam" and "Muslims," the highest-ranked links were still "overly political."

After the events of 9/11, the media highlighted how the hijackers deployed the web to facilitate the attacks.[16] Immediately after 9/11, the Justice Department under the Bush administration used the Patriot Act to scrutinize American Muslim activity online, enabling it to charge al-Hussayen, the IANA webmaster, with hosting content that encouraged "mass killings" in the first Internet terrorism prosecution.[17] American Muslim activity online continues to be associated with terrorism, thanks to a handful of high-profile cases. For example, "Azzam the American" (Adam Gadahn) used his Internet presence as al-Qaeda's YouTube spokesperson to attract followers from the English-speaking world.[18] Yet, many question whether the Internet alone can radicalize American Muslims,[19] noting that online training manuals have rarely resulted in the execution of successful attacks and that Internet interactions cannot single-handedly cause youth radicalization.[20] In 2009, the US government shut down Anwar Awlaki's website and killed him in a drone strike. Called the "Bin Laden of the Internet," Awlaki's YouTube sermons were thought to have been part of al-Qaeda's new decentralization strategy and were credited with inspiring the 2009 surge in "homegrown terrorism."[21]

Concurrently, American Muslims have sought to distance themselves from terrorism, to hold Muslims espousing violent behavior accountable, and to protest the erosion of American Muslims' civil liberties. In 2001, Shahed Amanullah launched *altMuslim*, an effort to foster dialogue between Muslims and non-Muslims.[22] Yet in 2003, when Facebook launched,[23] e-mail forwards of fatwas were circulated calling for Muslims to boycott American products in protest of the Iraq and Afghanistan invasions.[24]

Closer to home, since 9/11 American Muslims have grappled with how to develop inclusive mosque communities. In 2004, American Muslim activists established the *Progressive Muslim Union of North America* to facilitate these introspective discussions. They hosted lively Internet web forums discussing ways to reform Muslim communities.[25]

American Muslim organizations use new media both to address issues internal to their community and to counter growing anti-Muslim sentiment. For example, in 2005, *Wiki Islam* debuted, claiming to provide a "politically incorrect" alternative to Wikipedia.[26] In 2008, anti-Muslim documentaries such as Geert Wilders' *Fitna* and the Clarion Fund's *Obsession* became available online just before the presidential elections. In response, Muslims criticized the films in popular American blogs like the *Huffington Post, Religion Dispatches, Patheos, Washington Post's On Faith, CNN's Belief Blog*, and the *Immanent Frame*.

Yet Osama bin Laden's 2007 video upload upstaged American Muslim digital activists. In 2008, US Central Command launched the "Digital Engagement Team," which aspires to lower the "electronic curtain" by responding to jihadist rhetoric online and defending the Pentagon against "lies" that proliferate in "radical" forums.[27] Similarly, the US State Department initiated its own Digital Outreach Team to learn what motivates jihadists and to create online environments designed to counter extremism. [28]

Prosecutions related to American Muslim Internet use have continued. In 2009, Tarek Mehanna was charged for posting militant videos and translations of al-Qaeda's propaganda..[29] In response to how Mehanna's arrest seemed to criminalize free speech, some American Muslims complained that Robert Spencer's blogs inspired Anders Breivik's mass killing in July 2011, yet Spencer was not prosecuted for his postings.[30]

By 2009, American media outlets celebrated young pro-democracy Iranian digital activists who spearheaded the "Twitter revolution." Although the revolution did not oust President Ahmadinejad, Tunisian and Egyptian digital activists arguably assisted in toppling governments. During the "Arab Spring" of 2011, American Muslims eschewed CNN and ABC, turning directly instead to live streaming of Al-Jazeera and the tweets of antigovernment activists. As the uprising continued and spread into Syria in 2012, American Muslims raised money online to support Syria's opposition.

The Internet and American Muslim Religious Authority

Some observers argue that by democratizing religious authority, the Internet has opened "the cyber gates of *ijtihād.*"[31] They claim that the Internet can collapse distinctions in authority between lay Muslims and religious scholars. Access to classic sources online means American Muslims may forego visiting the local *imam*[32]; some dispute the *ulamas'* legal opinions and offer alternative interpretations of *Sharia* online.[33] The ability to engage in "do it yourself" jurisprudence has led to a rise in self-appointed charismatic amateur Islam experts[34] who lack formal religious training but publish interpretations online, drawing not only from classical texts but also from their own experiences.[35] Entrepreneurial individuals like Baba Ali upload *halaqas* [study circles] to YouTube, on topics that target young American Muslims.

American Muslims also use new media to hold their religious authority figures and institutions accountable. Those who are upset with how a leader represents the community can challenge her or him to a Twitter debate.[36] An *halal* restaurant that serves alcohol can be flagged over *Zabihah.*[37] Over *Salat-O-Matic,*[38] American Muslims rate mosques on their cleanliness, sermons, and how women-friendly they are, hence facilitating American Muslims to vote with their feet.[39]

Enhancing Religious Knowledge and Practice Online

For American Muslims who lack religious training, the overwhelming amount of online content about Islam and the "anarchy of the Internet"[40] can cause information overload, thereby exacerbating their efforts to make sense of the cacophony of disparate interpretive voices.[41] Moreover, American Muslims are tasked with determining which online voice to follow while institutions of religious learning attempt to instruct students on how to distinguish between legitimate online muftis and charlatans. For example, American Muslims searching for fatwas online are advised to eschew any website that calls a Muslim public figure a heretic and/or disbeliever or engages in argumentation over jurisprudential minutiae.[42] Moreover, American Muslim *ulama* caution that although digital anonymity allows American Muslims to confidentially raise sensitive questions,[43] the phenomenon of anonymous *fatwas* breaks with a tradition that calls for *fatwas* to be signed by *muftis,* a tradition that ensures that they are held accountable for their responsa.[44]

To address the challenges posed by self-appointed online *muftis* and online *fatwa*-shoppers, religious authorities are embracing social media in order to maintain relevance. Acknowledging that the vast majority of American Muslims do not regularly attend a mosque,[45] American Muslim *ulama* webcast their classes.[46] For example, in 2006, Imam Suhaib Webb launched a "virtual mosque" that aims to "synthesize" knowledge from classical texts with the circumstances of American Muslims. For those desiring traditional religious distance learning opportunities, the pioneer online Islamic Academy, *Qibla*, provides an elegant user interface and the chance for live interaction with scholars teaching classical texts for a fee. To accommodate those who cannot afford online tuition, *Seekers Guidance Deen Intensive* and the *Bayyinah Institute* offer online classes for free. Furthermore, *Celebrate Mercy* hosts global webcasts featuring Muslim scholars from around the world, including women.

Long sidelined to the mosque's "women's section," American Muslim women are capitalizing on the antipatriarchal structure of the Internet by claiming space online.[47] But new Internet and communications technologies can also be used to rebuild digital partitions. Those who wish to uphold traditional gender roles are able to monitor young womens' Facebook walls.[48] Nonetheless, American Muslim women are not relegated to "the sister's side" on websites but are authoring the content of their own homepages.[49] These sites range from how-to-wear *hijab* YouTube videos, to *AltMuslimah.com*, which is dedicated to providing a "unique space for compelling commentary on gender-in-Islam." *e-Khutba* is on Huffington Post webcasts, and YouTube videos include female preachers. These websites and the numerous acts of digital self-representation, such as digital profile pictures, allow American Muslim women to confront lingering orientalist characterizations of Muslim women as either oppressed victims or militant "Jihad Janes."[50]

Both American Muslim men and women go online to expand their knowledge through daily Hadith Twitter feeds or Quranic word-of-the-day e-mails. They search for "material for the next *khutba,*"[51] download activities for their children, and locate educational materials for non-Muslims online.

Some maintain that the Internet allows American Muslims to return to more traditional modes of religious learning. Digitized classical texts harken back to medieval manuscript culture as a single PDF can be uploaded, copied, and endlessly commented on by numerous students online.[52] Print technology interrupted "1200 years of oral transmission"[53] as knowledge was no longer always transmitted directly from teacher to student.[54] However, YouTube allows American Muslims access to the *majālis* of al-Azhar and other institutions of learning, where knowledge is still transmitted orally.[55] Despite the visual nature of the new media, Hirschkind argues that the "Islamic tradition of acoustically mediated piety" thrives on YouTube. He contends that videos that lack visual flourishes are sometimes more popular among Muslims since they emphasize the spoken word for its ability to elicit pious affects.[56] Even online fatwa services continue a tradition of scholarly responsa.[57]

Although there is consensus among American Muslim ulama that Internet use is permissible, some scholars maintain that the Internet is not conducive to spirituality. Muslim bloggers offer advice exhorting surfers to "catch up on all the unread messages in the Qur'an,"[58] to check their intention before posting when angry, and to avoid online plagiarism.

American Muslim web-surfers also encounter a lack of gender segregation online, where the sexes can interact online in seclusion without always observing adequate netiquette. For this reason, some American Muslims exhort each other to observe net-*adab*. Moreover, like other communities, Muslims struggle with Internet pornography. American Muslim leaders have responded by creating anonymous online programs that target addicts.

Other American Muslims have called for web fasting during Ramadan. Furthermore, Muslim religious retreats are going "off the grid" by barring WiFi-enabled devices. While some American Muslims recognize the dangers of Internet use, many embrace new forms of media that enhance religious practice. For example, the Internet provides resource guides for converts, allows mosque and MSA websites to market community activities online,[59] offers mobile applications that log supererogatory ritual prayers, showcases *hajj* tweets and Ramadan photographs, and allows Muslims to disperse charity online. American Muslims can "perform piety" online by using emoticons of religious invocations.[60] Furthermore, Charles Hirschkind observes that Muslims who leave comments on YouTube videos police each other to ensure that their comments on videos uphold a level of decorum similar to that found in a mosque, hence creating collective moral spaces online.[61]

Moreover, American Muslims have seized the opportunity to invite others to the faith online; they have taken advantage of the fact that 28 million Americans researched Islam online after 9/11,[62] that Christian missionaries have used the Internet to proselytize to Muslims,[63] and that many have become Muslim through Internet correspondence.[64] The Internet allows for *da'wa* to shift from an activity executed by centralized Muslim organizations to a decentralized activity in which ordinary Muslims call others to the faith.[65] Young American Muslims are often the most effective at using new media to spread Islam, sometimes in 140 characters or less.

THE INTERNET AND AMERICAN MUSLIM IDENTITY

Using new media, American Muslim youth have found a platform for expressing their hyphenated identity. Online, young American Muslims can forego the mosque politics of their parents and speak directly to each other and their fellow citizens. Countless sites satirize the way young people are treated by mosque elders as well as non-Muslims, while other blogs humanize American Muslims. For instance, in the "Guide to Halal (debatable) flirting," young Muslim women offers tips on how to stretch the limits of the permissible in order to attract suitors, while the blog *Hairinnewplaces* highlights how American Muslims have dealt with the awkwardness of puberty. Since American Muslims most likely spend more time online than in mosques, these virtual communities will continue to shape American Islam's future.[66]

The Internet has dramatically affected the issue of quasi-arranged marriages and the challenges faced by Muslims from smaller communities trying to meet spouses. Since the 1980s, the Internet has offered various matchmaking sites[67] that afford young American Muslims the independence of choosing a partner while at the same time reassuring parents by tailoring the process in a way that reflects traditional Muslim sensibilities.[68] In other ways, Muslim online dating sites reinforce divisions in the greater American Muslim community by asking participants to self-identify as "traditional" or "progressive," "fair," "seeking doctors only," etc.[69]

Apart from empowering women, youth and reformers, the Internet has also given other marginalized groups in Muslim communities a cyber-home. Sufi *shaykhs* regularly communicate with their disciples online. The *Muslims for Progressive Values* website provides alternative webcasts of Friday sermon where American Muslims who feel excluded at their local mosque can watch/attend. The Internet helps minority voices within the American Muslim community mobilize.

Some commentators have written about "radical Muslim clerics" using the Internet to attract a following among American Muslims who, at best, are seen through this framing as uncritical consumers of foreign religious education and who, at worst, are described as a "fifth column." Undoubtedly, some American Muslims use new media to reinforce their ties to the greater *ummah*. Foreign countries sometimes sponsor sites. For example, the Saudi Human Assistance and Development International (HADI) sponsored *IslamiCity*.[70] Furthermore, the transnational subjectivities of some American Muslims and their asymmetrical access to the Internet has allowed a minority to take a pivotal and often controversial role as digital interpreters[71] of foreign political developments.[72] Some digital entrepreneurs act as neoliberal "native Muslim informants" who profit from their seemingly subversive blogs to meet the demands of think tanks and government agencies who require "expert" testimony about Islam,[73] thereby assisting those in American policy circles to engage in "cyberimperialism."[74] While these digital activities contradict the claims of those who emphasize the Internet's democratizing qualities, they may be offset by the positive role diasporic American Muslims play abroad by sending remittances for development, mobilizing online after natural disasters, and keeping Americans abreast of the realities of their coreligionists abroad.[75]

In addition to engaging in diaspora politics online, the Internet allows American Muslims of immigrant origin to preserve their connection to the homeland."[76] Websites of international Muslim organizations and leaders often target American Muslim minorities, even though they may not grasp the localized cultural nuances of the American Muslim experience and may offer inappropriate guidance.[77]

While American Muslim Internet activities are enmeshed in international Muslim networks, they cannot be defined simply in relation to the greater *ummah*. Rather the loci of Muslim political and civic action are increasingly more domestic than international. For example, American Muslim websites collect alms for domestic nonprofit groups, collate resources that combat domestic violence in America, promote environmental awareness, and fundraise online to build Muslim institutions that benefit all Americans. Furthermore, American Muslim religious authorities are calibrating their religiolegal advice to American contexts to discourage their followers from seeking legal opinions from online muftis.

Due to the fact that historically Americans have much greater Internet access than those in Muslim majority countries and English has been a major web language,[78] large numbers of Muslim users are Americans. Moreover, the works of American Muslim scholars are being translated into other languages and made available online.[79] American Muslims represent the most frequent petitioners on online *fatwa* sites, and they produce a large portion of online content about Islam.[80] Garbi Schmidt found that some European Muslims emulate American Muslim institutions, particularly those with significant web presences.[81] Further research could explore whether the Internet shifts the center of Islamic education away from the Middle East to the American periphery.

AMERICAN MUSLIMS IN A SURVEILLANCE SOCIETY

In 2005, the National Security Agency's warrantless surveillance program was exposed. Intelligence agencies used the Internet to identify security threats, thereby chilling free speech online.[82] Although the First Amendment protects speech online that might "radicalize" Muslims, the Patriot Act allows the FBI to access American Muslim Internet records.[83] A relatively small number of American Muslims have changed their online behavior following 9/11, but a majority believes that the government tracks them online.[84] Other American Muslims have been deported simply because of their participation in online forums.[85]

Many American Muslims, long frustrated with their portrayal by the media, welcome the Internet as a powerful, financially accessible medium through which they can respond to stereotypes. [86] However, the tendency of anti-Muslim material to go viral online creates new challenges. In 2010, a New York bus ad campaign ran advertisements to encourage Muslims to leave Islam by directing them to the site *RefugefromIslam,* and[87] in 2011, one blogger single-handedly launched a web campaign that successfully convinced businesses to drop advertisements from the sitcom *All-American Muslim.*[88] In 2012, how-to-craft-your-own-anti-sharia bill YouTube videos surfaced widely, designed to train Tea Party activists.[89]

The repetitive talking points found in Islamophobic films from Europe and right-wing American websites rallying in support of anti-Muslim political candidates demonstrate how the Internet facilitates a "trans-Atlantic echo-chamber" for anti-Muslim messaging.[90] Anti-Muslim activists have built sophisticated online networks promoting "information terrorism" against the corporate reputation of American Muslims.[91] Today, growing constellations of websites smear academicians and other public figures sympathetic to Muslims in an attempt to reshape the policies of American institutions.[92] The messaging of anti-Muslim bloggers has even crept into non-Internet headlines—this is not surprising, given that many Americans receive information regarding religion online and journalists use the Internet to research stories.[93] Hence, American Muslim activists have launched a number of watchdog sites charged with challenging the statements of anti-Muslim e-activists.[94] Since 1994, the Council on American-Islamic Relations (CAIR) has alerted their subscribers of civil rights abuses and hate crimes. *Muslimah Media Watch* critiques how North American Muslim women are portrayed in the media and *Loonwatch* anonymously satirizes Islamophobes. Unaffiliated American Muslims have recourse to rebut bigoted content by posting comments, uploading their own video responses, and flooding the Facebook walls of bigoted politicians.

American Muslims have taken proactive steps to ensure that they develop their own narratives by taking advantage of new media. American Muslims hope new media will more accurately depict a broader segment of their views.[95] To promote the well being of the American Muslim blogosphere, the Brass Crescent Awards rewards skilled bloggers, while "the Muslim Blogger" offers tips on how to yield higher traffic. Hamza Yusuf encourages American Muslims to engage in online "perception management."[96] Some American Muslims heed his call by attempting to optimize search engine results that favor Muslims.

Conclusion

There is no question that the Internet has become a remarkable resource for American Muslims, at the same time that it has amplified certain voices among the American

Muslim community. However, such realities as the proliferation of search engine optimization technologies, the uneven distribution of Internet proficiency, the rise of online advertising and paid blogs, and the heavy lobbying and counter-mobilization by the American right all give reason for pause before wholeheartedly embracing the notion that new media can reverse asymmetries in traditional American print and broadcast media.[97] Despite their blogs, tweets, and posts, American Muslims continue to face negative public opinion. American Muslims will need to do more to outperform anti-Muslim bloggers to effectively counter claims from mainstream media outlets and, like Qasim Latif and countless others, attempt to retain some control over their own narrative.

NOTES

1. The actual name of the founder of the blogging community has been changed here.
2. "Martyrdom, God willing" in Arabic.
3. See Jeffrey Zaleski, *The Soul of Cyberspace* (Ann Arbor: HarperEdge, 1997): 79.
4. See Daniel Varisco, "Muslims and the Media in the Blogosphere" *Contemporary Islam* 4, 1 (2009): 157.
5. See Zaleski, *The Soul of Cyberspace*, 58–79.
6. See Peter Mandaville, "Reimagining the Ummah?" in Mohammadi Ali, ed., *Islam Encountering Globalisation* (New York: Routledge Curzon, 2002): 71.
7. See Larry Poston, "Da'wa in the West," in Yvonne Haddad, ed., *The Muslims of America* (New York: Oxford University Press, 1991): 133.
8. See Varisco, *Muslims and the Media*, 158.
9. See M. A. Sati, *"Internet Islam,"* (Proquest, Umi Dissertation Publishing, 2011): 84–6.
10. See Gary Bunt, *Virtually Islamic: Computer-Mediated Communication and Cyber-Islamic Environments* (Cardiff: University of Wales Press, 2000): 131.
11. See Peter Mandaville, *Transnational Muslim Politics: Reimagining the Umma* (New York: Routlege, 2001): 161.
12. See Jarret Brachman and Alix Levine. "You Too Can Be Awlaki!" *Fletcher Forum of World Affairs* 35, 1 (2011): 28.
13. See Mandaville, *"Reimagining the Ummah?"* 82.
14. See Jon Anderson, "Islam and the Globalization of Politics," presented to the Council on Foreign Relations Muslim Politics Study Group, New York City, June 25, 1996, p. 1.
15. A See Abdul Hamid Lotfi, "Spreading the Word: Communicating Islam in America," in Yvonne Haddad and Jane Smith, eds., *Muslim Minorities in the West: Visible and Invisible* (Oxford: AltaMira Press, 2002): 7–8.
16. See Anastasia Karaflogka, *E-Religion* (London: Equinox, 2006): 205.
17. See Paul Barrett, *American Islam: the Struggle for the Soul of a Religion* (New York: Farrar, Straus and Giroux, 2007): 231.
18. See Gary Bunt, *iMuslims: Rewiring the House of Islam* (Chapel Hill: University of North Carolina Press, 2009): 237.
19. See Alejandro Beutel, "Radicalization and Homegrown Terrorism in Western Muslim Communities," (Bethesda: Minaret of Freedom Institute, 2007): 6.

20. See Risa Brooks, "Muslim 'Homegrown' Terrorism in the United States," *International Security* 36, 2 (2011): 30–31

21. *Ibid.,* 42.

22. See Jacqueline Salmon, "An American Muslim Voice on the Internet." *Virginian-Pilot*, E3 (July 4, 2009).

23. See Varisco, *Muslims and the Media*, 158.

24. See Leor Halevi, "The Consumer Jihad: Boycott Fatwas and Nonviolent Resistance on the World Wide Web," *International Journal of Middle East Studies* 44, 1 (2012): 47.

25. See Karen Leonard, "American Muslims and Authority: Competing Discourses in a Non-Muslim State." *Journal of American Ethnic History* 25, 1 (2005): 17.

26. See Göran Larsson, "Cyber-Islamophobia? The Case of WikiIslam," *Contemporary Islam* 1, 1 (2007): 57–8.

27. See Thom Shanker and Eric Schmitt, "U.S. Military Goes Online to Rebut Extremists' Messages," *New York Times* (November 17, 2011).

28. See Michael Whine, "Cyberspace-a New Medium for Communication, Command, and Control by Extremists," *Studies in Conflict and Terrorism* 22, 3 (1999): 232.

29. See Adam Serwer, "Does Posting Jihadist Material Make Tarek Mehanna a Terrorist?," *Mother Jones*. Available at: http://www.motherjones.com/politics/2011/12/tarek-mehanna-terrorist. Accessed August 26, 2012.

30. See W. Ali, E. Clifton, M. Duss, L. Fang, S. Keyes, and F. Shakir, "Fear, Inc.," *Center for American Progress* (2011): 47.

31. See Alexis Kort, "Dar al-Cyber Islam: Women, Domestic Violence, and the Islamic Reformation on the World Wide Web," *Journal of Muslim Minority Affairs* 25, 3 (2005): 365.

32. See Smeeta Mishra and Gaby Semaan. "Islam in Cyberspace: South Asian Muslims in America Log In," *Journal of Broadcasting & Electronic Media*, 54, 1 (2010): 98.

33. See Mohammed el-Nanawy and Sahar Khamis, *Islam Dot Com: Contemporary Islamic Discourses in Cyberspace* (New York: Macmillan, 2009): 144.

34. See Lorne Dawson and Douglas Cowan, *Religion Online: Finding Faith on the Internet* (New York: Routledge, 2004): 2.

35. See Leonard, "American Muslims and Authority," 14.

36. See Suad Abdul-Khabeer in Amir Ahmad, ed., *The Future of Islam in the Age of New Media*. Available at: http://www.islamintheageofnewmedia.com/.

37. See Bunt, *iMuslims*, 123.

38. See Salmon, "An American Muslim," 2009.

39. See Mishra and Semaan, "Islam in Cyberspace," 96.

40. See el-Nanawy and Khamis, *Islam Dot Com*, 217.

41. See Peter Mandaville, "Globalization and the Politics of Religious Knowledge." *Theory, Culture & Society* 24, 2 (2007): 114.

42. See Muhammad Haq, "The 'Sheikh Google' Phenomenon." Available at: http://www.suhaibwebb.com/society/media/. Accessed August 26, 2012.

43. See Mishra and Semaan, "Islam in Cyberspace," 93.

44. See el-Nanawy and Khamis, *Islam Dot Com*, 207.

45. See Saminaz Zaman, "From Imam to Cyber—Mufti: Consuming Identity in Muslim America." *The Muslim World*, 98 (2008): 2.

46. See Dawson and Cowan, *Religion Online*, 5.

47. See Anna Piela, *Muslim Women Online* (New York: Routledge, 2011): 35.

48. See Mathangi, Subramanian. "New Modes of Communication," in Suad Joseph, ed., *Encyclopedia of Women & Islamic Cultures* (Leiden: Brill, 2012): 7.

49. See Piela, *Muslim Women*, 35.

50. See Anna Piela, "Challenging Stereotypes: Muslim Women's Photographic Self-Representations on the Internet," *Aesthetics* 4, 1 (2010): 100.

51. See Zaman, "Consuming Identity," 6.

52. See Muhsin Mahdi, "From the Manuscript Age to the Age of Printed Books," George Atiyeh, ed., *The Book in the Islamic World* (New York: SUNY Press, 1995): 13.

53. See Francis Robinson, "Technology and Religious Change," *Modern Asian Studies* 27, 1(1993): 247.

54. *Ibid.*, 238.

55. *Ibid.*, 250–1.

56. See Charles Hirschkind, "Experiments in Devotion Online: The YouTube Khuṭba." *International Journal of Middle East Studies* 44, 1 (2012): 13.

57. See Zaman, "Consuming Identity," 6.

58. See Naiyerah Kolkailah, "Avoiding a Harmful E-Diet." Available at: http://www.suhaibwebb.com/society/media/. Accessed August 26, 2012.

59. See Bunt, *Virtually Islamic*, 146.

60. See Piela, *Muslim Women*, 34.

61. See Charles Hirschkind, "Experiments in Devotion Online: The Youtube Khuṭba," *International Journal of Middle East Studies*, 44, 1 (2012): 13.

62. See Dawson and Cowan, *Religion Online*, 4.

63. See Leonard Bartlotti, "Open Access in Closed Societies: Theological Education in Muslim Contexts," *Transformation*, 18, 2 (2001): 104.

64. See Garbi Schmidt, "Dialectics of Authenticity," *The Muslim World*, 2 (2002): 13.

65. See Ghada Alakhdar in Amir Ahmad, ed., *The Future of Islam in the Age of New Media*. Available at: http://www.islamintheageofnewmedia.com/.

66. See el-Nanawy and Khamis, *Islam Dot Com*, 48.

67. See Alia Somani, "Online Dating," in Suad Joseph, ed., *Encyclopedia of Women & Islamic Cultures* (Leiden: Brill, 2012): 1.

68. *Ibid.*, 10.

69. *Ibid.*, 7.

70. See Dawson and Cowan, *Religion Online*, 128.

71. See Sima Shakhsari, "Weblogistan Goes to War: Representational Practices, Gendered Soldiers and Neoliberal Entrepreneurship in Diaspora," *Feminist Review*, 99, 1 (2011): 11–14.

72. *Ibid.*, 21.

73. *Ibid.*, 9–10.

74. See Karaflogka, *E-Religion*, 99.

75. See Jennifer Brinkerhoff, "Digital Diasporas and International Development," *Public Administration and Development*, 24, 5 (2004): 411.

76. See el-Nanawy and Khamis, *Islam Dot Com*, 117.

77. *Ibid.*, 120.

78. See Kort, "Dar al-Cyber Islam," 365.

79. See Bunt, *iMuslims*, 122.

80. See Zaman, "Consuming Identity," 3.

81. See Garbi Schmidt, "The Transnational Umma—Myth or Reality," *The Muslim World*, 95 (2005): 10.

82. See Steven Morrison, "Terrorism Online: Is Speech the Same as It Ever Was?" *Creighton Law Review*, 44 (2010): 9.
83. *Ibid.*, 8.
84. See Dawinder Sidhu, "Chilling Effect of Government Surveillance Programs on the Use of the Internet by Muslim-Americans," *University of Maryland Law Journal of Race, Religion, Gender and Class*, 7 (2007): 2
85. See Sunaina Maira, "Citizenship and Dissent: South Asian Muslim Youth in the US After 9/11." *South Asian Popular Culture*, 8, 1 (2010): 38.
86. See Sati, "Internet Islam," 16.
87. See Ali et al., "Fear, Inc.," 71.
88. See Samuel Freedman, "Waging a One-Man War on American Muslims," *The New York Times* (December 17, 2011).
89. See Ali et al., "Fear, Inc.," 40.
90. *Ibid.*, 67.
91. See Massimo Introvigne, "A Symbolic Universe: Information Terrorism and New Religions in Cyberspace," in Højsgaard and Warburg, eds., *Religion and Cyberspace* (New York: Routledge, 2005): 105. I am referring here to blogs like *Creeping Shariah, USA-Stop Shariah,* the pro-Israeli *MEMRI* blog, *Campus Watch, DiscoverTheNetworks, JihadWatch, FrontPageMagazine, Islamist Watch, Terrorism Awareness Project, NewsReal* blog, and *Atlas Shrugs.*
92. See Steven Salaita, "Curricular Activism and Academic Freedom," *Arab Studies Quarterly*, 30, 1 (2008): 1–2.
93. See Larsson, "Cyber-Islamophobia?" 54.
94. See Varisco, *Muslims and the Media*, 157.
95. See Roxanne Marcotte, "Gender and Sexuality Online on Australian Muslim Forums," *Contemporary Islam* 4, 1 (2009): 136.
96. See Introvigne, "A Symbolic Universe," 106.
97. See Stephen Marmura, "A Net Advantage?" *New Media & Society* 10, 2 (2008): 248.

References

Bunt, Gary, *iMuslims: Rewiring the House of Islam* (Chapel Hill: University of North Carolina Press, 2009).

Eickelman, Dale F., and Jon W. Anderson, eds., *New Media in the Muslim World: The Emerging Public Sphere* (Bloomington: Indiana University Press, 2003).

el-Nanawy, Mohammed, and Sahar Khamis, *Islam Dot Com: Contemporary Islamic Discourses in Cyberspace* (New York: Palgrave Macmillan, 2009).

Piela, Anna. *Muslim Women Online* (New York: Routledge, 2011).

CHAPTER 23

MUSLIM ARTISTS IN AMERICA

MUNIR JIWA

On January 19, 2002, an impressive event took place at the Cathedral of St. John the Divine in New York City; it was called *Reflections at a Time of Transformation: American Muslim Artists Reach out to New Yorkers in the Aftermath of September 11*. Hosted by the American Society for Muslim Advancement (ASMA), the event featuring the works of Muslim artists was aimed at "healing wounds" and "building interfaith and intercultural bridges." It was designed to celebrate the diversity of Muslim communities in New York, with and through its artists—visual artists, sculptors, musicians, poets, and filmmakers among others.[1] A first of its kind, the *Reflections* event has inspired numerous other such events and exhibits throughout the years, featuring contributions not only from the secular art worlds but also from Muslim communities who have begun including their artists/cultural producers to better represent themselves to the wider public.

From the Islamic Society of North America's annual conference (the largest annual gathering of Muslims in North America), where they now showcase an art exhibit and films, to the performers at the annual Muslim Parade in New York City as well as the comedy film/tours of *Allah Made Me Funny* produced by Michael Wolfe of Unity Productions, the US Department of State showcasing hip-hop group *Native Deen,* the MoMA exhibit *Without Boundary: Seventeen Ways of Looking* to countless online exhibits, the *Muslim Voices Festival* in New York City, the screening of *New Muslim Cool* at the San Francisco Film Festival, Wajahat Ali's *Domestic Crusaders*, and a major retrospective of the artist Zarina at the Guggenheim Museum in New York, it is clear that Muslim artists/cultural producers are being taken up in the art worlds and have become important to the representation of Muslim communities in the United States and globally.

Much has changed in the world, yet today, more than a decade since the events of 9/11, the national frames through which Muslims in America are identified and represented remain very much the same. Islam and Muslims are still framed through what I have been calling the five "media pillars" of Islam, namely: (1) the events of 9/11 as the predominant temporal lens through which to understand Muslims and Islamic history and theology; (2) violence and terrorism; (3) Muslim women and veiling; (4) Islam and "the West," including questions of compatibility and values as well as new debates on shar'ia; and (5) the Middle East as the geographical and spatial lens through which to understand Islam and Muslims, especially focusing on politics.

Exhibits and performances are not without their own politics. Too often Muslim artists are showcased as a means of projecting a more "cultured" and "civilized" Islam (Winegar, 2008). They are often paraded as "good Muslims" because they are likely to be more "spiritual" or more "Sufi" influenced and oriented and less tied to religious norms, or so the logic goes. If the artists are Muslim women, the art worlds often attempt to "save" them from Muslim men by liberating them from the shackles of "Islamic" patriarchy (Abu-Lughod, 2002). Assumed to be less "traditional," Muslim artists are likely to be more vocal in their denouncing of "Islamic" terrorism, more pluralistic, not very likely to attend a mosque, and have only a symbolic relationship to the Qur'an and the Sunna. Following this assumption, if one is a Muslim artist, religious norms are not likely to be very important to one's self-identity. In the American art worlds, the assumption is that it is because an artist is less religiously committed, she is artistically free and liberated. Nonetheless, the art worlds impose their own fundamentalisms, including limiting artistic genres and styles, gender bias, and racial privileging.

While there are numerous Muslims artists working in a variety of artistic genres, this chapter introduces four visual artists, "celebrities" who have made a significant contribution to and impact on the mainstream secular art worlds in the United States: Zarina Hashmi, Shirin Neshat, Ghada Amer, and Shahzia Sikander. After a brief sketch of each artist, I will turn to an analysis of why the study of Muslim artists is important, considering the questions these artists raise about the identification "Muslim," either as an externally imposed category they come to navigate or as a way of acknowledging their personal affiliation with Islam. Regardless of the fact that these four visual artists have "made it" in the American art establishment, they are fascinating for the ways in which they have dealt with issues of identity, even as they focus on the formal properties of art making.

ZARINA HASHMI (1937–)

Born in Aligarh, India in 1937, the artist Zarina Hashmi, known in the art world as Zarina, was perhaps among the first Muslim women to break into the otherwise very competitive and exclusive New York art scene. Educated at Aligarh Muslim University where she earned a B.Sc. Honors in 1958, she went on to study printmaking in India and then abroad in Paris at Atelier-17 with S. W. Hayter from 1963 to 1967. She continued her studies in woodblock printmaking on a Japan Foundation Fellowship at Toshi Yoshido Studio, Tokyo, in 1974.

For most of her life, Zarina has been traveling, and it is her life on the road that has become the very theme of her art works. Her central theme is the home, real and imagined, and it is reflected conceptually and formally through her work. Places of transit, borders, cities, countries, maps, migration—all are the subjects of her art and life. Her visually spare prints are dense with meaning, consistent not only with a formal minimalist aesthetic but also reflective of the nomadic life she has lived. Islam, including various Sufi traditions, alongside her love of mathematics and architecture, all ground her life and work. While Qur'anic passages, Urdu recall words, and Sufi meditations all provide the axis for her as a Muslim, she is also influenced by the many peoples and places that have been part of her life's journey. Both a practicing artist for many years and also a teacher of art, Zarina has a profound sense of what it means to make and reflect upon art. She has been awarded prestigious art residencies at Art-Omi in Omi, New York, at the Women's Studio Workshop in Rosendale, New York, and at Montalvo Residency in Saratoga, California, and has held faculty positions at the NY Feminist Art Institute, Bennington College, Cornell University, the University of California Santa Cruz, New York University, and the New School University, New York.

In a major retrospective of her work called *Weaving Memory 1990–2006*, exhibited at Bose Pacia Gallery in Mumbai in 2007, some of the seminal pieces of her vast body of work included *The House at Aligarh* (1990), *House With Four Walls* (1991), *House of Many Rooms* (1993), *Packed House* and *Journey to the Edge of Land* (1994), *Road Lines* (1996), *Santa Cruz* and *Homes I Made/A Life in Nine Lines* (1997), *Home is a Foreign Place* (1999), *Delhi* (2000), *Atlas of My World* (2001)... *These cities blotted into the wilderness* and *Countries* (2003), and *Letters from Home* (2004). Other solo retrospectives include *Silent Soliloquy* at Bodhi Art, Singapore (2006) and *Counting 1977–2005*, at Bose Pacia Modern, New York (2005). Solo shows include *Cities, Countries and Borders* at Chemould Gallery in Mumbai and Chawkandi Gallery in Karachi, (2004); *Maps, Homes, and Itineraries* at Gallery Lux in San Francisco (2003); *Home Is a Foreign Place* at Korn Gallery, Drew University, Madison (2002); *Homes I Made* at the Faculty Gallery, University of California, Santa Cruz (1994); and *House with Four Walls* at the Bronx Museum of the Arts, New York (1992).

Among Zarina's numerous group shows, an exhibit entitled *The Third Mind: American Artists Contemplate Asia, 1860–1989* at the Guggenheim Museum in New York, January to April 2009, included her works. She also participated in a show at the SH Contemporary in Shanghai in September 2007. Earlier groups shows included *Crossings: Contemporary Art of India* at Rutgers University, New Brunswick, New Jersey (2006), *Figures of Thinking—Convergences in Contemporary Cultures*,

University of Richmond, Virginia (2007–2008), *Fresh Talk Revisited: New York Artists from Fresh Talk/Daring Gazes* (2003), *From the Two Pens: Line and Color in Islamic Art*, Williams College Museum of Art, Williamstown, Massachusetts (2002), *India and Pakistan Contemporary Prints*, Victoria and Albert Museum, London (1997), and several other shows in Dubai, the United Arab Emirates, at the Asia Society, New York, a show in Krakow, Poland, and at the Bibliothèque Nationale in Paris.

Zarina's works are included in permanent collections of the Museum of Modern Art (MoMA) in New York, the Victorian and Albert Museum in London, the Bibliothèque Nationale in Paris, and the National Gallery of Modern Art in New Delhi, India. Her first retrospective exhibition in the United States, *Zarina Paper Like Skin*, was held at the Hammer Museum at UCLA, September 29 to December 30, 2012, at the Guggenheim Museum in New York, January 25 to April 21, 2013, and at the Art Institute of Chicago, June 26 to September 22, 2013. Zarina is represented by the gallery Luhring Augustine in New York City, where she lives.

SHIRIN NESHAT (1957–)

Arguably one of the most celebrated contemporary visual artists in the United States and globally, Shirin Neshat's photographs, video installations, and films explore themes of women, Iran, Islam, tradition and modernity, public and private, and the use of space and architecture to think about freedom and constraint, order and chaos.

Born to an upper-middle class family in Qazvin, Iran, on March 26, 1957, Neshat had a secular upbringing in Iran, where she also attended a Catholic school. She moved to the United States in 1974, prior to the Iranian Revolution, to pursue her education. She graduated from the University of California, Berkeley, with a B.A., M.A., and M.F.A. in painting in 1983. She moved to New York, where she worked at several different jobs, including at the nonprofit organization Storefront Art and Architecture. Although this gave her a lot of experience in the art world, it was not until she returned to her native Iran that she found a reason to make art again.

Inspired by the many postrevolutionary Iranian women she saw in Iran in the early 1990s, Neshat began a series of photographs entitled *Women of Allah*. This was a personal exploration for her, and she claims that the series had the naïveté of someone coming to terms with understanding the new Islamic Republic of Iran and its gendered spaces. Using Persian calligraphy, she explored the poetics and politics of the Revolution and women's participation in it.

As she continued with the theme of women, Islam, the Iranian Revolution, architecture, gendered spaces, and identity, Neshat also began experimenting with film, a medium she said was the most complete because it includes various other media, from photography to performance and music. She also called it a move toward becoming more philosophical, lyrical, and poetic, since she found that photography, through its single and still image, was often confining. Video and film called people into participating more intimately with her work. A number of her videos/ films appeared in the late 1990s, firmly establishing Neshat in the New York art scene. From there she became one of the most sought after artists in the United States and around the world. Her trilogy *Turbulent* (1998), *Rapture* (1999), and *Fervor* (2000)— followed by a fourth film, *Soliloquy* (2000)—has been shown around the world and has been the subject of many academic works on art.

Neshat's 2003 work *Tooba* was the first that neither included women in veils nor was filmed in Morocco and Turkey, as was the case with her previous films. Shot in Mexico, *Tooba* was an attempt to think more about meaning and less about the clichés of the veil. Inspired by the story called *Tooba and the Meaning of the Night* by Shahrnush Parsipur, Neshat's story was about the relationship of women, men, and a blessed tree in the garden of paradise. For Neshat, this work was a way of thinking about the events of September 11, 2001, and an attempt at bringing back beauty to the world. She called it her most Iranian, Islamic, and universal work.

Several more of Neshat's pieces, inspired by Parsipur's *Women Without Men*, were made into films. In March 2009 all five films of this series, *Mahdokh* (2004), *Zarin* (2005), *Munis* (2008), *Faezeh* (2008), and *Farokh Legha* (2008), were premiered together first at the ARoS Aarhus Kunstmuseum in Denmark (March–May, 2008) and then at the National Museum of Contemporary Art in Athens, Greece (March–May, 2009).

Shirin Neshat has received numerous awards for her work and has exhibited at all the major biennales and film festivals around the world. Her solo and group exhibits number into the hundreds all over the United States, Europe, Asia, and Africa. She was also a featured artist in the Museum of Modern Art's 2006 show called *Without Boundary: Seventeen Ways of Looking*, an exhibit on Islam and contemporary art/artists. A major retrospective of her work was shown at the Detroit Institute of Arts from April 7 to July 7, 2013. She continues to be represented by Barbara Gladstone Gallery in New York City, where she lives.

GHADA AMER (B. 1963–)

Ghada Amer was born in Cairo, Egypt. In 1974, her family relocated to France, where she later began her studies in art. She was trained first at L'École des Beaux-Arts in Nice, where she received her B.F.A. in 1986. She continued her studies at the School of the Museum of Fine Arts in Boston in 1987. Returning to Nice, France, she earned her M.F.A. in Painting at the L'École des Beaux-Arts in 1989. She completed her art studies at the Institut des Hautes Études en Arts Plastiques in Paris.

Amer's work includes paintings, embroidered canvases, textile installations, sculptures, and several multimedia urban art projects. Her art addresses themes of women, love, sex, sexuality, spirituality, religion, and war and peace. Amer's work came most fully to public attention after the events of September 11, 2001. Like many other visual artists identified as Muslim, she began explicitly speaking to issues relating to Muslim women, though this was not always her intention or necessarily apparent in her work.

Amer's initial interest in themes of women and women's bodies stemmed from an Egyptian magazine she came across in 1988, which she claimed became the inspiration for her art. The magazine, *Venus*, took photomontages of western models and superimposed on them more conservative and modest dress forms, including veils, making them more Islamically acceptable. These photos inspired Amer's art both in terms of themes and in the more formal aspects of art making, including the juxtaposition of various art forms, East and West boundaries, and male and female boundaries in western artistic practices, such as male-dominated painting, abstract expressionism, and women's art as craft.

Her early works in the 1990s explored themes of innocent and ideal love, while she continued questioning the formal aspects of art. The results included stitched and painted works such as *Happy End* (1992), *Barbie Loves Ken, Ken Loves Barbie* (1995), and *Les Mariés* (1995). Continuing with the theme of women and love, Amer began dealing with unrequited love through works such as *Majnun* (1997), based on the story of *Majnun Leila*. She created public works such as *Love Park* (1999) where she installed a bench in a park with a sign in French translated into English as, "In love, only conquest and breaking-up are important, the rest is filler." Keeping consistent with the themes of women and love, Ghada began exploring works which were sexually explicit. Sewing nude women in autoerotic and even lesbian sexual acts, she began exploring female sexuality as a way of repudiating first-wave feminism, which often sought to deny women the right to their bodies and pleasure, as Amer claimed. She also continued to think about what it means to use stitching and painting together to question high and low art forms. Numerous works were dedicated to these conceptual and aesthetic explorations, including *Big Drips* (1999), *Black Stripes* (2000), *The Little Girl* (2001), and *Big Black Kansas City Paining—RFGA* (2005), among many others.

From November to December 2001, Amer had a solo show at Deitch Projects entitled *Encyclopedia of Pleasures*, inspired by a twelfth-century text, *Jawami al-Ladha*, edited by Ali Ibn Nasr Al-Katib, which explored in detail female sexuality. Amer used this text as an example of how, over time, female sexuality became suppressed in the Muslim world as well as in the western world.

In numerous other works, Amer has pursued themes of peace. In a 2002 public installation work at Art Basel in Miami she created a garden with the peace symbol, questioning whether peace means just the absence of war and considering the difficulties of creating and promoting peace. In 2005, she presented a work called *Reign of Terror* at the Davis Museum and Cultural Center, Wellesley College.

A giant in the New York art world, Amer has exhibited in numerous solo and group shows at such venues such as Deitch Projects, New York; the Gagosian Gallery in London, New York, and Beverly Hills; the Whitney Biennale, New York; The Gwangju

Biennale, South Korea; the Venice Biennale; and the Johannesburg Biennale; and in exhibits all over Europe. She has exhibited works at Gallery Espace Karim Francis in Cairo, Egypt, and also at the Tel Aviv Museum of Art and at the Anadil Gallery in Jerusalem. In 2002, she exhibited her work at the P.S.1 Contemporary Art Center in Queens, New York in an exhibition titled *The Short Century: Independence and Liberation Movements in Africa, 1945–1994*. In 2003 Amer's work was included in *Looking Both Ways: Art of the Contemporary African Diaspora* at the Museum for African Art in Queens. In 2006, her work was exhibited at the MoMA in New York in a group show called *Without Boundary: Seventeen Ways of Looking*, a major exhibit exploring themes of Islam and contemporary art/artists. In 2008, a major retrospective exhibition of more than fifty of Ghada Amer's works, entitled *Love Has No End*, was held at the Brooklyn Museum of Art's Elizabeth A. Sackler Center for Feminist Art. She showed her works in a group exhibit called *Tea With Nefertiti* at Mathaf: Arab Museum of Modern Art, from November 2012 to March 2013; this is now on exhibit at the Institut du Monde Arabe in Paris. Amer is represented by the Cheim and Read Gallery in New York City, where she lives.

Shahzia Sikander (1969–)

A prominent artist in the United States and globally, Shahzia Sikander was named a John D. and Catherine T. MacArthur fellow in 2006, a prestigious award recognizing outstanding achievement in a variety of fields and disciplines. What has been dubbed the "genius" award recognized her contributions to the world as an artist, working in the painstaking and labor-intensive medium of Indo-Persian miniature painting. In addition to painting, Sikander's work traverses a variety of media, including drawings, large-scale wall installations, digital animation, and video. She was trained at the Department of Miniature Painting at Lahore's prestigious National College of Arts, where she received her B.F.A. in 1992, and she continued her studies at the Rhode Island School of Design, in Providence, Rhode Island, earning an M.F.A. in 1995. She was also a fellow of the Glassell School of Art's Core Program in Houston (1995–1997) and an artist in residence at Otis College of Art and Design in Los Angeles (2005).

In the mid-1980s in Lahore, Pakistan, Sikander experimented in the area of classical miniature painting. Her creative expressions combined the genre with contemporary art practices, launching a renewed commitment to the art of miniature painting and gaining her a substantial following. As a result the Department of Miniature Painting at the National College of Arts in Lahore has seen a dramatic increase in the number of young artists now pursuing majors in its fine arts program.

Sikander's work recasts the formal artistic debates about the conventional methods of addressing traditional miniature paintings. Using her various geographic locations creatively, she reassembles her miniature paintings both to expand the formal properties of the artistic practice often classified as craft and to question the materials and scale of the work. Using wit, irony, and paradox, Sikander's artworks draw upon a variety of media to push the boundaries of the miniature tradition. As much as she is interested in the formal aspects and properties of artistic practices, Sikander also addresses themes of Islam, Pakistan (where she was born in 1969), India, Hindu/Muslim relations, imagery and iconography, as well as notions of tradition and modernity, East and West, hybridity, and women.

Although based in New York City, Sikander works in various locations, and often these are visually reflected in her creations. Her works can be found in major collections at such New York institutions as the MoMA, the Whitney Museum of American Art, and the Solomon R. Guggenheim Museum. Collections in California include those at the Museum of Contemporary Art, Los Angeles, San Francisco Museum of Modern Art, and San Diego Museum of Art. Her work is also included in the Hirshhorn Museum, Washington, D.C.; Walker Art Center, Minneapolis; Philadelphia Museum of Art; Museum of Fine Arts, Boston; Houston Museum of Fine Arts; Art Gallery of New South Wales, Sydney; National Gallery of Canada; and at the Musée d'Art Moderne de la Ville de Paris.

Sikander's work has appeared in countless solo and group shows in the United States and around the world. It was featured in solo exhibitions at the Irish Museum of Modern Art, Dublin (2007); the Museum of Contemporary Art, Sydney (2007–2008); and Ikon Gallery in Birmingham, England (2008). Group shows include various exhibits and biennales around the world, including the First International Biennial of Contemporary Art—*The Joy of My Dreams,* Charterhouse of Santa Maria de las Cuevas, Seville, Spain (2004); *Translation,* Palais de Tokyo, Paris (2005); *Without Boundary: Seventeen Ways of Looking,* at the MoMA, New York (2006); *Shahzia Sikander Selects: Works from the Permanent Collection,* exhibited at the Cooper-Hewitt National Design Museum, New York (March–September 2009); Sharjah Biennale (2013), *Poetic Justice* in Istanbul, Turkey (2003) and again at the Istanbul Biennale (2013), and *Doris Duke Shangri La: Architecture, Landscape, and Islamic Art,* held at the Museum of Design in New York (September 2012–January 2013). In addition to the prestigious MacArthur award, Sikander was named a Young Global Leader by the World Economic Forum in Davos in 2006. She received the *Tamgha-e-Imtiaz,* National Medal of Honor from the Government of Pakistan (2005), and the Commendation Award by the Mayor's Office, New York City (2003). In 2012, she was awarded the inaugural US State Department Medal of Arts, presented by Hillary Clinton at the fiftieth anniversary celebration of Art in Embassies. In 2013 she was selected to serve on the Master Jury of the Aga Khan Award for Architecture, the largest architectural prize in the world. Her work has been reviewed in prestigious art and other publications including *Art Forum, Art News, The New York Times, The Wall Street Journal,* and *Time,* and in numerous academic journals and publications. She is represented by the gallery Sikkema Jenkins and Co. in New York City, where she lives.

Aestheticizing Politics, Politicizing Aesthetics

The framing by various institutions and curators renders the artist and art differently meaningful each time they come together at an event or exhibit. For artists, each time, it means having to enter a different relationship with their own work as well as being constantly creative and innovative—key features of modern art in the West. By taking up certain identities over others, like being Muslim post-9/11, artists show that they do not do their work in a vacuum. The art worlds with which they primarily identify professionally reproduce the hierarchies, boundaries, and questions of identity in the larger fields of power within the United States. For minority artists and Muslim artists more specifically, art and identity are intimately tied to national politics.

Studying Muslim artists in America is helpful in understanding the way identity and politics are played out in art worlds through art practices, including in artists' narratives, in the physical art object itself, and in the specific sites of galleries and museums and related art world sites, such as universities. In addition to the politics internal to the field of cultural production such as the hierarchies of difference among artists, the boundaries around art/nonart, and the questioning of Euro-American art history pitched as modern and universal and against which most art is judged and compared, art worlds and artistic practices localize the places and ways that people think about large notions like globalization, modernity and postcolonialism as they relate to identity and belonging. The study of Muslim artists also allows us to see more clearly the relationship between art worlds and the field of forces in which they are embedded (Bourdieu 1993). That artists and art are in conversation not only with cultural fields but also with national politics makes the case that modern art must be viewed as a sociopolitical production and not just "art for art's sake." Nowhere has this been clearer than in the impact the events of 9/11 have had on Muslim identity and representation in the United States. Tracking these shifts and changes by examining the American art worlds before and after 9/11 through the narratives and artworks of Muslim artists also allows us to see the ways that Muslim identity can be claimed, debated, discussed, and represented, relationally and circumstantially.

As Vera Zolberg, a prominent sociologist of art has reminded us, artists in the West do not often sustain communities over a long period of time and are also affiliated with many different individuals and communities, often at the same time. Indeed a key dimension of artistic life in the West is individual creativity and authenticity, and "the very character of art in Western societies makes it almost impossible to exclude individual artists from its purview" (Zolberg 1990, 109). While the four artists described above have most often been identified in terms of sex, gender, race, ethnicity, nationality, and region and often by art historical genres, they have rarely been seen in terms of the category or identification "Muslim." Such an identification became especially evident in the post-9/11 context and despite the fact that it is a discriminated against minority identity in the West, it is being increasingly claimed. My own framing of artists as Muslim provides one more reading of artists and art among the many readings by curators, gallerists, art critics, and art historians. But I also argue that being Muslim for many artists means understanding this identity in relation to other identities such as being Nigerian or Malaysian, or a woman, or Arab or South Asian or African American. As Metcalf has stated in the edited volume *Making Muslim Space* (1996), "singling out" Muslim identity does not "assume that anyone labeled Muslim focuses wholly on Islamic cultural expressions" (2). Similarly, Eickelman and Anderson (1999) have stated, "Muslims, of course, act not just as Muslims but according to class interests, out of a sense of nationalism, on behalf of tribal or family networks, and from all the diverse motivations that characterize human endeavor" (1). In addition to not singling out Muslim as a sole identity, but rather seeing it as relational, it is important to focus on the art, the artists' narratives around art, the disjunctures between various art world players, and the shifts in meaning brought on by different exhibits. Within these artistic landscapes, Appadurai (1996) reminds us, the "suffix-scape" in addition to pointing to the "fluid and irregular," changing, shifting contexts in which artists work and interact are not "objectively given relations that look the same from every angle of vision but, rather, that they are deeply perspectival constructs, inflected by the historical, linguistic, and political situatedness of different sorts of actors" (33).

Although the Muslim artists highlighted above might be involved with forging new networks related to identity inside and outside the art worlds, they view themselves first and foremost as artists, As cultural producers who see themselves as intellectuals and as privileged elites, artists make significant contributions to theoretical debates in the American and international art worlds. They do so by blurring insider/outsider boundaries in art worlds and by seeking out new places of exhibit, as evident in the plethora of Muslim artists' exhibits after 9/11, including online exhibits. Educated in fine arts, both in the East and the West—in diverse genres such as sculpting, printmaking, video, painting, photography, and calligraphy—these artists also insist on widening the definitions of the visual arts, just as they are thinking more creatively across artistic boundaries such as performance, poetry, and music. Much of this expansion is not just to secure themselves places of exhibit and success in the art worlds but also to provide a means of thinking creatively and innovatively about art and to express their identities through art, even as they often resist identity politics while focusing on the formal properties of art. Because the artists mentioned above are theologically, culturally, ethnically, nationally, and linguistically diverse, there is no predictability or aesthetic unity in their work based on being Muslim. Instead, artistic continuity is based on each artist's individual visual style and mark.

One of the great challenges of studying Muslim artists has been the academic literature within which they might be understood. Studying Muslim artists in the United States has been even more difficult, given that my own discipline of anthropology

rarely studies the West; when it does, it is usually through ethnic and cultural categories and rarely through the category "Muslim." Much of the literature in anthropology
addresses the non-West and refrains from "studying up." Working with postcolonial
Muslim artists in the West, a kind of elite group, confuses any stable notion of "culture" and blurs boundaries, both in art and Islam, of high/low, East/West, us/them,
and traditional/modern. Even as artists were identified as being Muslim post-9/11,
they hesitated to see this as the production of a "culture" or a stable aesthetic associated with being Muslim. Instead, through their own in-betweenness and through
their art and the many sites in which they have lived and worked, they have destabilized and even worked against any notion of a coherent, timeless culture. Working
"against culture" (Abu-Lughod, 1991) was seen both at the level of the material culture artists produced and at the level of culture as in "Muslim culture." Both were
refused on the grounds that Muslim identity and the art Muslims produce might be
essentialized. Although the artists spoke freely about such things as Iraqi culture, or
Malaysian culture, or African art, rarely did they refer to "Muslim/Islamic culture."

DO MUSLIM ARTISTS CREATE ISLAMIC ART?

As suggested above, because of the complexity of qualifying artists who are Muslim as
"Muslim artists," there is indeed a tendency to ask what is visually Islamic about the
works of these artists. When one uses the term, classification, and category "Muslim,"
which has now a worldwide geographical location, most often the assumption is that
Muslim artists create Islamic art, just as we might make similar correlations with
other categories. For example, if Egyptian-born Ghada Amer is exhibiting her work
in a show on African art, we might ask what is African about the art. If the same work
is exhibited in a show on Arab artists, we might ask about the Arabness of the art, and
if she is identified as a Muslim artist, we might ask what is visually "Islamic" about the
work. Of course, in the case of Ghada, the visuals do not correlate to the art-historical
category "Islamic art," but there are many nonvisual references to Islamic history as
there are to the formal properties of art making.

Islamic art as an art historical category and discipline does not necessarily correlate to the category of "Muslim artist." Although I have used it to convene artists
who are Muslims, I have also learned about the different ways and moments at which
these artists themselves called on the tradition of Islamic art. In the post-9/11context
in the United States, artists' works were often presented under the frames of "Islam"
and "America." Within these imposing categories along with their preconceived definitions, artists increasingly invoked and drew on "Islamic art" in different ways after
9/11: tying it to its various regional histories; exposing its influences on the arts of
Europe; highlighting its calligraphic splendor; looking at the relationship between
text and image; debating issues of representational art and labor, as found in the

miniature traditions of the Mughals, Safavids, Ottomans; and looking at the various theological arguments posited for abstract art and against figurative and/or representational art and the debates on the prohibition of images. These engagements revealed how Islamic art has shaped artists' thinking and also exposed the ways that histories (art histories), and practices are linked today. In a sense, artists were questioning as much about western modernist traditions (and their appropriations of other histories without referencing them) as they were trying to make sense of their own work in relationship, conceptually and experientially rather than formally, to Islamic art, including the questioning of Islamic art as a western art historical category. Yet they never classified their own art as Islamic—it was always classified by other art historical genres.

Islamic art departments at major museums usually exhibit works of an Islamic past, although they often make room for temporary exhibits that are contemporary (such as New York's Metropolitan Museum of Art's new galleries). Artists thus would have to be seen as contributing in some ways to a certain continuity in this Islamic art history, albeit in newer forms, including at minimum calligraphy, vegetal ornaments (arabesques), and geometric patterns, as found in ceramics, glass, miniature paintings, tiles, textiles, and architecture.

In an article published in the journal *RES: Anthropology and Aesthetics*, entitled "Beyond Islamic Roots—Beyond Modernism" by Fereshteh Daftari, a curator in the painting and sculpture department at the Museum of Modern Art, New York, the author demonstrates how three contemporary artists "refuse to inhabit a ghetto either Western or Islamic" by having "invented new orders alien to both." The article begins by showing how Islamic art has influenced and affected western art/artists, including giants like Matisse, Klee, Kandinsky, but also how it has affected contemporary artists from "Muslim lands" who are now "rooted in the West." The article goes on to say, "These artists are extending the Islamic vocabulary beyond its original framework, developing new narratives that reconfigure and subvert the original idioms. At the same time, they defy the assumptions of modernism." Daftari continues, "Elusive or transparent, the Islamic references are retained only to be superseded or altered, sometimes unrecognizably." She ends the opening paragraph with, "To expand our sense of the meaning of their work we must examine both the places where these artists are anchored and where they break loose and wander free" (175).

In her essay, "Islamic or Not?" accompanying the important 2006 show *Without Boundary: Seventeen Ways of Looking*, at the MoMA in New York, Daftari continues to think about the relationship of seventeen diverse artists, Muslim and non-Muslim, to Islamic art. Pointing to the fact that the contemporary artists exhibited in *Without Boundary* do not share any geographic, religious, linguistic, or aesthetic unity, Daftari makes a strong argument for working against essentialist notions of what constitutes contemporary art as "Islamic" especially since these artists aren't interested in such classification. Nonetheless, while these artists represent a range of diversity, they were brought together to discuss a single theme: "What is, or is not, Islamic?"

While many scholars and experts have written extensively about Islamic art, as an art-historical category its focus has been on the art works/objects themselves rather than on the artists across time and the vast expanse we call the "Islamic world." It is only very recently that discussions between those who consider themselves contemporary Muslim artists and others who are artists of the Islamic world, regarding Islamic art as an art-historical category, are being had. As a growing number of contemporary artists call on the various conceptual and visual traditions of Islamic art, as is evident among the artists in my study post-9/11, scholars will need to track the ways in which those traditions are being engaged today. This allows us to think not only about the constructed and changing nature of art and its social production but also about the merging of tradition and modernity. Such merging is often unrecognizable in visual forms, as illustrated in the new directions taken in the outstanding new book by Jamal Elias, *Aisha's Cushion: Religious Art, Perception, and Practices in Islam.*

My goal in my initial dissertation fieldwork and postdoctoral work with visual artists was to understand how they navigated the secular New York art world through the category "Muslim." More recently my research has considered a much wider artistic landscape engaging a range of younger Muslim cultural producers in America—including musicians, performers, poets, actors, and filmmakers—looking particularly at how they navigate both the art worlds and their relationship to the Islamic tradition. Some artists—such as comedians, hip-hop artists, and calligraphers, for example—are much more intentional about being Muslim, making sure their art works and performances are "halal"; while the visual artists often classify their work as Islamic art because of the visual links and methods associated with Islamic art history. Working with a wider range of Muslim cultural producers, beyond just the "normative" secular art world, also helps to displace the notion that Muslim artists are necessarily secular in nature simply because they are artists. Those who see themselves as practicing Muslims and artists deny the dichotomy between artistic creation and their commitment to their faith. In fact, these Muslim artists often find that it is the norms of the secular art world that are restrictive and that their art practices are enhanced because they are religiously observant.

A significant change is taking place in American Muslim communities. After 9/11, representing the "softer and gentler" side of Islam through art was a strategy to appease the general public as well as to provide solace and comfort to Muslims. Since then, the development of new Muslim networks, representing different persuasions and theological commitments, demonstrates the influence of external forces on the shaping of identity and communities. I argue that this process is really the domesticating of Islam and Muslims in the United States. The increasing visibility and presence of Islam and Muslims in the American public sphere shows both the impact that the United States is having on shaping Muslim identity and the creative and important ways in which Muslim artists are contributing to and shaping the United States.

NOTE

1. ASMA (the American Society for Muslim Advancement) is "a not-for-profit religious, cultural, and educational organization dedicated to building bridges between the American public and American Muslims in a myriad of fields, including various media and the arts." This description was taken from their website, http://www.asmasociety.org, back in 2004. They have since expanded their programs and reach, and their work is worth learning about. See their new and enhanced website at the same location.

SELECTED BIBLIOGRAPHY

Abu-Lughod, L. "Writing Against Culture," in *Recapturing Anthropology: Working in the Present*, ed. Richard Fox (Santa Fe, NM: School of American Research, 1991): 137–162.

———. "Do Muslim Women Really Need Saving? *American Anthropologist* 104.3 (2002): 783–790.

Ali, Wijdan. *Modern Islamic Art: Development and Continuity*. (Gainesville: University Press of Florida, 1997).

Amer, Ghada and Oguibe, Olu. *Ghada Amer* (Amsterdam: De Appel, 2003).

Anderson, Maxwell. 2001. *American Visionaries: Selections from the Whitney Museum of American Art* (New York: Harry N. Abrams, 2003).

Appadurai, Arjun. *Modernity at Large: Cultural Dimensions of Globalization* (Minneapolis: University of Minnesota Press, 1996).

Arthurs, Alberta and Wallach, Glenn, eds. *Crossroads: Art and Religion in American Life* (New York: New Press, 2001).

Asad, Talal. "The Idea of an Anthropology of Islam" (Washington, DC: Center for Contemporary Arab Studies of Georgetown University, 1986).

Bailey, David and Tawadros, Gilane, eds. *Veiling, Representation and Contemporary Art* (Cambridge, MA: MIT Press, 2003).

Becker, Howard. *Art World*. (Berkeley: University of California Press, 1982).

Bennett, Jill. *Practical Aesthetics: Events, Affects and Art after 9/11* (London: I. B. Tauris, 2012).

Bourdieu, Pierre. *The Field of Cultural Production: Essays on Art and Literature* (New York: Columbia University Press, 1993).

Chambers, Kristin. "Loose Threads," in *Threads of Vision: Toward a New Feminine Poetics* (Cleveland, OH: Cleveland Center for Contemporary Art, 2001).

Clifford, James. *The Predicament of Culture: Twentieth-Century Ethnography, Literature, and Art* (Cambridge, MA: Harvard University Press, 1988).

Dabashi, Hamid. "Shirin Neshat: Transcending the Boundaries of an Imaginative Geography," in *The Last Word* (San Sebastian, Spain: Museum of Modern Art, 2005).

Daftari, Fereshteh. "Beyond Islamic Roots—Beyond Modernism." *RES Anthropology and Aesthetics* 43 (2003): 175–186.

Daftari, Fereshteh. "Islamic or Not?" in *Without Boundary: Seventeen Ways of Looking* (New York: Museum of Modern Art, 2006).

Eickelman, D. F., & Anderson, J. W., eds., *New Media in the Muslim World*. (Bloomington: Indiana University Press, 1999).

Elias, Jamal. *Aisha's Cushion: Religious Art, Perception, and Practice in Islam* (Cambridge, MA: Harvard University Press, 2012).

Fabian, Johannes. *Remembering the Present* (Berkeley: University of California Press, 1996).

George, Kenneth. *Picturing Islam: Art and Ethics in a Muslim Lifeworld* (Malden, MA: Wiley-Blackwell, 2010).

Grabar, Oleg. *The Formation of Islamic Art* (New Haven, CT: Yale University Press, 1987).

——, ed. "What Should One Know About Islamic Art?" *RES: Anthropology and Aesthetics* 43 (2003): 5–12.

Homes, A. M. *Ghada Amer* (New York: Gagosian Gallery, 2006).

Jensen, Mona. *Shirin Neshat: Women Without Men* (Denmark: Narayana Press and the ARoS Kunstmuseum, 2008).

Jiwa, Munir. "Aestheticizing Politics and Politicizing Aesthetics: Visual Artists and the Production and Representation of Muslim Identities in the United States," Ph.D. dissertation (New York: Columbia University, 2004).

——. 2010. "Imaging, Imagining and Representation: Muslim Visual Artists in NYC." *Contemporary Islam* 4.1 (2010): 77–90.

——. "Ghada Amer, Zarina Hashmi, Shirin Neshat, Shahzia Sikander," in *Encyclopedia of Muslim-American History.* (New York: Fact on File, 2010).

Karp, Ivan, and Lavine, Steven. *Exhibiting Cultures: The Poetics and Politics of Museum Display* (Washington, DC: Smithsonian Institute Press, 1991).

Karp, Ivan, Kreamer, Christine, and Lavine, Steven. *Museums and Communities: The Politics of Public Culture* (Washington, DC: Smithsonian Institute Press, 1992).

Kim, Elaine, Margo Machida, and Sharon Mizoto. *Fresh Talk/Daring Gazes* (Berkeley: University of California Press, 2003).

Lawrence, Bruce and cooke, miriam. *Muslim Networks from Hajj to Hip Hop* (Chapel Hill: University of North Carolina Press, 2005).

Metcalf, B., ed. *Making Muslim Space in North America and Europe* (Berkeley: University of California Press, 1996).

Pesenti, Allegra. *Zarina Paper Like Skin* (New York: DelMonico Books/Prestel, 2012).

Ray, Sharmistha, ed. *Zarina: Weaving Memory 1990–2006* (Mumbai: Bodhi Art, 2007).

Shohat, Ella, and Fusco, Coco, eds. *Talking Visions: Multicultural Feminism in a Transnational Age* (Cambridge, MA: MIT Press, 1998).

Winegar, Jessica. *Creative Reckonings: The Politics of Art and Culture in Contemporary Egypt* (Stanford, CA: Stanford University Press, 2006).

——. "The Humanity Game: Art, Islam and the War on Terror." *Anthropology Quarterly* 81.3 (2008): 651–681.

Wolff, Janet. *The Social Production of Art* (London: Macmillan, 1981).

Zolberg, Vera. *Constructing a Sociology of the Arts* (Cambridge, UK: Cambridge University Press, 1990).

——, ed. *Outsider Art: Contesting Boundaries in Contemporary Culture* (Cambridge, UK: Cambridge University Press, 1997).

CHAPTER 24

AMERICAN MOSQUE ARCHITECTURE

AKEL ISMAIL KAHERA

ISLAM IN AMERICA

The scholarship on religious space in America from the 1940s through the 1960s exists at the intersection of several literatures, including history, religious studies, and material culture (Price, 2013). Furthermore, because of the increased mobility of people and beliefs and an increasingly worldwide diaspora, the scholarship asks whether cultural and political boundaries—both material and figurative—have been manufactured or dissolved as research is carried out. This essay focuses on the aesthetic features of the American mosque, a religious edifice caught in a temporal, cultural, and spatial nexus as academics (sociologists, anthropologists, historians, and so on) as well as architectural practitioners survey its unique set of urban architectural patterns and aesthetic development. Many motivations and sentiments mediate multicultural, multisensory, and/or multitemporal aesthetic features of mosques. Above all, the aesthetic features of the American mosque also define the way in which we experience the edifice, even if these features may be overly romantic or dissonant.

At the outset it is rewarding to consider the extent to which the previously noted assertions have proved influential in descriptions of American Muslim life in literary discourses, historical narratives, and religious practices, especially in the post-9/11 era. For example, the number of mosques built or planned since 9/11 has clearly declined, with some building being delayed for political reasons. Certain projects, such as Park 51 (the "ground zero mosque"), have gotten nationwide media attention. The link between the design and plan of the Park 51 mosque and the political climate in America is undeniable. Architects across the country and their Muslim clients are faced with increased anti-Muslim rhetoric, often specifically targeting the construction of new mosques.

Research has shown that the first antebellum community of African Muslim slaves in the American South and their descendants were not free to worship or openly build an edifice for communal worship. To highlight the presence of African Muslims in North America, Malcolm Bell Jr. (1913–2001) photographed and interviewed many coastal Georgia blacks as part of the Works Progress Administration (WPA) program; the results of this project were published in 1940 and entitled *Drums and Shadows: Survival Studies Among the Coastal Georgia Negroes*. Bell interviewed a number of coastal Georgia blacks who were descendants of former Muslim slaves. A few of them described the daily ritual prayer that was still being performed at the time of the interview. One interviewee mentioned a building that a slave master ordered to be torn down. From the description, it seems that it could have been intended to be a communal gathering place for Muslims (*musalla*) rather than a domicile.

With the passage of the US immigration quota laws in 1921 and 1924, Muslim and Christian immigrants from the Arab provinces of the former Ottoman Empire—Syria, Lebanon, and Jordan—began to arrive in North America. They were mainly Turks, Kurds, Albanians, and Arabs. From the early 1920s onward, immigrant communities were established at Ross, North Dakota, and, in the 1930s, in Rapid City, Iowa. Thus far, researchers have been unable to identify the earliest established mosque in the United States with any degree of certainty. We know that in 1915 an Albanian Muslim community existed at Biddeford, Maine, and that its members built at least one mosque (*masjid*) in the following few years.

Contrary to popular belief the "mother mosque" at RapidCity, Iowa, built circa 1934, is not the oldest mosque in America (Kahera 2002).

The "mother mosque" appeal became a means for expressing a simulacrum (a popular cultural idea) and of exploring a novel religious identity. Both Allan Austin and Sylviane Diouf present the idea of an original antebellum or post-bellum mosque intact, knowing that a clear identification of the first mosque continues to elude us. The cumulative oral interviews of members of indigenous communities such as those carried out by Bell provide strong suggestions of the communal existence of a *masjid* or *musalla*. More extensive literature exploring Muslim religious communities from the pre- and post–World War II era comes from the perspective of religion, sociology, and cultural studies. Works such as *The Muslims of America* (Haddad, 1991) and *Islam in America* (Smith, 2010) describe the fabric of communities that stretch across the American landscape; every adaptation of the religious community is clearly influenced by its multidimensional, multiethnic, and transnational identity.

In 1930 African American Muslims established the First Muslim Mosque in Pittsburgh, PA (Hakim). The first Cleveland mosque was founded in 1932 by al-Hajj Wali Akram (Dannin, 2005). The Ad-Deen Allah Universal Arabic Association and its leader, Muhammad Ez el-Deen, established a village at Camden, New Jersey, and another in Buffalo, New York, following the Great Depression from (1929–1945) (Dannin, 2005; Nash, 2008). In 1955, Shaykh Daud Ahmed Faisal established the State Street Masjid in Brooklyn, New York.

Many other indigenous American mosque communities came into existence in the 1960s through the 1970s, including the Dar-ul-Islam movement, mainly of Brooklyn, New York; the Mosque of Islamic Brotherhood (New York); the Islamic Party (Washington, D.C., and the Caribbean); and the Hanafi community (Washington D.C.). Almost every major American city on the East Coast of the United States had a mosque affiliated with one of these communities (Smith, 2010; Haddad and Smith, 1991; and others). Readers interested in pursuing this discussion and the forms of cultural representation related to it can also explore the work of Barbara Daly Metcalf and Kathleen Moore.

THE PRIMACY OF WORSHIP

The Mosque in America: A National Portrait, by Ihsan Bagbhy, Paul M. Perl, and Bryan T. Froehle (2001), estimates the total number of Muslims living in the United States at the time of publication as between 6 and 7 million. The same study estimates that more than half of the existing mosques (87 percent) were founded since 1970. Likewise approximately 64 percent of all mosques are located in urban areas, while 36 percent are established in rural or suburban locations.

Among North American Muslims there exist a number of different doctrinal traditions, as in the rest of the Muslim world. Nonetheless it is widely agreed that mosques everywhere owe their origin to the archetypal mosque of the Prophet Muhammad (*masjid an-nabi*), built in Medina around 622 CE. The etymology of the word *masjid* can be traced to the Arabic verb *sa-ja-da*, to prostrate or bow down to God in worship (Q.72:18; 24:36; 9:18). The primary functions that were accommodated in that mosque were those of congregational worship, religious education, and other types of communal activities. The *masjid an-nabi* reflected the importance of the Prophet's *Sunnah*, his daily religious practice (custom, tradition, model, law, habit, convention, and mannerisms), which were recorded and form the corpus of the *hadith*. Purpose-built American mosques generally try to provide for the same kind of communal activities that were accommodated in the Prophet's original structure.

Writing in the fifteenth century CE, Abu al-Hassan Abdallah al-Samhudi (d. 1505), in his *Wafa al-Wafa bi Akhbar Dar al-Mustafa*, informs us that the original edifice measured approximate 70 by 60 cubits (one cubit = approximately 18 inches); and that the edifice had two attached domestic chambers (later increased to nine) and a courtyard with three doors: the Door of Mercy, or *Bab ar-Rahmah*, to the west; the door of Gabriel, or *Bab Jibril*, and the Women's Door, or *Bab al-Nisa'*, to the east; there was also a shaded portico (*zullah*) to the north. The importance of keeping the *Sunnah* alive in public memory helps explain how later mosques outside of Madinah were built. Western art historians have tended to focus on individual patrons and stylistic details, treating the mosque primarily as a work of art. But they have essentially discounted the primordial relationship of the mosque to the Prophet's Sunnah.

The practice of Islam in America takes its religious precedents (Qur'an and Sunnah) and aesthetic traditions quite seriously, drawing heavily on the doctrinal understanding of iconography and architectural knowledge largely derived from extant styles in the Muslim world. This interpretation seeks to explain the long-standing influence of what is referred to as the "spatial Sunnah." Over time, five aesthetic principles have shaped the formative aesthetic principles of the spatial Sunnah: structure of belief, order, space, materials, and symbols (Kahera 2002). Thus in compliance with the Sunnah, all purpose-built American mosques face Makkah [Mecca]; typically, the plan of the prayer hall complies with the orientation of the *qiblah* axis. The most rudimentary expression of form in mosque architecture can be described as a "wall facing Makkah." This wall contains a niche (*mihrab*), which verifies the direction of Makkah, serving as a symbolic and ontological axis for the faithful, who must also follow the Sunnah by facing Makkah in the performance of prayer. The commitment of buildings everywhere to this basic orientation can be understood as a fundamental orientation of the heart of the believer. It provides a basic worldview or weltanschauung—the innate sense of devotion. Within the framework of the Qur'anic discourse on devotion we also find the word *mihrab* in connection to the Virgin Mary (Q 19:16–17; al-Tabari 8:320). Historian and exegete al-Tabari describes the mihrab in this context as a most honorable place. Allah commanded Mary to "bow down [in prayer] with those [the congregation] who bow down (Q 3:43; al-Tabari 3:246), indicating that in Mary's case the word corresponds simply to a place of pious devotion.

In North America the urban mosque operates under unique site constraints. Among these constraints is the accuracy of the qiblah. When a mosque is built, it is forced to conform to this canonical tenet. In keeping with the Prophet's Sunnah, social and religious practices are rooted in a long tradition of public gathering (the congregational five daily prayers), the *jum'ah* or Friday prayer, the nightly *taraweeh* prayers performed during the holy month of Ramadan, and other important religious events. While no prescriptive form for the urban mosque occurs in the Qur'an or Sunnah, the need for communal worship among adherents has led to the development of a particular American plan for these buildings.

Distinct site conditions continue to influence the form and function of the building. Urban and rural mosques usually differ in size and ancillary function; however, these differences can also be the result of construction costs or the availability of land. The musalla is the most common type of what is called "adaptive-reuse" for communal worship, because adapting an existing structure is far less costly than constructing a new building. For example, before the Park 51 controversy erupted, the congregants prayed in an adapted musalla for more than two decades; this is a building called Masjid al-Farah in the Tribeca neighborhood, at 245 West Broadway, New York City. Faced with the need to establish a place of communal worship, diaspora and indigenous communities began occupying alternative spaces (adaptive reuse) in urban and rural centers, from the earliest recorded period of the development of the urban community mosque (1930 to 1950s). The 1950s to 1980s saw an increase in the display of evocative features, aesthetics, and the use of specific cultural styles, which, with the influx of fresh immigrants, grew in influence, popularity, and scale from the late 1960s onward.

From the 1980s to 2000, architects responding to the needs of their clients made an effort to define the way in which the edifice was to be experienced, taking into consideration the cost of construction and the transglobal dimensions of Muslim culture. Above all, an architect's design strategy for the appropriation of space must take into account the religious values of the community that will worship there. Conversely, while architecture is obviously separate from exegesis and dogma, in the case of mosque construction it is nonetheless a by-product of religious belief and practice combined with technical design.

DIASPORA AESTHETICS

Today there are an estimated 1,500 to 3,000 mosques in North America, established over the last five or more decades. In the West in general, including Europe and America, there are some four stages in the development of the urban mosque and Islamic center: (1) an early period dating to the turn of the twentieth century, including such examples as La Mosquée de Paris (1926); (2) a second period from World War II to the 1960s, epitomized by the Islamic Cultural Center of Washington, D.C. (1957); (3) a third period witnessing the proliferation of mosques in the West, such as the London Central Mosque (1977), up to the 1990s and the Islamic Cultural Center of New York (1991); and (4) the period from 2000 to the present day, including the Islamic Cultural Center of Boston (2008) and al-Farooq masjid in Atlanta (2008). While the terms *Islamic center* (*markaz al-Islami*) and *mosque* (masjid) are often used interchangeably, the idea of using the term *Islamic cultural center* gained legitimacy in the early 1960s, when a host of ancillary functions were added to the typical edifice (masjid); these ancillary functions may include classrooms and facilities for social, educational, recreational, and civic activities for the entire community.

The North American mosque gives priority to a balanced mix of functions and aesthetic features. Because many cultural and religious traditions persist, urban mosques in North America have a two-tiered hybrid identity, which may differ according to the cultural tastes of émigrés and indigenous Muslims as well as available funds allocated for construction. Elements of culture such as dress, language, diet, and religious practice are also tied to cultural tastes. Cultural consciousness is an important mechanism for keeping alive various customs, making them meaningful to a community and easing fears of the loss of ethnic ties and familial bonds as well as spiritual affiliations. A host of planning issues must be taken into consideration when

FIGURE 24.1. The Al Farooq Mosque, Atlanta, Georgia, building exterior: main façade. (Photograph by Akel Ismail Kahera.)

the client, the architect, and the community come together to plan the construction of a mosque. How do the functions of an American mosque differ from those typical of of an émigré's homeland? When ideas borrowed from one's native land end up in the American melting pot (or salad bowl), do they become less important? In many Muslim countries women are not encouraged to attend the mosque. In America the First Amendment (promising freedom of worship) implicitly supports communal worship spaces and unfettered access for all persons regardless of gender, race, or religious faith. Do the client and architect understand these concepts, or are they lost in the development of a design concept? Given the First Amendment, how can we incorporate modes of practice and experience into a truly American context?

Recent scholarship has focused on the theory and design criteria of Muslim religious spaces which, as we have seen, can be problematic. Furthermore the number of mosques constructed in America during the past three decades clearly suggests an imminent need on the part of architects, planners, urban designers, researchers, and clients to embrace a deeper understanding of the religious values and norms that influence the design of mosques (Kahera, 2009). Architects and designers have sought to preserve meaning, religious practice, and social interaction in new ways. Robert Mugeraurer's *Interpreting Environments, Tradition, Deconstruction, Hermeneutics* explores various modalities of environment and ways to deconstruct different types of structures, landscapes, and images. But the difficulty lies in deciding what to select from a particular vocabulary of an émigré's place or history. This kind of diaspora aesthetic profile accounts for the vast majority of stylistic variations that exist today.

First, "Diaspora aesthetics" are cultural sentiments informed by the reminiscence of one's land of origin and cultural customs mixed with present-day beliefs. Cultural sentiments cause those attending the mosque to associate it with memories of their homeland. When there is commonality of memory, the result may be a style adapted from the land of origin. A good example is The Islamic Center of Washington D.C. (1957). Here arabesque patterns can be found in a myriad of versions. Typically arabesque designs are derived from vegetal motifs such as flowers, vines, and leaves. Arabic calligraphies were also part of the aesthetic theme—calligraphy is the most revered art form in Islam, featuring excerpts from the Holy Qur'an. Tessellation or the repetitive "ordering" of a geometric pattern makes up the third component of the arabesque. In the Islamic Center of Washington D.C., the architect and client invoked arabesque patterns largely because of the religious and cultural value associated with Egypt, Turkey, and Morocco. Historically Muslim aesthetics have been dominated (with few exceptions) by the written and the spoken word controlling the relationship of faith to communal worship.

FIGURE 24.2. The Al Farooq Mosque, Atlanta, Georgia, *mihrab* and *musalla* (sanctuary). (Photograph by Akel Ismail Kahera.)

Second, "diaspora aesthetics" is linked to the appeal for a simulacrum—a copy or applied replica. This appeal can be found in the Islamic Center of Toledo, Ohio (1983)—a simulacrum of the Ottoman style. This example is given full consideration in the later discussion. In sum, stylistically, the problem attendant upon interpretive meanings stands between three different ideologies of style:

1. Strict adherence to an aesthetic tradition containing disparate and mixed elements (hybridity). An architect or designer who quotes a mixed bag of formal elements, largely devoid of meaning, is an example of hybridity.
2. An attempt to copy or replicate a popular cultural idea from an aesthetic tradition using anachronism but not experimentation (simulacrum). This approach involves an architect or designer viewing fragments of aesthetics as precedent handed down through history, independent of the meaning of space or time. Both simulacrum and hybridity can cause a most intractable aesthetic problem for an untrained architect. Fundamentally the issue involves the inability of both architect and client to understand the true meaning of spatial form, as well as the inability to translate many types of corresponding modes of visual expression.
3. A faithful attempt to understand *genius loci*, modernity, tradition, and urbanism (contextualism). A fitting example is the Islamic Cultural Center of New York City (1991).

Over the last few decades, the identity of the American mosque has been the subject of considerable speculation among academics and researchers. Spanning the fields of architecture, urbanism, and art history, the debate provides us with a platform to discuss the analysis and study of religious aesthetics, and the broader implications of overcoming space and time (Kahera, 2002). The case studies presented here provide a thought-provoking overview of how hybridity, simulacrum, and contextualism.

HYBRIDITY

The cornerstone of the Islamic Center in Washington D.C., was laid in 1949. It was built primarily for the diplomatic community, and President Eisenhower formally inaugurated it in 1957. It is the first major mosque to be built in an American city. Artistic devices from Egypt, Turkey, and Morocco are employed in the aesthetic vocabulary. Arabesque themes, consisting of geometric patterns and calligraphy, display a common expression of aesthetic treatment. The affinity with the arabesque is common to Muslim religious and secular architecture as a kind of cosmological story that holds conscious or unconscious meaning. In addition, a number of hybrid architectural themes (derived from two or more regional styles) have resulted in the mixing of elements; these themes define the visual character of the edifice. It would seem

FIGURE 24.3. Islamic Cultural Center, Washington, D.C. (Photograph courtesy of the Library of Congress, Prints and Photographs Division, photograph by Carol M. Highsmith, LC-HS503-1306.)

that the client and the architect (Abdur-Rahman Rossi) wanted the visual character of the edifice to convey a bygone era. The building's hybrid vocabulary clearly recalls the past; it also makes a statement about "reminiscence" and the result is a simulacrum *image*. In this regard two important points are noteworthy: First, the building's hybrid vocabulary ignores the urban architectural context in which it was built, at 2551 Massachusetts Avenue, NW. It is clear that Rossi made no effort to address the prevailing architectural language or the urban context. Second, the masjid's simulacrum image is a mixture of visual compositions mostly influenced by the Mamluk architecture (1250–1517) of Cairo, Egypt.

Nevertheless, the stylized captions and the use of epigraphy from the Qur'an evoke a devotional theme; as an emotional device, these captions convey symbolic meaning purposely intended to instruct and to foster a quiet, devotional atmosphere. The use of epigraphy reinforces "reminiscence," further buoyed by the use of traditional crafts and materials from Turkey, Iran, and Egypt as employed by skilled craftsmen.

Rossi reproduced several simulacrum motifs; when seen as art, his design exhibits beauty and meaning. With regard to art and worship, two epigraphic inscription

FIGURE 24.4. Interior of the *musalla* (sanctuary), The Islamic Cultural Center Washington, D.C., Mosque. (Photograph © 2007, Mark Susman.)

bands run horizontally across the face of the prayer niche (mihrab). The upper band reads, "Verily we have seen the turning of your face to the heaven" and the lower band reads, "surely we shall turn you to a qiblah that shall please you" (Q. *Al-Baqara* 2:144). The mihrab's decorative treatment follows the Iznik and Bursa tradition of using glazed tiles—blue, red, and green—which are commonly found in Ottoman mosques.

An epigraph is a composition that transmits a message; each inscription is primarily intended to further knowledge and to instruct the community. The entry portal of the edifice runs parallel to the street; for added emphasis, it has an inscription band of Kufic Arabic script at the upper part of the facade, which reads, "In houses of worship which Allah has permitted to be raised so that His name be remembered, in them, [and] there extol His limitless glory at morning and evening" (Q. *Al-Nur* 24:36).

The plan of the masjid contains three halls (*iwan*) framed by an exterior double arcade (*riwaq*), which serves as an extra *muros* space or *ziyada*. The orthogonal arcade remains perpendicular to the street, but the main prayer hall is set out at a tangent to conform to the qiblah axis, which was calculated on the basis of the great circle—the shortest distance when facing Makkah. In the building there is a small court (*sahn*) open to the sky, but the whole central space of the masjid is covered with a modest clerestory dome. An arcade (*riwaq*) consisting of five contiguous arches serves as an entry portal and a key part of the façade.

On the interior of the main prayer hall (walls and ceilings), several verses of the Qur'an have been arranged in a symmetrical configuration. The Divine Names of Allah (*Al-Asma Allah Al-Husna*) and several familiar and often-quoted verses from the Qur'an such as *Al-Alaq* 96:1–5 are inscribed in large framed borders of Arabic (*thuluth*) script with smaller framed panels of ornamental Kufic script.

In this context the masjid's hybrid composition epitomizes both culture and tradition. While the concept of hybridity has been discussed chiefly to illustrate the cognitive differences between culture and tradition, which are sometimes difficult to reconcile, we should not ignore the importance to religious aesthetics. Such issues have become relevant across a range of disciplines. The Islamic Center of Washington, D.C., presents a diverse range of examples of such issues and provides direction for future study of religious architecture in an American context.

SIMULACRUM

The late Imam Khattab of the Islamic Center of Greater Toledo, Ohio (Toledo masjid, completed 1983), relates an interesting anecdote. He says that in the 1980s, when the building was under construction, truckers could be overheard on their shortwave radios as they drove by, obviously startled by the unfamiliar image of dome and minaret. One trucker remarked to another, "It must be a new Mexican restaurant!" While amusing, such an incident also helps us understand more accurately the significance of these iconic features in relation to the American landscape. But the picture is more complex; there is a ghostly residue of emotional and cultural feeling attached to the appearance and the image of an American mosque. From this perspective, if we accept the Toledo masjid as a representation of faith and community, the dome and minaret share a history of Muslim architecture. An alternative perspective of the anachronistic image of dome and minaret gives birth to the discussion of simulacra.

Simulacra help us to understand the extent to which an historical precedent can be considered as the basis for the American mosque, and whether it is entirely relevant to borrow in order to produce an architectural copy or replica. Imagine the response of the public if the Alamo or Chartres Cathedral were built today in Istanbul, Turkey, without the same attention to detail, craftsmanship, materials, and function. Clearly modern-day attitudes toward iconic architecture would not appreciate the value or special significance attached to the iconic image of the Alamo or Chartres. The power of simulacra is useful in this regard; it helps us to critically evaluate the Toledo masjid, and likewise the Islamic Center of Cleveland, Ohio (Cleveland masjid, completed 1995).

Despite the attempt to replicate the Ottoman style in America, there are glaring differences in time, place, and historical emphasis. The increasing awareness of form and function as well as the artistry of the Toledo masjid and the work of Mimar Sinan (1490–1588) are useful for comparison. Sinan was the most prominent Ottoman architect; he became construction officer in the janissaries and, at the age of forty-seven, the chief of the corps of royal architects of the empire. Over four hundred works were completed under his supervision. He constructed the Sulemaniye mosque (1550–1557) complex during the reign of Sulayman II, and later the Selimiye (1569–1575), considered his most mature work. Sinan was the unchallenged master builder of the classical period of Ottoman architecture. The single most important markers of the Toledo masjid and the Cleveland masjid are the pencil minarets and the large central dome, reminiscent of this Ottoman style.

Although the accent of these two elements distinguishes both buildings, they do not come close to capturing the visual language of Sinan's buildings. The double minaret and the large dome of the Toledo *masjid* employs had distinct political meaning in the Ottoman world: the patron of a double minaret building was often a high official, like a minister (*wazır*) or a prince or princess. In fact, the extraordinary breadth of the meaning of two minarets is never captured in America; mosques here contain only the slightest indication of a visual reference that was actively cultivated in Sinan's work. Even in the eighteenth-century Ottoman world, the architectural composition of a well-established visual language introduced by Sinan in the sixteenth century was subject to eclecticism coming from sentimental trends and Italian baroque influences (Kahera, 2010).

The term *simulacrum* may also be applied to a set of anachronistic features, apart from the dome, that occur in the composition of a mosque—namely, a sentimental display of ornament that is essentially responsive to an artistic movement. While the

Toledo and Cleveland masjids both share a referential identity with the Ottoman architectural style, the enigmatic features (minaret and dome) are direct simulacra. Simulacra here stand for feelings, sentiments, and attachment and for the misplaced time and geographic contexts. Another factor behind this emphasis is Sinan's octagonal baldachin, which produced two key effects: First, it established a duality between the dome and its supports by unifying all secondary spaces under the spell of the big dome. Second, it established the maximum dimensional effect, allowing for the movements of the body in a prayer space under a large canopy. In the Toledo masjid the particular dome simulacrum aims at situating this process within the wider cultural and visual context and public space.

Although the discipline of architecture upholds creative imagination, theory and practice, visual thinking, and criticism and research, little research has been done on the precedents that influence the American mosque. In North America there are, of course, several examples of simulacra, which are not detailed here for the sake of brevity. Manuel Toussaint has studied historical evidence of the Moorish style, which originated in medieval Andalusia and the Maghrib (modern-day Spain and North Africa). The emotional value placed on the Moorish revival style is evident in the Fox Theater in Atlanta (1929); the Isaac M. Wise Temple in Cincinnati (1866); the Murat Center in Indianapolis, (1862) and Opa Locka City Hall in Florida (1926). Opa Locka has the largest collection of Moorish revival buildings in the western world. American builders copied the original buildings in Andalusia and the Maghrib, illustrating the establishment of an elaborate art form in America in the nineteenth century. With important new emphasis, the Toledo and Cleveland masjids also demonstrate the cultural meaning attached to the fact that the dome and minaret were specifically selected in opposition to another visual genre. It should be noted that Prophet's mosque (circa 622 CE) had neither dome nor minaret.

Finally, a simulacrum means that an American mosque having mixed affiliations, romantic or otherwise, implicitly acknowledges reliance on an architectural precedent. What emerges from the visual language of the Toledo and Cleveland masjids affords us multiple interpretations and a keen understanding of a marked fondness for simulacra. These developments are defined by the increasing migration and mobility of communities, architectural themes, and beliefs across cultures and boundaries—a phenomenon that signals a need to address the exchange and the powers or anxieties produced in the process. In this sense beauty is a reflection of the aesthetic sensibility to other art forms; it is shared between building and object, empirically achieved through the visual treatment of the mosque. It is not an idée fixe. From a historical point of view, there are exhaustive categories of types and subtypes of mosques; yet in its simplest function, the Toledo masjid is a space for contemplation, repose, and communal worship. In the West, this formula holds true with the added proviso that the North American context has no exact parallel in the Muslim world.

Contextualism

By moving away from a simulacrum, the designers of the Islamic Center of New York (1991), Skidmore, Owings and Merrill (SOM), explored the use of modern technology without limitation. This approach provides a new framework for understanding contextualism in the urban experience. As we have seen in the previous two examples, imitative models demand traditional workmanship, materials, and skills that are not readily available in the United States. Architects and planners who discuss contextualism argue against hybridity and simulacra; they also argue about knowledge being related to the claim of context sensitivity.

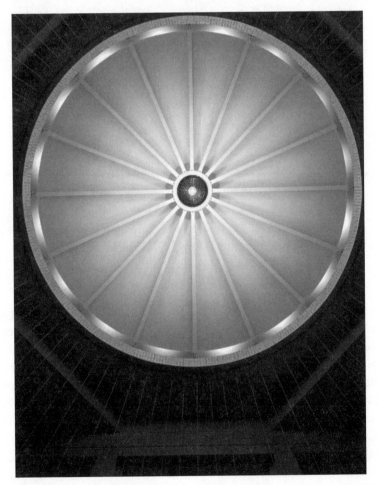

FIGURE 24.5. Islamic Cultural Center of New York, interior of the dome. (Photograph © Aga Khan Award for Architecture/Wolfgang Hoyt.)

FIGURE 24.6. Islamic Cultural Center of New York, interior /prayer hall (Photo©
Aga Khan Award for Architecture / AliyePekinCelik)

The production of contextual knowledge in architectural practices has for some
time been the subject of many debates; more recently it has been tied to research in
other interdisciplinary areas. While SOM's design for the Islamic Center of New York
gives us a renewed appraisal of design practices and the contextual debate, the Islamic
Center of New York is a good example of how to rethink aesthetic knowledge and the
production of space for an urban context. SOM's designer explains that the client's
design parameters for the building were dictated by two camps: one was the traditionalist, those who demanded a faithful adherence to a predetermined concept of
the building dictated by historical models; the other was the nontraditionalist camp,
those who allowed absolute freedom in the design vocabulary but were rigidly conscious of the need not to violate any religious principles (such as a simulacrum) even
in a minute detail (*Architectural Record*, 1992: 92–97).

FIGURE 24.7. **Cultural Center of New York, building exterior. (Photograph © Aga Khan Award for Architecture/AliyePekinCelik.)**

In recent decades, large-scale economics have had a profound impact on the practice of contextual architecture. While the impact of these phenomena on artistic production is acknowledged, the specific effects on our modes of analysis of those productions is exactly what SOM had to address—namely, finding ways to connect theoretical and methodological challenges within the study of architecture, faith, and culture. Finally, we must remember that New York City (where the mosque was built) exists as a complex historical and multicultural habitat; its architecture has always changed in concert with artistic trends, and the urban space is a fluid context.

In keeping with this notion, the architects explored the use of modern technology as a compositional device. In so doing, the Islamic Center of New York confronts both tradition and modernity, seeking to reinterpret various aesthetic themes associated with extant models found in the Muslim world. First, the surface motifs reflect geometric themes, which are employed as a unifying element throughout the mas-jid's interior and exterior. These motifs can be seen primarily in the carpet, where worshippers assemble for prayer in horizontal and parallel rows facing the qiblah. They also appear in the surface treatment of the *minbar*, the exterior façade, and several other interior elements as well. Geometry is a fundamental theme in Muslim cosmology, but in this instance it comes closer to a modernist, secular interpretation than a traditional, cosmological one.

The inscriptions, which are included in the decorative features of the masjid's inte-rior, are rendered in a geometric Kufic calligraphy style. They are set in straight, hori-zontal, and vertical arrangements to accommodate a modernist concept of order. For instance, around the *mihrab* the geometric Kufic script reads, "Allah is the Light of the Heavens and the Earth." The aesthetic needs of the faithful are therefore achieved through the words (of the Qur'an) and the meaning, which emanates when read or heard or transcribed. Thus, art of the script in the context of architecture is not an imitation of created form or a representation of nature but an aesthetic experience—a normative principle whose object, pattern, motif, and epigraphy is articulated in light of the ontological principle of *tawheed*, or monotheism.

Admittedly, the use of traditional inscriptions as a decorative element is in some respects incongruent with the idea of a secular, modernist interpretation of surface treatment. The significance of this translation and interpretation presents us with a model that is both explicit and experimental in a way that has no precedent in American mosque architecture. It legitimizes the use of well-known vocabulary and integrates it into the formal and defined theme of the liturgical space. From a theo-retical point of view, this possibility of an ensemble of interpretation structures into the space illustrates a shared vocabulary of elements, which have now found a new contextual expression.

SOM applied geometry as a spatial theme, with the aid of a corresponding, angular Kufic inscription, apparently to provide visual affinity; a less complementary script would have put the theme of composition and "order" at risk. The aesthetic treat-ment of the interior of the dome over the central prayer hall further illustrates this point. The dome's structural ribs have been left bare and rudimentary—providing a bold geometric texture to the dome's inner face when seen from below—as a way to define common spatial identity, establish order, and inscribe sense and meaning. The inner drum of the dome is covered with a band of angular Kufic inscription, but the pattern of concentric ribs clearly dominates the composition, especially since the text of the band is largely unreadable from the main prayer hall below. Both com-positional elements—epigraphy and geometry—were clearly intended by the archi-tect to be operative aesthetic devices. The repeated use of forms and compositional elements—epigraphy and geometry—stands at the center the building's design. Yet these concepts of compositional operative aesthetic devices also serve to highlight an expanded approach and an integral symmetry.

In another noteworthy example of contextualism—Dar al-Islam mosque in Abiquiú, New Mexico (1981)—the vernacular context is explored and the particular influence of site, edifice, and landscape are mutually reinforcing. The argument for contextualism supports the notion that knowledge of the landscape is vital—essentially the architect's delicate response to the site. Norberg-Schultz (1991) refers to this imaginative shift as the genius loci, or the spirit of place. In 1980, the late Hassan Fathy (d. 1989) was commissioned to design the mosque and master plan for a Muslim village at Abiquiu. Fathy's aesthetic themes for the master plan and the mosque retain some sense of the vernacular Nubian adobe construction, which is also ideal for the climate and topography of the region. The mesa site is framed by surrounding arid hills, and several snow-capped mountains are visible in the distance. Abiquiu, the Charma Valley, and its immediate surroundings were long populated by Native American peoples before the arrival of the Spanish (1598). The harsh environmental conditions at Abiquiu provided an ideal setting for using adobe construction. These conditions demonstrate how Fathy articulated these aspects in adobe. Fathy remained faithful to a long-established adobe building tradition that "small is beautiful"—its interpretation provides a connection to sustainability, the nature of tradition and art and the world of human existence, necessity, and contingency.

FIGURE 24.8. Mosque at Abiqui (*Dar al-Islam*), New Mexico. (Photograph courtesy of Ronald Baker.)

Since the 1940s adobe had become Fathy's technological passion. He remained loyal to it not only because of its durability over millennia—some adobe structures in Egypt are more than 3,000 years old—but also because of its thermal properties. In many desert climates, it maintains comfortable temperatures within a range of five to seven degrees Fahrenheit over a twenty-four-hour cycle. Furthermore, it is plentiful; approximately one third of the world's people already live in houses made of earth. Finally, the flexibility of the material, for which right angles and straight lines are not always essential, nourishes architectural creativity. The results of the Abiquiu mosque and village are captivating, simple, and beautiful. As Fathy puts it, "Tradition is a key element of culture when the craftsman was responsible for much of the work of building, traditional art came out of the subconscious of the community...it is held together by an accumulated culture, rather than by one individual's idea of harmony."[1]

In building the mosque, Fathy worked with local builders, adding a core of knowledge of the traditional Nubian building technique to their own and setting exemplars derived from the experience of his master mason. Today, the Dar al-Islam site has considerable appeal and it is perhaps favorably considered in terms of its psychological impulse. The Dar al-Islam organization emphasizes education first, and the mosque and madrassah provide a quiet retreat; it is now labeled as a sacred site. At the top of the mesa one can expect to experience the reflective aura of the mosque and madrassah upon viewing the contemplative landscape. The mosque and madrassah share an empathic relationship; Fathy's balanced sense of unity bears a close resemblance to Ruskin's *Seven Lamps of Architecture: sacrifice, truth, power, beauty, life, memory, and obedience* Ruskin argued that these seven appearances exist in sacred architecture of the world. Here again, a theoretical analysis of these properties is accompanied by heuristic knowledge as a device to understand the thinking intimately employed via contextualism.

WOMEN'S SPACE

For the untrained lay person, any number of interpretations could easily stymie the norm of practice allowed by the Sunnah, whose purpose is to unite the entire congregation in space and time. This discussion outlines the problem of religious practice and the right of women to attend the mosque, the key feature of which is the identification of what is commonly referred to as the "women's area." The Qur'an does not attribute a hermeneutical status to male or female worshipper. In fact, the Qur'an makes no distinction between the sexes: "I will not suffer the work of any worker among you to be lost whether male or female" (Q. 3:194). Over time a number of legal and theological interpretive claims—for example, the four major Sunni schools of law—and metaliterary disputes have emerged to form an opinion about a woman's

FIGURE 24.9. Muslim women praying (*in congregation*), Fayetteville, Georgia. (Photograph courtesy of AmirahKahera.)

right of entry to the mosque. In part this is an attempt to rework history, transposing modalities of historical time and preexisting space to adjudicate among conflicting legal opinions about what shapes the concept of communal worship.

Another explanation may be the usual troublesome influence of patriarchy. Such practices are not only ill founded but draw upon extant popular ideas and obvious male prejudices. Sayyid Mitawalli Darsh's essay "The Right of Women to Attend The mosque" and Asma Sayeed's critique "Early Sunni Discourses on Women's Mosque Attendance" highlight the source of the ambiguities that remain today.[2]

According to the CAIR 2001 report, *The American Mosque: A National Portrait*, in nearly two-thirds of mosques, 66 percent, of women make *salah* (prescribed prayer) behind a curtain or partition or in another room. One explanation of the common occurrence of this practice is the fact that segments of diaspora community in North America are inclined to subscribe to familiar cultural and social customs that originate in their home countries. This occurrence may be the result of male commentators who have long been accustomed to state that private worship for women is preferable. It may also result from the failure to embrace the principle of gender equity that is implicit in the text of the Qur'an. The ultimate justification for such an inquiry (and its architectural implications) still appears to be driven by the nature of interpretation, preferred social attitudes, and the tendency to consign hadith traditions to "norms" and "standards." We are therefore confronted with unlimited points of view about the concept of time and space, normative judgments, the value of collective worship, and the rules that govern places of public gathering within a community. In this case the hadith concerning women's right of entry to the mosque has dominated the debate, which also influences the formation of certain types of permanent and thematic architecture.

On the most basic level, patriarchy sanctions the values and perception of the community and provides a specific understanding of doctrinal ideas that is often ill founded or based solely on custom. This perception, together with the uncertainty of being transplanted in the middle of American society, may result in the inability to facilitate acceptance. At the same time many from the indigenous and the diaspora communities also rely on independent reasoning and in so doing welcome constructive forms of gender equity. That position is devoted to *ijtihad* or critical thinking. The Islamic Cultural Center of New York exemplifies the use of new approaches to planning and design that reject previous assumptions about a "woman's place' in the mosque. The elevated balcony above the men does not comply with convention; rather, it suggests the extent to which spatial stereotypes can be broken down. Besides relying on the overwhelming consensus of a majority of jurists who are consistently pragmatic, such work supports the merits of public worship because it is intended to undercut individual distinctions regarding positions of race, class, gender, or social status. It is also intended to return human piety to the center stage of belief through the performance of congregational prayer within the mosque.

Notes

1. Akel Ismail Kahera, *Deconstructing the American Mosque, Space, Gender and Aesthetics* (Austin, TX: University of Texas Press, 2002): 83.
2. S. M. Darsh, *Islamic Essays* (London: Islamic Cultural Center, 1979); Asma Sayeed, Early Sunni Discourses on Women's Mosque Attendance. *International Institute for the Study of Islam in the Modern World NewsLetter*, 7 (March 1, 2001). Available at www.isim.nl

References

Abdul Rauf, Muhammad. *Al Markaz al-Ismai bi Washington* (The Islamic Center of Washington) (Hyattsville MD: Colortone Press, 1978).

Al-Samhudi, Ali. *Wafa Al-Wafa: Bi Akhbar Dar Al-Mustafa* (Al-Furqan Publications, Heritage Foundation, 2002).

Austin, Allan. *African Muslims in Ante-Bellum America* (London: Routledge, 1997).

Architectural Record, 1992, 92–97.

Baghby, Ihsan. *The American Mosque 2011.* Available at: http://www.cair.com/Portals/0/pdf/ The-American-Mosque-2011-web.pdf

Baghby, Ihsan, P. M. Perl, and B. T. Froehle (eds.). *The Mosque in America: A National Portrait* (Washington, DC: Council on Islamic Relations, 2001).

Bell, Malcolm, Muriel Bell, and Charles Joyner. *Drums and Shadows: Survival Studies among the Coastal Georgia Negroes* (Atlanta: University of Georgia Press, 1986).

Dannin, Robert. *Black Pilgimage to Islam* (New York: Oxford University Press, 2005).

Darsh, S. M. *Islamic Essays* (London: Islamic Cultural Center, 1979).

Diouf, Sylvianne. *Servants of Allah: African Muslims Enslaved in the Americas* (New York: New York University Press, 1998).

Drums and Shadows: Survival Stories among the Coastal Georgia Negroes. Athens: University of Georgia Press, 1986.

Haddad, Yvonne Yazbeck. *The Muslims of America* (New York: Oxford University Press, 1991).

Haddad, Yvonne Yazbeck, Jane I. Smith, and Kathleen M. Moore, *Muslim Women in America: The Challenge of Islamic Identity Today* (New York: Oxford University Press, 2006).

Hakim, Jameela A. *History of the First Muslim Mosque of Pittsburgh, PA.*, n.d. n.p.

Kahera, Akel Ismail. "The Urban Mosque: Urban Islam, Activism and the Reconstruction of the Ghetto." *Studies in Contemporary Islam*, 3.2 (2001): 49–64.

Kahera, Akel Ismail. Urban Enclaves, Muslim Identity and the Urban Mosque in America. *Journal of Muslim Minority Affairs*, 22.2 (2002): 369–380.

Kahera, Akel Ismail. *Deconstructing the American Mosque: Space, Gender and Aesthetics* (Austin, TX: University of Texas Press, 2002).

Kahera, Akel Ismail. *A Mosque: Between Significance and Style* (Leiden: International Institute for the Study of Islam in the Modern World, 2005): 56–57.

Kahera, Akel Ismail. Art Is Not Created Ex-Nihilo: Order, Space & Form in the Work of Sinan and Palladio, *Journal of History & Culture* 1.3 (2010): 57–79.

Metcalf, Barbra, ed. *Making Muslim Space in North America and Europe* (Berkeley: University of California Press, 1996).

Moore, Kathleen. *Al-Mughtaribun: American Law and the Transformation of Muslim Life* (Albany, NY: State University of New York Press, 1995).

Mugeraurer, Robert. *Interpreting Environments: Tradition, Deconstruction, Hermeneutics.* Austin: University of Texas Press, 1995.

Nash, Michael. *Islam Among Urban Blacks: Muslims in Newark: A Social History* (Lanham, MD: University Press of America, 2008).

Norberg-Schultz, Christian. *Genius Loci: Towards a Phenomenology of Architecture* (Rome: Rizzoli, 1991).

Price, Jay M. *Temples for a Modern God: Religious Architecture in Postwar America* (New York: Oxford University Press, 2013).

Ruskin, John. *The Seven Lamps of Architecture.* Mineola, NY: Dover Publications, 1989.

Sayeed, Asma. Early Sunni Discourses on Women's Mosque Attendance. *International Institute for the Study of Islam in the Modern World NewsLetter, 7* (March 1, 2001). Available at: www.isim.nl

Ruskin, John. *The Seven lamps of Architecture* (Mineola, NY: Dover Publications, 1989).

Smith, Jane. *Islam in America* (New York: Columbia University Press, 2010).

Toussaint, Manuel. *Arte Mudejar in America* (Editorial Porrua, S.A., 1946).

CHAPTER 25

....

ISLAMIC DRESS AND FASHION IN THE UNITED STATES

....

RABIA KAMAL

INTRODUCTION
....

In every culture around the world, people use dress and fashion to express spiritual, aesthetic, and cultural values as well as to situate themselves in multiple ways within society. Communal traditions, social status, religious ethics, and political agendas are some of the major factors that have influenced dress and style through the ages. With the onset of globalization and the masscirculation of images through media, the sartorial choices of individuals and communities are now subject to an even more complex array of cultural, political, and personal factors that go into the making and wearing of contemporary apparel.

In the last several decades, a growing interest in Islamic dress and fashion has developed as a result of diasporic trends, mass mediated exposure, and shifts in global politics and the economy. In western countries, the notion of "Islamic fashion" has developed alongside rising social anxieties surrounding Islamic symbols relating to dress and signs such as "the veil." This chapter considers the multiple factors that have influenced how American Muslim men and women dress and how a growing Islamic fashion industry and new stylistic forms have evolved in the United States.

"Fashion" and "Islamic Dress" as Concepts

New interest in Islamic dress and Islamic fashion in contemporary academia and media often tends to privilege western definitions of "fashion," dehistoricizing and reasserting fixed perceptions of Islam and Muslim identities. Rather than looking at new kinds of Islamic fashion trends and clothing styles as "a dynamic, experiential process... involving the complicated negotiation of fashion and faith" (Landes 2012, 232), Muslim women's dress choices are often positioned within a framework whereby fashion and stylishness are seen as western standards linked to notions of individuality and choice. Often the underlying assumption is that while western fashion is very difficult to reconcile with Islamic standards, when Muslim women *do* choose to be fashionable, it is because residing in western society, they have become modernized and liberated. Even scholars aiming to dispel myths surrounding Muslim women's dress choices often end up inadvertently reinforcing the "modest and Islamic" *yet* "fashionable" dichotomy that pervades such discourse.

Furthermore, in considering "Islamic dress," it is important to note that there is no clear way to identify what such a concept entails. The sheer diversity and historical and cultural specificity of dress worn by Muslims around the world make it difficult to define what Islamic dress actually is. Forms of Muslim attire are manifold and differ greatly according to "social hierarchies, ethnic, and cultural backgrounds, and between urban and rural contexts even in a single country" (Dahlgren 1999, 90). Thus perhaps the simplest way to categorize such a large repertoire of cultural and material practices of dress as Islamic is through an understanding of modesty. Modesty, as mandated in the Qu'ran, is an ambiguous concept open to interpretation but applies equally to both women and men as an emotional and physical standard. As one scholar notes, while there are numerous interpretations of the concept of modesty, common to many understandings is the notion that Muslim dress "should please Allah" (El Guindi 1995, 1999). Aside from personal interpretation and piety, clothing that is loose and covers most of the body as a means of guarding one's sexuality is considered appropriately Islamic in reflecting a modest demeanor.

The negotiation of modest or Islamic dress by Muslims living in the West has gone through significant changes as a result of the conditions of diaspora, with dress being an integral way in which people connect to or leave behind previous affiliations and traditions. Second- and third-generation Muslims, in particular, are choosing new dress styles that not only reflect syncretism and innovation (Niessen 2003) but also signal new forms of religious and cultural consciousness. Often, their dress choices embody struggles over competing desires to realize "an ethnically transcendent, pure form of Islamic fashion"(Tarlo 2010) and to forge their own indigenous identities within western cultural contexts.

Immigrant Muslim and African-American Muslim Dress in the United States

The diversity of dress and sartorial styles in Muslim communities across the United States is immense. Muslims migrating to the United States often bring with them a rich cultural heritage of dress that is selectively maintained or gradually replaced, depending on a number of factors such as class, gender, generation, level of assimilation, and personal choice. Muslims of South Asian background, like their non-Muslim counterparts, often wear *shalwaar kameez* at home or on special occasions. Shalwaar kameez, a traditional outfit worn by both men and women, entails loose pajama-like trousers and a long shirt or tunic. This dress style meets cultural and religious standards of modesty, since it is loose-fitting and often long-sleeved, covering most of the body. In addition, some Muslim immigrant women may wrap a loose scarf around their heads—a sign of modesty maintained by many South Asian women regardless of religious affiliation.[1] In some immigrant Muslim communities, men and young boys will wear shalwaar kameez only within the privacy of their own homes, switching to western clothing when going to school or the workplace. On the other hand, women and young girls are often expected to wear shalwaar kameez both in and outside the home, not so much as a religious expectation but more so to uphold cultural tradition. Such gendered expectations surrounding traditional cultural dress are shifting over time, particularly among second- and third-generation Muslim Americans.

Other immigrant Muslim communities, such as those of Arab descent, are less likely to dress in traditional garb from the Middle East. Most often Arab Muslim men wear western pants and shirts, and women tend to wear long dresses or skirts and a headcovering or hijab. Immigrant Muslim women coming from parts of Africa, on the other hand, engage in dynamic dress practices that are now spreading across Muslim American communities, whereby individual and communal fashion references cultural and historical styles mixed with an Islamic universalism (Rabeeya 2007). Writing about fashion and piety among the Muslim Senegalese community in New York City, Buggenhagen describes the opulent attire of immigrant women from Africa: "The women…chose glossy fabrics, embroidered with shimmering metallic threads and accented with sparkling chokers, and stacks of bracelets" (2012, 86). Such attire not only reflects cultural heritage but also serves to display these Muslim immigrants' social status and the strength of their networks within a transnational and global Islamic community (Heath 1992).

AfricanAmerican Muslims also exhibit a wide array of dress-related choices. Many who convert to Islam acknowledge their Islamic faith socially through certain types of dress, wearing hijab or African-influenced clothing as a way to make a statement about their identity vis-à-vis other AfricanAmericans as well as mainstream society. As Rouse notes in her study on AfricanAmerican Muslims, women who choose to wear the hijab are "not only fulfilling a religious duty, but are also making statements of disagreement with the American mainstream culture, resisting Western middle-class hegemonic expectations of how a liberated American woman should look like and what she should wear" (2004, 8–9). Some AfricanAmerican Muslims, on the other hand, may choose not to dress in a way that visibly signals their Islamic identity, challenging social control and pressures to conform within Muslim communities dominated by immigrant standards. For example, often when people convert to Islam, they will practice and learn about the religion within an immigrant mosque or community center, where expectations or traditions of cultural dress may be conflated with Islamic laws on appropriate attire. Annual conventions held by such organizations as the Islamic Circle of North America as well as the Islamic Society of North America, which are often dominated by immigrant Muslims, also play an important role in promoting Islamic dress. Thousands of Muslim Americans flock to these conventions each year, where bazaars or souks have vendors selling scarves, *thobes*,[2] headdresses, and an array of "Islamic" clothing. In previous times most of the "Islamic" clothing sold at convention bazaars was from the Middle East or South Asia, essentially promoting the idea that shalwar kameez or long thobes may be considered more "authentically Islamic" than jeans and t-shirts. However, these culturally inflected and sometimes anti western expectations surrounding Islamic dress are now being challenged by the younger generation of Muslim Americans, who are seeking to create their own indigenous Islamic style that borrows from the culture in which they live.[3]

INTERNATIONAL TRENDS AND THEIR
IMPACT ON ISLAMIC FASHION

Islamic fashion and dress practices of Muslim American women and men have been significantly impacted by international and global trends. As a result of migration patterns, global capitalism, and the rise of new media and digital technologies, people's exposure and access to novel fashion trends has increased. While cosmopolitanism and engaging in a global economy dominated by the West has resulted in an unprecedented influence of western ideals through the commodification of culture, Islam has also become a powerful space of global social identification with respect to style and consumption (LeBlanc 2000, 445).

Growing patterns of transnational migration have caused significant shifts in gender roles, social expectations, intergenerational relations, and political orientations within diasporic communities. Such changes often manifest themselves in debates over religion and identity. An increase in migration from Muslim countries to the West in the last several decades has particularly positioned Muslim women and their clothing practices at the center of national and communal debates. For example, the visible increase in numbers of Muslim immigrant women who choose to wear the hijab, or the headscarf, demonstrates the local appropriation of transnational processes (Hansen 1995). The growth of political Islam and religious piety movements in recent times has thus influenced Islamic fashion trends in the West, discussed further below. In addition, the global circulation of images and information via the internet, satellite, and digital television channels has not only allowed Muslims in the United States to learn more about Islam, prompting changes in their dress, but has also facilitated their ability to follow fashion trends from beyond the western world.

Global consumerism and the commodification of women in the name of fashion has also led to interesting debates about the burgeoning of Islamic fashion around the world. While one recent report cites that the global Muslim fashion market is worth $96 billion (Ilyas 2012), consumers of Islamic fashion constantly negotiate what can be seen as two apparently contradictory phenomena—the rise in Islamic piety and a rise in consumerism (Jones 2007). The increasing popularity and global consumption of fashionable Islamic dress is critiqued by certain segments of the Muslim community as "commodity fetishism" that belies true piety (Jones 2010, 618), particularly targeting Muslim women. However, a number of recent studies have demonstrated that the consumption of Islamic fashion in fact allows Muslims to enact ethical lives in ways that not only challenge the alleged irreconcilability of consumption and devotion but also serve to deconstruct the false and sometimes forced divisions between western and Islamic fashion worlds (Akou 2007, Jones 2007, 2010, Kopp 2002, Koskennurmi-Sivonen, Koivula and Maijala 2004, Tarlo 2010). Thus the global commodification of Islamic dress and style becomes an important site where the relationship between gender, faith, and materiality are continually and productively negotiated.

ISLAMIC DRESS AND THE HIJAB: AGENCY AND GENDER

As mentioned above, Muslim women's pious dress is a particularly charged topic in contemporary western contexts. This is because signs typically connected with Islam have come to represent an important part of Muslim women's attire in the United States and elsewhere (Haddad 2007, Koskennurmi-Sivonen, Koivula and Maijala 2004). As a result of an increase in access to Islamic knowledge and a desire to distinguish themselves from previous generations' cultural or ethnically influenced dress, many young Muslim American women have chosen to wear the hijab. According to Islam, hijab is both the institution of covering and modesty and the veil itself (El Guindi 1995). However, the question of how this practice of modesty should materialize is debatable, with forms of cover ranging from headscarves, body cloaks, and face veils to an understanding of hijab as merely dressing in a "decent" manner (Tiilikainen 2003: 140–145). It is important to note here that until recently, the practice of face veiling or wearing a body cloak was not prevalent in most Muslim countries with the exception of places like Saudi Arabia. Thus although the range of interpretations of hijab is varied and shifting, contemporary western media and politics have reduced the "diverse array of modesty codes glossed as 'the veil' " (Ghodsee 2008) to a sign of the Islamic oppression of women.[4]

While much can be said regarding debates and controversies surrounding the Muslim veil, recent scholarly research addressing the various factors that determine the choice of veiling by Muslim American women serves to challenge simplistic accounts depicted in the media and often accepted by non-Muslims. According to many women interviewed in these studies, their decision to wear dress that marks them as "visibly Muslim" represents neither a sense of passive victimhood of patriarchal domination, nor an ideology that is "anti-Western and rejecting of the values of liberal democratic society" (Landes 2012, 232). Rather, ethnographic research that attempts to understand how Muslim American women construct their appearance demonstrates a high level of agency, individuality, and consciousness associated with wearing the hijab(Abu-Lughod 2002, Deeb 2006, El Guindi 1999, Mahmood 2001, 2005, Scott 2007). The choice of donning the headscarf is not only a sign of personal piety but can also be a means for young Muslim women to manage and subvert the reductionist gaze of members of their own community as well as those in mainstream American society (Tarlo 2010). The hijab thus serves a number of purposes, ranging from defining one's Islamic identity to resisting sexual objectification, affording respect, and providing freedom (Droogsma 2007, Williams and Vashi 2007).

As is demonstrated in the following section, the sartorial experimentation of young Muslim American men and women not only demonstrates an expression of communal and individual identity but also illustrates the agency of dress in facilitating new meanings and identities (Tarlo 2010) that defy conventional labels such as "modern," "traditional," "western," and "Islamic."

CONTEMPORARY MUSLIM AMERICAN DRESS: FUSING FASHION AND FAITH

As a new generation of Muslims come of age in an era of fast-paced change facilitated by the internet and social media, they demonstrate novel and proactive ways of bringing together their fashion and faith within the American context. While global

Muslim styles from the Middle East, Asia, and Africa continue to influence their choices of apparel, many Muslim American "fashionistas" are creating and choosing trends that reflect a uniquely *American* Muslim identity. Rather than pitting "Islamic" or "Arab" dress against "western" or "American" attire, young Muslims pick and choose from an array of cultural, ethnic, modern, and traditional clothing practices to create their own aesthetic. As one young Muslim American fashion designer and blogger explains:

> In America, we have a microcosm of the Muslim world. There are eighty different ethnicities. It's a cultural and spiritual buffet table. American Muslims pick and choose and create their own. But we put a Western twist to it. As American Muslims, we don't want to dress the way a girl in Turkey or the United Arab Emirates would. We have our own sense of fashion and style that is inspired by runways and the culture we live in. (Kasson 2010, 2)

Such shifts in approaches to dressing reflect a wider trend in the Muslim American community whereby individuals and groups are actively seeking to forge their own culturally *American* Muslim identity.

The mixing and matching of different elements in young Muslim American attire "are a tangible parallel to the way in which they commute between cultures much more fluently" than their parent's generation (Koskennurmi-Sivonen, Koivula, and Maijala 2004, 457). Such versatility can be witnessed in the diverse clothing choices of say, a young Muslim American man who can be seen wearing everything from a Banana Republic sweater and dress pants, a thobe, and a "hoodie" and Timberlands to a shalwaar kameez or tuxedo depending on the occasion. Young Muslim American girls will don dresses and long skirts, pair jeans with layered tops, and supplement their style with numerous accessories. They will often experiment with hijab styles, not just in terms of fabric and print but also in the ways that they wrap the garment around their heads. Not only does such sartorial diversity serve to challenge reductionist stereotypes about "what Muslims look like" but it can also embody expressions of sociocultural hybridity (Schoss 1996).

An increasing number of young Muslim American fashion designers are tapping into this modesty market (Rojas 2011, Taylor 2010), turning to an eclectic array of sources for their inspiration and style boards. Modesty standards are combined with high fashion as well as mainstream trends, bringing together an aesthetic that can range from punk/skater/reggae to urban hipster and preppychic (Davidson 2011, Rojas 2011). The burgeoning of the Islamic designer dress industry in the United States reflects a growing trend in many parts of the world where young independent entrepreneurs are seeking to fill a gap in the marketplace for practical, versatile, and well-designed Islamic clothing. Many young designers have found eager and loyal clients who are drawn to the "modernization" of such traditional garments as the *abaya*, a loose-fitting dress that covers the entire body. The success of these new designs includes innovation in style, cuts, and colors, whereby the garment caters to a fashion-conscious crowd that is still interested in practicality. Thus, some abayas are designed for nursing mothers or for maternity wear, while others are bedecked with crystals or high-end designer cuffs. In expanding their marketbase, Islamic fashion designers cater to a wide age and class range through the new ways in which they approach modest dress, using quality fabric and considering the needs of women in all walks of life. Strategic marketing of Islamic clothing has involved online advertising on websites such as Facebook, in local publications, on the street and by word of mouth. The importance of coming up with new ideas and paying attention to new needs and demands has been integral to business growth in the Islamic fashion industry. However, many designers and businesses emphasize that their success is measured not just by commercial results but also by the kind of support they are able to provide in promoting modest Muslim dress choices and spreading awareness about Islam in general.

An interesting example of innovation in meeting modest Muslim dress demands is the creation and marketing of Islamic swimwear. Many Muslim men and women wanting to swim or engage in water sports in public pools or on beaches have felt limited in the past by available swimsuits, which are neither loose-fitting nor cover the entire body. Thus a growing number of retailers and specialty shops have started to sell some version of the "burqini," a type of swimsuit for women that entails a full-length, loose-fitting wetsuit and built-in hood. Styles and colors of these swimsuits have diversified greatly, with growing competition between brands on the lightness of the fabric as well as designs that prevent the suit from sticking to the body on contact with water. While the wearing of burqinis in public places has incited some controversy in western nations, the trend has caught on with some outside the Islamic community, challenging the misconception that Islamic fashion is designed only for Muslims.

The internet has played a large part in facilitating and empowering young Muslim American fashion visionaries who combine high fashion with modest standards of dress (Taylor 2010). New websites, blogs, and online retailers catering to American Muslim women have emerged (Kasson 2010), becoming ways in which style, modesty, identity, creativity, and individuality are explored and sold. For example, one website that features a number of videos of American Muslim fashion shows exposes the world of "hijabistas"[5] by presenting women sashaying down the runway in everything from Diane Von Furstenberg maxis, six-inch Balenciaga stilettos, and Fendi scarves as hijabs" (Bose 2012) to urban street fashion. 'Hijabista', a word which fuses 'hijab' and 'fashionista', gained traction a few years ago when young Muslim women around the world realized they could follow the Islamic rules for modest dressing without stifling their need for creative expression" (Bose 2012, Shimek 2012).

Young bloggers and new magazines also signal a rising trend in the world of Islamic fashion, whereby a distinctly Muslim American style is constantly being negotiated by both men and women. One of North America's most popular women's magazines on Muslim American women, *Azizah*, focuses heavily on trends in Islamic dress through editorials on Islamic fashion shows, the rise in Muslim clothing companies, and Islamic influences on New York fashion week. *Emel*, a Muslim lifestyle magazine, features columns on building a stylish but modest wardrobe, ethical or environmentally conscious Muslim fashion, and Islamic work styles for the professional Muslim woman. Blogs with names like "Hijabulous," "We Love Hijab," "Muslim Style Queen," "Fashionably Modest," "Modest Plus," and "Hijabs High," which is the Muslim answer to the "Sartorialist" (Kasson 2010, 3), celebrate individual style and offer a wide variety of clothing choices while simultaneously challenging prevailing stereotypes about religiously observant Muslim American women. For example, the potential of dress and clothing choices to both define and subvert identities is powerfully demonstrated in a blog started by a young American Muslim entitled "Pictures of Muslims Wearing Things."[6] The blogger challenges stereotypes about Muslims through the use of clothing as a signifying practice in the media. What is particularly striking about the "archive" format of the blog is that it forms a collage of pictures of Muslims "wearing things" that are submitted over time. Scrolling down the page, the sheer diversity of apparel, ethnicity, race, activities, and styles that the pictures depict is thought-provoking, visually defying any easy categorization of "Muslim garb."

Finally, the contribution of internet commerce in the expansion of religious expression through fashion in the United States is ever-increasing. While previously, modest clothing available for Muslim women was predominantly imported from Arab and South Asian countries, stylish hijabistas can now order modest and fashionable clothing online, choosing from a wide variety of style, aesthetics, and fabrics (Kasson 2010). Combining trends from all over the globe in creating their own clothing lines, Muslim American fashion designers also serve to dispute the notion "that Islamic fashion is a world unto itself" (Tarlo 2010). A number of fashion designers seek to attract all Americans, regardless of religious affiliation. Potential clients who may not find adequately modest attire in mainstream fashion include members of the orthodox Jewish community, Mormons, evangelical Christians, and other individuals who prefer more conservative yet fashionable dress. The stylistic creations of Muslim fashion designers borrowing from western trends is no longer a one-way street. While high end fashion houses have always drawn inspiration from non-Western cultures, recent fashion shows by world-renowned designers such as Karl Lagerfeld are replete with looks that specifically reference ethnic South Asian Muslim dress.[7] While a "Chanel shalwar kameez is well beyond the budget of most young Muslim Americans, such design referencing becomes a subject of inspiration and identification for many Muslim American fashionistas. Thus the flow of fashion trends that determine both Muslim and non-Muslim dress in the West depends on increasingly entangled fashion worlds that thrive on cross-cultural and creative hybridity.

NOTES

1. This loose scarf is different from the Islamic *hijab* or headcovering. Writing about how second- and third-generation Muslims in the West who are learned in Islam make a clear distinction between their own use of a scarf and older forms of head covering associated with Muslim ethnic dress, Koskennurmi-Sivonen et al. note, "These women want to find their support in the religion itself, and they criticize those women of the older generation who dress in accordance with cultural tradition without knowing why" (2004, 448).
2. An ankle-length garment with long sleeves commonly worn by men in some Arab countries.
3. Some second- and third-generation Muslims of immigrant background, in an attempt to form an indigenous Muslim American identity, are turning to AfricanAmerican style and culture as a means of inspiration and appropriation (see, for example, Aidi 2002, Moghul 2010).
4. While the headscarf has become a central symbol in social and political discourse, equal expectations surrounding male modesty are mandated in Islam. Men are expected to meet standards of religious modesty by wearing loose and covering clothing. More religiously observant men will also don *kufis*, or traditional Islamic caps, as an additional sign of modesty.
5. http://www.kcet.org/arts/artbound/counties/orange/upcoming-muslim-american-fashion.html.
6. http://muslimswearingthings.tumblr.com
7. http://www.vogue.com/collections/fall-2012-rtw/chanel/review/

REFERENCES

Abaza, Mona, "Shifting Landscapes of Fashion in Contemporary Egypt," *Fashion Theory* 11, no. 2/3 (2007): 281–298.

Abu-Lughod, Lila, "Do Muslim Women Really Need Saving? Anthropological Reflections on Cultural Relativism and Its Others," *American Anthropologist* 104, no. 3 (2002): 783–790.

Aidi, Hisham, "Jihadis in the Hood: Race, Urban Islam and the War on Terror," *Middle East Report* 224 (2002): 36–43.

Ajrouch, Kristine J., "Global Contexts and the Veil: Muslim Integration in the United States and France," *Sociology of Religion* 68, no. 3 (2007): 321–325.

Akou, Heather M., "The Case of Somali Women's Dress in Minnesota: Evaluating Herbert Blumer's Theory on Fashion," Paper presented at Making an Appearance Conference,' Brisbane, Australia:, 2003a.

——, "Ethnic Dress? Understanding Somalis in Minneapolis-St. Paul," Paper presented at the ITAA Conference, Savannah, GA:, 2003b.

——, "'World Fashion': Islamic Dress in the Twenty-first Century," *Fashion Theory* 11, no. 4 (2007): 403–422.

Bose, Lilledeshan, "Hijabistas: Inside the World of Muslim-American Fashion," *KCET*. June 7, 2012. Available at http://www.kcet.org/arts/artbound/counties/orange/upcoming-muslim-american-fashion.html

Buggenhagen, Beth, "Fashioning Piety: Women's Dress, Money, and Faith among Senegalese Muslims in New York City," *City & Society* 24, no. 1 (2012): 84–104.

Dahlgren, Susanne, "The Multiple Interpretations of Islamic Female Images," in *Women of Pedigree and Feminists*, edited by Jaana Airaksinen and Tuula Ripatti(Tampere, Finland: Vastapaino, 1999): 87–110.

Davidson, Audrey-June, *Punk Islam? Muslim Punk?: Taqwacore as a Multivalent Means Through which to Counteract a Monolithic Image of Islam*(Portland, OR: Reed College, 2011).

Deeb, Lara, *Enchanted Modern: Gender and Public Piety in Shi'i Lebanon*(Princeton, NJ: Princeton University Press, 2006).

Droogsma, Rachel A., "Redefining Hijab: American Muslim Women's Standpoints on Veiling," *Journal of Applied Communication Research*35, no. 3 (2007): 294–319.

Dwyer, Claire, "Veiled Meanings: Young British Muslim Women and the Negotiation of Differences," *Gender, Place and Culture: A Journal of Feminist Geography* 6, no. 1 (1999): 5–26.

El Guindi, Fadwa, "Hijab," in *The Oxford Encyclopedia of the Modern Islamic World*, edited by John Esposito(New York: Oxford University Press, 1995): 108–111.

——, *Veil: Modesty, Privacy and Resistance*(Oxford, UK: Berg Publishers, 1999).

Ghodsee, Kristen, "The Miniskirt and the Veil: Islam, Secularism, and Women's Fashion in the New Europe," *Historical Reflections* 34, no. 3 (2008): 105–125.

Gökariksel, Banu, and Anna J. Secor, "New transnational geographies of Islamism, capitalism and subjectivity: the veiling-fashion industry in Turkey," *Area 41*, no. 1 (2008): 6–18.

Gole, Nilufer, *The Forbidden Modern: Civilization and Veiling*(Ann Arbor: University of Michigan Press), 1996.

Haddad, Yvonne Y., "The Post-9/11 *Hijab* as Icon," *Sociology of Religion* 68, no. 3 (2007): 253–267.

Hansen, Karen T., "Transnational Biographies and Local Meaning: Used Clothes Practices in Lusaka," *Journal of Southern African Studies* 21, no. (1995): 131–145.

Heath, Deborah, "Fashion, Anti-Fashion and Heteroglossia in Urban Senegal," *American Ethnologist* 19, no. 1 (1992): 19–33.

Huisman, Kimberly, and Pierrette Hondagneu-Sotelo, "Dress Matters: Change and Continuity in the Dress Practices of Bosnian Muslim Refugee Women," *Gender and Society* 9, no. 1 (2005): 44–65.

Ilyas, Sara, "Is Muslim Fashion Finally 'on Trend'?" *The Guardian*, April 26, 2012. Available at http://www.guardian.co.uk/fashion/fashion-blog/2012/apr/26/muslim-fashion-on-trend

Jones, Carla. "Fashion and Faith in Urban Indonesia," *Fashion Theory* 11, no. 2/3 (2007): 211–232.

——, "Materializing Piety: Gendered Anxieties about Faithful Consumption in Contemporary Urban Indonesia," *American Ethnologist* 37, no. 4 (2010): 617–637.

Kasson, Elisabeth G., "Wrapped up in Style," *Los Angeles Times*, June 6, 2010. latimes.com/features/image/la-ig-hijab-20100606,0,4885160.story.

Khan, Shahnaz, *Muslim Women: Crafting a North American Identity*. (Gainesville: University Press of Florida, 2000).

Kopp, Hollie, "Dress and Diversity: Muslim Women and Islamic Dress in an Immigrant/Minority Context," *The Muslim World* 92, no. 1–2 (2002): 59–78.

Koskennurmi-Sivonen, Ritva, Jaana Koivula, and Seija Maijala, "United Fashions—Making a Muslim Appearance in Finland," *Fashion Theory* 8, no. 4 (2004): 443–460.

Landes, David J., "Review of Visibly Muslim," *Journal of the Royal Anthropological Institute 18* (2012): 197–241.

LeBlanc, Marie N., "Versioning Womanhood and Muslimhood: 'Fashion' and the Life Course in Contemporary Bouaké, Côte D'Ivoire," *Africa 70*, no. 3 (2000): 442–481.

Mahmood, Saba, "Feminist Theory, Embodiment, and the Docile Agent: Some Reflections on the Egyptian Islamic Revival," *Cultural Anthropology* 16(2001): 202–236.

——, *Politics of Piety: The Islamic Revival and the Feminist Subject* (Princeton, NJ: University Press, 2005).

Mallouhi, Christine, *Mini-Skirts, Mothers and Muslims: Modeling Spiritual Values in Muslim Culture* (Carlisle, UK: Spear Publications, 1994).

McGinty, Anna M., "'Faith Drives Me to Be an Activist': Two American Muslim Women on Faith, Outreach, and Gender," *The Muslim World* 102(2012): 371–389.

Meneley, Anne, "Fashions and Fundamentalisms in fin-de-siècle Yemen: Chador Barbie and Islamic Socks," *Cultural Anthropology* 22 (2007): 214–243.

Metcalf, Barbara, "'Remaking Ourselves': Islamic Self-Fashioning in a Global Movement of Spiritual Renewal," in *Accounting for Fundamentalisms*, edited by Marty E. Marty and R.S. Appleby(Chicago: University of Chicago Press, 1994): 706–725.

Michelman, Susan O., "Reveal or Conceal? American Religious Discourse With Fashion," *Etnofoor* 16, no. 2 (2003): 76–87.

Moghul, Haroon, "Allah and the Los Angele Lakers," *The Huffington Post*, June 16, 2010. Available at http://www.huffingtonpost.com/hamid-moghul/allah-and-the-los-angeles_b_614481.html.

Moore, Kathleen M., "Visible through the Veil: The Regulation of Islam in American Law," *Sociology of Religion* 68, no. 3 (2007): 237–251.

Navaro-Yashin, Yael, *Faces of the State: Secularism and Public Life in Turkey*(Princeton, NJ: Princeton University Press, 2002).

Niessen, Sandra, "Three Scenarios from Batak Clothing History: Designing Participation in the Global Fashion Trajectory," in *Re-orienting Fashion: The Globalization of Asian Dress*, edited by Sandra Niessen, Ann Marie Leshkowich, and Carla Jones(Oxford, UK: Berg Publishers, 2003): 49–78.

Rabeeya, David, "Women's Dress in the West and Islam: Moral and Practical Implications," *The American Muslim (TAM)*, April 8, 2007.Available at http://theamericanmuslim.org/tam.php/features/articles/womens_dress_   in_the_west_and_islam_moral_and_practical_implications/0013677

Rojas, Leslie B., "The Right to Choose How We Dress:' American Muslim Women Speak Out on French Burqa Ban," *Multi-American*, April 12, 2011.Available at http://multiamerican.scpr.org/2011/04/the-french-burqa-ban-american-muslim-women-speak-out/

——, "Meet Jamesa Nikiema, Muslim Fashion Designer, Pure Southern California Girl," *Multi-American*, December 2, 2011.Available at http://multiamerican.scpr.org/2011/12/meet-jamesa-nikiema-muslim-fashion-designer-pure-southern-california-girl/

Rouse, Carolyn M., *Engaged Surrender: African American Women and Islam.* (Berkeley: University of California Press, 2004).

Sandikci, Ozlem, and Guliz Ger, "Fundamental Fashions: The Cultural Politics of the Turban and the Levis," *Advances in Consumer Research* 28 (2001): 146–150.

Schoss, Johanna, "'Dressed to Shine': Work, Leisure and Style in Malandi, Kenya," in *Clothing and Difference: Embodied Identities in Colonial and Post-colonial Africa*, edited by Ian H. Hendrickson(Durham, NC: Duke University Press, 1996): 157–188..

Scott, Joan Wallach Scott, *The Politics of the Veil*(Princeton, NJ: Princeton University Press, 2007).

Secor, Anna J., "The Veil and Urban Space in Istanbul: Women's Dress, Mobility and Islamic Knowledge," *Gender, Place & Culture: A Journal of Feminist Geography* 9, no. 1 (2002):5–22.

Shimek, Elizabeth D., "The Abaya: Fashion, Religion, and Identity in a Globalized World," Lawrence University Honors Projects, May 31, 2012. Available at http://lux.lawrence.edu/luhp/12

Tarlo, Emma, *Visibly Muslim: Fashion, Politics, Faith*. (New York: Berg Publishers, 2010).

Taylor, Jerome, "Beautiful *and* Islamic: the new look on the catwalk," *The Independent*, July 2, 2010.Available at http://www.independent.co.uk/life-style/fashion/news/beautiful-uandu-islamic-the-new-look-on-the-catwalk-2016293.html

Tiilikainen, Marja, *Islam in Everyday Life. Somali Women's Life in Finland*. (Tampere, Finland: Vastapaino, 2003).

Turner, Richard B., *Islam in the African-American Experience*(Bloomington: Indiana University Press, 2003).

"US Muslims Celebrate Islamic Fashion," *OnIslam & Newspapers*. March 23, 2012.Available at http://www.onislam.net/english/news/americas/456347-us-muslims-celebrate-islamic-fashion.html

Werbner, Pnina, "Veiled Interventions in Pure Space Honour, Shame and Embodied Struggles among Muslims in Britain and France," *Theory, Culture & Society* 24, no. 2(2007): 161–186.

Williams, Rhys H., and Gira Vashi, "Hijab and American Muslim Women: Creating the Space for Autonomous Selves," *Sociology of Religion* 68, no. 2 (2007): 269–287.

Zine, Jasmin, "Unveiled Sentiments: Gendered Islamophobia and Experiences of Veiling among Muslim Girls in a Canadian Islamic School," *Equity & Excellence in Education* 39(2006): 239–252.

CHAPTER 26

HEALTH AND MEDICINE AMONG AMERICAN MUSLIMS

LANCE D. LAIRD

INTRODUCTION

Texas oncologist Fazlur Rahman recalled an incident from his rural Bengali childhood in the medical journal *Lancet*. A local imam treated a painful boil on Rahman's head with holy water, an amulet, and a verse of scripture. His grandmother remarked on the scar, "You have a divine text in your head. It portends your good future." That future was marred by the inability of biomedical clinicians to prevent his mother's death or diagnose his own serious illness. Despite or because of these experiences, Rahman enrolled in medical school in Dacca, praying that his grandfather—as well as the imam who treated him as a child—might forgive him for the "act of desecration" involved: dissecting corpses (Rahman 1997).

Like Rahman, American Muslims—clinicians, imams and grandmothers—carry in their bodies elements of a long tradition of "Islamic medicine," rituals and healing ways from around the globe. Like most Americans (Barnes et al., 2004), Muslims also combine multiple complementary and alternative health practices and understandings in their daily lives. They draw on scripture, prophetic tradition, *shari`ah* principles, ritual practices, traditional herbal and physical remedies, biomedical science and technology, a range of alternative medical systems, and a religious emphasis on social justice and compassion to address their own health needs; assure proper care by non-Muslim health professionals; improve their professional medical practices; and promote the health of the public, both Muslim and non-Muslim.

GETTING TO THE ROOTS

Some historians of religion have seen contemporary Muslim contributions to international biomedicine flowing from both the heritage of Islamic medical science and the complementary use of "spiritual" healing practices in Muslim communities (Antes, 1989; Hermansen, 2004; Rahman, 1987). Muslims historically have adapted and integrated aspects of disparate healing systems (e.g., Galenic, Chinese, and Ayurvedic) into an Islamically framed moral universe, developing hospitals, clinics, pharmacological systems, and medical-education centers. The eclectic incorporation and adaptation of other medical systems, along with geographically diverse herbal and physical therapies, leads historians to characterize "Islamic medicine" of the medieval period as a mixture of religions, cultures, and healing practices among both physicians and patients (Pormann and Savage-Smith, 2007; Rahman, 1987). Sixteenth-century Spanish settlers brought humoral theories of hot-cold and dry-moist oppositions in diet, activity, and emotional states to the Americas. Enslaved West African Muslims brought their own traditions, which successive waves of immigrants and African Americans have modified and hybridized. Competing models of healing coexist, and Muslim Americans choose based on resource availability, nature of the symptoms, individual beliefs, and socioeconomic location (Hermansen, 2004).

Muslim leaders have encouraged the recovery and revival of both Islamic, or Unani, medicine, and "prophetic medicine" —the tradition of preventive medicine following the *sunnah* of the Prophet. Others have called for the "acculturation" or "Islamization" of biomedicine by investing it with moral-spiritual values (Rahman, 1987). Both Muslim and non-Muslim critics have questioned whether such "Islamization" provides an alternative to, or merely further entrenches, scientific rational medicine among Muslims (Adib, 2004; Morsy, 1988; Rehman, 2008; Stenberg, 1996).

From the Qu'ran and Hadith

The moral discourse on medicine often begins with a popular *hadith,* "Make use of medical treatment, for Allah has not made a disease without appointing a remedy for it, with the exception of one disease, namely old age" (Sunan Abu Dawud, 28.3846). God is thus Creator of both disease and cure. Ascribing illness to the will of God, Muslims exhort one another to show patience: illness provides a divine test, an opportunity to purify the heart of accumulated sins. Paradoxically, Muslims also must "seek the cure" that God has provided. For many, illness sparks renewed attention to Islam as a lifestyle of "right balance" and reliance on God. Healing prayers, the resumption of regular obligatory *salat* (five times daily prayer), and recitation of the Qur'an become adjunct or alternative "treatments" to biomedical or herbal remedies.

God declares in the Qur'an, "We send down (stage by stage) in the Qur'an that which is a healing and a mercy to those who believe" (17:82). The revealed word has special power to protect people from evil influences during times when they are vulnerable, to heal them when they are ill. As with Rahman's childhood experience, verses of the Qur'an may be recited, written and placed in amulets, or dissolved in water and drunk as a holy tonic.

Prevention and Purity

For religiously involved Muslims, submission to the will of God (*islam*) is the chief preventive "medicine." Through moral education, observation of God's precepts, accumulation of knowledge, and the creation of just and compassionate social structures, human beings maintain individual and public health (Antes, 1989). States of impurity—bodily, mental, spiritual, or environmental—make one vulnerable to disease, malfunction, and suffering. Hence, preserving and restoring purity is the foundation of Muslim health maintenance and healing practices as well as interactions with health-care personnel and facilities (Hermansen, 2004).

Personal and environmental hygiene is central in the Islamic tradition, with daily Muslim hygiene practices serving as assets for laypeople and health personnel alike (Allegranzi, et al., 2009): handwashing three times before each of five daily prayers, after toileting, before and after meals, and after touching anything soiled or dead; the required purifying bath (*ghusl*) after sexual intercourse or discharge of bodily fluids; the washing of genitals with water after toileting; and the washing of feet, nose, and ears during ablutions before prayers. Some of these activities (e.g., *wudu*) are focused on ritual purity, while others remove "filth." One study of *fiqh* related to the use of the *miswak* (stick toothbrush) highlights the debate over which priority should govern the choice of hand used to hold the brush—hygiene (related to the left hand, used for cleansing after toileting), or purity (associated with the right hand) (Cajee, 2012). Acts of daily living that keep one's body, mind, and soul pure are thus acts of worship. For Muslims who experience incontinence, bleeding, or other involuntary discharges, the ability to perform basic religious and social acts is compromised.

Fasting, Eating, and Medicinals

Diet is likewise part of a broader regime of self-discipline, with implications for cultivating moderation, balance, and healthy social relationships. The Prophet Muhammad's most basic dietary advice is often quoted on popular Muslim websites: "Nothing is worse than a person who fills his stomach. It should be enough for the son of Adam to have a few bites to satisfy his hunger. If he wishes more, it should be: One-third for his food, one-third for his liquids, and one-third for his breath"

(*Islamic Bulletin*, 1998). Following the Prophet's eating habits also means washing hands, saying prayers, eating slowly and graciously, eating together, and sharing food with others.

In mosques and at Muslim gatherings across the United States, vendors sell health products that contain ingredients such as "black seed" (*nigella sativa*), recommended by the Prophet Muhammad to boost the immune system and restore heat to a weakened body. Black seed oil is available in numerous combinations with other foods, even in capsules or throat lozenges. Honey and other sunnah or Qur'an recommended foods (e.g., olives, yogurt, dates, figs, grapes, pomegranates, and legumes) play a major role in the dietary practices of Muslims from various cultures. Muslim dietitians recommend incorporating these nutrient-rich foods into therapeutic diets for Muslim patients to build on the health assets and spiritual appeal of an Islamic lifestyle (al-Zibdeh, 2009). Muslim pharmacists and physicians have gathered scientific and clinical evidence in support of traditional Islamic remedies and foods (Wani, et al., 2011) for use in health promotion and education of their non-Muslim peers who serve Muslim patients and as a form of religious validation. South Asian and Arab pharmaceutical and health products companies also sponsor research on these religiously inspired traditional medicines as part of their marketing to an international Muslim market (Bode, 2008). In order for clinicians to tailor dietary and physical activity advice for Muslim patients, as in treating diabetes, they need to be aware of both prophetic and Unani medical foundations of diverse Muslim cuisines (Greenhalgh et al., 1998).

African Americans began to revive Islamic traditions of health care in the early twentieth century. Noble Drew Ali's Moorish Science Temple movement sold herbal remedies like Moorish Mineral and Healing Oil, and Moorish Body Builder and Blood Purifier as a tonic for "rheumatism, lung trouble, rundown constitutions, indigestion, and loss of manhood" (Curtis, 2009). Likewise, the Nation of Islam movement focused on healing the mind, body, and spirit of black Americans from the physical and mental poisoning of slavery and Jim Crow. In his two-volume *How to Eat to Live* (Muhammad and Fard, 1967) Elijah Muhammad prohibited "soul food," associated with slave culture, as well as pork and alcohol and advised eating one meal per day. Although Imam W. D. Mohammed led most followers to accept Sunni Islam in the late 1970s and questioned much of his father's diet advice, members who came through the Nation of Islam often incorporated the founder's emphasis on diet, hygiene, and prayer into their practice.

One of the most important aspects of Muslim dietary practice is consumption of *halal* foods. Alcohol, pork, and pork by-products (e.g., marshmallows, gelatin) and any meat from an animal not slaughtered according to *dhabiha* procedures are *haram*, or forbidden. Many major hospitals have adapted their menus to include halal options alongside kosher and vegetarian meals. Other facilities may not be prepared to offer substitutes that comply with halal standards, although several Muslim organizations offer certification for brand-name products, distributors, and food producers (e.g., the Islamic Food and Nutrition Council of America, at www.ifanca. org). Prohibitions against ingesting alcohol and pork products may inhibit acceptance of some medications, although many Islamic authorities indicate that medical "necessity overrides prohibition" in emergency cases.

The dawn-to-dusk pattern of Ramadan fasting presents both opportunities and challenges for Muslim health. While some take the opportunity to break habits of smoking or overeating to detoxify and lose weight, others find that sweet and fatty foods served at parties for the breaking of the fast offer additional temptation (al-Zibdeh, 2009). Ramadan fasting presents potential difficulties for those with chronic heart disease, hypertension, renal disease, or peptic ulcers (al-Zibdeh, 2009). Diabetics who must maintain their glycemic balance or who must maintain a strict diet along with their insulin and medication regimen may be able to make adjustments in order to fast (Benaji, et al., 2006). Muslims who are ill, pregnant, menstruating, traveling, or elderly may be exempt from fasting. Many, however, prefer to participate with family and community both in the regimen of fasting and in the festivities and must negotiate adjustments to diet and medication schedules with their physicians.

Behavioral Norms

Some Islamic behavioral norms have the effect of reducing risks to the individual's health. For example, an observant person is required to limit sexual contact strictly to the marriage relationship. If followed, such limits would reduce risky sexual behaviors. In many Muslim families and communities, gender segregation of social activities, proscription of dating and physical contact, and prescription of modest dress all protect against illicit relations. The possibility of dishonoring one's family by deviating from sexual norms or prescribed gender roles carries great psychological weight. Openly homosexual or sexually active, unmarried Muslim youth and young adults may risk alienating family and community (Dhami and Sheikh, 2000). In some communities it is acceptable for older adolescents to marry and parent children, with related implications for public health programs providing for the prevention of pregnancy (Higginbottom et al., 2006).

Cultural pressure among Muslims to marry and produce children often leads to difficulty in discussing sexual dysfunction, infertility, homosexuality, or sexual addiction. Killawi suggests that many will use folk remedies or traditional and multiple primary care physicians before accessing a sex therapist (Killawi, 2011). Inhorn and Fakih likewise address the cultural, financial, and social discrimination barriers that Arab Muslim men in Michigan face in addressing fertility issues. Islamic law prohibits the use of donated gametes or surrogates as well as adoption, thus limiting the range of therapies available to those offered by social service agencies or expensive private fertility clinics (Inhorn and Fakih, 2006). Major divisions have now arisen between Sunni and Shi'a authorities regarding the permissibility of third-party donation. Sunnis continue to forbid it, but many Shi'a authorities allow at least egg donation and surrogacy (Inhorn and Tremayne, 2012).

While Islamic religious beliefs and practices generally support healthy lifestyles and the avoidance of risky behaviors, many Muslim communities in the West have experienced a rise in domestic violence, divorce, smoking, drug and alcohol abuse, and sexually transmitted diseases. Organizations like the Virginia-based Peaceful Families Project provide counseling, refuge, and support for Muslim victims of domestic violence and conduct training for Muslim leaders and health-care providers (Abugideiri, 2011; Alkhateeb and Abugideiri, 2007). Several US communities have begun to establish domestic violence shelters specifically to serve Muslim women.

Proscriptions and Abstentions

Most reviews of alcohol use in Islam note that the use of intoxicants is a "major sin" (Ali-Northcott, 2011). As with other proscriptions, Islamic jurisprudence with regard to alcohol is not necessarily uniform. Reported alcohol consumption in Muslim-majority countries is extremely low relative to other countries, yet some World Health Organization statistics suggest that the proportion of "closeted" problem drinkers among the drinking population may be extremely high in Muslim communities (Michalak, 2006).

Abuse of other intoxicating or addictive substances proscribed by Islamic law may present a double bind for Muslims. The stigma and shame associated with addiction is difficult to share within the Muslim community, as the respect and piety of both individuals and their families may be at stake. Ali-Northcott relates a common pattern in immigrant Muslim families with an addicted member: offer *du'a* for healing, ignore the problem, forcibly detoxify the person, arrange a marriage, or send the person to a "culturally appropriate" addiction facility overseas (Ali-Northcott, 2011).

Most twelve-step or other rehabilitation programs (such as Alcoholics Anonymous) are unprepared for the unique ritual needs and theological concerns of Muslim addicts. The Millati Islami Twelve-Step program represents a Muslim adaptation, with an emphasis on intention and pleasing God by rebuilding an Islamic lifestyle and community (Ali-Northcott, 2011). Many recovering addicts have found in Islam the disciplined lifestyle, ritual, and community that provide a helpful structure for maintaining sobriety. Overcoming stigma and alienation for current users of intoxicants in Muslim communities and gaining access to religiously appropriate care remains a challenge for health-care providers.

ISLAM AND MENTAL HEALTH

Hermansen (2004) notes that American Muslims are more likely to seek traditional, private, religious treatments for psychological concerns, which may be stigmatized or treated as spiritual or moral problems. In Muslim societies from North Africa through South Asia, emotional distress commonly finds expression in bodily complaints (somatization) (Williams and Hunt, 1997). Many immigrant Muslim families, then, find interventions responding ostensibly to somatic complaints more acceptable than conventional (perceived as secular) psychotherapeutic techniques and psychopharmacological approaches to "mental illness."

While biological, psychological, and environmental causes of mental illness find support in both Qur'an and hadith, mental illness is often highly stigmatized. Muslims may understand symptoms of mental illness as evidence of spiritual disease ("diseases of the heart" or *qalb*)—that is, distance or punishment from God. Further, some consider mental illness to originate from supernatural forces or evil jinn who seek to harm humans or influence them negatively through whispering (*waswaas*) or possession. Some believe that magic and the "evil eye" or envious glance may cause mental difficulty for another person, with or without the mediation of jinn. Only a specialist in religious experience may perceive the distinctions and manage them properly, although a knowledgeable therapist could take these beliefs seriously and help the Muslim patient to consider religious and cultural constructs alongside clinical evaluation (Utz, 2011). Muslims often prefer to use religious coping methods for dealing with mental illness or to enlist imams to perform special *ruqyah* (recitation of verses and supplications) as a complement to psychotherapy (Loewenthal, et al., 2001; Utz, 2011). Religious coping in the face of mental illness involves strengthening essential Islamic practices like faith, prayer, increased mosque attendance and Qur'an reading, as well as involving family or community elders and religious leaders in mediating stressful marital and family conflict (Ali and Aboul-Fotouh, 2011).

The Role of Structural Violence

Racism and discrimination, often added to the effects of socio economic disparities, may create unique threats to the health of many minority groups (Geiger, 1996; James, 2003; Krieger, 2003; Lillie-Blanton and Hoffman, 2000; Williams, 1999). Racism, sexism, immigrant or refugee status, acculturation, current identity politics, homeland security policies, and socioeconomic status (Farmer, 1997) may all influence the self-understanding as well as the physical and psychological health of American Muslims. Scholars of culture and healing emphasize that "structural violence" (political, economic, and social systems that privilege some groups and disadvantage others) afflicts both personal and social bodies (Farmer, 1997). The current public focus on "fundamentalism" and "fanaticism" may serve to reinforce racist attitudes toward Muslim ethnic communities (Bywaters et al., 2003); both governmental and nongovernmental statistics document the overt rise in reported hate crimes against Muslims (Council on American Islamic Relations, 2005; Ibish, 2003; Singh, 2002). While it can be difficult to distinguish racial from religious discrimination, evidence suggests that religion-based bias figures strongly in violence and property crimes as well as in school bullying (Sheridan, 2006). Social psychological research suggests that physicians and other providers often contribute unwittingly to racial/ethnic health disparities by the ways in which they communicate with patients in clinical settings (Burgess et al., 2004; van Ryn, 2002).

The routine experience of overt and indirect prejudice has significant health effects. Workplace discrimination and "chronic daily hassles," including insults, can increase the risk of common mental disorders (Bhui et al., 2005). Arab Muslims in the United States experience higher degrees of acculturation stress and related symptoms than do Arab Christians (Amer and Hovey, 2005), while post-9/11 abuse correlates with symptoms of depression (Sheridan 2006) and anxiety (Abu-Ras and Suarez, 2009; Rippy and Newman, 2006) among Muslims (Laird et al., 2007).

MUSLIM PATIENTS AND AMERICAN BIOMEDICINE

In a study of the influence of Islam on health care for American Muslims, Padela et al. conclude that "patient-provider communication difficulties, mistrust, and perceived discrimination all play a part in minority healthcare disparities and contribute to a poorer quality of healthcare in general." They suggest that Muslim patients may delay access to allopathic medicine and conceal their use of alternative medicines as a result (Padela et al., 2011a).

Given the cultural diversity and medical pluralism within individual, family, and community health traditions among American Muslims, health-care providers should recognize that being "Muslim" provides a person with an identity that informs motivations and decisions regarding medical issues. Overly simplified summaries of Islam in "cultural competency" literature risk reinforcing stereotypes and prejudices. At its best, however, this literature provides necessary contextual frameworks for understanding Muslim patients (Sheikh and Gatrad, 2000) and their views, needs, and concerns. While one may formulate a tentative hypothesis about how "Islam" influences a patient's health-care decisions, one should never assume that a particular Muslim patient is like all other Muslim patients.

A more helpful alternative to cultural and religious "trait lists" is the cultural transformation of care provision, so that cultural, religious, and individual diversity is genuinely accepted, encouraged, and accommodated (Betancourt, 2004). The philosophy of "holism" in nursing certainly holds promise in this regard. However, even here, challenges persist. For example, a study of nursing care for hospitalized Pakistani Muslim patients found that nurses who valued patient "spirituality" had little specific knowledge of Muslim religious life and thus had difficulty in conceptualizing spirituality outside the western cultural norms of the institution (Cortis, 2004). "Cultural humility" and an ethnographic curiosity on the part of providers can go a long way toward improving care.

One successful effort to reduce nonattendance rates of immigrant Muslim patients, for instance, combined education about religious practices, outreach to religious communities, and practical adjustments for multiple cultural, social, and linguistic barriers (Gatrad, 2000). Eliminating discrimination and increasing the employment and education of Muslim health care providers and community outreach workers may be one of the most effective ways to reduce health-care disparities for Muslims.

Culturally Humble Care for Muslim Patients

From a theological point of view, medical professionals collaborate with Muslim belief in God's revelation of signs to all creation as an act of mercy, requiring of humans pious worship and service to others, regulated by the boundaries of Islamic teachings and the principle of preservation of life. This principle governs bioethical issues such as abortion and palliative care for dying patients. The doctor-patient relationship of mutual confidence is integral to the holistic healing process. Medical treatments should also enable Muslims to fulfill their religious duties of prayer and fasting and the maintenance of purity.

Most observant Muslims include ritual requirements—along with ethical and legal obligations to self, family and community—as part of healing, childbearing, and childrearing. Examples include sensitivities about sexual conduct, the significance of purity and hygiene for the normal performance of daily prayer, and periodic rituals (after the age of "maturity") (Gatrad and Sheikh, 2001a; Hedayat and Pirzadeh, 2001). Issues of incontinence and bodily fluid discharges may also have implications for a Muslim's ability to perform basic ritual activities (Khot et al., 2005). Health professionals may need to have some familiarity with birth customs,(Gatrad and Sheikh, 2001b), male circumcision (Gatrad et al., 2002), and Islamic ethical positions on pregnancy termination, prenatal screening (Gatrad and Sheikh, 2001a), disability, (Bywaters et al., 2003), end-of-life care, and organ donation (Gatrad and Sheikh, 2002a,2002b; Sachedina, 2005).

Modesty

Perhaps the most consistent concern expressed in studies of Muslim patients is modesty. Segregation of space and activities by gender to prevent potential illicit contact between the sexes leads many Muslim postpubertal adolescents to prefer same-sex providers, especially for genital examination. One should therefore consult with parents and/or the patient regarding preferences. Providers also need to consider how much bodily exposure is necessary in order to care sensitively for Muslim women. Even simple adjustments may overcome barriers. The use of new hospital gowns that more effectively guard patient modesty has shown significant results (Stover 2004). Cultural and religious barriers to breast and cervical cancer screening among Muslim women have enlisted the involvement of at least two Muslim-initiated charitable clinics: the University Muslim Medical Association (Los Angeles) and Arab Community Center for Economic and Social Services (Dearborn, Michigan) clinics (Alford et al., 2009; Schwartz et al., 2008). These and others studies have recommended accommodations to make these screenings more acceptable to Muslim and other women from Middle Eastern and South Asian cultures (Salman 2011; Underwood et al., 1999).

Ethnic minorities are sometimes viewed as not accessing particular health services because of a religiously based explanation for illness or disability—an explanation that attributes the cause entirely to the patient or family. However, Bywaters and colleagues demonstrate that "institutional and structural racism" (i.e., a history of social and economic inequalities affecting racially defined minorities in a given population) also lies behind parents' poor economic status and lack of access to appropriate services for their children. These structural conditions are further compounded by the fear of being misunderstood by "out-group professionals" (Cinnirella and Loewenthal, 1999). Authors likewise contrast the importance of extended family in Muslim societies with the more individually centered model that often structures clinical practice. Parents and extended family may be involved in medical decision making, speaking on behalf of even older youth. Parents also play an important role in modeling positive health behaviors, which can help decrease risk behaviors among Muslim adolescents (Frank, 2001).

For instance, clinicians commonly encounter girls who wear headscarves and ask for a same-gender provider or consult with a male relative in making decisions; in such instances the clinician may incorrectly assume that the girl as oppressed, abused, or "traditional" (understood negatively) in her understanding of sexuality, gender roles, and morality. Suspicion, cautious behavior, and perceived misunderstanding in relation to health-care professionals may be a learned response to discrimination, harassment, and chronic stereotyping. As with racism, clinicians need to know that religious discrimination exists in order to recognize its effects.

MUSLIM BIOMEDICAL PROVIDERS/ PROFESSIONALS IN THE UNITED STATES

The creation of Medicare and Medicaid in 1965 led American-born physicians to establish private practices in wealthier suburbs. The government sought to fill major gaps in inner-city and rural areas by encouraging immigration of medical professionals from other countries. By 1972, 46 percent of all newly licensed physicians in the United States were trained abroad. By 1974, one-fifth of all US physicians were international medical graduates (IMGs), as were one-third of all hospital resident trainees (Ginzberg, 1982). Many of these IMGs came from India, Pakistan, Syria, Lebanon, Iran, and other countries with majority Muslim populations.

In 1967, a small group of Muslim physicians associated with the Muslim Students Association formed the Muslim Medical Association, which later became the Islamic Medical Association of North America (IMANA). IMANA now provides resources to Muslim medical professionals, promotes Islamic ethics and values, and organizes international relief work. Endocrinologist Shahid Athar, a prominent international speaker on Islamic medical ethics, spirituality and medicine, is a former IMANA president who graduated from medical school in India and completed his graduate medical education in Chicago and Indiana in the early 1970s (Athar, 1989). Physicians on IMANA's Medical Ethics Committee publish position papers and articles reflecting "an Islamic perspective" on patient care guidelines. Former IMANA president Faroque Khan, a Pakistani American pulmonologist in Long Island, New York, became the first international medical graduate elected to the Board of Regents for the American College of Physicians (ACP) in 1995. In 1997, the ACP held a joint convention with IMANA in Amman, Jordan. Khan celebrated this milestone when "IMANA enter[ed] the mainstream of American Medicine" with the phrase, "we moved from the outhouse to the main house" (Khan, 2008). IMANA's leaders initiated international humanitarian relief missions in response to the Indonesian tsunami of 2004 and the Pakistan earthquake of 2005. IMANA Medical Relief has become an important part of the organization's mission, providing Muslim physicians with opportunities to fulfill Islamic obligations of charity and service.

IMANA also provides a platform for collecting historical material and educating both Muslims and non-Muslims about the heritage of Islamic healing through the International Institute of Islamic Medicine, founded by surgeon Husain Nagamia in 1992. While less concerned with the current practice of traditional medicines, the institute represents yet another way in which Muslim Americans have celebrated their cultural contribution in the health-care field.

The so-called brain drain of medical professionals who left the Middle East and South Asia for the United States beginning in the 1950s and expanding significantly since

1965 spurred several organizations to provide medical aid for their homelands. The National Arab American Medical Association (NAAMA) was formed in 1975 to provide medical humanitarian aid in the Middle East, continuing education, and networking for health professionals of Arabic descent in the United States. During the past three decades, NAAMA has provided support for medical work and health-care workers in Palestine, Egypt, Lebanon, Iraq, and Syria. Similarly, the Association of Physicians of Pakistani Descent in North America (APPNA) began to develop medical and educational assistance programs in Pakistan in 1977. As the organization has grown to include North American alumni associations of Pakistani medical schools, APPNA has played a major role in connecting international medical graduates with US residency programs. Through free clinics, volunteer service opportunities in disaster relief both in the United States and abroad, APPNA also seeks to channel the charitable activity of Muslim physicians. The North American Arab Medical Association, APPNA, and IMANA all provide continuing medical education and specific ways for American Muslims to improve health-care services and education in the United States and abroad.

American Muslim physicians have assumed leadership in mainstream health care. Abdel Rahim Omran has led World Health Organization projects among Muslims throughout the world since the publication of his *Family Planning in the Legacy of Islam* (Omran, 1992). Pakistani American Muhammad Akhter, director since 2011 of the Washington, D.C., Department of Health, was president of the American Public Health Association from 1997 to 2002 and director of the National Medical Association, which represents 30,000 African American physicians. Elias Zerhouni, an Algerian American radiologist, served as director of National Institutes of Health from 2002 to 2008 and as a "medical ambassador" to Muslim countries.

A new generation of young Muslim health professionals is taking leadership of the older organizations and creating new ones. African American social worker Aneesah Nadir helped to found the Islamic Social Service Association in 1999. Nurse Rose Khalifa founded the National American Arab Nurses Association in 2003, and health finance professional Arshia Wajid formed a listserv in 2004 that has grown rapidly to become the Association of Muslim Health Professionals (AMHP). The AMHP has coordinated and advised independent Muslim charitable clinics nationwide, lobbied for health-care reform at the state and national levels, and promoted public health initiatives. Even more recently, Sara Elnakib formed the Muslims in Dietetics and Nutrition group in 2009 as a forum for discussing the unique needs of Muslim patients and professionals. Mental health professionals founded Muslim Mental Health, Inc., in 2004 to advance outreach to Muslim communities and study the mental and physical health effects of increased discrimination and harassment. The emergence of new ethnically and religiously identified professional organizations and clinics and the transformation of older ones will provide a wealth of research material on the integration of Islamic norms and values, cultural customs, traditional practices, medicine, public health, health policy, and humanitarian relief activity over the coming decades (Laird and Cadge, 2010).

The younger generation of Muslim physicians, along with Muslim and non-Muslim scholars from several disciplines, has also drawn attention to the need for critical interdisciplinary collaboration in bioethics and *fiqh* (Islamic jurisprudence). Many Muslim physicians are asked to provide authoritative guidance on Islamic perspectives to hospital ethics committees without receiving any formal training that would qualify them to make such judgments. (Padela et al. 2011c; Shanawani and Khalil, 2008). In her concluding essay for Brockopp and Eich's volume *Muslim Medical Ethics*, anthropologist Marcia Inhorn pleads for greater local specificity in studying the moral worlds of Muslim patients and physicians who may or may not observe normative practices of their religion; recognition of divergent and contested fatwas on everything from abortion to organ transplantation; and allowance for the heterogeneity and fluidity of Islamic tradition over space and time (Inhorn, 2008).

AMERICAN MUSLIMS AND ALTERNATIVE MEDICINES

More difficult to assess is the local and supralocal significance of Muslim complementary and alternative medicine use. Since the 1970s, complementary and alternative therapies have gained popularity in the dominant Euro-American community alongside advances in medical health care. Some therapies are appropriated from indigenous or ethnic communities in an exploitative manner (Laplante, 2010), while some minority religious figures play to the spiritual marketplace of holistic healing (Bowman, 1999).

Prophetic Medicine

In the late 1970s, Sufi healer and naturopath Hakim Ghulam Moinuddin Chishti (formerly Robert Thomson) published *Natural Medicine* (Chishti, 1978) and began promoting a two-year training program in Tucson, Arizona, for people who wanted to practice "prophetic medicine." Chishti's *The Book of Sufi Healing* (Chishti, 1991a) laid out the principles of Sufi life, the practices of Sufi meditation, the healing powers contained in the five pillars of Muslim life, and formulas for various herbal remedies. In *The Traditional Healer's Handbook* (Chishti, 1991b), he asserts that humoral medicine and Sufi spirituality are able to combine Ayurvedic, Chinese, Persian, and Greek medical wisdom to provide practical remedies and guidance regarding diet and lifestyle.

The distribution of English translations of Ibn Qayyim al-Jawziyya's *Medicine of the Prophet*, a fourteenth-century compendium, throughout the United States in

Islamic bookstores testifies to the continued popularity and the perceived longing among many American Muslims to unite healing of the body with healing of the soul, or as Seyyid Hossein Nasr puts it in his introduction, to deny the absolute claims of any human medicine and to make it "subservient to the tenets of religion which cure the ailments of the soul and to the world of nature itself which reflects directly the wisdom of the Creator" (Ibn Qayyim al-Jawzīyah 1998, xix). Hakima Karima Kristie Burns, N. D., began offering advice and consultations on herbal therapies in 1989, creating the Herb'n Muslim website, among others. Originally from Iowa, she reportedly "healed herself from asthma, allergies, panic attacks, depression, hypoglycemia, and dysmenorrhea using only natural therapies and herbs." She began a pilgrimage in search of traditional medical knowledge in Egypt and formal training in therapies like iridology and reflexology. She has also written numerous articles about the Islamic basis of acupuncture and herbal medicines and offers courses through the Avicenna Institute for Natural Healing (the BEarth Institute). Another interesting figure in the integration of Unani and Sufi healing perspectives with other complementary and alternative medicines is Hakim Archuletta, who gives lectures at Islamic centers around the country and participates in a working group on MysticMedicine. com with American Shadhiliyya Shaykh Nuh Ha Mim Keller.

Spiritual Healers

Hermansen (2004) notes that various spiritual healers offer ritual healing modalities in a number of American cities to immigrant and US-born constituencies In some East African immigrant and refugee communities, women may perform rituals to appease *zar* spirits (spirits, often of "foreign" personages, who possess and demand sacrifices and ceremonial appeasement) (cf. (Boddy, 1988). Other Muslims may consult healers from their own ethnic group to mediate with or exorcise jinn (supernatural beings created by God from fire, who may assume multiple forms and meddle in human affairs) in order to recover spiritual and mental health (Utz, 2011). Kassamali explored the rituals of Muslim immigrant women from several different countries who called on Bibi Fatima, daughter of the Prophet, to help protect the emotional and physical health of their families (Kassamali, 2004). Among immigrant and refugee women, these gatherings may offer important connections to their culture and provide strength for daily family duties.

   Spiritual healers deal with a wide range of financial, relationship, homeopathic, and Unani medical issues. They also focus on immigrants' concerns with rebellious children and business matters. Sufi healers and religious scholars may do the same. Imams, Sufi shaykhs, or spiritual healers may be consulted when illness or misfortune is attributed to jinn possession, evil eye, curses or magic (Hoffer, 1992). Each healer may have degrees of comfort or expertise in one particular area of healing or may refer to other traditional or professional healers. Padela et al. point out both opportunities and challenges of coordinating local imams with health-care professionals and institutions, although these religious leaders play an important role in therapeutic choice (Padela et al., 2011b). Further ethnographic, community-based studies are needed to clarify how American Muslims integrate various healing modalities with roots within and outside of "Islamic" tradition.

Sufi Psychologies

One prominent area of resurgence in "Islamic medicine" in the United States is known as "Sufi psychology." Pir Vilayat Khan and the Sufi Order of the West incorporate Jung's and Corbin's interpretations of active or creative imagination. The Golden Sufi Center of British Naqshbandi uses dream workshops, lucid dreaming, and collective interpretation of dreams. Combining traditional Sufi master-disciple relationships with western psychotherapeutic traditions, notable popular authors like Idries Shah and Robert Frager integrate particularly Jungian theories and transpersonal psychology with traditional Sufi theories of spiritual development (Frager, 1999). The Frithjof Schuon and Seyyid Hossein Nasr school of the Maryamiyya Sufi movement tries to "retraditionalize science as a sacred discipline," rejecting modernism (Hermansen, 2004). The Shah Maghsoud Angha line and its two sublines, International Association of Sufism and Maktab Tarighat Oveyssi, have both established associations for Sufi psychology. The range of Sufi psychology groups ranges from shariah-oriented, explicitly Muslim groups to perennialist, universalist groups with broad appeal outside the Muslim community. Joining yoga, Buddhist forms of meditation, Reiki, and other forms of religiously inspired therapies that are experiencing broadening acceptance in mainstream and biomedical cultures, Sufi psychology represents one influential stream of Muslim healing traditions in American culture.

CONCLUSIONS

The healing practices, beliefs, and concerns of American Muslims are as diverse as the geographical and cultural landscape of the American Muslim community. Muslims integrate moral discourses about health, purity, right living, moderation, personal responsibility, and reliance on God into their daily lives. Muslim health professionals practice contemporary medical science in research and clinical institutions, lead secular organizations, and engage in humanitarian relief, charitable work, and advocacy through ethnic and religious networks and clinics. They engage in debates about how to interpret the ethical imperatives, dietary restrictions, and prescriptions of Islam in a biomedical context. Religious leaders, alternative healers, and local markets offer spiritual healing, psychological advice, herbal therapies, and dietary supplements. Muslim patients choose from a variety of options in their health care and voice concerns about guarding modesty, the stress of discrimination, and the ethics of reproductive and end-of-life care. American Muslims are reviving, renewing, reforming, questioning, blending, and abandoning healing traditions past and present as they seek to follow the way of Islam. The "sustained argument" that is the Islamic tradition emerges in the fabric of everyday life as it fluctuates between illness and health.

References

Abu-Ras, W. M., and Z. E. Suarez, "Muslim Men and Women's Perception of Discrimination, Hate Crimes, and PTSD Symptoms Post 9/11," *Traumatology* 15.3 (2009): 48–63.

Abugideiri, Salma Elkadi. 2011 "Domestic Violence," in *Counseling Muslims: Handbook of Mental Health Issues and Interventions*, eds. S. Ahmed and M.M. Amer (New York, NY: Brunner-Routledge, 2011): 309–328.

Adib, Salim M., "From the Biomedical Model to the Islamic Alternative: A Brief Overview of Medical Practices in the Contemporary Arab World," *Social Science & Medicine* 58.4 (2004): 697.

al-Zibdeh, Nour, "Understanding Muslim Fasting Practices," *Today's Dietitian* 11.8 (2009): 56.

Alford, S. H., K. Schwartz, A. Soliman, C. C. Johnson, S. B. Gruber, and S. D. Merajver, "Breast Cancer Characteristics at Diagnosis and Survival Among Arab-American Women Compared to European—and African-American Women," *Breast Cancer Research and Treatment* 114.2 (2009): 339–346.

Ali-Northcott, Lynne, "Substance Abuse," in *Counseling Muslims: Handbook of Mental Health Issues and Interventions*, eds. S. Ahmed and M. M. Amer (New York, NY: Brunner-Routledge, 2011): 355–381.

Ali, Osman M., and Frieda Aboul-Fotouh, "Traditional Mental Health Coping And Help-Seeking," in *Counseling Muslims: Handbook of Mental Health Issues and Interventions*, eds. S. Ahmed and M. M. Amer (New York, NY: Brunner-Routledge, 2011): 33–47.

Alkhateeb, Maha Buthayna, and Salma Elkadi Abugideiri, *Change from Within: Diverse Perspectives on Domestic Violence in Muslim Communities* (Great Falls, VA: Peaceful Families Project, 2007).

Allegranzi, B., Z. A. Memish, L. Donaldson, and D. Pittet, "Religion and Culture: Potential Undercurrents Influencing Hand Hygiene Promotion in Health Care," *American Journal of Infection Control* 37.1 (2009): 28–34.

Amer, M. M., and J. D. Hovey, "Examination of the Impact of Acculturation, Stress, and Religiosity on Mental Health Variables for Second-Generation Arab Americans," *Ethnicity and Disease* 15 (Suppl 1, 2005): 111–112.

Antes, Peter, "Medicine and the Living Tradition of Islam," in *Healing and Restoring: Health and Medicine in the World's Religious Traditions*, ed. L. Sullivan (New York, NY: Macmillan, 1989): 173–202.

Athar, Shahid, *Islamic medicine* (Karachi, Pakistan: Pan-Islamic Publishing House, 1989).

Barnes, Patricia M., Eve Powell-Griner, Kim McFann, and Richard L. Nahin, *Complementary and Alternative Medicine Use Among Adults: United States, 2002. Advance Data from Vital and Health Statistics*, no. 343 (National Center for Health Statistics:, 2004).

BEarth Institute, The Avicenna Institute of Natural Healing, Website: http://earthschooling. info/thebearthinstitute/?page_id=757. Accessed Nov. 6, 2013.

Benaji, B., N. Mounib, R. Roky, N. Aadil, I. E. Houti, S. Moussamih, "Diabetes and Ramadan: Review of the Literature," *Diabetes Research and Clinical Practice* 73.2 (2006): 117–125.

Betancourt, J. R., "Cultural Competence—Marginal or Mainstream Movement?" *New England Journal of Medicine* 351.10 (2004): 953–954.

Bhui, K., S. Stansfeld, K. McKenzie, S. Karlsen, J. Nazroo, and S. Weich,. "Racial/Ethnic Discrimination and Common Mental Disorders among Workers: Findings from the EMPIRIC Study of Ethnic Minority Groups in the United Kingdom," *American Journal of Public Health* 95.3 (2005): 496–501.

Boddy, Janice, "Spirits and Selves in Northern Sudan: The Cultural Therapeutics of Possession and Trance," *American Ethnologist* 15.1 (1988): 4–27.

Bode, Maarten, *Taking Traditional Knowledge to the Market: The Modern Image of the Ayurvedic and Unani Industry, 1980–2000* (Hyderabad: Orient Longman, 2008}.

Bowman, M., "Healing in the Spiritual Marketplace: Consumers, Courses and Credentialism," *Social Compass* 46.2 (1999): 181–189.

Burgess, D. J., S. S. Fu, and M. van Ryn, "Why Do Providers Contribute to Disparities and What Can Be Done About It?" *Journal of General Internal Medicine* 19.11 (2004): 1154–1159.

Bywaters, P., Z. Ali, Q. Fazil, L. M. Wallace, and G. Singh, "Attitudes Towards Disability Amongst Pakistani and Bangladeshi Parents of Disabled Children in the UK: Considerations for Service Providers and the Disability Movement," *Health & Social Care in the Community* 11.6 (2003): 502–509.

Cajee, Na'eel, "Oral hygiene in the Shari`ah:A Thousand-Year Old Conversation between Islam's Schools of Legal Thought," *Journal of the History of Dentistry* 60.3 (2012): 148–157.

Chishti, G. M., *Natural Medicine* (New York, NY: McGraw-Hill, 1978).

Chishti, G. M., *The Book of Sufi Healing* (Rochester, VT: Inner Traditions International, 1991a).

Chishti, G. M., *The Traditional Healer's Handbook: A Classic Guide to the Medicine of Avicenna* (Rochester, VT: Healing Arts Press, 1991b).

Cinnirella, M., and K. M. Loewenthal, "Religious and Ethnic Group Influences on Beliefs about Mental Illness: A Qualitative Interview Study," *British Journal of Medical Psychology* 72 (Pt 4, 1999): 505–524.

Cortis, J. D., "Meeting the Needs of Minority Ethnic Patients," *Journal of Advanced Nursing* 48.1 (2004): 51–58.

Council on American Islamic Relations (CAIR), *Unequal Protection: The Status of Muslim Civil Rights in the United States 2005* (Washington, DC: Author, 2005).

Curtis, Edward E., "Debating the Origin of the Moorish Science Temple: Toward a New Cultural History," in *The New Black Gods: Arthur Huff Fauset and the Study of African American Religions*, Eds. E. E. Curtis and D. B. Sigler (Bloomington: Indiana University Press, 2009): 70–90.

Dhami, S., and A. Sheikh, "The Muslim Family: Predicament and Promise," *Western Journal of Medicine* 173.5 (2000): 352–356.

Farmer, Paul, "On Suffering and Social Violence: A View from Below," in *Social Suffering*, eds. A. Kleinman, V. Das, and M. M. Lock. (Berkeley: University of California Press, 1997): 261–284.

Frager, Robert, *Heart, Self & Soul: The Sufi Psychology of Growth, Balance, and Harmony*, (Wheaton, IL: Quest Books, 1999).

Frank, Natalie C., "Religion, Risk Prevention and Health Promotion in Adolescents: A Community-Based Approach," *Mental Health, Religion and Culture 4.2* (2001): 132–147.

Gatrad, A. R., "A Completed Audit to Reduce Hospital Outpatients Non-Attendance Rates," *Archives of Disease in Childhood 82.1* (2000): 59–61.

Gatrad, A. R., and A. Sheikh, "Medical Ethics and Islam: Principles and Practice" [see comment], *Archives of Disease in Childhood 84.1* (2001a): 72–75.

Gatrad, A. R., and A. Sheikh, "Muslim Birth Customs" [see comment], *Archives of Disease in Childhood: Fetal & Neonatal Edition 84.1* (2001b): F6–F8.

Gatrad, A. R., and A. Sheikh, "Palliative Care for Muslims and Issues Before Death," *International Journal of Palliative Nursing 8.11* (2002a): 526–531.

Gatrad, R., and A. Sheikh, "Palliative Care for Muslims and Issues After Death," *International Journal of Palliative Nursing 8.12* (2002b): 594–597.

Gatrad, A. R., A. Sheikh, and H. Jacks, "Religious Circumcision and the Human Rights Act," *Archives of Disease in Childhood 86.2* (2002):76–78.

Geiger, H. J., "Race and Health Care—An American dilemma?" *New England Journal of Medicine 335.11* (1996): 815–816.

Ginzberg, Eli, "The Future Supply of Physicians: From Pluralism to Policy," *Health Affairs 1.3* (1982): 6–19.

Greenhalgh, T., C. Helman, and A. M. Chowdhury, "Health Beliefs and Folk Models of Diabetes in British Bangladeshis: A Qualitative Study," *British Journal of Medicine 316.7136* (1998): 978–983.

Hedayat, K. M., and R. Pirzadeh, "Issues in Islamic Biomedical Ethics: A Primer for the Pediatrician," *Pediatrics 108.4* (2001): 965–971.

Hermansen, Marcia, "Dimensions of Islamic Religious Healing in America," in *Religion and Healing in America*, eds. L. Barnes and S. Sered (New York, NY: Oxford University Press, 2004): 407–422.

Higginbottom, G. M., N. Mathers, P. Marsh, M. Kirkham, J. M. Owen, and L. Serrant-Green, "Young People of Minority Ethnic Origin in England and Early Parenthood: Views from Young Parents and Service Providers," *Social Science and Medicine 63* (4): 858–870.

Hoffer, C.B.M., "The Practice of Islamic Healing," in *Islam in Dutch Society: Current Developments and Future Prospects*, eds. W.A.R. Shadid and P. S. Koningsveld (Kampen, The Netherlands: Kok Pharos Publishing House, 1992): 40–53.

Ibish, Hussain, *Report on Hate Crimes and Discrimination Against Arab Americans: The post September 11 Backlash* (Washington, D.C.: American-Arab Anti-Discrimination Committee, 2003).

Ibn Qayyim al-Jawzīyah, Muhammad ibn Abī Bakr, *Medicine of the Prophet*, transl. P. Johnstone (Cambridge, UK: Islamic Texts Society, 1998).

Inhorn, Marcia C., "Conclusion," in *Muslim Medical Ethics: From Theory to Practice*, eds. J. E. Brockopp and T. Eich (Columbia, SC: University of South Carolina Press): 252–255.

Inhorn, Marcia C., and Michael Hassan Fakih, "Arab Americans, African Americans, and Infertility: Barriers to Reproduction and Medical Care," *Fertility and Sterility 85.4* (2006): 844–852.

Inhorn, Marcia Claire, and Soraya Tremayne, *Islam and Assisted Reproductive Technologies: Sunni and Shia Perspectives* (New York, NY: Berghahn Books, 2012).

Islamic Bulletin, "Islamic Diet and Manners," 1998. Available at: http://www.islamicbulletin.org/newsletters/issue_16/diet.aspx

James, S. A., "Confronting the Moral Economy Of US Racial/Ethnic Health Disparities," *American Journal of Public Health* 93.2 (2003): 189.

Kassamali, Noor, "Healing Rituals and the Role of Fatima," in *Religious Healing in Boston: Body, Spirit, Community*, ed. S. Sered (Cambridge, MA: Center for the Study of World Religions, Harvard University): 43–45.

Khan, Faroque, "Islamic Medical Association of North America: A Brief History," Vol. 2012 (Lombard, IL: IMANA, 2008).

Khot, U. P., K. D. Vellacott, and K. J. Swarnkar, "Islamic Practices: Informed Consent for Stoma," *Colorectal Disease* 7.5 (2005): 529–530.

Killawi, Amal, "Sexuality and Sexual Dysfunctions," in *Counseling Muslims: Handbook of Mental Health Issues and Interventions*, eds. S. Ahmed and M. M. Amer (New York, NY: Brunner-Routledge, 329–351): 329–351.

Krieger, N., "Does Racism Harm Health? Did Child Abuse Exist Before 1962? On Explicit Questions, Critical Science, and Current Controversies: An Ecosocial Perspective," *American Journal of Public Health* 93.2 (2003): 194–199.

Laird, Lance D, M. M. Amer, E. D. Barnett, and L. L. Barnes, Muslims and Health Disparities in the US & UK, *Archives of Disease in Childhood* 92.10 (2007): 922–926.

Laird, Lance D., and Wendy Cadge, "Negotiating Ambivalence: The Social Power of Muslim Community-Based Health Organizations in America," *PoLAR: Political and Legal Anthropology Review* 33.2 (2007): 225–244.

Laplante, Line Denise, Lillie-Blanton, M., and C. Hoffman, "Racial and Ethnic Inequities in Access to Medical Care: Introduction, *Medical Care Research and Review* 57 (Suppl 1, 2000): 5–10.

Loewenthal, K. M., M. Cinnirella, G. Evdoka, and P. Murphy "Faith Conquers All? Beliefs About the Role of Religious Factors in Coping with Depression Among Different Cultural-Religious Groups in the UK," *British Journal of Medical Psychology* 74(Pt 3, 2001): 293–303.

Michalak, Laurence, "Alcohol and Islam: An Overview," *Contemporary Drug Problems* 33.4 (2006): 523.

Morsy, Soheir A., "Islamic Clinics in Egypt: The Cultural Elaboration of Biomedical Hegemony," *Medical Anthropology Quarterly* 2.4 (1998): 355–369.

Muhammad, Elijah, and Muhammad Fard, *How to Eat to Live. Book One* (Atlanta, GA: Messenger Elijah Muhammad Propagation Society, 1967).

Omran, Abdel R., *Family Planning in the Legacy of Islam* (London and New York: Routledge, 1992).

Padela, A. I., Katie Gunter, and Amal Killawi, *Meeting the Healthcare Needs of American Muslims: Challenges and Strategies for Healthcare Settings* (Clinton TWP, MI: Institute for Policy and Understanding, 2011a).

Padela, A. I., Katie Gunter, and Amal Killawi, "The Role of Imams in American Muslim Health: Perspectives of Muslim Community Leaders in Southeast Michigan," *Journal of Religion & Health* 50.2 (2011b): 359–373.

Padela, A. I., H. Shanawani, and A. Arozullah, "Medical Experts & Islamic Scholars Deliberating over Brain Death: Gaps in the Applied Islamic Bioethics Discourse," *Muslim World* 101.1 (2011c): 53–72.

Pormann, Peter E., and Emilie Savage-Smith, "Medieval Islamic Medicine" (Washington, DC: Georgetown University Press, 2007).

Rahman, F., "Amulets and Poems: One Healer's Beginnings," *Lancet* 350.9094 (1997): 1848–1849.

Rahman, Fazlur, *Health and Medicine in the Islamic Tradition: Change and Identity* (New York, NY: Crossroads, 1987).

Rehman, Jalees, "Oversimplifying the Relationship Between Religion and Biomedicine: Does It Serve Either?" *Journal of the Islamic Medical Association* 40 (2008): 54–55.

Rippy, Alyssa E., and Elana Newman, "Perceived Religious Discrimination and Its Relationship to Anxiety and Paranoia Among Muslim Americans." *Journal of Muslim Mental Health* 1.1 (2006): 5–20.

Sachedina, A., "End-of-Life: The Islamic View," *Lancet* 366.9487 (2005): 774–779.

Salman, Khlood Faik, "Health Beliefs and Practices Related to Cancer Screening Among Arab Muslim Women in an Urban Community," *Health Care for Women International* 33.1 (2011): 45–74.

Schwartz, K., M. Fakhouri, M. Bartoces, J. Monsur, and A. Younis, Mammography screening among Arab American women in metropolitan Detroit. *Journal of Immigrant and Minority Health / Center for Minority Public Health* 10.6 (2008): 541–549.

Shanawani, Hasan, and Mohammad Hassan Khalil, "Reporting on 'Islamic bioethics' in the Medical Literature: Where Are the Experts?" in *Muslim Medical Ethics: From Theory to Practice*, eds. J. E. Brockopp and T. Eich (Columbia, SC: University of South Carolina Press, 2008): 214–228.

Sheikh, Aziz, and Abdul Rashid Gatrad, eds., *Caring For Muslim Patients* (Abingdon, UK: Radcliffe Medical Press, 2000).

Sheridan, L. P., "Islamophobia pre- and post-September 11th, 2001," *Journal of Interpersonal Violence* 21.3 (2006): 317–336.

Singh, A., "'We Are Not the Enemy': Hate Crimes Against Arabs, Muslims, and Those Perceived to Be Arab or Muslim after September 11" [Research Report], *Human Rights Watch* 14.6 (2002).

Stenberg, Leif, "Seyyed Hossein Nasr, and Ziauddin Sardar on Islam and Science: Marginalization or Modernization of a Religious Tradition," *Social Epistemology* 10.3–4 (1996): 273–287.

Stover, Kathy, "Hospital Gowns Break Down a Cultural Barrier to Health Care," *AHA News* 40.22 (2004): 5.

Underwood, S. M., L. Shaikha, and D. Bakr, "Veiled Yet Vulnerable—Breast Cancer Screening and the Muslim Way of Life," *Cancer Practice* 7.6 (1999): 285–290.

Utz, Aisha, "Conceptualizations of Mental Health, Illness, and Healing," in *Counseling Muslims: Handbook of Mental Health Issues and Interventions*, eds. S. Ahmed and M. M. Amer (New York, NY: Brunner-Routledge, 2011) 15–31.

van Ryn, M., "Research on the Provider Contribution to Race/Ethnicity Disparities in Medical Care," *Medical Care* 40 (1 Suppl, 2002): I140–I151.

Wani, Bilal Ahmad, Fida Mohammad Wani, Amina Khan, R. H. Bodha, F. A. Mohiddin, and Aadil Hamid, "Some Herbs Mentioned in the Holy Quran and Ahadith and Their Medicinal Importance in Contemporary Times," *Journal of Pharmacy Research* 4,11 (2011): 3888–3891.

Williams, David R., "Race, Socioeconomic Status, and Health: The Added Effects of Racism and Discrimination," *Annals of the New York Academy of Sciences* 898 (1999): 173–188.

Williams, R., and K. Hunt, "Psychological Distress Among British South Asians: The Contribution of Stressful Situations and Subcultural Differences in the West of Scotland Twenty-07 Study," *Psychological Medicine* 27.5 (1997): 1173–1181.

CHAPTER 27

MUSLIMS IN FILM AND MUSLIM FILMMAKING IN THE UNITED STATES

HUSSEIN RASHID

INTRODUCTION

Plato says that the person who tells stories is the person who rules society. In thinking about the modern film industry in America, we have to understand it as part of the new modern way of storytelling. Therefore the film industry is instrumental in defining how Muslims are seen as part of American society and we must look at the film industry as a way of understanding Muslims and America simultaneously in conversation with one another. We can look at Muslims and filmmaking through four distinct lenses. The first is how movie studios in America have traditionally represented Muslims. The second is how the film industry defines America using Muslims. The third is understanding the role Muslims play in the film industry now. And finally, the fourth is how all these components interact with one another to create a national narrative.

THE ORIENTALIST GAZE

Perhaps the person most closely associated with the depiction of Arabs in film is Jack Shaheen. His seminal work *Reel Bad Arabs* (2001) formally introduced a way of categorizing and looking at films that filter Arabs through the Orientalist lens. By virtue of his extensive research, he argues that in many places *Arab* and *Muslim* become synonymous in the filmic imaginary.[1] His initial work takes him to see similar developments in the television industry and a much more jingoistic form of Orientalism after 9/11.

Shaheen divides the Orientalist stereotypes into four basic categories: villains, sheikhs, maidens, and cameos.[2] One sees the strong gendered quality in representation of Arabs/Muslims in film. Women are invariably presented as silent and helpless, and their bodies are eroticized. They are presented in two basic fashions, as sexual nymphs, often in the dress of belly dancers, or as veiled, with the Orientalist gaze demanding that they be seen. This question of sight is representative of both an "unveiling" of the Orient as well as a different type of control as the female figure is subjected to a western gaze.

The representation of the male figure as interpreted by Shaheen is antithetical to the conceptions of the American male. In the case of the villian/terrorist, the conflict is clearly established and direct. In this binary, there is an American hero battling an Arab/Muslim villain. The figure of the sheikh is a more implicit challenge and constructs American virtues negatively. For Shaheen, the depiction of the sheikh has consistently relied on the presentation of a lecherous man looking to conquer the West through its women. He is obsessed with sex, both with his own women and with the beautiful blonde who comes under his sway or whom he takes by force. National honor is tied intimately to the control of women and is further racialized by depicting the good woman as obviously white. Shaheen argues that the figure of the sheikh is further developed to be someone who is explicitly immoral, if not amoral, and relies on undeserved wealth (from oil money) and the power it brings. These characteristics are often shared with the villian. However, the sheikh is not necessarily opposed to America so much as he is self-absorbed and may do things that unintentionally or incidentally damage American interests.

These stereotypical traits have a long pedigree predating the filmic Arab. Sexuality, and the threat to the "American woman," was an important way of characterizing slaves, who were often portrayed as sexual predators. That motif continues to be attached to African Americans today and, in addition, is further applied to other dark-complected men, including Latinos. Furthermore, the idea of indolent rich men is a variation of the anti-Jewish theme of the moneylender. In many respects, the presentation of the Arab/Muslim is simply an updating of stereotypical images given to other minority subjects in the American imagination, some of which were inherited from Europe. What makes The imagery is so damaging because it collapses the worst attributions from numerous communities and projects them onto a single community. Thus Muslims are cast with racist, anti-Semitic, and uniquely anti-Muslim prejudices.[3]

The characteristics that are given to individual actors are part of a larger system that impugns the entire group. Because we see the individual acting in a stereotypical manner, it creates a negative feedback that proves true the prejudice against the group. In the visual canvas of film, the nation also becomes a site of tropes. Shaheen speaks of "Instant Ali Baba Kits," where actors are invariably given scimitars, hijabs, beards, and belly dance outfits, and the land always has camels and oil wells.[4] So we see in the representation of "reel Arabs" individual, community, and national configurations of the Other.

Tim Semmerling, following the work of Stuart Hall, notes that the Other and the Self are in a dialogic relationship, constantly defining each other.[5] The Self is the site of power, which constructs the Other. There are only a limited number of ways in which the Other can be created. Generally the Muslim Other has been cast as barbaric, and that barbarianism can be subdivided into roughly five broad categories. The Other is violent and/or does not have any concept of the value of human life. The Other prizes possessions or power over life. The Other is dirty and his presence defiles the cleanliness of the Self. The Other possesses nothing that can be understood as culture. He has no art, poetry, music, dance, or appreciation of any of these things. He is essentially an animal with weapons. The Other is illogical and superstitious. His religion, if he has one, is false, and his ritual life is in opposition to the true religion/belief of the Self. If the Other had any logical ability, he would not believe in something so obviously untrue, but he lacks the intellect of the Self. Finally, the Other is unable to show any respect to women. He treats women as objects and property that exist solely for the pleasure of men, and this offends the sensibility of the Self.

This pattern of crafting the Other holds true in stereotyping all minority subjects. In an interesting twist, the film *The 13th Warrior* (1999), a fictional tale of an actual Arab nobleman by the name of Ahmad ibn Fadlan, takes all of the above stereotypes and applies them to Vikings. This inversion highlights an important aspect of the Othering process: it is dependent on power, and as such is inherently contextual. This conditionality means that in America, there will be negative portrayals of Muslims. However, that does not remove agency from the Muslim outside of America, nor should it be seen as limiting possibilities for American Muslims.

THE HOMEMADE MOVIE INDUSTRY

This filmic conversation is perhaps most clearly seen in the post-9/11 homemade movie industry. American servicemen, stationed overseas, take video footage of their missions, including taping the death of locals. The videos are then circulated to other service members and posted online. Commentaries embedded with these files compare the excursions of the military to what the individuals have seen in movies. These films are reinforcing and making real the stereotypes present in Hollywood movies. On the other side, violent extremists use clips from Hollywood movies and homemade military movies to create recruitment videos for their causes.[6] Each side is then defining itself against the other, with the American film industry playing a pivotal mediating role in each community's sense of itself.

THE ORIENTALIST FEAR

Semmerling, in extending the work of Shaheen, sees Hollywood film as being implicitly conscious of the dialogic of each group defining itself against the other. Therefore the point of creating the Other through Muslims is to define a vision of America. Specifically, Semmerling argues that "Our filmic villains are narrative tools used for self-presentation and self-identity to enhance our own stature, our own meaning, and our own self-esteem in times of our own diffidence. Therefore, are the 'evil' Arabs in American film actually oblique depictions of ourselves: the insecure Americans?"[7]

According to Semmerling, one can clearly see a demarcation in the types of stereotypical narratives assigned to Muslims in the 1970s. This time period coincides with an oil crisis, the Iranian Revolution, the Soviet invasion of Afghanistan, and other international events that involve Muslim communities.

Semmerling coins the term *Orientalist fear* to talk about how films are made that show "evil Arabs" destabilizing American notions of Self. In particular, this Self is constructed by treating Orientalist myths as fact, so that any destabilization of "American conceptual discipline" of the Arab/Muslim is a threat to America. He states "The potential exposure of the destabilized Self causes anxiety and fear in the Orientalist audience, which are then projected back onto the Arabs," thereby creating further attempts at controlling the Muslim.[8] This "Orientalist fear" is based on stereotypes that are integral in defining America's understand of its national character and treated as fact. When these stereotypes are challenged, the audience's understanding of what it means to be an "American" and "good" is also challenged. The result is that the audience seeks to exert more control over Muslims in order to bring back a semblance of control and stability to what it means to be American.

The implications for this reading of film are potentially disastrous, not only from the perspective of foreign affairs but also for defining who belongs to America. There is no neat dividing line that says the Muslim "over there" is different from the American Muslim. In other words, by casting an entire people as suspect, a group of Americans are also suspect and are told that they do not belong. Thus, the Orientalist gaze and fear are functional components of Islamophobia, contributing to the assumption that a return to a strong and virile America is at least partially dependent on expelling the foreign bodies.

While it is important to note that this rhetoric of belonging has been applied to other minority groups, there is a difference in degree and in the sustained nature of the caricatures applied to Muslims. For example, the film *Rules of Engagement* (2000) is singled out for its portrayal of Muslims in Yemen as inherently violent. During one particular court scene, when a key Yemeni witness is on the stand, the script is crafted so as to make him state that all Muslims are potential terrorists in all places and all times. Another film, *The Siege* (1998), while including a relatively complex portrayal of an Arab with Tony Shalhoub's character, generally plays into the idea of the Orientalist fear, where all Muslims in New York must be suspect. The film also portrays New Yorkers coming out to protest the racial profiling of Arabs in the film. However, despite small scenes like this in many movies, the overwhelming effect is to show Muslims as a dangerous Other.

BREAKING THE STEREOTYPE

While not highly nuanced in its characterizations of individuals, *The Siege* is part of a larger change in filmmaking that seeks to bring complexity to issues of Muslim identity and belonging in America. After a brief reactionary period that saw films trading in the worst stereotypes of Muslims, the post-9/11 era actually seemed to accelerate the use of complex story lines. The response to negative stereotyping is not a pendulum swing to only positive representations, with Muslims as a contrasting "model minority." Rather, it is the humanizing quality of seeing diverse, involved, characters that show the breadth of normalcy of Muslims.

Implicitly, *The Siege*, through the protesting of racial profiling, shows that Muslims were integral parts of their communities, mirroring the variety of their neighborhoods. Tommy Lee Jones, who starred in the previously mentioned *Rules of Engagement*, also stars *In the Valley of Elah* (2007). In this film, the cost of war on American troops returning home is explored. Again, implicitly, the questions of America's engagement with an Orientalist fear is investigated. Perhaps the film most challenging of the Orientalist fear is *Rendition* (2007), which questions the practice of extraordinary rendition—the practice of the US government transferring prisoners from the War on Terror, usually covertly, to countries where torture could be conducted on them. The film is an explicit critique of suspecting all Muslims, particularly those in America.

This change did not come about as a result of Muslim involvement in the film industry. During the 1990s some Muslims were involved in the making of films. Egyptian Muslim Dodi al-Fayad (1955–1997) financed several major Hollywood pictures, including *Hook* (1991), *The Scarlet Letter* (1995), and *Chariots of Fire* (1981), which won four Academy Awards. Yet during this same period, films like *The Siege* and *Rules of Engagement* were also produced. Fahrid Murray Abraham, Academy Award–winning actor for his role as Salieri in *Amadeus* (1984), is of Arab descent but does not use his first name for fear of being typecast. The situation of having prominent Arabs and Muslims present in Hollywood while negative portrayals of Arabs and Muslims persist is not without parallel. In the mid-twentieth century there were influential Jews in the film industry, but Hollywood continued to produce anti-Semitic films.[9]

While changes in narrative will come with familiarity with Arabs and Muslims, there is another element, that of backlash. As movies become more extreme in their stereotyping of Muslims, the specter of earlier racist films becomes apparent. Therefore it is no surprise that many of the first responses to stereotyping are satirical, as satire is used to point out the absurdity of stereotypes. The film *Team America: World Police* (2004) is difficult to make sense of, as it lampoons American interventionism and the Orientalist fear, but at a superficial level it also appears to valorize American militarism. Perhaps the clearest instance of the mockery of Muslim stereotypes occurs on the television show *The Simpsons*. In the episode "Mypods and Boomsticks" (2008, season 20, episode 7), Bart makes a Muslim friend, Bashir. Although there are some elements of the life of this friend that show the audience how a Muslim may live, the main point of the story is to mock Homer's paranoia regarding Muslims. The episode parodies another show, *24*, that features story lines indicating that one can never trust a Muslim.

In 2011, *The Simpsons* aired another episode involving an American Muslim the well-known basketball player Kareem Abdul-Jabbar. However, in this episode, entitled "Love Is a Many Strangled Thing" (season 22, episode 17), the question of faith is never explicitly raised. Abdul-Jabbar's faith is no secret to the American viewing audience; his presence simply normalizes a Muslim. In a similar vein, the TV show *Bones*, about a forensic anthropologist, has a recurring Muslim character, Arastoo Vaziri. He is shown praying and openly discussing his faith when asked. His conversations with his colleagues address many popular misconceptions of Muslims. All three shows, *The Simpsons*, *24*, and *Bones* appear on Fox Television, highlighting the evolving nature of representations of Muslims on screen.

CONFLICTING READINGS OF FILM

Television is an important bellwether for film, as the turnaround times are faster, and with the possibility of longer story arcs, many of the complexities one might hope to see in movies appear first on the small screen. *Aliens in America* (2007–2008), focusing on the presence of a Pakistani foreign exchange student in small town America, features the type of wit and sensitivity that we hope will appear in film. However, one of the implications of the introduction of nuanced characters is disagreement over how to read them. For example, Shaheen objects to the show *NCIS* on CBS.[10] The show is a police procedural focusing on federal agents investigating crimes against US Navy personnel. Shaheen's primary objection is that one of the characters, Ziva David, is a former Mossad agent who is seen arresting Arabs and Muslims.

However, the message of the show is that the US government is overly focused on threats coming from Muslim majority countries. More importantly, David is instrumental in defending Muslims against false accusations ("Suspicion," 2007, series 4, episode 12) and explaining that Jews, Christians, and Muslims are part of the same family. She is also shown as exposing Mossad plots against American interests, so that duplicitousness is not limited to Muslims. The show offers a fairly nuanced reading of Muslim worship in the episode "Tribes" (2008, series 5, episode 11), where it is revealed that Muslim marines are being killed for not joining al-Qaeda. They are being targeted by a non-Muslim who has betrayed his country for money. In addition, the father of one of the Muslim marines is an imam at a local mosque; he criticizes the US government for its foreign policy while recognizing that he has a responsibility to work against violent extremism.

With a long series of complicated presentations of Muslims on a serial like *NCIS*, it is not surprising that there are many readings of the show. The more limited presentation of movies can also lend itself to multilayered presentations. *The Siege*, while not without its share of Muslim stereotypes, offers a vision of a city where Muslims are an important part of the social fabric. In addition, Tony Shalhoub's character, an FBI agent of Arab descent whose son is detained without probable cause, offers a subversive critique of the stereotypes presented in the movie. Shaheen and Semmerling disagree about the value of the film *Three Kings* (1999), whose subject is the first Gulf War. Shaheen sees it as a positive representation of human motivations for Muslim characters, whereas Semmerling sees it as a further portrayal of Muslims interfering with American "victory culture."

Both Shaheen and Semmerling are clearly invested in their own methodological perspectives. However, the fact that both arguments are supported by the film is a testament to the depth of the film and a sign that nuance is possible. Semmerling's broadly negative review of the movie hints at a problem that exists in reading films with Muslim characters. When movies treat all Arabs/Muslims as suspect, all movies with Arabs/Muslims become suspect for stereotypes. Furthermore, if the category of cameo exists to tangentially disparage Muslims, then it is possible that all films have these cameos. The problem with this sort of reading of the movies is that it creates a culture of victimhood and potentially exacerbates and perpetuates a problem rather than actually addressing it.

In particular, I wish to highlight two films that are characterized as having negative depictions of Middle Easterners but which I believe are readings based in the culture of victimhood. The two are *The Prince of Egypt* (1998) and *The Lord of the Rings: The Return of the King* (2003). The first is based on the story of Moses and his conflict with Pharaoh. It is possible to read the representation of the Egyptians as falling into the Orientalist mold stereotype. However, doing so ignores the context of the film. The story is based on a scriptural story that predates the idea of Egyptians as Arabs. Although the makers of the film are clearly producing it in the era of "Egyptian = Arab," they do not make that elision as easily. In fact, when Moses is in the desert, the people who show him the most generosity are ones who are more easily marked as Arab. Further, the story borrows elements from the Qur'anic telling of the Moses story, making it even more difficult to argue an anti-Muslim element to the story.

Deciphering the Haradrim race in *The Return of the King* is more difficult. The characters dress in black, with masks covering their faces, similar to the way in which Bedouins are presented in movies like *The Mummy* (1999). However, it seems more likely that Haradrim represent a different group of people than Arabs, both in the book and in the film. They are from the south, indicating that they are most likely symbolic of southern and eastern Europeans, who are viewed as being different from northern Europeans. One can also argue that they represent Africa, the "dark continent," since the dress of the Haradrim resembles that of the Tuareg of North Africa. In other words, the Haradrim are most likely enmeshed in the racial discourse of the time, but to read them as simply anti-Muslim obfuscates a longer tradition of exclusion in both literature and film.

Participatory Culture

The role of the critic is to see through a particular lens. However, film, as we have seen with respect to homemade movies, is a part of a participatory culture. That is, both the producers and consumers have an impact on what is seen. Being a participant implies a different role than being a critic. It means being part of a process instead of being an observer and an analyst of the process. A participant may not recognize the Orientalism or Islamophobia present in a film, because these stereotypes have become cognitive facts for the audience. However, we have discussed how filmmakers have satirized the most extreme forms of stereotypes. I argue that consumers can recognize non-Islamophobic types of discrimination. By tying the Orientalist gaze to the racist history of the film industry, it is placing the Muslim experience within the broader American experience, and exposes the discrimination implicit in these stereotypes.

If we focus on Orientalism as a unique phenomenon in film as opposed to a unique manifestation of a larger phenomenon of stereotyping and racial marginalization, I do not believe we can properly understand the forces at play for American Muslims engaged in the film industry. Wajahat Ali, an American Muslim playwright, speaks of two different types of cultural production: by Muslims for Muslims and by Muslims for everyone. This structure is useful for understanding the ways in which Muslims are engaged with filmmaking. By adopting this framing, we can discuss intent, audience, and cultural impact more clearly.

In this section I propose to look at the ways in which commercially available films and DVDs are used to construct a vision of an American Islam, to look at some actors and producers who are involved in the film industry, and to understand how all of these elements are instrumental in crafting a new national narrative that integrates Muslims, as opposed to marking Muslims at "outsiders" and as the Other.

DEFINING AN ISLAM IN AMERICA?

The DVD series *Adam's World*, which focuses on a young boy growing up in America, is an obvious entry point into looking at productions by Muslims for Muslims. Using puppets and live actors in a manner reminiscent of *Sesame Street*, the film allows Adam to learn about Muslims in other parts of the world and about the Muslim values he should be living by. The series is produced by Chicago-based Sound Vision enterprises, started by Abdul Malik Mujahid. Ostensibly, anyone can learn something about Muslims from these videos, but the intended audience is clearly Muslim.[11]

Two movies about the life of the Prophet Muhammad occupy an indeterminate space. They are works created by Muslims but were arguably designed for a larger audience. These two films are *The Message* (1976), and *Muhammad: The Last Prophet* (2004). Moustapha Akkad directed and produced *The Message*, for which he had to raise money from outside the United States, as he could not get Hollywood support. The film was actually nominated for an Academy Award for its soundtrack. Akkad is best known for producing the horror movie *Halloween* (1978). His involvement in that franchise allowed him to continue to work on films that represent Muslims and Muslim history. The animated feature *Muhammad* did not receive as broad a theatrical release as *The Message*, and it has achieved its greatest success among Muslims. However, the high production values and emphasis on morals means that the film could easily be geared toward a more diverse audience.

Freek Bakker argues that *The Message* and to a certain extent *Muhammad* craft a story that emphasizes the place of Islam among the Abrahamic religions and the inherent interfaith nature of the early Muslim community.[12] This emphasis allows Muslim viewers to understand their role within the American context and gives them tools for explaining their faith to non-Muslims. There is direct pressure to respond to the Orientalist gaze and in the case of *Muhammad* to the "War on Terror." These films seek to educate their Muslim audiences not just by providing history but by crafting the meaning that should be taken from that history.

In both situations, whether the primary intended audience is Muslim or non-Muslim, a vision is presented of what an American Islam could look like. This vision is embedded in the discourse of the Orientalist gaze and is a response to it. *Adam's World* is explicitly interested in creating a normative discourse around dress and ritual. Although cultural discussion is present, the goal of the series seems to be to preserve and articulate a visible Muslim identity. Naif al-Mutawa's television/ movie series of animated super heroes, *The 99*, is a different approach to an American identity that seeks to emphasize values and ethics over observable markers of identity.

Unity Production Films (UPF) is an example of work done primarily by Muslims for everyone.[13] UPF is known for a variety of well-produced documentaries relating to Islam. In addition, they produce resources for classroom use, including dialogues centered on these films. They have recently begun offering advice to producers of both screen and television, as well as trying to create resource packets of information from their documentaries for policymakers.[14]

UPF also offers a selective reading of Muslim history to create a narrative of an American Islam. Two films, *Muhammad: Legacy of a Prophet* (2002) and *Islamic Art: Mirror of the Invisible World* (2012), offer a cultural approach to understanding Islam. Rather than looking at theology, these pieces seek to showcase the contributions of Muslims to world civilization and counter the narrative of Islam as an austere, nihilistic religion as portrayed by Orientalist fear. *Inside Islam: What a Billion Muslims Really Think* (2009) continues this refutation by turning polling data from the Gallup organization into a documentary. The point of the film is to take the information present in the poll and explain that Muslims are not scary, nor do they all wish to kill indiscriminately. There is also a focus on the compatibility of democracy and Islam. Other documentaries produced by UPF focus more directly on the American Muslim experience. These films include a Star Wars-obsessed son of a halal butcher in Queens, New York (*A Son's Sacrifice*, 2007), a manager of a shari'a-compliant fund who wants to learn how to fly after 9/11 (*On a Wing and a Prayer*, 2008), an interfaith push to build a mosque (*Talking through Walls*, 2008), and a multiethnic Muslim comedy tour (*Allah Made Me Funny*, 2008). All offer a vision of Muslims being the "people next door," through the normalcy of their lives. They also articulate for Muslims that it is acceptable to be normal, that normalcy is derived through a particular performance of Americaness that does not challenge the status quo.[15]

It is not entirely clear if the movies mentioned here would have been produced in the same way were it not for the reality of the Orientalist gaze. UPF has another documentary called *A Prince Among Slaves* (2007), which highlights the presence of Muslims in America during the slave period. This film embeds Muslims in the American historical narrative and allows them to see themselves in America. Well done as the movie is, however, it is not entirely clear that the story has had much of an appeal outside an particular audience. As a result, it is shown on PBS and not in theaters. This lack of mass attraction raises an issue I have discussed before, which is the artificial nature of having foundations produce movies about Muslims.[16] There is no doubt that these are important stories to tell, and they are well told, but it is not clear that they have the impact that organic integration into mainstream media would have had.

Muslims in Film

Although the presence of Muslims in Hollywood is not a guarantee of better depictions of Muslims, it does have an impact. Organic integration is the way in which

Muslims can be normalized, both by their presentation as Muslims and when they are acting in ways that are not necessarily marked as Muslim. Faran Tahir (b. 1964) speaks of being cast to play the short-lived Captain Robau in *Star Trek* (2009) as a color-blind decision, and Iqbal Theba (b. 1963) of the TV show *Glee* plays a character that does not require him to discuss his faith.[17]

There are now many young actors of Muslim heritage performing both in film and television. Rizwan Manji (b. 1974), Asif Mandvi (b. 1966), Sarah Shahi (b. 1980), and Noureen DeWulf (b. 1984) are all well-known figures, and although they may not consider themselves Muslim, they all talk about coming from a Muslim background. The 2003 film *The House of Sand and Fog* featured two prominent actors with Muslim backgrounds: Shohreh Aghdashloo (b. 1952) and Ben Kingsley (né Krishna Bhanji, b. 1943 of Khoja descent). Alexander Siddig (b. 1965), like Kingsley, is English and appears in complex stories like *Syriana* (2005) that are enmeshed in Hollywood. Perhaps the best-known American Muslim comedic actor is Dave Chappelle (b. 1973) and he talks of his faith openly.

These actors are capable of changing the way Muslims are discussed in the entertainment industry. Just as important, their celebrity allows them to directly address Islamophobia. For example, Rizwan Manji appeared in a satirical web short to protest the home improvement chain Lowe's.[18] The company pulled advertising from the nationally broadcast reality show *All-American Muslim* (2011) because of pressure from a small conservative group, The Florida Family Association, which threatened a boycott.[19]

Films about Muslims are also important avenues for changing the perception of Muslims. Anisa Mehdi wrote, produced, and directed *Inside Mecca* (2003), a film about *hajj*, for *National Geographic*. One of the people she chose to follow is an American Muslim woman, giving us insight into the spiritual lives of American Muslims. There are also films that focus on American cultural icons who are Muslim, like *Malcolm X* (1992) and *Ali* (2001). In both these films, the faith of the figures is a prominent part of the story.

Behind the scenes, UPF is involved with a project called Muslims on Screen and Television (MOST). Their goal is to work with people in the film and television industries to achieve better representations of Muslims. While they do not generally publicize their work, a producer and writer for *24*, Howard Gordon, is on their website, and it is public knowledge that because of the work of MOST, representation of Muslims on the show changed for the better.[20] Kamran Pasha, a writer and producer for several shows and movies, is believed to have brought about more nuanced portrayals of Muslims on his projects.

In considering Muslims in film or the film industry, we need to think broadly. There are actors, producers, directors, writers, consultants, and stories that are all part of an ecosystem. At any point, the presence of Muslims, or someone of Muslim descent, can alter the perception or representation of Muslims. All of the films discussed in this section contribute to the way in which a national narrative is constructed to make room for Muslims.

Crafting the National Narrative

One of UPF's projects, web-based, is called "My Fellow American."[21] It is a series of testimonials of people talking about Muslims that they know and the positive impact that they have had on the speakers' lives. This series highlights the fact that in a participatory culture, production can be more widespread and, with the right catalyst, can help change the story. The impetus for this venture is clearly a rise in Islamophobia, but the stories reflect a variety of experiences and interactions with Muslims.

The approach is direct, one that personalizes Muslims and makes them active agents in creating an American story, as opposed to being looked at and described. The historical pieces, like *Prince Among Slaves*, then extend this agency back through history to show that America was positively shaped by interactions with Muslims. These interactions became nonthreatening challenges to the American sense of Self, thereby avoiding triggering an Orientalist fear.

I have written about the idea of "media capitalism" as an update to Benedict Anderson's idea of "print capitalism."[22] Although print is no longer the primary means of information delivery in the United States, the narrative that ties the nation-state is still very much operative.

We see a narrative of exclusion in the Orientalist gaze, which posits the Muslim as inherently the Other. In the Orientalist fear, we witness that Muslims as the Other are marginalized further when they are used to help define American notions of Self. However, after a period of excess, a natural counternarrative emerges that attempts to mitigate the dominant exclusionary narrative. With the involvement of individuals of Muslim descent in the film industry, we expect to see a narrative of inclusion, moving beyond tolerance. Of course, these forces remain in a dialogic relationship, constantly changing the terms of belonging. Ultimately, we should see an equilibrium that allows Muslims to comfortably call America "home."[23]

Conclusion

This process of creating a narrative of inclusion, one that establishes Muslim belonging, is not without problems,[24] but it is also not new. The tool in question, filmmaking, is simply a new one for cultural production. In previous generations, cultural production was used to define the community and locate it within a broader national context. American Muslims are going through many of the stages of integration, but they face a more sustained exclusionary narrative. In combating that narrative, it is easy to fall into a culture of victimhood, even when there are generally positive approaches to presenting Muslims. True transformation will happen through participatory culture and producing a narrative of inclusion and belonging.

NOTES

1. Cf. Amir Hussain, "(Re)presenting: Muslims on North American television," *Contemporary Islam* 4 (2010): 55–74; Rubina Ramji, "From "Navy SEALs" to "The Siege": Getting to Know the Muslim Terrorist, Hollywood Style," *Journal of Religion and Film* 9, no. 2 (2005).

2. Jack G. Shaheen, *Reel Bad Arabs: How Hollywood Vilifies a People* (New York: Olive Branch Press, 2001): 20–34. Also see Jack G. Shaheen, *Guilty: Hollywood's Verdict on Arabs after 9/11* (Northampton, MA: Olive Branch Press, 2008): 25–33.

3. See, for example, Peter Gottschalk and Gabriel Greenberg. *Islamophobia: Making Muslims the Enemy* (Lanham, MD: Rowman & Littlefield, 2008); Bruce B. Lawrence, *New Faiths, Old Fears: Muslims and Other Asian Immigrants in American Religious Life* (New York; Columbia University Press, 2004); Andrew Shyrock, ed., *Islamophobia/ Islamophilia: Beyond the Politics of Enemy and Friend* (Bloomington: Indiana University Press, 2010). In addition, there is a rich literature in American immigration studies and in critical race studies that examines some of these issues in an indirect way.

4. Jack G. Shaheen, *Reel Bad Arabs*, 14.

5. Tim Jon Semmerling, *"Evil" Arabs in American Popular Film: Orientalist Fear* (Austin: University of Texas Press, 2006), 81. and Stuart Hall, "Ethnicity: Identity and difference," *Radical America* 23, no. 4 (1991), 15–17.

6. Jack G. Shaheen, *Guilty*, 22–23.

7. Tim Jon Semmerling, *"Evil" Arabs*, 2.

8. Tim Jon Semmerling, "Those "Evil" Muslims! Orientalist Fears in the Narratives of the War on Terror," *Journal of Muslim Minority Affairs* 28, no. 2 (2008), 207–208.

9. Jack G. Shaheen, *Reel Bad Arabs*, 5.

10. Jack G. Shaheen, *Guilty*, 48–49.

11. For a detailed discussion on *Adam's World* and identity formation amongst American Muslim children, please see: Moll, Yasmin. "Screening Faith, Making Muslims: Islamic Media for Muslim American Children and the Politics of Identity Construction." In *Educating the Muslims of America*, edited by Yvonne Yazbeck Haddad (155–177), Farid Senzai, and Jane I Smith. New York: Oxford University Press, 2009.

12. Freek L. Bakker, "The Image of Muhammad in The Message, the First and Only Feature Film About the Prophet of Islam," *Islam & Christian-Muslim Relations* 17, no. 1 (2006): 77–92.

13. In the interests of disclosure, I wish to state that I have been invited to and participated in UPF dialogue trainings, and conducted dialogues for their campaigns.

14. http://upf.tv; Accessed April 13, 2013.

15. John Tehranian, *Whitewashed: America's invisible Middle Eastern Minority* (New York: New York University Press, 2009), 17.

16. Hussein Rashid, "Allah Made Me Funny: Borscht Belt Goes Halal," 2008. (http://religion-dispatches.org/archive/culture/600/allah_made_me_funny%3A_borscht_belt_goes_halal_%7C_culture_%7C_/); Accessed April 13, 2013.

17. Kalsoom Lakhani, "Tackling Stereotypes in Hollywood: An Interview with Faran Tahir," 2009. (https://changinguppakistan.wordpress.com/2009/07/29/tackling-stereotypes-in-hollywood-an-interview-with-faran-tahir/); Accessed April 13, 2013.

18. Hussein Rashid, "Creators of Missing Lowe's Ad Tell All," 2011. (http://religiondispatches.org/archive/culture/5518/creators_of_missing_lowe%E2%80%99s_ad_tell_all_%7C_culture_%7C_/); Accessed April 13, 2013.

19. Hussein Rashid, "Islam meets reality TV," 2011. (http://www.washingtonpost.com/blogs/guest-voices/post/islam-meets-reality-tv/2011/11/11/gIQAI1rhCN_blog.html); Hussein Rashid, "What's So Threatening About "All-American Muslim"?," 2011. (http://blog.britishcouncil.org/oursharedfuture/2011/12/13/whats-so-threatening-about-all-american-muslim/); Accessed April 13, 2013.

20. John Feffer, "Interview with Cynthia Schneider," 2011. (http://www.fpif.org/articles/interview_with_cynthia_schneider).

21. Again, in the interests of full disclosure, there is a testimonial about me on the site.

22. Benedict R. O'G Anderson, *Imagined Communities: Reflections on the Origin and Spread of Nationalism* (New York: Verso, 1991); Hussein Rashid, "Nation and Narrative," in *The Power of Words and Images*, ed. Emmanuel Kattan, Acknowledging a Shared Past to Build a Shared Future: Rethinking Muslim/ non-Muslim Relations (Cambridge, UK: Our Shared Future, British Council, 2012).

23. Hussein Rashid, "A Handful of Dust: Reading South Asian (Im)migrant Identity in Islamicate Literatures" (PhD, Harvard University, 2010).

24. Urmila Seshagiri, "At the Crossroads of Two Empires: Mira Nair's Mississippi Masala and the Limits of Hybridity," *Journal of Asian American Studies* 6, no. 2 (2004): 177–198.

BIBLIOGRAPHY

Anderson, Benedict R. O'G., *Imagined Communities: Reflections on the Origin and Spread of Nationalism* (New York: Verso, 1991).

Bakker, Freek L., "The Image of Muhammad in the Message, the First and Only Feature Film About the Prophet of Islam," *Islam & Christian-Muslim Relations* 17, no. 1 (Jan. 2006): 77–92.

Feffer, John. March 25, 2011. Interview with Cynthia Schneider. Available at http://www.fpif.org/articles/interview_with_cynthia_schneider (Accessed September 3, 2012.)

Hall, Stuart, "Ethnicity: Identity and difference," *Radical America* 23, no. 4 (1991): 9–20.

Hussain, Amir. "(Re)presenting: Muslims on North American television," *Contemporary Islam* 4 (2010): 55–74.

Lakhani, Kalsoom, July 29, 2009. Tackling Stereotypes in Hollywood: An Interview with Faran Tahir. Available at https://changinguppakistan.wordpress.com/2009/07/29/tackling-stereotypes-in-hollywood-an-interview-with-faran-tahir/ (Accessed Sep. 3, 2012.)

Moll, Yasmin, "Screening Faith, Making Muslims: Islamic Media for Muslim American Children and the Politics of Identity Construction," in *Educating the Muslims of America*, edited by Yvonne Yazbeck Haddad, Farid Senzai, and Jane I Smith (New York: Oxford University Press, 2009): 155–177.

Ramji, Rubina, "From "Navy SEALs" to "The Siege": Getting to Know the Muslim Terrorist, Hollywood Style," *Journal of Religion and Film* 9, no. 2 (2005).Available at http://www.unomaha.edu/jrf/Vol9No2/RamjiIslam.htm

Rashid, Hussein, October 9, 2008. Allah Made Me Funny: Borscht Belt Goes Halal. Available at http://religiondispatches.org/archive/culture/600/allah_made_me_funny%3A_borscht_belt_goes_halal_%7C_culture_%7C_/ (Accessed September 3, 2012.)

——, "A Handful of Dust: Reading South Asian (Im)migrant Identity in Islamicate Literatures," Ph.D. dissertation, Harvard University:, 2010.

——, November 11, 2011, Islam meets reality TV. Available at http://www.washingtonpost. com/blogs/guest-voices/post/islam-meets-reality-tv/2011/11/11/gIQAI1rhCN_blog.html (Accessed Sep. 3, 2012.)

——, December 13, 2011, What's So Threatening About "All-American Muslim"? Available at http://blog.britishcouncil.org/oursharedfuture/2011/12/13/whats-so-threatening-about- all-american-muslim/ (accessed Sep. 3, 2012).

——, December 20, 2011. Creators of Missing Lowe's Ad Tell All. Available at http://religion- dispatches.org/archive/culture/5518/creators_of_missing_lowe%E2%80%99s_ad_tell_ all_%7C_culture_%7C_/ (Accessed Sep. 3, 2012.)

——, "Nation and Narrative," In the Power of Words and Images, edited by Emmanuel Kattan (Cambridge, UK: Our Shared Future, British Council, 2012): 10–11.

Semmerling, Tim Jon, "Evil" Arabs in American Popular Film: Orientalist Fear (Austin: University of Texas Press, 2006).

——, "Those "Evil" Muslims! Orientalist Fears in the Narratives of the War on Terror," Journal of Muslim Minority Affairs 28, no. 2 (2008): 207–223.

Seshagiri, Urmila, "At the Crossroads of Two Empires: Mira Nair's Mississippi Masala and the Limits of Hybridity," Journal of Asian American Studies 6, no. 2 (2004/02/03): 177–198.

Shaheen, Jack G., Reel Bad Arabs: How Hollywood Vilifies a People (New York: Olive Branch Press, 2001).

——, Guilty: Hollywood's Verdict on Arabs after 9/11 (Northampton, MA: Olive Branch Press, 2008).

Tehranian, John, Whitewashed: America's Invisible Middle Eastern Minority (New York: New York University Press, 2009).

CHAPTER 28

....

AMERICAN MUSLIMS AND GLOBAL ISLAM

....

PETER MANDAVILLE

LIKE the members of any world religious community, the nearly 3 million Muslims currently living in the United States continually negotiate and adapt the universalist dimensions of their faith to the specific contexts and local settings in which their lives play out.[1] Globally, Islam is a religious tradition whose adherents number some 1.6 billion, with enormous regional variations that—in its majoritarian form—encompasses diverse societies and cultures ranging from West Africa to the Middle East and to Central, South, and Southeast Asia. Seeking to capture the nature of the dynamic between these two worlds—American Muslims and global Islam—Kathleen Moore (1995, 13) asserts:

> The global implications of Muslims' experiences in and observations of North America have been profound. The rising popularity of Islamic revival and the intensification of Islamic identity abroad have, in turn, affected the goals and identity of the Muslim community remaining in the United States. Muslims who stay permanently and those who are North American converts are encouraged by the global resurgence of Islam to assert their religious identity more publicly and to be more religiously observant.

Although the picture today—some two decades after this statement was made and in the context of several intervening geopolitical events and demographic shifts of major significance—is somewhat more complicated, the broader phenomenon that Moore points to remains highly relevant but relatively understudied.[2]

The primary purpose of this chapter is hence to achieve a better understanding of the relationship and interplay between Muslims living in the United States and broader Islamic trends in the world at large.[3] Such an effort is immediately complicated by the fact that the aforementioned diversity that characterizes the Muslim world makes it very difficult to speak meaningfully about any such thing as a distinct and singular "global Islam." That said, it is certainly the case that many American Muslims today are aware of and have had some engagement with ideas, thinkers, and, in some cases, Muslim groups and organizations outside the United States —even if such linkages often occur through narrower ethnic, national, and sectarian channels. Likewise, it is possible to find some presence in the United States today of nearly every major global Islamic trend and movement whose origins lie in the Muslim majority world. This process of transplantation, as we will see, has entailed some considerable adaptation and evolution, as groups whose vision and goals were initially elaborated in very different settings seek relevance in the unique circumstances of Muslim minority life in the West. And despite the endless variety of "Islams" found around the world, it is increasingly possible today to speak meaningfully about such a thing as a global Muslim public sphere. This concept refers to the idea of a set of interlinked discursive spaces—often defined by the internet, social media, and satellite television—in which Muslims of many ethnonational backgrounds and theological orientations, including American Muslims, debate the meaning, nature, and future of their faith.

This chapter begins by framing some of the larger conceptual and political challenges naturally thrown up by any inquiry into the relationship between Muslims in the United States and global Islam more broadly. It goes on to briefly explore some early examples of interplay between American Muslim communities and global Islamic trends, as the former emerged and consolidated in the first half of the twentieth century, before turning to look at several major movements and organizations from the Muslim majority world that established a presence in the United States during the second half of the twentieth century. The emphasis here is on understanding the processes and implications of domestic adaptation alongside ongoing transnational activity. The next section focuses specifically on the question of intellectual-legal debates by profiling four prominent Islamic scholars who have served in various ways as conduits between American Muslims and global Islam and who represent distinct currents in contemporary transnational Islamic discourse. The concluding section seeks to move beyond the conventional framework of viewing American Islam as being influenced and shaped by global Muslim trends by asking whether and to what extent it is possible to discern any impact of American Muslim voices on Islam outside the United States. We should note that this chapter does not pretend to be comprehensive in its coverage. Inevitably there are many forms and vectors of American Muslim engagement with Islam in the world that go untreated here. Rather, the goal here is—through a more selective set of reference examples—to identify the major issues, themes, and questions entailed in understanding the global Islamic ties of American Muslims.

WHO AND WHAT? PRIVILEGING MUSLIMNESS, SECURITIZING TRANSNATIONALISM

Before delving into the substance of American Muslim engagement with global Islam, it is important to consider some of the unspoken assumptions that may inform the way we frame our underlying questions. Two distinct issues here need to be addressed. The first relates to our very usage of the term *American Muslim* and the question of what is at stake in focusing primarily on religion rather than on other dimensions of what are invariably highly complex and multifaceted identities. The answer to this will also help to define the scope of our focus here. The second issue pertains to the need to be cognizant of the fact that we are asking questions about American Muslim connectivity to the wider Islamic world during a time of heightened political sensitivity to this very phenomenon. This sensitivity can be found in multiple strains of contemporary political discourse in the United States, ranging from those who question the loyalty of American Muslims with overseas ties (Toplansky 2010), to some who view American Muslims as agents and conduits for foreign groups seeking to propagate Islamic law. Because the idea of transnational or global Islam is frequently viewed first and foremost through the lens of Al-Qaeda and the global jihadi movement (Colbaugh et al. 2010), the idea of Islam crossing international borders carries an inherent sense of danger for many Americans unfamiliar with the history and nature of the Islamic faith.

It is important to recognize that by primarily figuring the individuals whose world views and motivations we seek to understand as "Muslims" we are to some extent foreclosing from consideration other aspects of their identities that may be equally (or even more) relevant to both understanding who they are and assessing their transnational engagements. Take, for example, a hypothetical Muslim factory worker in the American Midwest. There are many facets to this person's identity—for example, being Arab American, being a lower-middle-class unionized worker—that might help to contextualize him alongside a focus on his religion affiliation (which may or may not be a relevant identity for him). This person might closely follow developments in, and have strong opinions about, Middle East politics, since this is the world region from which his parents emigrated decades ago—perhaps even informed by direct access to regional media forums. To regard this as a prime example of an American Muslim with ties to global Islam, however, would clearly be problematic. The conceptual danger is twofold: that of working with an overly ascriptive conception of Muslimness that constructs religion as the predominant category of identity and of deploying a reductionist understanding of global Islam that views any activity in the Muslim majority world—be it social, political, economic, or cultural— as somehow a function of religion. It thus helps to clarify the scope of the phenomenon under consideration in this chapter to explain that our focus here lies not with understanding how those in America who happen to be Muslim engage the broad affairs of the Muslim majority world. Rather, we are seeking to answer a much more specific question: *How and to what extent are the religious lives of American Muslims shaped by—and, in turn, able to shape—Islamic ideas, doctrines, organizations and movements that circulate beyond the United States?*

The need to provide this admittedly somewhat belabored clarification is a function of the changing discursive environment that surrounds Islam in America today. Muslims in the United States have received unprecedented levels of public attention and scrutiny in the aftermath of 9/11, and this has been accompanied by a reifying effect whereby Muslim communities in America have increasingly been defined, analyzed, and addressed in terms of their religious identity—and sometimes exclusively so. This "racialization" of Muslims in America (Mandaville 2013) has occurred in parallel with similar developments surrounding Muslim communities in Europe (Amiraux 2011). Over the course of the 2000s, Muslim immigrant communities in both Europe and North America that in the past had commonly been differentiated along ethnonational lines in public discourse (e.g., with an emphasis on "hyphenated" identities such as Arab-American or British–South Asian) came increasingly to be captured under religious labels and referents (e.g., Islam, Muslims). Inevitably this shift in nomenclature also signaled at some level a privileging—and sometimes an over-privileging—of religious identity at the expense of other relevant factors. In sum, just as any analysis of Latino communities in the United States that sought to explain that population exclusively with reference to its Christianity would be regarded as severely anemic, any effort to capture the lives of America's diverse and multifaceted "Muslim" population (which comprises Arabs, South Asians, African Americans, Africans, etc.) primarily through reference to Islam suffers from similar problems.

Another important dimension of the particular discursive environment that surrounds Islam in America today relates quite directly to the question of the relationship between American Muslims and "global Islam." Just as American Catholics have been the object of considerable scrutiny—which reached a fever pitch during the presidential candidacy of John F. Kennedy—owing to their supposed allegiance to religious authorities in the Vatican (Jenkins 2003), so have Muslims today become the target of similar suspicion on account of "foreign ties" both real and imagined. Sometimes this sentiment takes the form of a vague and generalized suspicion about whether Muslims can be regarded as loyal Americans who "belong," with its more intense manifestations drawing linkages between American Muslim ties to global Islam and efforts by various foreign Muslim groups to infiltrate the United States in the name of spreading Islamic law, or shari'a (Center for Security Policy 2010). In the aftermath of 9/11, court cases such as the charges made against the Holy Land Foundation in connection with funding groups like HAMAS—designated by the US government as terrorist organizations—gave rise to a belief in some quarters that American Muslim organizations should be viewed as components of a global network that undertakes fundraising work on behalf of Islamic militants (Vidino 2010). Various incidents in recent years involving lone individuals or small groups who sought to undertake acts of violence in the United States in the name of Islam have also sustained a debate about the extent to which American Muslims are susceptible to influence or "radicalization" at the hands of militant Islamic preachers encountered through the internet or in the course of overseas travel and study.[4]

It is of course these more sensational and spectacular engagements with "global Islam" that tend to grab US media headlines and, by extension, to frame public understanding. In fact, the vast majority of American Muslim transnational connectivity is thoroughly mundane and very distant in its nature and purposes from violent activism. It might take the form, for example, of a Pakistani American doctor in Chicago whose family members have for centuries been devotees of the thoroughly transnational Chishtiyya Sufi mystical order but who has of late been reading works of feminist exegesis of the Qur'an that lead her to question some of the teachings promulgated by the order's traditional leaders. Or it might involve a recent convert to Islam who, in an effort to make sure that he is embracing a correct understanding of his new religion, gravitates towards the austere and highly conservative Salafi doctrine, emanating from Saudi Arabia (readily available in many American mosques), which he imagines to be the heartland of Islamic authenticity. Or the young African American Muslim who undertakes the ritual pilgrimage to Mecca in hopes of of participating in a cosmopolitanism of shared belief in which national and racial differences have no meaning—only to return disillusioned after learning that narrow-mindedness and chauvinism are alive and well in the *umma* (world community of Muslims).

These are the idioms of American Muslim engagement with global Islam that primarily inform the subsequent sections of this chapter. It is a story of the interplay between the phenomenon of Muslim immigration to the United States (juxtaposed against an African American Muslim population with deeper roots in the country and a complex relationship with global Islamic tradition), the presence of transnational and transplanted Islamic religious organizations, and the emergence of a new global Muslim public sphere. This schema closely mirrors John Bowen's (2004) account of "three transnational dimensions of Islam" that encompass *demographic movements, transnational religious institutions,* and *the field of Islamic reference and debate.* In subsequent sections this framework is elaborated on with reference to specific examples and forms of American Muslim engagement with global Islam. Throughout the ensuing discussion, an effort is made to show how—as Peggy Levitt (2007) argues—that the presence of religion in the transnational lives of immigrant communities is increasingly commonplace under conditions of globalization that ease communication, movement, and engagement across borders. In other words, there is an effort being made here to gesture at the idea that in the globalized world of the twenty-first century, we should view transnationalism on the part of any given communities—particularly immigrant communities—to be the new norm (Basch et al. 1994). Viewed in this light, American Muslim engagement with global Islam represents a natural extension into the realm of religion of a transnational orientation that pervades the everyday lives of these communities.

GLOBAL ISLAM AND THE MAKING OF AMERICAN MUSLIM COMMUNITY

A brief survey of the evolution of American Muslim engagement with global Islam over the last century will serve to illustrate the complex and multifaceted nature of this phenomenon and also permit us to identity and draw out a number of cross-cutting features and patterns.

At the outset we need to stress the importance of African American Islam and its engagement with the wider Muslim world in the early formation of American Muslim consciousness. This is not only because the current emphasis on Islam in the United States as an "immigrant religion" often leaves African American Muslims—by some estimates (Pew Research Center 2007) the largest group of American-born Muslims in the United States —out of the picture but also because paying attention to legacies associated with earlier vectors of forced labor transmigration—the slave trade—allows us to see how American Islam has always been part of a larger global story. By the late nineteenth century, for example, Edward Wilmot Blyden was already engaged in an effort to "Islamize" the Pan-Africanist ideology that served as a touchstone of black political consciousness in a rapidly changing world (Turner 2003). African American religious leaders, such as Noble Drew Ali, developed their own idioms of syncretic religion, borrowing heavily from Islamic symbols and teaching in the development of the Moorish Science Temple of America (Allen 1998). Even as America developed its own unique idioms of Islamic belief and organization, such as Elijah Muhammad's Nation of Islam, an ongoing if fraught relationship to mainstream global Islam continued to be part of that picture. Indeed, as Edward Curtis (2007) has shown, Arab religious leaders specifically targeted major black American Muslim leaders such as Malcolm X in their outreach efforts during the Cold War era. And as W. D. Muhammad steered the Nation of Islam into the fold of Sunni orthodoxy in the latter twentieth century, following the death of his father, he often found himself walking a fine line between aligning the movement with influences emanating from the Muslim majority world and preserving the unique character of the Nation of Islam as a distinctly African American religious movement.

The story of latter-day immigrant Islam in the United States begins with another account of minorities seeking respite from persecution, in this case the Ahmadiyya community from India. The Ahmadiyya movement, viewed as heterodox by many Sunnis in South Asia and other regions where they reside, began initial missionary work in the United States in the third decade of the twentieth century; they have been a small but active and influential part of the American Muslim community ever since. Some of their earliest interactions were with African American Muslims, whom they helped sensitize to wider currents of thinking in the Muslim world outside (Haddad and Smith 1993).

The more conventional account of contemporary Muslim immigration to the United States begins in the 1960s with the arrival of several waves of students from the Arab world seeking higher education qualifications. Some of these figures—such as Jamal Barzinji, Ahmad Totonji, and Hisham al-Talib—came out of Middle East circles heavily influenced by the ideas of the Muslim Brotherhood. Together with fellow Muslims from South Asia who were similarly influenced by the Islamist Jama'at-i Islami movement, they founded the Muslim Students Association (MSA) in 1963 (Ahmad 2005). The MSA, which continues to exist and be active today, served as the lodestone source for many of the organizations that became mainstays of the American Muslim scene over the subsequent decades. As they left university, settled in the United States and entered professional life, many of these same early MSA leaders were key figures in the founding in 1982 of the Islamic Society of North America (ISNA). While the same Muslim Brotherhood influences were present at the founding of ISNA, that organization developed rapidly in terms of its diversity and demographic composition (mirroring similar shifts in the composition of the American Muslim community). As ISNA took on a more generically Muslim tenor by the early 1990s, those figures within the organization who wanted to reflect the vision of the Muslim Brotherhood in their work left to establish a new organization, the Muslim American Society (MAS), which became the main focal point of Muslim Brotherhood-inspired activity in the United States. In recent years, as Islamism has come under increased scrutiny, MAS leaders have sought to play down their ties to the Muslim Brotherhood, preferring to emphasize the organization's identity as a civil rights group (Nimer 2010, Vidino 2010, Pargeter 2010).

Even as these groups proliferated in the United States —resulting in the founding of the Council on American-Islamic Relations and the Muslim Public Affairs Council, among others—some of them sought to develop extensive transnational networks and to establish themselves as players on the global Muslim stage. For example, another by-product of the networks created by the early MSA was the International Institute of Islamic Thought (IIIT), founded in 1980 by the Palestinian scholar Ismail al-Faruqi. In the pursuit of the "Islamization of knowledge"—a vision inspired by the Muslim Brotherhood background of some of its founders—IIIT built a vast international network of financial, scholarly, and religious ties, with branch offices in over a dozen countries. In this respect, its tendrils had some overlap with organizations and networks funded out of Saudi Arabia. For example, the Muslim World League and World Assembly of Muslim Youth, founded on petrodollar wealth in the 1960s as vehicles for the propagation of Saudi Salafism (often termed Wahhabism), were early supporters of efforts to build mosques and provide religious education for American Muslims, and it is natural that they would begin to collaborate with some of the groups that grew out of US MSA circles even when their longer-term goals did not exactly coincide (Schulze 1990). While IIIT continues to be active today, its recent publication record reflects a shift away from the Islamization of knowledge agenda in favor of a focus on identifying and showcasing new, modernist approaches to Islamic jurisprudence and ethics. In this regard it stands as an interesting example of a Muslim organization that sought relatively early to establish the United States as a major hub of global Islamic intellectual production.

American Muslim engagement with global Islam is not exclusively a story of professional organizations inspired by the modern Islamic movement, however. Alongside and often quite distinct from the ecosystem outlined here are to be found all manner of other American Islamic institutions and networks with global ties. Some, such as the activities of the Naqshbandi Sufi leader Muhammad Hisham Kabbani, represent the US branch of centuries-old and inherently transnational mystical orders. Indeed, almost all of the major global Sufi *tariqat*—such as the Qadiriyya, Chishtiyya, and Tijaniyya—are well represented in North America.[5] While the relative affluence of their North American devotees makes the United States a lucrative site for fundraising, these orders regard their disciples as just another piece of a global operation characterized by devotional practices and traditions that have endured for centuries; even when the far flung shaykhs of these groups are encountered via videoconference.

The idea of personalized transnational religious authority structures also points to the presence in the United States of a significant Shi'i Muslim community. It is common for followers of Shi 'i Islam to elect to follow one of a handful of preeminent religious scholars as a model for their religious lives. Most members of this elite circle of Grand Ayatollahs, known as the *marja'iyya*, have deputies (*waqil*) based in the United States who can represent and provide guidance on behalf of their principals back in Lebanon, Iraq, or Iran (Takim 2002).

One example of a global movement that combines elements of traditionalist (Sufi) and modernist (reformist) Islam and has a growing presence in the United States is the network of followers and institutions inspired by the Turkish religious teacher Fethullah Gülen. Gülen, who today lives in Pennsylvania, initiated a Sufi-based movement in the 1970s, which sought to reconcile modern values and knowledge with religious belief. The Gülen movement is best known for the thousands of schools it operates around the world, including in the United States. These institutions offer a modern curriculum—heavy in math, science, and languages—rather than religious instruction. In some settings, however, the religious dimensions of the Gülen movement can be found alongside the schools. Stressing the importance of intercultural and interfaith dialogue, the movement has also established various research centers and think tanks in a number of western countries, including the Rumi Forum in Washington, D.C., and the Pacifica Institute, which has several branches in

California. Interestingly, American Muslims are not the primary audience for their activities. Rather, these organizations seek primarily to bring the teachings and message of Fethullah Gülen to a broader American audience. The semisecretive nature of the movement, however, has meant that its activities in the United States—and elsewhere—sometimes generate controversy among those who view their work with suspicion (Hendrick 2013).

We can thus see that manifestations of global Islam in the United States vary widely and that they have evolved significantly over time. From the preceding discussion it is also possible to identify several patterns and trends that characterize the role and influence of transnational Muslim influences in the United States. First, currents of religious thought or Islamic movements transplanted to the United States from elsewhere generally adapt and transform over time. The Muslim Brotherhood is an illustrative example. Where it was possible for the founders of the MSA in the early 1960s to infuse their work with the Brotherhood's vision, it became clear over time that an Islamist project to create an Islamic social, political, and legal order had only limited relevance in settings where Muslims lived as minorities. Therefore, over time, as the relevant organizations evolved and came to be led by a new generation of Muslims born and raised in the United States, their mission and focus came to be governed first and foremost by the imperatives of America's Muslim community. This is not to say that their Islamist roots are not relevant, only that they do not necessarily tell us that much about the priorities of these organizations in their contemporary forms. Second, it is clear that what we have been calling "global Islam" is often very local—even parochial—insofar as some of its manifestations in the United States take the form of religious institutions and structures organized along relatively narrow ethnic, national, or sectarian lines. For example, the transnational *tijaniyya* Sufi order finds few adherents outside America's West African diaspora. And the religious dimensions of Fethullah Gülen's movement are mainly found in Turkish-American communities. Transnational, in other words, does not necessarily always mean broad-based. Some global influences travel today in very narrow and exclusivist channels. Finally, it is worth noting that among young Muslim Americans today, the boundaries that separate particular theological, sectarian, or ideological orientations in Islam seem less important than they were for their parents' generation (Mandaville 2001). In this regard we have to ask whether even well-established and long-standing movements such as the Muslim Brotherhood are regarded as relevant by the current generation of young American Muslims, given the range of global Islamic voices they are able to access today via the internet, social media, and satellite television. Is it not perhaps appropriate, as we suggest below in the conclusion, to see American Muslims as increasingly part of a global Muslim public sphere that they have a role in shaping just as much as it shapes them?

CONDUITS OF GLOBAL ISLAM: FOUR PROTOTYPICAL INTELLECTUAL FIGURES

One way of gaining a better understanding of how "global Islam" shapes the religious lives of American Muslims even as it becomes reshaped itself is to look more closely at some of the modalities through which Muslims in the United States access religious ideas from the wider Muslim world. This section does this by providing a portrait of four exemplary intellectual figures representing distinct approaches to the problem of how to make religious knowledge available and relevant to Muslims in America. The four scholars profiled below represent a range of Islamic tendencies, currents, and movements, including some of the groups and organizations dealt with in the previous section. What they share in common is an effort to connect Muslims in the United States to broader Islamic legal, theological, and intellectual traditions by serving as conduits and "translators" for contemporary American Muslims of Islamic ideas first articulated in very different settings and historical periods. Of particular note is the fact that several of these thinkers have done considerably more than simply arrange for the wholesale "importation" into American Muslim discourse of ideas from the Middle East or South Asia. At least a couple of them have crafted significant original works of their own that bear clear traces of their unique American Muslim provenance. This latter point gestures forward to something that we address in the conclusion: namely the question of whether it is now possible to begin speaking of American Islam having some impact on global Islam.

The Orthodox Centrist: Shaykh Taha Jabir al-Alwani

A former president of the North American Fiqh Council and a member of several other regional and international juridical bodies organized under the auspices of the Organization of Islamic Cooperation (previously the Organization of the Islamic Conference), Taha Al-Alwani is a religious scholar of Iraqi background trained at the famed Al-Azhar University who has been living and teaching in the United States since 1985. His religious discourse is characterized by three major themes: (1) the need for a new *ijtihad* (independent legal reasoning) among Muslims in the West in recognition of the reality that the circumstances and challenges faced by this community cannot be addressed by shari'a unless its interpretation is adapted to local conditions; (2) related to this, Al-Alwani has been a central figure in the broader project to establish what is generally known as a minority jurisprudence (*fiqh al-aqaliyyat*)—that is, a body of thought focused on the special circumstances that apply to legal reasoning regarding Muslims living as minorities; and (3) the importance of integrating non-Islamic knowledge and science with *fiqh* (Islamic jurisprudence) in order to help the latter adapt to modern conditions while simultaneously seeking to bring the former into line with Islamic reasoning and normativity, a project commonly known as the "Islamization of knowledge."[6] This approach characterizes the chief enterprise of the IIIT—briefly discussed above—with which Al-Alwani has had a long affiliation. In terms of the overall gist of his jurisprudence, Al-Alwani is thoroughly orthodox but resistant to both overly conservative and unduly liberal interpretations of shari'a. In this regard he can be seen more broadly as part of the *wasatiyya* (centrist) movement whose chief figure is the Egyptian Shaykh Yusuf al-Qaradawi, a luminary global figure in Sunni jurisprudence. Indeed, Al-Alwani represents an important conduit for the dissemination in the United States of the general current of thought around figures such as Qaradawi. We saw the importance of this relationship very clearly around the time of the commencement of US military action in Afghanistan. Having been asked whether American Muslims are permitted to take part in military action against another Muslim country, Al-Alwani deferred the question to Qaradawi—who ruled that American Muslims could indeed fight as part of a non-Muslims army.[7]

The Neotraditionalist: Shaykh Hamza Yusuf Hanson

Hamza Yusuf is an American convert to Islam based in northern California who spent a decade studying Islamic sciences in the Middle East and Africa. In the 1990s he founded the Zaytuna Institute outside San Francisco to serve as the epicenter of an effort to rejuvenate traditional models of Islamic intellectual and moral inquiry strongly informed by traditional mysticism. Hamza Yusuf is extremely popular with younger Muslims in both the United States and Europe. Beyond his own relatively young age and comfort with idioms of American popular culture, Hamza Yusuf's religious discourse is appealing because it is not—in contrast to Al-Alwani's—framed primarily in terms of the "mechanics" of jurisprudence. Rather, Hamza Yusuf addresses themes of spiritual vitality, religious consciousness, and multiple identities through allegory and metaphor. While his own religious orientation is quite orthodox, it is also possible to detect the strong influence of Sufism in aspects of his teaching—particularly the traditional currents emanating from theological centers in Yemen and Mauritania. Hamza Yusuf has recently completed an annotated translation into English of the Aqeeda al-Tahawiyeen, an early-tenth-century creedal text, which many regard as the best single statement of core Islamic beliefs, seeking to explain its relevance to contemporary issues faced by Muslims in America and elsewhere (Yusuf 2009).

The Scholar Activist: Tariq Ramadan

A Swiss-Egyptian philosopher, Ramadan is the maternal grandson of Hassan al-Banna, the founder of the Muslim Brotherhood. Tariq Ramadan first came to prominence in Europe in the mid- to late 1990s, when his ideas crystallized a new social and intellectual current emphasizing the need for the second- and third-generation of immigrant Muslims in the West to become engaged with the majority societies around them (unlike their parents' more "ghettoized" tendencies). Ramadan emphasizes civic participation and the responsibilities of holding western citizenship while denying that these are in any way incompatible with remaining true to Islam. Also an advocate of ijtihad (albeit as an intellectual rather than a jurist), Ramadan—like Al-Alwani—insists that Muslims need to draw on other forms of knowledge in order to enrich and reform their tradition (Ramadan 1999). At the same time he insists on the importance of remaining connected to and working within the boundaries of this tradition. In this regard, he may be seen in some regards as the social and political aspect of the orthodoxy promulgated by figures such as Al-Alwani and Qaradawi (both of whom he respects greatly). At the same time, however, he also has certain disagreements with orthodox ulama, advancing views the latter sometimes find too progressive. For example, Ramadan has for some time now been calling for a moratorium on the application of *hudud* (capital) punishment in the Muslim world and has entered into debate on the subject with figures such as Shaykh Ali Juma'a, the grand mufti of Egypt.[8] Ramadan also emphasizes the importance of reform and ijtihad, placing particular importance on the idea that religious law must always be interpreted in ways that allow it to best serve the common public good (*maslaha*), with the implicit assumption that what constitutes the public good may well vary between time and place. "In addition to scholars of texts," he writes, "we need scholars of contexts." Ramadan has been the center of considerable controversy. In Europe he has been repeatedly accused of operating with a "double discourse" (Fourest 2010)—taking one position on an issue in the western media and then modifying it when addressing Muslim audiences—although the evidence mustered in support of this claim, it must be said, has generally failed to substantiate it. In 2004 he was denied a US work permit under the terms of the USA Patriot Act (and several visitor's visas thereafter) and excluded from the country until 2010. Since then, Ramadan has continued to be an active and influential voice in European and Canadian circles, and his popularity among American Muslims remains high.

The Critical Modernist: Khaled Abou El-Fadl

A legal scholar (of both the Islamic sciences and a juris doctor), Abou El-Fadl is a Kuwaiti-Egyptian teaching at the UCLA Law School. His version of ijtihad emphasizes the need for Muslims and non-Muslims alike to recognize and engage the long tradition of sophisticated critical, philosophical and legal thought to be found in the Islamic tradition. On the one hand, he rejects what he sees as the rigid anti-intellectualism of the Wahhabis and Salafis but, on the other, also a tendency among many western observers of Islam to characterize the tradition in equally inflexible terms. In a number of books written over the past ten years, he has addressed a range of subjects including tolerance, authority, and aesthetics (e.g., Abou El Fadl 2001, 2005). His works demonstrate a thorough command of both the western liberal scholarly idiom and a mastery of Islamic legal sciences. In that sense, there is a certain "hybridity" to his writing that allows it to speak to both kinds of audiences and create a unique dialogue between American academic and legal norms and Islamic tradition. Implicit in his discourse is a condemnation of what he regards as the stultified practices of many conservative religious scholars today; this has made him the subject of considerable controversy in certain quarters in the Muslim community. His texts are voluminous, dense, and philosophically complex, meaning that—in contrast to figures such as Hamza Yusuf and Tariq Ramadan—his ideas generally tend to reach only the most highly educated Muslim audiences.

It is worth emphasizing that even as we hold these four figures out as representatives of diverse approaches to creating some interface between the American Muslim experience and broader global Islamic tradition, the scholars profiled above should be viewed merely as indicative of the varying and multidirectional pathways that link Muslims in the United States to broader intellectual currents in the umma. These figures are by no means the only relevant players, and the approaches they represent should be regarded as ideal types rather than precise representations of social reality. Nonetheless, their unique approaches to bridging the tension between religious universalism and the specific life conditions of Muslim minorities in local American contexts help us to understand the multifaceted nature of American Muslim engagement with global Islam.

CONCLUSION: AMERICAN ISLAM IN THE GLOBAL MUSLIM PUBLIC SPHERE

If there is one insight that arises from the preceding discussion it is surely that the relationship between American Muslims and religious currents in the wider Islamic world has been complex, multifaceted, and continually evolving. While global Muslim trends were clearly important in the early formation of American Muslim communities, these relationships changed over time as Muslims in the United States became settled and confident about their place in American society. Global Islam continued to be significant but in forms adapted to the specific requirements of American society. Religious currents and movements originating in very different Muslim majority contexts found themselves having to continually evolve to remain relevant. But global Islam's presence in America, as we have also seen, is not exclusively a story of transformation and adaptation. Some religious practices and structures of personalized spiritual authority—such as the traditional Sufi orders (globalized, by now, for centuries)—have proven themselves capable of thriving under conditions of transnationalism and remarkably capable of weaving themselves largely unchanged into American Muslim religious lives.

As a primarily immigrant population, it is natural that the religious lives of American Muslims continue to engage with and draw inspiration and resources from the broader Islamic world. However, as American Islam enters a predominantly "postimmigrant" phase—with more and more US Muslims being born and raised exclusively in America—we should expect to see a further evolution in these transnational relationships. Where older generations of Muslim immigrants tended to take their religious pointers from leaders and institutions in the countries from which they originally emigrated, young American Muslims today see themselves as part of a global Muslim public sphere. This means not only that young Muslims can access and feel free to draw on a much wider range of religious ideas and reference points as they curate individualized Islamic experiences but also that they are also no longer passive consumers of Islamic knowledge generated elsewhere or the subjects of religious imperatives mandated from Islam's supposed heartlands. Rather, as more and more Muslims around the world find their way onto the internet and social media—frequently using English as a lingua franca—American Muslims are finding new opportunities to be active contributors to, and even shapers of, these religious debates.

Moreover, we can now point to a number of western-based Islamic thought leaders such as Hamza Yusuf and Tariq Ramadan who have developed small but growing followings in the Muslim majority world. It is too early yet to discern any significant influence of these figures on mainstream religious debates in countries such as Egypt and Pakistan where local structures and traditions of religious authority are deep and enduring. However, as the old world Islamic "religious establishment"—such as the scholars of Al-Azhar, leaders of traditional Sufi orders, insular pietist movements— finds itself increasingly forced to contend with upstart Muslim voices claiming the right to speak on behalf of Islam, it is highly likely that some of them will be American.

NOTES

1. Estimates of the size of the American Muslim population vary significantly from just under a million on the low end to upwards of seven million. I rely here on population figures (as well as other demographic data) from the Pew Forum (2011), which estimated the U.S. Muslim population in 2010 as 2.6 million and forecasted a doubling in size to 6.2 million by 2030.
2. See Leonard (2009) for one effort to capture some of the broad transnational currents among Muslims in the West.
3. The author wishes to acknowledge the invaluable research assistance provided by Emily Smith in the preparation of this chapter.
4. Relevant examples here include Major Nidal Hasan and the 2009 Ft. Hood shooting, the alleged "underwear bomber" Umar Farouk Abdulmutallab later that same year, Faisal Shahzad and the attempted Times Square bombing in 2010, and the Chechen brothers accused of the 2013 Boston Marathon bombings.

5. See, for example, www.magma.ca/~mkalsi/ (Chishtiyya); hishamkabbani.net (Naqshbandiyya); www.tijani.org/tijani-future/(Tijaniyya)
6. See Al-Faruqi 1986 for a representative example of this genre.
7. See http://www.unc.edu/~kurzman/Qaradawi_et_al.htm for a translation of Qaradawi's *fatwa* on this question.
8. See http://www.tariqramadan.com/spip.php?article264&lang=fr for the full text of Ramadan's call for a moratorium on *hudud* punishments.

REFERENCES

Abou El Fadl, Khaled, *And God Knows the Soldiers: The Authoritative and Authoritarian in Islamic Discourses* (Lanham, MD: Rowman & Littlefield, 2001).
——, *The Search for Beauty in Islam: A Conference of the Books* (Lanham, MD: Rowman & Littlefield, 2005).
Ahmad, Irfan, "Between moderation and radicalization: transnational interactions of Jamaat-e-Islami of India," *Global Networks* 5, 3 (2005): 279–299.
Al-Faruqi, Ismail, *Toward Islamic English* (Herndon, VA: International Institute of Islamic Thought, 1986).
Allen, Ernst Jr., "Identity and Destiny: The Formative Views of the Moorish Science Temple and the Nation of Islam," in *Muslims on the Americanization Path?* edited by Yvonne Yazbeck Haddad and John L. Esposito (Atlanta: Scholars Press, 1998): 201–266.
Amiraux, Valérie, "Burka Bashing in the European Union: The Racialization of Muslims," *Religious Norms in the Public Sphere* May 6 (2011). Available at http://rps.berkeley.edu/content/burka-bashing-european-union-racialization-muslims
Basch, Linda, et al., *Nations Unbound: Transnational Projects, Postcolonial Predicaments, and Deterritorialized Nation-States* (New York: Psychology Press, 1994).
Bowen, John, "Beyond Migration: Islam as a Transnational Public Space." *Journal of Ethnic and Migration Studies* 30, 5 (2004): 879–894.
Center for Security Policy, *Shariah: The Threat to America* (Washington DC: Center for Security Policy, 2010).
Colbaugh, Richard, et al., *Transnational Islamic Activism and Radicalization: Patterns, Trends, and Prognostications* (Albuquerque, NM: Sandia National Laboratories, 2010).
Curtis, Edward E. IV, "Islamism and Its African-American Muslim Critics: Black Muslims in the Era of the Arab Cold War," *American Quarterly* 59, 3 (2007): 683–709.
Fourest, Caroline, *Frère Tariq: Le Double Discours de Tariq Ramadan* (Paris: Livre Poche, 2010).
Haddad, Yvonne Y., and Jane I. Smith, *Mission to America: Five Islamic Sectarian Communities in North America* (Gainesville, FL: University Press of Florida, 1993).
Hendrick, Joshua, *Gülen: The Ambiguous Politics of Market Islam in Turkey and the World* (New York: New York University Press).
Jenkins, Philip, *The New Anti-Catholicism: The Last Acceptable Prejudice* (New York: Oxford University Press, 2003).
Leonard, Karen, "Transnational and Cosmopolitan Forms of Islam in the West," *Harvard Middle Eastern and Islamic Review* 8 (2009): 176–199.
Levitt, Peggy, *God Needs No Passport: Immigrants and the Changing American Religious Landscape,* (New York: The New Press, 2007).

Mandaville, Peter, "Islam and Exceptionalism in American Political Discourse," *PS: Political Science & Politics* 46, 2 (2013): 235–239.

——, *Transnational Muslim Politics: Reimagining the Umma* (London: Routledge, 2001).

McCloud, Aminah B. 2006. *Transnational Muslims in American Society*. Gainesville, FL: University Press of Florida.

Moore, Kathleen, *Al-Mughtaribun: American Law and the Transformation of Muslim Life in the United States* (Albany, NY: SUNY Press, 1995).

Nimer, Mohamed, "The Muslim Brotherhood in America: Citizens with Foreign Attachments?" *Middle East Policy* 17, 4 (2010): 144–156.

Pargeter, Alison, *The Muslim Brotherhood: The Burden of Tradition* (London: Saqi Books, 2010).

Pew Forum, *The Future of the Global Muslim Population* (Washington, DC: Pew Research Center, 2011).

Pew Research Center, *American Muslims: Middle Class and Mostly Mainstream* (Washington DC: Pew Research Center, 2007).

Ramadan, Tariq, *To Be a European Muslim: A Study of Islamic Sources in the European Context* (Leicester, UK: The Islamic Foundation, 1999).

Schulze, Reinhard, *Islamischer Internationalismus Im 20. Jahrhundert: Untersuchungen Zur Geschicte Der Islamischen Weltliga* (Leiden: Brill, 1999).

Smith, Jane I., *Islam in America*, 2nd ed. (New York: Columbia University Press, 2nd Edition 2010).

Takim, Liyakat, "Multiple Identities in a Pluralistic World: Shi'ism in America," in *Muslims in the West: From Sojourners to Citizens*, edited by Yvonne Yazbeck Haddad (New York: Oxford University Press, 2002).

Toplansky, Eileen F., "American Muslims Debate Loyalty to America." *American Thinker* (August 15, 2010). Available at http://www.americanthinker.com/2010/08/american_muslims_debate_loyalt.html

Turner, Richard Brent, *Islam in the African-American Experience*, 2nd ed. (Bloomington: Indiana University Press, 2003).

Vidino, Lorenzo, *The New Muslim Brotherhood in the West* (New York: Columbia University Press, 2010).

Yusuf, Hamza, *The Creed of Imam al-Tahawi* (Louisville, KY: Fons Vitae, 2009).

CHAPTER 29

....

THE WAR ON TERROR AND ITS EFFECTS ON AMERICAN MUSLIMS

....

CHARLES KIMBALL

THE world most US citizens thought they knew changed on September 11, 2001. Ordinary daily activities like opening one's mail, boarding a commercial airliner, or attending a public event where large crowds assembled were no longer simple or routine. While Americans were frequently reminded of dangers posed by individuals lashing out violently and sometimes indiscriminately against innocent people, the new threat was not that of a disgruntled former employee or an unstable adolescent in high school. Now, the threat of attack came from seemingly intelligent people who claimed inspiration from Islam, the world's second largest religion. The stunning attacks on 9/11 were carefully planned and skillfully executed by zealots operating as part of an international organization called *al-Qaeda* ("the group") under the leadership of a Saudi Arabian millionaire, Osama bin Laden, and an Egyptian physician, Ayman al-Zawahiri.

A lengthy handwritten letter left behind by the ringleader of the nineteen hijackers, Muhammad Atta, revealed how they were fighting in defense of Islam and were preparing "to meet God" as martyrs.[1] Subsequent communications by Osama bin Laden and other extremists provided additional details attempting to justify as "holy war" behavior that virtually everyone else denounced as terrorism. For many months following 9/11 and the beginning of the US war in Afghanistan (October 7, 2001), intense and nonstop swirl of media attention included mixed images of Islam. While some highly visible politicians, pundits and preachers repeatedly portrayed Islam as somehow inherently violent and menacing, many others emphasized Islam as a "religion of peace." Numerous Muslim leaders and organizations—in the United States and internationally—denounced violent extremism as a perversion of Islam. President George W. Bush publicly supported this view on several occasions, stating: "We have no quarrel with Islam, which is a good and peaceful religion."[2] In a visible effort to add substance to his words and offset those who framed unfolding events as a conflict between Christianity and Islam, the US president visited the Islamic Center in Washington, D.C., and later invited Muslim leaders to the White House.

DECLARING A "WAR ON TERROR"

Nine days after the 9/11 attacks, President George W. Bush addressed a joint session of Congress to identify the threat and make clear the US resolve:

> Tonight, we are a country awakened to danger and called to defend freedom. Our grief has turned to anger and anger to resolution. Whether we bring our enemies to justice or bring justice to our enemies, justice will be done... The enemy of America is not our many Muslim friends. It is not our many Arab friends. Our enemy is a radical network of terrorists and every government that supports them.[3]

Even as President Bush made these distinctions, he also spoke about "this war on terror." The designation stuck. The "war on terror" or the "war on terrorism" became the umbrella under which all kinds of actions were implemented in subsequent months and years. These included military interventions in Afghanistan and Iraq; holding suspected individuals indefinitely without bringing charges or providing legal counsel; enhanced interrogation techniques; dispatching pilotless drone aircraft to bomb suspected individuals in Pakistan, Yemen, and elsewhere; and various types of surveillance focused on Americans and non-Americans both in the United States and abroad.

Despite the verbal distinction separating Islam and the actions of extremists claiming inspiration from Islam, President Bush also defined a larger narrative that was framed in his September 20, 2001, address to Congress and the nation. He drew heavily on religious imagery by repeatedly speaking of the conflict between "good and evil" and making clear that those who were not "for us" were "against us." The "good versus evil" and "us versus them" framework was further reinforced by another ubiquitous question posed repeatedly in all forms of media: Why do they hate us? While many analysts and experts from various fields offered constructive responses to that question—including the insistence that a simplistic question that presumes the monolithic categories of "us" and "them" is bound to be misleading—the most common response was articulated time and time again: They hate us because of our freedom. This explanation was also prominently emphasized in Bush's September 20 address to Congress:

> All of this was brought upon us in a single day, and night fell on a different world, a world where freedom itself its under attack.... The course of this conflict is not yet known, yet its outcome is certain. Freedom and fear, justice and cruelty, have always been at war, and we know that God is not neutral between them.[4]

Linking the attacks on America to a hatred of freedom added to the perception of Islam as rigid and authoritarian. Images of the most extreme manifestation of Islamic rule under the Taliban in Afghanistan—who, even before they provided safe haven to Osama bin Laden and al-Qaeda, were notorious for the severe restrictions on and harsh treatment of women—reinforced this stereotype.

Terrorism is a tactic that is employed both to draw attention to a cause and strike fear among the populace. A war on terror is far more difficult to define than is a war against a nation-state. But the attitude of "us versus them" and "good versus evil" combined with the refrain that "they" hate our "freedom" gave shape to the post-9/11 war on terror. The religious leaders and political pundits who believed the violence and extremism per-petrated by al-Qaeda represented "true" Islam found an audience. Foiled attempts by would-be terrorists determined to detonate a shoe bomb on a plane bound for Detroit and a car laden with explosives in New York City heightened the fear of extremist Muslim individuals or cell groups at large. Even more, successful terrorist attacks by al-Qaeda inspired zealots in various settings—on London's underground trains and buses on July 7, 2005; on a nightclub in Bali on October 1, 2005; and at the end of the Boston Marathon on April 15, 2013; for example—reinforced the connection of Islam with terrorism for those who embraced uncritically an "us versus them" narrative.

Well over a decade after the attacks of 9/11 and the start of the multifaceted war on terror, it is possible to identify several prominent ways these momentous devel-opments have affected Muslims in America. While not exhaustive, the examples described below represent both negative and positive ways the experiences of American Muslims have been directly impacted. They may also provide some insight on obstacles and opportunities to help shape a more hopeful and healthy future in the religiously diverse and increasingly interdependent world of the twenty-first century.

INCREASED US GOVERNMENT SURVEILLANCE ON MUSLIMS IN AMERICA

In the immediate aftermath of 9/11, the FBI and various other local, state and federal bodies charged with law enforcement began an intensive process of surveillance and intelligence gathering activities focused largely on Muslims in America. The fear of additional attacks from al-Qaeda–related extremist cell groups was both understandable and widespread. The shock of what a small number of dedicated extremists had been able to accomplish within the United States did not dissipate. On the contrary, as more details emerged about who knew what prior to 9/11, it was clear that many pieces of information were available but only a few people had been able to connect the dots. In an effort ostensibly to coordinate information and strengthen security measures at airports, ports, and so on, an enormous new branch of the federal government—Homeland Security—was created just nine days after 9/11. Forty-five days after the attacks, Congress passed the USA Patriot Act.

From its inception, the Patriot Act was sharply criticized by many civil libertarians for severely limiting the rights of citizens and legal immigrants. While Muslim leaders and mosques across the country were the primary targets, no one was exempt. Law enforcement agencies now had wide latitude not only to engage in phone and internet surveillance but also to mine, store, and process data from libraries, medical records, credit cards, and so forth. The range and scope of various types of surveillance became clearer over time. For example, shortly after 9/11 President George W. Bush issued an executive order authorizing the National Security Agency (NSA) to pursue a warrantless wiretapping program. Thus, a phone call from someone in the United States to someone outside the country could be monitored without a warrant. But this turned out to be only a small portion of an extensive secret surveillance initiative by the government. *The New York Times* reported in late 2005 that NSA was monitoring phone calls and emails by Americans within the country and had been assisted by large telecommunications companies. Many people—including some congressional representatives—believed that the NSA's "special collection program" was in direct violation of federal statutes and rights protected by the US Constitution.[5]

In addition to the secretive eavesdropping programs, the FBI conducted extensive interrogations of Muslim leaders and closely scrutinized activities at hundreds of mosques and Islamic centers across America. This intense and visible scrutiny centered largely on Muslims. It was also coupled with other new policies, such as the government's ability to designate anyone, including American citizens, as "enemy combatants" and to imprison them indefinitely. Not surprisingly, men and women whose name or appearance seemed to be Islamic were subjected to additional screening at airports within the United States and on flights bound for the United States. As one American Imam told a university audience in 2011, "I always get the VIP treatment at airports. TSA [Transportation Security Administration] officials provide special services for me as a 'Very Islamic Person'!" This type of special attention along with periodic congressional hearings on the dangers posed by Islamic extremists fueled an ongoing controversy about "profiling" particular racial or religious groups.

While Muslims in America were keenly aware of various types of surveillance, the full extent of covert activities aimed at their communities became public when investigative journalists at the Associated Press published detailed accounts linking the FBI and CIA with the New York City Police Department (NYPD) in an extensive domestic spying program. Highlights of the reports, which earned the AP journalists a coveted Pulitzer Prize, include the following:

> The NYPD dispatched undercover officers into minority neighborhoods as part of a human mapping program. Police also used informants, known as "mosque crawlers," to monitor sermons, even when there was no evidence of wrongdoing.... Police subjected entire neighborhoods to surveillance and scrutiny, often because of the ethnicity of the residents, not because of any accusations of crimes. Hundreds of mosques and Muslim student groups were investigated and dozens were infiltrated. Many of these operations were built with help from the CIA, which is prohibited from spying on Americans but was instrumental in transforming the NYPD's intelligence unit after 9/11.[6]

All of the above directly affected Muslims in America. One can easily understand the chilling effect of various forms of visible and covert surveillance. Anxiety and fear rise dramatically with the knowledge that something you say on the phone or to a colleague in a mosque or something you put in an email might be interpreted negatively by an invisible person working in some form of law enforcement. It goes much further. A simple trip to the country of your (or your parents') birth may be the cause of intense scrutiny for months or years. Listening to sermons or purchasing religious materials may be interpreted as a flag warranting government eavesdropping. Many thousands of Muslims in America, for instance, purchased sermons and lectures by American-born imam Anwar al-Awlaki while he was a highly visible and articulate Imam in the United States. When he later became overtly radicalized and left the United States for a presumed safe haven in Yemen, he became a high-priority target in the war on terror. Anwar al-Awlaki was killed in an attack by an unpiloted drone aircraft on September 30, 2011. While freedom of speech and the right to read or listen to whatever one wants are protected in the United States, owning a lecture by Anwar al-Awlaki or mentioning something he said about a biblical prophet in an email to a friend could be cited as evidence against a Muslim in America.[7]

CONSEQUENCES OF ISLAMOPHOBIA

The August 19, 2010, cover story for *Time* magazine posed the question bluntly: "Is America Islamophobic?" The lengthy article centered on many elements linked to the central focus of a month-long national controversy swirling around proposed plans to build an Islamic community center (including a place for Muslims to perform the required five daily prayers) at 51 Park Place in New York City, a location some 2 ½ blocks from Ground Zero. The plans for this center had been approved by all the appropriate officials in New York City and were strongly supported by Mayor Michael Bloomberg. But several national politicians subsequently instigated a firestorm of controversy not about the right of Muslims to build such a facility on privately owned land but on the proximity of the site to the former World Trade Towers. The opponents dubbed the Islamic proposed center with the misleading but politically charged moniker the "Ground Zero Mosque."[8]

The generic association of Islam with the terrorist attacks on 9/11 was evident throughout the heated debate. The *Time* story sought to clarify the issues informing the controversy even as it highlighted a range of bitterly anti-Muslim protests and activities that had occurred in at least six different mosque projects during the previous year.[9] One of the more heated confrontations centered in Murfreesboro, Tennessee, the home of Middle Tennessee State University. Having outgrown their small mosque in the town of 100,000, located thirty-five miles south of Nashville, the Muslim community bought fifteen acres of land south of town and developed plans to build a new Islamic center that would include the mosque, a school, a gym, and a swimming pool. Hostile opposition was visible, vocal, and active in a city that has at least 140 churches and one mosque. After construction began, a fire started by arson at the construction site destroyed a bulldozer and damaged three other vehicles. A sign announcing the new building project was vandalized with the message, "Not welcome." Over 500 people marched to protest the construction, some wearing T-shirts bearing the word *Infidel*, while others carried placards reading "Stop TN Homegrown Terrorism." At one point, a local judge halted the process of building permits after some residents filed a lawsuit to stop the project. A federal judge finally stepped in and ordered that construction be allowed to continue. The new facilities finally opened two years later, in August 2012. But the entire process took a toll on Muslims in Murfreesboro (and others), some of whom had lived and raised families in that college town for more than thirty years.[10]

Another unmistakable and direct consequence of increasing Islamophobia emerged with a ballot initiative in Oklahoma. On November 2, 2010, Oklahoma voters passed State Question No. 755 with a 70 percent plurality. The measure, which immediately drew national and international attention, required that Oklahoma courts rely exclusively on state or federal laws and specifically prohibited "*shariah* and international law" from being employed when making rulings. From the outset, the "Save our State" initiative was fraught with problems. The way it presumed shari'a law to be clearly defined and the generic inclusion of all "international law" raised dozens of legal and practical problems. Shortly after the public vote to amend the state constitution, it was challenged in court and struck down by a federal judge; therefore the law was never implemented. Even so, in the two years following the Oklahoma ballot initiative, the Pew Forum on Religion and Public Life reported that 32 of the 50 states had introduced legislation aimed at limiting religious and international laws in state court decisions.[11]

The Pew Forum analysis points out how religious courts are part of the American landscape:

> Across the United States, religious courts operate on a routine, everyday basis.... The Roman Catholic Church alone has nearly 200 diocesan tribunals that handle a variety of cases, including an estimated 15,000 to 20,000 marriage annulments each year. In addition, many Orthodox Jews use rabbinical courts to obtain religious divorces, resolve business conflicts and settle other disputes with fellow Jews. Similarly, many Muslims appeal to Islamic authorities to resolve marital disputes and other disagreements with fellow Muslims.[12]

Islam has been singled out repeatedly on the basis of a widespread fear that Muslims are seeking to take over the world and impose Islamic law (shariʿa) on everyone. Roger Cohen, a columnist for the *New York Times*, documented the impact of Islamophobia on Oklahoma voters in a humorous and poignant article entitled "Shariah at the Kumback Café." Cohen's analysis of the rationale that led 70 percent of Oklahomans to vote in favor of banning shariʿa and international law in order to "Save our State" is compelling. Although Muslims make up less than 1 percent of the population in Oklahoma and the people he interviewed had no direct experience with Muslims, they had strong opinions on the dangerous threat Islamic law posed to the US Constitution.[13]

In addition to the direct impact linked to Islamophobia, many Muslims have been affected in ways that are difficult to measure or document. As Americans from various ethnic, religious, and national groups know all too well, discrimination comes in many forms: employment opportunities, housing options, competition for college admission or scholarships, and the like. Some social science research on attitudes toward Muslims post-9/11 has helped move beyond anecdotal evidence. While more research should help to clarify specific components related to prejudice toward Muslims and a dread or fear of Islam, several research projects have demonstrated the role of demographic and situational factors. The Pew Forum, for instance, found that Republicans expressed an unfavorable opinion toward Islam two times more often than Democrats, and that college graduates' view of Islam was 19 percent more positive than the view of those who had not graduated from college. Research conducted by psychologists Kathryn Ecklund and Mussarat Khan documented the particular situations—such as boarding an airplane or buying a used car or the ethnic diversity present in a community—as tangible ways to assess bias.[14]

Is America Islamophobic? More than a decade after the terrorist attacks of 9/11, this much is clear: A substantial and vocal segment of the wider population has been gripped by fear of having an Islamic center nearby and profoundly worried that Muslims constitute a threatening monolithic entity committed to world domination and imposing Islamic law on everyone. Precisely how American Muslims, who make up only 1 to 2 percent of the population, will be able to accomplish these presumed goals is never clearly explained.

HATE SPEECH AND HATE CRIMES

In the United States, a society that values and protects freedom of speech, it is not always obvious how to distinguish between free speech and hateful speech that may incite violence. The First Amendment is not absolute. One cannot yell "Fire!" in a crowded theater or issue threats and claim protection under freedom of speech. But, there is a great deal more latitude in the United States than one finds in many other countries. It is illegal to deny the Holocaust, for instance, in many European countries. Canada, the Netherlands, South Africa, India, and Australia have laws banning hate speech. Laws in France and Israel prohibit selling Nazi swastikas and flags. And many predominantly Muslim countries may impose severe punishment for speech that is deemed to violate one or another version of "blasphemy laws."

Numerous examples of hostile or hateful anti-Muslim sentiment have been evident in the United States since 9/11. Three of the most widely publicized efforts provoked storms of controversy in the United States and internationally: advertisements placed on New York City subways by Pamela Geller[15]; a thirteen-minute video (purporting to be a trailer for a feature film) posted on YouTube in September 2012 entitled *The Innocence of Muslims*; and the attempts of a Florida minister who, through the use of social media, promoted a "Burn the Qur'an" event to mark the nine-year anniversary of 9/11. *The Innocence of Muslims* video depicted the Prophet Muhammad as a sinister, bloodthirsty charlatan with an insatiable sexual appetite. After going viral on the internet, riots broke out in Egypt and elsewhere as rumors spread that this vile portrayal of Muhammad and the beginning of Islam was made by Jews and was soon to be released in American theaters. It turned out that a disgruntled Coptic Christian living in California had produced this offensive and amateurish video.

The Innocence of Muslims episode illustrates the potential for hateful speech leading to destructive behavior. This was even more visible with the controversy swirling around the Rev. Terry Jones, the independent fundamentalist Pentecostal Florida minister serving a church of less than fifty people. Jones's plan to hold a three-hour "Burn the Qur'an" event was augmented by inflammatory signs outside his church declaring "Islam is of the Devil." When his plans were reported in various media, anti-Christian and anti-American demonstrations erupted in Pakistan, India, Indonesia, and Afghanistan. In less than two days, President Barack Obama, Secretary of State Hillary Clinton, General David Petraeus (who was in charge of US troops in Iraq and Afghanistan), and Pope Benedict XVI had all made public and personal appeals to Jones urging him to cancel the Qur'an burning event. The event was canceled; in the following year, however, Jones carried out his plan.

While Terry Jones was a previously obscure figure, since 9/11 many other highly visible Christian leaders have repeatedly spewed hostile rhetoric about Muhammad, Islam, mandates prescribed in the Qur'an, and the nefarious goals of contemporary

Muslims. Prominent televangelists Pat Robertson in Virginia, John Haggee in Texas, and Rod Parsley in Ohio have proudly led the way among a host of high-profile preachers who seem to be certain that Islam is the focus of evil in the twenty-first century.[16]

Hostile rhetoric about Islam long preceded the attacks of 9/11. Whether or not such derogatory speech increased dramatically is not clear. What is certain, however, is that dramatic changes have taken place in modes of communication. Social media, electronic mail, and the ability of virtually anyone to post videos or opinions online marks a sea change in the way information can spread. With few safeguards or means of vetting information, almost anything posted on the internet (such as *The Innocence of Muslims* video) has the potential for going viral and inciting people to act—sometimes in violent and destructive ways.

Hate crimes are defined as criminal acts motivated by race, color, religion, or national origin. In addition to crimes committed against people, hate crimes may be directed at property or at the larger society. One of the most horrific post 9/11 hate crimes occurred in Norway but had close ties to hate speech in the United States. On July 22, 2011, Anders Behring Breivik, a trhirty-two-year-old Norwegian Christian, bombed buildings in Oslo (killing eight people) and then attacked and killed sixty-nine more people—mostly teenagers—at a Norwegian summer camp. Describing himself a "100 percent Christian," his rationale for this slaughter of innocents was to call attention to the deeply held views articulated in a manifesto he released the day of the attacks. The peril posed by Islam and multiculturalism were at the top of his grievances. He called for the expulsion of all Muslims from Europe. The *New York Times* highlighted the direct connection between anti-Muslim writings, blogs in the United States, and Breivik's violent assaults. Specifically, Breivik's manifesto cited Robert Spencer, the prolific anti-Islamist American, sixty-four times, quoting his writings at great length. Breivik also referenced high-profile Americans such as the aforementioned Pamela Geller and neoconservative scholar Daniel Pipes as primary sources of inspiration.[17]

The FBI keeps records and since 1992 has issued annual reports on hate crimes in America. The categories include crimes directed against various ethnic groups, gangs, people in particular religions, and so forth. Hate crimes against Muslims peaked in the year after 9/11, when the FBI documented 481 anti-Muslim crimes. This represented a 1,600 percent increase from the year before 9/11. In 2010, when national attention swirled around the "Ground Zero mosque" and efforts to ban shari'a in some states were gaining momentum, the FBI reported 160 hate crimes against Muslims—a 50 percent rise over the 106 reported in 2009.[18]

A number of organizations collect and publish information on hate crimes directed against Muslims in America, including the Southern Poverty Law Center (SPLC), the Muslim Public Affairs Council (MPAC), the American-Arab Anti-Discrimination Committee (ADC), and the Council on American-Islamic Relations (CAIR). Each of these organizations suggests that the FBI figures substantially underestimate the actual number of Anti-Muslim hate crimes. The ADC, for instance, documented more than 700 violent crimes against Arab Americans in the weeks after 9/11. And, as is often the case with some other types of crimes such as sexual assault, each of the organizations emphasizes that a significant but unknown number of crimes are never reported officially.[19]

While many anti-Islamic hate crimes involve arson or other forms of destruction or defacing of property, some include physical threats and murder. A few examples from 2012 illustrate the point. The Center for American Progress issued a report on a sharp spike in violent attacks on mosques—ten total—all across America during the month of Ramadan (from July 20 to August 18, 2012).[20] A man in Queens, New York, was stabbed multiple times in front of a mosque on November 10 while the attackers shouted anti-Muslim epithets; three weeks later, a seventy-year-old man was brutally beaten by two teenagers who asked repeatedly if he was a Muslim or a Hindu.[21] On December 27, 2012, just weeks after Pamela Geller's hateful ads appeared in New York subway stations, a thirty-one-year-old woman, Erika Mendendez, pushed forty-six-year-old Sunando Sen onto the subway tracks in front of an oncoming train because she thought he was a Muslim. Charged with second-degree murder, she told police, "I pushed a Muslim off the train tracks because I hate Hindus and Muslims ever since 2001 when they put down the twin towers."[22] Menendez was not alone in conflating Hindus with Muslims as she lashed out. On several occasions Sikhs have been attacked or killed by individuals who assumed they were Muslims because they wore a "turban."

In response to various murderous attacks on Muslims in the New York City area, Muneer Awad, a spokesperson for CAIR's New York office, urged people to respond to such hate crimes by being vocal and productive, serving in the local communities, hosting interfaith events, and inviting people to Muslim community events: "Personal contact (with neighbors, other faith communities and elected officials) will alleviate any phobia derived from ignorance... the challenge we face is creating that personal contact in an organized and united manner."[23]

Awad's plea highlights important and effective antidotes to fear and ignorance of Islam: education and personal engagement. Major strides in these areas arguably reflect the most positive consequences for American Muslims after 9/11 and the "war on terror."

EDUCATION, INTERFAITH DIALOGUE AND COOPERATION

In the months following 9/11, college professors with expertise in Islamic studies as well as Muslim leaders throughout the United States were in high demand. A wide variety of universities, seminaries, civic organizations, and churches were eager to organize lectures, seminars, panel discussions, and other events in order to learn more about Islam and the forces at work in the world's second largest religion. This hunger for accurate information and longer-term educational programs continued for several years. Many university professors and local imams participated in dozens or even hundreds of educational programs in different venues. In many instances, a church sponsoring an evening lecture and Q&A or a dialogue between Christian and Muslim leaders energized the clergy and congregation to organize additional events or even semester long study programs. People in different settings clearly knew that they had far too little understanding of Islam, the Qur'an, what had motivated violent extremists, and how representative they were of the larger Muslim community in the United States and globally.

As one with a history of involvement in such educational efforts for twenty-five years prior to 2001—in churches, universities, and with civic organizations—I know that the sustained interest and demand for information following 9/11 was qualitatively different. My direct engagement began with doctoral studies in comparative religion at Harvard in 1975 and continued while I was living and studying Islam in Cairo in 1977–1978. It shifted experientially when I was one of a small number of American clergy directly involved in the Iranian hostage conflict, and I later directed the Middle East Office (from 1983–1990) at the National Council of Churches, based in New York. This position involved traveling throughout the Middle East several times a year and working closely with Christian, Jewish, and Muslim leaders and organizations in the United States. Interest in the mix of Islam, conflict, and political upheaval in the Middle East spiked with the Iran hostage crisis (1979–1981), Israel's war and the rise of Hizbollah ("Party of God") in Lebanon in the 1980s, and the Gulf War against Saddam Hussein's Iraq in 1991. In each case, other international and domestic developments subsequently shifted attention away from changing dynamics and the role of religion in various Muslim majority lands. This was not the case in the decade after 9/11. Upheavals in predominantly Muslim countries, periodic stories of "homegrown" terrorists whose plans were thwarted, the fear of secret terrorist cells in our midst, and the ever-present awareness that another attack could occur at any time kept the attention level high.

The various educational initiatives—particularly in churches and church-related organizations such as local, state and national councils of churches—connected naturally to organized efforts in interfaith dialogue as well as practical manifestations of interfaith cooperation in local settings. For many, the history of focused initiatives in Jewish–Christian relations provided a helpful foundation for developing Christian–Muslim and Jewish–Christian–Muslim dialogue. The face-to-face encounter organized by churches, synagogues and mosques as well as a large number of local, state, and national church-related organizations signified the importance of education and interfaith relations in post 9/11 America. While numerous examples of intentional Christian–Muslim engagement can be cited, two larger initiatives—one international that involved many in the United States and one focused domestically in the United States —serve to illustrate the energy and urgency fueling this movement.

In September 2006, Pope Benedict XVI delivered a speech in Regensburg, Germany, that shocked and angered Muslims everywhere. The speech implied that Muhammad preached spreading Islam by the sword and that the Qur'anic declaration that "There is no compulsion in religion" (Qur'an 2:256) was superseded by later revelations concerning "holy war." Thirty-eight prominent Muslim scholars sent the pontiff a letter within weeks detailing their reasons for strong disagreement. A year after the controversial speech, a group of 138 Muslim leaders—including academics, government leaders, *muftis*, and prominent authors—sent an open letter to the leaders of the world's major Christian churches. The letter stressed how Christians and Muslims comprise almost half of the world's population and that the future peace of the world depends on peace between these religious communities. Most important, the open letter emphasized that the basis for peaceful coexistence and cooperation already exists at the heart of both the Bible and Qur'an, namely: the two great commandments to love God and love your neighbor. [24]

In the United States, more than 300 evangelical and mainline Christian leaders and scholars responded to the Muslim-led initiative by signing a full-page statement that appeared in the *New York Times* entitled, "Loving God and Neighbor Together." Soon, the original 138 Muslim leaders who endorsed "A Common Word" increased to more than 300 while more than 450 Islamic organizations also officially added their support. Additional conferences and interfaith education and dialogue projects to facilitate understanding and build trust across religious lines have continued under the auspices of this new type of interfaith venture. Clearly the rationale and urgency for such efforts relate to the potential for disaster in an increasingly interdependent world community that includes many types of weapons of mass destruction.

The American Baptist Convention (ABC) organized a three-day symposium on Baptist-Muslim relations in January 2009. This gathering included six plenary sessions where papers were presented by a Christian and a Muslim, common meals, and small group discussion sessions each day. The papers presented at the symposium were later published in the *American Baptist Quarterly*. More important, the three-day event produced a statement, "A Declaration of Our Common Will," which all forty participants signed. The declaration underscores commitments to eradicate stereotypes and develop friendships, affirm the dignity of one another's faith while honoring the differences and building upon common values, educate the respective faith communities, cooperate on projects that contribute to justice, peace, and the common good, and pray for one another. [25]

This type of national dialogue has been replicated in numerous local settings across the United States. While some people and institutions remained wary or even visibly opposed to such interfaith efforts, many others in major urban communities and mid-sized cities have pursued ongoing commitments to meet, develop educational programs and seek ways to cooperate on projects in their local settings. In numerous communities, for example, people from neighboring churches, mosques, and often synagogues have joined forces to build Habitat for Humanity homes. It is clear to me, having studied the history of the interfaith dialogue movement and participated personally in local, national, and international programs for four decades,[26] that the scope of and urgency motivating such endeavors shifted to an entirely different level as a result of 9/11, the "war on terror," and the dangers posed by violent extremists as well as those who are gripped by fear of the "other."

Another measure of the strong growth in educational efforts following 9/11 can be seen in the demand for college courses and the development of new departments and programs. In many colleges and universities (and some divinity schools and theological seminaries) the demand for courses on comparative religion, Islam, the Qur'an, Islamic law, women in Islam, religion and politics in the Middle East, and the like rose exponentially. Academic jobs for people with expertise in Arabic, Islamic studies, and Middle Eastern history, for example, were plentiful when compared to pre-9/11 tenure-track openings.

Some American universities developed new academic centers and programs in the first decade of the twenty-first century. The University of North Carolina-Chapel Hill, for instance, responded to what it called "the overwhelming demand for information" by launching the Carolina Center for the Study of the Middle East and Muslim Civilizations.[27] The University of Oklahoma (UO) inaugurated a new, interdisciplinary Religious Studies Program beginning in 2002. In the first decade, the program hired seven full-time faculty members and drawing in twenty more faculty lodged in the departments of history, philosophy, sociology, anthropology, and so on. By the 2012–2013 academic year, the UO Religious Studies Program included more than sixty majors and forty minors; its courses were fully integrated into the general education curriculum of students from the different colleges and majors across the campus. In the 2009, a newly established College for International and Area Studies at UO included a vibrant Center for Middle East Studies. In addition, an intentional initiative added faculty and secured new funding as UO was selected by the US Department of Education as a "flagship" school for Arabic language instruction.

INTENTIONAL INITIATIVES BY MUSLIMS

Many American Muslims responded constructively to the increasingly challenging issues shaping perceptions in the era of the US "war on terror." In addition to the types of programs focused on education, dialogue, and interfaith cooperation in community mentioned above, individuals, communities who gathered in local mosques, and different national organizations have issued statements condemning violent extremists, written books, articles, opinion pieces, and letters to the editor to clarify what is Islam means and requires of faithful adherents. Since Islam is not monolithic, these intentional efforts took many forms and varied a great deal in their focus. Selected examples serve to illustrate the scope and substance of the multifaceted endeavors.

Among the several hundred books published by Muslims for an American audience, many since 9/11 have focused on an accessible introduction to Islam, the hijacking of Islam by extremists, the meanings and approaches to the life of faith (including shari'a law), the roles of women in Islam, and specific ways Muslims today can and must integrate constructively into non-Muslim majority western societies. Examples of best-selling books illustrating these respective foci include the following: *No god but God*, by Reza Aslan; *The Great Theft: Wrestling Islam from the Extremists*, by Khaled Abou el Fadl; *Why I Am a Muslim: An American Odyssey*, by Asma Gull Hasan; *Mecca and Main Street: Muslim Life in America after 9/11*, by Geneive Abdo; *What's Right with Islam: A New Vision for Muslims and the West*, by Imam Feisal Abdul Rauf; and *Western Muslims and the Future of Islam*, by Tariq Ramadan.

A discernible pattern here goes well beyond distinguishing Islam as practiced by the large majority of Muslims from the interpretations proffered by extremists such as the late Osama bin Laden. Many American Muslims have focused energies on the freedom and opportunities available as citizens in the United States —particularly in comparison to the upheavals and uncertainties visible in many predominantly Muslim lands in the aftermath of the wars in Afghanistan and Iraq and the revolutionary movements inspired by dramatic changes in Tunisia and Egypt in late 2010 and early 2011. Imam Feisal Abdul Rauf was an articulate spokesperson, as he argued in his book that American laws and values are highly compatible with Islam. Rauf's prominence as a leading figure in interfaith work morphed in 2010 when his efforts to develop an Islamic center at 51 Park Place in New York City became ensnared in the political controversy noted above. It was more than a little ironic that he was not available to defend the project when the controversy erupted because he was traveling on a State Department trip to several countries in order to promote the image of the United States as a great country for Muslims.

Imad Enchassi, the imam of a large mosque in Oklahoma City, completed a doctoral dissertation in Beirut, Lebanon, in 2010 entitled "The Constructive Effects of 9/11 on the Muslim Community in the United States." Enchassi, who was raised in a Palestinian refugee camp in Beirut, initially came to the United States as a student in the early 1980s. His research acknowledges and documents many negative consequences experienced by Muslims flowing from 9/11 and the "war on terror." But, he argues, the pressures and dynamics engendered by these events have spurred American Muslims to constructive action on numerous fronts. Complacency and semi-isolation were not options. Rather, American Muslims have been energized to speak out, to work at education both within their communities and in the larger society, to become involved in community projects, to stand up for their rights to freedom of worship, including the right to build and enlarge mosques and Islamic schools. Imam Enchassi modeled these constructive activities as a highly visible figure giving lectures and educational programs throughout the state of Oklahoma. He was the prime mover in a successful project to enlarge the mosque and to build an Islamic school, the Mercy School Institute, in another area of Oklahoma City.

Imad Enchassi goes further. His research suggests large increases in ways American Muslims perceive themselves as more integrated into American society, increased involvement and support for healthy Islamic institutions in local communities, substantial increases in the percentage of Muslims engaging in the political processes (at local, state, and national levels), the emergence of Muslim comedians, and so forth. In short, Enchassi argues that the crises following 9/11 and multiple problems flowing from the decade plus "war on terror" not only created serious problems but have opened up many important opportunities for Muslims in America to enter a new and more positive era.[28]

In the coming decade or two, more detailed analyses of the various ways the "war on terror" challenged and changed the experiences of American Muslims will be forthcoming. More than a decade after the world most Americans knew changed on 9/11, it is possible to discern several prominent negative and positive consequences. Hopefully, in a world that is not only laden with many weapons of mass destruction but also increasingly interdependent, people of good will will be able to look back and identify many enduring positive developments that were rooted in responses to the shocking events that marked the first decade of the twenty-first century.

NOTES

1. The complete English translation of Muhammad Atta's five-page document was published in *The Washington Post*, September 28, 2001.
2. George W. Bush, quoted in *The New York Times*, September 21, 2001.
3. "President Bush's Address to Congress and the Nation," full text in *The Washington Post*, September 21, 2001.
4. Ibid.
5. "Bush Lets U.S. Spy on Callers without Courts," *The New York Times*, December 16, 2005.
6. The various 2011 Associated Press reports are available online in archives maintained by the AP.
7. In addition to reading various accounts of domestic trials for alleged terrorists, I experienced this at first hand. As a consultant to court appointed lawyers defending two young men charged with conspiring to engage in *jihad* ("holy war") abroad, the presence of lectures by Anwar al-Awlaki on a computer and an email (sent to a friend while Awlaki was functioning as a Muslim leader in the United States) commending his lectures was offered as evidence against the young men. While I have more than thirty hours of Awlaki's lectures on a computer and have accessed online the speeches and other communications by the late Osama bin Laden, my status as a non-Muslim specialist on Islam and the Middle East does not raise any red flags. The same is not true for Muslims in America.
8. The proposed community center was not a mosque; nor was its location at "Ground Zero." Rather, it was to function more like a YMCA or a Jewish community center with a variety

of meeting rooms and facilities for a range of physical and other activities like weddings, performances, and lecture series. The organizers planned for interfaith dialogue and cooperation to be major components of the multiple uses for the community center.

9. "Islamophobia: Does America Have a Muslim Problem?" *Time*, August 30, 2010.

10. The two-year saga of the Murphreesboro Islamic Center was chronicled in a nationally broadcast CNN program on August 12, 2012. The program, "Unwelcome: The Muslims Next Door," was hosted by Soledad O'Brien.

11. For a summary of this trend and the likelihood that issues connected to the various state initiatives will eventually be presented to the U.S. Supreme Court, see the article published by Michael Kirkland III, the United Press International senior legal affairs writer, "Under the U.S. Supreme Court: Islamic Law in U.S. Courts," May 19, 2013.

12. "Applying God's Law: Religious Courts and Mediation in the U.S.," an analysis published by The Pew Forum on Religion and Public Life, April 8, 2013. The analysis includes detailed reviews of many religious communities (e.g., Hindus, Buddhists, Jews, and Muslims) as well as many Christian denominations (Assemblies of God, Southern Baptists, Lutherans, Presbyterians, Roman Catholics, Mormons, etc.).

13. Roger Cohen, "Shariah at the Kumback Café," *The New York Times*, December 10, 2010.

14. Mussarat Khan and Kathryn Ecklund, "Attitudes Toward Muslim Americans Post-9/11," University of Michigan: *Journal of Muslim Mental Health*, 7, 1 (2012).

15. Pamela Geller's mission to stop what she labeled the "Islamization of America," was paid for by a group called the American Freedom Defense Initiative. The most notorious billboards featured a photo of the burning and collapsing World Trade Towers with a quotation from the Qur'an: "Soon we shall cast terror into the hearts of unbelievers" (Qur'an 3:151).

16. For a detailed overview of the activities of these anti-Muslim Christian ministers, see Charles Kimball, *When Religion Becomes Lethal: The Explosive Mix of Politics and Religion in Judaism, Christianity, and Islam* (San Francisco: Jossey-Bass, 2011), pp. 96–97 and 168–170.

17. "Killings in Norway Spotlight Anti-Muslim Thought in the U.S.," *The New York Times*, July 24, 2011.

18. Annual statistics of hate crimes in America can be found at the official website of the FBI: www.fbi.gov/about-us/investigate/civilrights/hate_crimes

19. Data and reports from the SPLC, MPAC, ADC, CAIR and other human/civil rights organizations are easily accessed via their respective websites or various internet search engines.

20. "Young Muslim American Voices: Attacks on Muslim American Houses of Worship on the Rise." Available at http://americanprogress.org, September 26, 2012

21. "Queens Man, 70, Beaten After He Was Asked if He Was a Muslim or Hindu," *New York Daily News*, November 30, 2012.

22. "Woman Is Charged with Murder in a Hate Crime in a Fatal Subway Push," *New York Times*, December 29, 2012.

23. "Hate Crimes Against Muslims Only Escalating 10 Years after 9/11." Available at http://arabamericannews.com, January 4, 2013.

24. For the complete letter and multiple additional initiatives by hundreds of prominent Muslim and Christian leaders, see www.acommonword.com

25. "The Declaration of Our Common Will" and the proceedings from the Baptist-Muslim Dialogue meeting can be found in *American Baptist Quarterly* (Spring 2009).

26. My doctoral dissertation at Harvard Divinity School explored the history and accomplishments flowing from the first twenty years of intentional Christian-Muslim dialogue programs organized through the World Council of Churches and the Vatican, particularly through the experiences and perspectives of key Muslim participants. From the 1980s onward, I have been a consultant to and involved directly with a wide variety of Christian-Muslim, Christian-Jewish, and Jewish-Christian-Muslim programs and projects within the United States and internationally.

27. UNC professors Charles Kurzman and Carl Ernst detailed the process leading to the creation of the new academic center in a paper on "Islamic Studies in U.S. Universities," delivered on September 30, 2009, at a Social Sciences Research Council workshop on "The Production of Knowledge on World Religions: The Middle East."

28. Imad Enchassi's dissertation was completed in Arabic. His plans as of 2013 include a reworked English version of his research to be published as a book.

BIBLIOGRAPHY

Abdul Rauf, Imam Feisal, *What's Right with Islam: A New Vision for Muslims and the West* (San Francisco: HarperSanFrancisco, 2004).

Abdo, Geneive, *Mecca and Main Street: Muslim Life in America after 9/11* (New York: Oxford University Press, 2007).

Abou el Fadl, Khaled, *The Great Theft: Wrestling Islam from the Extremists* (San Francisco: HarperSanFrancisco, 2005).

Aslan, Reza, *No God but God: The Origins, Evolution, and Future of Islam* (New York: Random House, 2005).

Curtis, Edward E. IV, ed., *The Columbia Sourcebook on Muslims in America* (New York: Columbia University Press, 2008).

Esposito, John, *The Future of Islam* (New York: Oxford University Press, 2010).

Haddad, Yvonne Y., Farid Senzai, and Jane I. Smith, eds., *Educating the Muslims in America* (New York: Oxford University Press, 2009).

Hasan, Asma Gull, *Why I am a Muslim: An American Odyssey* (Rockport, MA: Element Books, 2004).

Kimball, Charles, *When Religion Becomes Evil: Five Warning Signs*, rev. ed. (San Francisco: HarperOne, 2008).

——, *When Religion Becomes Lethal: The Explosive Mix of Politics and Religion in Judaism, Christianity, and Islam* (San Francisco: Jossey-Bass, 2011).

Patel, Eboo, *Acts of Faith: The Story of an American Muslim, the Struggle for the Soul of a Generation* (Boston: Beacon Press, 2007).

Ramadan, Tareq, *Western Muslims and the Future of Islam* (New York: Oxford University Press, 2005).

Smith, Jane I., *Islam in America*, 2nd ed. (New York: Columbia University Press, 2009).

Volf, Miroslav, Ghazi bin Muhammad, and Melissa Yarrington, eds., *A Common Word: Muslims and Christians on Loving God and Neighbor* (Grand Rapids, MI: Eerdmanns, 2010).

Zogby, James, *Arab Voices: What They Are Saying to Us and Why It Matters* (New York: Palgrave Macmillan, 2010).

CHAPTER 30

ISLAMOPHOBIA AND ANTI-MUSLIM SENTIMENT IN THE UNITED STATES

PETER GOTTSCHALK

ACCORDING to the Federal Bureau of Investigation, in 2010, nearly 20 percent of offenses described as hate crimes in the United States stemmed from religious bias. Of those, 13.2 percent targeted Muslims. In more meaningful terms, the FBI recorded 197 Muslims victimized because of their religion. While the bureau had reported even more hate crimes for 2000, it recorded only 36 Muslim victims. Although these numbers do not evidence the many incidents that went unreported to law enforcement officials and may reflect the increasing willingness of Muslims to identify hate crimes as such, they nevertheless indicate the surge in anti-Muslim and anti-Islamic discrimination and violence that followed the attacks by Islamist terrorists on September 11, 2001. Indeed, in that year Muslims went from being the second least victimized religious group in America to the second most (the numbers of victimized Jews have far surpassed those of any other group throughout the decade) (Federal Bureau of Investigation, 2001, 2011).

Although many journalists and scholars have investigated this unfortunate change, too often their efforts have focused on the recent or near recent past, suggesting that the rise of active discrimination derives from twentieth-century American confrontations with Middle Eastern Muslims over issues involving oil and Israel. In hindsight, the loss of US lives, position, and pride in such incidents as the Iranian hostage crisis (1979–1980), the Beirut bombing of Marine barracks (1983), the destruction of Pan Am flight 103 over Scotland (1988), and the bombing of US barracks in Saudi Arabia (1996) might appear to have primed Americans for the explosion of anti-Muslim sentiments following 9/11. Yet in only some of these instances did Americans, at the time these events occurred, explicitly identify the perpetrators as Muslims and associate their motivations with Islam. Moreover, the allegations, stereotypes, and anxieties expressed in the wake of the 9/11 attacks had parallels in anti-Muslim stereotypes found among Americans from the beginning of the European settlement of North America. Therefore an examination of Islamophobia and anti-Muslim sentiment in the United States must simultaneously consider the continuities of prejudice across five centuries of European and European-American presence while appreciating the particularities of specific events and circumstances.

While the FBI statistics hint at the seriousness of the issue, their numerical quality cannot reflect the nuances implicit in understanding Islamophobia and anti-Muslim sentiment. For instance, the 2012 vandalization of a mosque in Harrisonburg, Virginia, would undoubtedly be classified by the FBI as an "anti-Islamic" hate crime. But among the graffiti obscenities and the images of genitalia on the mosque walls were slurs against "Irakis" and racial epithets usually reserved for Arabs and African Americans, all apparently meant to underline the spray-painted proclamation "This is America, bitches." This interweaving of racial, ethnic, gendered, and nationalist prejudice demonstrates the multidimensionality of many Islamophobic and anti-Muslim expressions and the necessity to explore these nuances in order to determine whether there is a single, larger phenomenon or multiple, occasionally interrelated phenomena.

In the current discourse about Islamophobia, some critics have argued that Muslims and Islamophiles use the term as a screen to protect Islam from critique. They contend that the threat of censure curtails the legitimate investigation of Islam's sanction of violence, intolerance, misogyny, and tyranny. These critics are right to chafe at overzealous accusations; to whatever degree, some have used the notion to chastise commentators who ask questions uncomfortable to them. American public and academic discourse has long made space for the critical examination of the beliefs and practices of religious—as well as nonreligious—communities. However, when these critics refer to Islam in the singular as an actor, the wording of their very complaint evidences the weakness of their argument. While Muslims understandably may refer to an ideal, singular Islam to which they belong, just as Christians may do with Christianity and Jews with Judaism, the outside observer must acknowledge something different. For many if not most Muslims, "Islam" acts as a uniform horizon whereby to align their behavioral, moral, cultural, and personal compasses. But the world's more than a billion Muslims neither start from the same cultural position nor hold the same views of how best to strive for that horizon. Any non-Muslim's criticism of a supposedly singular "Islam" impeaches itself from the start. For example, professional critic David Yerushalmi has claimed that shari'a "is effectively sedition when advocated from within our borders and an act of war from without." Defending his accusation—that collapses more than a millennium of Islamic legal traditions manifested in scores of different cultural contexts into one powder keg—he protests that "to argue that discriminating between legitimate religious expression and worship on the one hand and a violent doctrine seeking our destruction on the other is "racist" or "Islamophobic" is absurd in the extreme" (Society of Americans for National Existence, 2009). As another scholar and I have argued elsewhere, Islamophobic arguments often proceed from the assumption that Islam is a uniform whole and overlook the inherent divergences among the fifth of the human population who identify as Muslim (Gottschalk and Greenberg, 2008, 54–56).

THE TERMS

Any consideration of the topics of Islamophobia and anti-Muslim sentiment must first contend with the terms themselves. Although used in English as early as 1923, the word *Islamophobia* has found widespread academic and popular use only since the middle of the first decade of the twenty-first century. Its prevalence soared with the backlash against Muslim Americans that followed 9/11. The use of the term has not been without criticism, and this controversy has—among other effects—helped scholars, journalists, and others map the many contours of the phenomena of anti-Muslim sentiment even as they question its origins, aggravating factors, continuities, and discontinuities among various cultures.

The Oxford English Dictionary cites the earliest Anglophone use of the term in a 1923 review of a French book by E. Dinet and Sliman ben Ibrahim, apparently adapting the word from the original French. Dinet and ben Ibrahim used it in their plea for a more complex approach to the history of religions and a less reductive attitude toward Islamic traditions. Instances of the English use of *Islamophobia* remained sparse until 1995, when debates about the place of Islam and Muslims in Europe began to culminate following significant migrations from India, Pakistan, Bangladesh, Turkey, Morocco, and Algeria. Subsequent marginalization of, discrimination against, and sometimes violence against these migrants in their host countries led many non-Muslim Europeans to critically examine native sentiments. British references to Islamophobia particularly peaked in conjunction with the controversy and protests regarding the publication of Salman Rushdie's *Satanic Verses* in 1988. Although the widely reported book burnings and death threats responding to Rushdie's book only reconfirmed some Britons' suspicions, endeavors to understand their less proximate causes led others to probe the larger socioreligious background of these responses. A 1997 report by the Runnymede Trust—entitled *Islamophobia: A Challenge for Us All*—particularly helped popularize the term in the United Kingdom. In the United States, academic use of the word soared following 2001, while popular use climbed later in the decade.

The Runnymede report offered a particularly well-defined view of *Islamophobia*. The authors explained that the term "refers to unfounded hostility toward Islam." Furthermore, "it refers also to the practical consequences of such hostility in unfair discrimination against Muslim individuals and communities, and to the exclusion of Muslims from mainstream political and social affairs" (Runnymede Trust 1997, 4). In other words, the report draws a straight causal line between anti-Islamic attitudes and anti-Muslim discrimination. While in many instances this has certainly been the case, in others the connections become less convincing. For example, during the 1973 oil embargo, many Americans used the Muslim stereotype of the scimitar-wielding thug to express their anger at the Arab-majority Organization of Petroleum Exporting Countries. They did so without any overt suggestion that members' Islamic commitments informed their decision to sharply decrease exports to the United States. Nevertheless, a historical connection has long existed in American perceptions between the scimitar, forced conversions to Islam, and the aggressive violence of Muslims. Such examples suggest the need for a different—though not entirely distinct—term to encapsulate racist, ethnic, and linguistic biases toward Muslims not connected with their religion.

The term *anti-Muslim* came into use as early as the 1930s and gained particular prominence in discussions about Hindu–Muslim antagonism in 1940s India. Some would strongly prefer that the notion of anti-Muslim sentiment displace the use of *Islamophobia*, arguing that non-Muslim Americans (and Europeans) see Muslims as more the enemy than Islam. To this end, Fred Halliday has argued that the prejudice "involves not so much hostility to Islam as a religion . . . but hostility to *Muslims*" (Halliday 1996, 160). Of course Halliday is partly correct in that the biases and violence that prompted most of the initial and subsequent uses of the term responded to the presence of Muslims and had the concrete aim of engaging them. Indeed, in many instances, those who discriminate target their victims due to their presumed Muslim qualities, which often entail racial, ethnic, and linguistic qualities hardly stemming from the religion. Other scholars dispute claims that a perennial Islamophobia has infused the West, drawing attention to the discontinuities between many of today's antithetical attitudes and medieval Christian antagonisms to Islam that helped propel the Crusades and Reconquista on their respective ends of the Mediterranean (Paley, 2010). While acknowledging both the need to recognize less religiously motivated biases and the historical variations in attitudes, it would be a serious mistake to overlook the potency of anti-Islamic attitudes with their attendant universalizing and simplistic understandings of a singular "Islam."

All of these considerations, then, might suggest that Islamophobia and anti-Muslim sentiments represent only a set of disunited attitudes—which may or may not involve fear—expressed in different ways by different actors in different contexts. The only continuity among them would be an antagonistic view of Muslims. However, the repetition of various allegations, the reuse of specific language, and the insistent return of particular stereotypes indicate how in the American context—and, in all likelihood, in any other—these represent a historically lingering phenomenon but one that has no singularly perpetual form. The religious, racial, ethnic, linguistic, and nationalist dimensions shift in their centrality and potency depending on the specific context of prejudice, with some perhaps even disappearing in importance, but with social anxieties about the nature of Islam and the actions of Muslims remaining a near constant. A colonial era rendition of Voltaire's play *Mahomet the Imposter*, the schoolchild's jibe that a hijab-wearing classmate is "Arab," and the extra airport screening demanded of a dark-complexioned man all may appear quite disconnected from one another yet each ultimately has its roots in an enduring, self-reinforcing legacy of American social fears about Muslims. Following a reflection on how Muslim discrimination results from acts of comparison, we will examine some of the types of comparison and how they lead to both this constancy and malleability.

THE LOGIC OF DISCRIMINATION

The phenomena of Islamophobia and anti-Muslim sentiment have permeated too deeply into and found too many expressions among Americans over five centuries of nonnative settlement to allow for a comprehensive overview here. At best we can try to develop a methodical, hermeneutical approach to a set of claims that demonstrate the variability yet contingency of prejudices against Muslims. Specifically we will consider the most publicly circulated expressions: those uttered by politicians, scholars, and journalists. Such references neither represent the entirety of negative depictions nor are they completely lacking in nuanced and balanced portrayals of Muslims and Islam.

We must begin by distinguishing two types of claims about Islam and Muslims and understanding how both have served as acts of comparison. The first type of claim makes assertions about specific Muslims and the second about generic Muslims and Islam in general. Thomas Jefferson's view of the Barbary states, popular attitudes toward the Ayatollah Khomeini, and Republican Party insinuations about Barack Obama's secret Muslim identity should be distinguished from Hannah Adams's thoughts on Muslim licentiousness, Samuel Huntington's ideas on Islamic civilization, and Franklin Graham's understandings of Islamic family life. The latter sets of claims rely upon either a view of all Muslims as a collective of essentially identical individuals or of a generic Muslim meant to singly represent them all. Both types of claims stem from an urge to compare that, in turn, derives from a simultaneous declaration of similarity and difference.

Most of the time, this declaration does not amount to a complete "othering" that casts Muslims and Islam as irreconcilably different from other Americans and religions in the United States. In the extreme cases when this does occur, non-Muslims no longer attempt to "make sense of them" and Muslims are relegated to a sub- or nonhuman position.[1] Instead, Islamophobic and anti-Muslim discourse more commonly has attempted to position Islam and Muslims in some comparative schema that establishes similarity as the foundation for discerning difference. The conclusion depends on the basis of comparison. For instance, using religion as a basis, a commentator might refer to a universalized, generic Muslim, comparing him[2] with a generic member of the commentator's religious group (e.g., "they have a religion and so do we: mine is loving while the Muslim's is violent.") Taking secularism as the comparative basis would foster a different result (e.g., "Islamic law requires the Muslim American to extend shari'a into all segments of US society, but a non-Muslim American respects the separation of church and state"). Discerning the basis helps reveal both the comparative logic and the self-understanding implicit in Islamophobic perspectives.

One of the key components of the comparative logic that informs most forms of Islamophobia—and sometimes of anti-Muslim sentiment—is that people who happen to be Muslim are assumed *only ever to be Muslim*. Often this arises from the claim that Islam is not just a religion but a way of life, thus leaving no facet of a Muslim's life Islamically undefined. In other cases, it results from repeated exposure to stereotypes that reduce individuals to two-dimensional caricatures defined only by their religion. Although most Americans recognize that Christians, Jews, Hindus, and atheists may consider themselves as neighbors, fellow citizens, family members, charity boosters, and team supporters, those promoting Islamophobic perspectives reduce the interests, attitudes, and agendas of people who happen to be Muslim to a singular, all-enveloping Muslim identity. Hence even claims about specific Muslim groups may ultimately derive from generic stereotypes of all Muslims because those operating under such a totalistic vision cannot comprehend departures from the universal archetype. In these cases, particular individuals or communities are understood deductively based on received stereotypes that have become accepted as unquestioned common sense.

Such commonsensical conclusions illustrate well how many instances of Islamophobia and anti-Muslim sentiment derive not from conscious derision but from received attitudes. Sadly, most Americans have been socialized into Islamophobic views. Films depicting Muslim men as terrorists, news accounts of political violence in Muslim majority countries, and magazine articles about oppressed Muslim women have long served as mass media staples with few counterbalancing representations of Muslims or their traditions. Although this situation has lessened in the new century, pressures remain to continue it, as demonstrated in 2012, when efforts by the Florida Family Association led to the cancellation of a well- reviewed docuseries about five Lebanese American Muslim families. The association described the show as "propaganda that riskily hides the Islamic agenda's clear and present danger to American liberties and traditional values" (Davidson, 2011). Without alternative perspectives such as those offered by this show, negative stereotypes remain unchallenged. Issues of intentionality are usually difficult to resolve, but certainly a distinction must be made between those who repeat ill-informed claims about Muslims or Islam because of their lack of alternative perspectives and those who propagate—without consideration of available evidence to the contrary—the most malicious slurs for their personal and/or professional profit. As we shall see again at the end of this chapter, examples of the latter are unfortunately easy to find in the twenty-first century.

The Comparisons

As mentioned above, Islamophobic and anti-Muslim views—like most forms of anthropological knowledge (however contested)—result from efforts to understand that necessarily involve the process of comparison. Their conclusions depend on the basis from which the comparison proceeds. Theology, development, and nationalism represent three themes that non-Muslim Americans commonly have taken as bases of comparison in their attempts to understand (or at least describe) Muslims and Islam.

Theological comparison has informed the oldest expressions of American Islamophobia and the clearest manifestations of antagonism to Islam. Colonial Puritan theologian Jonathan Edwards (d. 1758) contrasted Christianity with Islam, which he found indulgent of the lascivious and luxury-loving, reliant on forced conversions, and "not propagated by light and instruction, but by darkness; not by encouraging reasoning and search, but by discouraging knowledge and learning; by shutting out those things, and forbidding inquiry; and so, in short, by blinding, the eyes of mankind" (Edwards, 1839, 492). Hannah Adams (d. 1831), historian and relation of patriot John Adams, similarly argues in her dictionary of religions that Islam's success depended on Muhammad's use of conversion by the sword and of "poligamy and concubinage to make his creed palatable to the most depraved of mankind" (Adams, 1817, 157). Such descriptions implicitly staked Christianity as the religion of truth and of the American norm. Indeed, during the constitutional convention in the late eighteenth century, many of the delegates who disagreed with provisions for a religious test of potential candidates mollified concerns that non-Protestants could be elected to office by pointing out the unlikelihood of this occurring. As delegate Samuel Johnston explained, a "Jew, a Mahometan or a pagan could get into office only in one of two ways: either the American people would have to lay aside the Christian religion altogether" or the individual would have to prove his or her virtuosity (Lambert, 2008, 34). The unspoken assumption among most of the delegates was that the new republic held few if any Muslims other than recently arrived African captives, whose Islamic practices and beliefs seldom survived the terrible oppressions of the slave system. Hence their perspectives did not arise from a fear of any immanent Islamic presence; instead, Muslims represented an abstract, absent outlier used to define the limits of domestic tolerance.

These early American antagonisms to Islam as a religion undoubtedly stemmed from medieval European Christian antipathies imported into the North American colonies by Spanish, French, and English settlers. Arab Muslim military conquests beginning in the seventh century opened the way to widespread, mostly voluntary conversions of Christians in North Africa and the Iberian Peninsula, challenging Christian teleological expectations of a gradually universalizing church. While the Reconquista may have achieved success in 1492, after four centuries of warfare, the multiple waves of crusaders found no permanent victory in the eastern Mediterranean despite at least as many years of bloody endeavor. Indeed, their declining efforts only preceded (if not helped enable) the Ottomans' conquest of Constantinople that preceded their surge through southeastern Europe, which peaked in 1683 with the failed siege of Vienna. Although European Christian attitudes toward Islam and Muslims were not uniformly negative and varied across time and among various westerners, they could not but inform New World colonists, who had even less opportunity for the intercultural encounters with Muslims that eventually helped challenge many inherited European notions.

Despite the increase in competing perspectives, similar sentiments of Christian normativity and Muslim violence and decadence remain apparent in twenty-first-century America. Proponents, often using a deeply inflected Christian tone, warn that Islam endangers both Muslims and non-Muslims. Columnist Ann Coulter responded to the 9/11 attacks by opining about terrorists, "we should invade their countries, kill their leaders and convert them to Christianity" (*Washington Monthly*, 2001). Among the arguments made against the purported "shariaization" of US law courts, some maintain that it makes Muslim women and children vulnerable to the discriminations and cruelties of Islamic law. In 2010, national evangelical leader Franklin Graham declared that "true Islam cannot be practiced in this country. You can't beat your wife. You cannot murder your children if you think they've committed adultery or something like that" (Vu, 2010). Many who oppose any use of shari'a in the courts—despite existing allowances for Jewish and Christian forms of arbitration—argue that doing so imperils further the Christian basis of American society already undermined by liberal secularists. To this end, also in 2010, former congressional leader Newt Gingrich approvingly quoted President Franklin Delano Roosevelt and British Prime Minister Winston Churchill, who separately invoked Christianity as the basis of their societies as distinct from their Nazi German enemy.

Developmental comparisons of Islamophobia and anti-Muslim sentiments represent the second oldest strain found in the United States. Many Americans have projected a secularized developmental arc on which Muslim-majority countries fare less well than western ones. The developmental trajectory projected might be political, social, civilizational, and/or economic. Its similarity to older, though still popular, Christian salvation teleologies suggests at least a parallel, if not an origin, although its secular nature tends to downplay this (Gingrich's speech demonstrates as much when he quotes Roosevelt regarding the interconnection between democracy and Christianity). As one of the enduring qualities of Islamophobia, critics have repeatedly connected the backwardness and arrested development of contemporary "Muslim" societies to the fateful mandates Muhammad instituted in the original Islamic community.

Islamic states—or even just those presumed to be "Islamic" because their countries have Muslim majorities—have long served as targets of comparative criticism if not fear. Allegations of "Oriental despotism" figured prominently in nineteenth-century depictions, although Americans have applied this label in non-Muslim Asian contexts as well. The term commonly served as an uncritically examined marker of difference between the presumably progressive political systems of the United States—if not also of some European states—and supposedly tyrannical, brutal, and pompous (even overly sensual) Asian ones. So, for instance, in 1802 Thomas Jefferson helped translate a French book popular enough already to have been translated twice into English in the decade since it was first published. Its discussion of the decline of empires offered particular attention to how the despotism and fanaticism supposedly rooted in Muhammad's original vision provided the ruinous seed that repeatedly doomed subsequent Muslim empires (Allison, 1995, 50). In this work and many others, the far-removed, phantom figureheads of the Ottoman sultan and Chinese emperor particularly served as icons of this notion. This demonstrates again how absent Muslims can act as generic figures of negative comparison, sometimes even reduced to a persona-less abstraction. Indeed, an abolitionist lamented on July 4, 1833, that slavery marred the celebratory day for a nation "in the bosom of which a worse than oriental despotism is exercised" (Cushing, 1833, 252). The notion lasted as late as 1957, when American historian Karl Wittfogel published *Oriental Despotism*, in which he likened Communist Russia and China to ancient despotisms while unfavorably contrasting them with both the historic and current West.

More contemporarily, Samuel Huntington rebreathed life into nineteenth-century notions of civilizational development and difference. First stated in a 1993 essay and elaborated upon in a book three years later, Huntington's argument postulated a post–Cold War metapolitics in which "civilizational identity" would define international conflicts. His indices of success measured economic development, population growth, national cohesion, and democratization. At first blush, his description of an Islamic resurgence seems eerily prescient when he warns that it is likely to power in "the early years of the twenty-first century . . . an ongoing resurgence of non-Western power and culture and the clash of the peoples of non-Western civilizations with the West and with each other" (Huntington, 1996, 121). Yet closer examination reveals the same Islamophobic impulse to posit a single, totalized Islamic realm (religiously defined) apart from the western (described in neutral geographic terms). Reinforcing views of Muslims as never defined in other than religious terms, Huntington allowed this ultimate simplification to trump his own careful description of divergences among Muslim-majority cultures and to ignore the transnational flows of Muslims and their cultures into the West (and elsewhere) and the reciprocal flow of western cultural products into "the Islamic world." Sadly, scholars, journalists, and broader audiences around the world have fastened on Huntington's paradigm to frame specific conflicts as emblematic of a global clash between starkly and essentially defined oppositional civilizations.

Most recently, Muslim-majority nations have drawn popular and media concern when helmed by states steered by Islamic ideologies. While few US administrations have hesitated to ally with undemocratic, oppressive dictatorships such as those of

Mohammed Shah Reza Pahlavi of Iran, Saddam Hussein of Iraq, and Anwar Sadat and Hosni Mubarak of Egypt, the ascent of Islamist states often has triggered immediate handwringing and negative uses of developmental comparison. Significantly, administrations have tended to publicly celebrate dictators favored for their secular and economic accomplishments, especially the holding at bay of Islamic energies. The State Department's surprise at the success of the 1979 Iranian revolution demonstrates to what degree the notions of secular and industrial progress have been taken as symptomatic of a nation's advancement and stability. Contemporary commentators struggled to reconcile the evidently "modern" technological, educational, and industrial success of many Iranians with their "medieval" decision to establish a semidemocratic theocracy. The adoption of this language demonstrates a shift in the developmental comparison from a contrast of an alien, Oriental despotism with a familiar, western democracy to a more singular timeline of (religiously) medieval to (secularly) modern political development. Meanwhile, the debacle that ensued when Iranian revolutionary students subsequently took the US embassy staff hostage solidified any vague American concerns about Islamist governments into a well-practiced alarm that has lingered into the new millennium.

Nineteenth-century Islamophobic social comparisons often combined with Orientalist erotic and romantic fascinations to criticize the place of women in Muslim-majority societies in titillating pictorial and verbal portrayals. Following first-wave feminist criticisms of women's legal inequalities in the United States, twentieth-century American critics increasingly took their measure of Muslim women's public freedoms as a litmus test of a government's worth. In the next century, the administration of George W. Bush drew on this enduring sentiment when it sought to mobilize public support for two invasions by linking his (Muslim) enemies not only to terrorist violence but also to a politics of developmental decline and women's rights. For instance, despite broad acceptance for the invasion of Afghanistan to dislodge al Qaeda in the wake of 9/11, the Bush administration sought to shore support by also casting the war as aiding the liberation of women. Only a month after the war began, First Lady Laura Bush proclaimed, in November 2001, "the fight against terrorism is also a fight for the rights and dignity of women" because "the brutal oppression of women is a central goal of the terrorists." In a rhetorical effort to confirm the president's claim that the United States was not at war with Islam, Laura Bush explained "the severe repression and brutality against women in Afghanistan is not a matter of legitimate religious practice" (von der Lippe, 2012, 157). By doing so, she sought to strengthen the justification for the invasion by positioning the United States as arbitrator regarding the proper position not only of Afghan women on a trajectory of comparative development but also of Afghan Muslim praxis relative to "legitimate" Islam. Although American news sources reciprocated with bountiful stories celebrating the liberation of Afghans—particularly women—from Taliban rule, they have offered fewer overall comparisons of Afghans' quality of life under the Taliban's erstwhile extreme rule with that during the decade-long war to expel them.

This hints at how media sources often suspend their interest in Muslim women's development once secular governments displace Islamist ones. In contrast to the extensive coverage of women's issues in Afghanistan preceding the American invasion, reporting a decade later on the US standoff with Iran regarding its nuclear ambitions has largely ignored the progressive advances Iran's women have made since the 1979 revolution. The higher enrollment of women than men in universities does not fit the themes of regression and threat usually employed to depict the semidemocratic theocracy. Conversely, the success of Iran's last shah in promoting secularism deflected American media concerns for women's rights, even as his secret police publicly tore headscarves off women to enforce their ban.

Nationalist comparisons attempt to measure the patriotism of Muslim Americans relative to their fellow citizens. Islamophobia and anti-Muslim sentiment work from suspicions of nonallegiance that allege mixed commitments to outright sedition, as David Yerushalmi's comments above suggest. Practical security concerns about the presence of militants in the United States have been allowed to become opportunities for blanket suspicion of all Muslims, with particular use of profiling based on ethnic and racial stereotypes. The nationalist normativity of whiteness and Christian identity becomes very apparent, for instance, when law enforcement encounters with violent militia groups—many motivated by Christian ideologies—do not result in subsequent white racial profiling or suspicions of all Christians. In the case of the 1995 bombing of the Murrah Federal Building in Oklahoma City, news reporting brought immediate allegations of Muslim terrorism, but the eventual prosecution of perpetrator Timothy McVeigh and the revelation of his association with the racist, anti-Semitic, and antisecular Christian Identity movement did not stir larger concerns regarding whites or militant Christians despite the rising numbers of such extremists.

The Southern Poverty Law Center (SPLC) estimates that hate groups have increased by 69 percent since 2000, motivated by a weakening economy and shrinking white majority. (Surely the enduring suspicions both about the nation's first African American president's "Muslim identity" and about his status as an American citizen are not coincidental.) The SPLC points particularly to the role of politicians and mainstream media figures in exacerbating fears about immigrant and other minority groups (SPLC, 2012b). This finding reinforces the invaluable 2012 report by the Center for American Progress that outlines a new twenty-first-century dynamic of mutually reinforcing Islamophobic actors who have been responsible for a chilling surge in prejudice. The report concludes that a cycle of incrimination has developed that creates an echo chamber of false accusations. This involves professional Islamophobes who advance allegations, media representatives who help propagate them, conservative politicians who make them into causes, and wealthy donors who subsidize much of this activity.

The attempt to establish an Islamic center two blocks from the site of Manhattan's former World Trade Center provides a sad example of the success of this Islamophobic combine. A 2010 effort to obtain building permits for the center had proceeded uneventfully until professional critic Pamela Geller used her Stop Islamicization of America organization to rally against it. Under the headline "Mosque Madness at Ground Zero," a *New York Post* columnist promoted Geller's cause (euphemistically describing her organization as a "human-rights group," which the SPLC identifies as a hate group) as the first step in bringing a media spotlight on the effort. While other conservative journalists weighed in, media stars Rush Limbaugh, Glenn Beck, Sarah Palin, and Newt Gingrich joined them. As the year came to a close, Republican candidates from across the country used the misleadingly labeled "Ground Zero mosque" controversy to position themselves as patriots as compared with insensitive Muslims who wanted to build a "victory mosque," in the words of North Carolina congressional candidate Renee Ellmers. As Kathleen E. Foley has detailed, this represented only one in a number of mosque construction conflicts that began as minor local concerns and ended as regional if not national causes célèbres as a result of Islamophobic machinations.

The results of these efforts have been telling this century. In their efforts to portray Muslims and Islam as unpatriotic if not virulently anti-American, professional critics such as Pamela Geller, David Horowitz, Daniel Pipes, Jonathan Spencer, and David Yerushalmi have joined politicians like Renee Ellmers, Michele Bachmann, and Peter T. King in promoting unsubstantiated fears regarding the presence of Muslim communities, the construction of mosques, and the use of shari'a in American courtrooms.

Polls show that deliberate provocations can aggravate Islamophobia and anti-Muslim sentiment and create concrete consequences for Muslim Americans. They demonstrate that experiences of discrimination have continued to rise even a decade after 9/11, with a quarter of respondents in 2011 saying that their mosque has been the target of controversy or hostility. Nevertheless, polls also indicate that Muslim Americans hold strong American identities, are as likely as Christians to identify with their religion before their nation, and are far more likely than other Americans to think that Muslims who come to the United States want to adopt American customs and ways of life (Pew 2011, 2, 7, 10).

Notes

1. Ironically, "Musulman" in concentration camp jargon referred to prisoners so exhausted and famished that they appeared as walking dead (an insight offered by my colleague Ulrich Plass).
2. In popular American discourse, the generic Muslim commonly is envisioned as male when described as an Islamic decision-maker but as female when described as a victim of Islam.

References

Adams, Hannah, *A Dictionary of All Religions and Religious Denominations: Jewish, Heathen, Mahometan, and Christian, Ancient and Modern* (Boston: James Eastburn, 1817).

Ali, Wajahat, Eli Clifton, Matthew Duss, Lee Fang, Scott Keyes, and Faiz Shakir, *Fear, Inc.: The Roots of the Islamophobia Network in America* (Center for American Progress, August 2011). Available at: http://www.americanprogress.org/issues/religion/report/2011/08/26/10165/fear-inc/

Allison, Robert J., *The Crescent Obscured: The United States and the Muslim World, 1776–1815* (New York, NY: Oxford University Press, 1995).

Bakalian, Anny, and Mehdi Bozorgmehr, *Backlash 9/11: Middle Eastern and Muslim Americans Respond* (Berkeley: University of California Press, 2009).

Cushing, Caleb, "An Oration Pronounced at Boston before the Colonization Society of Massachusetts, on the Anniversary of American Independence, July 4, 1833," *The New England Magazine*, Volume 5, 1833, Boston: J. T. Buckingham.

Davidson, Amy, "The Attack on "All-American Muslim,"" in *The New Yorker*, December 14, 2011. Available at: http://www.newyorker.com/online/blogs/comment/2011/12/the-attack-on-all-american-muslim.html#ixzz2FlvhDMCf (Accessed December 22, 2012).

Edwards, Jonathan, *The Works of Jonathan Edwards, A. M.*, Vol. 2, ed. Edward Hickman (London: William Ball, 1839).

Esposito, John, and Ibrahim Kalin, eds. *Islamophobia: The Challenge of Pluralism in the 21st Century* (New York: Oxford University Press, 2011).

Federal Bureau of Investigation, "Foreword," in *Hate Crime Statistics 2001* (Washington, DC: Author, 2001).

Federal Bureau of Investigation, *Hate Crime Statistics 2011* (Washington, DC: Author, 2011.) Available at: http://www.fbi.gov/about-us/cjis/ucr/hate-crime/2011/narratives/victims (Accessed December 22, 2012).

Foley, Kathleen E., ""'Not In Our Neighborhood': Managing Opposition to Mosque Construction" (Institute for Social Policy and Understanding, October 2010).

Gottschalk, Peter, *American Heretics: Catholics, Jews, Muslims, and the History of Religious Intolerance* (New York: Palgrave Macmillan, 2013).

Gottschalk, Peter, and Gabriel Greenberg, *Islamophobia: Making Muslims the Enemy* (Lantham, MD: Rowman & Littlefield, 2008).

Halliday, Fred, *Islam & the Myth of Confrontation: Religion and Politics in the Middle East* (New York: I. B. Tauris, 1996).

Huntington, Samuel L., *The Clash of Civilizations: Remaking of World Order* (New York: Touchstone, 1996).

Lambert, Frank, *Religion in American Politics: A Short History* (Princeton, NJ: Princeton University Press, 2008).

Paley, Naamah, "The Khalil Gibran International Academy: Diasporic Confrontations with an Emerging Islamophobia" in *Islamophobia, Islamophilia: Beyond the Politics of Enemy and Friend*, ed. Andrew Shryock (Bloomington: Indiana University Press, 2010): 53–75.

Peek, Lori, *Behind the Backlash: Muslim Americans after 9/11* (Philadelphia: Temple University Press, 2011).

Pew Research Center, "No Signs of Growth in Alienation or Support For Extremism" (Washington, DC: Author, August 30, 2011).

Runnymede Trust, *Islamophobia: A Challenge for Us All* (London: Author, 1997).

Said, Edward W., *Orientalism* (New York: Vintage, 1978).

Said, Edward W., *Covering Islam: How the Media and the Experts Determine How We See the Rest of the World* (New York: Vintage, 1979).

Shaheen, Jack G., *Guilty: Hollywood's Verdict on Arabs After 9/11* (Northampton, MA: Olive Branch Press, 2008).

Shaheen, Jack G., *Reel Bad Arabs: How Hollywood Vilifies a People*, rev. ed. (Northampton, MA: Olive Branch Press, 2009).

Shryock, Andrew, ed., *Islamophobia, Islamophilia: Beyond the Politics of Enemy and Friend* (Bloomington: Indiana University Press, 2010).

Society of Americans for National Existence, "The Truth and Nothing But the Truth." Available at: http://www.saneworks.us/indexnew.php (Accessed December 22, 2012).

Southern Poverty Law Center, 2012a. "Anti-Muslim." Available at: http://www.splcenter.org/get-informed/intelligence-files/ideology/anti-muslim (Accessed September 19, 2012).

Southern Poverty Law Center, 2012b. "Hate and Extremism." Available at: http://www.splcenter.org/what-we-do/hate-and-extremism (Accessed September 19, 2012).

von der Lippe, Berit, "Rhetoric of War, Rhetoric of Gender" in *Rhetorical Citizenship and Public Deliberation*, ed. Christian Kock and Lisa S. Villadsen (University Park, PA: Pennsylvania State University Press, 2012): 153–168.

Vu, Michelle A., "Franklin Graham: Islam Is Not Faith of America," *The Christian Post*, May 6, 2010. Available at: http://m.christianpost.com/news/franklin-grahamislam-is-not-faith-of-america-45041/ (Accessed December 22, 2012).

Washington Monthly, "The Wisdom of Ann Coulter." October 2001. Available at: http://www.washingtonmonthly.com/features/2001/0111.coulterwisdom.html (Accessed December 22, 2012).

INDEX

....

"n." indicates material in notes. "f" indicates material in figures. "t" indicates material in tables.

on house of worship, 229

How to Eat to Live, 442

imprisonment of, in WWII, 65, 288

international visits of, 36

as NOI leader, 24–26, 35–37, 91

on prayers, 228–29

"preachments" of, 25, 290

Muhammad, Fard, 35, 228. *See also* Fard, Wallace D.

Muhammad, Salahuddin, 51

Muhammad, Wallace (Warith), 37, 230, 479. *See also* Mohammed, Warith Deen

Muhammadan Anglo-Oriental College, 271

Muhammad: Legacy of a Prophet (film), 246, 468

Muhammad: The Last Prophet (film), 467

Muharram, 168

Mujahid, Abdul Malik, 280, 467

Mummy, The (film), 466

Murfreesboro Islamic Center, 495, 505n.10

Murid Order, 127–28

murids, 119

murshidas, 58, 120

al-Murtada, al-Sharif, 117n.17

musallas, 238, 405, 407, 413f

Musawah, 205n.12

music

African slaves and, 1, 21–22

Ahmadiyya Movement and, 147

blues, 22, 238

call to prayer and, 22, 238

doo-wop, 2

in Druze services, 143

at "Great Muslim Adventure Day," 72

hip-hop, 2, 95, 389

from ICNA, 72

jazz, 2, 147

Nakshabendi brotherhood and, 83n.9

nasheeds, 72

of Nizaris, 139

Qur'anic recitation and, 22, 238

Qur'anists on, 153

rap, 2, 72

Sufism and, 120, 130, 134n.30

Muslim Advocates, 194, 195t, 202

Muslimah Media Watch (website), 384

Muslimah Pride Day, 198

Muslim American Public Opinion Survey (MAPOS), 337n.16

Muslim American Society (MAS), 65, 86n.1, 245, 262, 480

Muslim Brotherhood, 73, 78, 81, 273, 480, 482, 484. *See also* Society of the Muslim Brothers

Muslim Chaplaincy Program, 56

Muslim Children of North America, 261

Muslim Community Center for Human Services (MCCHS), 311

Muslim Community School, 241

Muslim Congress, 111

Muslim Endorsement Council of Connecticut, 53

Muslim Family Days, 262

Muslim Home School in America (journal), 243

Muslim Home School Network and Resource, 243

Muslim Medical Association, 449

Muslim Medical Ethics (Brockopp & Eich), 451

Muslim Mental Health, Inc., 450

Muslim Mosque, Inc., 25, 89

Muslim Public Affairs Council (MPAC)

on hate crimes, 498, 505n.19

ICNA and, 71

lobbying by, 77

Al-Marayati's appointment to, 81

on "Muslim block vote," 329

South Asian American Muslims and, 39

transnational networks of, 480

women on, 194

Young Leaders National Summits, 263

Muslim Scouts (film), 246, 261–62

Muslim Spiritual Care Services, 56

Muslim Sports Days, 262

Muslim Student Association (MSA)

background and history of, 36, 256–57, 480

COMPASS, 319n.1

da'wa in, 256–59

FCNA and, 178

history of, 308–9

iftars at, 168, 259

IMANA and, 449

interfaith activities of, 259–260

ISNA and, 3, 66, 67

leadership development in, 315

media and, 260

membership of, 257

modernism and, 3

Muslim Brotherhood and, 480, 482

NAIT and, 68

Salafi movement and, 481

secularism and, 3

September 11 terrorist attacks and, 259–260

services provided by, 257–59

Shi'i-Sunni divisions within, 205n.10

socialism and, 3

Sufism and, 125

website of, 381

women in, 316

Muslim Teachers' College, 241

Muslim Women Resource Center, 195t

prisons (*Cont.*)
  civil rights movements and, 290
  da'wa in, 281, 290
  headdress in, 47
  history of Islam in, 288
  ICNA activities in, 70
  "Levee Camp Holler" in Mississippi, 22
  Lindh's freedom of religion lawsuit on, 301n.16
  pat searches in, 47
  race and rates of incarceration in, 91
  religious programs in, 293
  September 11 terrorist attacks and, 294
  Shi'i outreach to, 111
  statistics on Muslims in, 293
  threat of extremism in, 297–99
  TTQ Qur'ans for, 111
  Useem on terrorism and, 300n.1
  Van Baalen on Islam in, 6, 286–314
  Wahhabi movement outreach in, 113
profiling, 336n.5, 463, 493, 517
progressive Muslim movement, 78–80, 83n.8, 150
Progressive Muslims (Safi), 79
Progressive Muslim Union of North America (PMUNA), 79–80, 378
progressive reformism, 5, 192–93
progressivism, 96
Project Downtown, 319
Project MAPS, 337n.18
prophetic medicine, 440, 442, 451–52
proselytizing
  by Ahmadiyya Movement, 23, 144–48, 276
  by Christians, after emancipation, 21
  da'wa. See da'wa/dawah
  Druze and, 142
  ICNA and, 69
  Moore's study of, 5–6, 274–282
  online, 381
  in prisons, 298
  by Shi'ites, 110
Protestants. *See also individual denominations*
  congregationalism on, 41
  on depriving Muslims constitutional rights, 327, 336n.6
  dialogue with Muslims, 368–370
  discrimination by, 259–260
  immigration and, 1
  ministers, 57–58, 497–98, 505n.16
  opposition and mob violence by, 205n.11
  pastors, 50
  religious courts of, 505n.12
proto-American Islamic movements, 26, 112, 127, 228
psychology, 129–130, 445, 453
purdah, 148

Qaddafi, Muammar, 37
Qadiani movement, 145, 149. *See also* Ahmadiyya Movement
Qadiri Boutchichiyya Order, 126
Qadiriya Order, 16, 120, 481
qadr, 155n.43
al-Qa'ida. *See* Al-Qaeda
qalb, 445
al-Qaradawi, Yusuf, 377, 484, 485, 488n.7
Qasid Center, 132–33
Qasimi dynasty, 102
al-Qatami, Laila, 194
qawwamun 'ala, 348
Qibla, 161, 380
qiblah, 161, 407, 413, 414, 420
qiyas, 175
Qom, 377
Quakers, 291
al-Quds, 170. *See also* Jerusalem
Quraishi, Sima, 195
Qur'an. *See also* Koran
  on adoption, 184
  on afterlife, 347
  Ahmadiyya Movement and, 23, 144–46, 149
  Asani on pluralism and, 140
  Bible and, 94, 354, 501
  "Burn the Qur'an Day," 365, 372, 497
  on charity, 140, 166
  context and history of, 343, 345, 347–48
  on creation, 347
  da'wa and, 269–272
  definition of, 159
  on diversity, 152
  on divorce, 217–18
  Druze and, 142
  fasting and, 167
  FCNA and, 179
  feminism and, 88, 347
  fiqh and, 175
  on foods in healthy diet, 442
  healing through reading/recitation of, 440–41, 445
  ICNA literature on, 69, 72
  imam's knowledge of, 51–52
  on injustice, 196
  interpreting, 92, 159, 235, 341–43, 346–353
  ISNA on, women and, 69
  Khalifa's analysis of, 150–51
  legal reasoning based on, 5
  on marriage and family life, 93, 210, 214–17, 222–23n.13, 348, 356n.41
  on mental health, 445
  Moses story in, 465
  music and recitation of, 22, 238